Contents

II Travel information

II	Driving abroad – a cautionary tale
IV	Driving regulations
VII	Ski resorts

1 Route planning maps

| 1 | Key map · Distance table |

17 Road maps

| 17 | Key map |

121 City plans and urban area maps

| 121 | Legends to city plans and urban area maps |

Alicante C	121	Madrid U	135
Amsterdam CU	122	Madrid C	136
Antwerpen Antwerp C	121	Málaga C	136
Athina Athens U	122	Marseille Marseilles C	136
Athina Athens C	123	Milano Milan CU	137
Barcelona CU	123	Moskva Moscow CU	138
Basel C	123	München Munich CU	138
Beograd Belgrade C	125	Nápoli Naples CU	139
Berlin CU	124	Oslo U	139
Bordeaux CU	125	Oslo C	140
Bruxelles Brussels U	125	Paris C	140
Bruxelles Brussels C	126	Paris U	141
Budapest CU	126	Praha Prague CU	142
Dublin CU	127	Roma Rome CU	143
Düsseldorf C	127	Rotterdam C	142
Düsseldorf (Ruhrgebiet) U	128	Sankt Peterburg	
Edinburgh C	127	St Petersburg U	142
Firenze Florence C	129	Sevilla Seville C	144
Frankfurt C	129	Stockholm CU	145
Genève Geneva C	129	Strasbourg CU	144
Génova Genoa C	129	Stuttgart C	144
Göteborg Gothenburg C	130	Torino Turin U	146
Granada C	130	Torino Turin C	147
Hamburg CU	130	Venézia Venice C	146
Helsinki CU	131	Warszawa Warsaw CU	147
İstanbul U	131	Wien Vienna U	147
København Copenhagen CU	132	Wien Vienna C	148
Köln Cologne C	132	Zagreb C	148
Lisboa Lisbon CU	133	Zürich C	148
London C	133		
London U	134	**C City street plan**	
Luxembourg C	135	**U Urban area map**	
Lyon CU	135		

149 Index to road maps

www.philips-maps.co.uk
First published in 1998 as **Philip's Multiscale Europe** by
Philip's, a division of Octopus Publishing Group Ltd
www.octopusbooks.co.uk
Carmelite House,
50 Victoria Embankment
London EC4Y 0DZ
An Hachette UK Company
www.hachette.co.uk

Twentieth edition 2018
First impression 2018

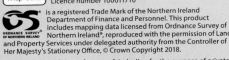
The maps of Ireland on pages 18 to 21 and the urban area map and town plan of Dublin are based upon the Crown Copyright and are reproduced with the permission of Land & Property Services under delegated authority from the Controller of Her Majesty's Stationery Office, © Crown Copyright and database right 2018, PMLPA No 100503, and on Ordnance Survey Ireland by permission of the Government © Ordnance Survey Ireland / Government of Ireland Permit number 9130.

Cartography by Philip's
Copyright © Philip's 2018

Printed in China

*Independent research survey, from research carried out by Outlook Research Limited, 2005/06.

Photographic acknowledgements:
Pages II and III: all photographs by Stephen Mesquita

Legend to route planning maps — pages 2–16

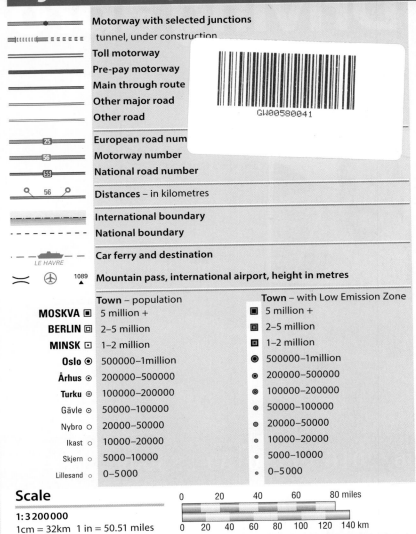

| Motorway with selected junctions |
| tunnel, under construction |
| Toll motorway |
| Pre-pay motorway |
| Main through route |
| Other major road |
| Other road |
| 25 European road number |
| 56 Motorway number |
| 55 National road number |
| 56 Distances – in kilometres |
| International boundary |
| National boundary |
| Car ferry and destination LE HAVRE |
| Mountain pass, international airport, height in metres 1089 |

	Town – population		Town – with Low Emission Zone
MOSKVA	5 million +		5 million +
BERLIN	2–5 million		2–5 million
MINSK	1–2 million		1–2 million
Oslo	500000–1million		500000–1million
Århus	200000–500000		200000–500000
Turku	100000–200000		100000–200000
Gävle	50000–100000		50000–100000
Nybro	20000–50000		20000–50000
Ikast	10000–20000		10000–20000
Skjern	5000–10000		5000–10000
Lillesand	0–5000		0–5000

Scale

1:3 200 000
1cm = 32km   1 in = 50.51 miles

0 20 40 60 80 miles
0 20 40 60 80 100 120 140 km

Legend to road maps — pages 18–120

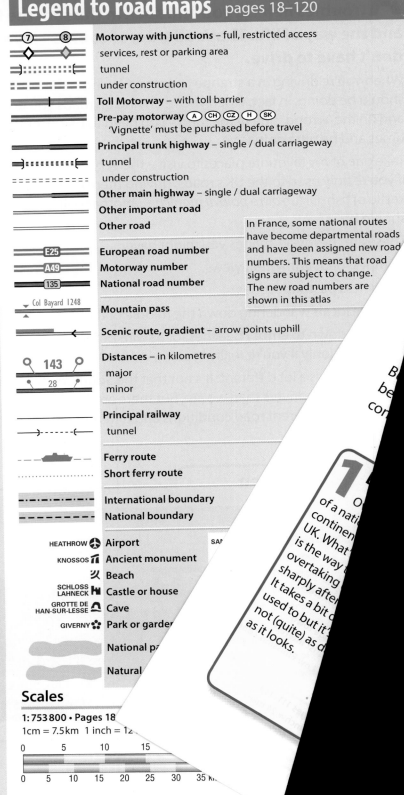

| 7 8 Motorway with junctions – full, restricted access |
| services, rest or parking area |
| tunnel |
| under construction |
| Toll Motorway – with toll barrier |
| Pre-pay motorway A CH CZ H SK |
| 'Vignette' must be purchased before travel |
| Principal trunk highway – single / dual carriageway |
| tunnel |
| under construction |
| Other main highway – single / dual carriageway |
| Other important road |
| Other road |
| E25 European road number |
| A49 Motorway number |
| 135 National road number |
| Col Bayard 1248 Mountain pass |
| Scenic route, gradient – arrow points uphill |
| 143 Distances – in kilometres |
| 28 major |
| minor |
| Principal railway |
| tunnel |
| Ferry route |
| Short ferry route |
| International boundary |
| National boundary |
| HEATHROW Airport |
| KNOSSOS Ancient monument |
| Beach |
| SCHLOSS LAHNECK Castle or house |
| GROTTE DE HAN-SUR-LESSE Cave |
| GIVERNY Park or garden |
| National p... |
| Natural ... |

In France, some national routes have become departmental roads and have been assigned new road numbers. This means that road signs are subject to change. The new road numbers are shown in this atlas

Scales

1:753 800 · Pages 18
1cm = 7.5km   1 inch = 12...

0 ... 10 ... 15
0 5 10 15 20 25 30 35 km

Driving abroad –
a cautionary tale

by Stephen Mesquita,
Philip's On the Road Correspondent

5/06/2016 07:10:39 LS300W   *******

At last, you're on holiday. You can relax, leave your troubles behind you and soak in the sun, the food and the way of life. That's all true, of course – if you don't have to drive.

When you're driving in a strange country, relaxing is the last thing you should be doing. In fact, when you're driving on roads you don't know – and on the 'wrong' side of the road – you need to pay attention at all times and be ultra defensive.

Take one of my favourite places to visit – the very end of the heel of Italy. If you're only used to the UK's roads, driving there is a whole different kettle of fish. Or 'un altro paio di maniche' (another pair of sleeves), as it should be.

These are the idyllic images you might have :

- Empty roads with great views.
- Timeless pastoral scenes.
- Village locals wandering down the middle of the street.
- Driving down to empty beaches for a swim before breakfast (only if you're really keen).

But the reality's a lot different. It's not that the Southern Italians are any better or worse drivers than we are. But there are different laws, different conventions, different road conditions and different driving styles.

5/06/2016 07:05:10 LS300W   ******* Timeless pastoral scenes

2016 08:54:36 LS300W   ** Wandering down middle of street

15/06/2016 07:01:38 LS300W   *******   Empty beaches

So here is my survival guide. Of course, this is only one small region of Europe. But I'm sure that wherever you're driving, some of this may ring bells – and perhaps even be useful.

Here are my Top 10 Tips from last year's holiday, illustrated with real-time dashcam video...

1 Being overtaken

Overtaking is more national sport on the [roa]t than it is in the [UK. It]s disconcerting [... t]hat the [...]car pulls in so [...]overtaking. [...]f getting [...]s generally [... d]angerous

13/06/2016 08:43:35 LS300W   *******

2 Tailgating

It's probably no worse than in the UK; but tailgating can still be intimidating and distracting. If you feel threatened, try to pull off the road if it's safe to do it. Or try my favourite ploy – go round a roundabout twice to escape your tailgater.

3 Motorway Slip Roads

Beware short slip roads on to motorways. They give merging motorists little chance to join the traffic at anything other than a snail's pace, leading them into narrow lanes of fast traffic. Not for the faint-hearted. Check your mirror as often as you can.

4 Oncoming traffic driving on your side of the road

On narrow country roads, this is a hazard everywhere. It's probably worse in the UK than it is in Southern Italy. But, as the picture shows, it can produce some heart-stopping moments.

5 Pulling out of side roads and hoping

Pulling out of side roads and hoping. A lot of this goes on at crossroads in small towns and villages. Given the configuration of the roads, there's not much you can do about it – except be very cautious, even when it's your right of way or, as here, the traffic lights only work at certain times of day

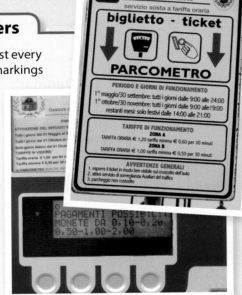

6 Petrol stations

Many country petrol stations are unmanned. Those that are manned sometimes charge you more for the privilege of having someone serve you. It may be worth it: the unmanned ones are not easy to operate. In a richly comic episode, I had to seek assistance to discover that I had paid for €40 of petrol at a pump some distance from the one at which my car was parked.

7 Parking Meters

In this region, almost every town has the blue road markings which indicate that, if you want to park here, you'll need to buy a ticket. You'll need coins – many don't accept notes or credit cards. No change is given. If you're lucky, as you put the coins in, the expiry time is shown. If you're unlucky, this panel will be dirty or scratched so that you can't read it. The times you need to pay for vary from town to town, depending on the time of year (always in the tourist season) and the time of day (siesta time is sometimes not charged). A crash course in the language is recommended. In 11 days, I spent over €65 on meters.

8 Sat Nav – beware of speed limits

Even though I'm an atlas publisher, I would strongly recommend you take a sat nav – as well as this atlas, of course. It really reduces the stress of navigating on unfamiliar roads (it's not so good for route planning). But beware if your sat nav tells you the speed limit – those on the screen seem to bear little resemblance to the signs at the side of the road.

9 Speed limits Part 2

Even relying on the roadside signs, it can be hard to work out the speed limits. Can you work out what's happening here (answer at the foot of the page)?

10 Cameras

These pictures cost me €200. They show me at the wheel of my stylish Fiat 500 (that's what the website said anyway) being distracted by two cyclists as they went through a red light. The red light is hidden in the hedge. This deserted spot in the middle of the countryside boasts the only traffic camera ever seen in the region. I stupidly had my eye on the cyclists, not the light. First I received a bill from Hertz for €47.90 – which I innocently thought was for the 'offence'. But no, it was for supplying my name and address (with almost every word misspelt) to the local authority. A year later, a bill arrived from said local authority, for €145 if paid within 5 days (or €220 if not).

And I haven't even got to that most thrilling part of your holiday 'At the Car Hire Desk' (damage waiver rip-off's, not getting the car you ordered, should you photograph the car, and is it worth having another driver), documentation (the code you have to get now from the DVLA if you're hiring a car) and taking a spare pair of glasses. And do watch how much you drink. See the next section for all the rules and regulations for each country, including the alcohol limits. If in doubt, don't drink and drive. Now turn over and read the driving laws of the country you're going to. Buon Viaggio.

Answer to point 9: the speed limit is normally 90kph but it's 50kph when it's foggy or visibility is less than 100m.

Driving regulations

Vehicle

A national vehicle identification plate is always required when taking a vehicle abroad.

Fitting headlamp converters or beam deflectors when taking a right-hand drive car to a country where driving is on the right (every country in Europe except the UK and Ireland) is compulsory.

Within the EU, if not driving a locally hired car, it is compulsory to have either Europlates or a country of origin (eg GB) sticker. Outside the EU (and in Andorra) a sticker is compulsory, even with Europlates.

Documentation

All countries require that you carry a valid passport, vehicle registration document, hire certificate or letter of authority for the use of someone else's vehicle, full driving licence/International Driving Permit and insurance documentation (and/or green card outside the EU). Some non-EU countries also require a visa. Minimum driving ages are often higher for people holding foreign licences. New exit checks at the Eurotunnel and ferry terminals mean that drivers taking vehicles from the UK should allow extra time. Drivers of vehicles over three years old should ensure that the MOT is up to date and take the certificate with them.

EHIC cards are free and give you entitlement to healthcare in other EU countries and Switzerland. *www.gov/european-health-insurance-card.*

Licence

A photo licence is preferred; with an old-style paper licence, an International Driving Permit (IDP) should also be carried. In some countries, an IDP is compulsory, whatever form of licence is held. Non-EU drivers should always have both a licence and and IDP. UK (except NI) drivers should check in advance whether a hire company will wish to check for endorsements and vehicle categories. If so, visit *https://www.gov.uk/view-driving-licence* to create a digital code (valid for 72 hours) that allows their details to be shared. For more information, contact the DVLA (0300 790 6802, *www.dft.gov.uk/dvla*).

Insurance

Third-party cover is compulsory across Europe. Most insurance policies give only basic cover when driving abroad, so you should check that your policy provides at least third-party cover for the countries in which you will be driving and upgrade it to the level that you require. You may be forced to take out extra cover at the frontier if you cannot produce acceptable proof that you have adequate insurance. Even in countries in which a green card is not required, carrying one is recommended for extra proof of insurance.

Motorcycles

It is compulsory for all motorcyclists and passengers to wear crash helmets. In France it may become compulsory for all motorcyclists and passengers to wear a minimum amount of reflective gear.

Other

In countries in which visibility vests are compulsory one for each person should be carried in the passenger compartment, or panniers on a motorbike, where they can be reached easily.

Warning triangles should also be carried in the passenger compartment.

The penalties for infringements of regulations vary considerably from one country to another. In many countries the police have the right to impose on-the-spot fines (ask for a receipt). Penalties can be severe for serious infringements, particularly for exceeding the blood-alcohol limit; in some countries this can result in immediate imprisonment.

In some countries, vignettes for toll roads are being replaced by electronic tags. See country details.

Please note that driving regulations often change, and that it has not been possible to cover all the information for every type of vehicle. The figures given for capitals' populations are for the whole metropolitan area.

The symbols used are:

- 🛣 Motorway
- ⚠ Dual carriageway
- ⚠ Single carriageway
- 🚗 Surfaced road
- 🚙 Unsurfaced or gravel road
- 🏙 Urban area
- ⏱ Speed limit in kilometres per hour (kph). These are the maximum speeds for the types of roads listed. In some places and under certain conditions they may be considerably lower. Always obey local signs.

🦺 Seat belts	🛂 Additional documents required
🧒 Children	📱 Mobile phones
🍷 Blood alcohol level	LEZ Low Emission Zone
△ Warning triangle	🔦 Dipped headlights
⊞ First aid kit	❄ Winter driving
🔧 Spare bulb kit	★ Other information
🧯 Fire extinguisher	
⊖ Minimum driving age	

The publishers have made every effort to ensure that the information given here was correct at the time of going to press. No responsibility can be accepted for any errors or their consequences.

Andorra Principat d'Andorra AND

Area 468 sq km (181 sq miles)
Population 85,500 **Capital** Andorra la Vella (44,000)
Languages Catalan (official), French, Castilian and Portuguese
Currency Euro = 100 cents
Website http://visitandorra.com

⏱	🛣	⚠	⚠	🏙
	n/a	90	60/90	50

- 🦺 Compulsory
- 🧒 Under 10 and below 150 cm must travel in an EU-approved restraint system adapted to their size in the rear. Airbag must be deactivated if a child is in the front passenger seat.
- 🍷 0.05%
- △ Compulsory
- ⊞ Recommended
- 🔧 Compulsory
- 🧯 Recommended
- ⊖ 18
- 📱 Not permitted whilst driving
- 🔦 Compulsory for motorcycles during day and for other vehicles during poor daytime visibility.
- ❄ Winter tyres recommended. Snow chains compulsory in poor conditions or when indicated.
- ★ On-the-spot fines imposed
- ★ Visibility vests compulsory

Austria Österreich A

Area 83,859 sq km (32,377 sq miles)
Population 8,794,000
Capital Vienna / Wien (1,868,000)
Languages German (official)
Currency Euro = 100 cents
Website www.bka.gv.at

⏱	🛣	⚠	⚠	🏙
	130	100	100	50

If towing trailer under 750kg / over 750 kg

⏱				
	100	100	100/80	50

- 🦺 Compulsory
- 🧒 Under 14 and under 150cm cannot travel as a front or rear passenger unless they use a suitable child restraint; under 14 over 150cm must wear adult seat belt
- 🍷 0.049% • 0.01% if licence held less than 2 years
- △ Compulsory
- ⊞ Compulsory
- 🔧 Recommended
- 🧯 Recommended
- ⊖ 18 (20 for motorbikes over 50cc)
- 📱 Only allowed with hands-free kit
- LEZ Several cities and regions have LEZs affecting HGVs that ban non-compliant vehicles, impose speed restrictions and night-time bans.
- 🔦 Must be used during the day by all road users. Headlamp converters compulsory
- ❄ Winter tyres compulsory 1 Nov–15 Apr
- ★ On-the-spot fines imposed
- ★ Radar detectors and dashcams prohibited
- ★ To drive on motorways or expressways, a motorway sticker must be purchased at the border or main petrol station. These are available for 10 days, 2 months or 1 year. Vehicles 3.5 tonnes or over must display an electronic tag.
- ★ Visibility vests compulsory

Belarus BY

Area 207,600 sq km (80,154 sq miles)
Population 9,499,000
Capital Minsk (2,101,000)
Languages Belarusian, Russian (both official)
Currency Belarusian ruble = 100 kopek
Website www.belarus.by/en/government

⏱	🛣	⚠	⚠	🏙
	110	90	90	60*

If towing trailer under 750kg

⏱			
	90	70	70

*In residential areas limit is 20 km/h • Vehicle towing another vehicle 50 kph limit • If full driving licence held for less than two years, must not exceed 70 kph

- 🦺 Compulsory in front seats, and rear seats if fitted
- 🧒 Under 12 not allowed in front seat and must use appropriate child restraint
- 🍷 0.00%
- △ Compulsory
- ⊞ Compulsory
- 🔧 Recommended
- 🧯 Compulsory
- ⊖ 18
- 🛂 Visa, vehicle technical check stamp, international driving permit, green card, health insurance. Even with a green card, local third-party insurance may be imposed at the border
- 📱 Use prohibited
- 🔦 Compulsory during the day Nov–Mar and at all other times in conditions of poor visibility or when towing or being towed.
- ❄ Winter tyres compulsory; snow chains recommended
- ★ A temporary vehicle import certificate must be purchased on entry and driver must be registered
- ★ It is illegal for vehicles to be dirty
- ★ On-the-spot fines imposed
- ★ Radar-detectors prohibited
- ★ Road tax imposed at the border
- ★ To drive on main motorways and on-board unit must be acquired at the border or a petrol station in order to pay tolls. See **www.beltoll.by/index.php/en**

Belgium Belgique B

Area 30,528 sq km (11,786 sq miles)
Population 11,251,000 **Capital** Brussels/Bruxelles (1,175,000) **Languages** Dutch, French, German (all official)
Currency Euro = 100 cents **Website** www.belgium.be/en

⏱	🛣	⚠	⚠	🏙
	120[1]	120[1]	90[2]	50[3]

If towing trailer

⏱				
	90	90	60	50[3]

Over 3.5 tonnes

⏱				
	90	90	60	50

[1]Minimum speed of 70 kph may be applied in certain conditions on motorways and some dual carriageways.
[2]70 kph in Flanders. [3]20 kph in some residential areas, 30 kph near some schools, hospitals and churches.

- 🦺 Compulsory
- 🧒 All under 18s under 135 cm must wear an appropriate child restraint. Airbags must be deactivated if a rear-facing child seat is used in the front
- 🍷 0.049% △ Compulsory
- ⊞ Recommended 🔧 Recommended
- 🧯 Compulsory ⊖ 18
- 👕 Motorcyclists must wear fully protective clothing
- 📱 Only allowed with a hands-free kit
- LEZ LEZs in operation in Antwerp, Brussels and areas of Flanders. Preregistration necessary and fees payable for most vehicles.
- 🔦 Mandatory at all times for motorcycles and advised during the day in poor conditions for other vehicles
- ★ Cruise control must be deactivated on motorways where indicated
- ★ On-the-spot fines imposed
- ★ Radar detectors prohibited
- ★ Sticker indicating maximum recommended speed for winter tyres must be displayed on dashboard if using them
- ★ Visibility vest compulsory

Bosnia & Herzegovina

Bosna i Hercegovina BIH

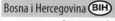

Area 51,197 km² (19,767 mi²) **Population** 3,872,000
Capital Sarajevo (643,000)
Languages Bosnian/Croatian/Serbian
Currency Convertible Marka = 100 convertible pfenniga
Website www.fbihvlada.gov.ba/english/index.php

⏱	🛣	⚠	⚠	🏙
	130	100	80	50

- 🦺 Compulsory if fitted
- 🧒 Under 12s must sit in rear using an appropriate child restraint. Under-2s may travel in a rear-facing child seat in the front only if the airbags have been deactivated.
- 🍷 0.03% △ Compulsory ⊞ Compulsory
- 🔧 Compulsory 🧯 Compulsory for LPG vehicles ⊖ 18
- 🛂 Visa, International Driving Permit, green card
- 📱 Prohibited 🔦 Compulsory for all vehicles at all times
- ❄ Winter tyres compulsory 15 Nov–15 Apr; snow chains recommended
- ★ GPS must have fixed speed camera function deactivated; radar detectors prohibited.
- ★ On-the-spot fines imposed
- ★ Visibility vest, tow rope or tow bar compulsory
- ★ Spare wheel compulsory, except for two-wheeled vehicles

Bulgaria Bulgariya BG

Area 110,912 sq km (42,822 sq miles)
Population 7,102,000 **Capital** Sofia (1,682,000)
Languages Bulgarian (official), Turkish
Currency Lev = 100 stotinki
Website www.government.bg

⏱	🛣	⚠	⚠	🏙
	130	90	90	50

If towing trailer

⏱				
	100	70	70	50

- 🦺 Compulsory in front and rear seats
- 🧒 Under 3s not permitted in vehicles with no child restraints; 3–10 year olds must sit in rear in an appropriate restraint. Rear-facing child seats may be used in the front only if the airbag has been deactivated
- 🍷 0.049% △ Compulsory ⊞ Compulsory
- 🔧 Recommended 🧯 Compulsory ⊖ 18
- 🛂 Photo driving licence preferred; a paper licence must be accompanied by an International Driving Permit. Green card or insurance specific to Bulgaria.
- 📱 Only allowed with a hands-free kit 🔦 Compulsory
- ❄ Winter tyres compulsory. Snow chains should be carried 1 Nov–1 Mar. Max speed with chains 50 kph
- ★ Fee at border ★ On-the-spot fines imposed
- ★ GPS must have fixed speed camera function deactivated; radar detectors prohibited
- ★ Road tax stickers (annual, monthly or weekly) must be purchased at the border and displayed prominently with the vehicle registration number written on them.
- ★ Visibility vest compulsory

Croatia Hrvatska HR

Area 56,538 km² (21,829 mi²)
Population 4,191,000 **Capital** Zagreb (1,113,000)
Languages Croatian **Currency** Kuna = 100 lipa
Website https://vlada.gov.hr/en

⏱	🛣	⚠	⚠	🏙
	130	110	90	50

Under 24

⏱				
	120	100	80	50

If towing

⏱				
	90	90	80	50

Czechia Česko CZ

Area 78,864 sq km (30,449 sq miles)
Population 10,554,000 **Capital** Prague/Praha (2,157,000)
Languages Czech (official), Moravian
Currency Czech Koruna = 100 haler
Website www.vlada.cz/en/

⏱	🛣	⚠	⚠	🏙
	130	90	90	50

If towing

⏱				
	80	80	80	50

- 🦺 Compulsory in front seats and, if fitted, in rear
- 🧒 Children under 36 kg and 150 cm must use appropriate child restraint. Only front-facing child retrains are permitted in the front in vehicles with airbags fitted. Airbags must be deactivated if a rear-facing child seat is used in the front.
- 🍷 0.00% △ Compulsory ⊞ Compulsory
- 🔧 Compulsory 🧯 Compulsory
- ⊖ 18 (17 for motorcycles under 125 cc)
- 📱 Only allowed with a hands-free kit
- LEZ Two-stage LEZ in Prague for vehicles over 3.5 and 6 tonnes. Permit system.
- 🔦 Compulsory at all times
- ❄ Winter tyres compulsory Nov–Mar, roads are icy/snow-covered or snow is expected. Max speed 50 kph.
- ★ GPS must have fixed speed camera function deactivated; radar detectors prohibited
- ★ On-the-spot fines imposed
- ★ Replacement fuses must be carried
- ★ Spectacles or contact lens wearers must carry a spare pair in their vehicle at all times
- ★ Vignette needed for motorway driving, available for 1 year, 60 days, 15 days. Toll for lorries introduced 2006: those over 12 tonnes must buy an electronic tag
- ★ Visibility vest compulsory

Denmark Danmark DK

Area 43,094 sq km (16,638 sq miles)
Population 5,749,000 **Languages** Danish (official)
Capital Copenhagen / København (2,037,000)
Currency Krone = 100 øre **Website** www.denmark.dk/en

⏱	🛣	⚠	⚠	🏙
	110-130	80-90	80	50*

If towing

⏱				
	80	70	70	50*

*Central Copenhagen 40 kph

- 🦺 Compulsory front and rear
- 🧒 Under 135cm must use appropriate child restraint; in front permitted only in an appropriate rear-facing seat with any airbags disabled.
- 🍷 0.05% △ Compulsory ⊞ Recommended
- 🔧 Recommended 🧯 Recommended ⊖ 17
- 📱 Only allowed with a hands-free kit
- LEZ Aalborg, Arhus, Copenhagen, Frederiksberg and Odense. Proofs of emissions compliance or compliant filter needed to obtain sticker. Non-compliant vehicles banned.
- 🔦 Must be used at all times
- ❄ Spiked tyres may be fitted 1 Nov–15 Apr, if on all wheels
- ★ On-the-spot fines imposed
- ★ Radar detectors prohibited
- ★ Tolls on Storebaeltsbroen and Oresundsbron bridges.
- ★ Visibility vest recommended

Estonia Eesti EST

Area 45,100 sq km (17,413 sq miles)
Population 1,316,000 **Capital** Tallinn (543,000)
Languages Estonian (official), Russian
Currency Euro = 100 cents **Website** www.valitsus.ee

⏱	🛣	⚠	⚠	🏙
	n/a	90*	90	50

If full driving licence held for less than two years

⏱				
	90	90	90	50

*In summer, the speed limit on some dual carriageways may be raised to 100/110 kph

- 🦺 Compulsory if fitted
- 🧒 Children too small for adult seatbelts must wear a seat restraint appropriate to their size. Rear-facing safety seats must not be used in the front if an air bag is fitted, unless this has been deactivated.
- 🍷 0.00% △ 2 compulsory ⊞ Compulsory
- 🔧 Recommended 🧯 Compulsory ⊖ 18
- 📱 Only allowed with a hands-free kit
- 🔦 Compulsory at all times
- ❄ Winter tyres are compulsory from Dec–Mar. Studded winter tyres are allowed from 15 Oct–31 Mar, but this can be extended to start 1 October and/or end 30 April
- ★ A toll system is in operation in Tallinn
- ★ On-the-spot fines imposed
- ★ Two wheel chocks compulsory
- ★ Visibility vest compulsory

Finland Suomi (FIN)

Area 338,145 sq km (130,557 sq miles)
Population 5,506,000 **Capital** Helsinki (1,442,000)
Languages Finnish, Swedish (both official)
Currency Euro = 100 cents
Website http://valtioneuvosto.fi/en/frontpage

	🛣	⩓	▲	🏘
⏲	120	100	80/100*	20/50
Vans, lorries and if towing				
⏲	80	80	60	20/50

*100 in summer • If towing a vehicle by rope, cable or rod, max speed limit 60 kph • Maximum of 80 kph for vans and lorries • Speed limits are often lowered in winter

◈ Compulsory in front and rear
☻ Below 135 cm must use a child restraint or seat
🍸 0.05% △ Compulsory ⊞ Recommended
💡 Recommended 🧯 Recommended
⊖ 18 (motorbikes below 125cc 16)
📱 Only allowed with hands-free kit
🔦 Must be used at all times
❄ Winter tyres compulsory Dec–Feb
★ On-the-spot fines imposed
★ Radar-detectors are prohibited
★ Visibility vest compulsory

France (F)

Area 551,500 sq km (212,934 sq miles)
Population 66,991,000 **Capital** Paris (12,405,000)
Languages French (official), Breton, Occitan
Currency Euro = 100 cents
Website www.diplomatie.gouv.fr/en/

	🛣	⩓	▲	🏘
⏲	130	110	90	50
On wet roads or if full driving licence held for less than 3 years				
⏲	110	100	80	50
If towing below / above 3.5 tonnes gross				
⏲	110/90	100/90	90/80	50

50kph on all roads if fog reduces visibility to less than 50m • Licence will be lost and driver fined for exceeding speed limit by over 50kph

◈ Compulsory in front seats and, if fitted, in rear
☻ In rear, 4 or under must have a child safety seat (rear facing if up to 9 months); if 5–10 must use an appropriate restraint system. Under 10 permitted in the front only if rear seats are fully occupied by other under 10s or there are no rear safety belts. In front, if child is in rear-facing child seat, any airbag must be deactivated.
🍸 0.049% • If towing or with less than 2 years with full driving licence, 0.00% • All drivers/motorcyclists must carry an unused breathalyser to French certification standards, showing an NF number.
△ Compulsory ⊞ Recommended
💡 Recommended ⊖ 18 (16 for motorbikes up to 80cc)
📱 Use not permitted whilst driving
LEZ An LEZ operates in the Mont Blanc tunnel and such zones are being progressively introduced across French cities. Non-compliant vehicles are banned during operating hours. See http://certificat-air.gouv.fr
🔦 Compulsory in poor daytime visibility and at all times for motorcycles
❄ Winter tyres recommended. Carrying snow chains recommended in winter as these may have to be fitted if driving on snow-covered roads, in accordance with signage.
★ GPS must have fixed speed camera function deactivated; radar-detection equipment is prohibited
★ It is compulsory to carry a French-authority-recognised (NF) breathalyser.
★ Motorcyclists and passengers must have four reflective stickers on their helmets (front, back and both sides) and wear CE-certified gloves.
★ On-the-spot fines imposed
★ Tolls on motorways. Electronic tag needed if using automatic tolls.
★ Visibility vests, to be worn on the roadside in case of emergency or breakdown, must be carried for all vehicle occupants and riders.
★ Wearers of contact lenses or spectacles or lenses should carry a spare pair

Germany Deutschland (D)

Area 357,022 sq km (137,846 sq miles)
Population 82,176,000
Capital Berlin (6,005,000) **Languages** German (official)
Currency Euro = 100 cents
Website www.bundesregierung.de

	🛣	⩓	▲	🏘
⏲	*	*	100	50
If towing				
⏲	80	80	80	50

*no limit, 130 kph recommended

◈ Compulsory
☻ Aged 3-12 and under 150cm must use an appropriate child seat or restraint and sit in the rear. In the front, if child under 3 is in a rear-facing seat, airbags must be deactivated
🍸 0.049% • 0.0% for drivers 21 or under or with less than two years full licence △ Compulsory ⊞ Compulsory
💡 Recommended 🧯 Recommended
⊖ 18 (motorbikes: 16 if under 50cc)
📱 Use permitted only with hands-free kit – also applies to drivers of motorbikes and bicycles
LEZ More than 60 cities have or are planning LEZs. Proof of compliance needed to acquire sticker. Non-compliant vehicles banned.
🔦 Compulsory during poor daytime visibility and tunnels; recommended at other times. Compulsory at all times for motorcyclists.
❄ Winter tyres compulsory in all winter weather conditions; snow chains recommended
★ GPS must have fixed speed camera function deactivated; radar detectors prohibited
★ On-the-spot fines imposed
★ Tolls on autobahns for lorries
★ Visibility vest compulsory

Greece Ellas (GR)

Area 131,957 sq km (50,948 sq miles)
Population 10,955,000
Capital Athens / Athina (4,174,000)
Languages Greek (official)
Currency Euro = 100 cents
Website www.primeminister.gr/english

	🛣	⩓	▲	🏘
⏲	130	110	90	50
Motorbikes, and if towing				
⏲	90	70	70	40

◈ Compulsory in front seats and, if fitted, in rear
☻ Under 12 or below 135cm must use appropriate child restraint. In front if child is in rear-facing child seat, any airbags must be deactivated.
🍸 0.05% • 0.00% for drivers with less than 2 years' full licence and motorcyclists
△ Compulsory ⊞ Compulsory
💡 Recommended 🧯 Compulsory
⊖ 17
📱 Not permitted.
🔦 Compulsory during poor daytime visibility and at all times for motorcycles
❄ Snow chains permitted on ice- or snow-covered roads. Max speed 50 kph.
★ On-the-spot fines imposed
★ Radar-detection equipment is prohibited
★ Tolls on several newer motorways.

Hungary Magyarország (H)

Area 93,032 sq km (35,919 sq miles)
Population 9,798,000
Capital Budapest (3,304,000)
Languages Hungarian (official)
Currency Forint = 100 filler
Website www.kormany.hu/en

	🛣	⩓	▲	🏘
⏲	130	110	90	50*
If towing				
⏲	80	70	70	50*

*30 kph zones have been introduced in many cities

◈ Compulsory
☻ Under 135cm and over 3 must be seated in rear and use appropriate child restraint. Under 3 allowed in front only in rear-facing child seat with any airbags deactivated.
🍸 0.00% △ Compulsory ⊞ Compulsory
💡 Compulsory 🧯 Recommended ⊖ 17
📱 Only allowed with a hands-free kit
LEZ Budapest has vehicle restrictions on days with heavy dust and is planning an LEZ.
🔦 Compulsory during the day outside built-up areas; compulsory at all times for motorcycles
❄ Snow chains compulsory where conditions dictate. Max speed 50 kph.
★ Many motorways are toll and operate electronic vignette system with automatic number plate recognition, tickets are available for 10 days, 1 month, 13 months
★ On-the-spot fines issued
★ Radar detectors prohibited
★ Tow rope recommended
★ Visibility vest compulsory

Iceland Ísland (IS)

Area 103,000 sq km (39,768 sq miles)
Population 333,000
Capital Reykjavík (210,000)
Languages Icelandic
Currency Krona = 100 aurar
Website www.government.is/

	🛣	🚗	🚙	🏘
⏲	n/a	90	80	50

◈ Compulsory in front and rear seats
☻ Under 12 or below 150cm not allowed in front seat and must use appropriate child restraint.
🍸 0.05% △ Compulsory ⊞ Compulsory
💡 Compulsory 🧯 Compulsory
⊖ 17; 21 to drive a hire car; 25 to hire a jeep
📱 Only allowed with a hands-free kit
🔦 Compulsory at all times
❄ Winter tyres compulsory c.1 Nov–14 Apr (variable)
★ Driving off marked roads is forbidden
★ Highland roads are not suitable for ordinary cars
★ On-the-spot fines imposed

Ireland Eire (IRL)

Area 70,273 sq km (27,132 sq miles)
Population 4,762,000
Capital Dublin (1,905,000)
Languages Irish, English (both official)
Currency Euro = 100 cents
Website www.gov.ie/en/

	🛣	⩓	▲	🏘
⏲	120	60–100	60–100	50*
If towing				
⏲	80	60	60	50*

*Dublin and some other areas have introduced 30 kph zones

◈ Compulsory where fitted. Driver responsible for ensuring passengers under 17 comply
☻ Children 3 and under must be in a suitable child restraint system. Airbags must be deactivated if a rear-facing child seat is used in the front. Those under 150 cm and 36 kg must use appropriate child restraint.
🍸 0.05% • 0.02% for novice and professional drivers
△ Compulsory
⊞ Recommended
💡 Recommended
🧯 Recommended
⊖ 17 (16 for motorbikes up to 125cc; 18 for over 125cc; 18 for lorries; 21 bus/minibus)
📱 Only allowed with a hands-free kit
🔦 Compulsory for motorbikes at all times and in poor visibility for other vehicles
★ Driving is on the left
★ GPS must have fixed speed camera function deactivated; radar detectors prohibited
★ On-the-spot fines imposed
★ Tolls are being introduced on some motorways; the M50 Dublin has barrier-free tolling with number-plate recognition.

Italy Italia (I)

Area 301,318 sq km (116,338 sq miles)
Population 60,600,000 **Capital** Rome / Roma (4,356,000)
Languages Italian (official) **Currency** Euro = 100 cents
Website www.italia.it

	🛣	⩓	▲	🏘
⏲	130	110	90	50
If towing				
⏲	80	70	70	50
Less than three years with full licence				
⏲	100	90	90	50
When wet				
⏲	110	90	80	50

Some motorways with emergency lanes have speed limit of 150 kph

◈ Compulsory in front seats and, if fitted, in rear
☻ Under 12 not allowed in front seats except in child safety seat; children under 3 must have special seat in the back. For foreign-registered cars, the country of origin's legislation applies.
🍸 0.05% • 0.00% for professional drivers or with less than 3 years full licence
△ Compulsory
⊞ Recommended
💡 Compulsory
🧯 Recommended
⊖ 18 (14 for mopeds, 16 up to 125cc, 20 up to 350cc)
📱 Only allowed with hands-free kit
LEZ Most northern and several southern regions operate seasonal LEZs and many towns and cities have various schemes that restrict access. There is an LEZ in the Mont Blanc tunnel
🔦 Compulsory outside built-up areas, in tunnels, on motorways and dual carriageways and in poor visibility; compulsory at all times for motorcycles
❄ Snow chains compulsory where signs indicate 15 Oct–15 Apr. Max speed 50 kph
★ On-the-spot fines imposed
★ Radar-detection equipment is prohibited
★ Tolls on motorways. Blue lanes accept credit cards; yellow lanes restricted to holders of Telepass pay-toll device.
★ Visibility vest compulsory

Kosovo Republika e Kosoves / Republika Kosovo (RKS)

Area 10,887 sq km (4203 sq miles)
Population 1,908,000 **Capital** Pristina (504,000)
Languages Albanian, Serbian (both official), Bosnian, Turkish, Roma
Currency Euro (Serbian dinar in Serb enclaves)
Website www.kryeministri-ks.net/?page=2,1

	🛣	⩓	▲	🏘
⏲	130	80	80	50

◈ Compulsory
☻ Under 12 must sit in rear seats in an appropriate restraint.
🍸 0.00%
△ Compulsory
⊞ Compulsory
💡 Compulsory
🧯 Compulsory
⊖ 18 (16 for motorbikes less than 125 cc, 14 for mopeds)
🪪 International driving permit, locally purchased third-party insurance (green card is not recognised), documents with proof of ability to cover costs and valid reason for visiting. Visitors from many non-EU countries require a visa.
📱 Only allowed with a hands-free kit
🔦 Compulsory at all times
❄ Winter tyres or snow chains compulsory in poor winter weather conditions

Latvia Latvija (LV)

Area 64,589 sq km (24,942 sq miles)
Population 1,953,000 **Capital** Riga (1,018,000)
Languages Latvian (official), Russian
Currency Euro = 100 cents **Website** www.mk.gov.lv/en

	🛣	⩓	▲	🏘
⏲	n/a	100	90	50
If towing				
⏲	n/a	80	80	50

In residential areas limit is 20kph • If full driving licence held for less than two years, must not exceed 80 kph

◈ Compulsory in front seats and if fitted in rear
☻ If under 12 years and 150cm must use child restraint in front and rear seats
🍸 0.05% • 0.02% with less than 2 years experience
△ Compulsory ⊞ Compulsory
💡 Recommended 🧯 Compulsory ⊖ 18
📱 Only allowed with hands-free kit
🔦 Must be used at all times all year round
❄ Winter tyres compulsory for vehicles up to 3.5 tonnes Dec–Feb, but illegal May–Sept
★ On-the-spot fines imposed
★ Pedestrians have priority
★ Radar-detection equipment prohibited
★ Visibility vests compulsory

Lithuania Lietuva (LT)

Area 65,200 sq km (25,173 sq miles)
Population 2,822,000 **Capital** Vilnius (805,000)
Languages Lithuanian (official), Russian, Polish
Currency Euro = 100 cents **Website** http://lrvk.lrv.lt/en

	🛣	⩓	▲	🏘
⏲	130	110	70–90	50
If towing				
⏲	n/a	70	70	50
If licence held for less than two years				
⏲	130	90	70	50

In winter speed limits are reduced by 10–20 km/h

◈ Compulsory
☻ Under 12 or below 135 cm not allowed in front seats unless in a child safety seat; under 3 must use appropriate child seat and sit in rear
🍸 0.04% • 0.00% if full licence held less than 2 years
△ Compulsory ⊞ Compulsory
💡 Recommended 🧯 Compulsory ⊖ 18
🪪 Licences without a photograph must be accompanied by photographic proof of identity, e.g. a passport
📱 Only allowed with a hands-free kit
🔦 Must be used at all times
❄ Winter tyres compulsory 10 Nov–1 Apr
★ On-the-spot fines imposed
★ Visibility vest compulsory

Luxembourg (L)

Area 2,586 sq km (998 sq miles)
Population 576,000 **Capital** Luxembourg (107,000)
Languages Luxembourgian / Letzeburgish (official), French, German **Currency** Euro = 100 cents
Website www.luxembourg.public.lu/en/

	🛣	⩓	▲	🏘
⏲	130/110	90	90	50*
If towing				
⏲	90	75	75	50*

If full driving licence held for less than two years, must not exceed 75 kph • *30 kph zones are progressively being introduced.

◈ Compulsory
☻ Children under 3 must use an appropriate restraint system. Airbags must be disabled if a rear-facing child seat is used in the front. Children 3–18 and/or under 150 cm must use a restraint system appropriate to their size. If over 36kg a seatbelt may be used in the back only
🍸 0.05%, 0.02 for young drivers, drivers with less than 2 years experience and drivers of taxis and commercial vehicles
△ Compulsory ⊞ Compulsory (buses)
💡 Compulsory ⊖ 18
🧯 Compulsory (buses, transport of dangerous goods)
📱 Use permitted only with hands-free kit
🔦 Compulsory for motorcyclists and in poor visibility for other vehicles
❄ Winter tyres compulsory in winter weather
★ On-the-spot fines imposed
★ Visibility vest compulsory

Macedonia Makedonija (MK)

Area 25,713 sq km (9,927 sq miles)
Population 2,074,000 **Capital** Skopje (507,000)
Languages Macedonian (official), Albanian
Currency Denar = 100 deni **Website**

	🛣	⩓	▲	🏘
⏲	120	100	80	50
Newly qualified drivers or if towing				
⏲	100	80	60	50

◈ Compulsory
☻ Under 12 not allowed in front seats
🍸 0.05% • 0.00% for business, commercial and professional drivers and with less than 2 years experience
△ Compulsory ⊞ Compulsory
💡 Compulsory ⊖ 18 (mopeds 16)
🧯 Recommended; compulsory for LPG vehicles
🪪 International driving permit; visa
📱 Use not permitted whilst driving
🔦 Compulsory at all times
❄ Winter tyres or snow chains compulsory 15 Nov–15 Mar. Max speed 70 kph
★ GPS must have fixed speed camera function deactivated; radar detectors prohibited
★ Novice drivers may only drive between 11pm and 5am if there is someone over 25 with a valid licence in the vehicle.
★ On-the-spot fines imposed
★ Tolls apply on many roads
★ Tow rope compulsory
★ Visibility vest must be kept in the passenger compartment and worn to leave the vehicle in the dark outside built-up areas

Moldova (MD)

Area 33,851 sq km (13,069 sq miles)
Population 299,000 **Capital** Chisinau (736,000)
Languages Moldovan / Romanian (official)
Currency Leu = 100 bani **Website** www.moldova.md

⊙	90	90	90	60
If towing or if licence held under 1 year				
⊙	70	70	70	60

- Compulsory in front seats and, if fitted, in rear seats
- Under 12 not allowed in front seats
- 0.00% Compulsory Compulsory
- Recommended Compulsory
- 18 (mopeds and motorbikes, 16; vehicles with more than eight passenger places, taxis or towing heavy vehicles, 21)
- International Driving Permit (preferred), visa
- Only allowed with hands-free kit
- Must use dipped headlights at all times
- Winter tyres recommended Nov–Feb

Montenegro Crna Gora (MNE)

Area 14,026 sq km, (5,415 sq miles)
Population 679,000 **Capital** Podgorica (187,000)
Languages Serbian (of the ijekavian dialect)
Currency Euro = 100 cents
Website www.gov.me/en/homepage

⊙	n/a	100	80	50

80kph speed limit if towing a caravan

- Compulsory in front and rear seats
- Under 12 not allowed in front seats. Under-5s must use an appropriate child seat.
- 0.03 % Compulsory Compulsory
- Compulsory Compulsory
- 18 (16 for motorbikes less than 125cc; 14 for mopeds)
- Prohibited
- Must be used at all times
- From mid-Nov to March, driving wheels must be fitted with winter tyres
- ★ An 'eco' tax vignette must be obtained when crossing the border and displayed in the upper right-hand corner of the windscreen
- ★ On-the-spot fines imposed
- ★ Tolls on some primary roads and in the Sozina tunnel between Lake Skadar and the sea
- ★ Visibility vest compulsory

Netherlands Nederland (NL)

Area 41,526 sq km (16,033 sq miles)
Population 17,000,000
Capital Amsterdam 2,431,000 • administrative capital 's-Gravenhage (The Hague) 1,051,000
Languages Dutch (official), Frisian
Currency Euro = 100 cents **Website** www.government.nl

⊙	130	80/100	80/100	50

- Compulsory
- Under 3 must travel in the back, using an appropriate child restraint; 3–18 and under 135cm must use an appropriate child restraint. A rear-facing child seat may be used in front only if airbags are deactivated.
- 0.05% • 0.02% with less than 5 years experience or moped riders under 24
- Compulsory Recommended
- Recommended Recommended
- 18
- Only allowed with a hands-free kit
- LEZ About 20 cities operate or are planning LEZs.
- Recommended in poor visibility and on open roads. Compulsory for motorcycles.
- ★ On-the-spot fines imposed
- ★ Radar-detection equipment is prohibited

Norway Norge (N)

Area 323,877 sq km (125,049 sq miles)
Population 5,267,000 **Capital** Oslo (1,718,000)
Languages Norwegian (official), Lappish, Finnish
Currency Krone = 100 øre
Website www.norway.no/en/uk

⊙	90–100	80	80	30/50
If towing trailer with brakes				
⊙	80	80	80	50
If towing trailer without brakes				
⊙	60	60	60	50

- Compulsory in front seats and, if fitted, in rear
- Children less than 150cm tall must use appropriate child restraint. Children under 4 must use child safety seat or safety restraint (cot). A rear-facing child seat may be used in front only if airbags are deactivated.
- 0.01% Compulsory Recommended
- Recommended Recommended
- 18 (heavy vehicles 18/21)
- Only allowed with a hands-free kit
- LEZ Oslo and Bergen (administered through national road-toll scheme), with plans for other cities
- Must be used at all times
- Winter tyres or summer tyres with snow chains compulsory for snow- or ice-covered roads
- ★ On-the-spot fines imposed
- ★ Radar-detectors are prohibited
- ★ Tolls apply on some bridges, tunnels and access roads into Bergen, Oslo, Trondheim and Stavangar. Several use electronic fee collection only.
- ★ Visibility vest compulsory

Poland Polska (PL)

Area 323,250 sq km (124,807 sq miles)
Population 38,634,000 **Capital** Warsaw / Warszawa (3,106,000) **Languages** Polish (official)
Currency Zloty = 100 groszy
Website www.premier.gov.pl/en.html

Motor-vehicle only roads[1], under/over 3.5 tonnes				
⊙	130[2]/80[2]	110/80	100/80	n/a
Motor-vehicle only roads[1] if towing				
⊙	n/a	80	80	n/a
Other roads, under 3.5 tonnes				
⊙	n/a	100	90	50/60[3]
Other roads, 3.5 tonnes or over				
⊙	n/a	80	70	50/60[3]
Other roads, if towing				
⊙	n/a	60	60	30

[1]Indicated by signs with white car on blue background
[2]Minimum speed 40 kph • [3]50 kph 05.00–23.00; 60 kph 23.00–05.00; 20 kph in marked residential areas

- Compulsory in front seats and, if fitted, in rear
- Under 12 and below 150 cm must use an appropriate child restraint. Rear-facing child seats not permitted in vehicles with airbags.
- 0.02% Compulsory Recommended
- Recommended Compulsory
- 18 (mopeds and motorbikes under 125cc – 16)
- Only allowed with a hands-free kit
- Compulsory for all vehicles
- Snow chains permitted only on roads completely covered in snow
- ★ On-the-spot fines imposed
- ★ Radar-detection equipment is prohibited
- ★ Vehicles over 3.5 tonnes (including cars towing caravans) must have a VIAbox for the electronic toll system
- ★ Visibility vests compulsory

Portugal (P)

Area 88,797 sq km (34,284 sq miles)
Population 10,310,000 **Capital** Lisbon / Lisboa (2,822,000) **Languages** Portuguese (official)
Currency Euro = 100 cents
Website www.portugal.gov.pt/en.aspx

⊙	120*	90/100	90	50/20
If towing				
⊙	100*	90	80	50

*50kph minimum; 90kph maximum if licence held under 1 year

- Compulsory in front seats and, if fitted, in rear
- Under 12 and below 135cm must travel in the rear in an appropriate child restraint; rear-facing child seats permitted in front for under 3s only if airbags deactivated
- 0.049% • 0.019% if full licence held less than 3 years
- Compulsory Recommended
- Recommended Recommended 17
- MOT certificate for vehicles over 3 years old, photographic proof of ID must be carried at all times.
- Only allowed with hands-free kit
- LEZ An LEZ prohibits vehicles without catalytic converters from certain parts of Lisbon. There are plans to extend the scheme city-wide
- Compulsory for motorcycles, compulsory for other vehicles in poor visibility and tunnels
- ★ On-the-spot fines imposed
- ★ Radar detectors and dash-cams prohibited
- ★ Tolls on motorways; do not use green lanes, these are reserved for auto-payment users. Some motorways require an automatic toll device.
- ★ Visibility vest compulsory
- ★ Wearers of spectacles or contact lenses should carry a spare pair

Romania (RO)

Area 238,391 sq km (92,042 sq miles)
Population 19,511,000 **Capital** Bucharest / Bucuresti (2,403,000) **Languages** Romanian (official), Hungarian
Currency Romanian leu = 100 bani **Website** www.gov.ro

Cars and motorcycles				
⊙	120/130	100	90	50
Vans				
⊙	110	90	80	40
Motorcycles				
⊙	100	80	80	50

For motor vehicles with trailers or if full driving licence has been held for less than one year, speed limits are 20kph lower than those listed above • Jeep-like vehicles: 70kph outside built-up areas but 60kph in all areas if diesel. For mopeds, the speed limit is 45 kph.

- Compulsory
- Under 12s not allowed in front and must use an appropriate restraint in the rear
- 0.00% Compulsory Compulsory
- Compulsory Compulsory 18
- Only allowed with hands-free kit
- Compulsory outside built-up areas, compulsory everywhere for motorcycles
- Winter tyres compulsory Nov–Mar if roads are snow- or ice-covered, especially in mountainous areas
- ★ Compulsory road tax can be paid for at the border, post offices and some petrol stations. Price depends on emissions category and length of stay
- ★ It is illegal for vehicles to be dirty
- ★ On-the-spot fines imposed
- ★ Visibility vest compulsory

Russia Rossiya (RUS)

Area 17,075,000 sq km (6,592,800 sq miles)
Population 144,463,000 **Capital** Moscow / Moskva (17,100,000) **Languages** Russian (official), and many others
Currency Russian ruble = 100 kopeks
Website government.ru/en/

⊙	110	90	90	60/20
If licence held for under 2 years				
⊙	70	70	70	60/20

- Compulsory if fitted
- Under 12s permitted only in an appropriate child restraint
- 0.03 % Compulsory Compulsory
- Compulsory Compulsory 17
- International Driving Permit with Russian translation, visa, green card endorsed for Russia, International Certificate for Motor Vehicles
- Only allowed with a hands-free kit
- Compulsory during the day
- Winter tyres compulsory 1 Dec–1 Mar
- ★ On-the-spot fines imposed
- ★ Picking up hitchhikers is prohibited
- ★ Radar detectors/blockers prohibited
- ★ Road tax payable at the border

Serbia Srbija (SRB)

Capital Belgrade / Beograd (1,167,000)
Area 77,474 sq km, 29,913 sq miles **Population** 7,058,000
Languages Serbian **Currency** Dinar = 100 paras
Website www.srbija.gov.rs

⊙	120	100	80	60
If towing				
⊙	80	80	80	60

Novice drivers limited to 90% of speed limit and not permitted to drive 11pm–5am.

- Compulsory in front and rear seats
- Age 3–12 must be in rear seats and wear seat belt or appropriate child restraint; under 3 in rear-facing child seat permitted in front only if airbag deactivated
- 0.029% • 0.0% for commercial drivers, motorcyclists, or if full licence held less than 1 year
- Compulsory Compulsory Compulsory
- Compulsory Compulsory
- 18 (16 for motorbikes less than 125cc; 14 for mopeds)
- International Driving Permit, green card or locally bought third-party insurance
- Winter tyres compulsory Nov–Apr for vehicles up to 3.5 tonnes. Carrying snow chains recommended in winter as these may have to be fitted if driving on snow-covered roads, in accordance with signage.
- ★ 3-metre tow bar or rope
- ★ Spare wheel compulsory
- ★ On-the-spot fines imposed
- ★ Radar detectors prohibited
- ★ Tolls on motorways and some primary roads
- ★ Visibility vest compulsory

Slovakia Slovenska Republika (SK)

Area 49,012 sq km (18,923 sq miles)
Population 5,435,000 **Capital** Bratislava (660,000)
Languages Slovak (official), Hungarian
Currency Euro = 100 cents **Website** www.vlada.gov.sk

⊙	130/90	90	90	50

- Compulsory
- Under 12 or below 150cm must be in rear in appropriate child restraint
- 0.0% Compulsory Compulsory
- Compulsory Recommended
- 18, 17 for motorbikes over 50cc, 15 for mopeds
- International driving permit, proof of health insurance
- Only allowed with a hands-free kit
- Compulsory at all times Winter tyres compulsory
- ★ On-the-spot fines imposed
- ★ Radar-detection equipment is prohibited
- ★ Tow rope recommended
- ★ Vignette required for motorways, car valid for 1 year, 30 days, 7 days; lorry vignettes carry a higher charge.
- ★ Visibility vests compulsory

Slovenia Slovenija (SLO)

Area 20,256 sq km (7,820 sq miles)
Population 2,066,000 **Capital** Ljubljana (280,000)
Languages Slovene **Currency** Euro = 100 cents
Website www.vlada.si/en

⊙	130	110[1]	90[1]	50[2]
If towing				
⊙	80	80[1]	80[1]	50[2]

[1] 70 kph in urban areas, [2] 30 kph zones are increasingly common in cities

- Compulsory
- Below 150cm must use appropriate child restraint. A rear-facing baby seat may be used in front only if airbags are deactivated.
- 0.05% • 0.0% for commercial drivers, under 21s or with less than one year with a full licence
- Compulsory Compulsory
- Compulsory Recommended
- 18 (motorbikes up to 125cc – 16, up to 350cc – 18)
- Licences without photographs must be accompanied by an International Driving Permit
- Only allowed with hands-free kit
- Must be used at all times
- Snow chains or winter tyres compulsory mid-Nov to mid-March, and in wintery conditions at other times. Max speed 50 kph. This limit also applies if visibility is below 50m.
- ★ On-the-spot fines imposed
- ★ Radar detectors prohibited
- ★ Vignettes valid for variety of periods compulsory for vehicles below 3.5 tonnes for toll roads. Write your vehicle registration number on the vignette before displaying it. For heavier vehicles electronic tolling system applies; several routes are cargo-traffic free during high tourist season.
- ★ Visibility vest compulsory

Spain España (E)

Area 497,548 sq km (192,103 sq miles)
Population 46,468,000 **Capital** Madrid (6,530,000)
Languages Castilian Spanish (official), Catalan, Galician, Basque **Currency** Euro = 100 cents
Website www.lamoncloa.gob.es/lang/en/Paginas/index.aspx

⊙	120*	100*	90	50*
If towing				
⊙	80	80	70	50*

*Urban motorways and dual carriageways 80 kph. 20 kph zones are being introduced in many cities

- Compulsory
- Under 135cm and below 12 must use appropriate child restraint
- 0.049% • 0.029% if less than 2 years full licence or if vehicle is over 3.5 tonnes or carries more than 9 passengers
- Two compulsory (one for in front, one for behind)
- Recommended Compulsory Recommended
- 18 (21 for heavy vehicles; 16 for motorbikes up to 125cc)
- Hands-free only
- Compulsory for motorcycles and in poor daytime visibility for other vehicles.
- Snow chains recommended for mountainous areas in winter
- ★ Drivers who wear spectacles or contact lenses must carry a spare pair.
- ★ On-the-spot fines imposed
- ★ Radar-detection equipment is prohibited
- ★ Spare wheel compulsory
- ★ Tolls on motorways
- ★ Visibility vest compulsory

Sweden Sverige (S)

Area 449,964 sq km (173,731 sq miles)
Population 10,053,000 **Capital** Stockholm (2,227,000)
Languages Swedish (official), Finnish
Currency Swedish krona = 100 ore
Website www.sweden.gov.se

⊙	90–120	80	70–100	30–60
If towing trailer with brakes				
⊙	80	80	70	50

- Compulsory in front and rear seats
- Under 15 or below 135cm must use an appropriate child restraint and may sit in the front only if airbag is deactivated; rear-facing baby seat permitted in front only if airbag deactivated.
- 0.019% Compulsory Recommended
- Recommended Recommended 18
- Licences without a photograph must be accompanied by photographic proof of identity, e.g. a passport
- LEZ Gothenberg, Helsingborg, Lund, Malmo, Mölndal and Stockholm have LEZs, progressively prohibiting older vehicles.
- Must be used at all times
- 1 Dec–31 Mar winter tyres, anti-freeze, screenwash additive and shovel compulsory
- ★ On-the-spot fines imposed
- ★ Radar-detection equipment is prohibited

Switzerland Schweiz (CH)

Area 41,284 sq km (15,939 sq miles)
Population 8,401,000 **Capital** Bern (407,000)
Languages French, German, Italian, Romansch (all official)
Currency Swiss Franc = 100 centimes / rappen
Website www.admin.ch

⊙	120	80	80	30/50
If towing up to 1 tonne / over 1 tonne				
⊙	80	80	60/80	30/50

- Compulsory
- Up to 12 years or below 150 cm must use an appropriate child restraint. Children 6 and under must sit in the rear.
- 0.05%, but 0.0% for commercial drivers or with less than three years with a full licence
- Compulsory Recommended
- Recommended Recommended
- 18 (mopeds up to 50cc – 16) Compulsory
- Only allowed with a hands-free kit
- Winter tyres recommended Nov–Mar; snow chains compulsory in designated areas in poor winter weather
- ★ GPS must have fixed speed camera function deactivated; radar detectors prohibited
- ★ Motorways are all toll and for vehicles below 3.5 tonnes a vignette must be purchased at the border. The vignette is valid for one calendar year. Vehicles over 3.5 tonnes must have an electronic tag for travel on any road.
- ★ On-the-spot fines imposed
- ★ Pedestrians have right of way

- ★ Picking up hitchhikers is prohibited on motorways and main roads
- ★ Spectacles or contact lens wearers must carry a spare pair in their vehicle at all times

Turkey Türkiye (TR)

Area 774,815 sq km (299,156 sq miles)
Population 79,815,000
Capital Ankara (5,271,000)
Languages Turkish (official), Kurdish
Currency New Turkish lira = 100 kurus
Website www.mfa.gov.tr/default.en.mfa

	120	90	90	50
If towing				
	80	80	80	40
Motorbikes				
	80	70	70	50

- Compulsory if fitted
- Under 150 cm and below 36kg must use suitable child restraint. Under 3s can only travel in the front in a rear facing seat if the airbag is deactivated. Children 3–12 may not travel in the front seat.
- 0.00%
- Two compulsory (one in front, one behind)
- Compulsory Compulsory
- Compulsory 18
- International driving permit advised, and required for use with licences without photographs; note that Turkey is in both Europe and Asia, green card/UK insurance that covers whole of Turkey or locally bought insurance, e-visa obtained in advance.
- Prohibited
- Compulsory in daylight hours
- ★ Spare wheel compulsory
- ★ On-the-spot fines imposed
- ★ Several motorways, and the Bosphorus bridges are toll roads
- ★ Tow rope and tool kit must be carried

Ukraine Ukraina (UA)

Area 603,700 sq km (233,088 sq miles)
Population 42,542,000
Capital Kiev / Kyviv (3,375,000)
Languages Ukrainian (official), Russian
Currency Hryvnia = 100 kopiykas
Website www.kmu.gov.ua/control/en

	130	110	90	60
If towing				
	80	80	80	60

If driving licence held less than 2 years, must not exceed 70 kph

- Compulsory in front and rear seats
- Under 12 and below 145cm must use an appropriate child restraint and sit in rear
- 0.02% – if use of medication can be proved. Otherwise 0.00%
- Compulsory
- Compulsory
- Optional
- Compulsory
- 18
- International Driving Permit, visa, International Certificate for Motor Vehicles, green card
- No legislation
- Compulsory in poor daytime and from Oct–Apr
- Winter tyres compulsory Nov–Apr in snowy conditions
- ★ A road tax is payable on entry to the country.
- ★ On-the-spot fines imposed
- ★ Tow rope and tool kit recommended

United Kingdom (GB)

Area 241,857 sq km (93,381 sq miles)
Population 65,648,000
Capital London (13,880,000)
Languages English (official), Welsh (also official in Wales), Gaelic
Currency Sterling (pound) = 100 pence
Website www.direct.gov.uk

	112	112	96	48
If towing				
	96	96	80	48

Several cities have introduced 32 kph (20 mph) zones away from main roads

- Compulsory in front seats and if fitted in rear seats
- Under 3 not allowed in front seats except with appropriate restraint, and in rear must use child restraint if available; in front 3–12 or under 135cm must use appropriate child restraint, in rear must use appropriate child restraint (or seat belt if no child restraint is available, e.g. because two occupied restraints prevent fitting of a third).
- 0.08% (England, Northern Ireland, Wales) • 0.05% (Scotland)
- Recommended
- Recommended
- Recommended
- Recommended
- 17 (16 for mopeds)
- Only allowed with hands-free kit
- LEZ London's LEZ operates by number-plate recognition; non-compliant vehicles face hefty daily charges. Foreign-registered vehicles must register.
- ★ Driving is on the left
- ★ On-the-spot fines imposed
- ★ Smoking is banned in all commercial vehicles
- ★ Some toll motorways, bridges and tunnels

Ski resorts

The resorts listed are popular ski centres, therefore road access to most is normally good and supported by road clearing during snow falls. However, mountain driving is never predictable and drivers should make sure they take suitable snow chains as well as emergency provisions and clothing. Listed for each resort are: the atlas page and grid square; the resort/minimum piste altitude (where only one figure is shown, they are at the same height) and maximum altitude of its own lifts; the number of lifts and gondolas (the total for lift-linked resorts); the season start and end dates (snow cover allowing); whether snow is augmented by cannon; the nearest town (with its distance in km) and, where available, the website and/or telephone number of the local tourist information centre or ski centre ('00' prefix required for calls from the UK).

Walking with snow shoes, La Plagne, France blickwinkel / Alamy

The ❄ symbol indicates resorts with snow cannon

Andorra

Pyrenees

Pas de la Casa / Grau Roig 91 A4 ❄ 2050–2640m • 31 lifts • Dec–Apr • Andorra La Vella (30km) www.pasdelacasa.com • *Access via Envalira Pass (2407m), highest in Pyrenees, snow chains essential.*

Austria

Alps

Bad Gastein 72 A3 ❄ 1050/1100–2700m • 50 lifts • Dec–Mar • St Johann im Pongau (45km) +43 6432 3393 0 www.gastein.com

Bad Hofgastein 72 A3 ❄ 860–2295m • 50 lifts • Dec–Mar • St Johann im Pongau (40km) +43 6432 3393 0 www.gastein.com/en/region-villages/bad-hofgastein

Bad Kleinkirchheim 72 B3 ❄ 1070–2310m • 27 lifts • Dec–Mar • Villach (35km) +43 4240 8212 www.badkleinkirchheim.at

Ehrwald 71 A5 ❄ 1000–2965m • 24 lifts • Dec–Apr • Imst (30km) +43 5673 2501 www.wetterstein-bahnen.at/en

Innsbruck 71 A6 ❄ 574/850–3200m • 59 lifts • Dec–Apr • Innsbruck + 43 512 56 2000 www.innsbruck.info/en/ • *Motorway normally clear. The motorway through to Italy and through the Arlberg Tunnel are both toll roads.*

Ischgl 71 A5 ❄ 1340/1400–2900m • 101 lifts • Dec–May • Landeck (25km) +43 50990 100 www.ischgl.com • *Car entry to resort prohibited between 2200hrs and 0600hrs.*

Kaprun 72 A2 ❄ 885/770–3030m, • 25 lifts • Nov–Apr • Zell am See (10km) +43 6542 770 www.zellamsee-kaprun.com

Kirchberg in Tirol 72 A2 ❄ 860–2000m • 197 lifts • Nov–Apr • Kitzbühel (6km) +43 57507 2100 www.kitzbueheler-alpen.com/en • *Easily reached from Munich International Airport (120 km)*

Kitzbühel (Brixen im Thale) 72 A2 ❄ 800/790–2000m • 197 lifts • Dec–Apr • Wörgl (40km) +43 57057 2000 www.kitzbueheler-alpen.com/en

Lech/Oberlech 71 A5 ❄ 1450–2810m • 87 lifts • Dec–Apr • Bludenz (50km) +43 5583 2161 0 www.lechzuers.com • *Roads normally cleared but keep chains accessible because of altitude. Linked to the other Arlberg resorts.*

Mayrhofen 72 A1 ❄ 630–2500m • 57 lifts • Dec–Apr • Jenbach (35km) +43 5285 6760 www.mayrhofen.at • *Chains rarely required.*

Obertauern 72 A3 ❄ 1740/1640–2350m • 26 lifts • Dec–Apr • Radstadt (20km) +43 6456 7252 www.obertauern.com • *Roads normally cleared but chain accessibility recommended. Camper vans and caravans not allowed; park these in Radstadt*

Saalbach Hinterglemm 72 A2 ❄ 1000/1030–2100m • 52 lifts • Nov–Apr • Zell am See (19km) +43 6541 6800-68 www.saalbach.com • *Both village centres are pedestrianised and there is a good ski bus service during the daytime*

St Anton am Arlberg 71 A5 ❄ 1300–2810m • 87 lifts • Dec–Apr • Innsbruck (104km) +43 5446 22690 www.stantonamarlberg.com • *Linked to the other Arlberg resorts.*

Schladming 72 A3 ❄ 745–1900m • 45 lifts • Dec–Mar • Schladming + 43 36 87 233 10 www.schladming-dachstein.at

Serfaus 71 A5 ❄ 1427/1200–2820m • 68 lifts • Dec–Apr • Landeck (30km) +43 5476 6239 www.serfaus-fiss-ladis.at • *Private vehicles banned from village. Use Dorfbahn Serfaus, an underground funicular that runs on an air cushion.*

Sölden 71 B6 ❄ 1380–3250m, • 33 lifts • Oct–Apr • Imst(50km) +43 57200 200 www.soelden.com • *Roads normally cleared but snow chains recommended because of altitude. The route from Italy and the south over the Timmelsjoch via Obergurgl is closed Oct–May and anyone arriving from the south should use the Brenner Pass motorway.*

Zell am See 72 A2 ❄ 750–1950m • 53 lifts • Dec–Mar • Zell am See +43 6542 770 www.zellamsee-kaprun.com • *Low altitude, so good access and no mountain passes to cross.*

Zell im Zillertal (Zell am Ziller) 72 A1 ❄ 580/930–2410m • 2 lifts • Dec–Apr • Jenbach (25km) +43 5282 7165–226 www.zillertalarena.com

Zürs 71 A5 ❄ 1720/1700–2450m • 87 lifts • Dec–Apr • Bludenz (30km) +43 5583 2245 www.lechzuers.com • *Roads normally cleared but keep chains accessible because of altitude. Village has garage with 24-hour self-service gas/petrol, breakdown service and wheel chains supply. Linked to the other Arlberg resorts.*

France

Alps

Alpe d'Huez 79 A5 ❄ 1860–3330m • 85 lifts • Dec–Apr • Grenoble (63km) www.alpedhuez.com • *Snow chains may be required on access road to resort.*

Avoriaz 70 B1 ❄ 1800/1100–2280m • 35 lifts • Dec–May • Morzine (14km) +33 4 50 74 02 11 www.avoriaz.com/en • *Chains may be required for access road from Morzine. Car-free resort, park on edge of village.*

Chamonix-Mont-Blanc 70 C1 ❄ 1035–3840m • 49 lifts • Dec–Apr • Martigny (38km) +33 4 50 53 99 98 www.chamonix.com

Chamrousse 79 A4 ❄ 1700/1420–2250m • 26 lifts • Dec–Apr • Grenoble (30km) www.chamrousse.com • *Roads normally cleared, keep chains accessible because of altitude.*

Châtel 70 B1 ❄ 1200/1110–2200m • 41 lifts • Dec–Apr • Thonon-Les-Bains (35km) +33 4 50 73 22 44 www.chatel.com

Courchevel 70 C1 ❄ 1300–2470m • 67 lifts • Dec–Apr • Moûtiers (23km) www.courchevel.com • *Roads normally cleared but keep chains accessible. Traffic 'discouraged' within the four resort bases.*

Flaine 70 B1 ❄ 1600–2500m • 26 lifts • Dec–Apr • Cluses (25km) +33 4 50 90 80 01 www.flaine.com • *Keep chains accessible for D6 from Cluses to Flaine. Car access for depositing luggage and passengers only. 1500-space car park outside resort. Near Sixt-Fer-á-Cheval.*

La Clusaz 69 C6 ❄ 1100–2600m • 55 lifts • Dec–Apr • Annecy (32km) www.laclusaz.com • *Roads normally clear but keep chains accessible for final road from Annecy.*

La Plagne 70 C1 ❄ 2500/1250–3250m • 109 lifts • Dec–Apr • Moûtiers (32km) www.la-plagne.com • *Ten different centres up to 2100m altitude. Road access via Bozel, Landry or Aime normally cleared. Linked to Les Arcs by cablecar*

Les Arcs 70 C1 ❄ 1600/1200–3230m • 77 lifts • Dec–May • Bourg-St-Maurice (15km) +33 4 79 07 12 57 www.lesarcs.com • *Four base areas up to 2000 metres; keep chains accessible. Pay parking at edge of each base resort. Linked to La Plagne by cablecar*

Les Carroz d'Araches 70 B1 ❄ 1140–2500m • 69 lifts • Dec–Apr • Cluses (13km) http://winter.lescarroz.com

Les Deux-Alpes 79 B5 ❄ 1650/1300–3600m • 55 lifts • Dec–Apr • Grenoble (75km) +33 4 76 79 22 00 www.les2alpes.com/en • *Roads normally cleared, however snow chains recommended for D213 up from valley road (D1091).*

Les Gets 70 B1 ❄ 1170/1000–2000m • 52 lifts • Dec–Apr • Cluses (18km) +33 4 50 74 74 74 www.lesgets.com

Les Ménuires 69 C6 ❄ 1815/1850–3200m • 40 lifts • Dec–Apr • Moûtiers (27km) www.lesmenuires.com • *Keep chains accessible for D117 from Moûtiers.*

Les Sept Laux Prapoutel 69 C6 ❄ 1350–2400m, • 24 lifts • Dec–Apr • Grenoble (38km) www.les7laux.com (in French only) • *Roads normally cleared, however keep chains accessible for mountain road up from the A41 motorway. Near St Sorlin d'Arves.*

Megève 69 C6 ❄ 1100/1050–2350m • 79 lifts • Dec–Apr • Sallanches (12km) www.megeve.com

Méribel 69 C6 ❄ 1400/1100–2950m • 61 lifts • Dec–May • Moûtiers (18km) +33 4 79 08 60 01 www.meribel.net • *Keep chains accessible for 18km to resort on D90 from Moûtiers.*

Morzine 70 B1 ❄ 1000–2460m • 67 lifts, • Dec–Apr • Thonon-Les-Bains (30km) +33 4 50 74 72 72 http://en.morzine-avoriaz.com

Pra Loup 79 B5 ❄ 1500–2600m • 53 lifts • Dec–Apr • Barcelonnette (10km) www.praloup.com • *Roads normally cleared but chains accessibility recommended.*

Risoul 79 B5 ❄ 1850/1650–2750m • 59 lifts • Dec–Apr • Briançon (40km) +33 4 92 46 02 60 www.risoul.com • *Keep chains accessible. Near Guillestre. Linked with Vars Les Claux*

St-Gervais Mont-Blanc 70 C1 ❄ 850/1150–2350m • 27 lifts • Dec–Apr • Sallanches (10km) +33 4 50 47 76 08 www.saintgervais.com/en

Serre Chevalier 79 B5 ❄ 1350/1200–2800m • 77 lifts • Dec–Apr • Briançon (10km) + 33 4 92 24 98 98 www.serre-chevalier.com • *Made up of 13 small villages along the valley road, which is normally cleared.*

Tignes 70 C1 ❄ 2100/1550–3450m • 87 lifts • Jan–Dec • Bourg St Maurice (26km) +33 4 79 40 04 40 www.tignes.net • *Keep chains accessible because of altitude. Linked to Val d'Isère.*

Val d'Isère 70 C1 ❄ 1850/1550–3450m • 87 lifts • Dec–Apr • Bourg-St-Maurice (30km) +33 4 79 06 06 60 www.valdisere.com • *Roads normally cleared but keep chains accessible.*

Val Thorens 69 C6 ❄ 2300/1850–3200m • 29 lifts • Dec–Apr • Moûtiers (37km) +33 4 79 00 08 08 www.valthorens.com • *Chains essential – highest ski resort in Europe. Obligatory paid parking on edge of resort.*

Valloire 69 C6 ❄ 1430–2600m • 34 lifts • Dec–Apr • Modane (20km) +33 4 79 59 03 96 www.valloire.net • *Road normally clear up to the Col du Galbier, to the south of the resort, which is closed from 1st November to 1st June. Linked to Valmeinier.*

Valmeinier 69 C6 ❄ 1500–2600m • 34 lifts • Dec–Apr • St Michel de Maurienne (47km) +33 4 79 59 53 69 www.valmeinier.com • *Access from north on D1006 / D902. Col du Galbier, to the south of the resort closed from 1st November to 1st June. Linked to Valloire.*

Valmorel 69 C6 ❄ 1400–2550m • 90 lifts • Dec–Apr • Moûtiers (15km) www.valmorel.com • *Near St Jean-de-Belleville. Linked with ski areas of Doucy-Combelouvière and St François-Longchamp.*

Vars Les Claux 79 B5 ❄ 1850/1650–2750m • 59 lifts • Dec–Apr • Briançon (40km) +33 4 92 46 51 31 www.vars.com/en/winter • *Four base resorts up to 1850 metres. Keep chains accessible. Linked with Risoul.*

Villard de Lans 79 A4 ❄ 1050/1160–2170m • 28 lifts • Dec–Apr • Grenoble (32km) +33 4 76 95 10 38 www.villarddelans.com

Pyrenees

Font-Romeu 91 A5 ❄ 1800/1600–2200m • 25 lifts • Nov–Apr • Perpignan (87km) www.font-romeu.fr • *Roads normally cleared but keep chains accessible.*

Saint-Lary Soulan 77 D3 ❄ 830/1650/1700–2515m • 31 lifts • Dec–Mar • Tarbes (75km) +33 5 62 39 50 81 www.saintlary.com • *Access roads constantly cleared of snow.*

Vosges

La Bresse-Hohneck 60 B2 ❄ 600–1370m • 33 lifts • Dec–Mar • Cornimont (6km) +33 3 29 25 41 29 www.labresse.net

Germany

Alps

Garmisch-Partenkirchen 71 A6 ❄ 700–2830m • 38 lifts • Dec–Apr • Munich (95km) ☎ +49 8821 180 700 • 🖥 www.gapa.de • *Roads usually clear, chains rarely needed.*

Oberaudorf 62 C3 ❄ 480–1850m • 30 lifts • Dec–Apr • Kufstein (15km) 🖥 www.oberaudorf.de • *Motorway normally kept clear. Near Bayrischzell.*

Oberstdorf 71 A5 820/830–2200m • 26 lifts • Dec–Apr • Sonthofen (15km) ☎ +49 8322 7000 • 🖥 www.oberstdorf.de/en

Rothaargebirge

Winterberg 51 B4 ❄ 700/620–830m • 19 lifts • Dec–Mar • Brilon (30km) ☎ +49 2981 925 00 • 🖥 www.winterberg.de (German and Dutch only) • *Roads usually cleared, chains rarely required.*

Greece

Central Greece

Mount Parnassos: Kelaria-Fterolakka 116 D4 1640–2260m • 14 lifts • Dec–Apr • Amfiklia • 🖥 www.parnassos-ski.gr

Mount Parnassos: Gerondovrahos 116 D4 1800–1900m • 3 lifts • Dec–Apr • Amfiklia • ☎ +30 29444 70371

Peloponnisos

Mount Helmos: Kalavrita Ski Centre 117 D4 1650–2100m • 7 lifts • Dec–Mar • Kalavrita ☎ +30 276920 24451-2 • 🖥 www.kalavrita-ski.gr (in Greek only)

Mount Menalo: Ostrakina 117 E4 1500–1600m • 4 lifts • Dec–Mar • Tripoli ☎ +30 27960 22227

Macedonia

Mount Falakras: Agio Pnevma 116 A6 1720/1620–2230m • 7 lifts • Dec–Mar • Drama ☎ +30 25210 23691

Mount Vermio: Seli 116 B4 1500–1900m • 8 lifts • Dec–Mar • Kozani ☎ +30 23310 26237 • 🖥 www.seli-ski.gr (in Greek)

Mount Vermio: Tria-Pente Pigadia 116 B3 ❄ 1420–2005m • 5 lifts • Dec–Mar • Ptolemaida ☎ +30 23320 44464

Mount Verno: Vigla 116 B3 1650–1900m • 5 lifts • Dec–Mar • Florina ☎ +30 23850 22354 • 🖥 www.vigla-ski.gr (in Greek)

Mount Vrondous: Lailias 116 A5 1600–1850m • 4 lifts • Dec–Mar • Serres ☎ +30 23210 53790

Thessalia

Mount Pilio: Agriolefkes 116 C5 1300–1500m • 5 lifts • Dec–Mar • Volos ☎ +30 24280 73719

Italy

Alps

Bardonecchia 79 A5 ❄ 1312–2750m • 21 lifts • Dec–Apr • Bardonecchia 🖥 www.bardonecchiaski.com • *Resort reached through the 11km Frejus tunnel from France, roads normally cleared.*

Bórmio 71 B5 ❄ 1200/1230–3020m • 24 lifts • Dec–Apr • Tirano (40km) 🖥 www.bormio.com • *Tolls payable in Ponte del Gallo Tunnel, open 0800hrs–2000hrs.*

Breuil-Cervinia 70 C2 ❄ 2050–3500m • 21 lifts • Jan–Dec • Aosta (54km) ☎ +39 166 944311 🖥 www.cervinia.it • *Snow chains strongly recommended. Bus from Milan airport.*

Courmayeur 70 C1 ❄ 1200–2760m • 21 lifts • Dec–Apr • Aosta (40km) 🖥 www.courmayeurmontblanc.it • *Access through the Mont Blanc tunnel from France. Roads constantly cleared.*

Limone Piemonte 80 B1 ❄ 1000/1050–2050m • 29 lifts • Dec–Apr • Cuneo (27km) 🖥 www.limoneturismo.it • *Roads normally cleared, chains rarely required.*

Livigno 71 B5 ❄ 1800–3000m • 31 lifts • Nov–May • Zernez (CH) (27km) 🖥 www.livigno.com • *Keep chains accessible. The traffic direction through Munt la Schera Tunnel to/from Zernez is regulated on Saturdays. Check in advance.*

Sestrière 79 B5 ❄ 2035/1840–2840m • 92 lifts • Dec–Apr • Oulx (22km) 🖥 www.sestriere-online.com • *One of Europe's highest resorts; although roads are normally cleared keep chains accessible.*

Appennines

Roccaraso – Aremogna 103 B7 ❄ 1285/1240–2140m • 24 lifts • Dec–Apr • Castel di Sangro (7km) • 🖥 www.roccarasoturismo.it (Italian only)

Dolomites

Andalo – Fai della Paganella 71 B5 ❄ 1042/1050/2125m • 17 lifts • Dec–Apr • Trento (40km) • 🖥 www.visitdolomitipaganella.it ☎ +39 461 585836

Arabba 72 B1 ❄ 1600/1450–2950m • 29 lifts • Dec–Mar • Brunico (45km) ☎ +39 436 79130 🖥 www.arabba.it • *Roads normally cleared but keep chains accessible.*

Cortina d'Ampezzo 72 B2 ❄ 1224/1050–2930m • 37 lifts • Dec–Apr • Belluno (72km) ☎ +39 436 869086 • 🖥 www.dolomiti.org/it/cortina • *Access from north on route 51 over the Cimabanche Pass may require chains.*

Corvara (Alta Badia) 72 B1 ❄ 1568–2500m • 56 lifts • Dec–Apr • Brunico (38km) 🖥 www.altabadia.it • *Roads normally clear but keep chains accessible.*

Madonna di Campiglio 71 B5 ❄ 1550/1500–2600m • 72 lifts • Dec–Apr • Trento (60km) ☎ +39 465 447501 • 🖥 www.campigliodolomiti.it/homepage • *Roads normally cleared but keep chains accessible. Linked to Folgarida and Marilleva.*

Moena di Fassa (Sorte/Ronchi) 72 B1 ❄ 1184/1450–2520m • 8 lifts • Dec–Apr • Bolzano (40km) ☎ +39 462 609770 • 🖥 www.fassa.com

Selva di Val Gardena/Wolkenstein Groden 72 B1 ❄ 1563/1570–2450m • 81 lifts • Dec–Apr • Bolzano (40km) ☎ +39 471 777777 🖥 www.valgardena.it • *Roads normally cleared but keep chains accessible.*

Norway

Hemsedal 32 B5 ❄ 700/640–1450m • 24 lifts • Nov–May • Honefoss (150km) ☎ +47 32 055030 🖥 www.hemsedal.com • *Be prepared for extreme weather conditions.*

Slovakia

Chopok (Jasna-Chopok) 65 B5 ❄ 900/950–1840m • 17 lifts • Dec–Apr • Jasna ☎ +421 907 886644 🖥 www.jasna.sk

Donovaly 65 B5 ❄ 913–1360m • 17 lifts • Nov–Apr • Ruzomberok ☎ +421 48 4199900 🖥 www.paksnow.sk/zima/en

Martinské Hole 65 A4 1250/1150–1456m • 8 lifts • Nov–May • Zilina ☎ +421 43 430 6000 🖥 http://leto.martinky.com/sk (Slovak only)

Plejsy 65 B6 470–912m • 9 lifts • Dec–Apr • Krompachy ☎ +421 53 429 8015 🖥 www.plejsy.sk

Strbske Pleso 65 A6 1380–1825m • 7 lifts • Dec–Mar • Poprad ☎ +421 917 682 260 🖥 www.vt.sk

Slovenia

Julijske Alpe

Kanin (Bovec) 72 B3 460/1690–2293m • 5 lifts • Dec–Apr • Bovec 🖥 www.boveckanin.si

Kranjska Gora 72 B3 ❄ 800–1210m • 19 lifts • Dec–Mar • Kranjska Gora ☎ +386 4 5809 440 🖥 www.kranjska-gora.si

Vogel 72 B3 570–1800m • 8 lifts • Dec–Apr • Bohinjska Bistrica ☎ +386 4 5729 712 🖥 www.vogel.si

Kawiniške Savinjske Alpe

Krvavec 73 B4 ❄ 1450–1970m • 10 lifts • Dec–Apr • Kranj ☎ 386 4 25 25 911 🖥 www.rtc-krvavec.si

Pohorje

Rogla 73 B5 1517/1050–1500m • 13 lifts • Dec–Apr • Slovenska Bistrica ☎ +386 3 75 77 100 🖥 www.rogla.eu

Spain

Pyrenees

Baqueira-Beret/Bonaigua 90 A3 ❄ 1500–2500m • 33 lifts • Dec–Apr • Vielha (15km) ☎ +34 902 415 415 🖥 www.baqueira.es • *Roads normally clear but keep chains accessible. Near Salardú.*

Sistema Penibetico

Sierra Nevada 100 B2 ❄ 2100–3300m • 24 lifts • Dec–May • Granada (32km) ☎ +34 902 70 80 90 🖥 http://sierranevada.es • *Access road designed to be avalanche safe and is snow cleared.*

Sweden

Idre Fjäll 115 F9 590–890m • 33 lifts • Nov–Apr • Mora (140km) ☎ +46 253 41000 🖥 www.idrefjall.se • *Be prepared for extreme weather conditions.*

Sälen 34 A5 360m • 100 lifts • Nov–Apr • Malung (70km) ☎ +46 771 84 00 00 🖥 www.skistar.com/salen • *Be prepared for extreme weather conditions.*

Switzerland

Alps

Adelboden 70 B2 1353m • 94 lifts • Dec–Apr • Frutigen (15km) ☎ +41 33 673 80 80 🖥 www.adelboden.ch • *Linked with Lenk.*

Arosa 71 B4 1800/1740–2650m • 16 lifts • Dec–Apr • Chur (30km) ☎ +41 81 378 70 20 🖥 www.arosa.ch • *Roads cleared but keep chains accessible due to high altitude.*

Crans Montana 70 B2 ❄ 1500–3000m • 34 lifts • Dec–Apr, Jul–Oct • Sierre (15km) ☎ +41 848 22 10 12 • 🖥 www.crans-montana.ch • *Roads normally cleared but keep chains accessible for ascent from Sierre.*

Davos 71 B4 ❄ 1560/1100–2840m • 38 lifts • Nov–Apr • Davos. ☎ +41 81 415 21 21 🖥 www.davos.ch

Engelberg 70 B3 ❄ 1000/1050–3020m • 26 lifts • Nov–May • Luzern (39km) ☎ +41 41 639 77 77 🖥 www.engelberg.ch • *Straight access road normally cleared.*

Flums (Flumserberg) 71 A4 ❄ 1400/1000–2220m • 17 lifts • Dec–Apr • Buchs (25km) ☎ +41 81 720 18 18 🖥 www.flumserberg.ch • *Roads normally cleared, but 1000-metre vertical ascent; keep chains accessible.*

Grindelwald 70 B3 ❄ 1050–2950m • 39 lifts • Dec–Apr • Interlaken (20km) ☎ +41 33 854 12 12 🖥 www.jungfrauregion.ch • *Linked with Wengen.*

Gstaad – Saanenland 70 B2 ❄ 1050/950–3000m • 74 lifts • Dec–Apr • Gstaad ☎ +41 33 748 81 81 🖥 www.gstaad.ch • *Linked to Anzère.*

Klosters 71 B4 ❄ 1191/1110–2840m • 52 lifts • Dec–Apr • Davos (10km). ☎ +41 81 410 20 20 🖥 www.davos.ch/klosters • *Roads normally clear but keep chains accessible.*

Leysin 70 B2 ❄ 2260–2330m • 16 lifts • Dec–Apr • Aigle (6km) ☎ +41 24 493 33 00 🖥 www.leysin.ch

Mürren 70 B2 ❄ 1650–2970m • 12 lifts • Dec–Apr • Interlaken (18km) ☎ +41 33 856 86 86 🖥 www.mymuerren.ch • *No road access. Park in Strechelberg (1500 free places) and take the two-stage cable car.*

Nendaz 70 B2 ❄ 1365/1400–3300m • 20 lifts • Nov–Apr • Sion (16km) ☎ +41 27 289 55 89 🖥 www.nendaz.ch • *Roads normally cleared, however keep chains accessible for ascent from Sion. Near Vex.*

Saas-Fee 70 B2 ❄ 1800–3500m • 23 lifts • Jan–Dec • Brig (35km) ☎ +41 27 958 18 58 🖥 www.saas-fee.ch/en/ • *Roads normally cleared but keep chains accessible because of altitude.*

St Moritz 71 B4 ❄ 1856/1730–3300m • 24 lifts • Nov–May • Chur (89km) ☎ +41 81 837 33 33 🖥 www.stmoritz.ch • *Roads normally cleared but keep chains accessible.*

Samnaun 71 B5 ❄ 1846/1400–2900m • 40 lifts • Dec–May • Scuol (30km) ☎ +41 81 861 88 30 🖥 www.engadin.com/ferienorte/engadin-Åsamnaun. • *Roads normally cleared but keep chains accessible.*

Verbier 70 B2 ❄ 1500–3330m • 17 lifts • Nov–Apr • Martigny (27km) ☎ +41 27 775 38 38 🖥 www.verbier.ch • *Roads normally cleared.*

Villars-Gryon 70 B2 ❄ 1253/1200–2100m • 16 lifts • Dec–Apr, Jun–Jul • Montreux (35km) ☎ +41 24 495 32 32 🖥 www.villars.ch • *Roads normally cleared but keep chains accessible for ascent from N9. Near Bex.*

Wengen 70 B2 ❄ 1270–2320m • 39 lifts • Dec–Apr • Interlaken (12km) ☎ +41 33 856 85 85 🖥 http://wengen.ch • *No road access. Park at Lauterbrunnen and take mountain railway. Linked with Grindelwald.*

Zermatt 70 B2 ❄ 1620–3900m • 40 lifts, • all year • Brig (42km) ☎ +41 27 966 81 00 🖥 www.zermatt.ch • *Cars not permitted in resort, park in Täsch (3km) and take shuttle train.*

Turkey

North Anatolian Mountains

Uludag 118 B4 1770–2320m • 15 lifts • Dec–Mar • Bursa (36km) ☎ +90 224 285 21 11 • 🖥 http://skiingturkey.com/resorts/uludag.html

To the best of the Publisher's knowledge the information in this table was correct at the time of going to press. No responsibility can be accepted for any errors or their consequences.

Skiing near Valmorel, France
Jacques Pierre / hemis.fr / Alamy

1 : 3 200 000 map pages

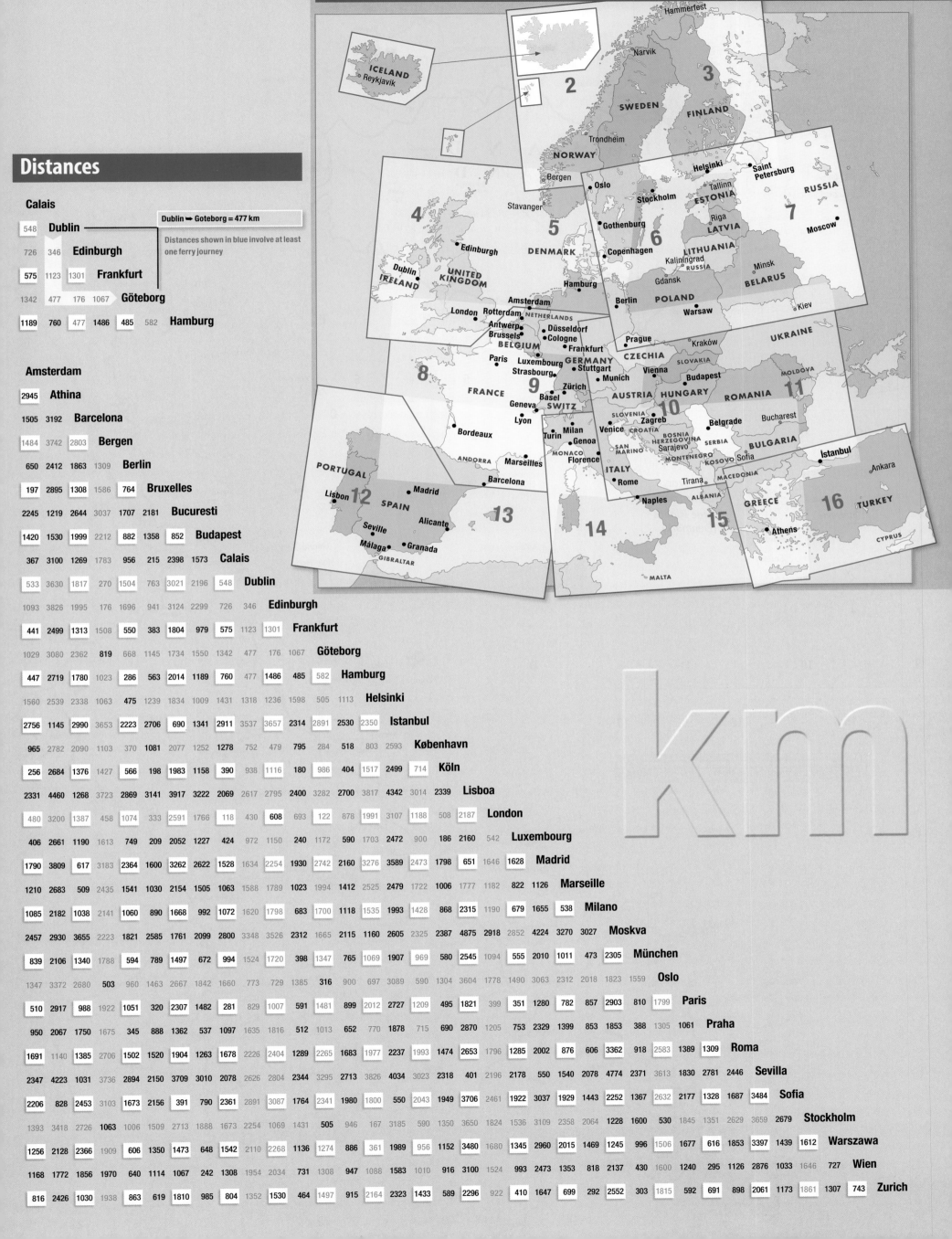

Distances

Calais

548	**Dublin**
726	346	**Edinburgh**
575	1123	1301	**Frankfurt**
1342	477	176	1067	**Göteborg**
1189	760	477	1486	485	582	**Hamburg**

Dublin ➡ Goteborg = 477 km

Distances shown in blue involve at least one ferry journey

Amsterdam

2945 **Athina**

1505 3192 **Barcelona**

1484 3742 2803 **Bergen**

650 2412 1863 1309 **Berlin**

197 2895 1308 1586 764 **Bruxelles**

2245 1219 2644 3037 1707 2181 **Bucuresti**

1420 1530 1999 2212 882 1358 852 **Budapest**

367 3100 1269 1783 956 215 2398 1573 **Calais**

533 3630 1817 270 1504 763 3021 2196 548 **Dublin**

1093 3826 1995 176 1696 941 3124 2299 726 346 **Edinburgh**

441 2499 1313 1508 550 383 1804 979 575 1123 1301 **Frankfurt**

1029 3080 2362 819 668 1145 1734 1550 1342 477 176 1067 **Göteborg**

447 2719 1780 1023 286 563 2014 1189 760 477 1486 485 582 **Hamburg**

1560 2539 2338 1063 475 1239 1834 1009 1431 1318 1236 1598 505 1113 **Helsinki**

2756 1145 2990 3653 2223 2706 690 1341 2911 3537 3657 2314 2891 2530 2350 **Istanbul**

965 2782 2090 1103 370 1081 2077 1252 1278 752 479 795 284 518 803 2593 **København**

256 2684 1376 1427 566 198 1983 1158 390 938 1116 180 986 404 1517 2499 714 **Köln**

2331 4460 1268 3723 2869 3141 3917 3222 2069 2617 2795 2400 3282 2700 3817 4342 3014 2339 **Lisboa**

480 3200 1387 458 1074 333 2591 1766 118 430 608 693 122 878 1991 3107 1188 508 2187 **London**

406 2661 1190 1613 749 209 2052 1227 424 972 1150 240 1172 590 1703 2472 900 186 2160 542 **Luxembourg**

1790 3809 617 3183 2364 1600 3262 2622 1528 1634 2254 1930 2742 2160 3276 3589 2473 1798 651 1646 1628 **Madrid**

1210 2683 509 2435 1541 1030 2154 1505 1063 1588 1789 1023 1994 1412 2525 2479 1722 1006 1777 1182 822 1126 **Marseille**

1085 2182 1038 2141 1060 890 1668 992 1072 1620 1798 683 1700 1118 1535 1993 1428 868 2315 1190 679 1655 538 **Milano**

2457 2930 3655 2223 1821 2585 1761 2099 2800 3348 3526 2312 1665 2115 1160 2605 2325 2387 4875 2918 2852 4224 3270 3027 **Moskva**

839 2106 1340 1788 594 789 1497 672 994 1524 1720 398 1347 765 1069 1907 969 580 2545 1094 555 2010 1011 473 2305 **München**

1347 3372 2680 503 960 1463 2667 1842 1660 773 729 1385 316 900 697 3089 590 1304 3604 1778 1490 3063 2312 2018 1823 1559 **Oslo**

510 2917 988 1922 1051 320 2307 1482 281 829 1007 591 1481 899 2012 2727 1209 495 1821 399 351 1280 782 857 2903 810 1799 **Paris**

950 2067 1750 1675 345 888 1362 537 1097 1635 1816 512 1013 652 770 1878 715 690 2870 1205 753 2329 1399 853 1853 388 1305 1061 **Praha**

1691 1140 1385 2706 1502 1520 1904 1263 1678 2226 2404 1289 2265 1683 1977 2237 1993 1474 2653 1796 1285 2002 876 606 3362 918 2583 1389 1309 **Roma**

2347 4223 1031 3736 2894 2150 3709 3010 2078 2626 2804 2344 3295 2713 3826 4034 3023 2318 401 2196 2178 550 1540 2078 4774 2371 3613 1830 2781 2446 **Sevilla**

2206 828 2453 3103 1673 2156 391 790 2361 2891 3087 1764 2341 1980 1800 550 2043 1949 3706 2461 1922 3037 1929 1443 2252 1367 2632 2177 1328 1687 3484 **Sofia**

1393 3418 2726 1063 1006 1509 2713 1888 1673 2254 1069 1431 505 946 167 3185 590 1350 3650 1824 1536 3109 2358 2064 1228 1600 530 1845 1351 2629 3659 2679 **Stockholm**

1256 2128 2366 1909 606 1350 1473 648 1542 2110 2268 1136 1274 886 361 1989 956 1152 3480 1680 1345 2960 2015 1469 1245 996 1506 1677 616 1853 3397 1439 1612 **Warszawa**

1168 1772 1856 1970 640 1114 1067 242 1308 1954 2034 731 1308 947 1088 1583 1010 916 3100 1524 993 2473 1353 818 2137 430 1600 1240 295 1126 2876 1033 1646 727 **Wien**

816 2426 1030 1938 863 619 1810 985 804 1352 1530 464 1497 915 2164 2323 1433 589 2296 922 410 1647 699 292 2552 303 1815 592 691 898 2061 1173 1861 1307 743 **Zurich**

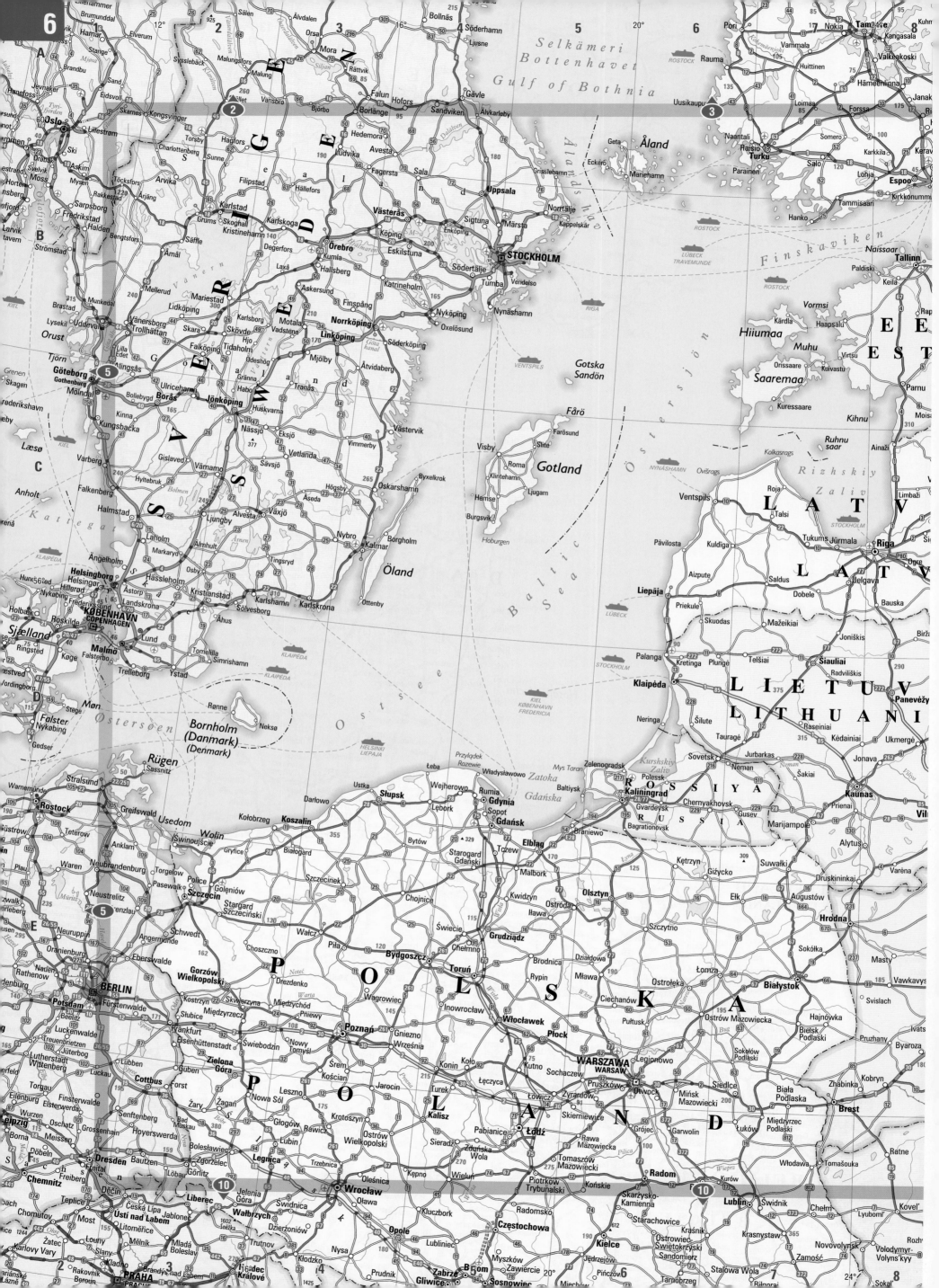

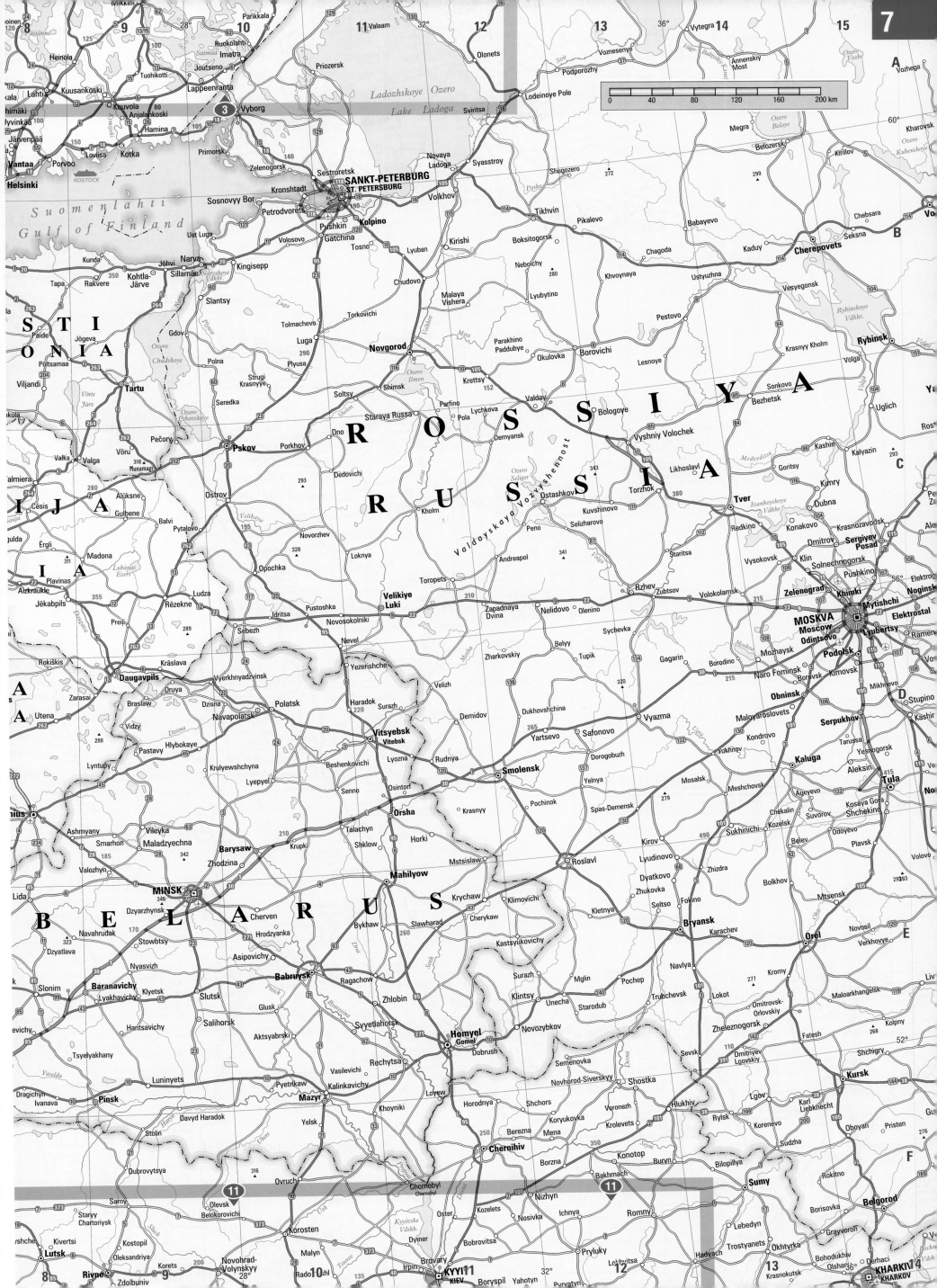

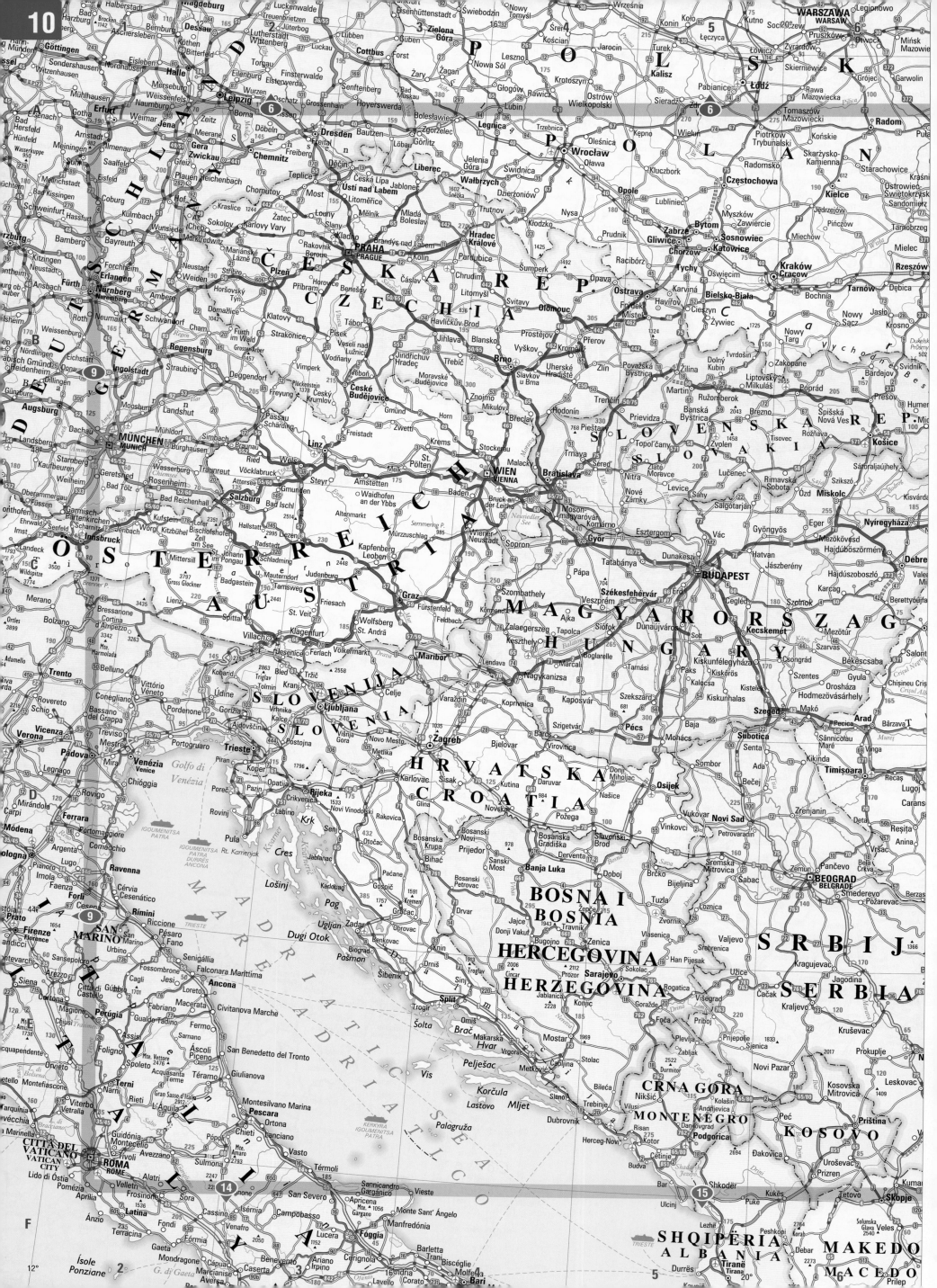

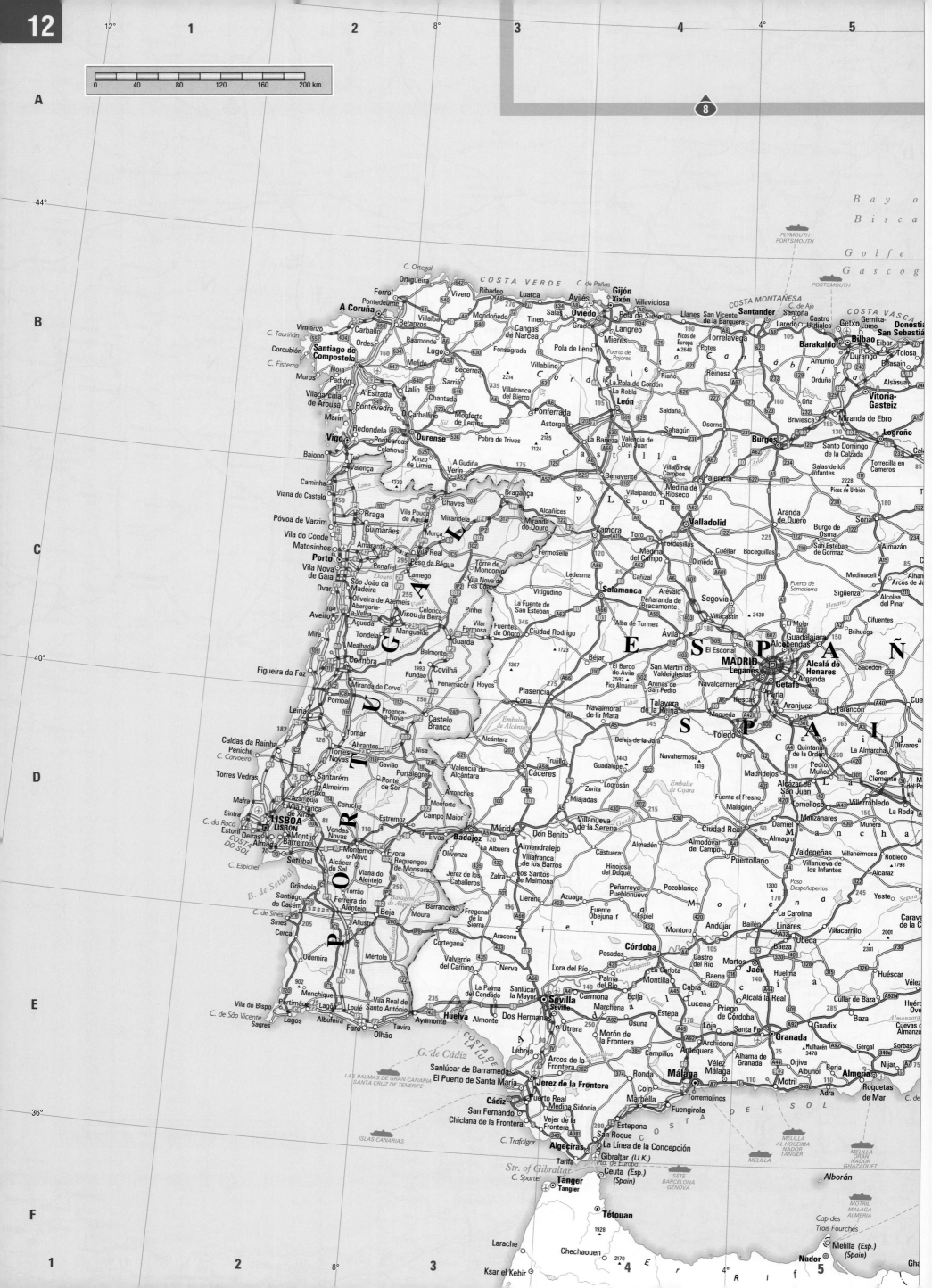

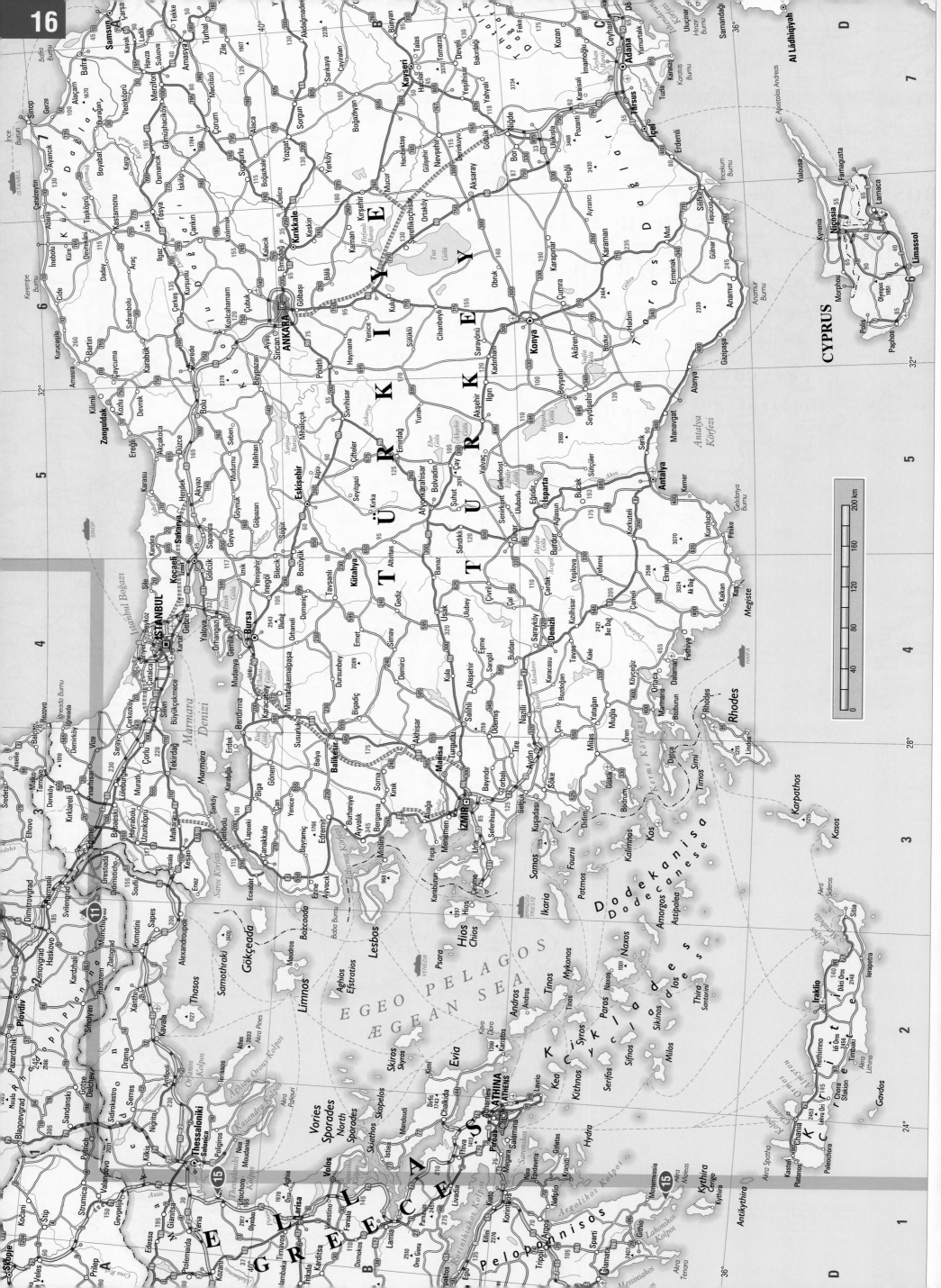

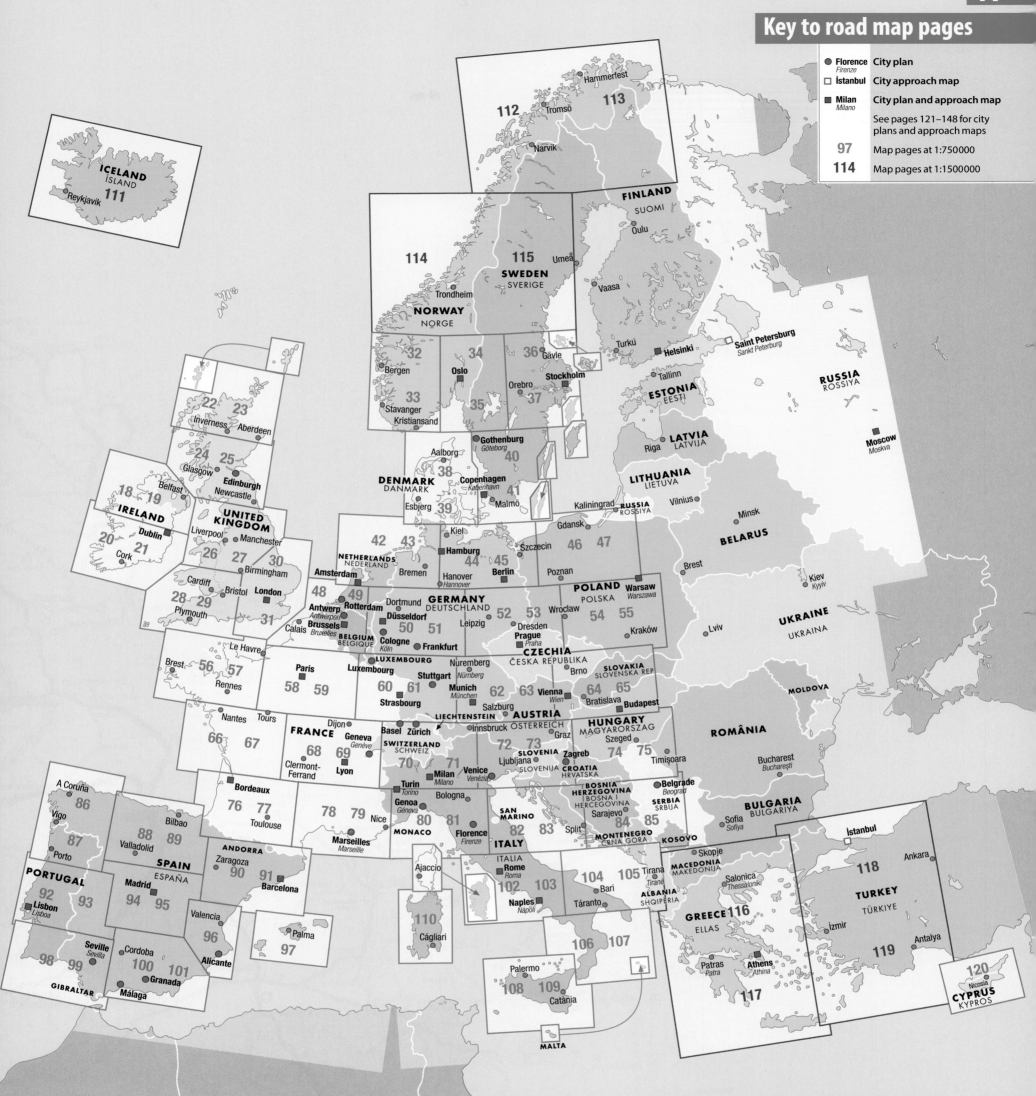

Key to road map pages

- ● **Florence** *Firenze* City plan
- □ **İstanbul** City approach map
- ■ **Milan** *Milano* City plan and approach map

See pages 121–148 for city plans and approach maps

97 Map pages at 1:750000

114 Map pages at 1:1500000

Motorway vignettes

Some countries require you to purchase (and in some cases display) a vignette before using motorways.

In Austria you will need to purchase and display a vignette on the inside of your windscreen. Vignettes are available for purchase at border crossings and petrol stations. More details from www.asfinag.at/toll/toll-sticker

In Belarus all vehicles over 3.5 tonnes and cars and vans under 3.5 tonnes registered outside the Eurasion Economic Union are required to have a BelToll unit installed. This device exchanges data with roadside gantries, enabling motorway tolls to be automatically deducted from the driver's account. http://beltoll.by/index.php/en/

In Czechia, you can buy a vignette at the border and also at petrol stations. Make sure you write your vehicle registration number on the vignette before displaying it. The roads without toll are indicated by a traffic sign saying "Bez poplatku". More details from www.motorway.cz

In Hungary a new e-vignette system was introduced in 2008. It is therefore no longer necessary to display the vignette, though you should make doubly sure the information you give on your vehicle is accurate. Vignettes are sold at petrol stations throughout the country. Buy online at http://toll-charge.hu/

In Slovakia, an electronic vignette must purchased before using the motorways. Vignettes may be purchased online, via a mobile app or at Slovak border crossings and petrol stations displaying the 'eznamka' logo. More details from https://eznamka.sk/selfcare/home/

In Switzerland, you will need to purchase and display a vignette before you drive on the motorway. Bear in mind you will need a separate vignette if you are towing a caravan. www.ezv.admin.ch/ezv/en/home/information-individuals/documents-for-travellers-and-road-taxes/motorway-charge-sticker--vignette-.html

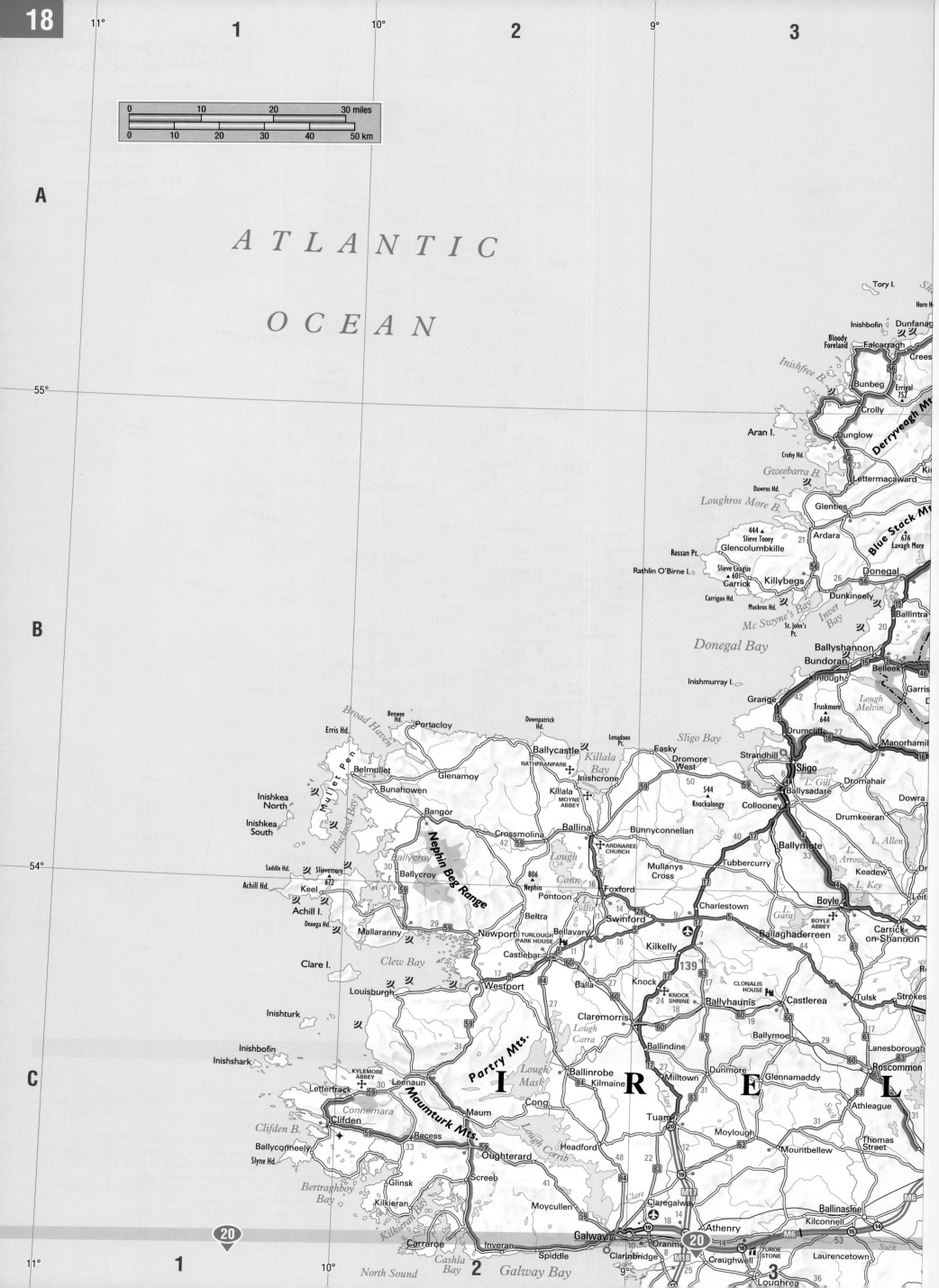

11°   1   10°   2   9°   3

0   10   20   30 miles
0   10   20   30   40   50 km

A

ATLANTIC

OCEAN

55°

Tory I.

Horn Hd.

Inishbofin   Dunfanag
Bloody
Foreland   Falcarragh
Crees
Bunbeg   42
Errigal
752
Crolly
Aran I.   Dunglow
Derryveagh Mts.
Crohy Hd.   Lettermacaward   Ki
Gweebarra B.
Dawros Hd.   Glenties   Blue Stack Mts.
Loughros More B.
444   Ardara   676
Slieve Tooey   21   Lavagh More
Rossan Pt.   Glencolumbkille
Slieve League   56   Donegal
Rathlin O'Birne I.   601   Killybegs   26
Carrick   Muckros Hd.   Dunkineely   15
Carrigan Hd.   Ballintra
St. John's   Mc Swyne's Bay   Inver
Pt.   Bay   20

B   Inishmurray I.   Ballyshannon   7
Donegal Bay   Bundoran   15   Belleek   46
Kinlough   Garris
Grange   42   Lough
Melvin
Truskmore   15
Sligo Bay   644   Drumcliff   Manorhamil
16
Benwee   Downpatrick   Lenadoon   Easky   Strandhill   Sligo   16
Hd.   Portacloy   Hd.   Pt.   Dromore   8   L. Gill   Dromahair
Broad Haven   Ballycastle   West   4   Ballysadare
Erris Hd.   RATHFRANPARK   Killala   Inishcrone   50   544   Colllooney   Dowra
Belmullet   Glenamoy   Bay   Knockalongy   Ballymote   L. Allen
Killala   59   Tubbercurry   33   Keadew
Bunahowen   MOYNE   Bunnyconnellan   40   17   L.
Inishkea   ABBEY   Ballina   Mullanys   17   Arrow   Drumkeeran   Leit
North   Bangor   ARDNAREE   Cross   Boyle   L. Key
Crossmolina   42   59   CHURCH   806   17   32
Inishkea   30   Lough   26   Foxford   Charlestown   5   BOYLE
South   Ballycroy   Conn   16   Swinford   9   17   ABBEY   Carrick-
Saddle Hd.   Nephin   Pontoon   14   26   Ballaghaderreen   on-Shannon
Slievemore   677   Ballycroy   Beltra   Cullin   11   Kilkelly   5   44   61
Achill Hd.   Keel   Nephin Beg Range   Newport   TURLOUGH   Knock   CLONALIS
Achill I.   29   59   PARK HOUSE   5   Balla   16   139   HOUSE   Castlerea   Strokes
Dooega Hd.   Mallaranny   Castlebar   11   24   Ballyhaunis   33
Clare I.   Clew Bay   84   60   KNOCK   18   Ballymoe   29   Lanesborough
Westport   27   Knock   SHRINE   5
Louisburgh   Balla   60   Clonmel   Castlerea   Roscommon
Inishturk   27   Claremorris   Ballindine   63
Partry Mts.   Lough   60   Dunmore   31   Athleague
Inishbofin   Carra   Milltown   Glennamaddy   L
Inishshark   KYLEMORE   31   Ballinrobe   84   Kilmaine   19   Tuam   Moylough
ABBEY   Leenaun   Lough   Cong   20   63   Mountbellew   Thomas
Letterfrack   30   59   Mask   Headford   48   Street
Connemara   Maumturk Mts.   Maum   Lough   22   31
Clifden B.   Clifden   Recess   Oughterard   Corrib   84   83   19   M17
Ballyconneely   59   33   Screeb   59   Claregalway   Ballinasloe   M6
Slyne Hd.   Glinsk   Moycullen   18   Athenry   Kilconnell   14   Suck
Bertraghboy   Kilkieran   Moycullen   Oranmore   TUROE   53   Laurencetown
Bay   Kilkieran Bay   Spiddle   Galway   19   STONE   15
20   Carraroe   Inveran   Clarinbridge   M18   Craughwell   36
North Sound   Cashla   Galway Bay   25
Bay   Loughrea

54°

C

I   R   E   L

1   10°   2   9°   3

11°   1

20

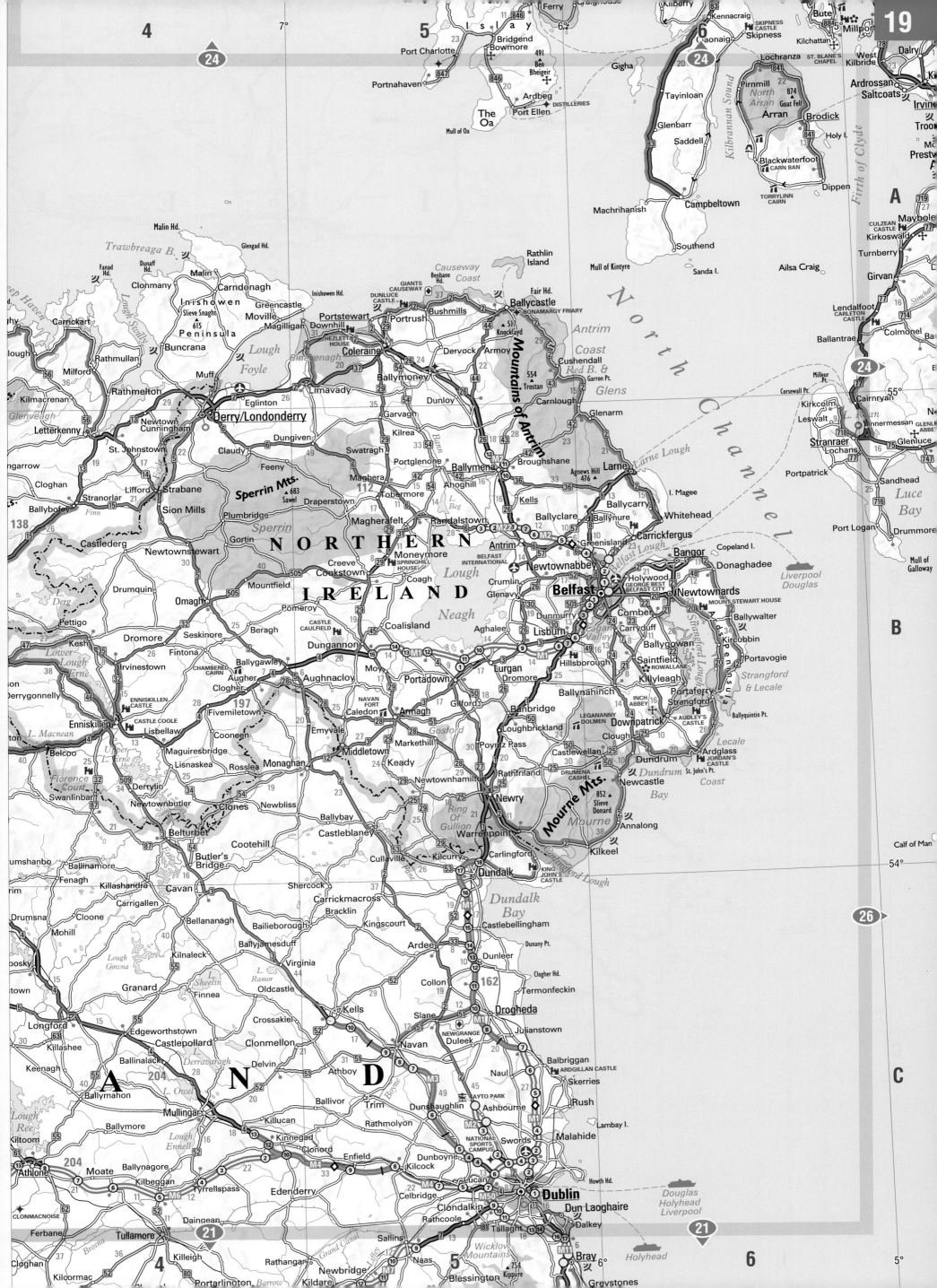

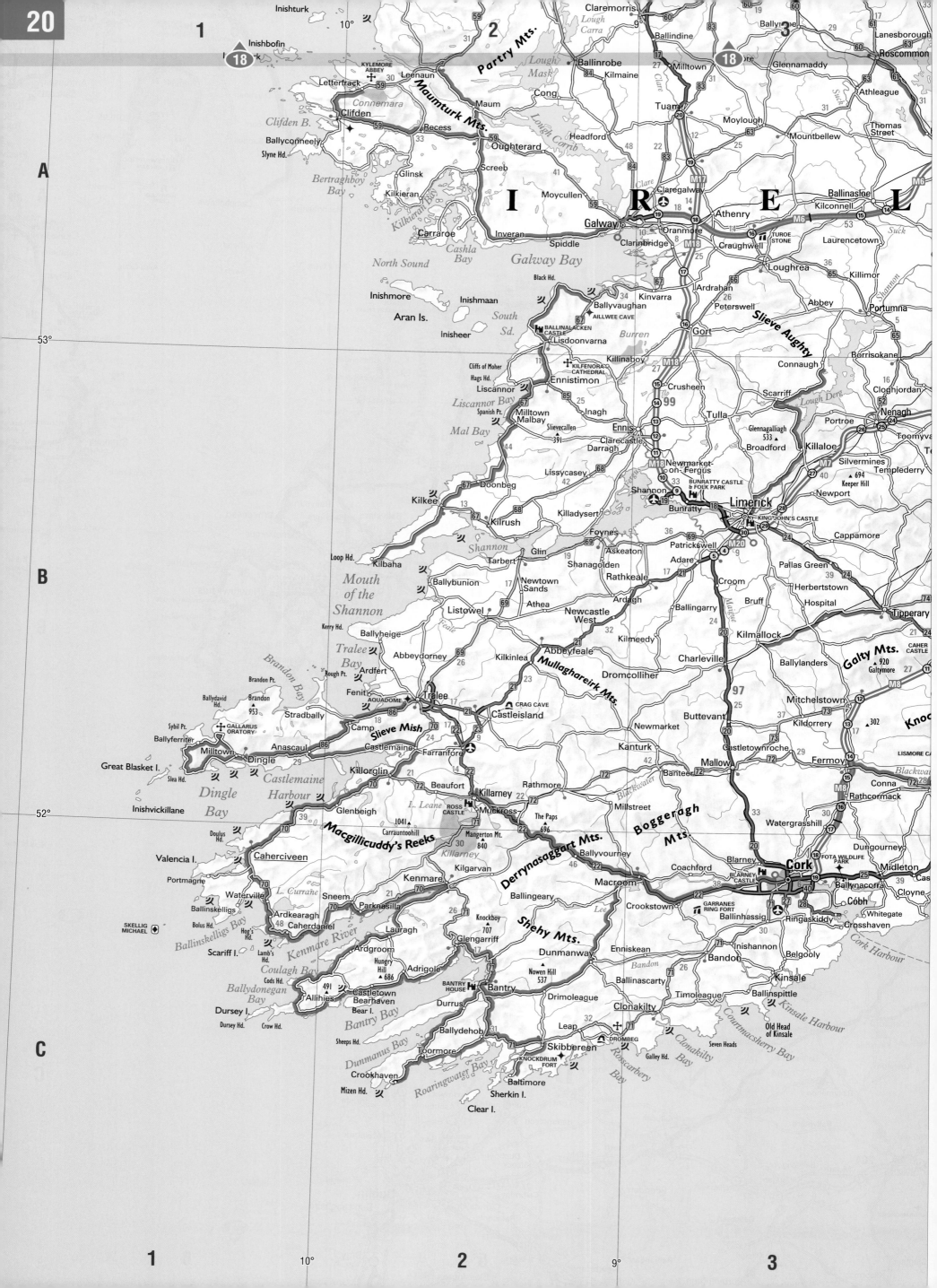

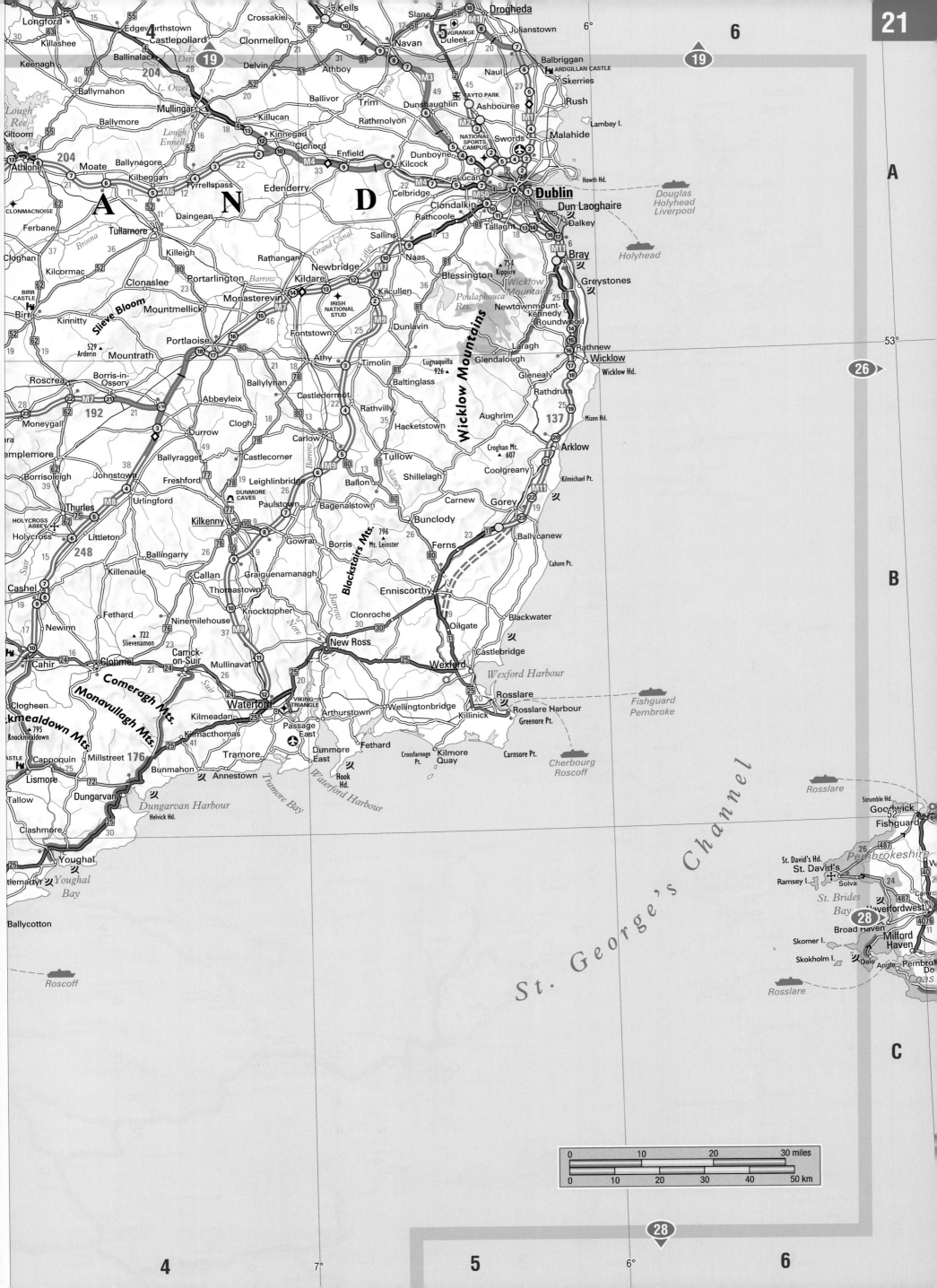

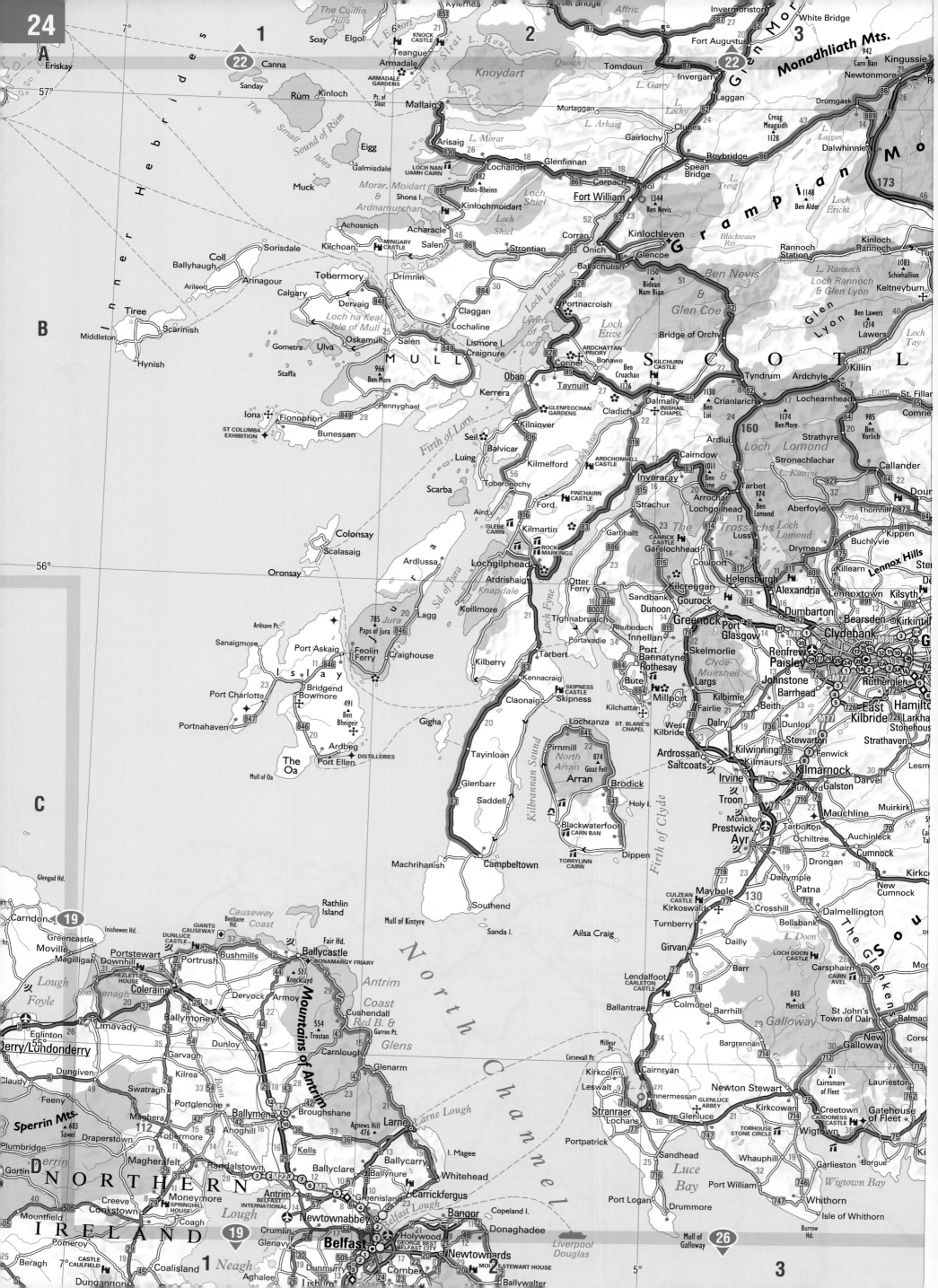

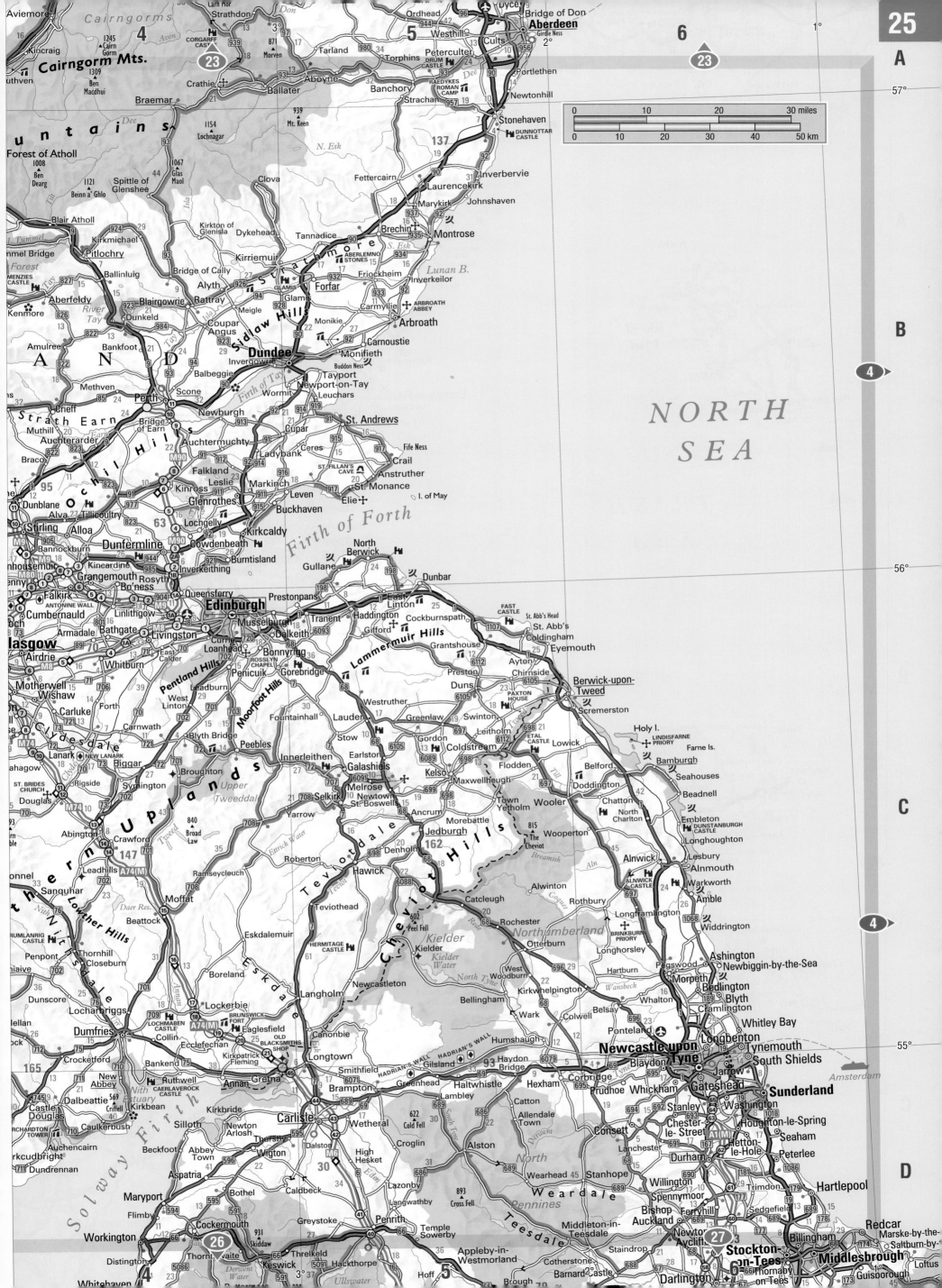

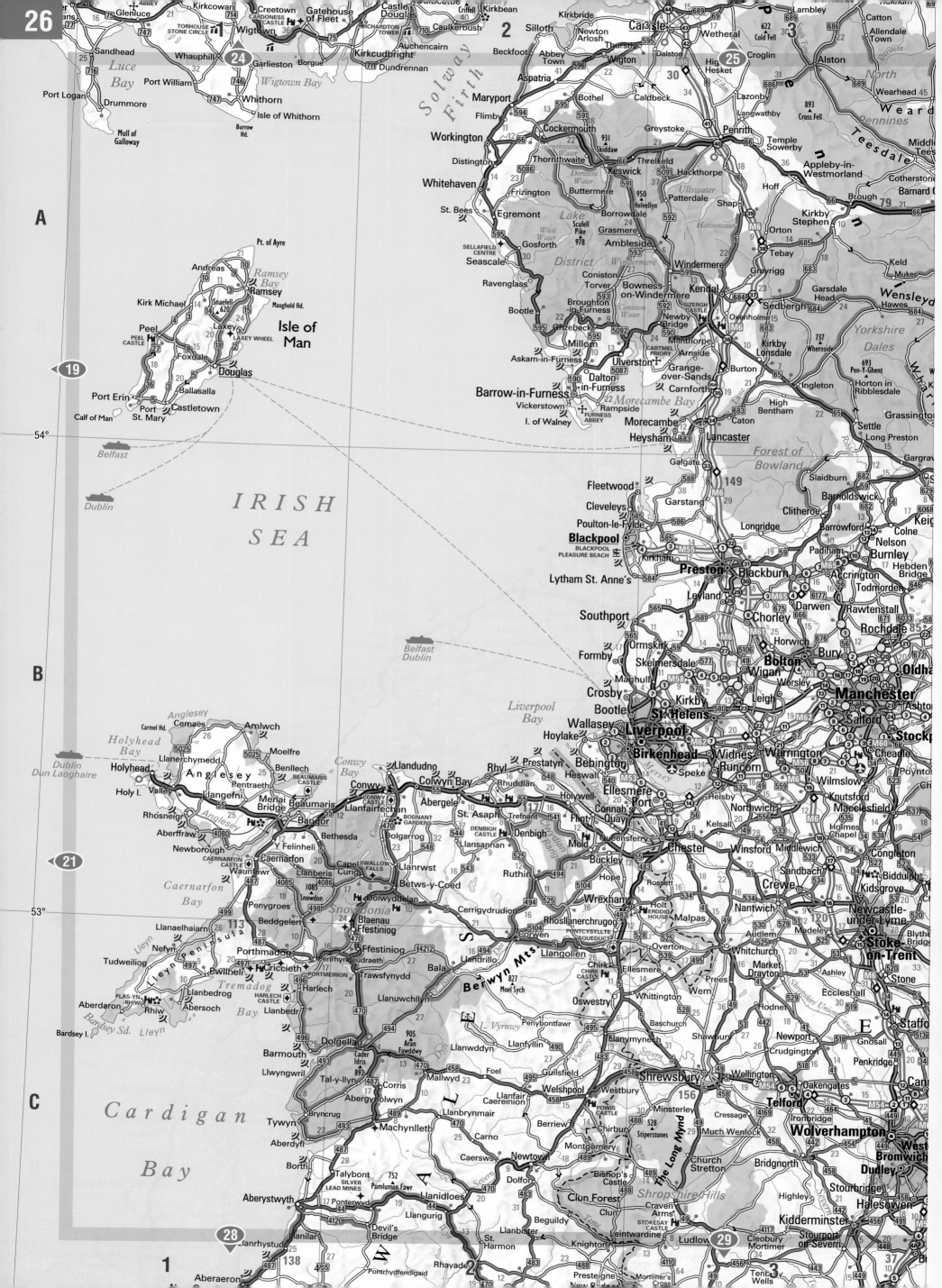

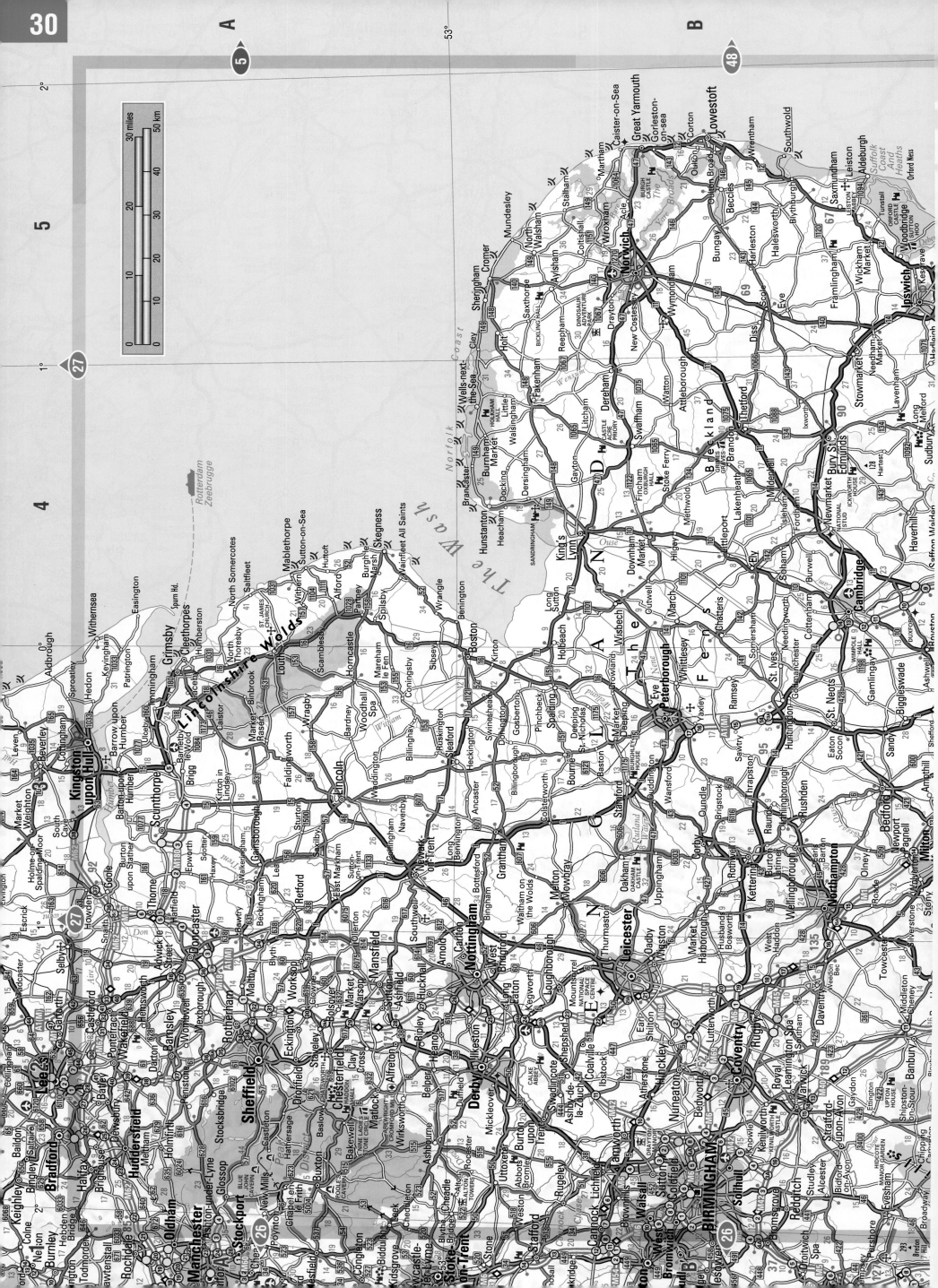

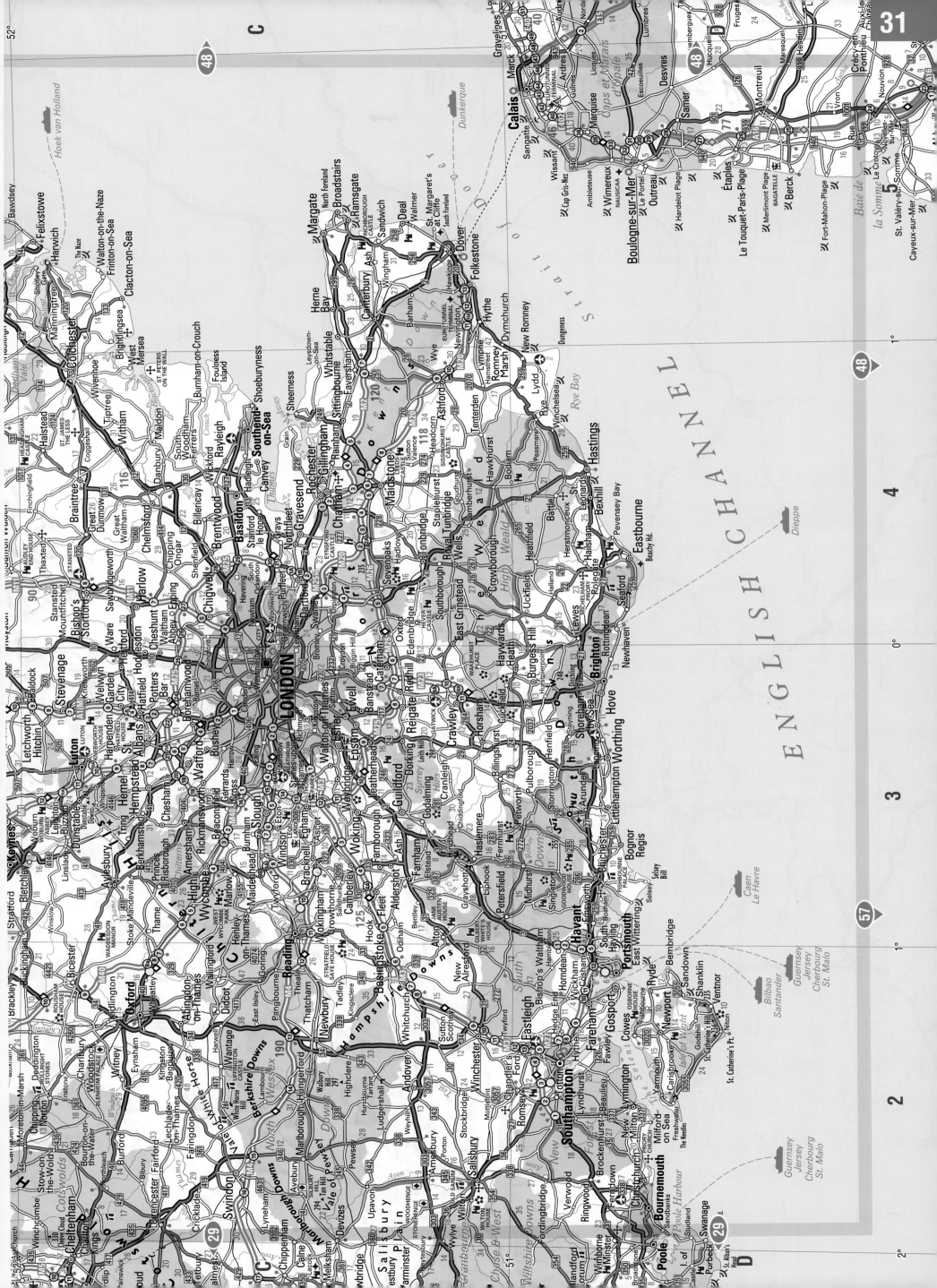

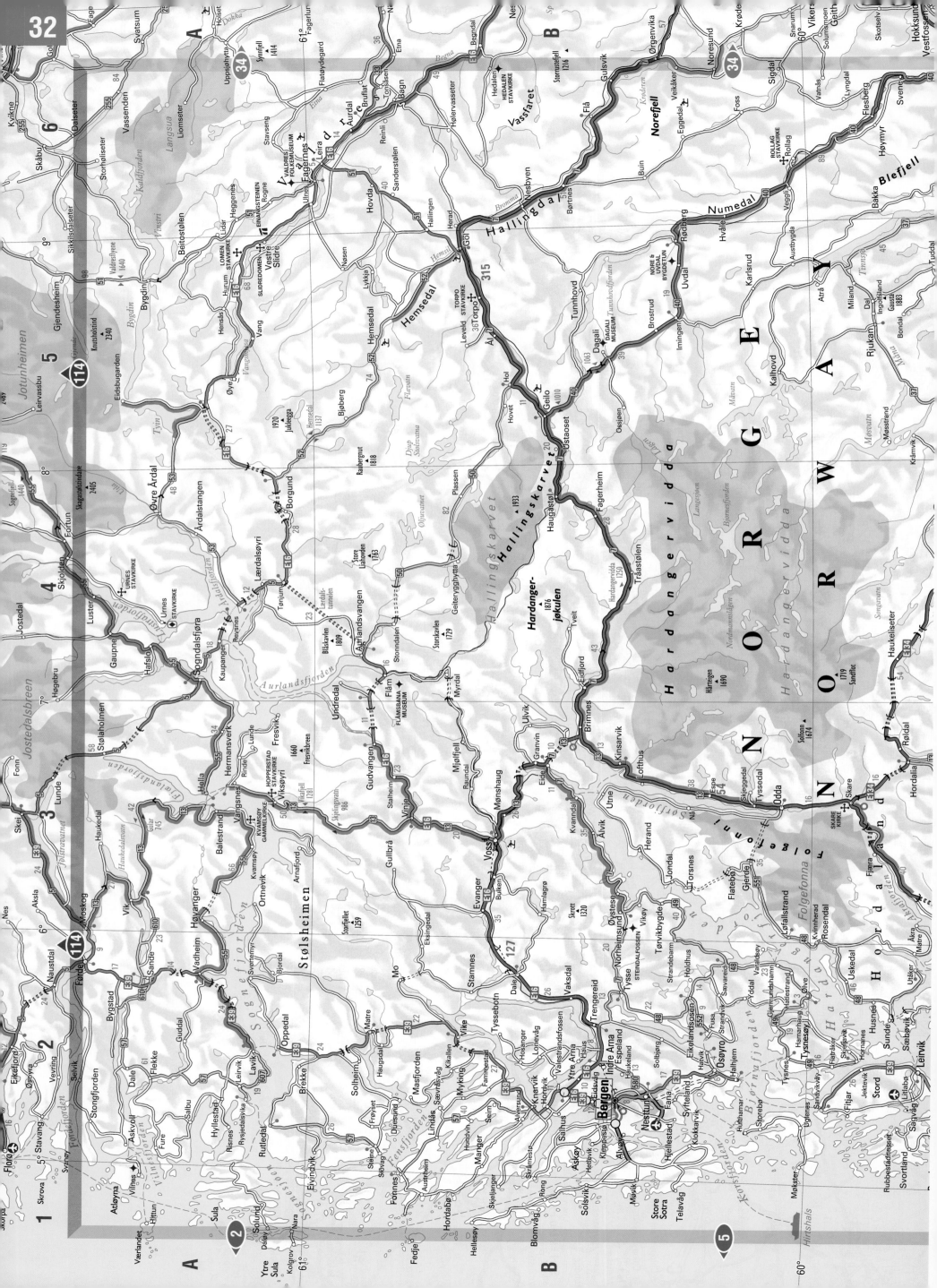

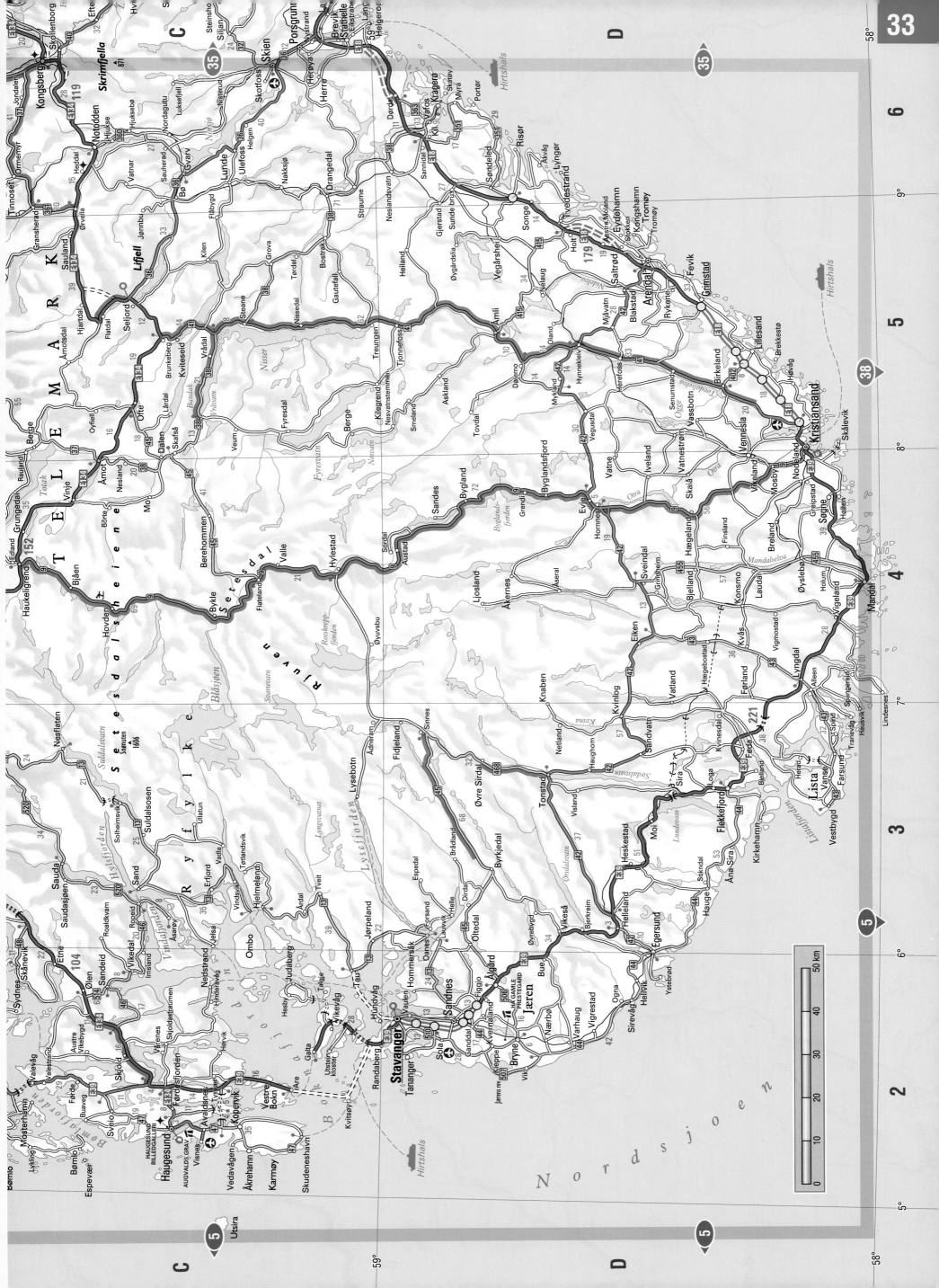

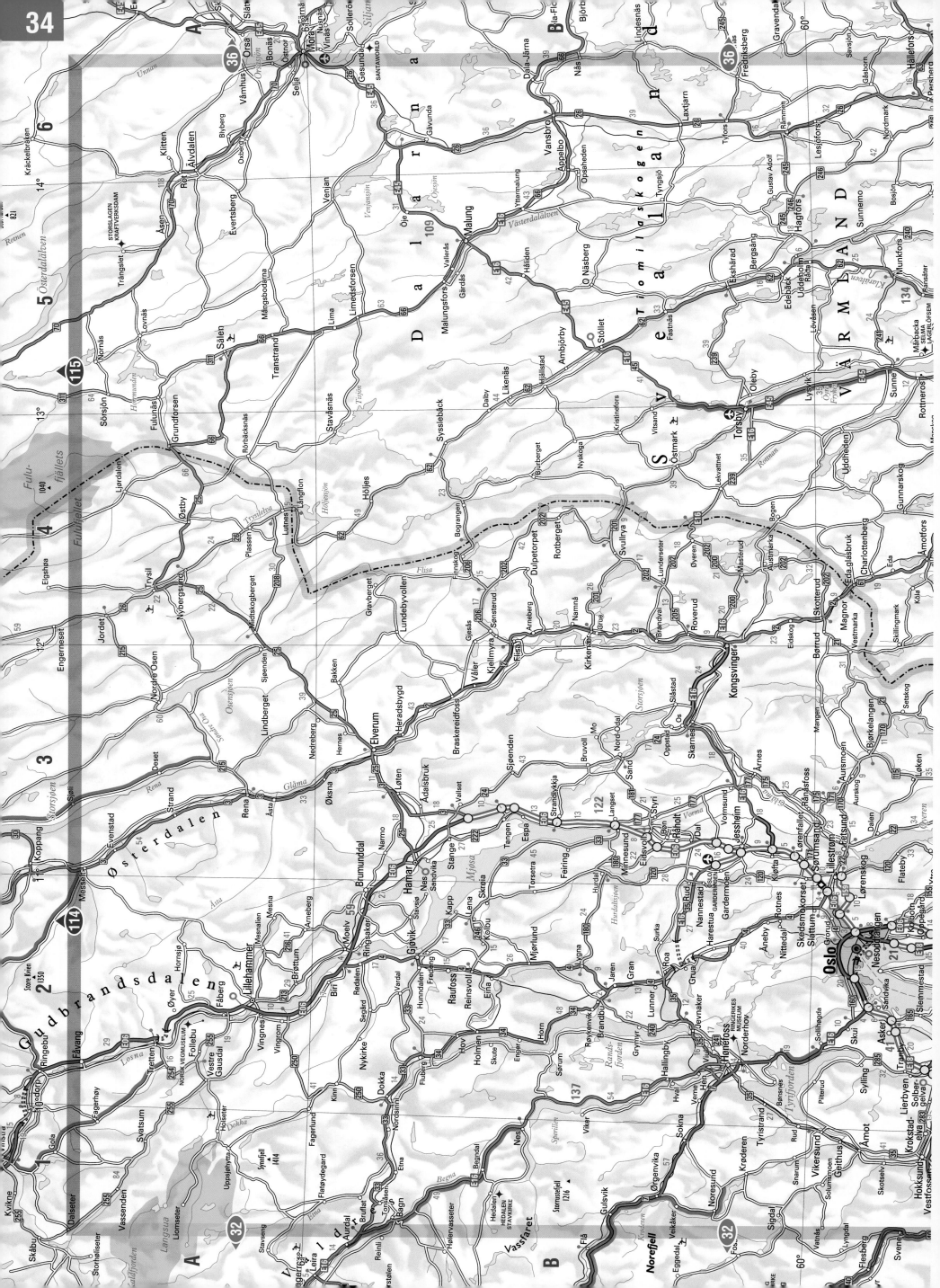

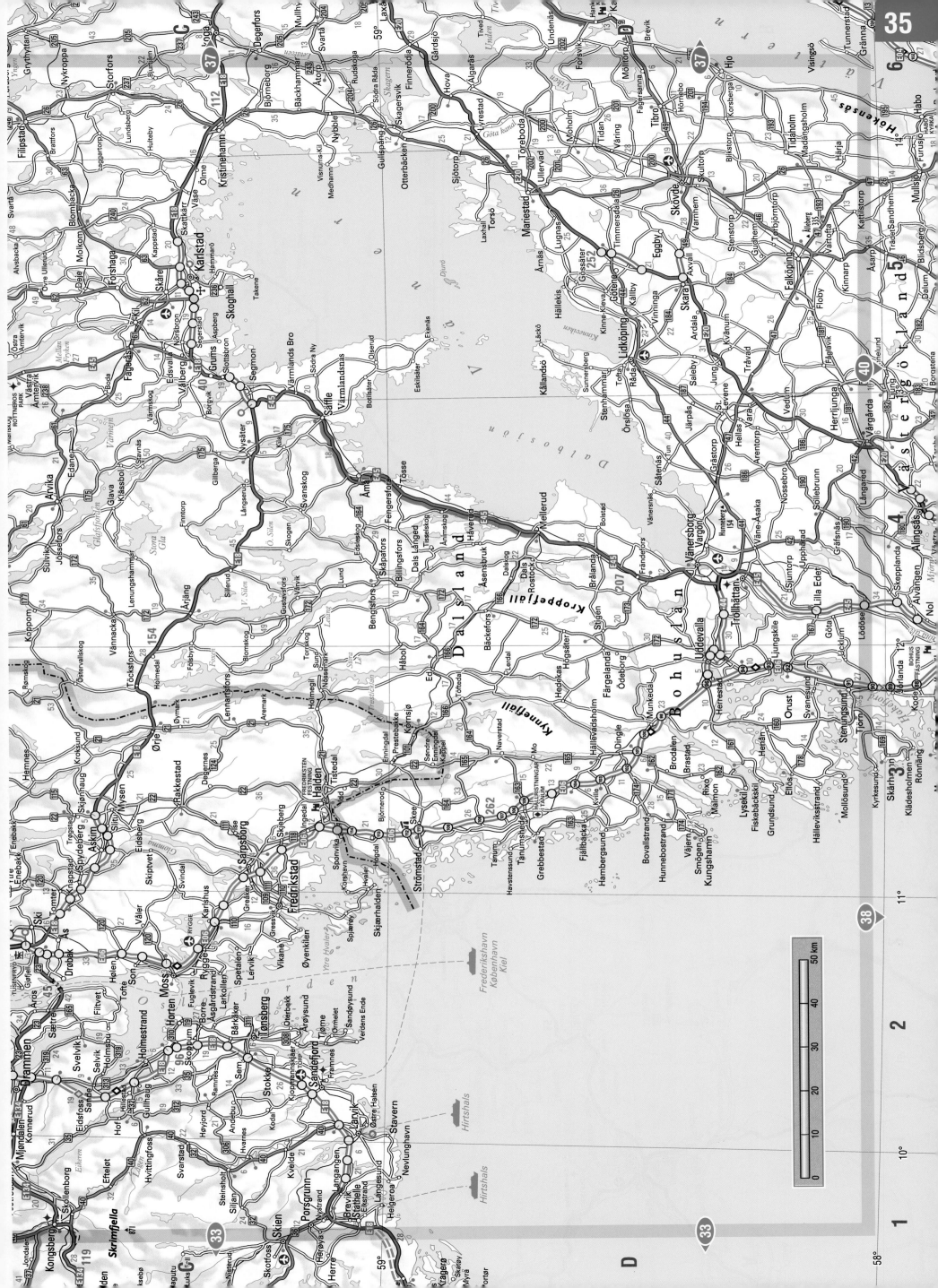

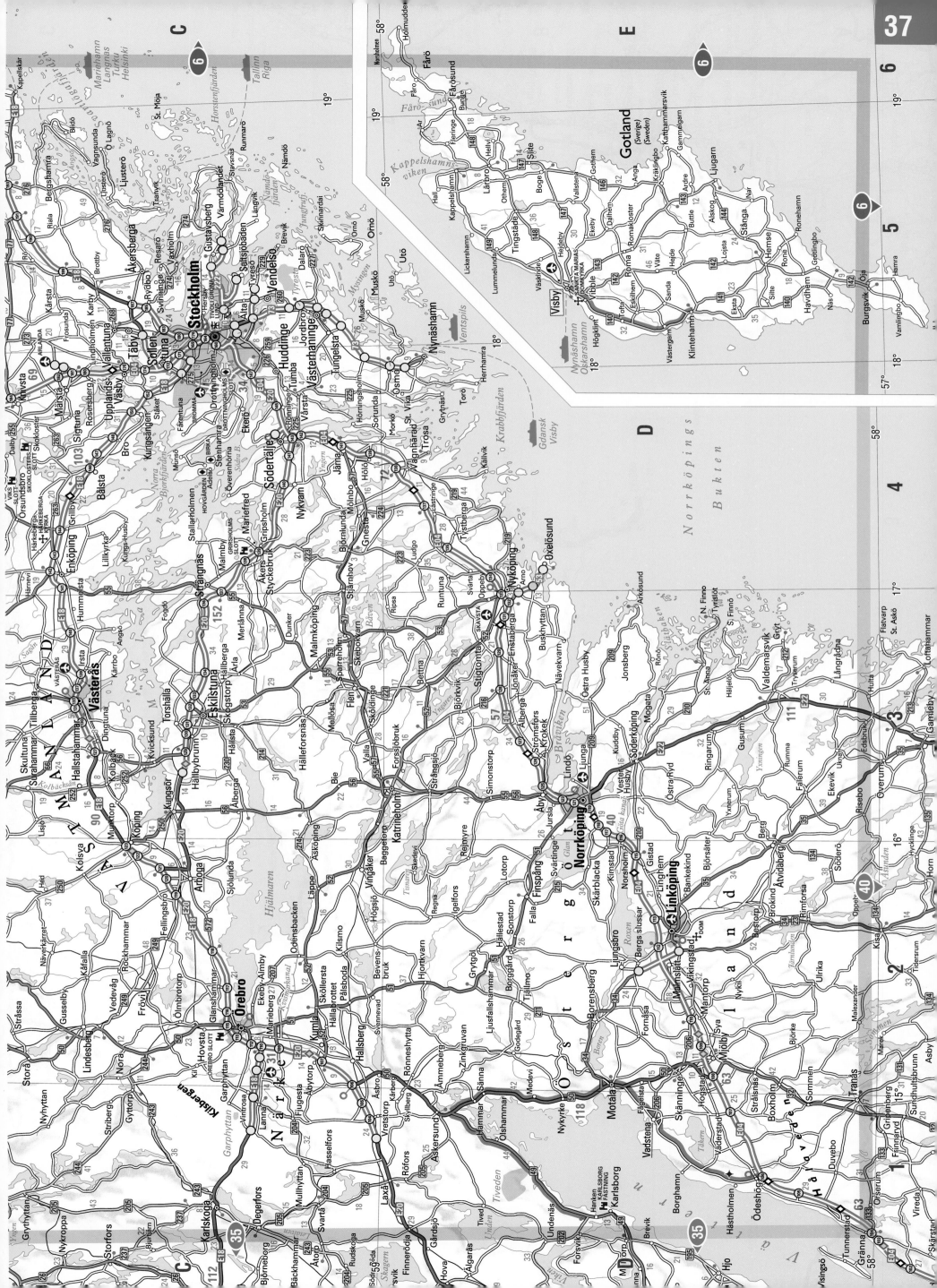

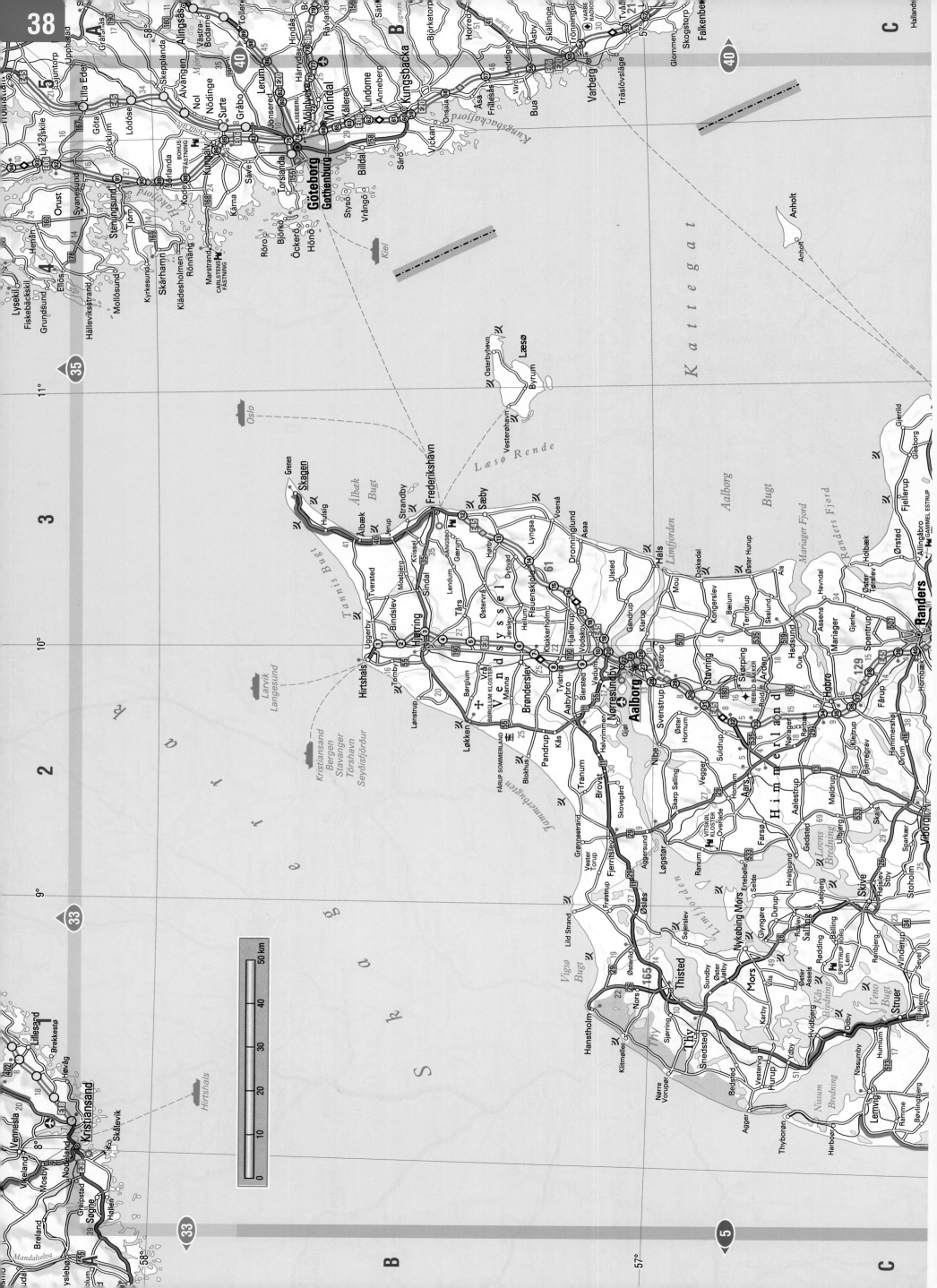

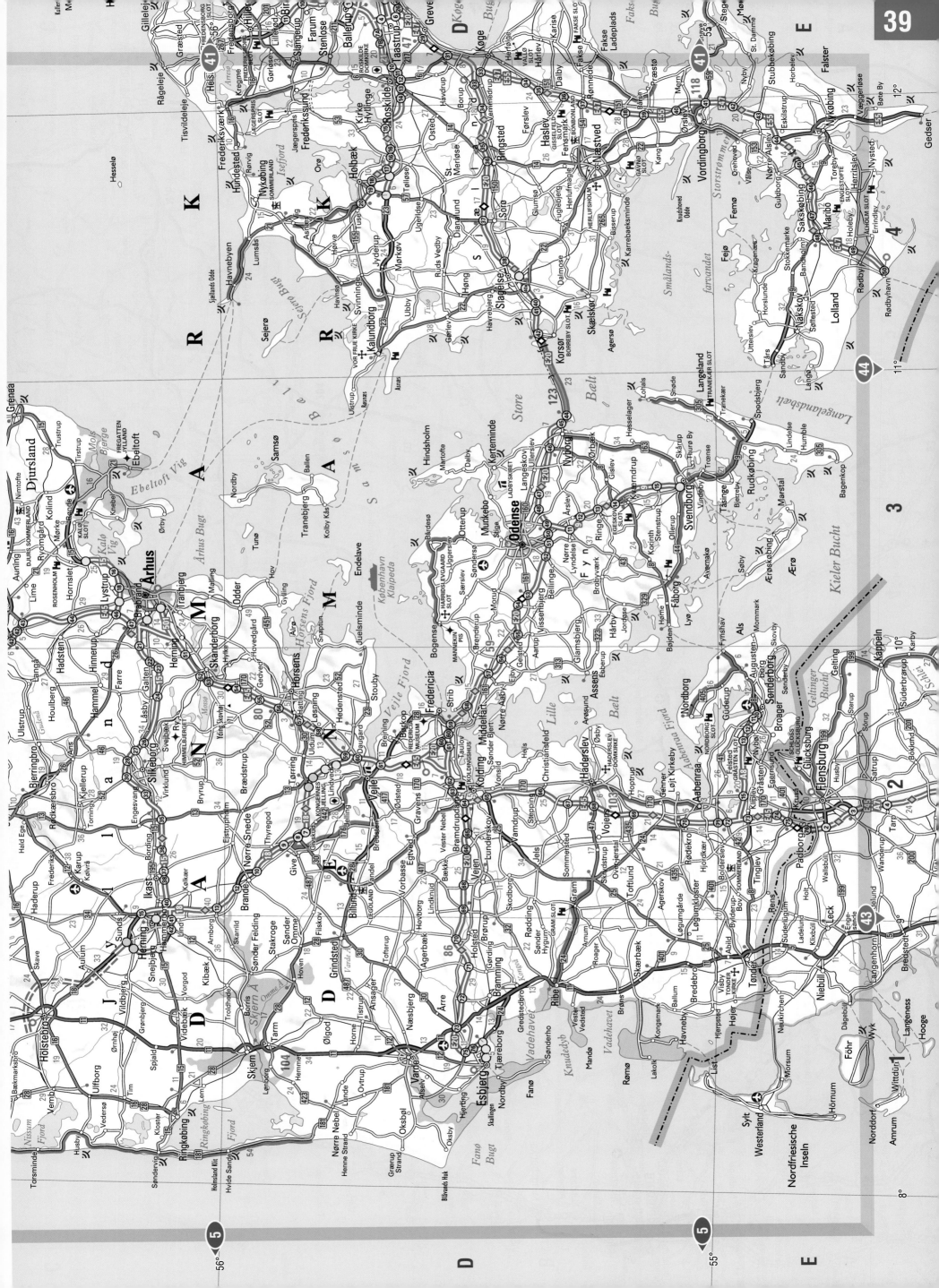

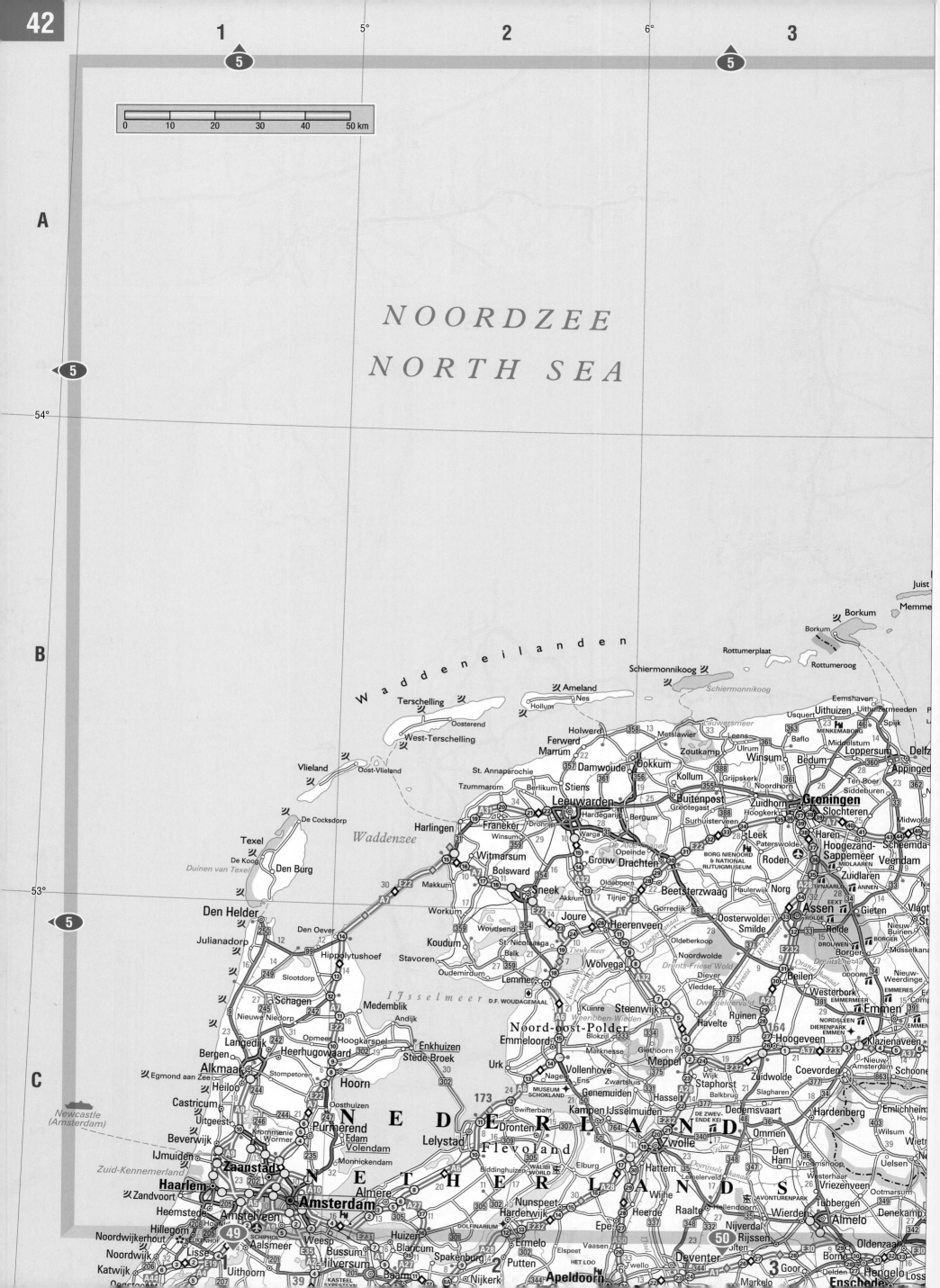

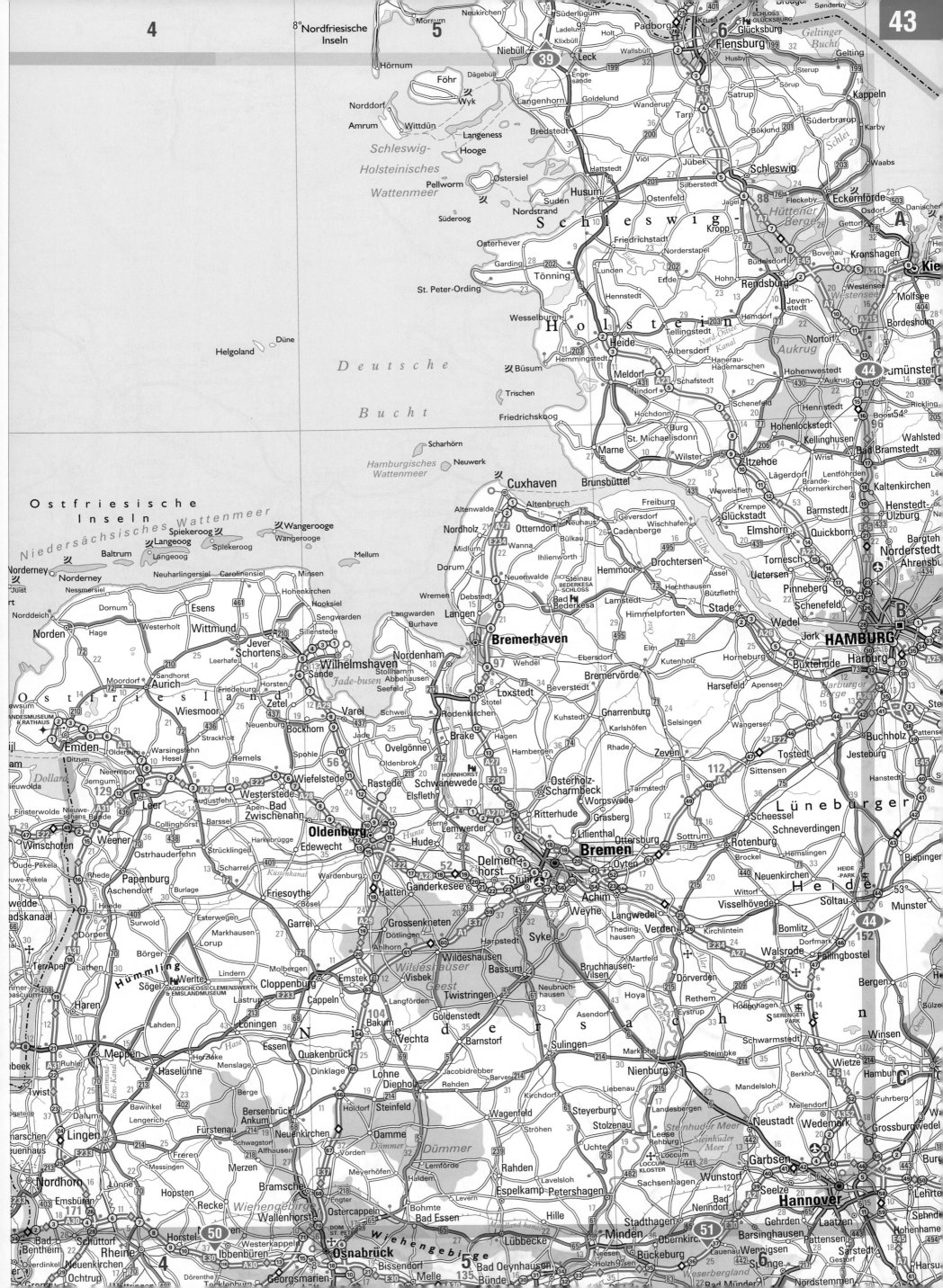

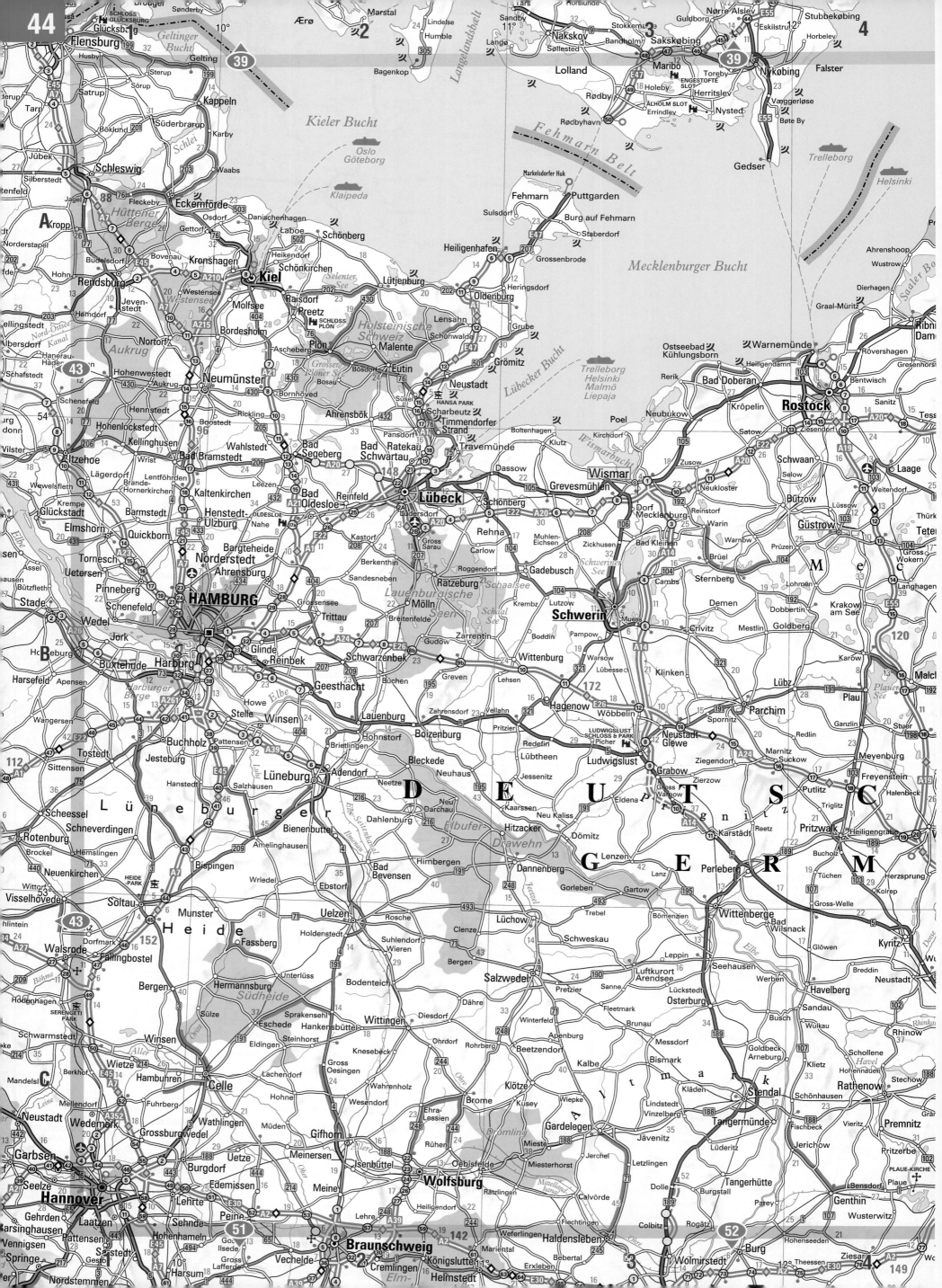

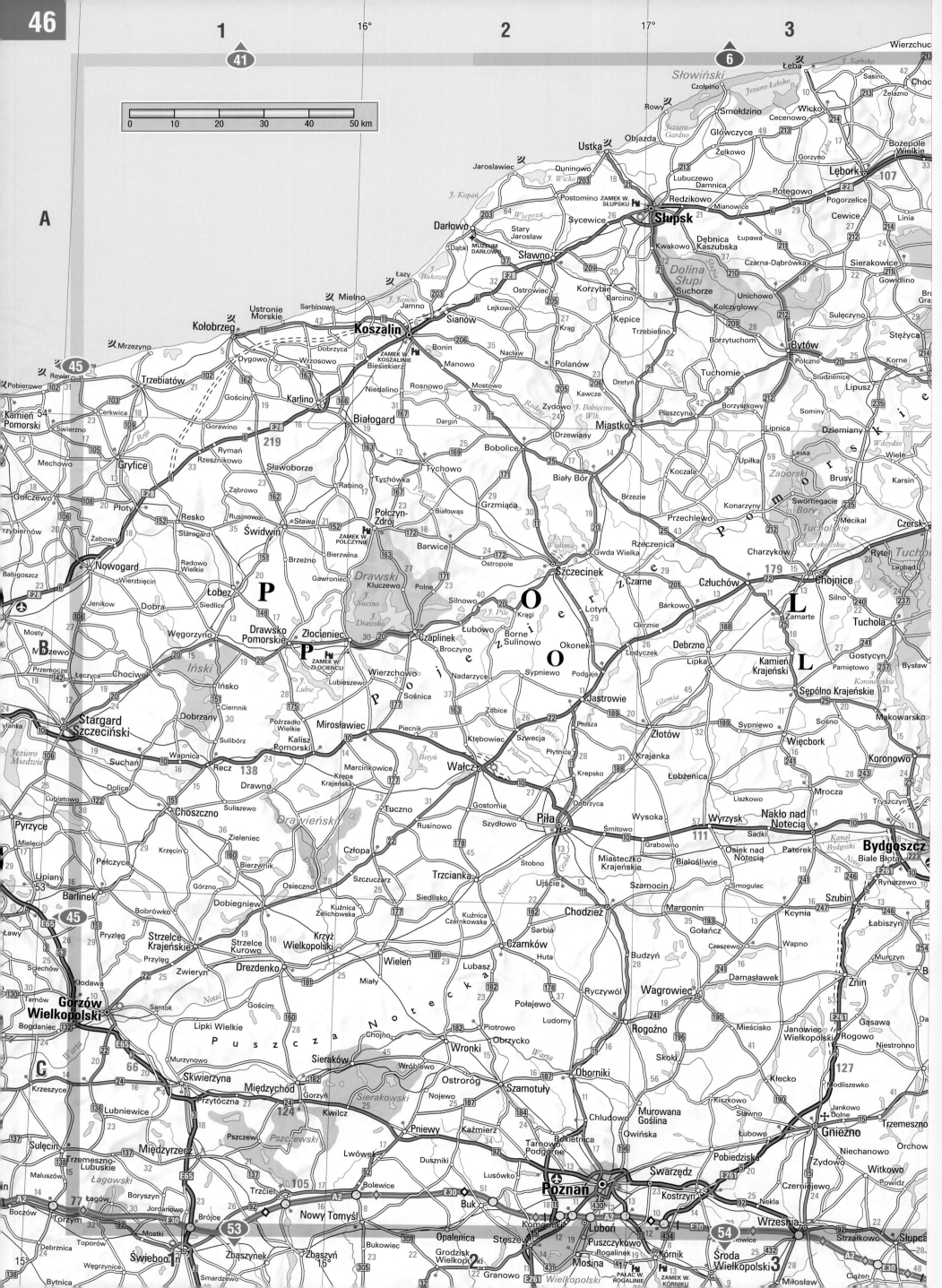

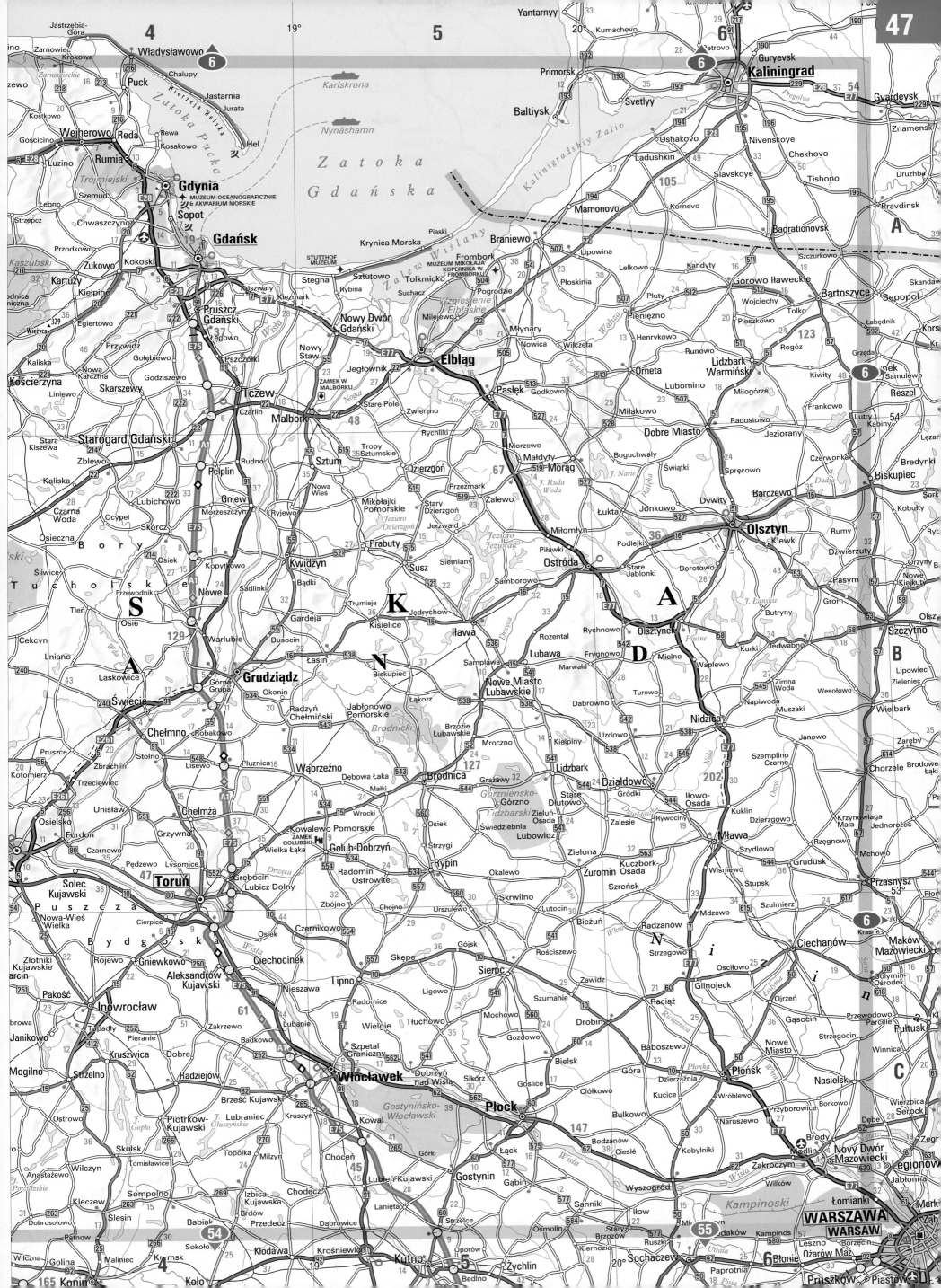

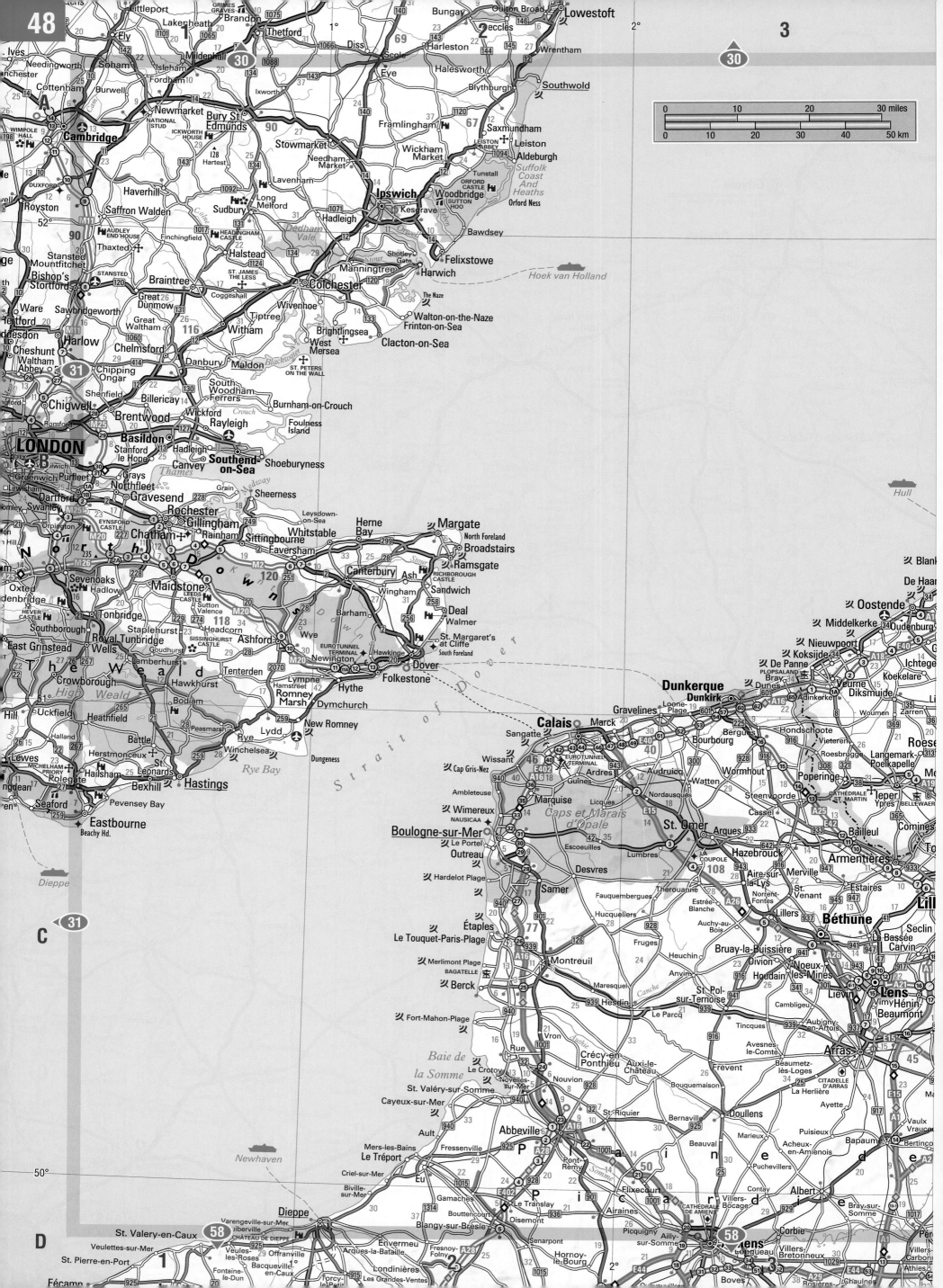

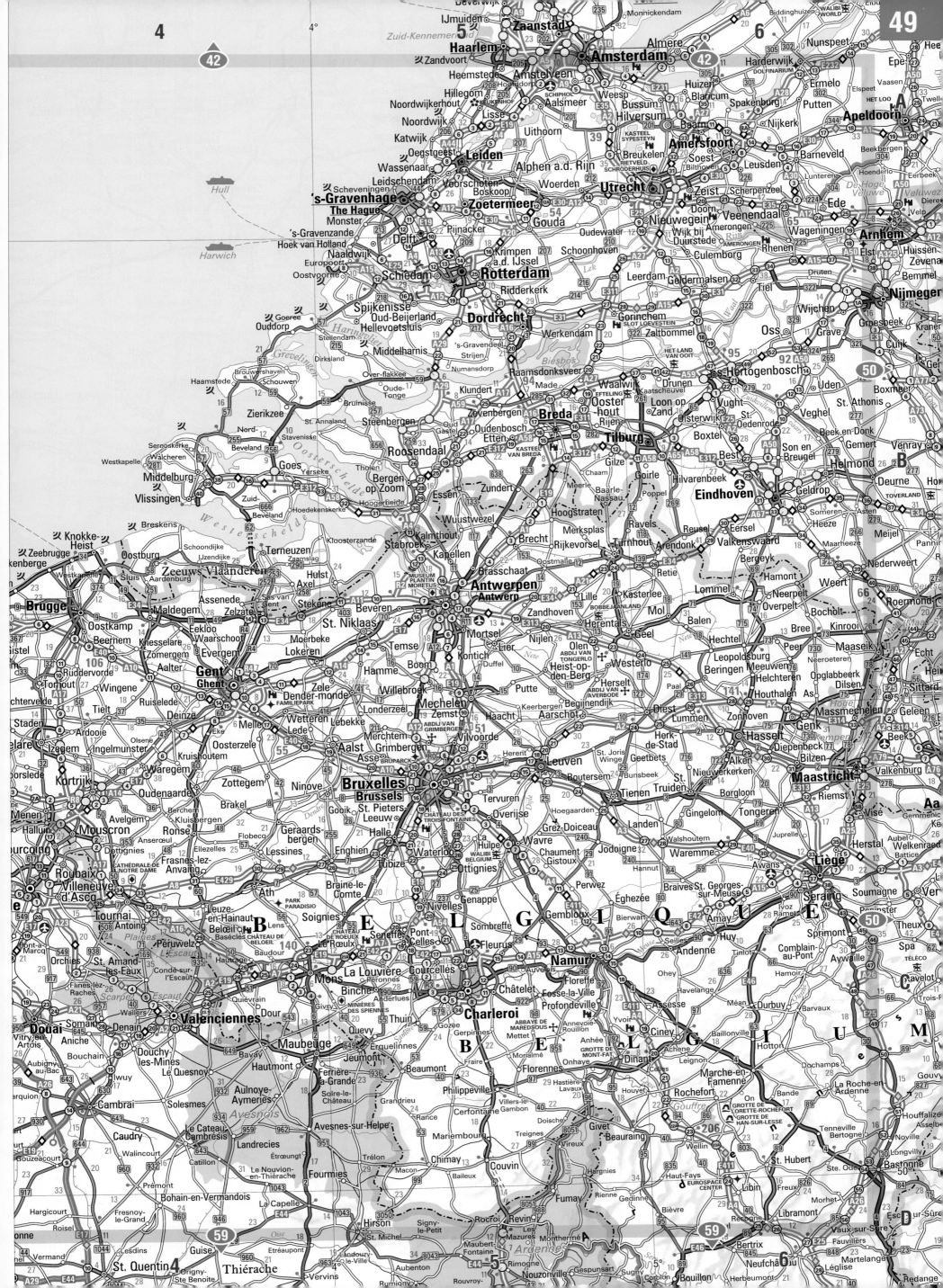

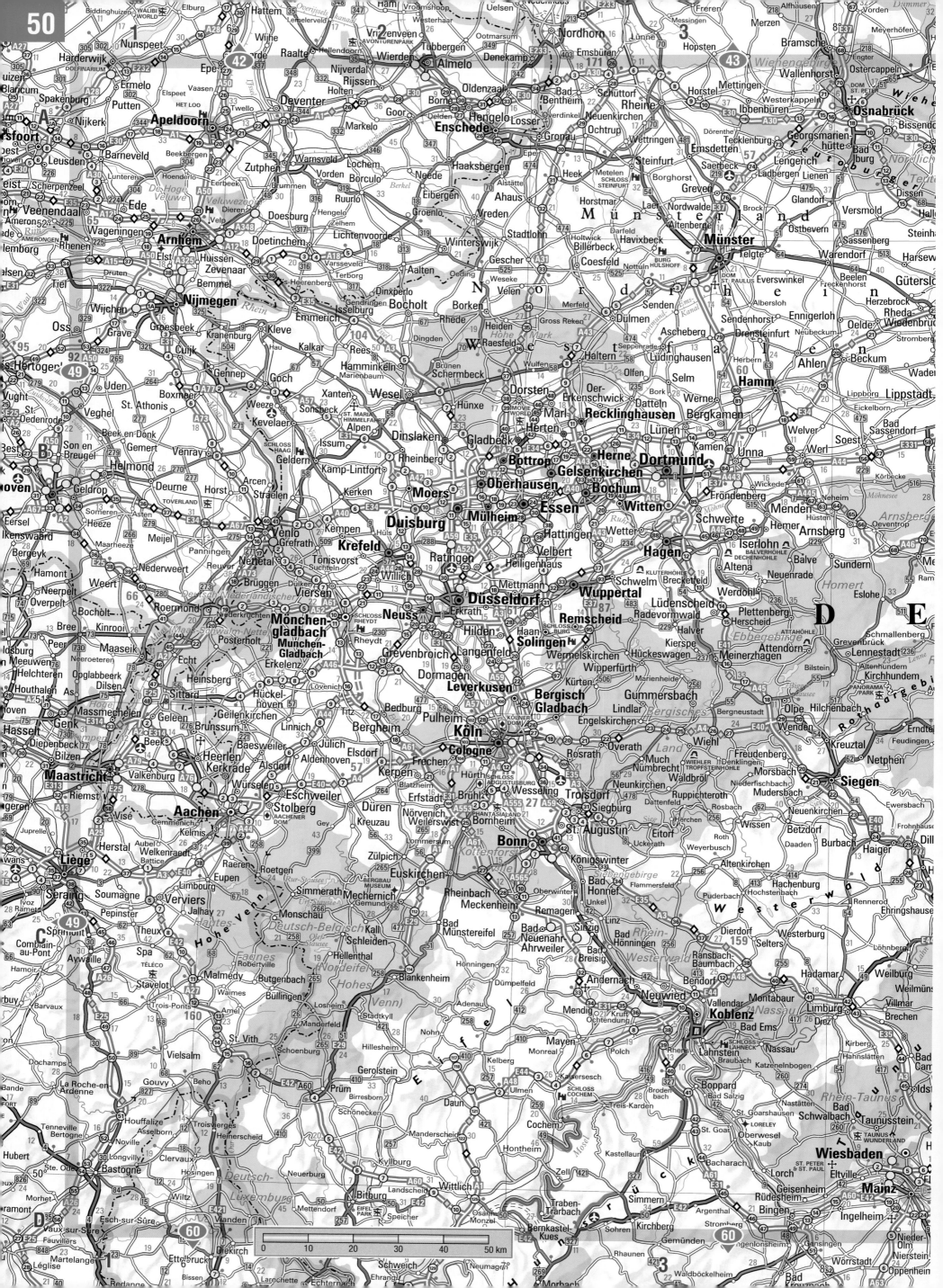

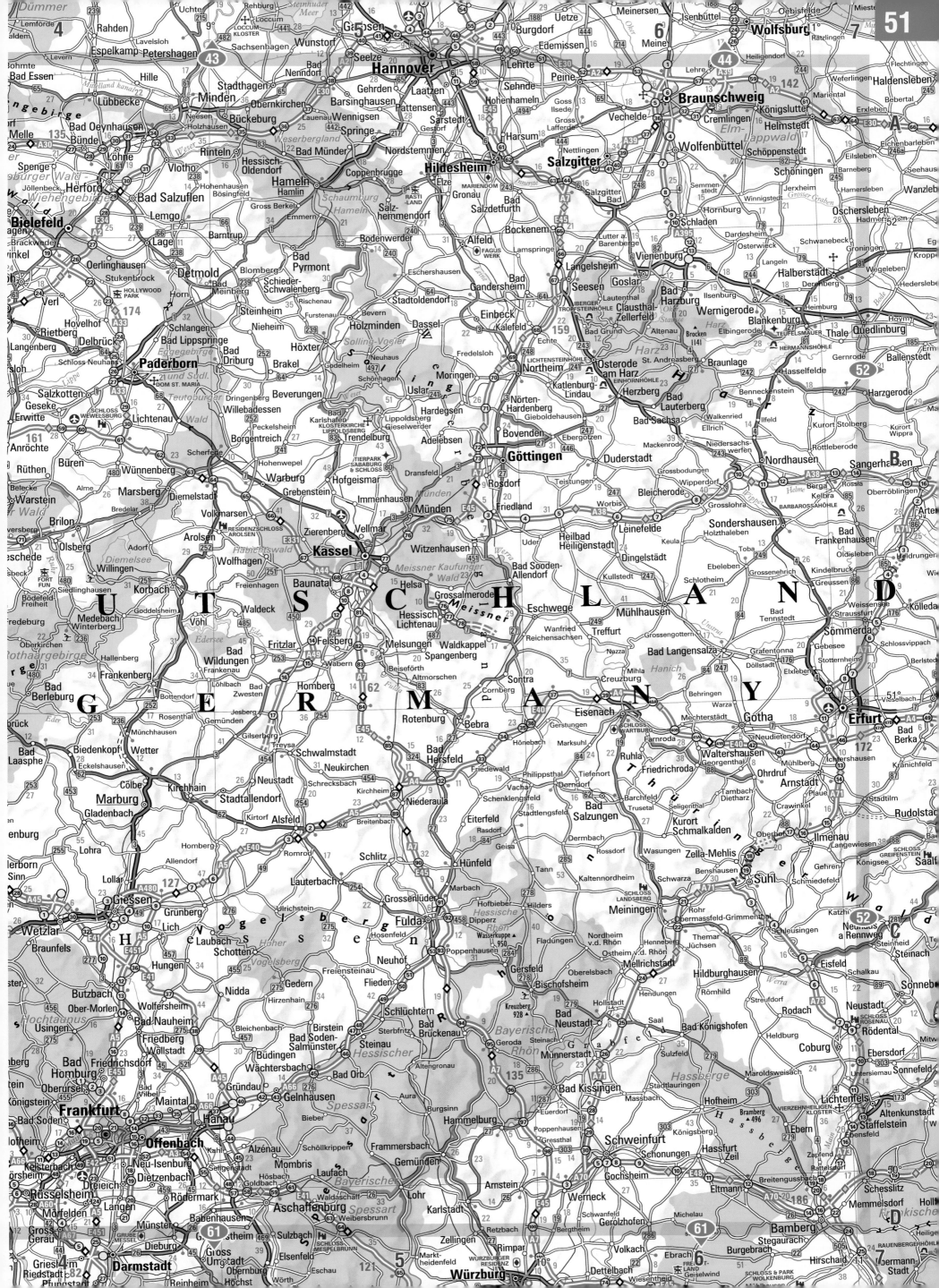

DEUTSCHLAND / GERMANY

Sachsen-Anhalt

Wolfsburg · Braunschweig · Magdeburg · Potsdam · Halle · Leipzig · Chemnitz · Erfurt · Jena · Gera · Zwickau · Plauen · Hof · Bayreuth · Coburg · Bamberg · Karlovy Vary · Chomutov

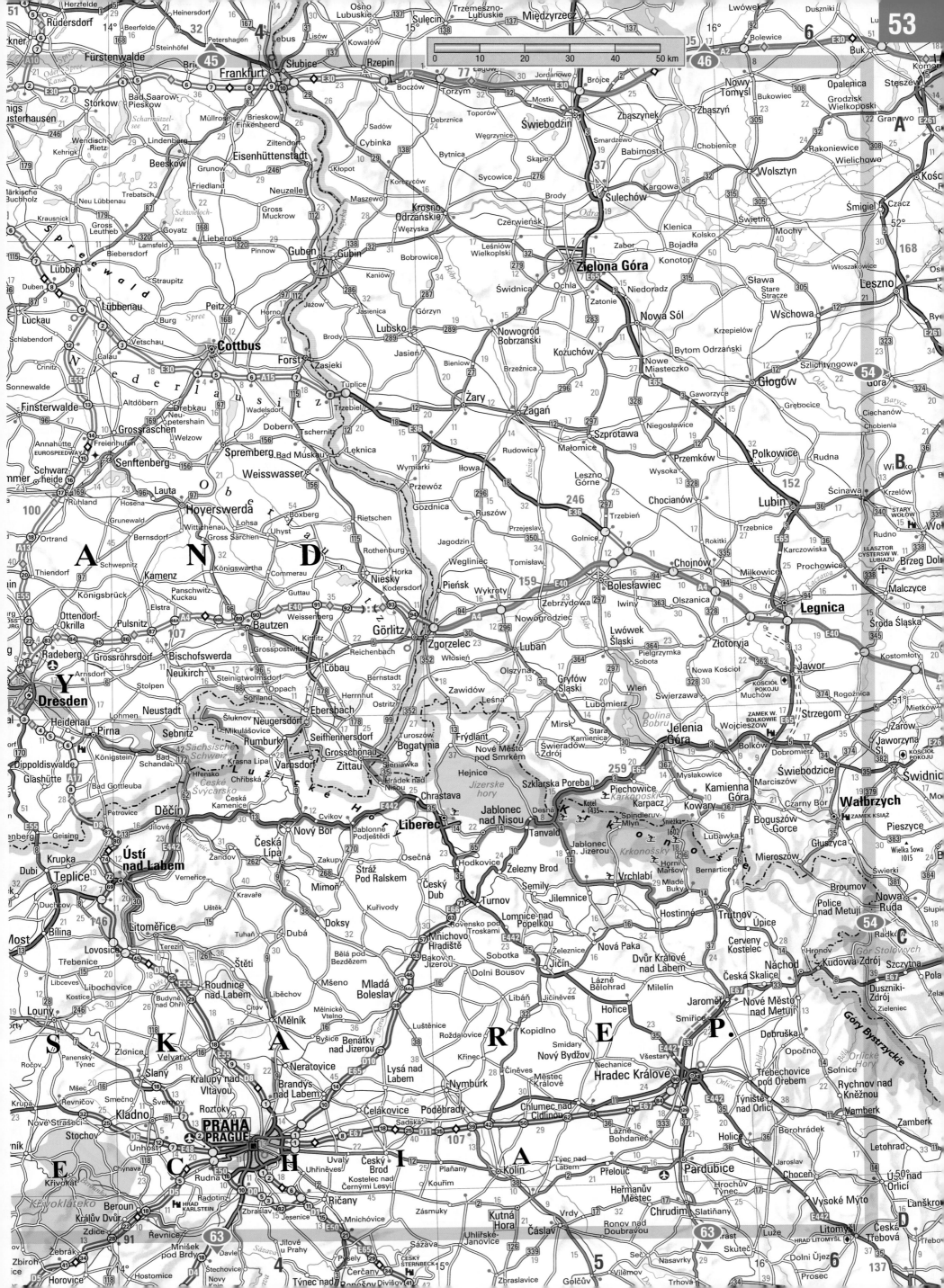

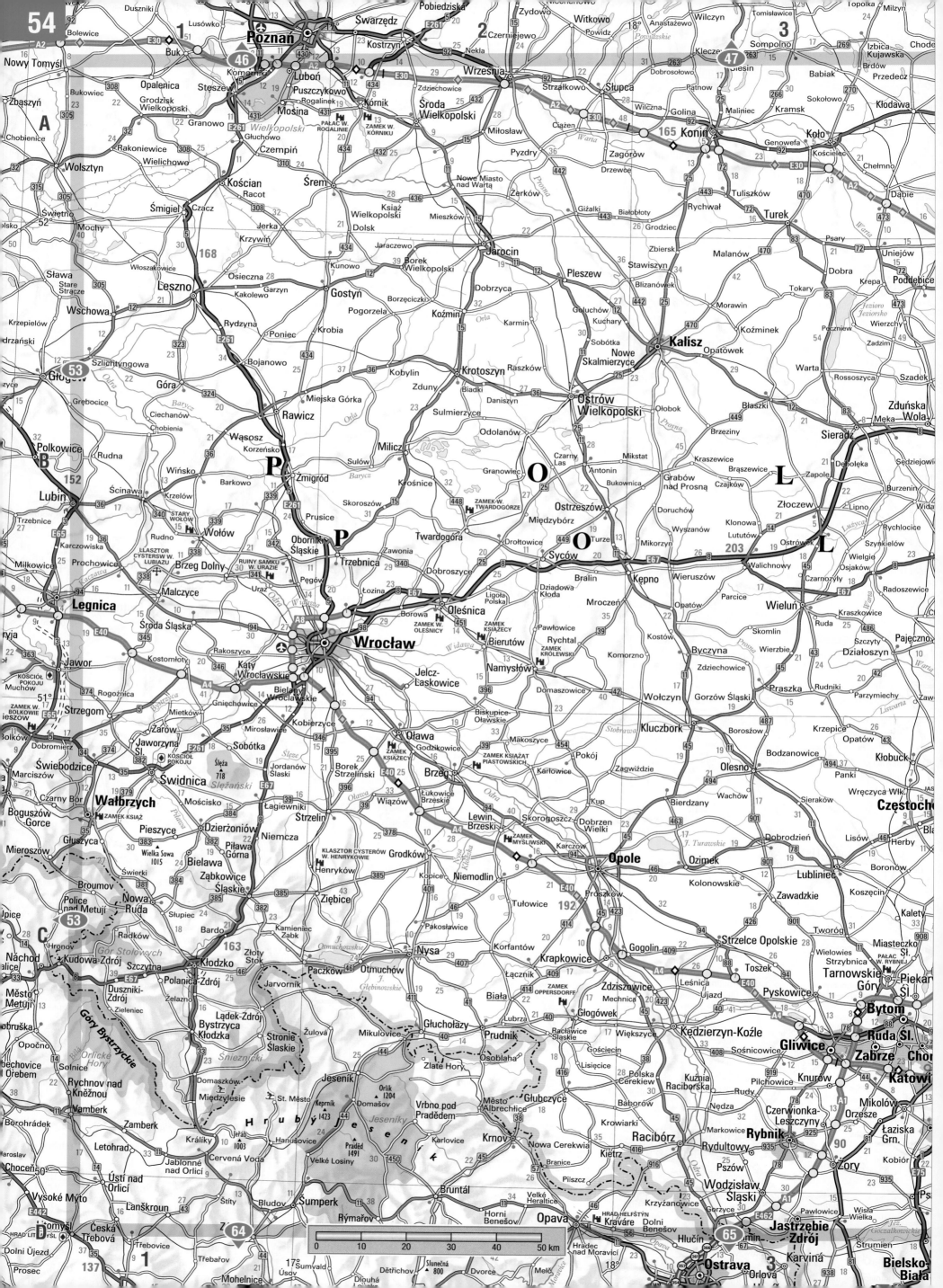

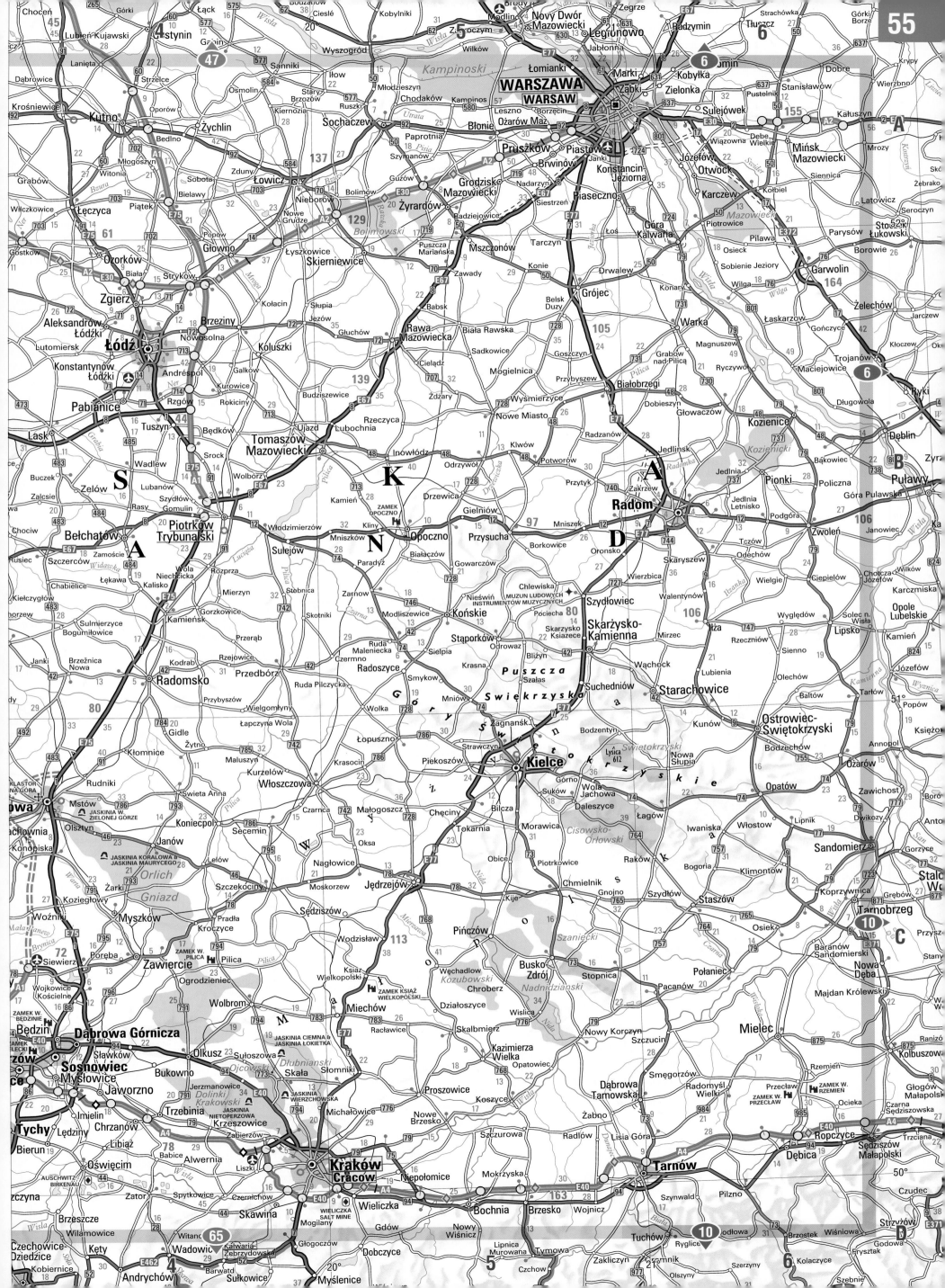

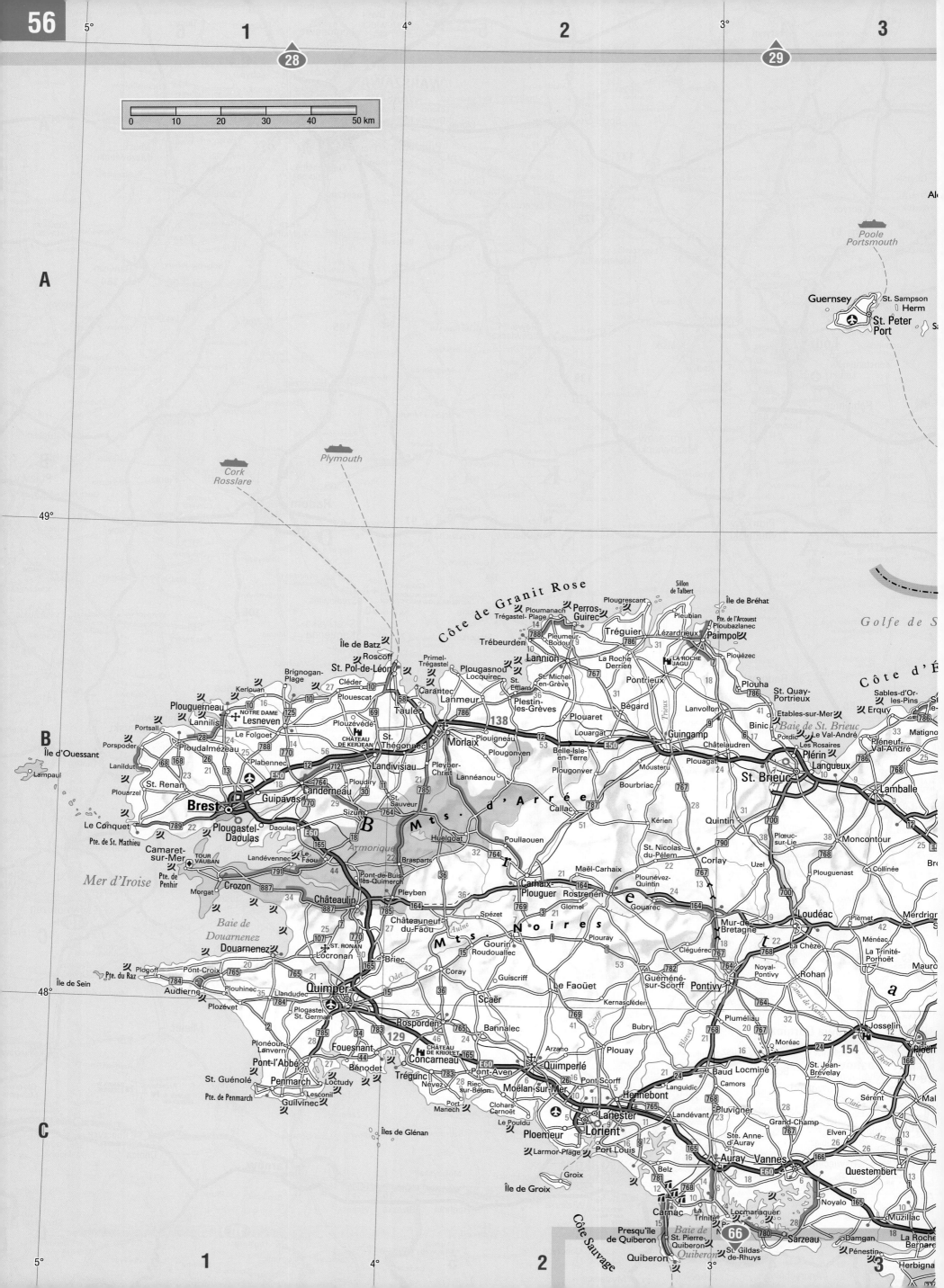

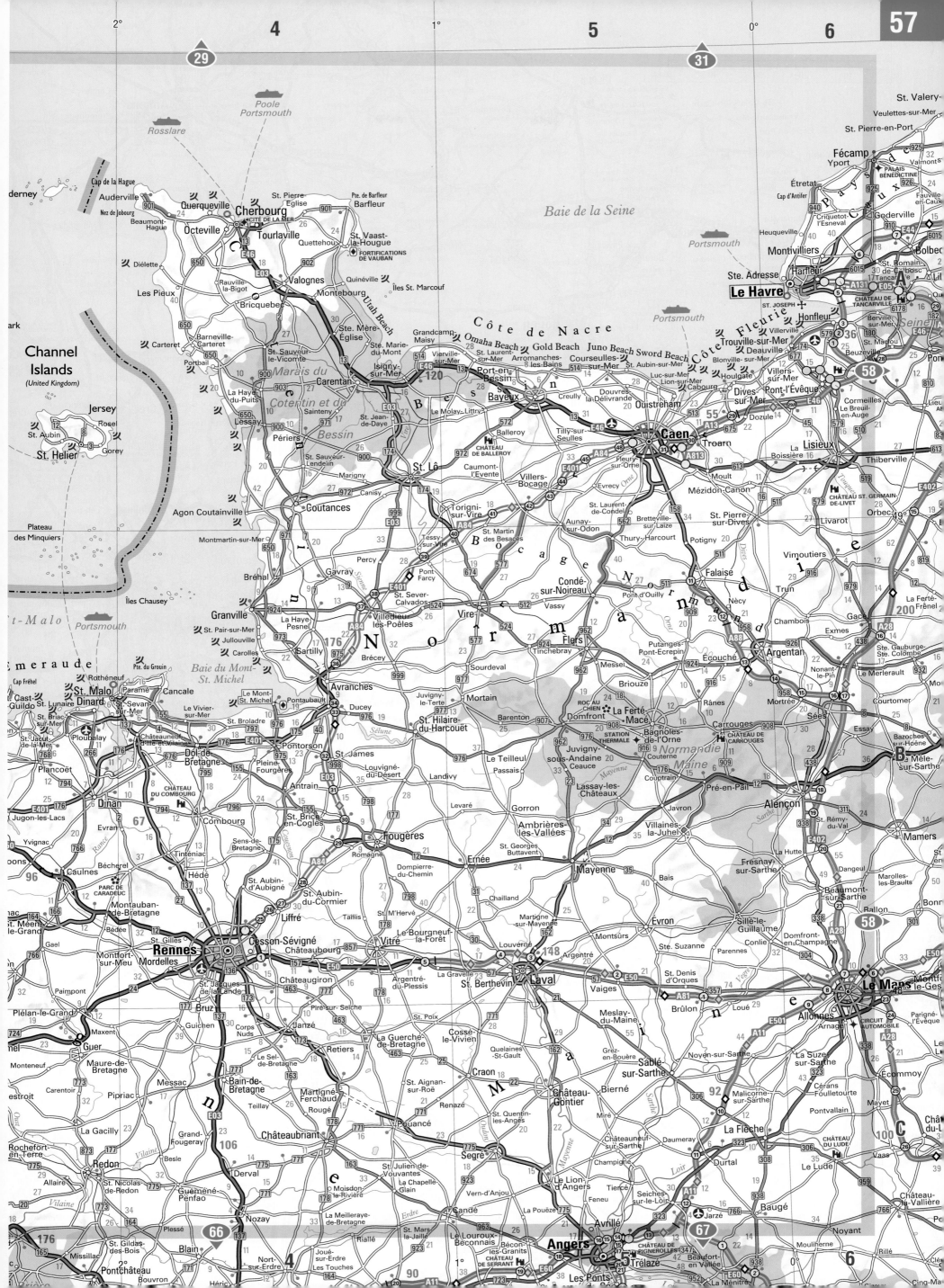

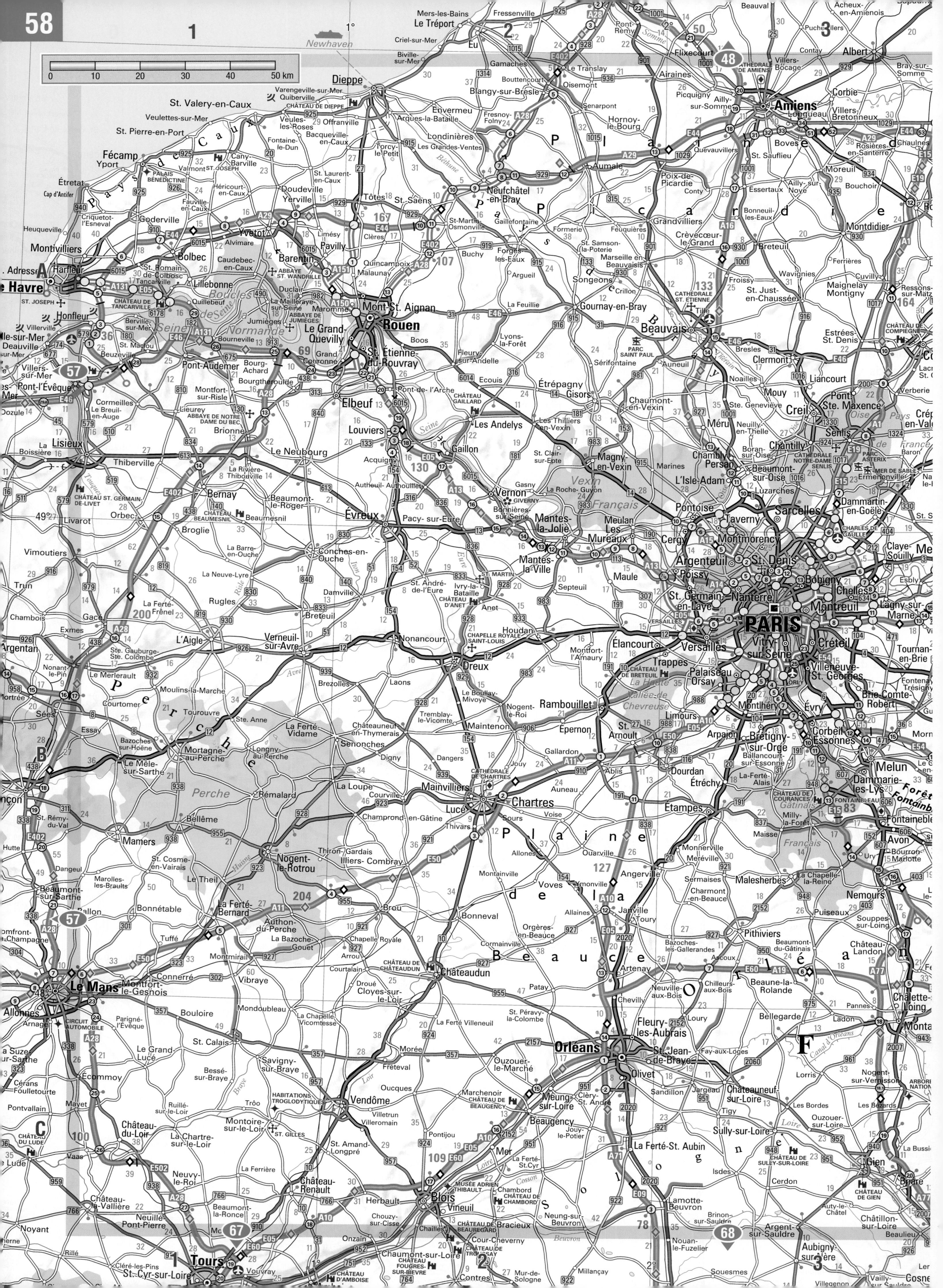
1
2
3
Newhaven
0
10
20
30
40
50 km
Mers-les-Bains
Le Tréport
Fressenville
Beauval
Acheux-en-Amiénois
Criel-sur-Mer
Eu
Pont-Remy
Flixecourt
Albert
Biville-sur-Mer
Gamaches
Le Translay
Airaines
Villers-Bocage
Bray-sur-Somme
Dieppe
Blangy-sur-Bresle
Oisemont
Picquigny
Ailly-sur-Somme
Amiens
Corbie
Varengeville-sur-Mer
Quiberville
CHÂTEAU DE DIEPPE
St. Valery-en-Caux
Envermeu
Arques-la-Bataille
Fresnoy-Folny
Senarpont
Hornoy-le-Bourg
Longueau
Villers-Bretonneux
Veulettes-sur-Mer
Veules-les-Roses
Offranville
Bacqueville-en-Caux
Londinières
St. Pierre-en-Port
Pays de Caux
Fontaine-le-Dun
Torcy-le-Petit
Les Grandes-Ventes
Quevauvillers
Boves
Rosières-en-Santerre
Chaulnes
Fécamp
Yport
Cany-Barville
Valmont
ST. JOSEPH
PALAIS BÉNÉDICTINE
St. Laurent-en-Caux
Aumale
St. Saufliec
Moreuil
Étretat
Cap d'Antifer
Héricourt-en-Caux
Doudeville
Tôtes
St. Saëns
Neufchâtel-en-Bray
Poix-de-Picardie
Essertaux
Ailly-sur-Noye
Bouchon
Criquetot-l'Esneval
Fauville-en-Caux
Yerville
Pays de Bray
Plateau de Picardie
Goderville
Yvetot
Limésy
Pavilly
Clères
St. Martin-Osmonville
Gaillefontaine
Formerie
Feuquières
Grandvilliers
Bonneuil-les-Eaux
Montdidier
Heuqueville
Alvimare
Buchy
Forges-les-Eaux
St. Samson-la-Poterie
Crèvecœur-le-Grand
Breteuil
Montivilliers
Bolbec
Caudebec-en-Caux
Barentin
Quincampoix
Marseille-en-Beauvaisis
Ferrières
Harfleur
Le Havre
Ste. Adresse
St. Romain-de-Colbosc
Tancarville
Lillebonne
ABBAYE DE ST. WANDRILLE
Malaunay
Argueil
Songeons
Crillon
Wavignies
Cuvilly
ST. JOSEPH
CHÂTEAU DE TANCARVILLE
Quillebeuf
Boucles de la Seine Normande
Duclair
La Mailleraye-sur-Seine
Maromme
Mont-St. Aignan
Froissy
St. Just-en-Chaussée
Maignelay Montigny
Ressons-sur-Matz
Honfleur
Villerville
Jumièges
ABBAYE DE JUMIÈGES
Berville-sur-Mer
Rouen
La Feuillie
Gournay-en-Bray
CATHÉDRALE ST. ÉTIENNE
Tillé
Beauvais
Trouville-sur-Mer
Deauville
St. Maclou
Bourneville
Le Grand-Quevilly
Lyons-la-Forêt
PARC SAINT PAUL
Bresles
Estrées-St. Denis
CHÂTEAU DE COMPIÈGNE
Villers-sur-Mer
Beuzeville
Pont-Audemer
Bourg-Achard
Grand Couronne
St. Étienne-du-Rouvray
Boos
Fleury-sur-Andelle
Sérifontaine
Auneuil
Clermont
Pont-l'Évêque
Bourgtheroulde
Montfort-sur-Risle
Ecouis
Étrépagny
Gisors
Noailles
Liancourt
Cormeilles
Le Breuil-en-Auge
Lieurey
ABBAYE DE NOTRE DAME DU BEC
Elbeuf
Pont-de-l'Arche
CHÂTEAU GAILLARD
Chaumont-en-Vexin
Mouy
Pont Ste. Maxence
Verberie
Dozulé
Brionne
Louviers
Les Andelys
Les Thilliers-en-Vexin
Ste. Geneviève
Méru
Creil
Crépy-en-Valois
Lisieux
La Boissière
Thiberville
Le Neubourg
Acquigny
Gaillon
St. Clair-sur-Epte
Magny-en-Vexin
Neuilly-en-Thelle
Chantilly
Senlis
CATHÉDRALE NOTRE-DAME SENLIS
PARC ASTÉRIX
MER DE SABLE
Ermenonville
La Rivière-Thibouville
Bernay
Beaumont-le-Roger
Autheuil-Authouillet
Vernon
GIVERNY
Gasny
La Roche-Guyon
Vexin Français
Chambly
Persan
Marines
L'Isle-Adam
Boran-sur-Oise
Beaumont-sur-Oise
Luzarches
Dammartin-en-Goële
CHÂTEAU ST. GERMAIN-DE-LIVET
Livarot
Orbec
CHÂTEAU BEAUMESNIL
Beaumesnil
Évreux
Pacy-sur-Eure
Bonnières-sur-Seine
Mantes-la-Jolie
Meulan
Les Mureaux
Pontoise
Cergy
Taverny
Sarcelles
Montmorency
CHARLES DE GAULLE
Broglie
La Barre-en-Ouche
Conches-en-Ouche
Mantes-la-Ville
Argenteuil
St. Denis
Claye-Souilly
Vimoutiers
La Neuve-Lyre
St. Martin
Ivry-la-Bataille
Septeuil
Maule
Poissy
Bobigny
Chelles
Esbly
Trun
Rugles
Damville
St. André-de-l'Eure
CHÂTEAU D'ANET
Anet
St. Germain-en-Laye
Nanterre
Montreuil
Lagny-sur-Marne
Chambois
Gacé
La Ferté-Frênel
Breteuil
PARIS
VERSAILLES
Exmes
L'Aigle
Verneuil-sur-Avre
Nonancourt
CHAPELLE ROYALE SAINT-LOUIS
Houdan
Élancourt
Versailles
Vitry-sur-Seine
Créteil
Tournan-en-Brie
Argentan
Ste. Gauburge-Ste. Colombe
Dreux
Montfort-l'Amaury
CHÂTEAU DE BRETEUIL
Trappes
Palaiseau
Orsay
Villeneuve-St. Georges
Nonant-le-Pin
Le Merlerault
Brezolles
Laons
La Haute Vallée de Chevreuse
Fontenay-Trésigny
Moulins-la-Marche
Le Boullay-Mivoye
Nogent-le-Roi
Rambouillet
Brie-Comte-Robert
Sées
Courtomer
Perche
Tourouvre
Ste. Anne
Châteauneuf-en-Thymerais
Tremblay-le-Vicomte
Limours
Montlhéry
Évry
Essay
Bazoches-sur-Hoëne
La Ferté-Vidame
Senonches
Maintenon
Épernon
St. Arnoult
Arpajon
Brétigny-sur-Orge
Corbeil-Essonnes
Mortagne-au-Perche
Longny-au-Perche
Digny
Dangers
Gallardon
Ballancourt-sur-Essonne
Le Mêle-sur-Sarthe
Jouy
Ablis
Dourdan
Étréchy
La Ferté-Alais
Melun
Dammarie-les-Lys
Forêt de Fontainebleau
Alençon
La Loupe
CATHÉDRALE DE CHARTRES
Mainvilliers
Auneau
CHÂTEAU DE COURANCES
Gâtinais Français
Rémalard
Courville
Chartres
Étampes
Milly-la-Forêt
Fontainebleau
St. Rémy-du-Val
Champrond-en-Gâtine
Lucé
Voise
Maisse
Bellême
Thivars
Sours
Plaine de la Beauce
Avon
Mamers
Thiron-Gardais
Illiers-Combray
Nogent-le-Rotrou
Allonnes
Monnerville
Méréville
Ury
Bourron-Marlotte
St. Cosme-en-Vairais
Ouarville
Angerville
Sermaises
Malesherbes
La Chapelle-la-Reine
Marolles-les-Braults
Le Theil
Montainville
Voves
Ymonville
Charmont-en-Beauce
Nemours
Dangeul
Beaumont-sur-Sarthe
Ballon
Bonnétable
La Ferté-Bernard
Brou
Bonneval
Allaines
Janville
Toury
Puiseaux
Souppes-sur-Loing
Authon-du-Perche
La Bazoche-Gouet
Chapelle Royale
Orgères-en-Beauce
Pithiviers
Beaumont-du-Gâtinais
Château-Landon
Montfront-la-Champagne
Tuffé
Montmirail
Arrou
Cormainville
Bazoches-les-Gallerandes
Ascoux
Le Mans
Connerré
Vibraye
CHÂTEAU DE CHÂTEAUDUN
Courtalain
Châteaudun
Artenay
Chilleurs-aux-Bois
Beaune-la-Rolande
Montfort-le-Gesnois
Droué
Cloyes-sur-le-Loir
Patay
Neuville-aux-Bois
Chevilly
Châlette-sur-Loing
Allonnes
Arnage
CIRCUIT AUTOMOBILE
Bouloire
Mondoubleau
La Chapelle-Vicomtesse
St. Péravy-la-Colombe
Fleury-les-Aubrais
Loury
Bellegarde
Ladon
Montargis
Parigné-l'Évêque
La Ferté Villeneuil
St. Calais
Orléans
St. Jean-de-Braye
Fay-aux-Loges
Canal d'Orléans
La Suze-sur-Sarthe
Le Grand-Lucé
Morée
Fréteval
Ouzouer-le-Marché
Olivet
Cérans-Foulletourte
Écommoy
Bessé-sur-Braye
Savigny-sur-Braye
Oucques
Marchenoir
Lorris
Nogent-sur-Vernisson
ARBORETUM NATIONAL
HABITATIONS TROGLODYTIQUES
Vendôme
CHÂTEAU DE BEAUGENCY
Meung-sur-Loire
Cléry-St. André
Sandillon
Jargeau
Châteauneuf-sur-Loire
Pontvallain
Mayet
Ruillé-sur-le-Loir
Trôo
Villetrun
Villeromain
Tigy
Les Bordes
Les Bézards
Montoire-sur-le-Loir
ST. GILLES
Beaugency
Jouy-le-Potier
Ouzouer-sur-Loire
Château-du-Loir
La Chartre-sur-le-Loir
Pontijou
Sully-sur-Loire
CHÂTEAU DU LUDE
Le Lude
Vaas
St. Amand-Longpré
Mer
La Ferté-St. Cyr
La Ferté-St. Aubin
CHÂTEAU DE SULLY-SUR-LOIRE
La Bussière
Neuvy-le-Roi
La Ferrière
Château-Renault
MUSÉE ADRIEN THIBAULT
Chambord
CHÂTEAU DE CHAMBORD
Sologne
Cerdon
Gien
CHÂTEAU DE GIEN
Briare
Isdes
Château-la-Vallière
Neuillé-Pont-Pierre
Beaumont-la-Ronce
Herbault
Blois
Vineuil
Lamotte-Beuvron
Auty-le-Châtel
Noyant
Chouzy-sur-Cisse
Chailles
CHÂTEAU DE BEAUREGARD
Bracieux
Neung-sur-Beuvron
Brinon-sur-Sauldre
Argent-sur-Sauldre
Châtillon-sur-Loire
Beaulieu
Onzain
Cour-Cheverny
Nouan-le-Fuzelier
Aubigny-sur-Nère
Rillé
Chaumont-sur-Loire
CHÂTEAU DE TROUSSAY
Tours
Cléré-les-Pins
St. Cyr-sur-Loire
Vouvray
CHÂTEAU D'AMBOISE
CHÂTEAU FOUGÈRES-SUR-BIÈVRE
Contres
Mur-de-Sologne
Millançay
Souesmes
Vailly-sur-Sauldre
Villegenon
Cosne
48
57
67
68
83
A
B
C
F

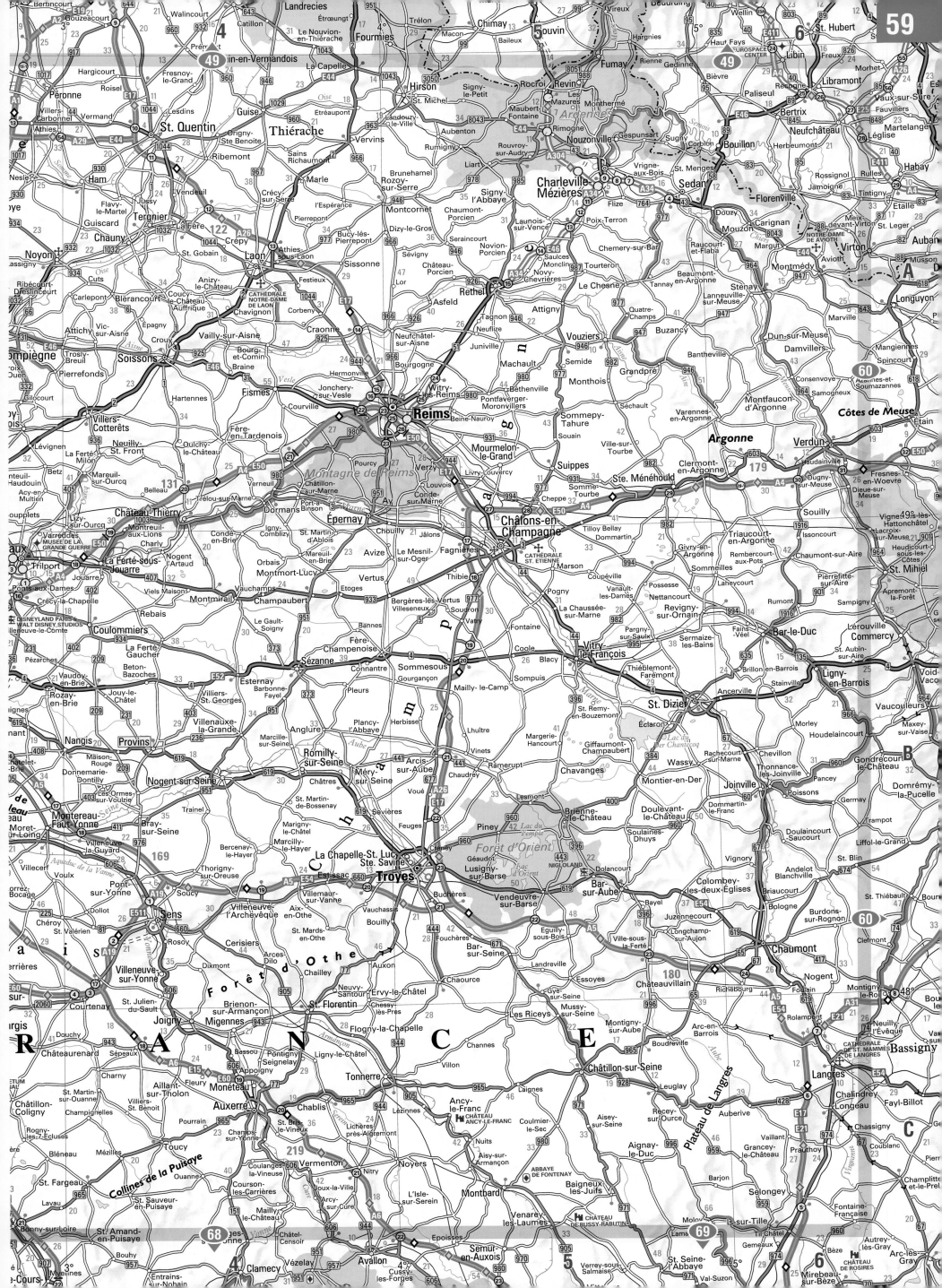

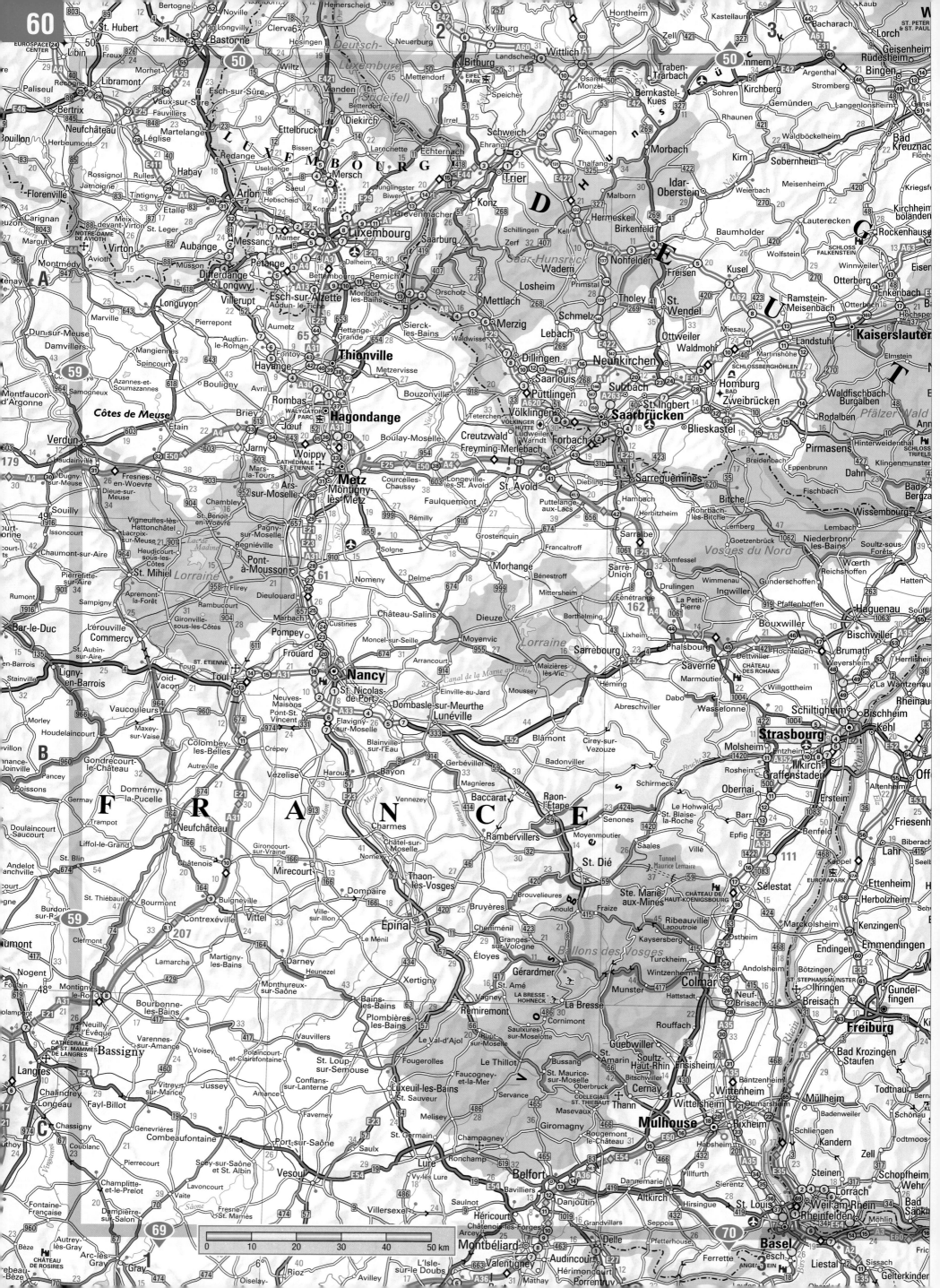

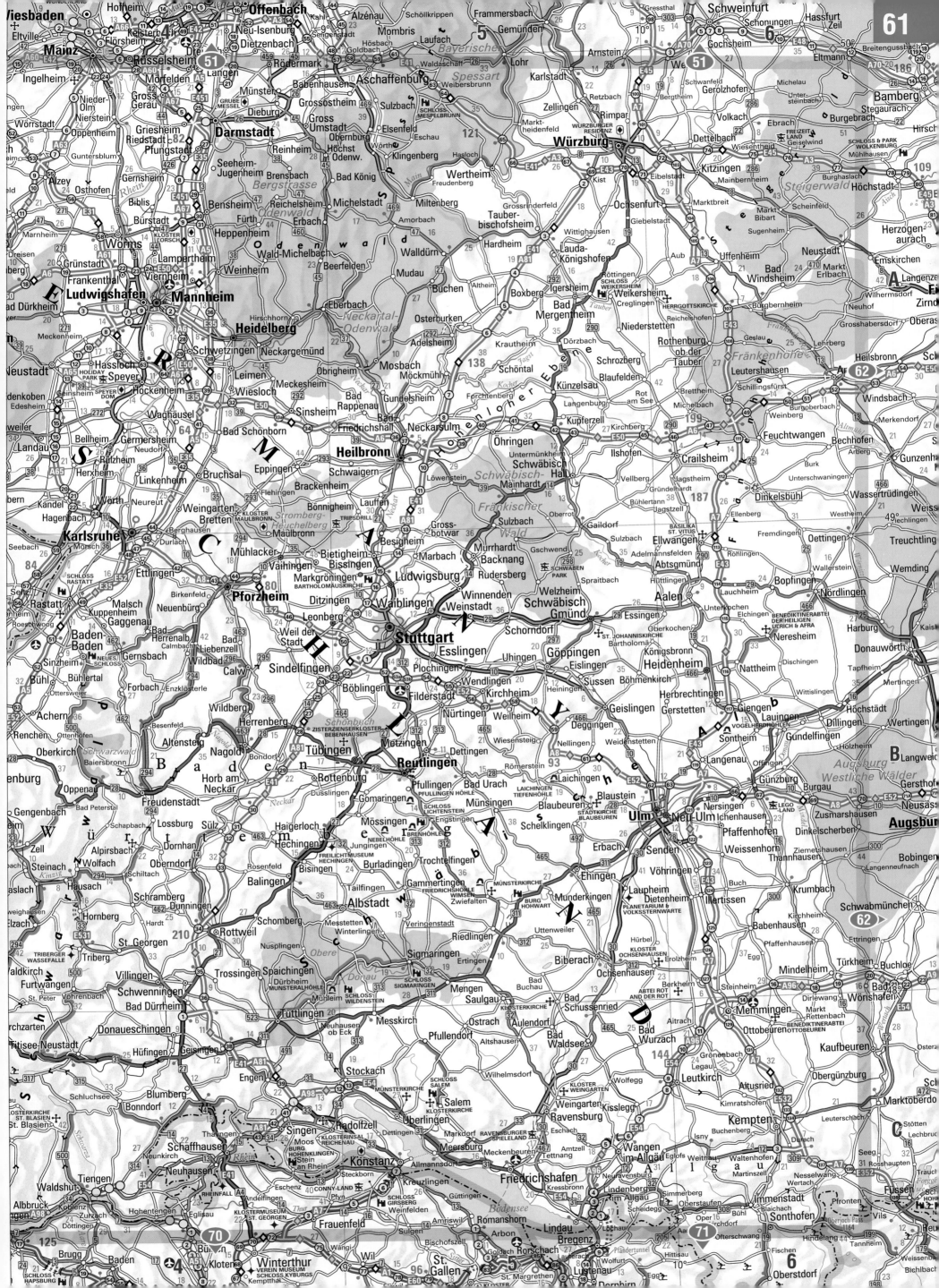

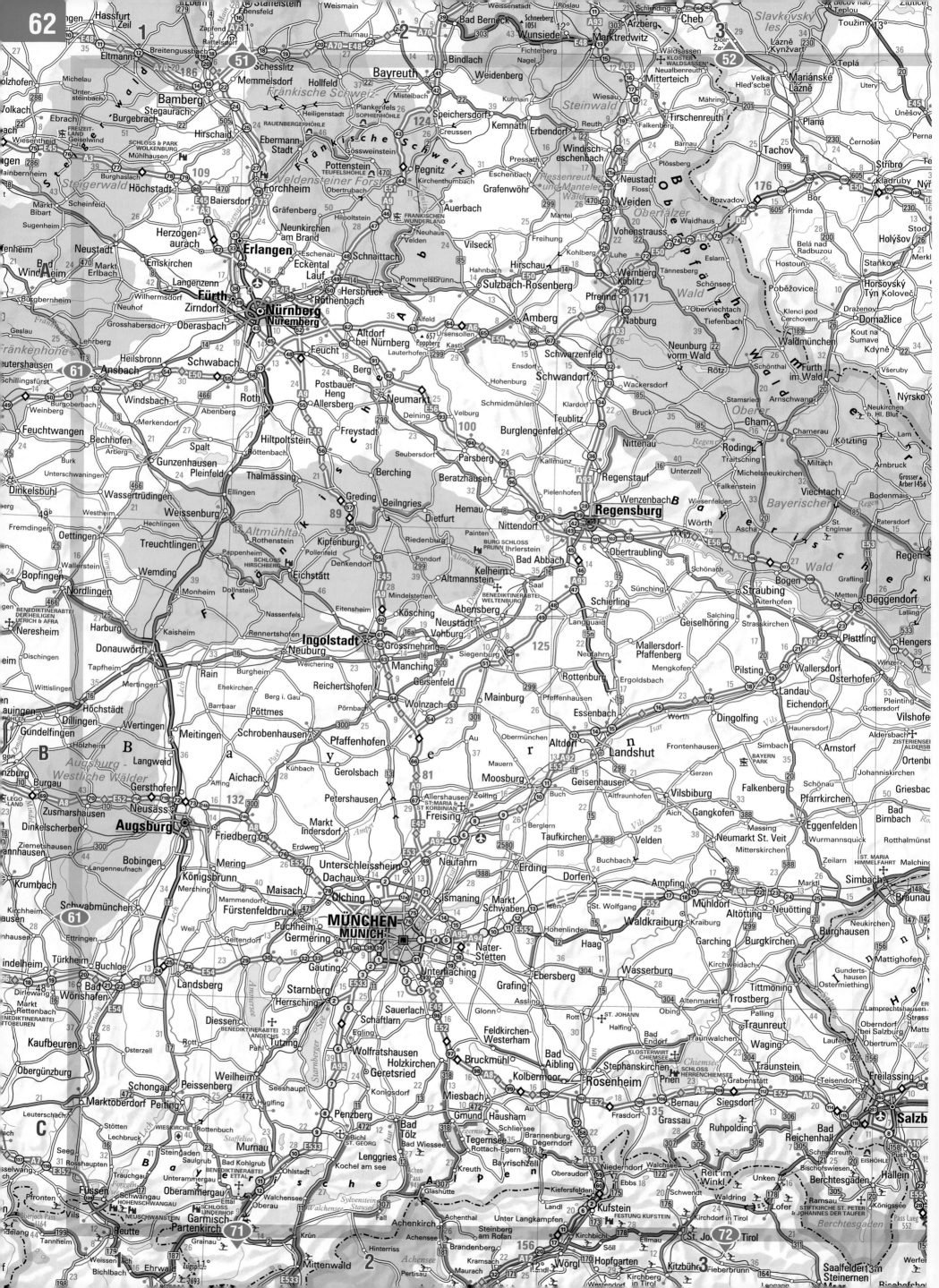

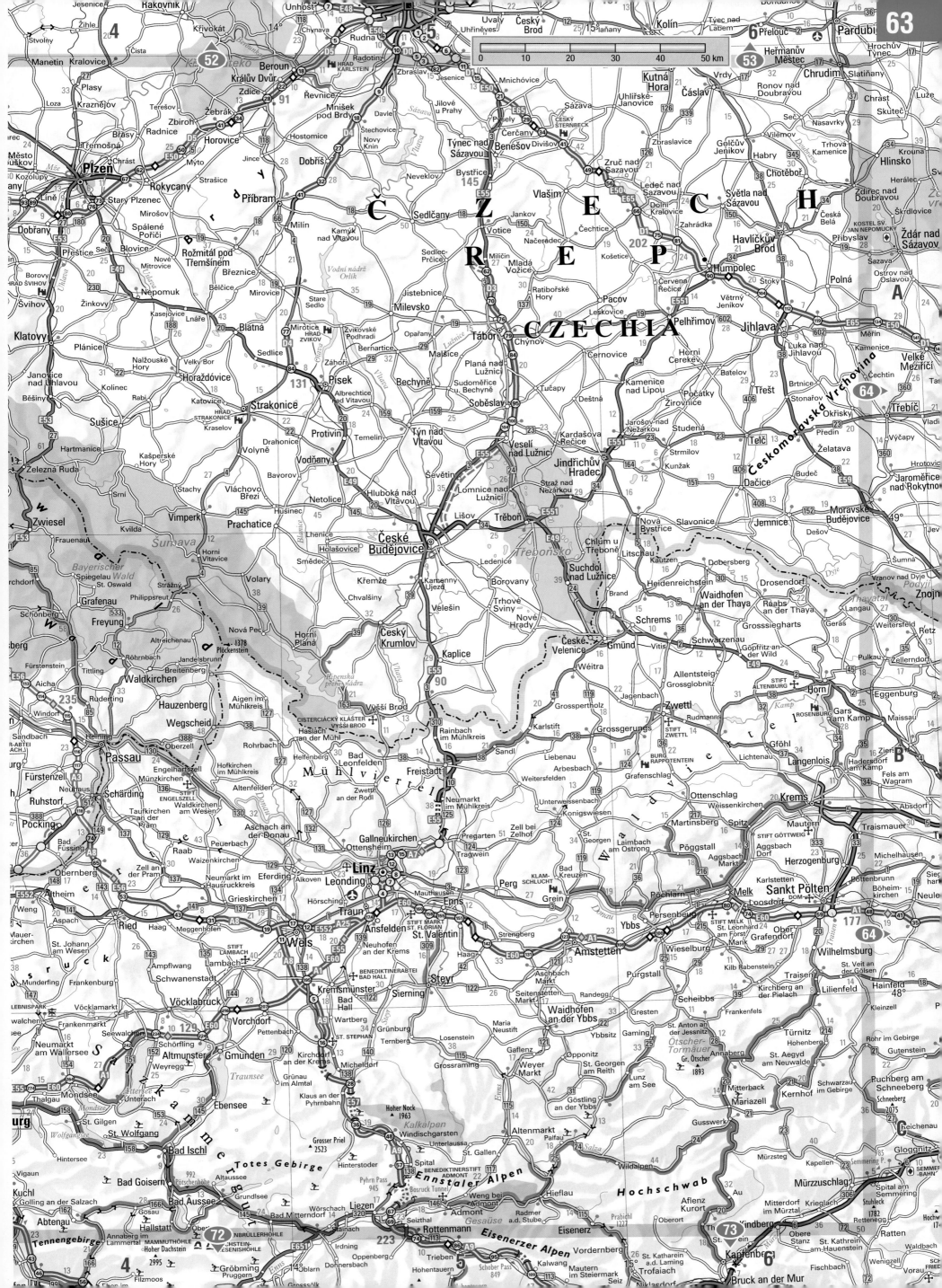

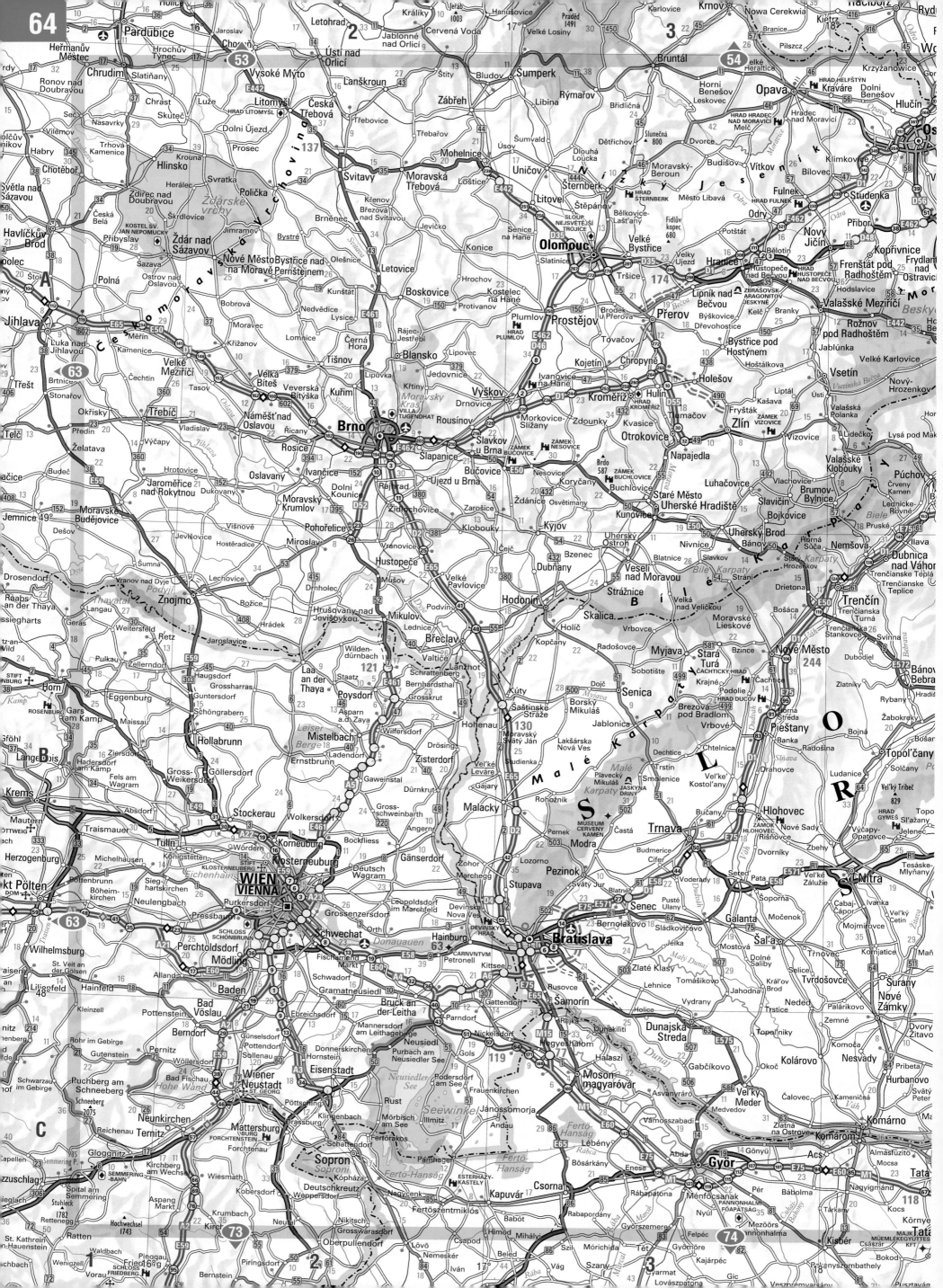

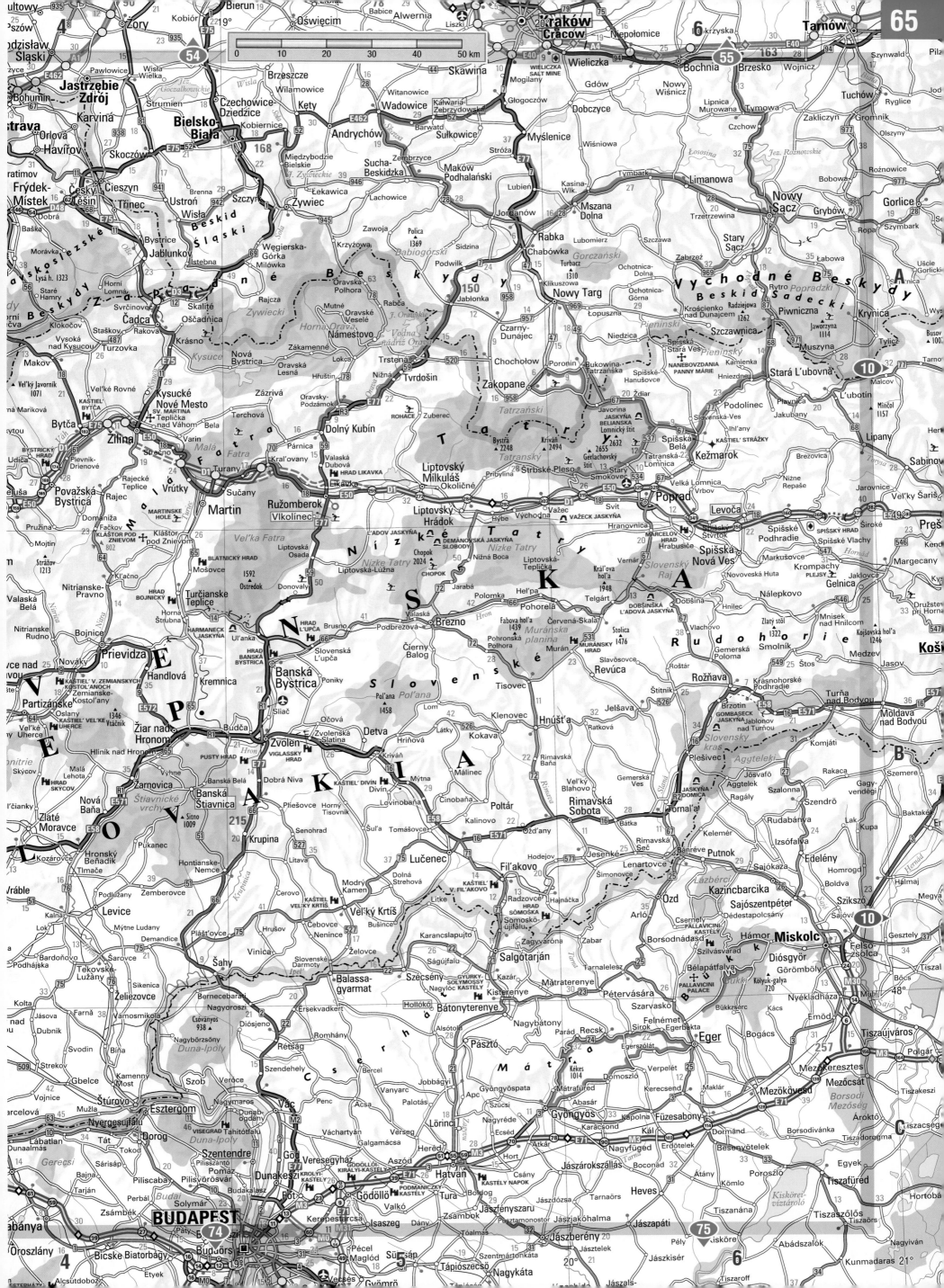

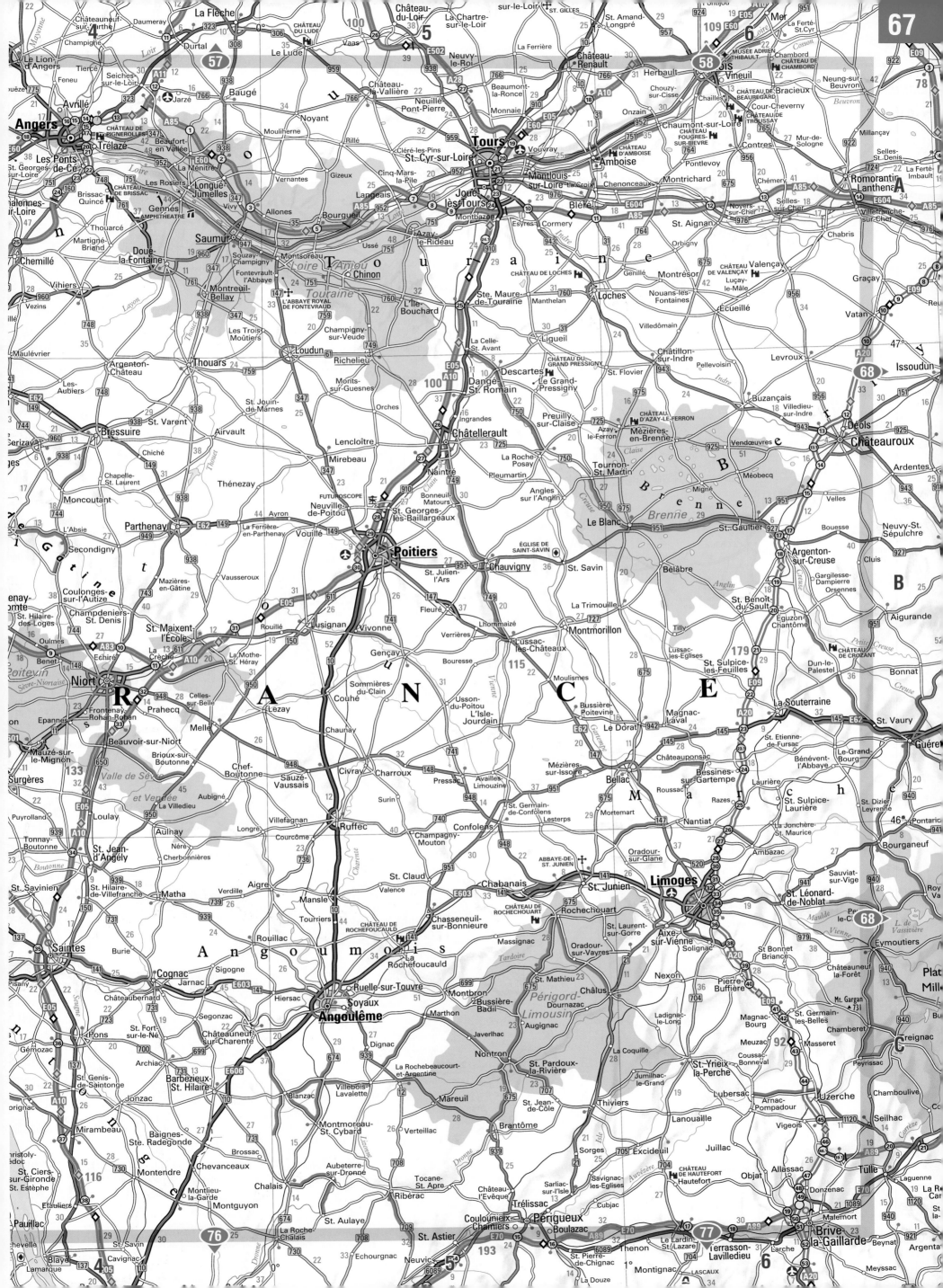

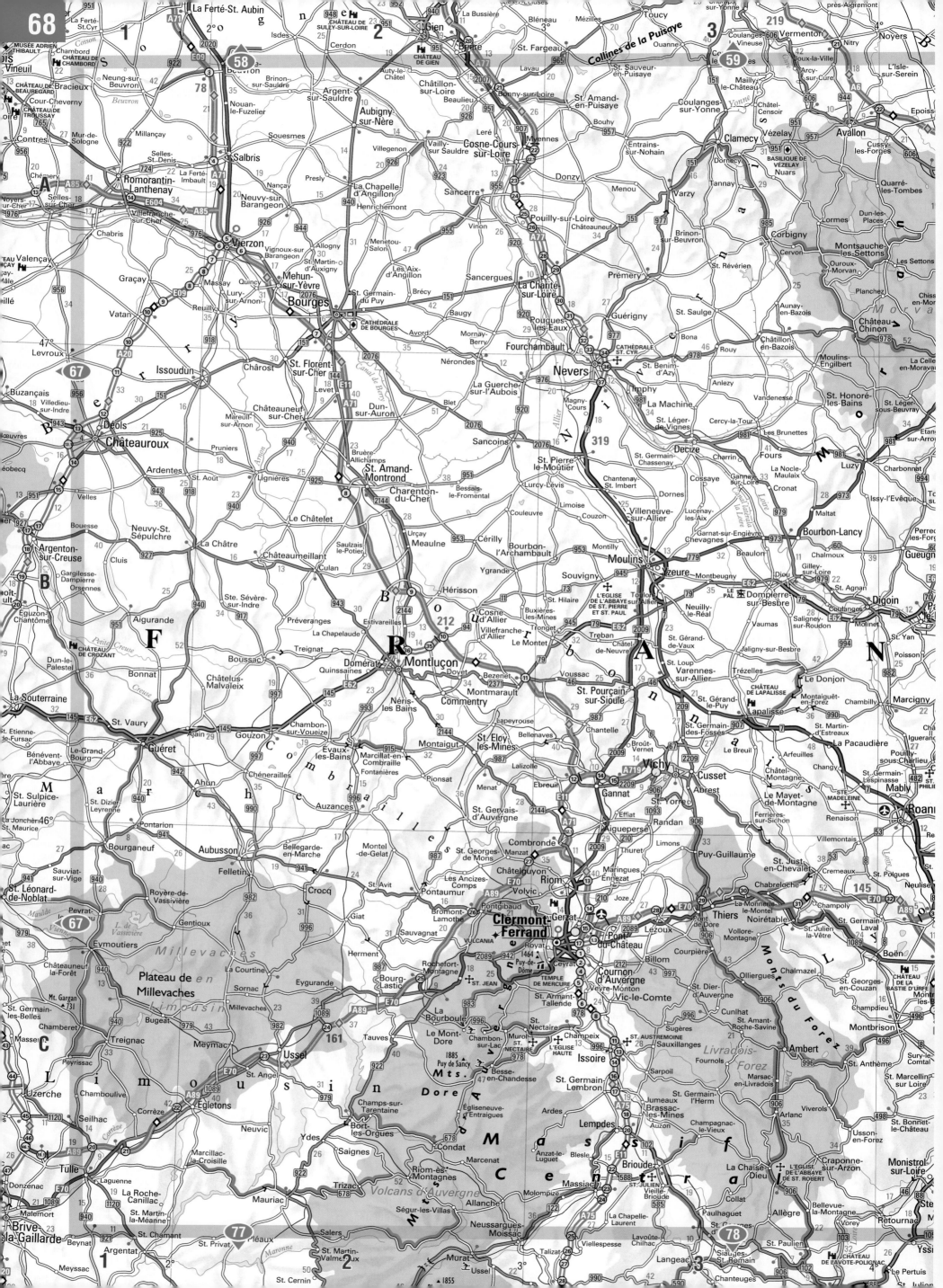

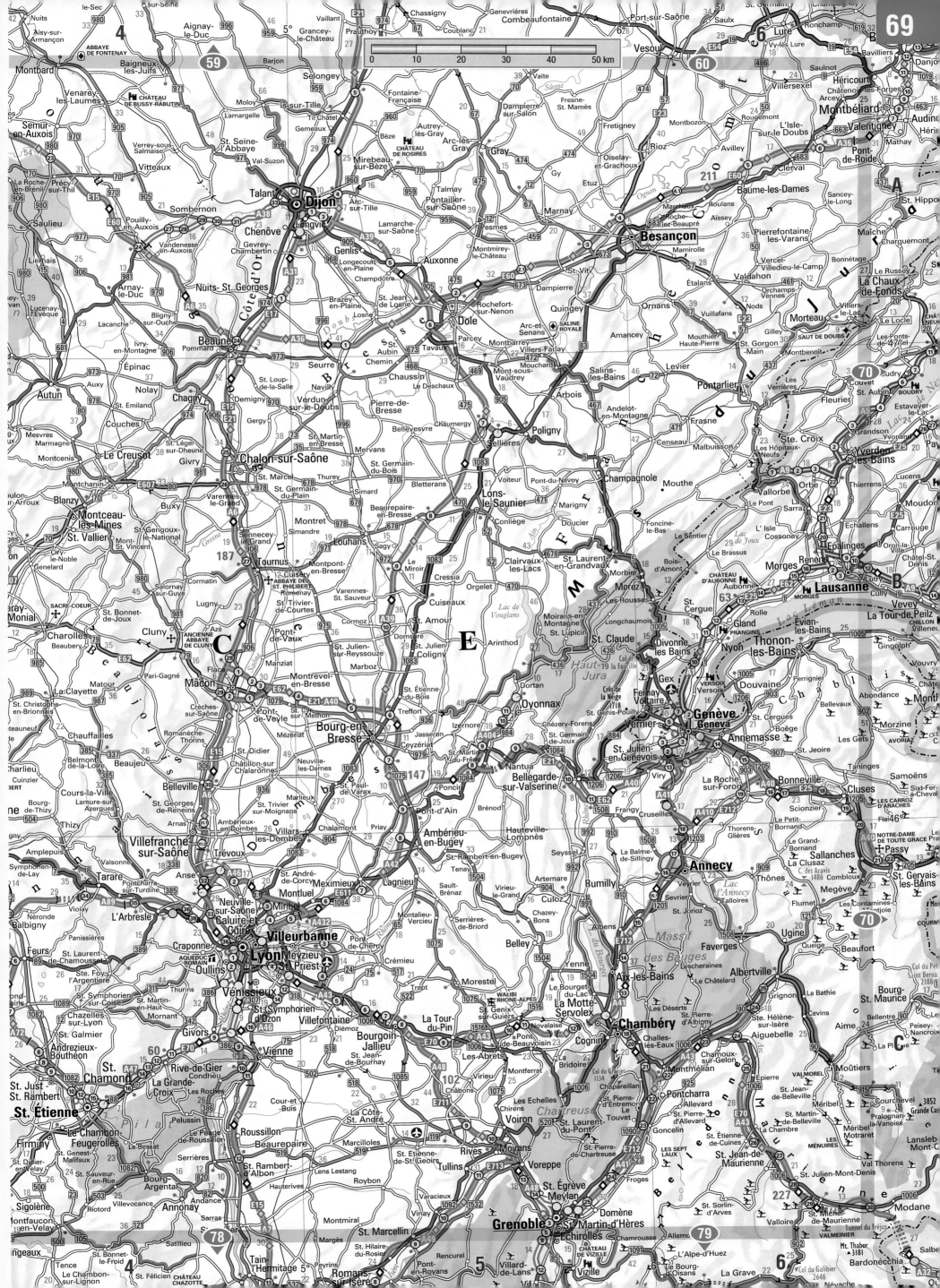

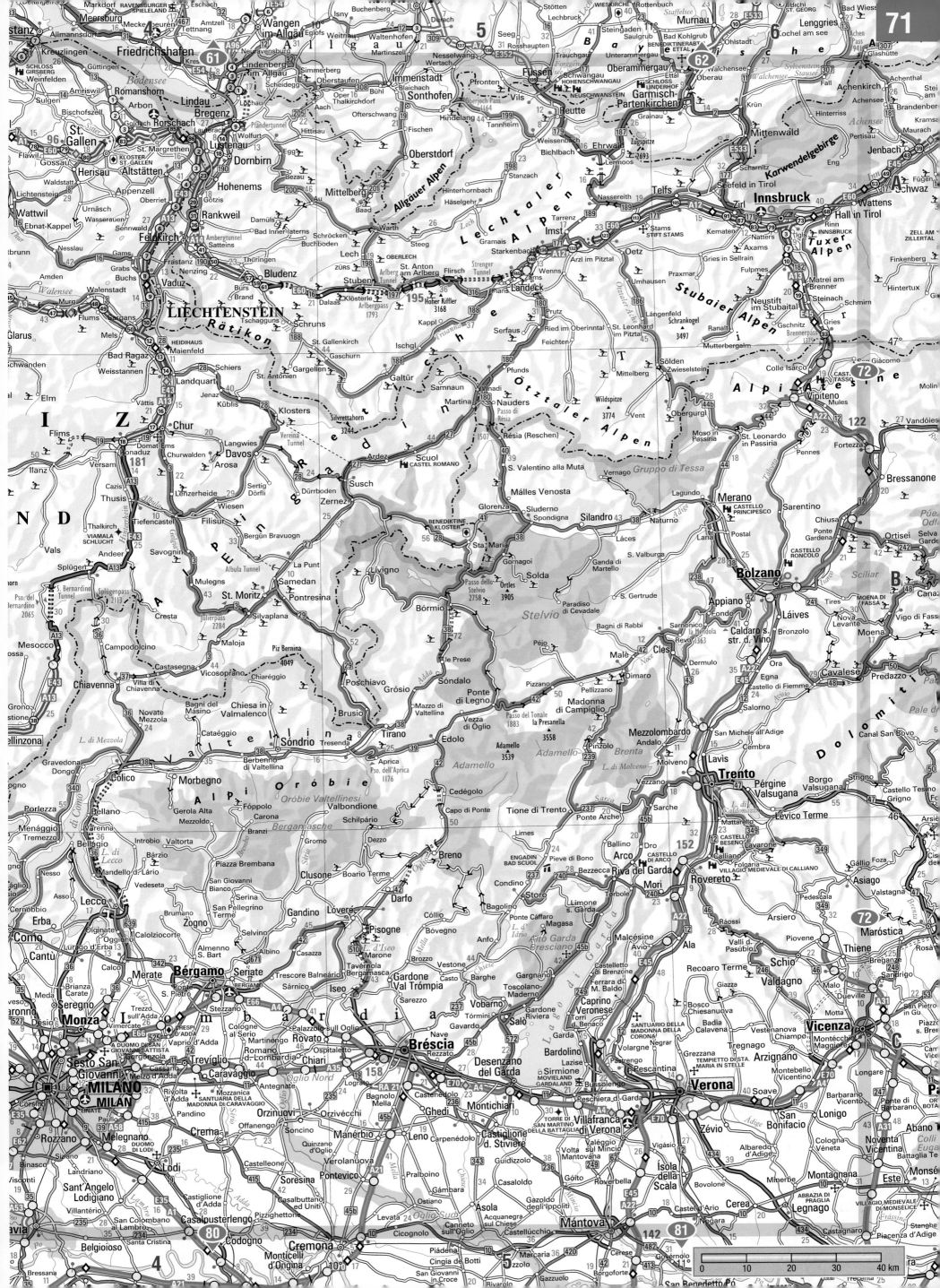

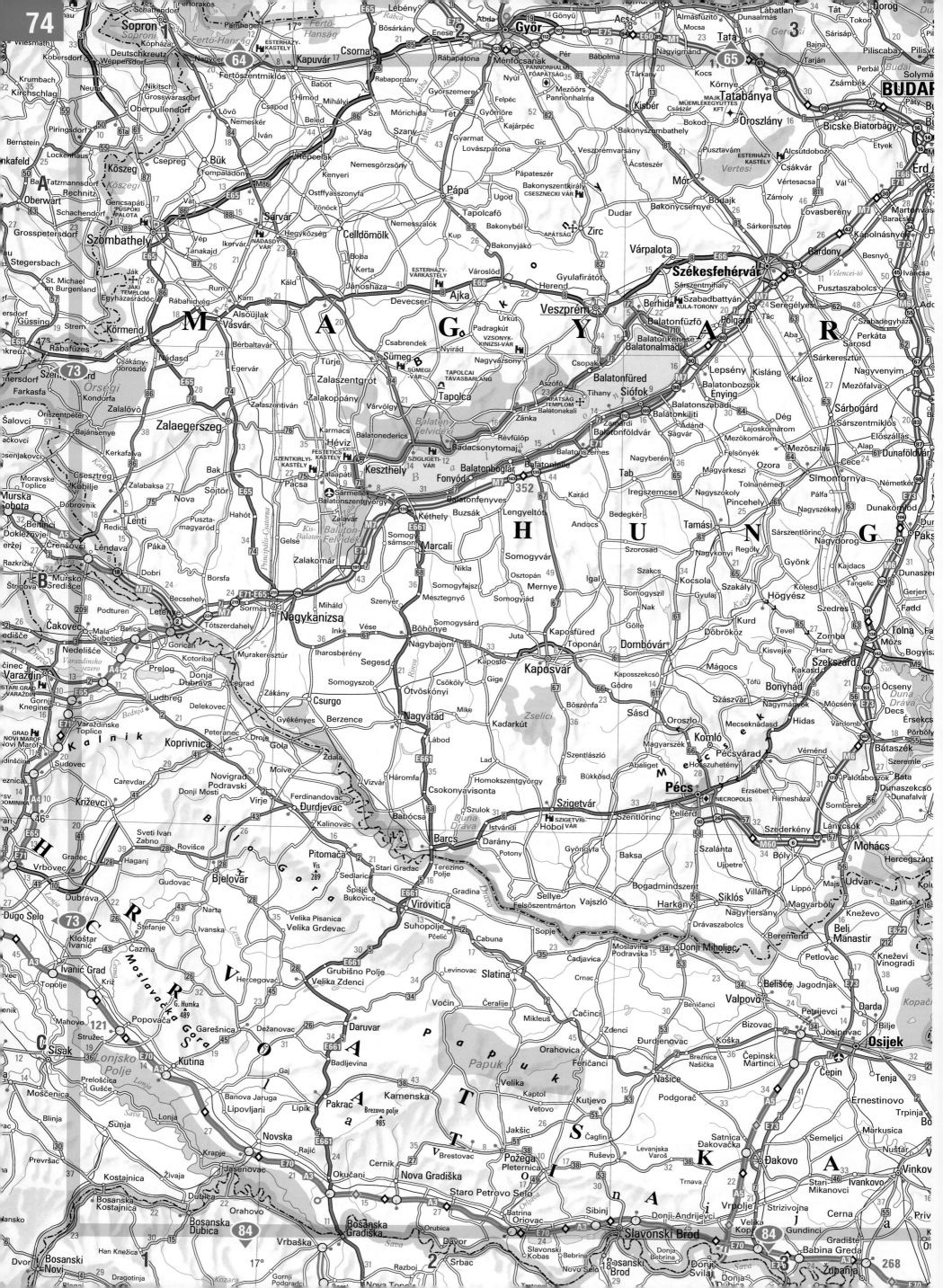

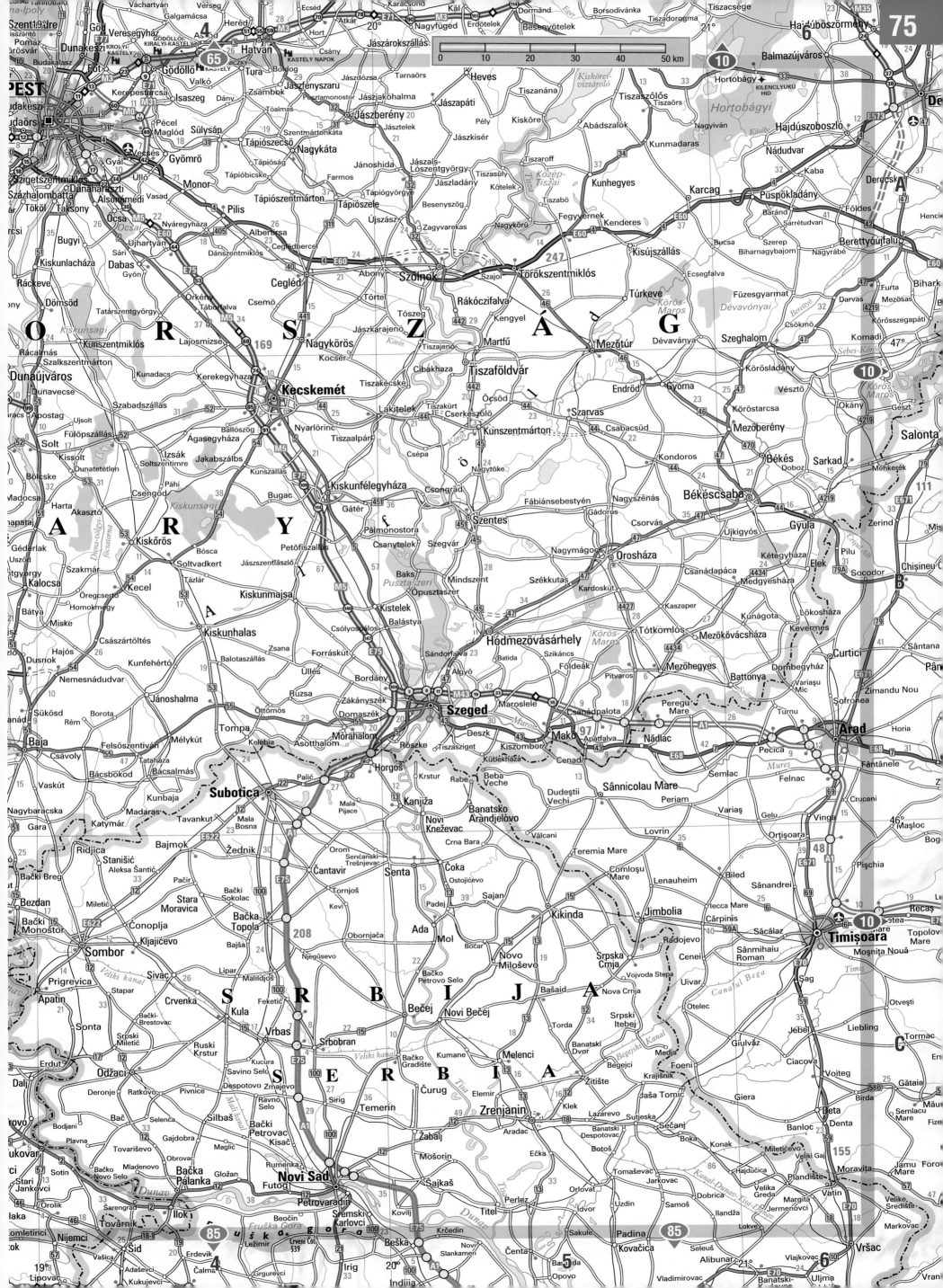

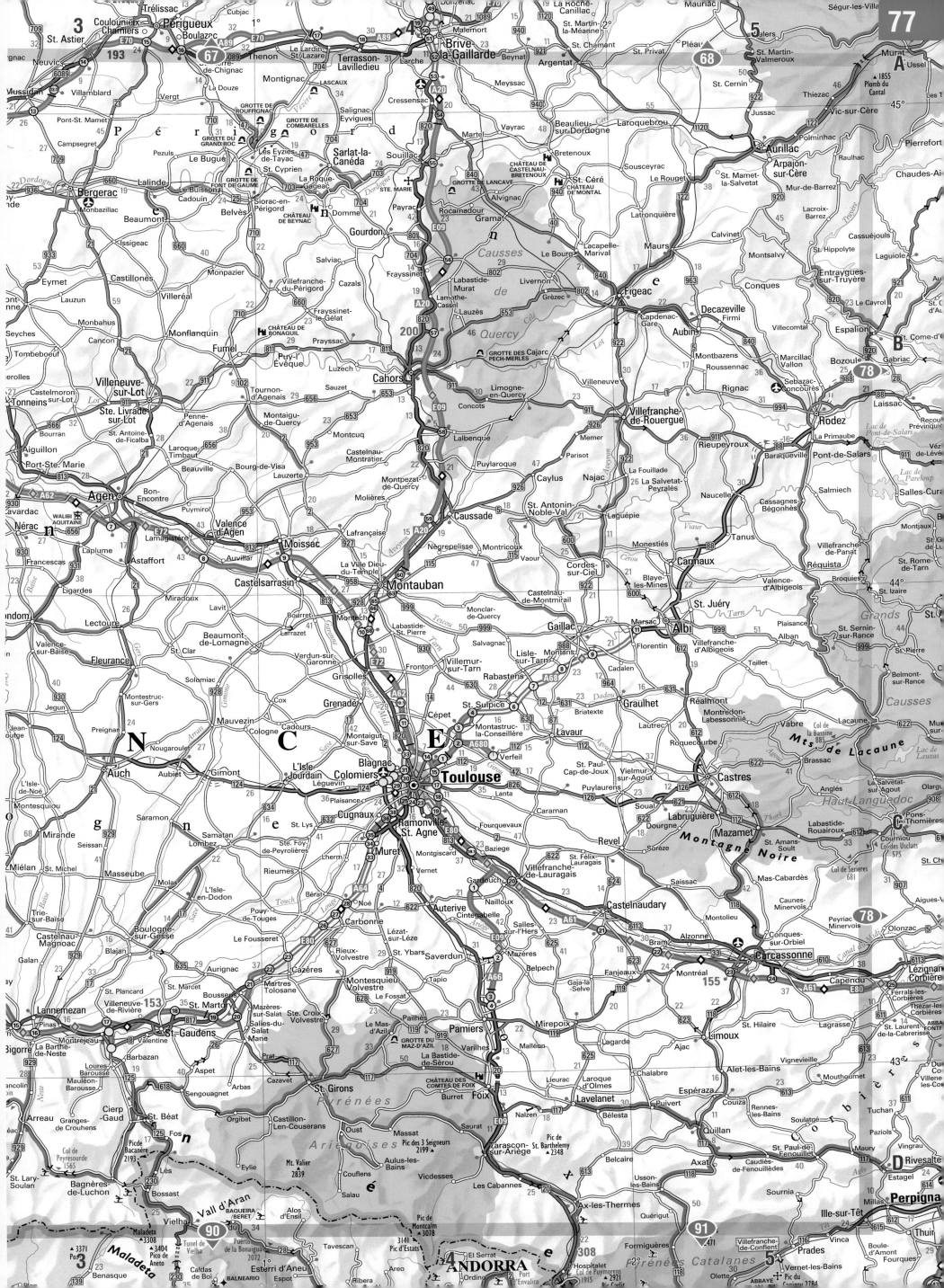

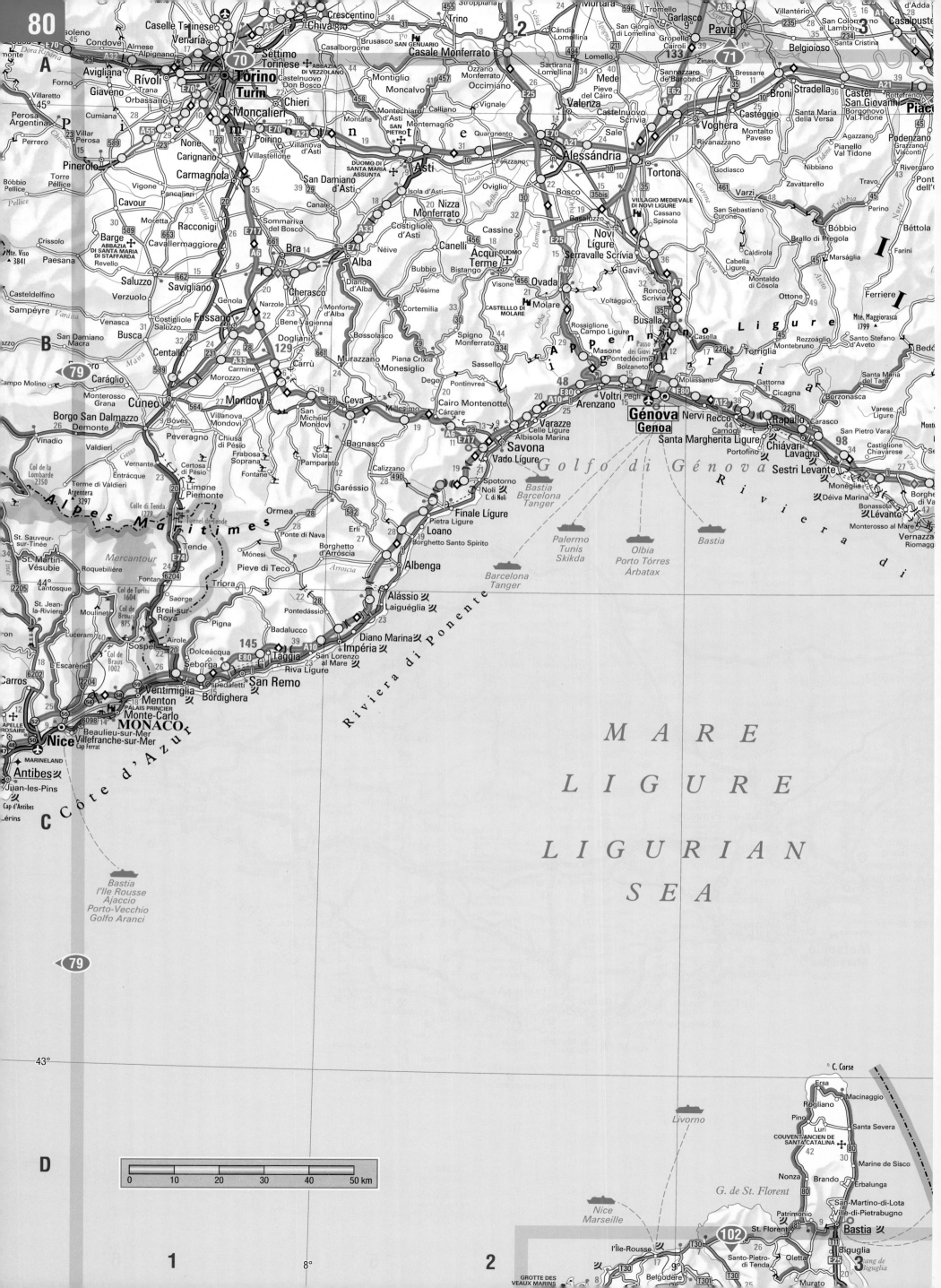

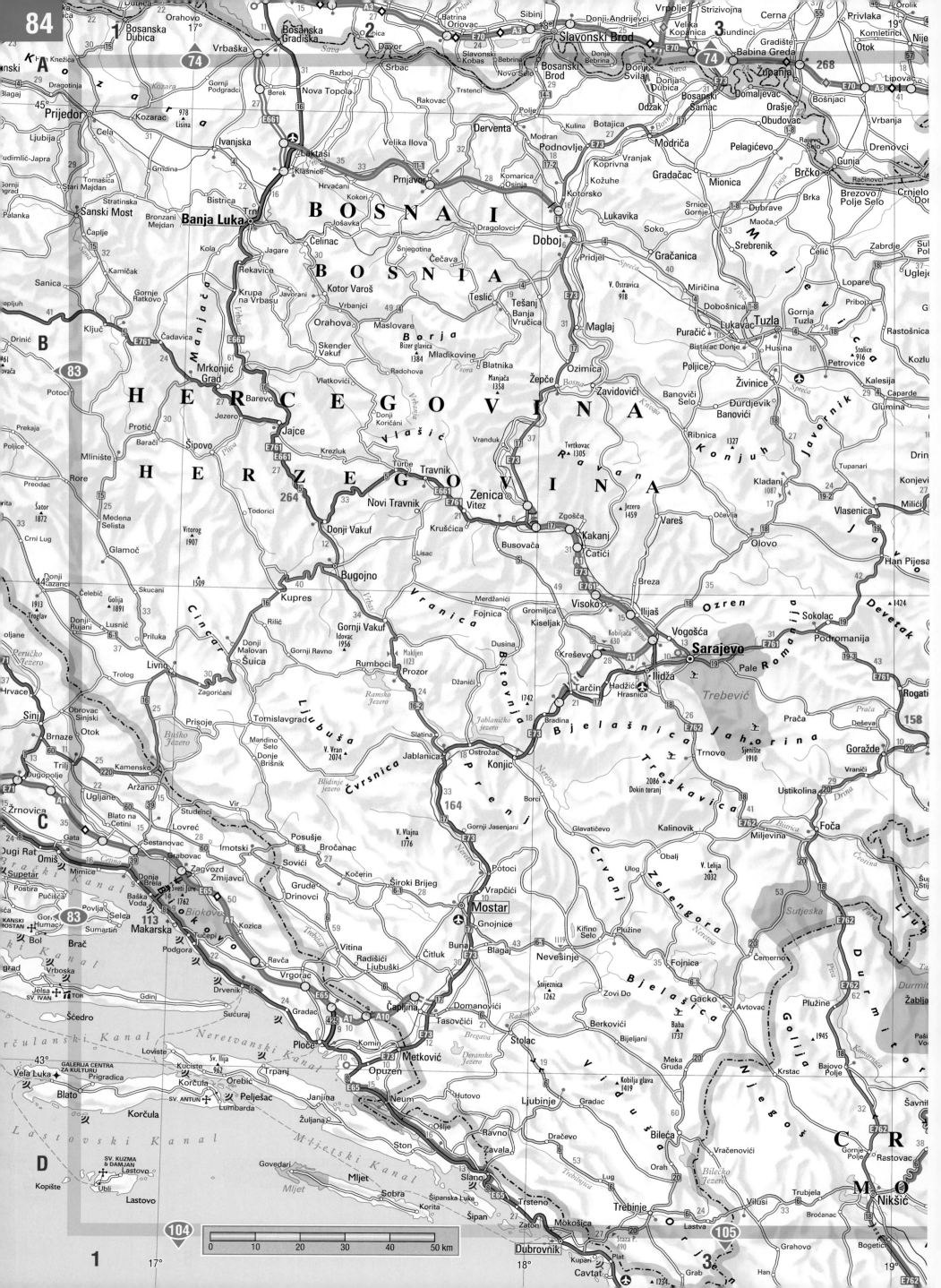

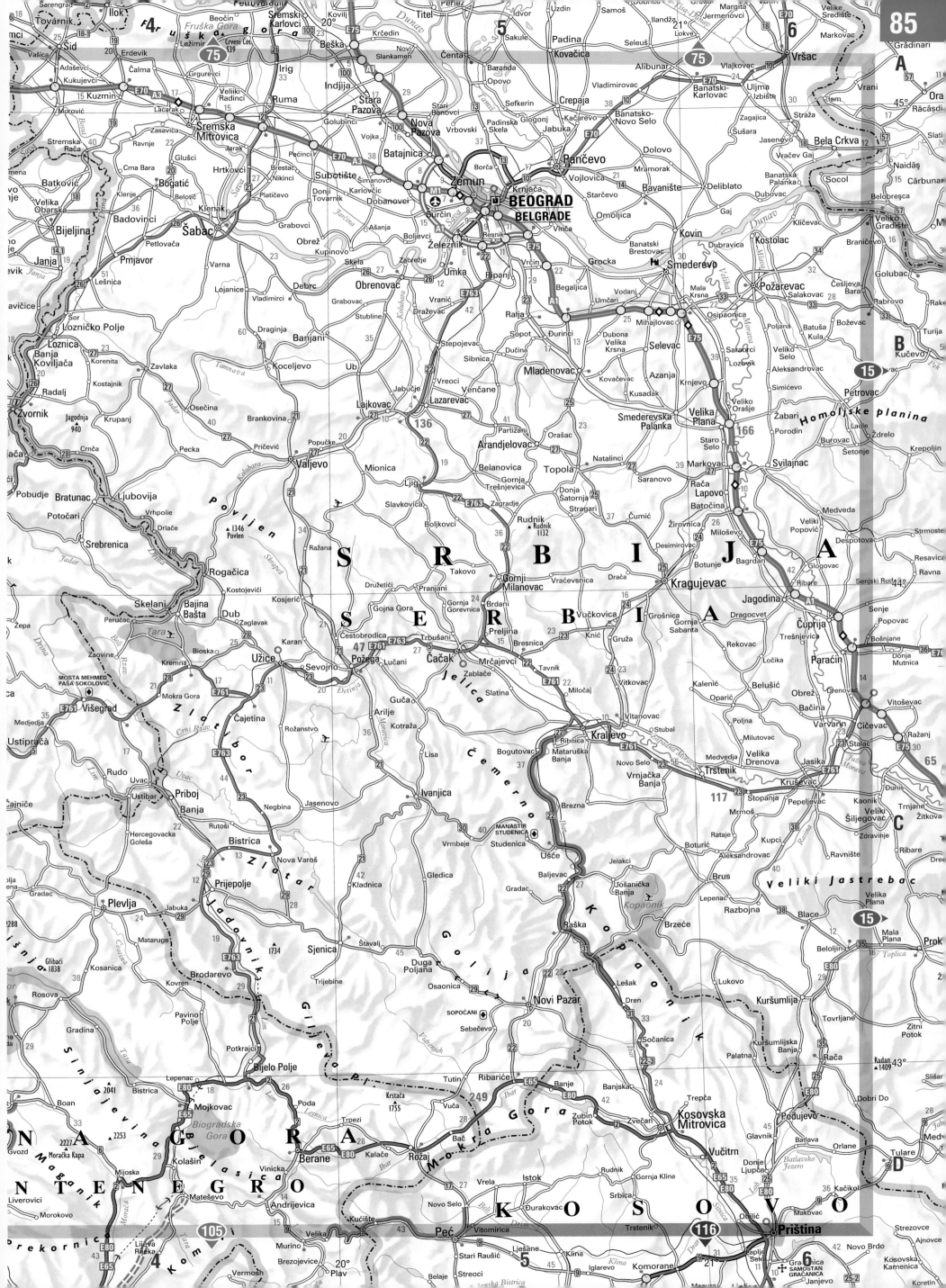

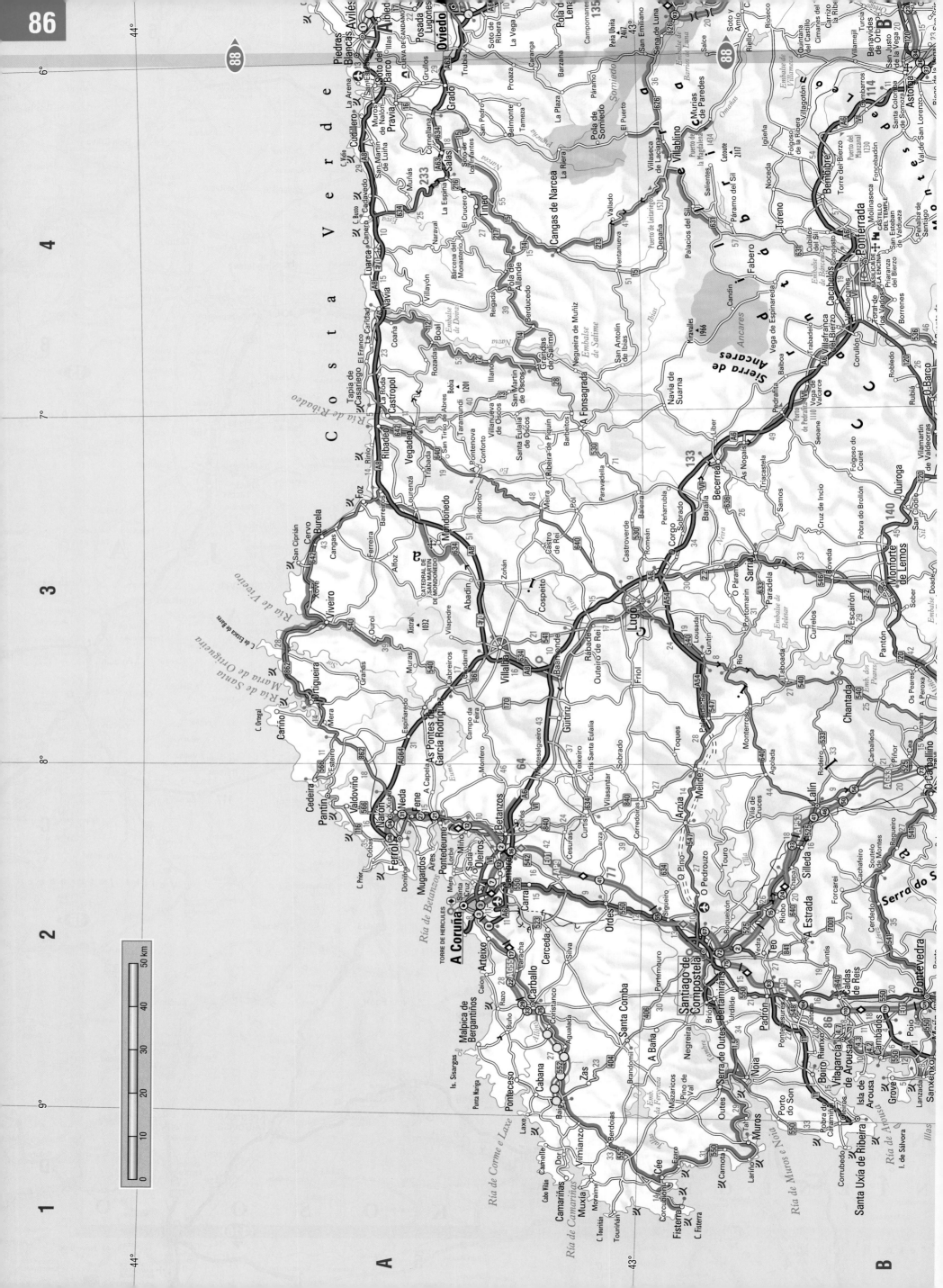

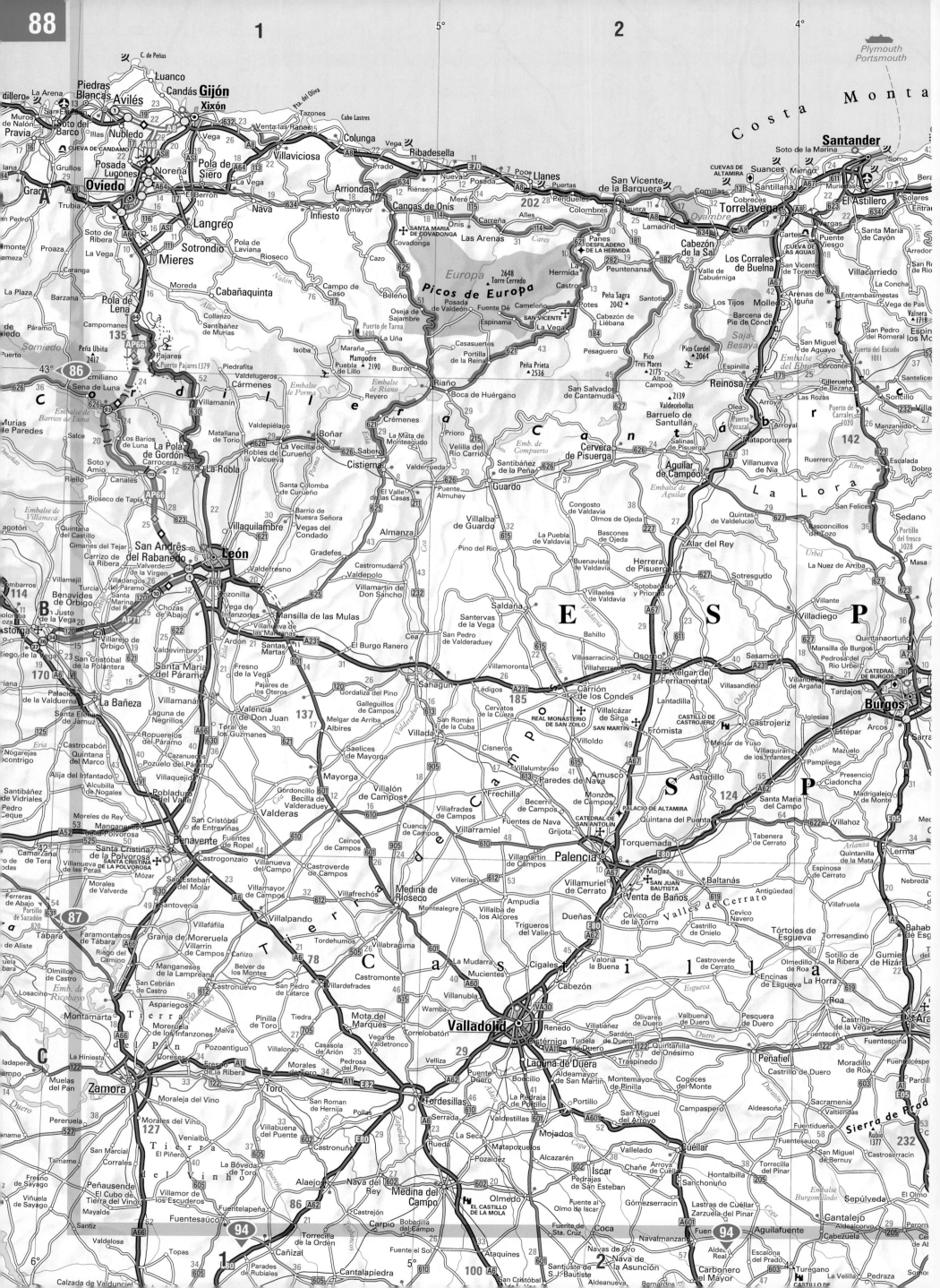

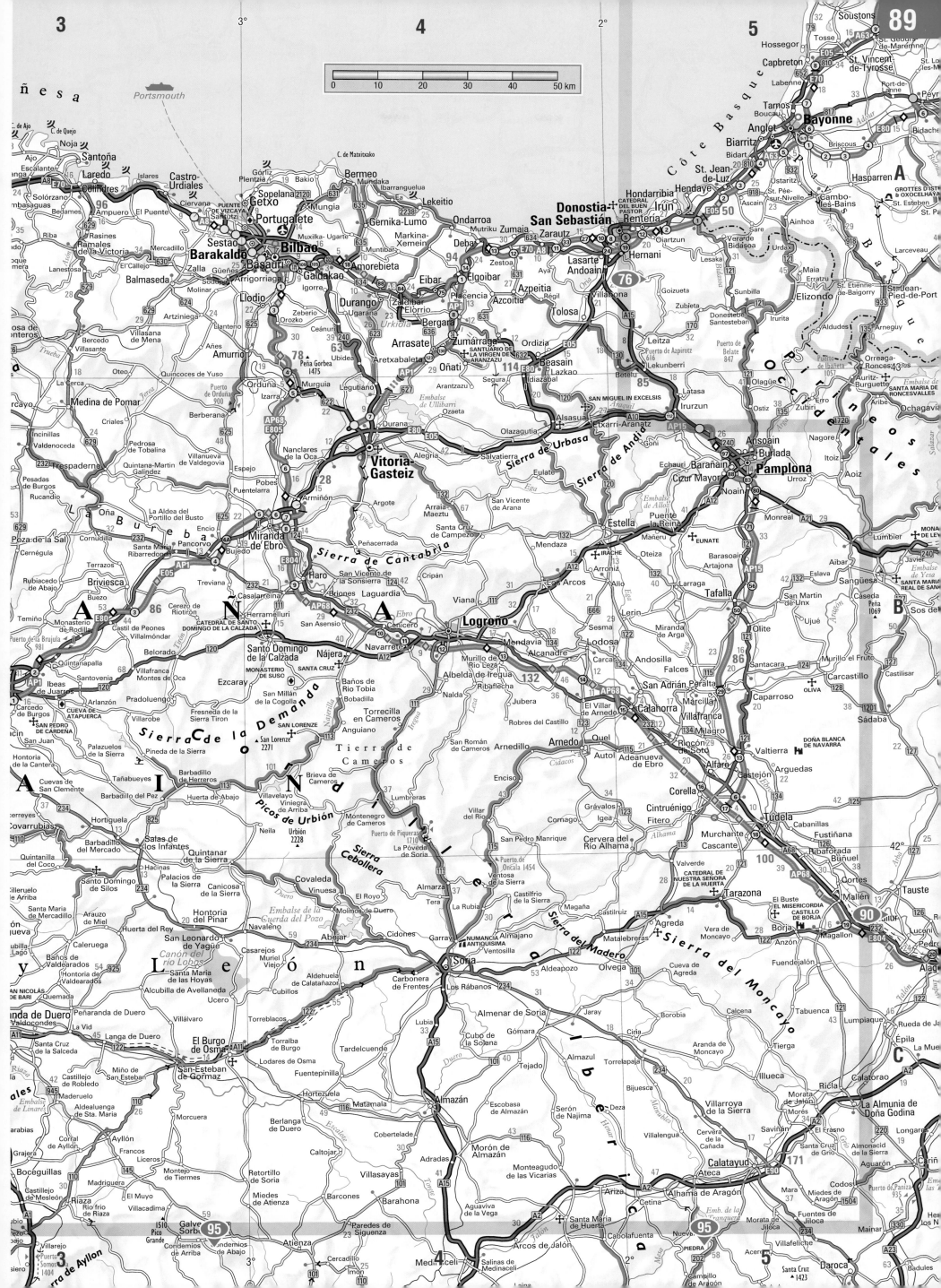

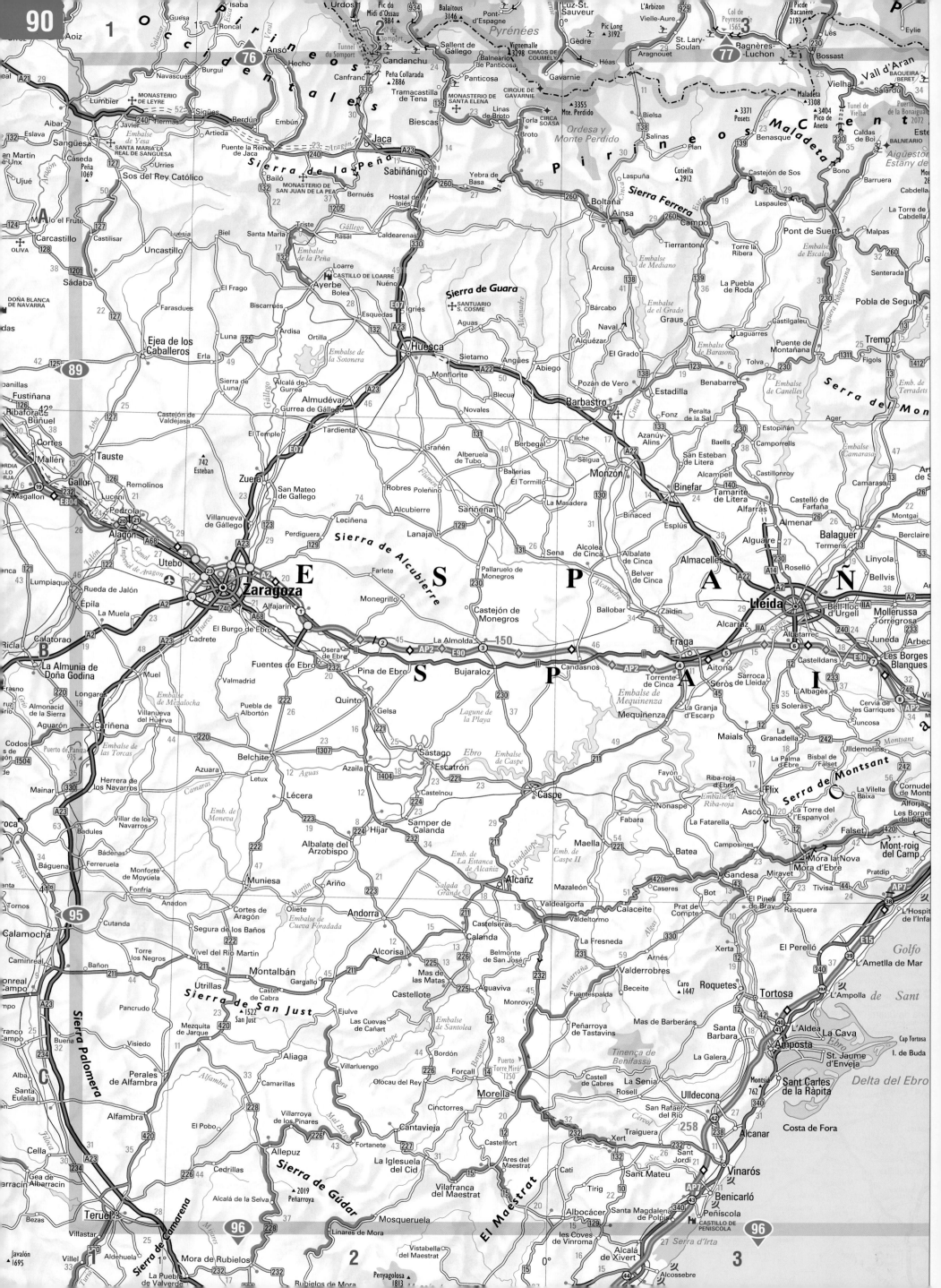

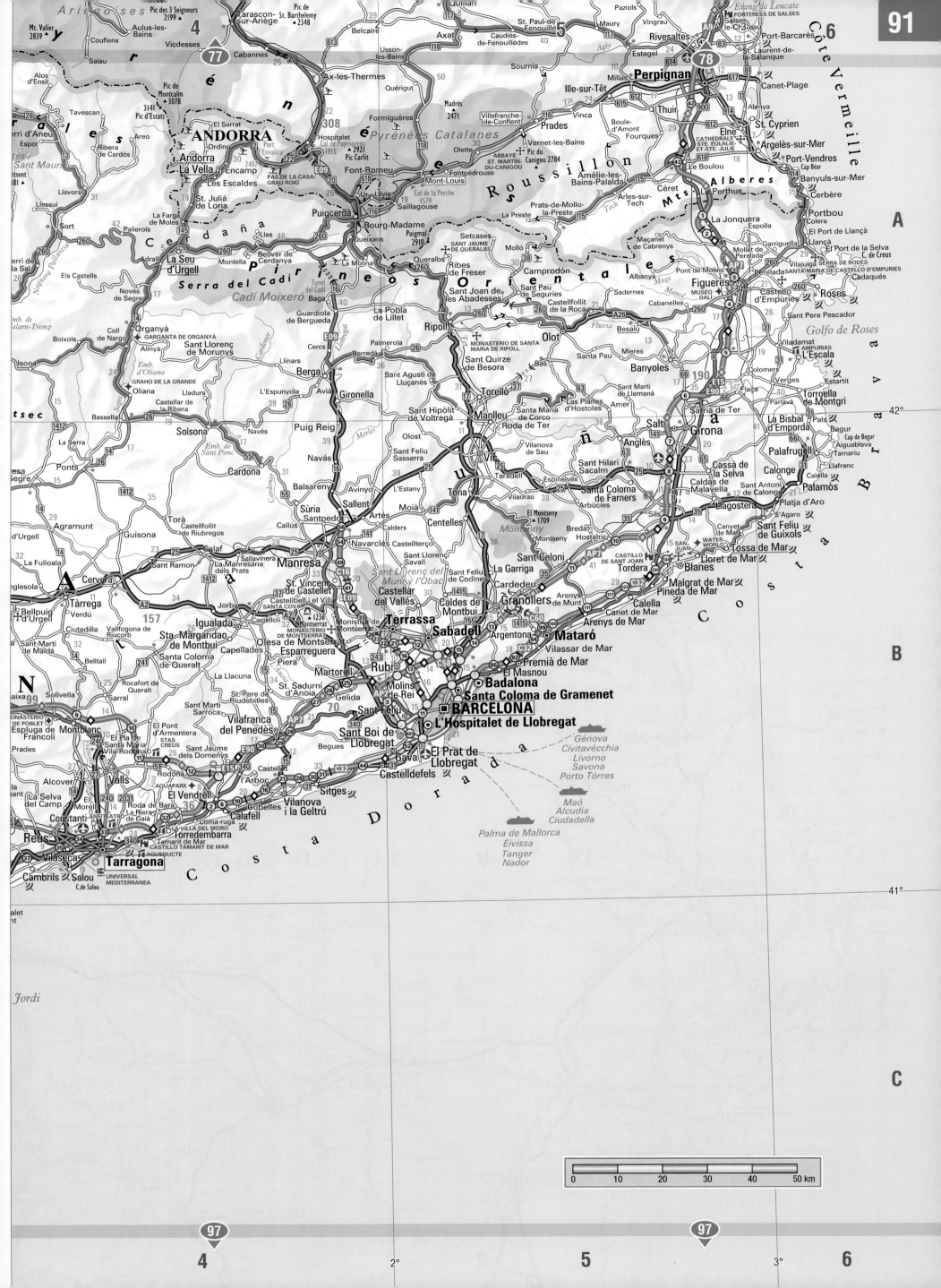

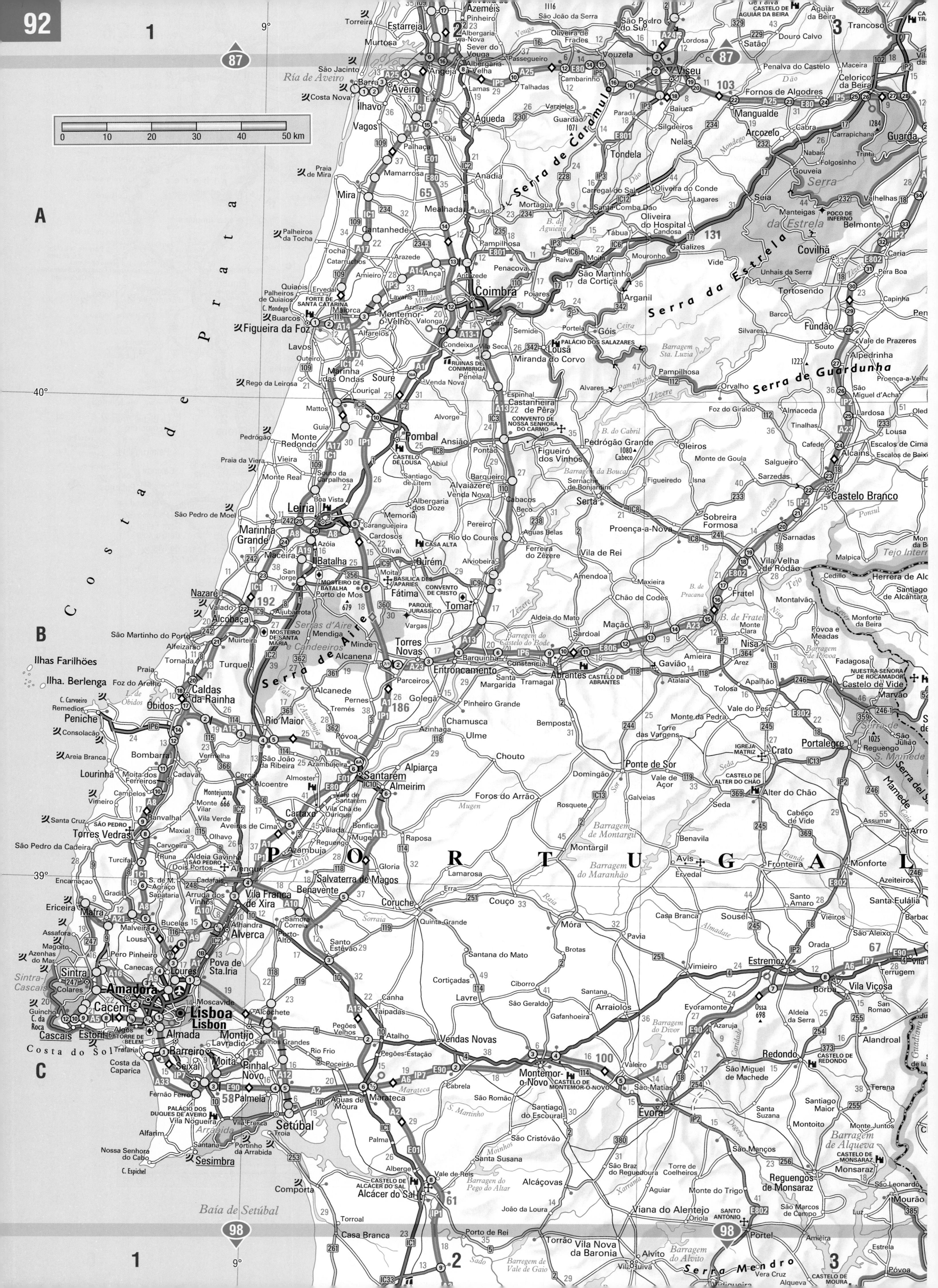

1

87

Ría de Aveiro
Costa de Prata

A

Coimbra

Figueira da Foz

40°

B

Ilhas Farilhões
Ilha Berlenga

Leiria

Nazaré

Peniche

Caldas da Rainha
Óbidos

Santarém

Torres Vedras

39°

Mafra

Sintra-Cascais
Sintra

Amadora
Cacém

LISBOA
Lisbon

Cascais
Estoril
Costa do Sol

Almada
Barreiro
Seixal
Moita
Pinhal Novo
Palmela
Setúbal
Sesimbra
C. Espichel

Baía de Setúbal

C

1

98

9°

P O R T U G A L

Serra de Caramulo
Viseu
Guarda
Serra da Estrela
Covilhã
Serra de Guardunha
Castelo Branco

Tomar
Fátima
Abrantes
Portalegre
Crato
Marvão
Castelo de Vide

Évora
Estremoz
Vila Viçosa
Borba
Redondo
Monsaraz

Serra Mendro

2

98

3

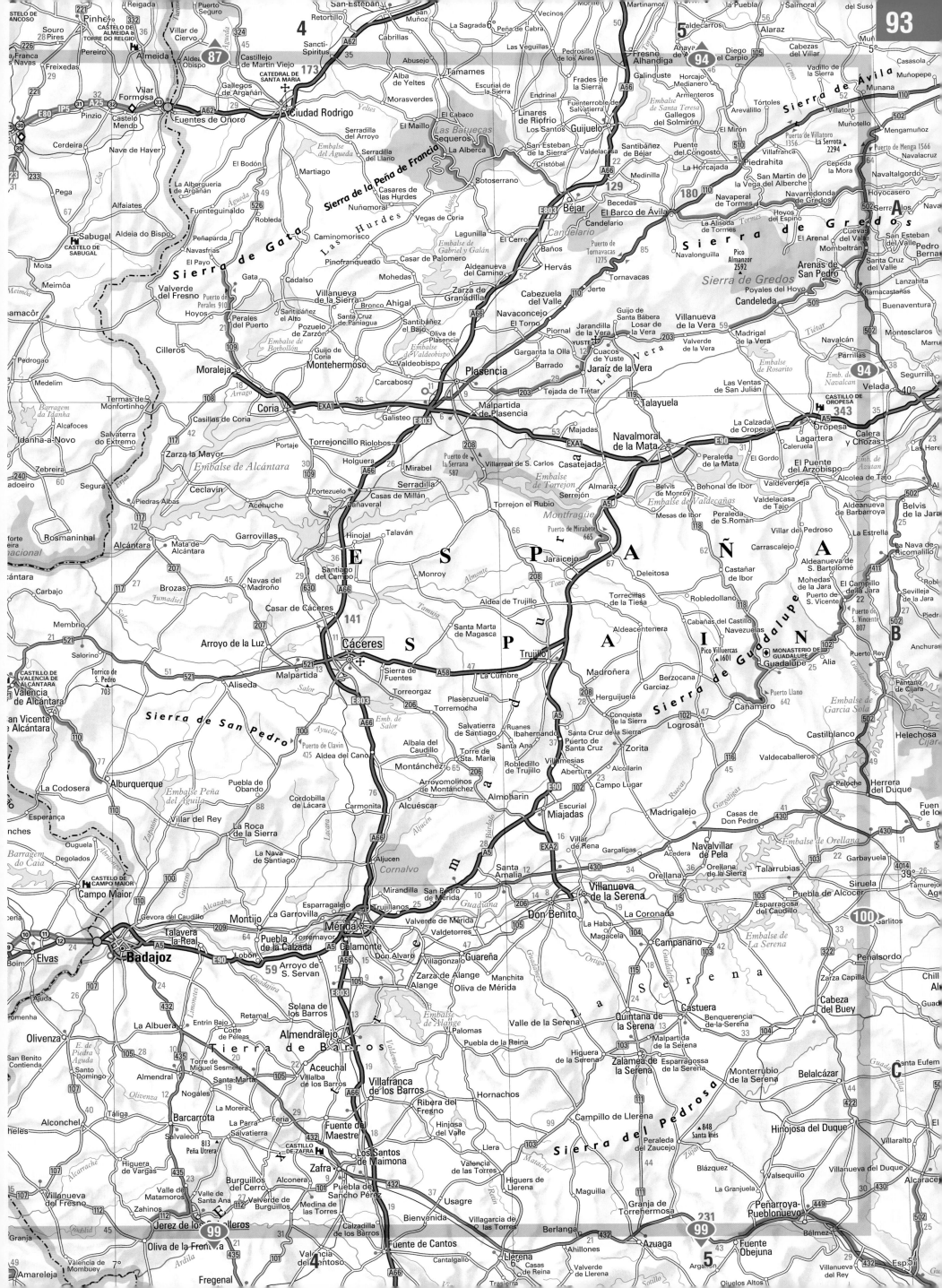

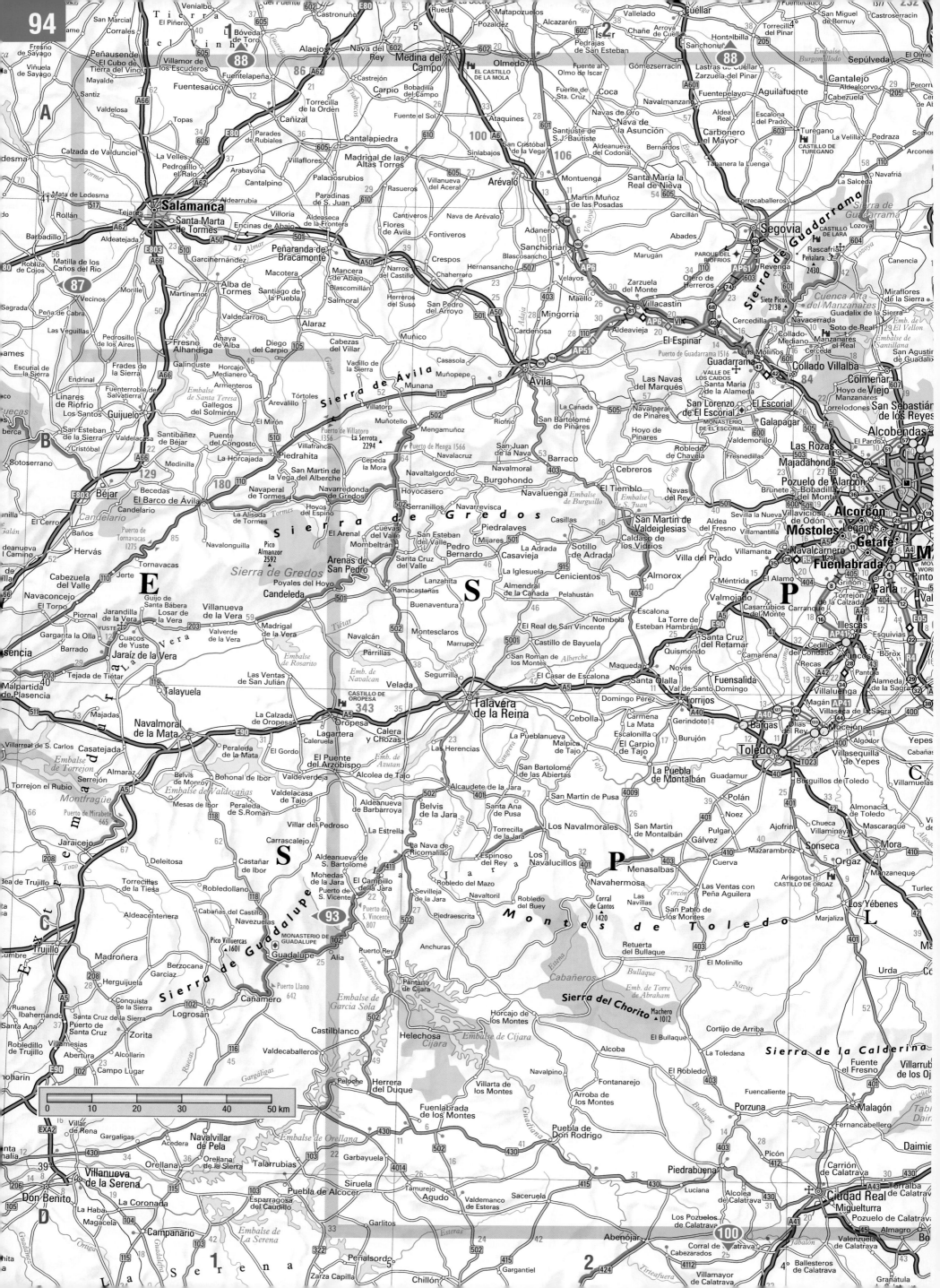

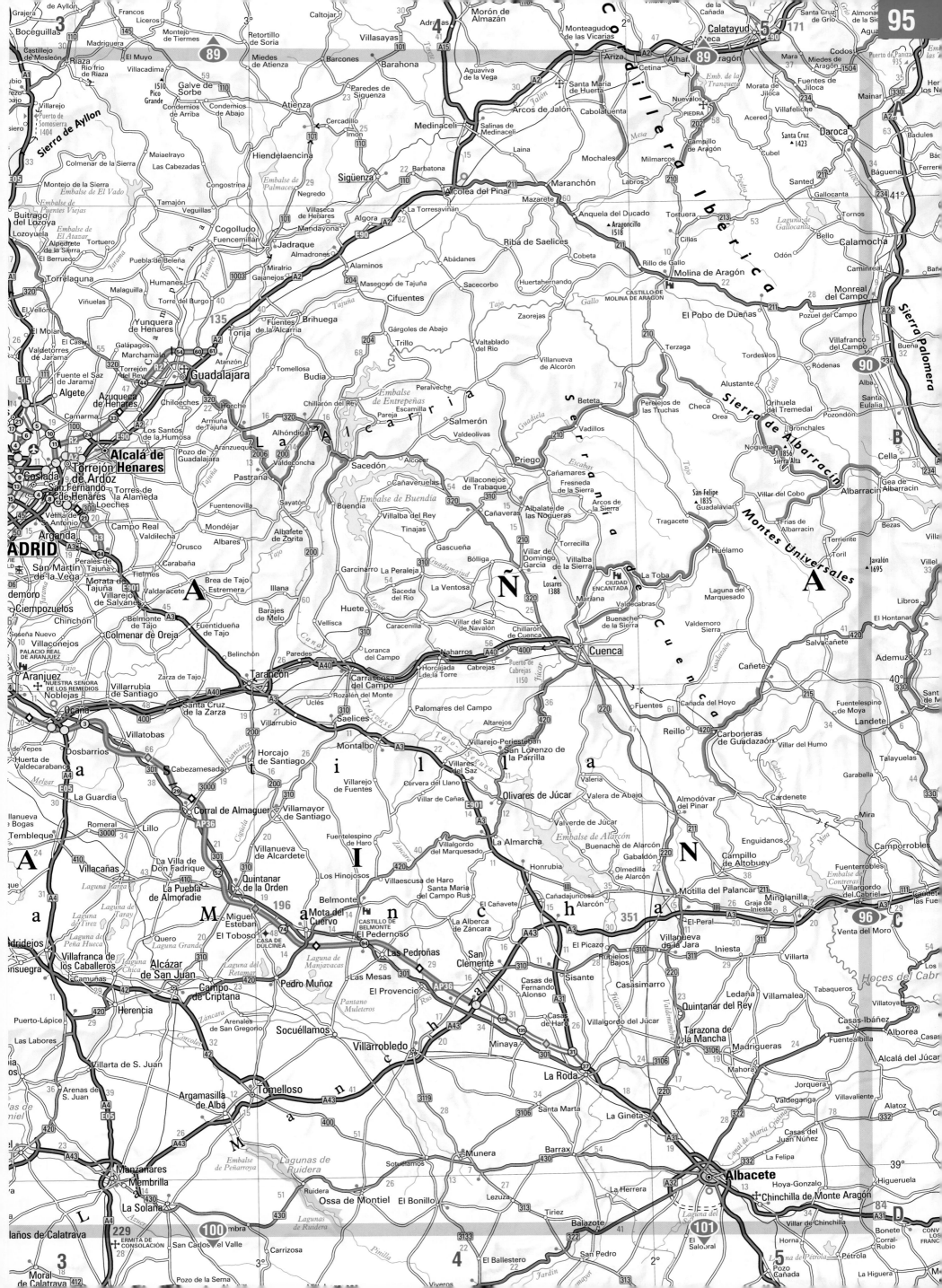

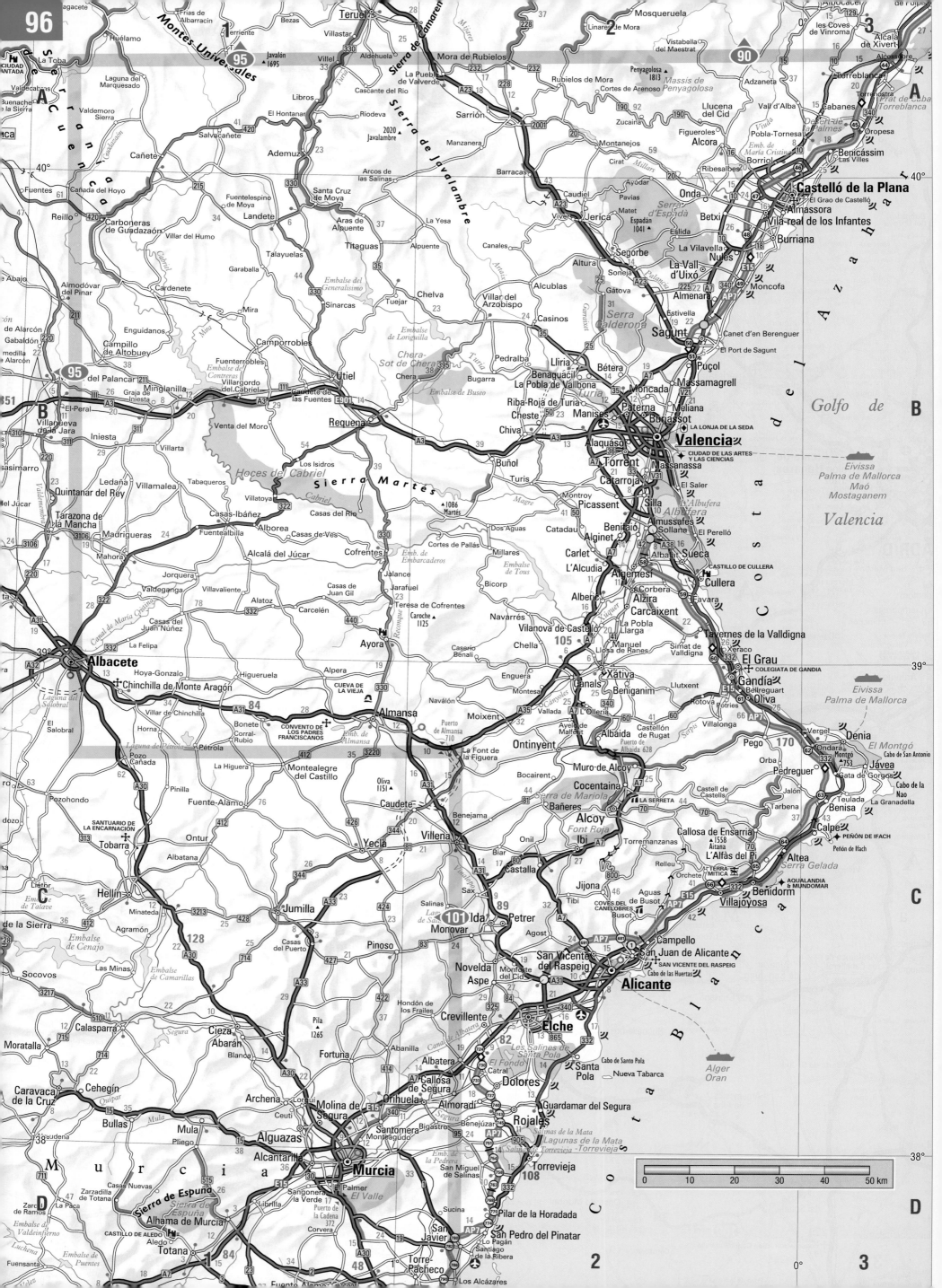

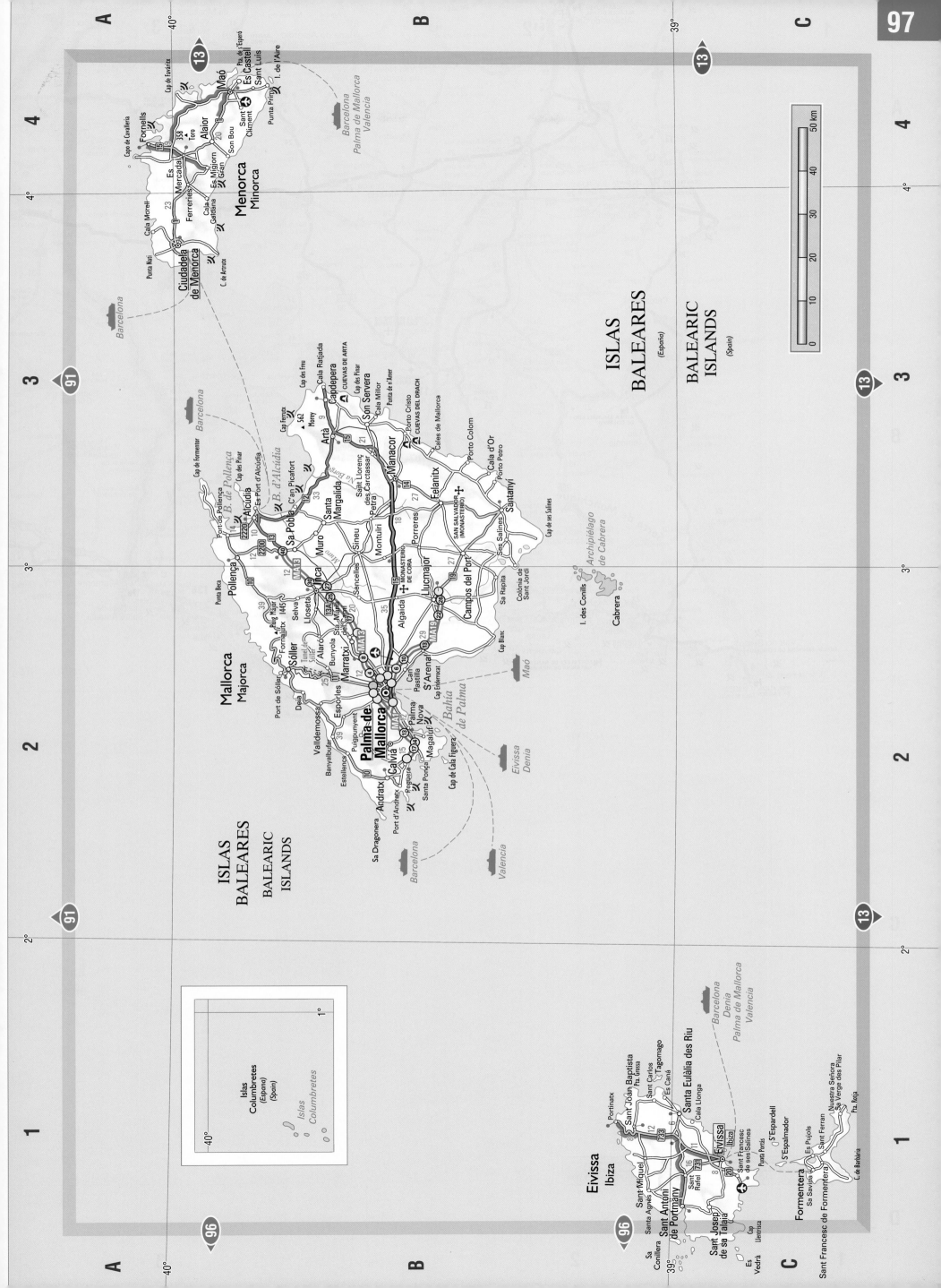

ISLAS BALEARES (España)
BALEARIC ISLANDS (Spain)

Menorca Minorca

Ciudadela de Menorca

Maó
Es Castell
Sant Luis

ISLAS BALEARES
BALEARIC ISLANDS

Mallorca Majorca

Palma de Mallorca
Calvià

Eivissa Ibiza

Formentera

Sant Francesc de Formentera

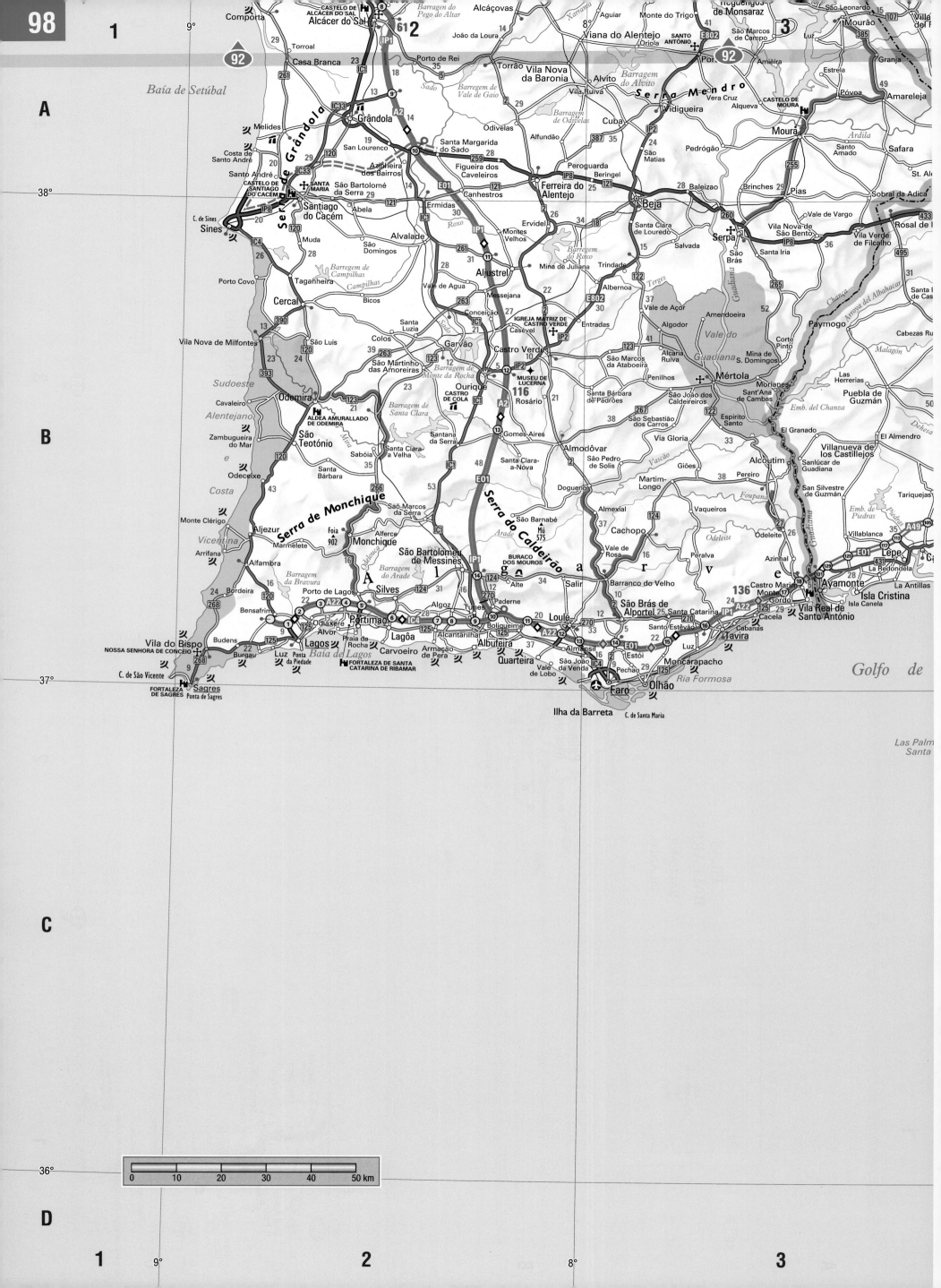

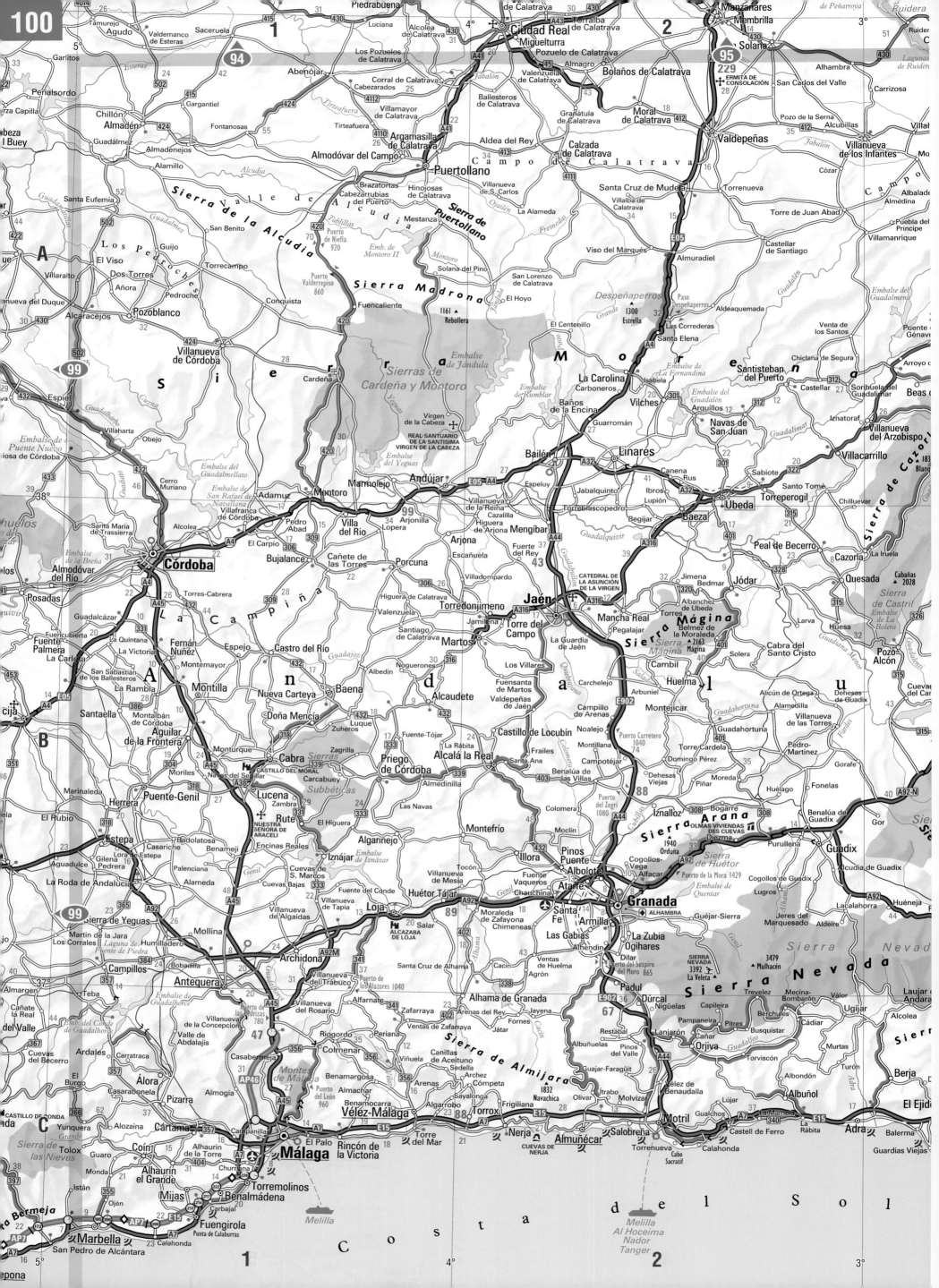

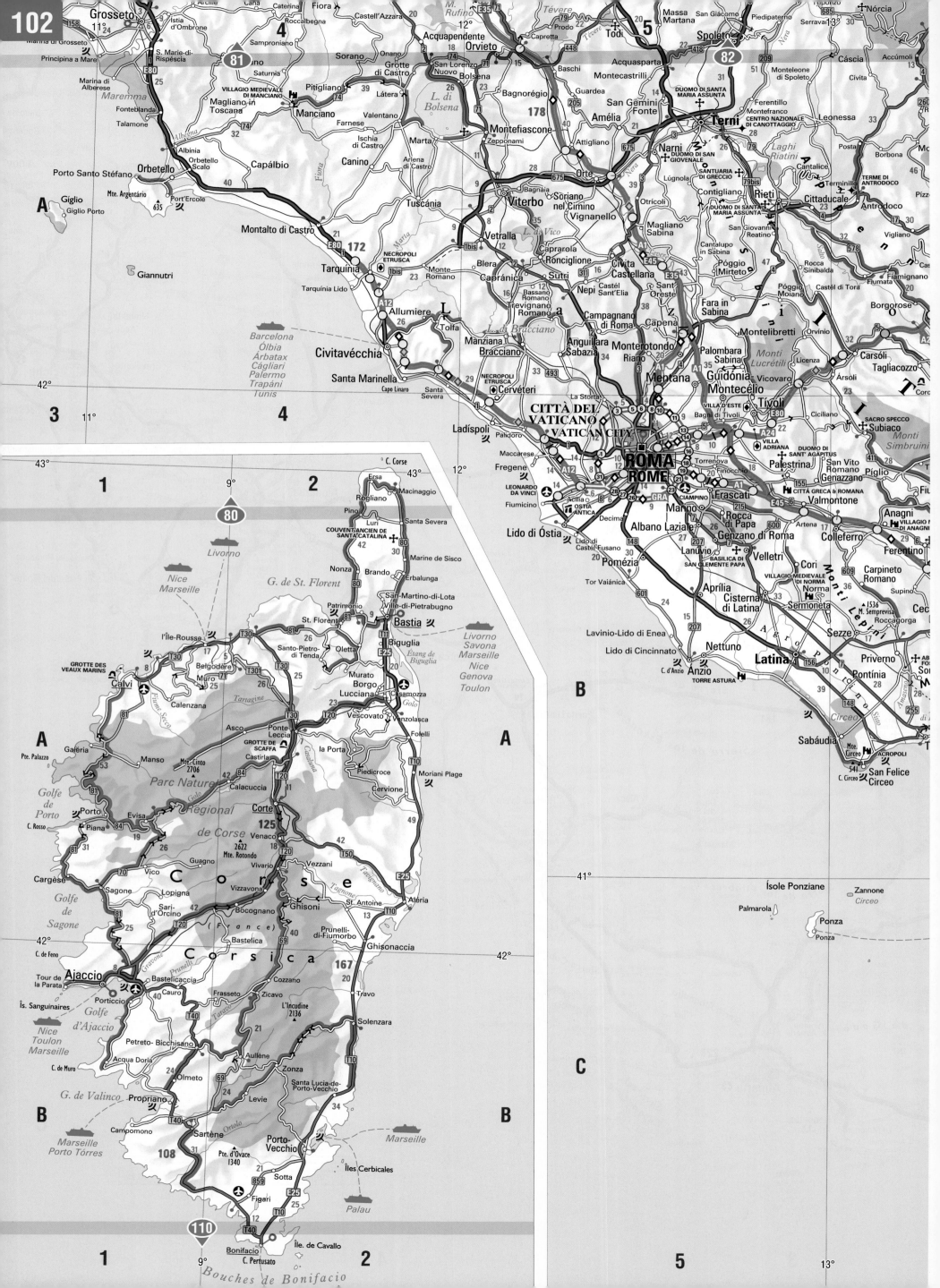

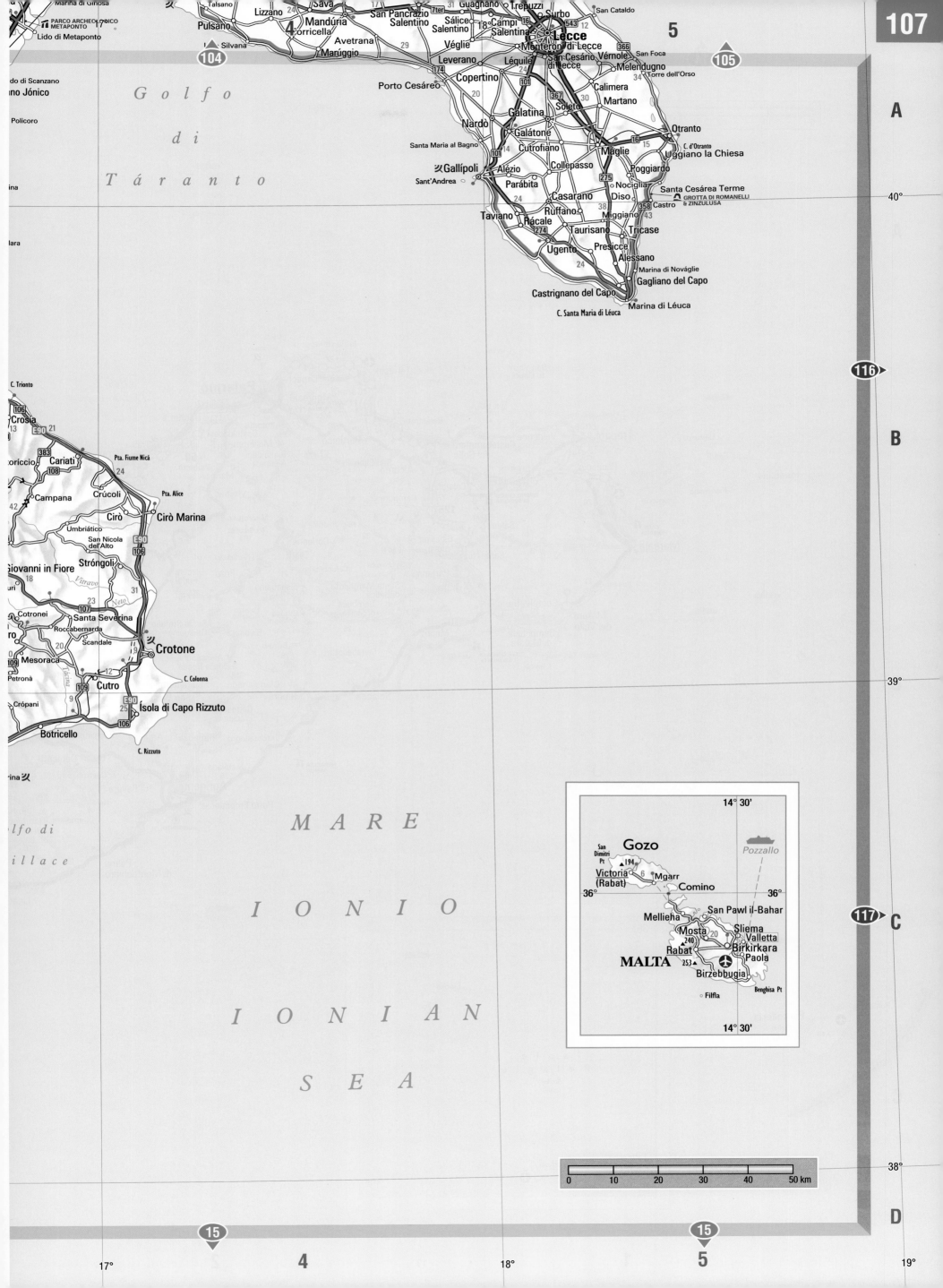

Parco Archeologico METAPONTO
Lido di Metaponto
do di Scanzano
ano Jónico
Policoro

San Cataldo

Talsano
Lizzano 24
Sáva
Guagnano
Trepuzzi Surbo
Pulsano
Mandúria Sálice
Campi Salentina
Lecce
San Pancrazio Salentino
Salentino
Monteroni di Lecce
San Foca
Torricella
Avetrana
Véglie
San Cesário di Lecce
Melendugno
Torre dell'Orso
Marúggio
Leverano
Léquile
Vérnole
Copertino
Calimera
Galatina
Martano
Porto Cesáreo
Soleto
Nardò
Galátone
Otranto
Santa Maria al Bagno
Cutrofiano
C. d'Otranto
Gallípoli
Máglie
Uggiano la Chiesa
Sant'Andrea
Aléezio
Collepasso
Poggiardo
Parábita
Nociglia
Santa Cesárea Terme
Casarano
Diso
Castro
GROTTA DI ROMANELLI & ZINZULUSA
Ruffano
Miggiano
Taviano
Taurisano
Tricase
Rácale
Presicce
Ugento
Alessano
Marina di Nováglie
Gagliano del Capo
Castrignano del Capo
Marina di Léuca
C. Santa Maria di Léuca

Golfo di Táranto

C. Trionto
Crosia
E90
Cariati
Pta. Fiume Nicá
oríccio
Crúcoli
Pta. Alice
Campana
Cirò
Cirò Marina
Umbriático
San Nicola dell'Alto
E90
Giovanni in Fiore
Stróngoli
Víravo
Neto
Cotronei
Santa Severina
Roccabernarda
Mesoraca
Scandale
Crotone
Petronà
C. Colonna
Crópani
Cutro
Ísola di Capo Rizzuto
Botricello
C. Rizzuto

Golfo di illace

MARE

IONIO

IONIAN

SEA

Pozzallo

Gozo
San Dimitri Pt
194
Victoria (Rabat)
Mgarr
Comino
Mellieha
San Pawl il-Bahar
Mosta
240
Sliema
Valletta
Rabat
Birkirkara
MALTA
253
Paola
Birzebbugia
Filfla
Benghisa Pt

14° 30'

36°

14° 30'

0 10 20 30 40 50 km

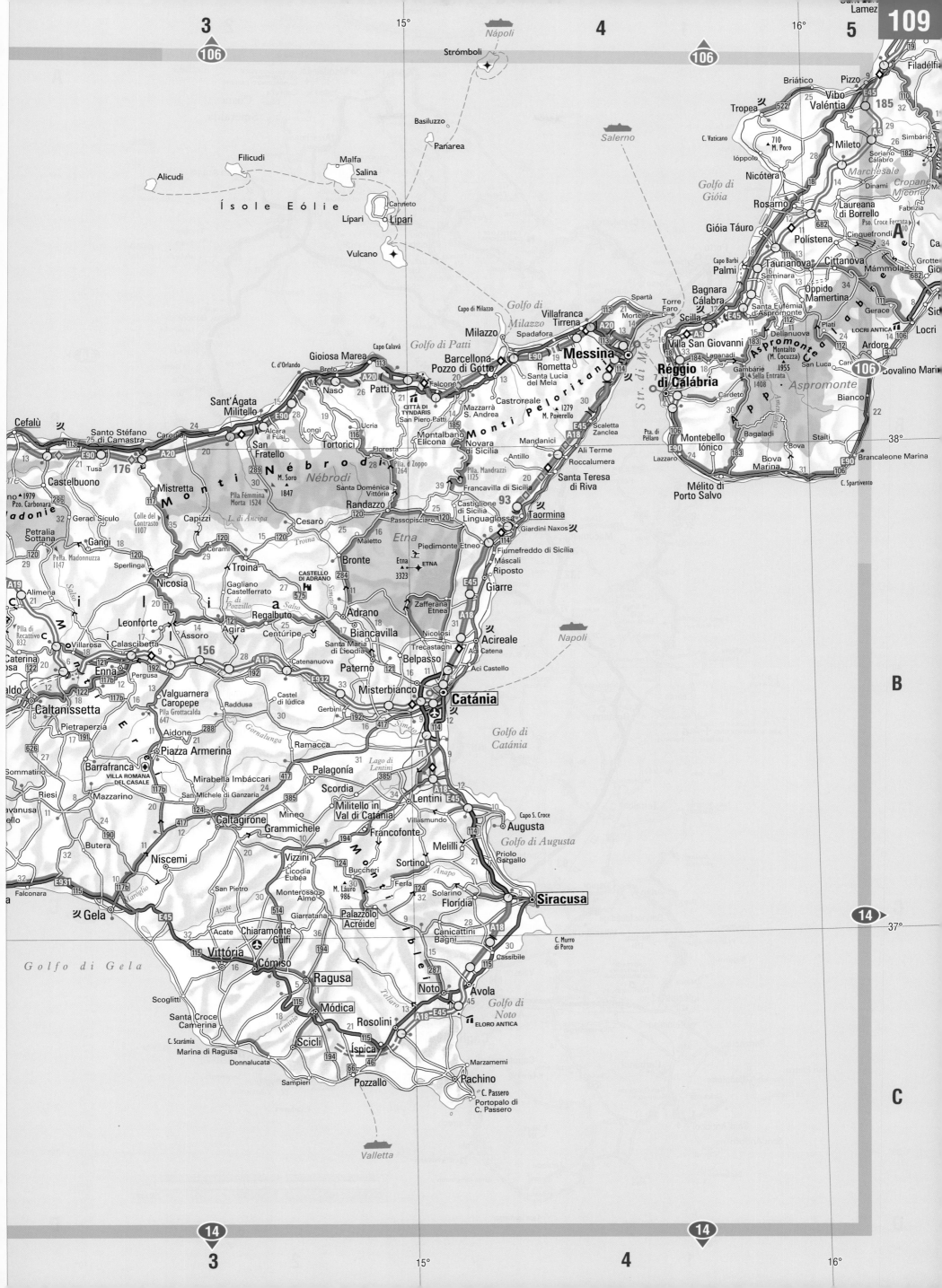

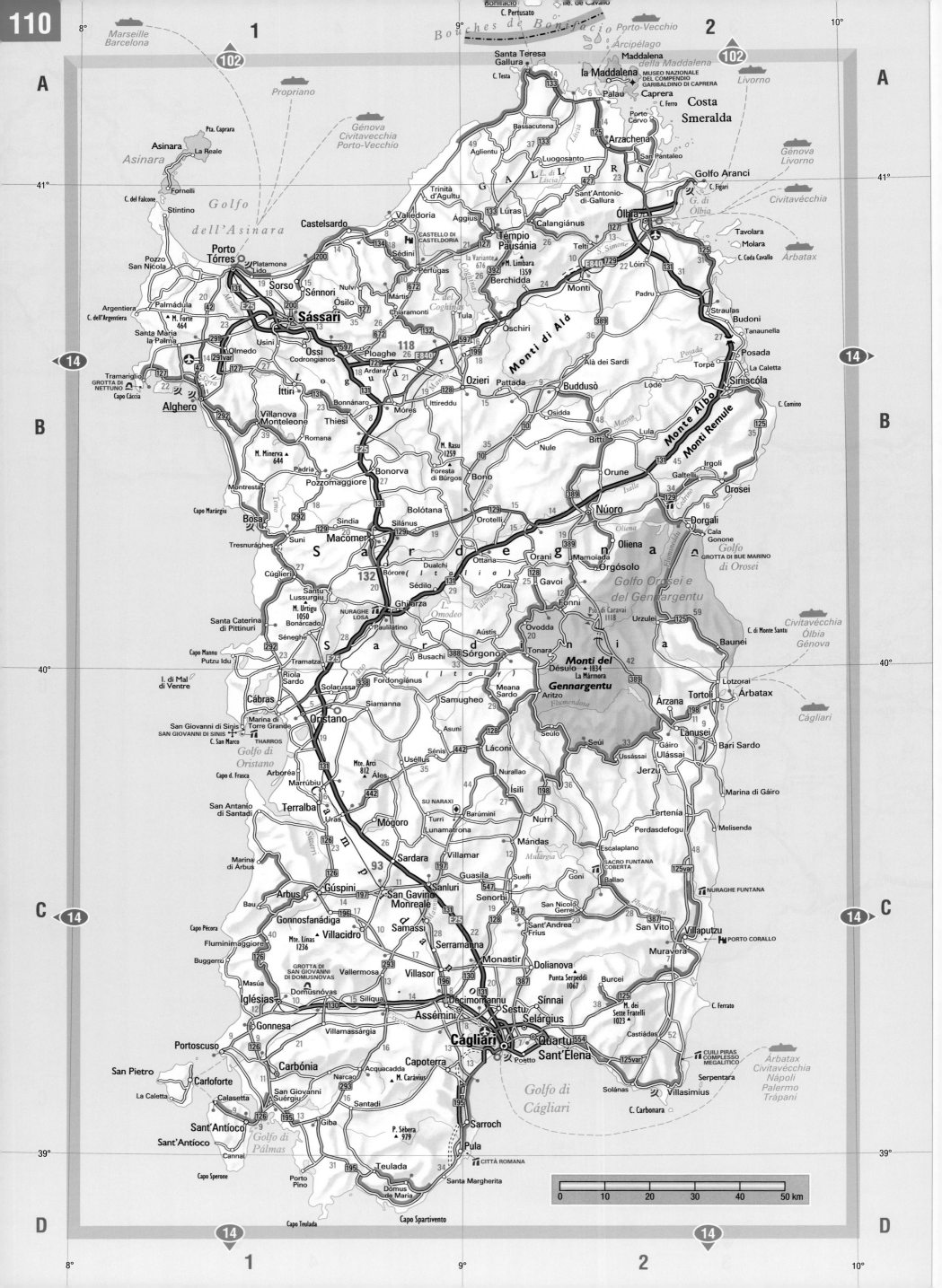

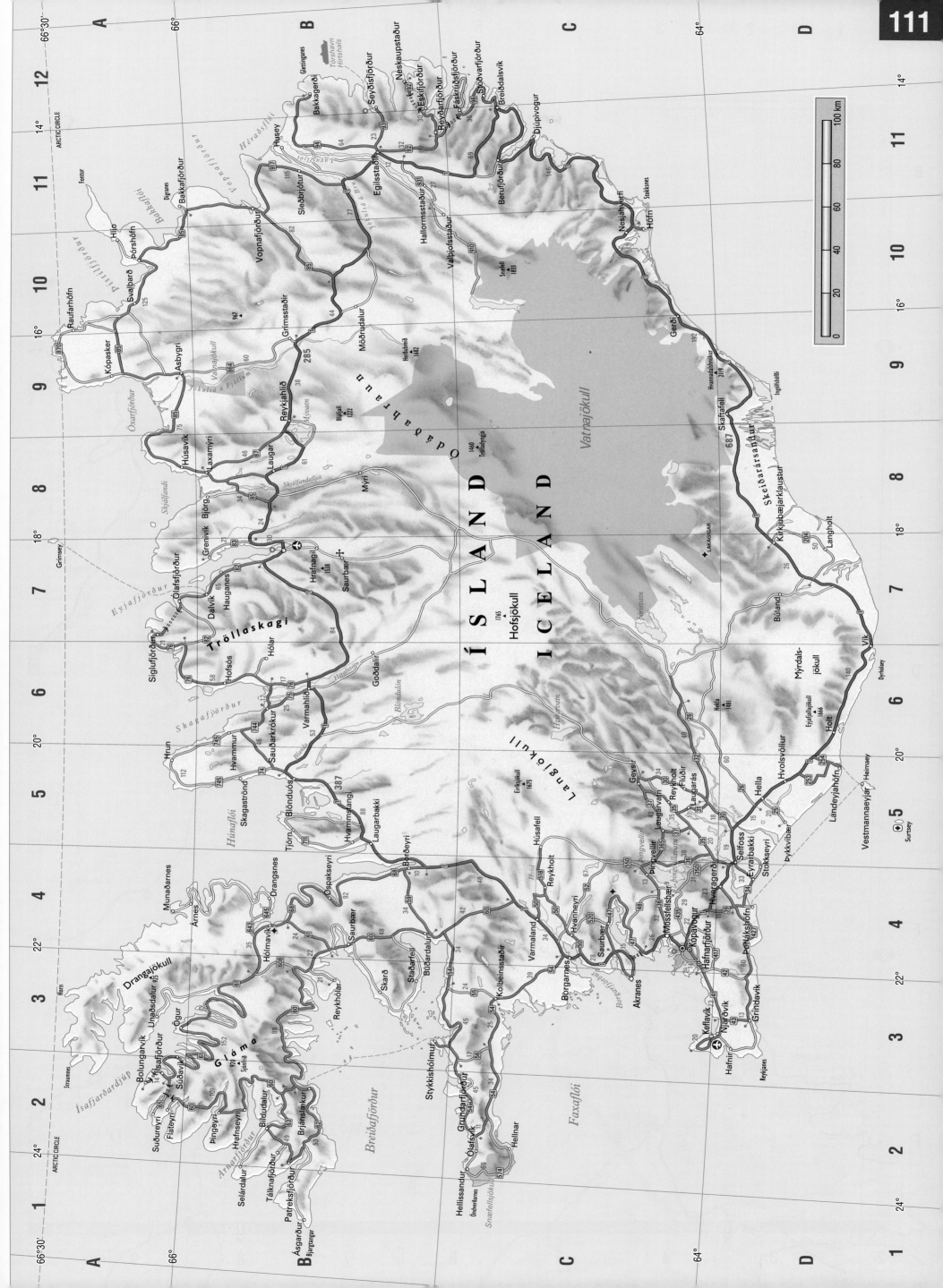

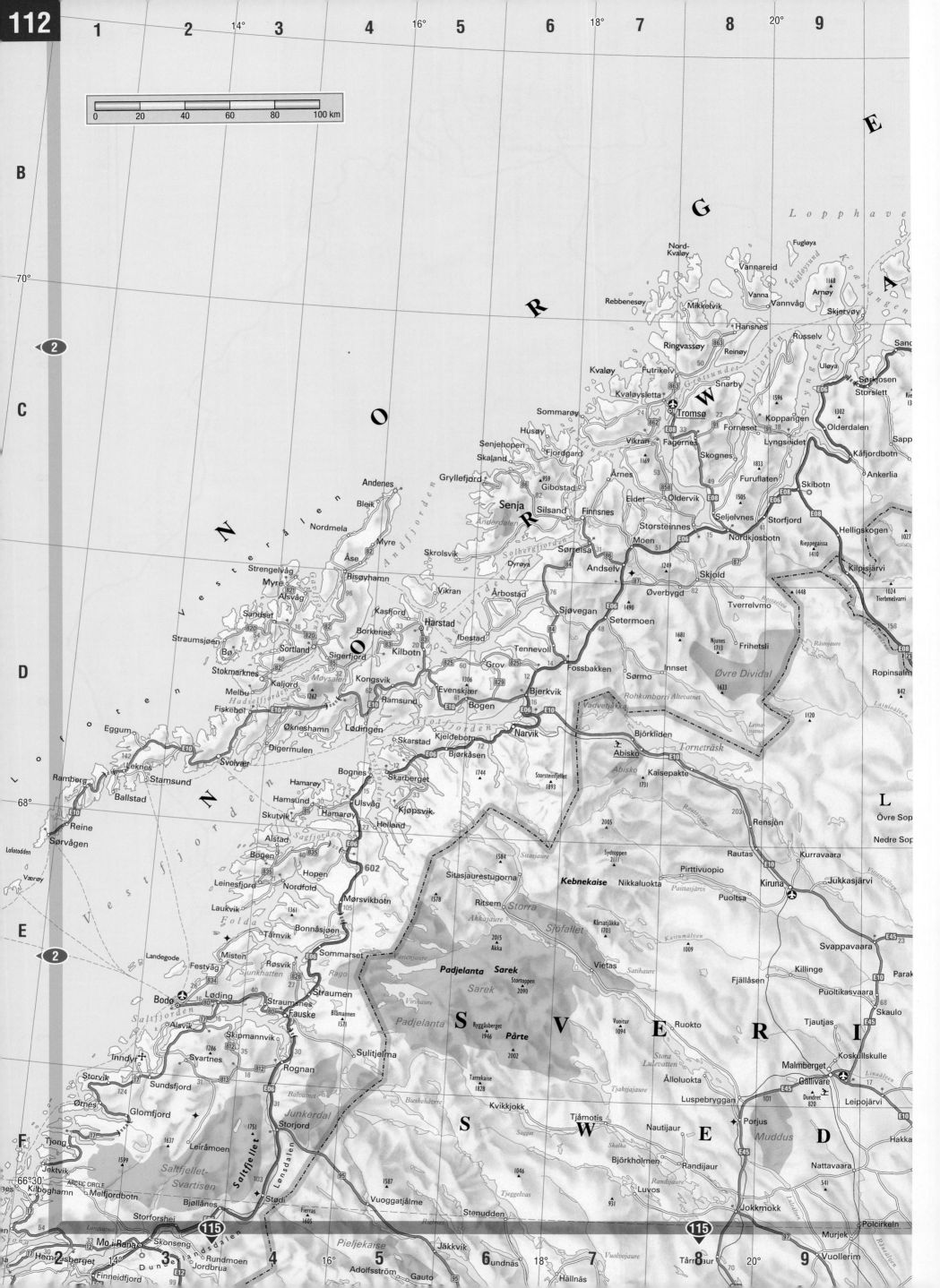

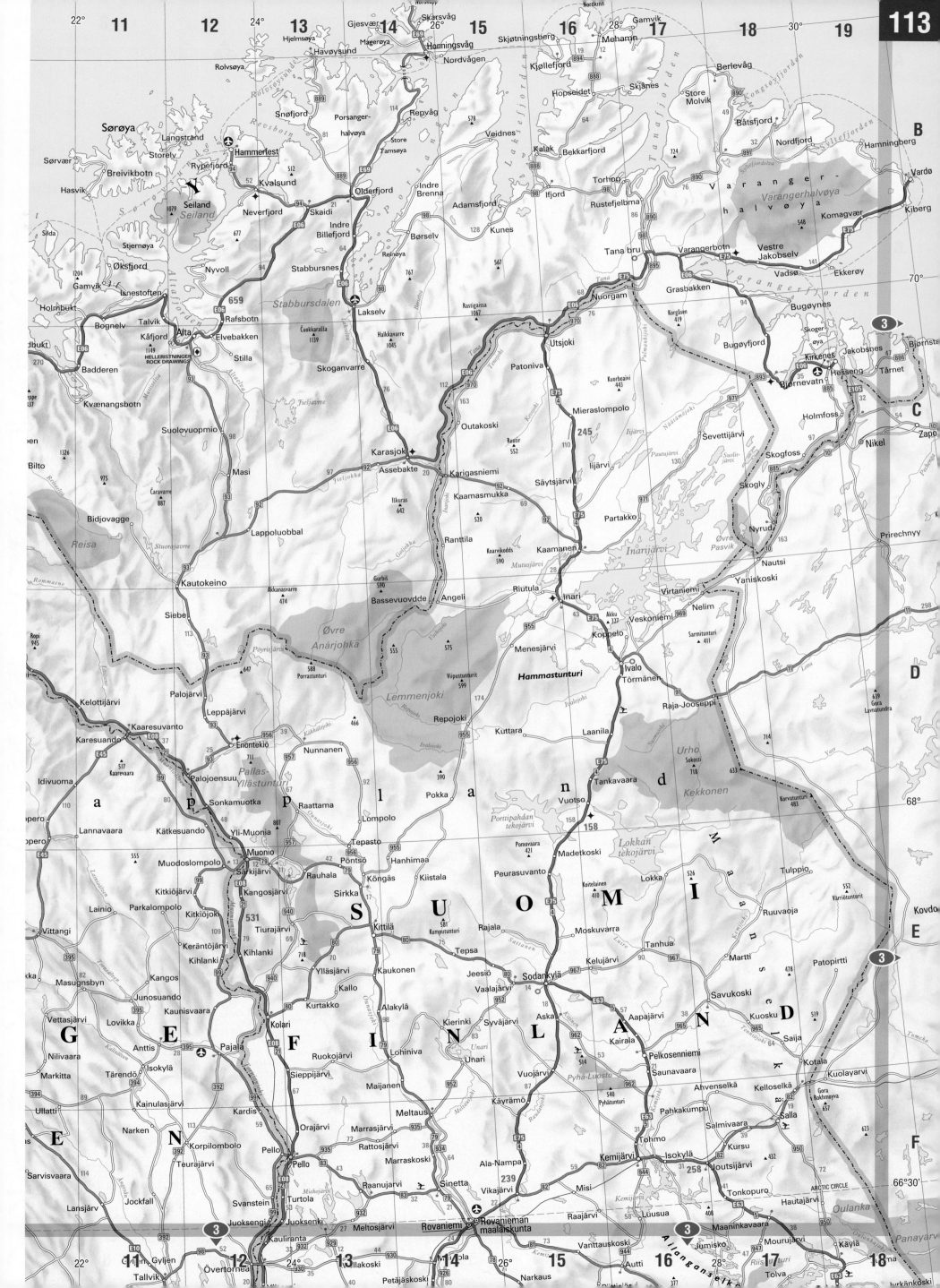

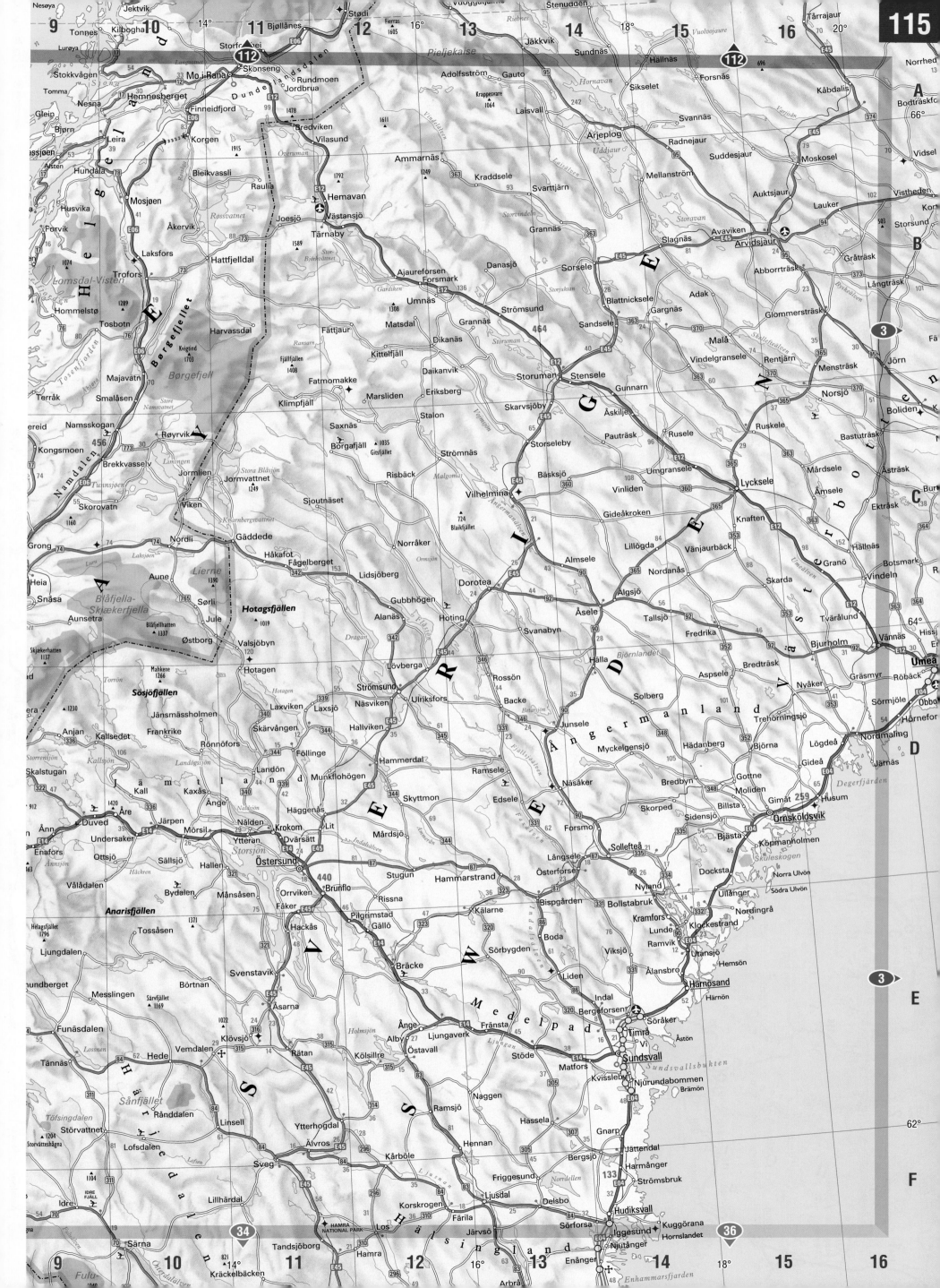

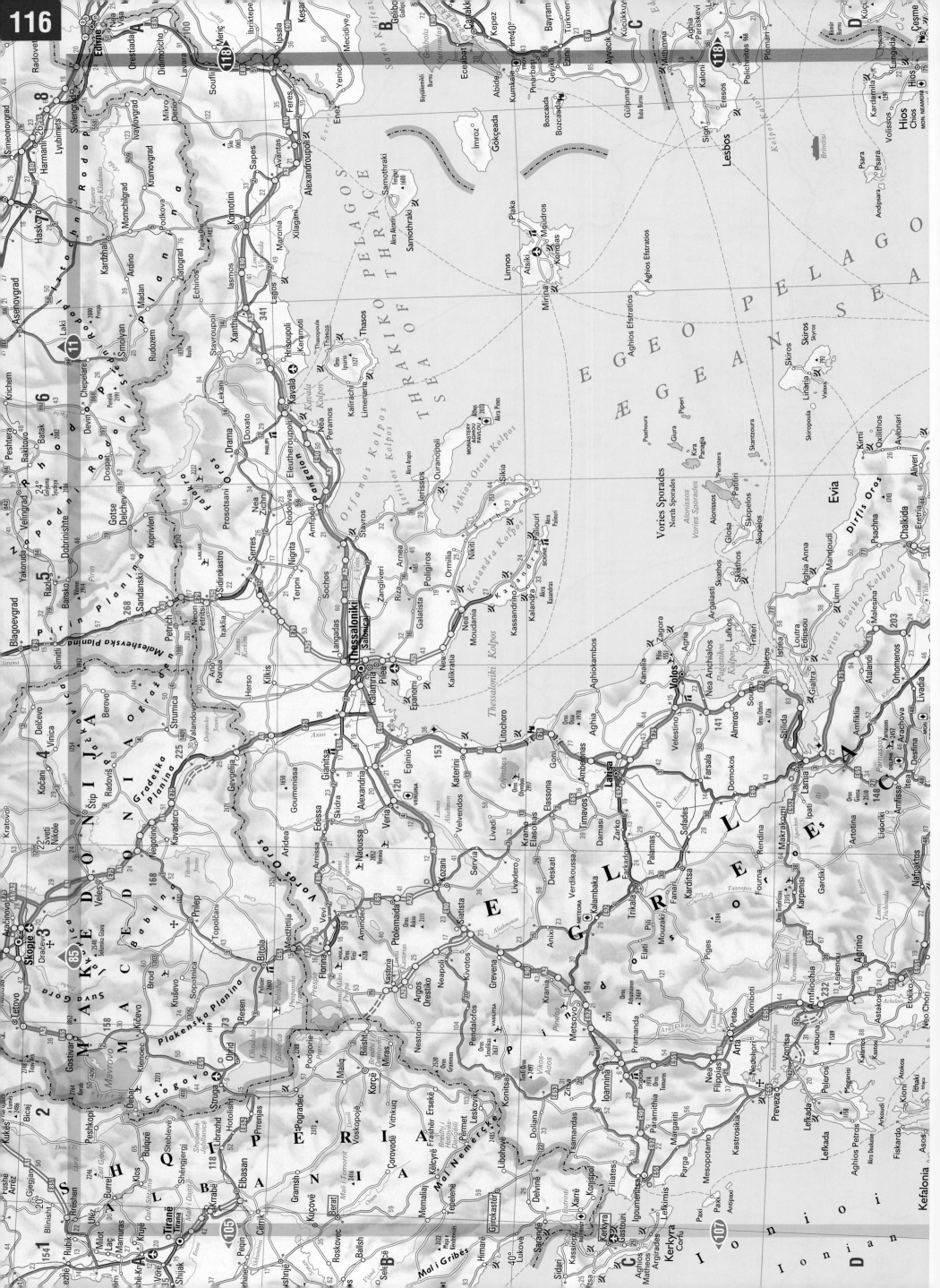

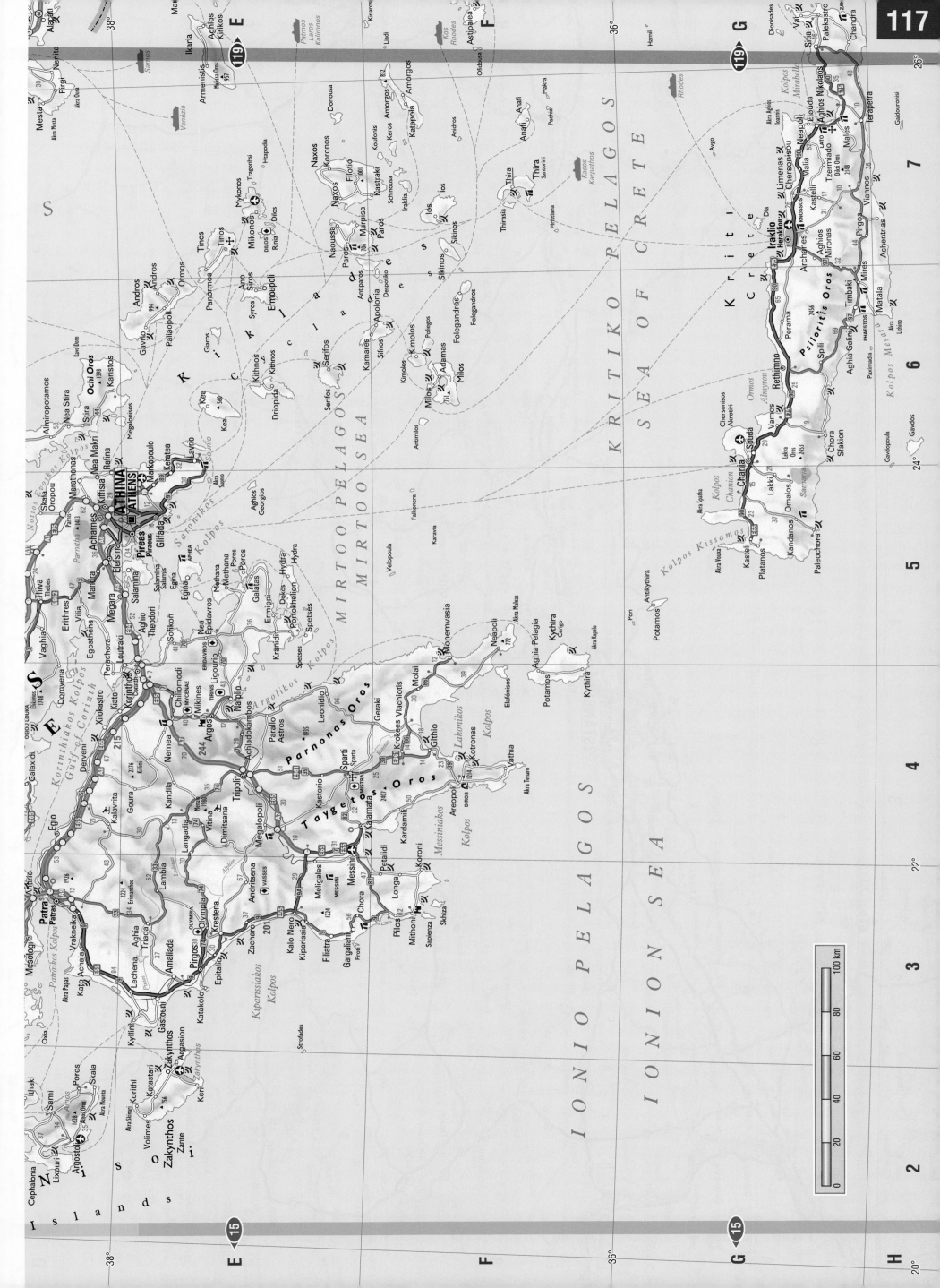

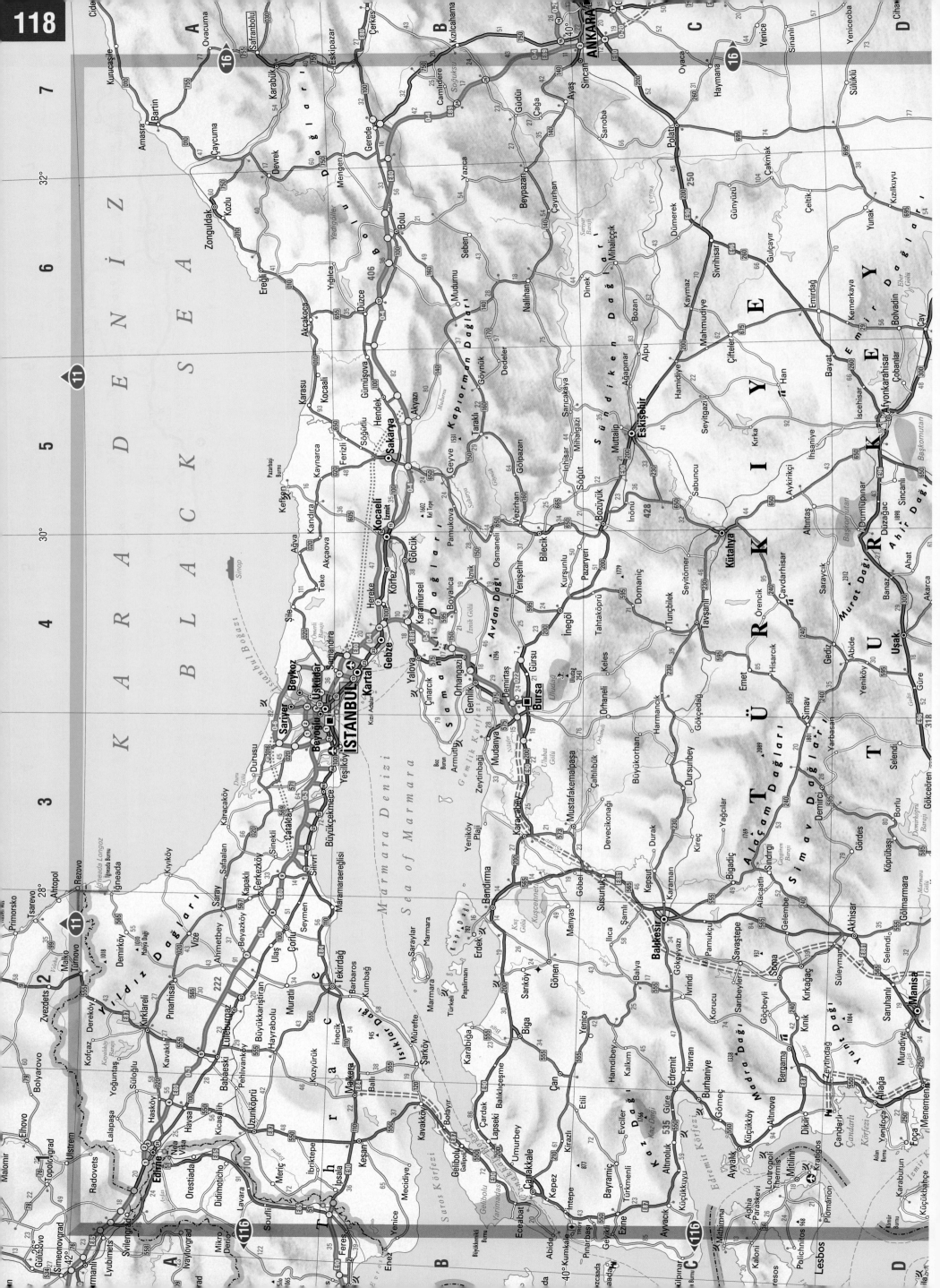

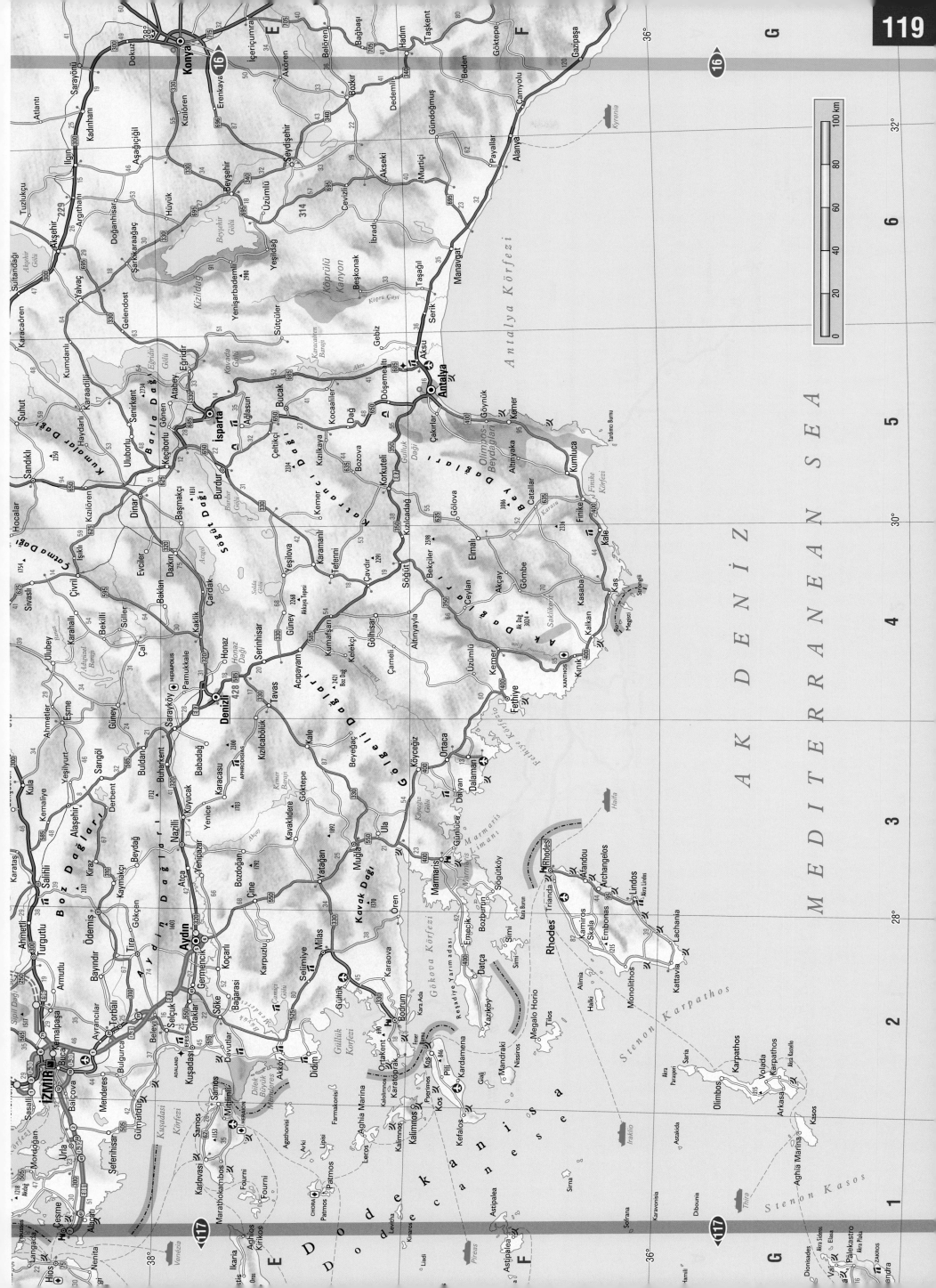

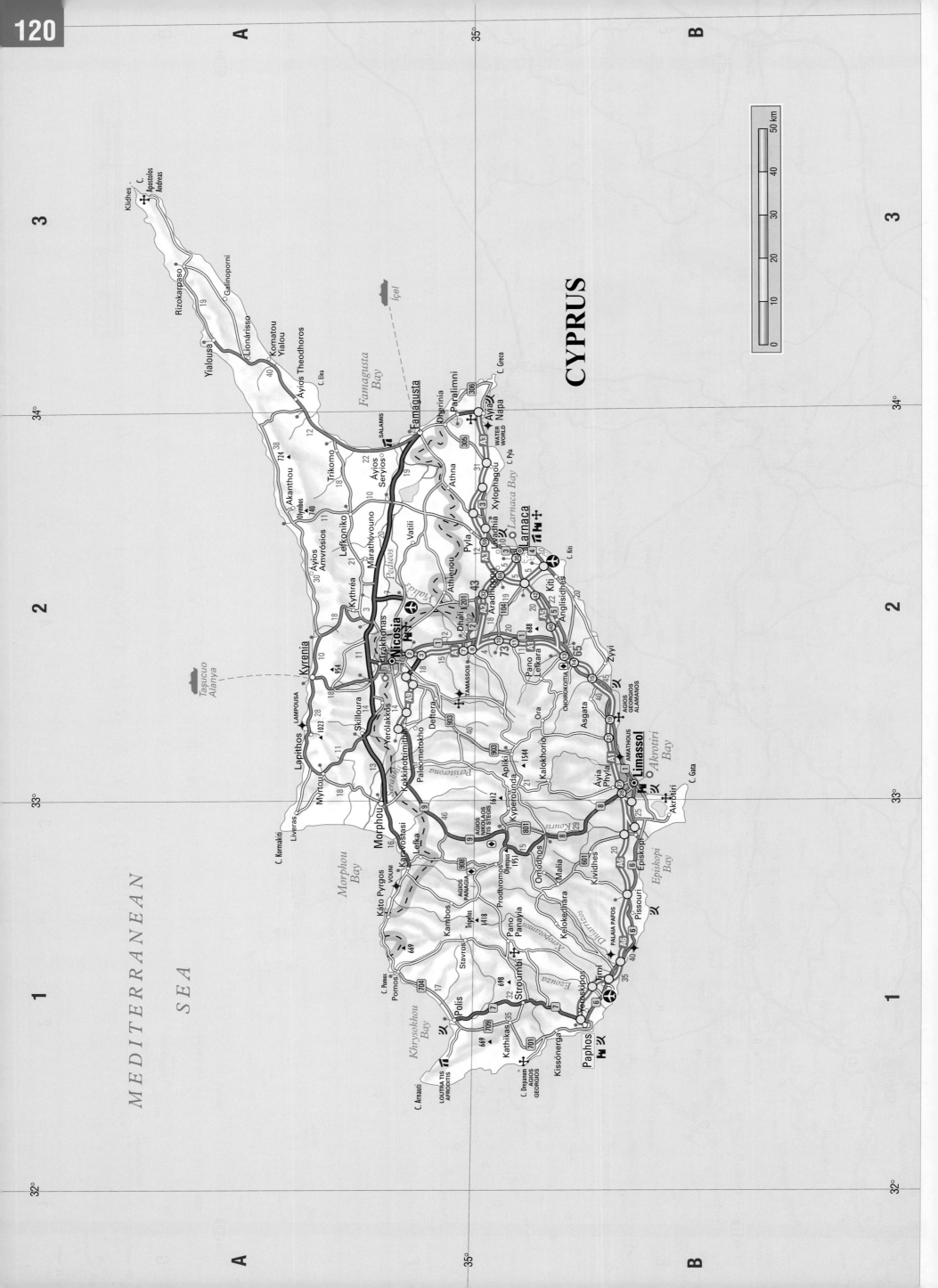

CYPRUS

City plans • Plans de villes
Stadtpläne • Piante di città

Motorway	Autoroute	Autobahn	Autostrada
Major through route	Route principale majeur	Hauptstrecke	Strada di grande communicazione
Through route	Route principale	Schnellstrasse	Strada d'importanza regionale
Secondary road	Route secondaire	Nebenstrasse	Strada d'interesse locale
Dual carriageway	Chaussées séparées	Zweispurig Schnellstrasse	Strada a carreggiate doppie
Other road	Autre route	Nebenstrecke	Altra strada
Tunnel	Tunnel	Tunnel	Galleria stradale
Limited access / pedestrian road	Rue réglementée / rue piétonne	Beschränkter Zugang/ Fussgängerzone	Strada pedonale / a accesso limitato
One-way street	Sens unique	Einbahnstrasse	Senso unico
Parking	Parc de stationnement	Parkplatz	Parcheggio
Motorway number A7	Numéro d'autoroute	Autobahnnummer A7	Numero di autostrada
National road number 447	Numéro de route nationale	Nationalstrassen-nummer 447	Numero di strada nazionale
European road number E45	Numéro de route européenne	Europäische Strassennummer E45	Numero di strada europea
Destination GENT	Destination	Ziel GENT	Destinazione
Car ferry	Bac passant les autos	Autofähre	Traghetto automobili
Railway	Chemin de fer	Eisenbahn	Ferrovia
Rail/bus station	Gare / gare routière	Bahnhof/ Busstation	Stazione ferrovia / pullman
Underground, metro station	Station de métro	U-Bahnstation	Metropolitano
Cable car	Téléférique	Drahtseilbahn	Funivia
Abbey, cathedral	Abbaye, cathédrale	Abtei, Kloster, Kathedrale	Abbazia, duomo
Church of interest	Église intéressante	Interessante Kirche	Chiesa da vedere
Synagogue	Synagogue	Synagoge	Sinagoga
Hospital	Hôpital	Krankenhaus	Ospedale
Police station POL	Police	Polizeiwache POL	Polizia
Post office	Bureau de poste	Postamt	Ufficio postale
Tourist information	Office de tourisme	Informationsbüro	Ufficio informazioni turistiche
Place of interest Theatre	Autre curiosité	Sonstige Sehenswürdigkeit Theatre	Luogo da vedere

Approach maps • Agglomérations
Carte régionale • Regionalkarte

Toll motorway – with motorway number A10	Autoroute à péage – avec numéro d'autoroute	Gebührenpflichtige Autobahn – mit Autobahnnummer A10	Autostrada a pedaggio – con numero
Toll-free motorway – with European road number E51	Autoroute – avec numéro de route européenne	Gebührenfreie Autobahn – Europäische Strassennummer E51	Autostrada – con numero di strada europea
Pre-pay motorway – vignette required	Autoroute 'vignette'	Autobahn – 'vignette'	Autostrada – 'vignette'
Motorway services	Aire de service	Autobahnservice	Area di servizio autostradale
Motorway junction full access, restricted access	Échangeur d'autoroute accès libre, accès reglémenté	Autobahnkreuz – voller/begrenzter Zugang	Raccordi autostradali – completo/parziali
Under construction	En construction	Im Bau	In construzione
Tunnel	Tunnel	Tunnel	Galleria stradale
Major route dual carriageway 14 single carriageway 14	Route principale chausées séparées chausée sans séparation	Hauptstrecke – zweispurige 14 Schnellstrasse 14	Strada di grande communicazione carreggiata doppia carreggiata unica
Secondary route dual carriageway 96 single carriageway 96	Route secondaire chausées séparées chausée sans séparation	Nebenstrasse – zweispurige 96 Schnellstrasse 96	Strada d'interesse locale – carreggiata doppia carreggiata unica
Other road	Autre route	Nebenstrecke	Altra strada
Car ferry	Bac passant les autos	Autofähre	Traghetto automobili
Destination GIRONA	Destination	Ziel GIRONA	Destinazione
Railway	Chemin de fer	Eisenbahn	Ferrovia
Railway station Estación Central	Gare	Hauptbahnhof Estación Central	Stazione ferrovia
Height – in metres 234	Altitude – en mètres	Höhe – über dem Meeresspiegel 234	Altezza in metri
Airport	Aéroport principal	Flughafen	Aeroporto
Airfield	Autre aéroport	Flugplatz	Aerodromo/ campo d'aviazione
City plan coverage area	Région de plan de ville	Vom Stadtplan abgedecktes Gebiet	Area della pianta della città

Alicante
0 km 0.5

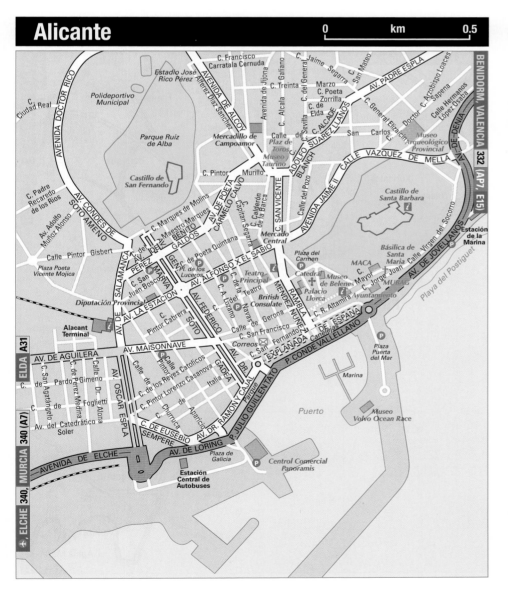

Antwerpen Antwerp
0 km 1

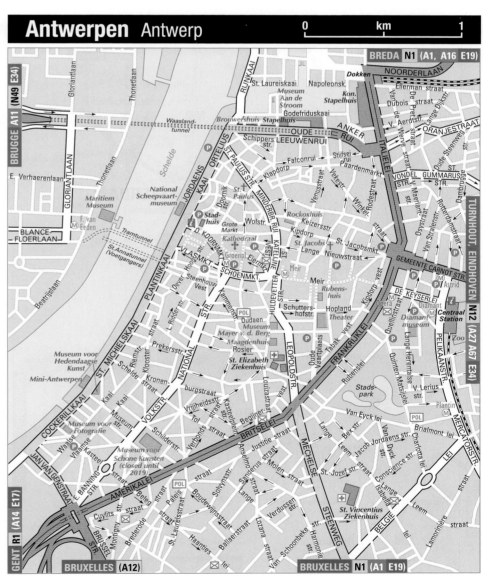

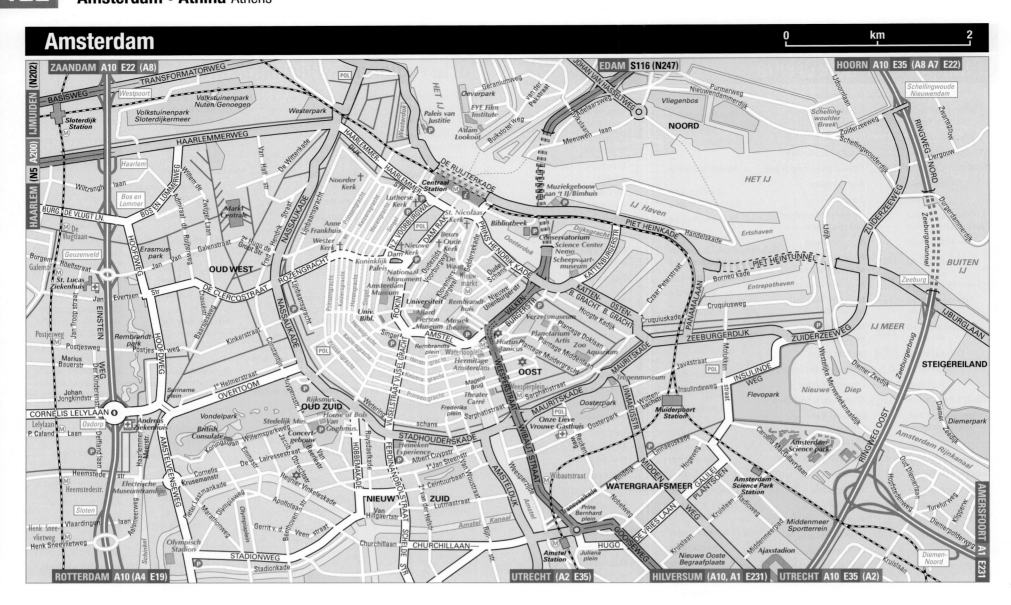

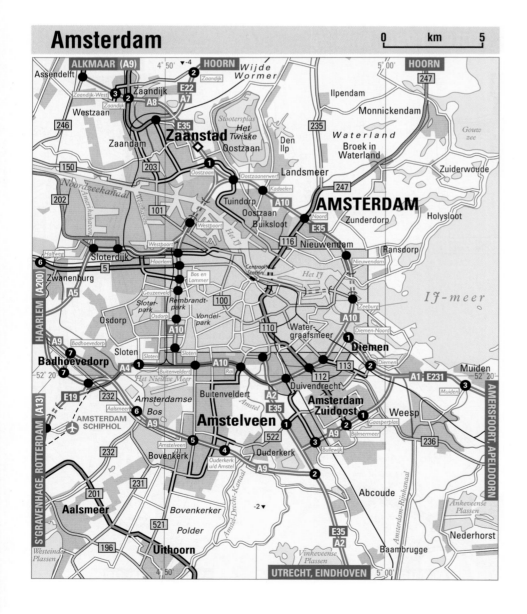

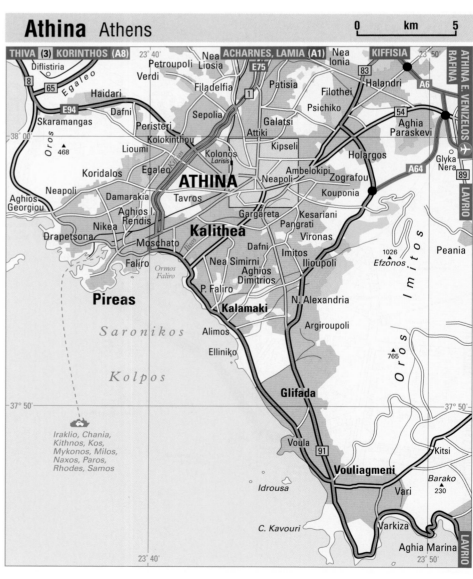

Athina Athens

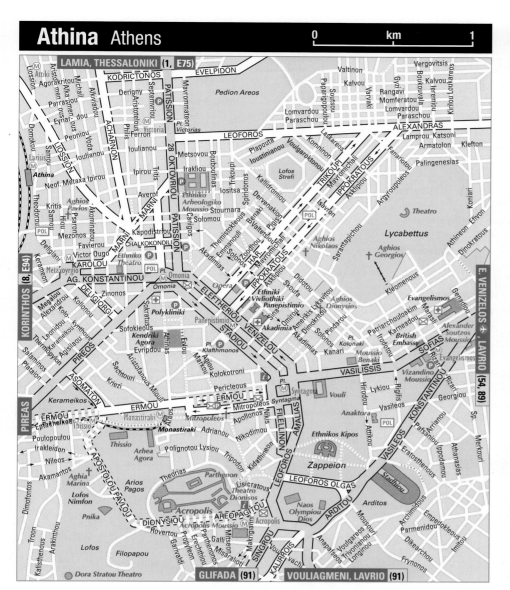

Basel

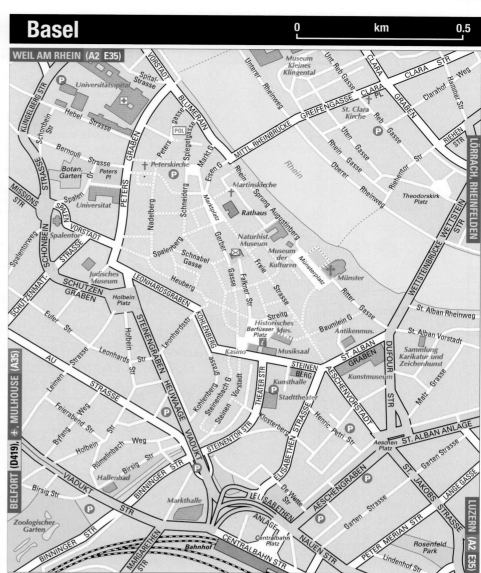

Barcelona

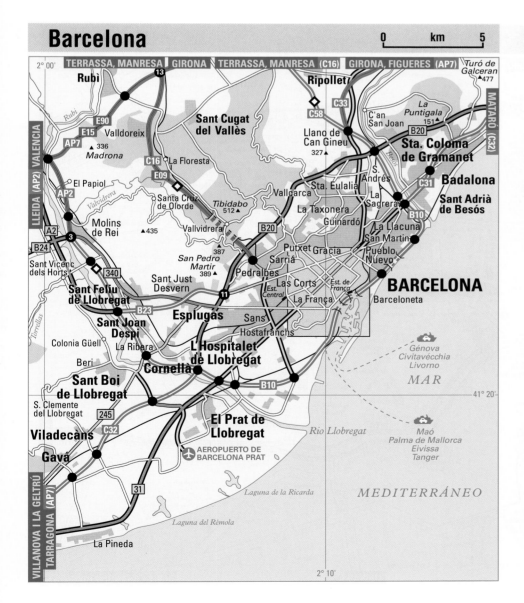

Barcelona

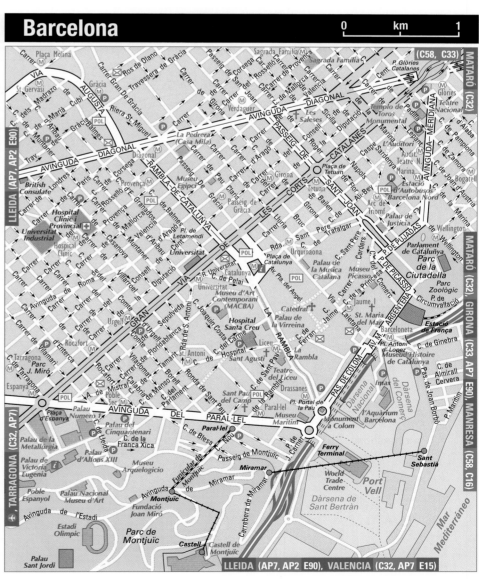

Berlin

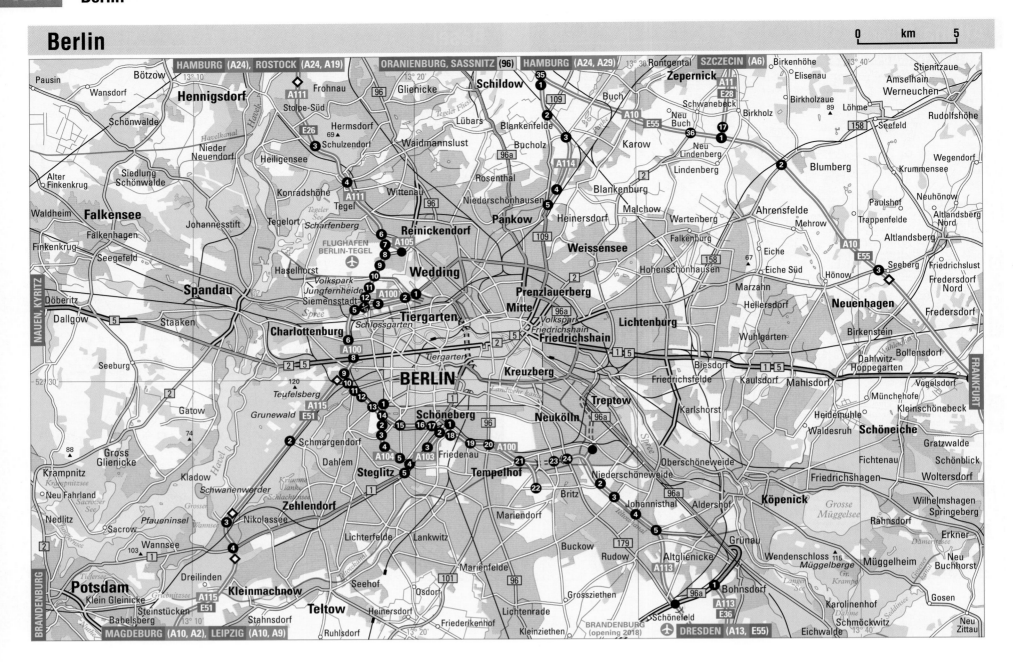

Berlin

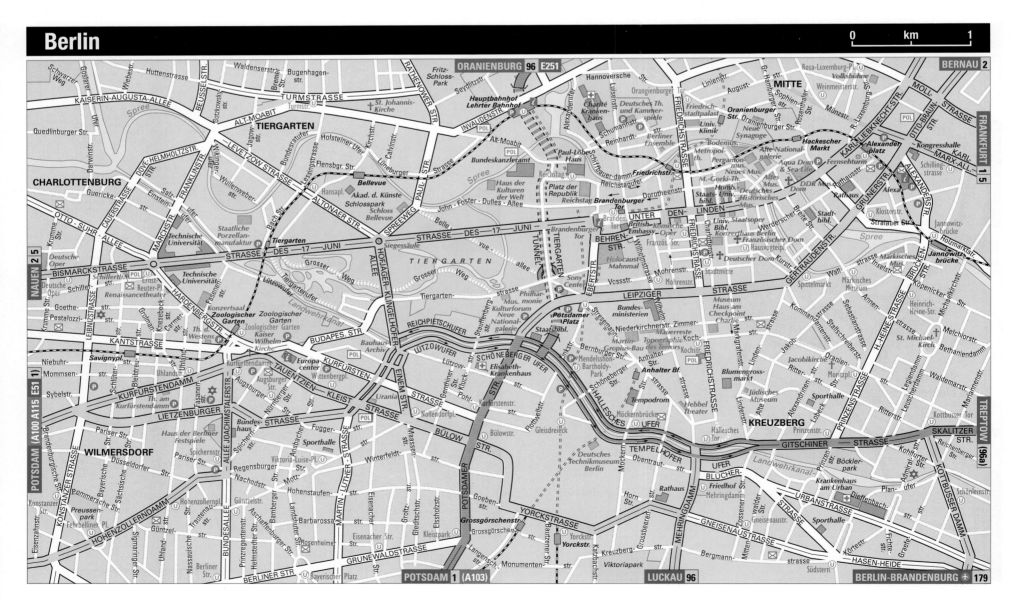

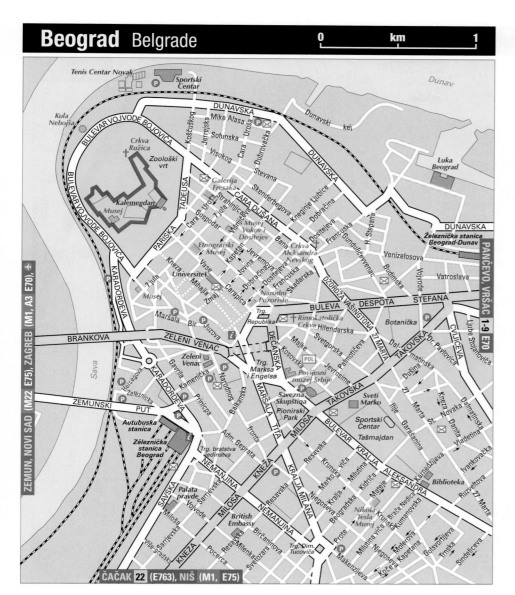

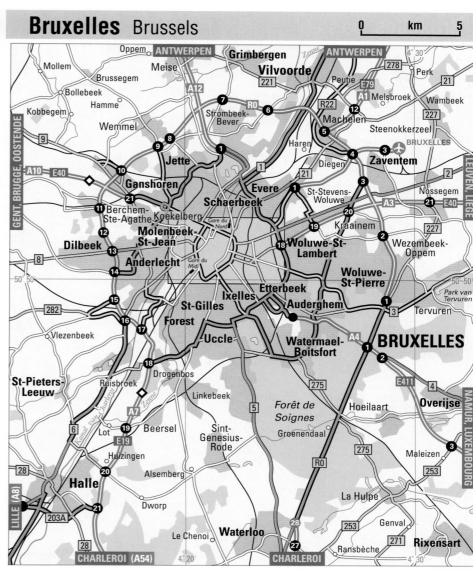

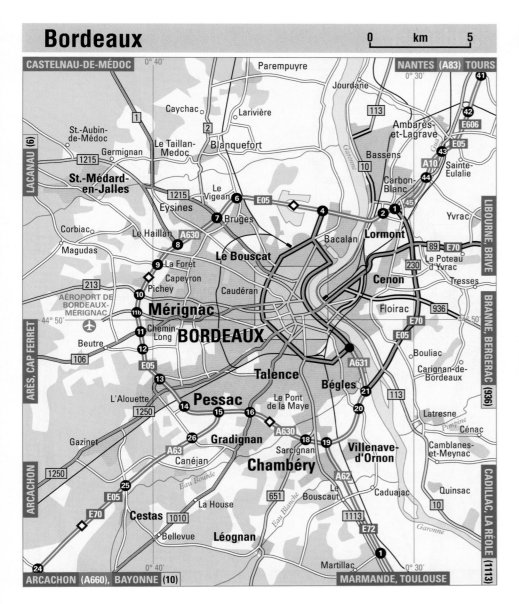

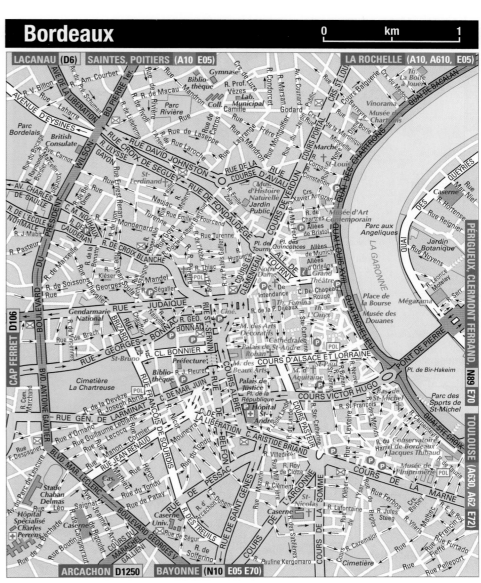

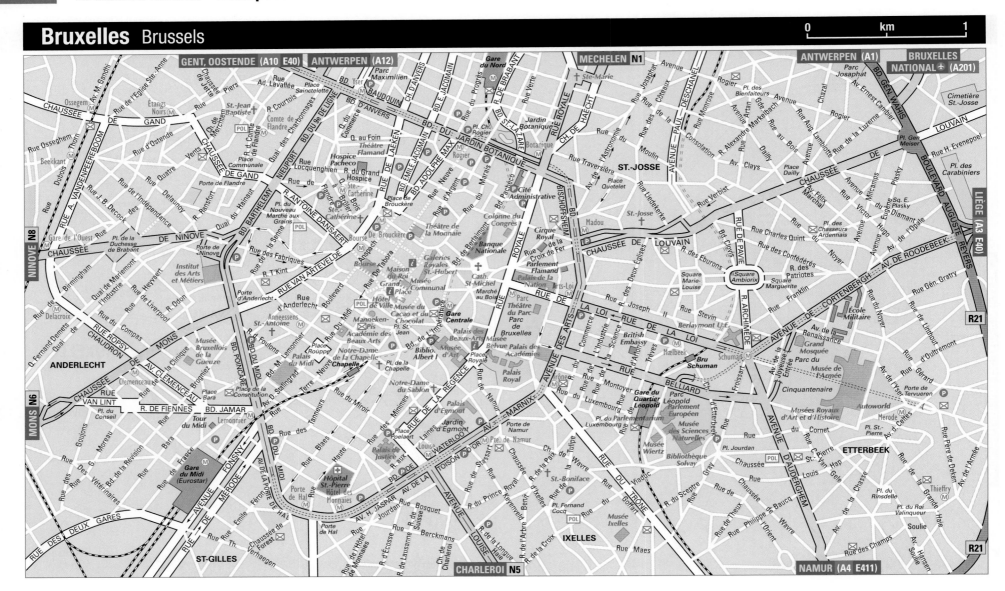

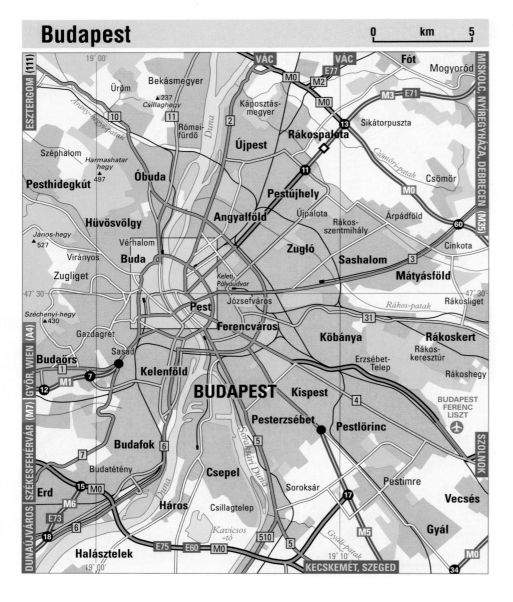

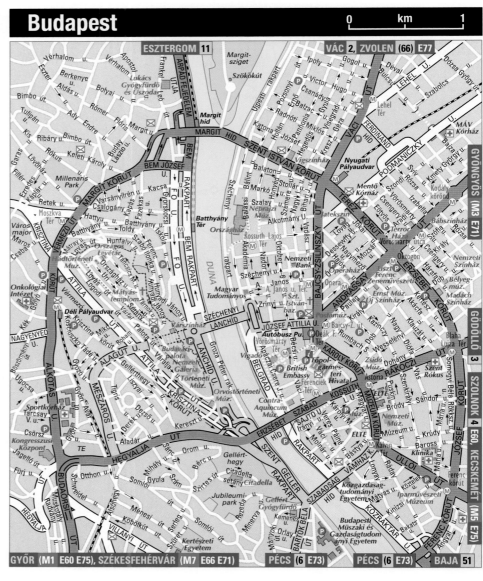

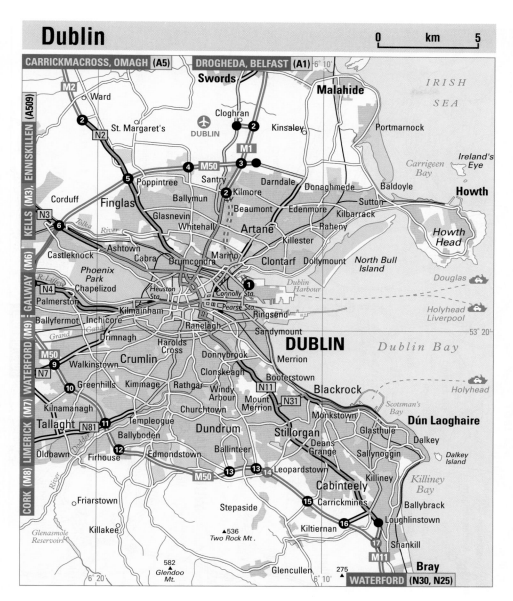

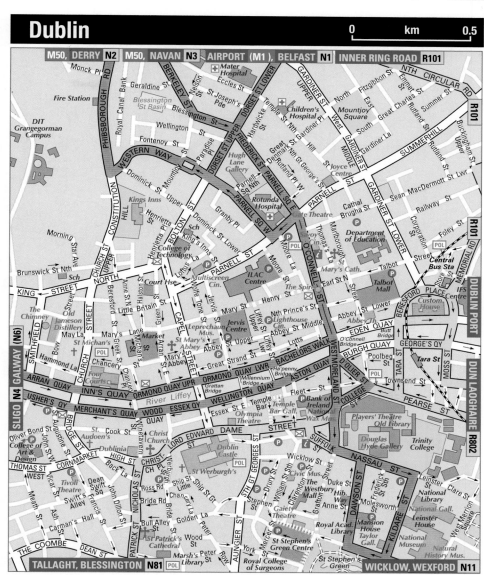

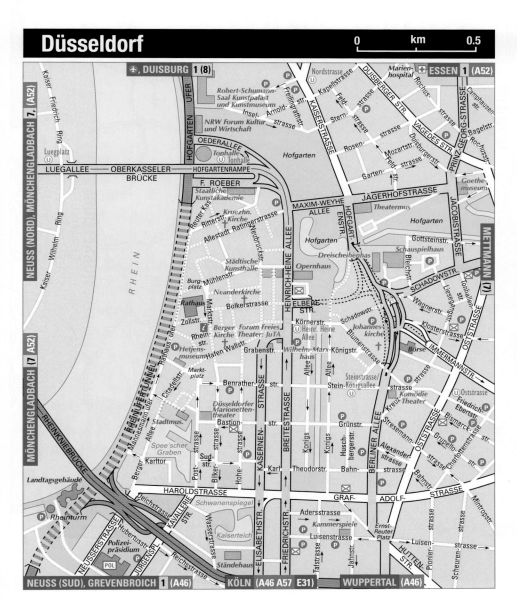

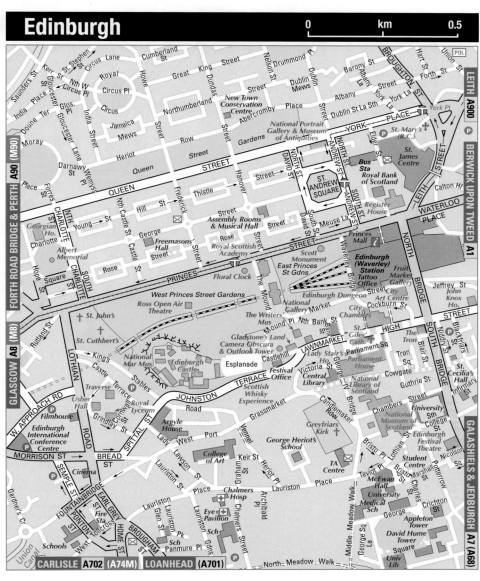

For **Cologne** see page 132
For **Copenhagen** see page 132

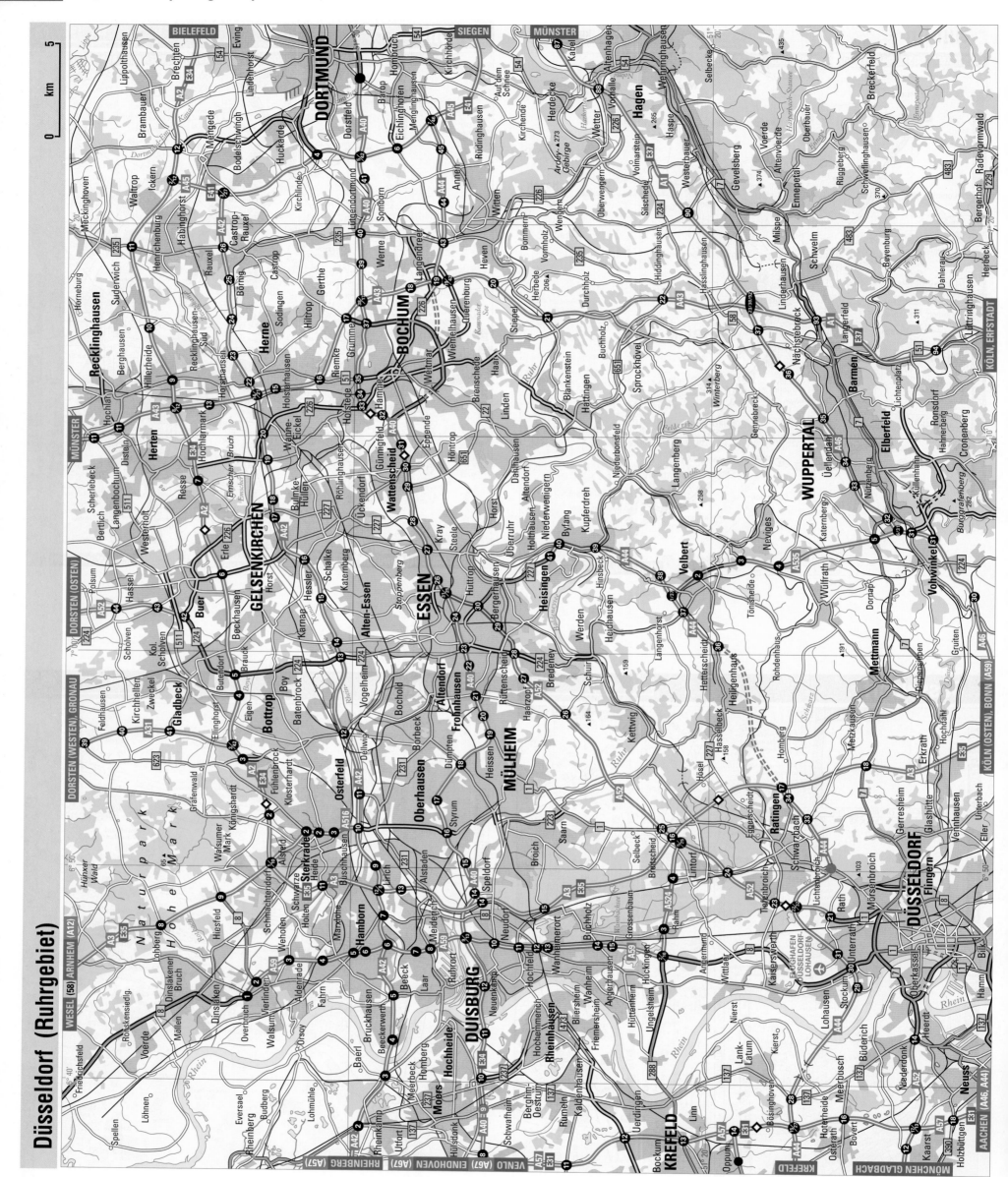

Firenze Florence

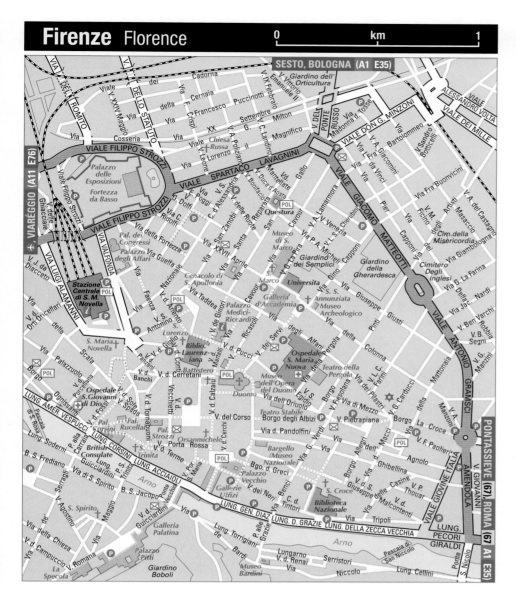

Frankfurt

Genève Geneva

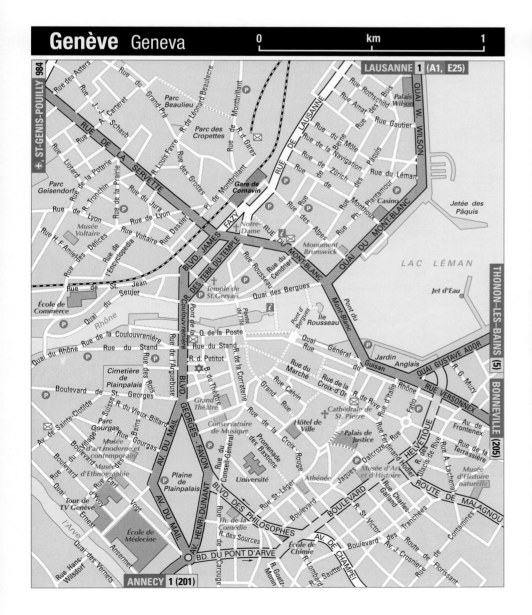

Génova Genoa

Granada

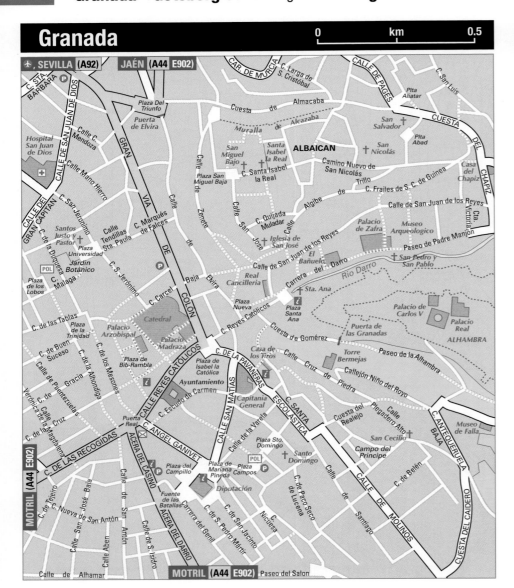

Göteborg Gothenburg

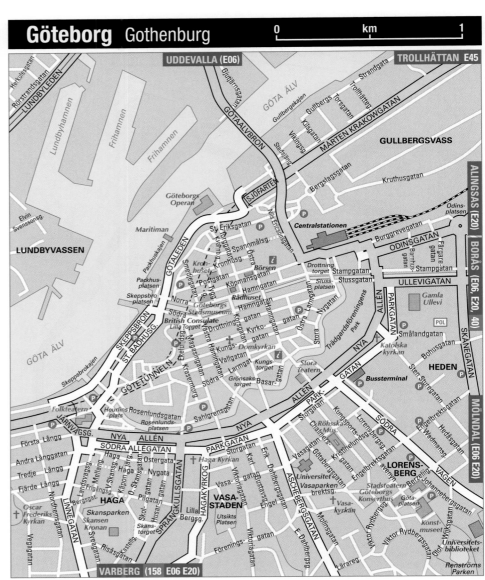

Hamburg

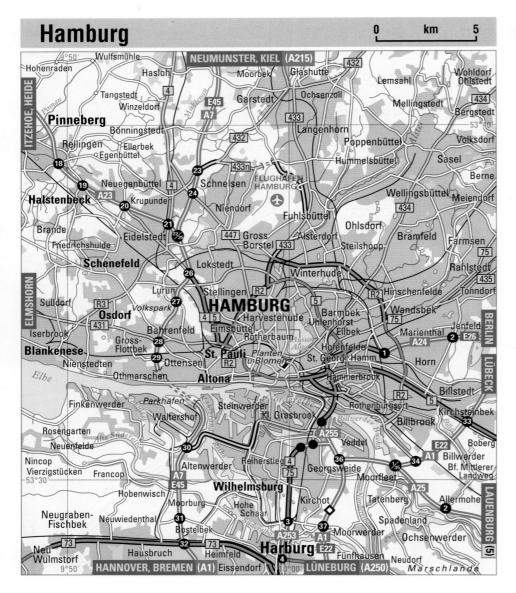

Hamburg

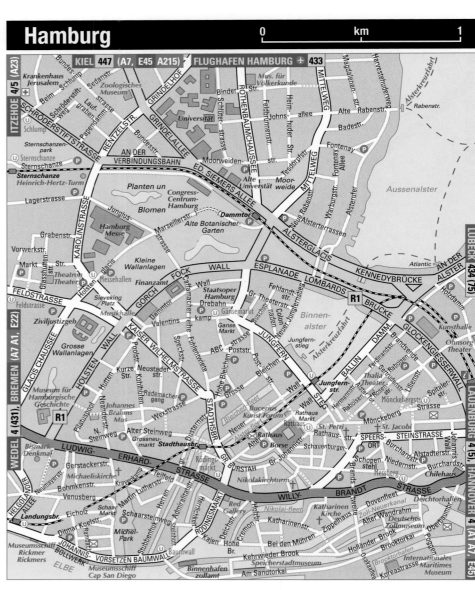

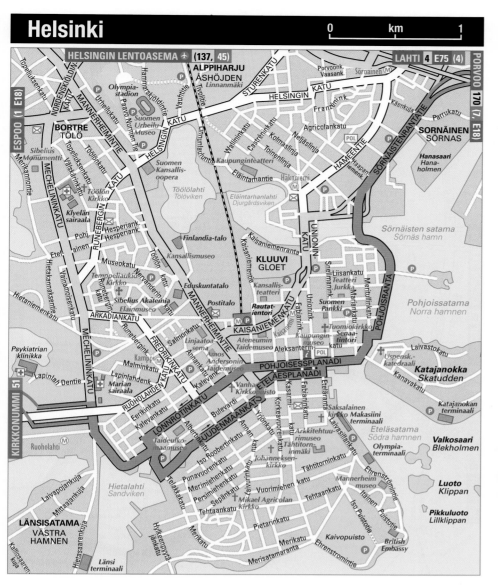

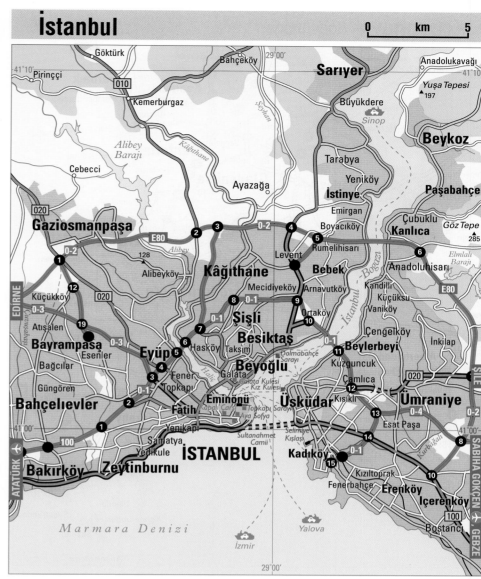

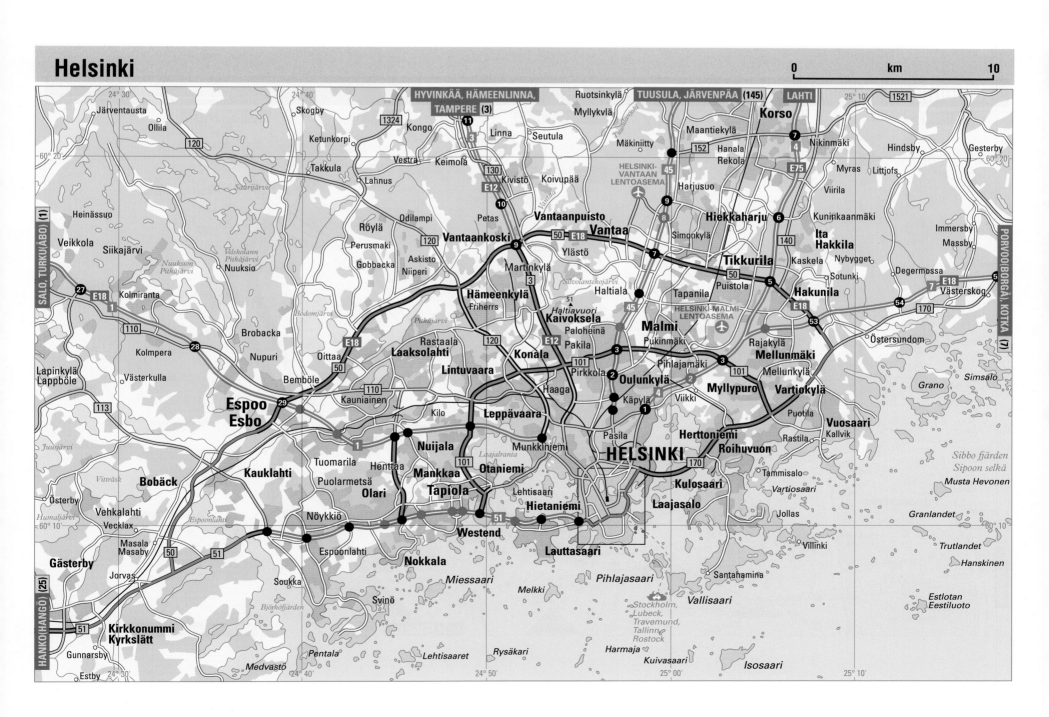

København Copenhagen

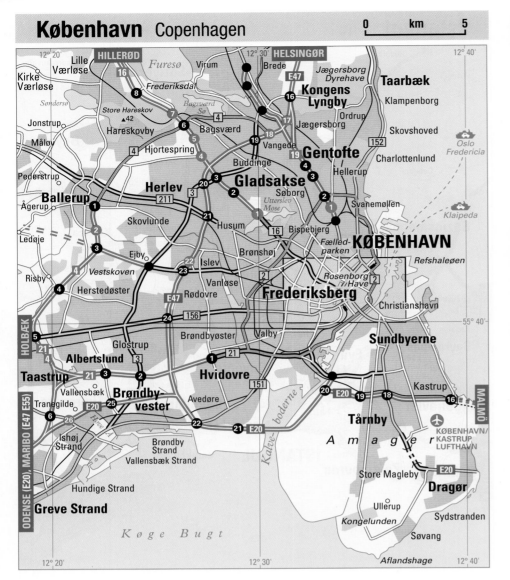

Köln Cologne

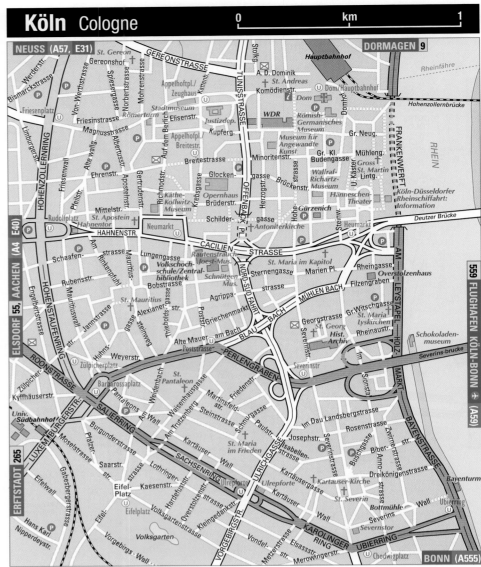

København Copenhagen

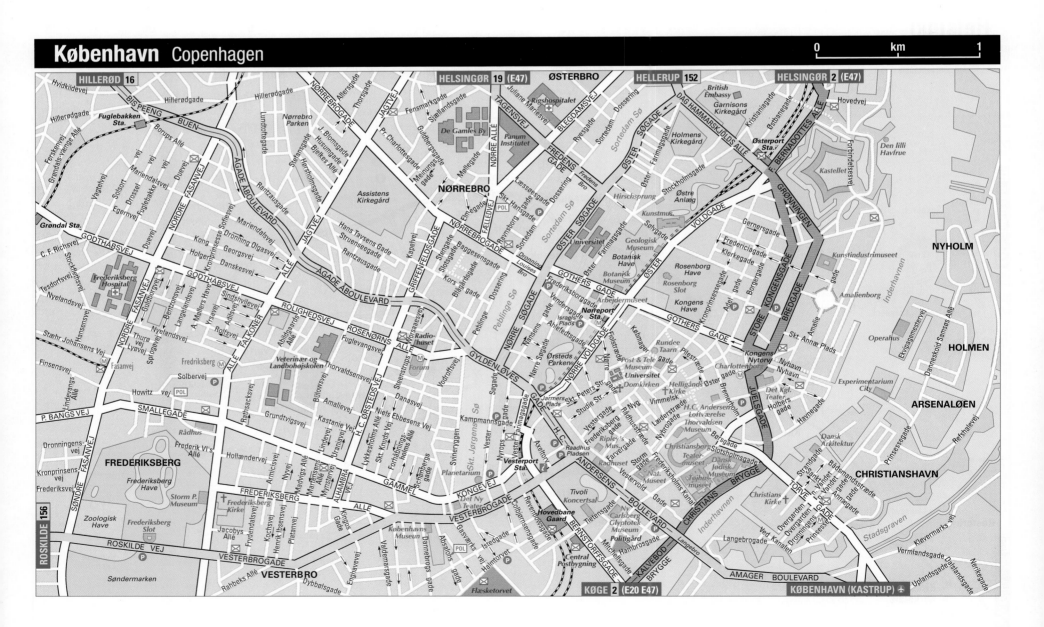

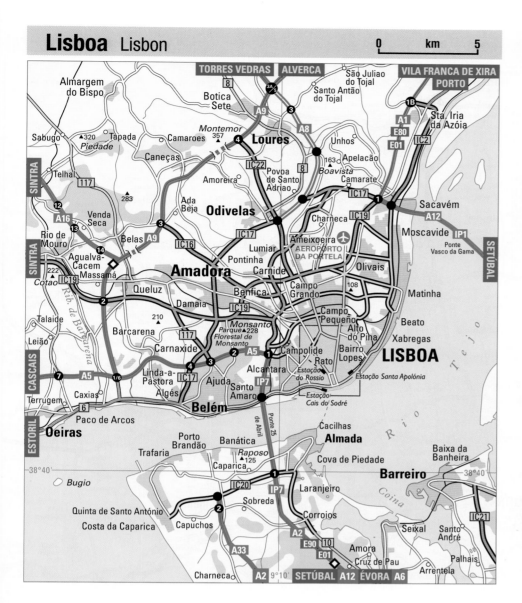

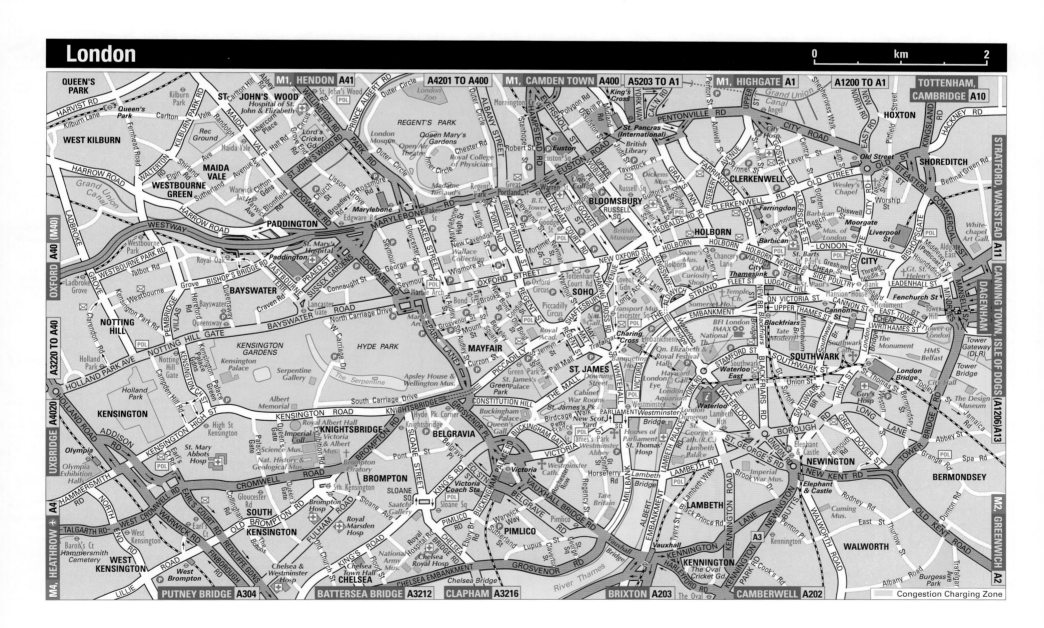

London

0 km 10

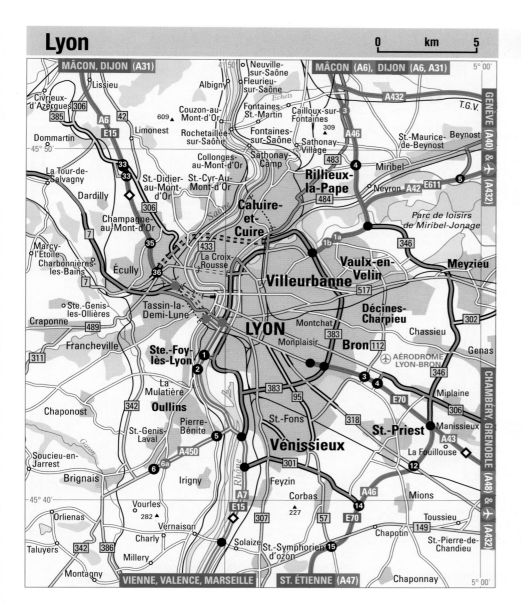

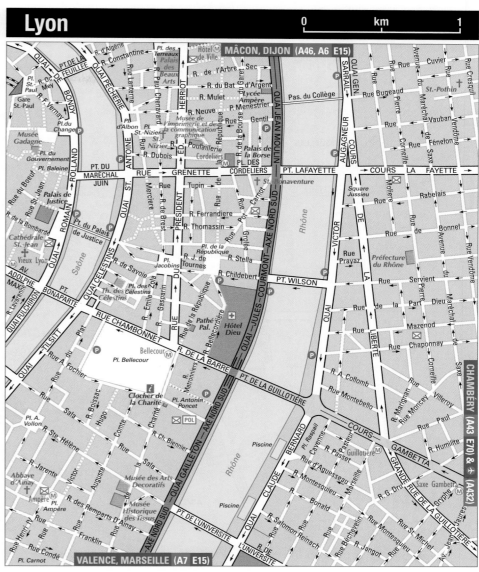

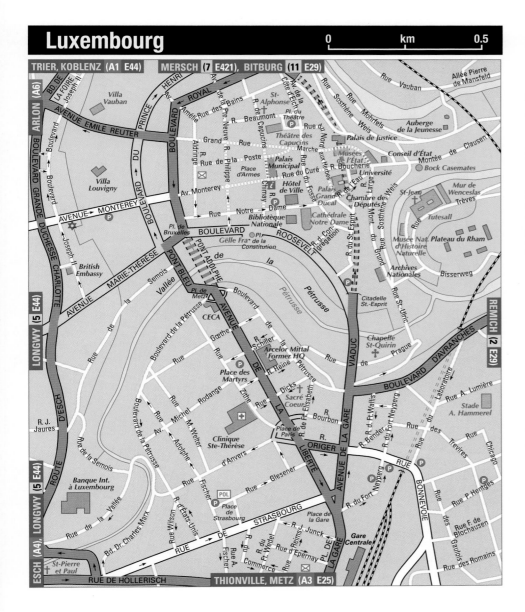

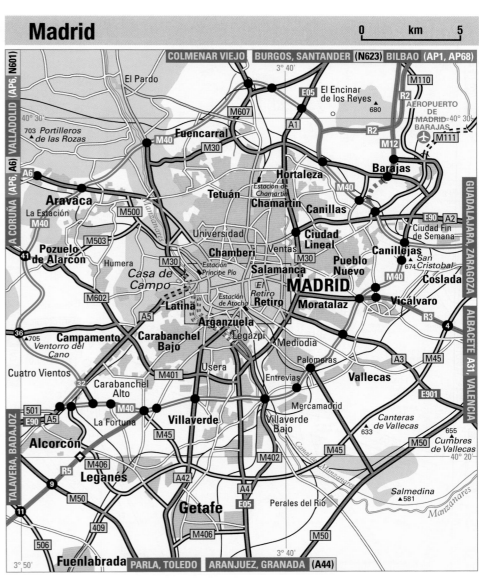

Madrid

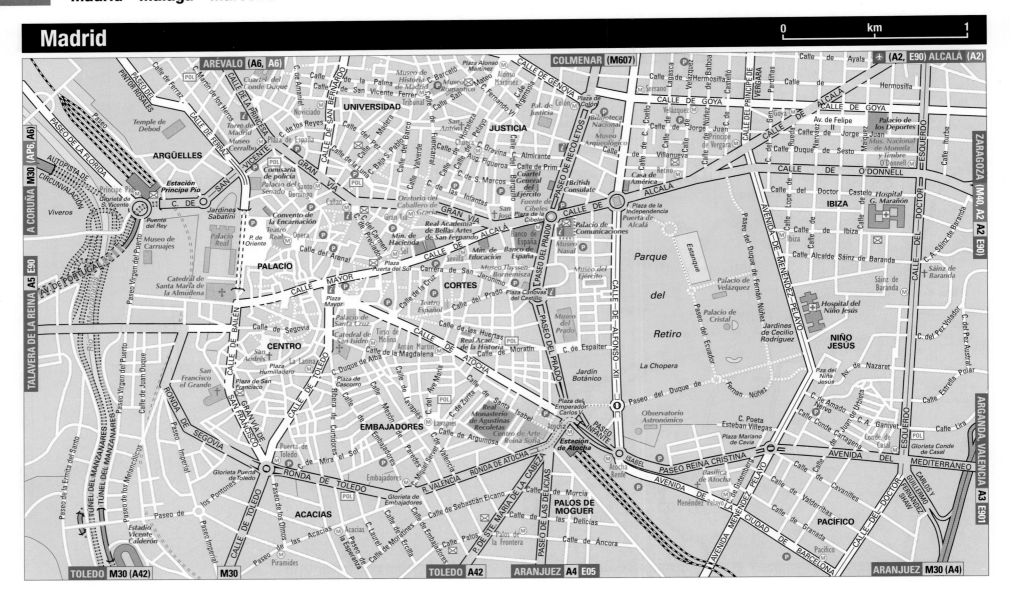

Málaga

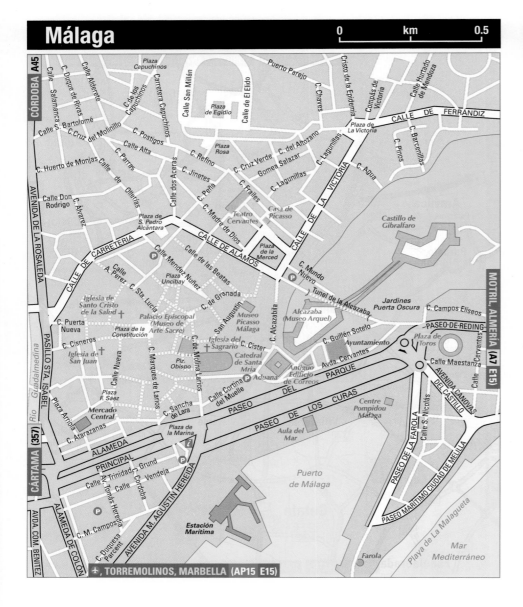

Marseille / Marseilles

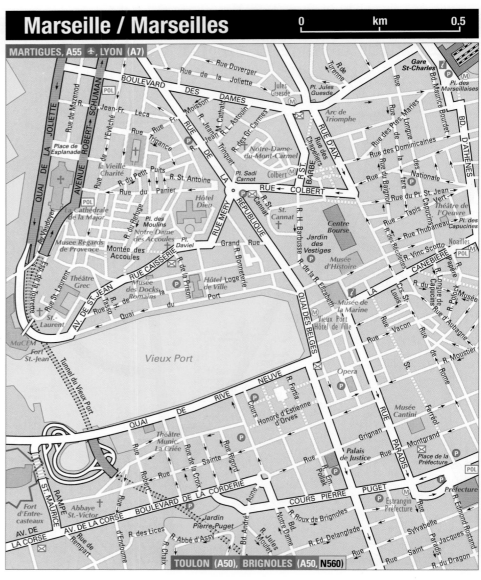

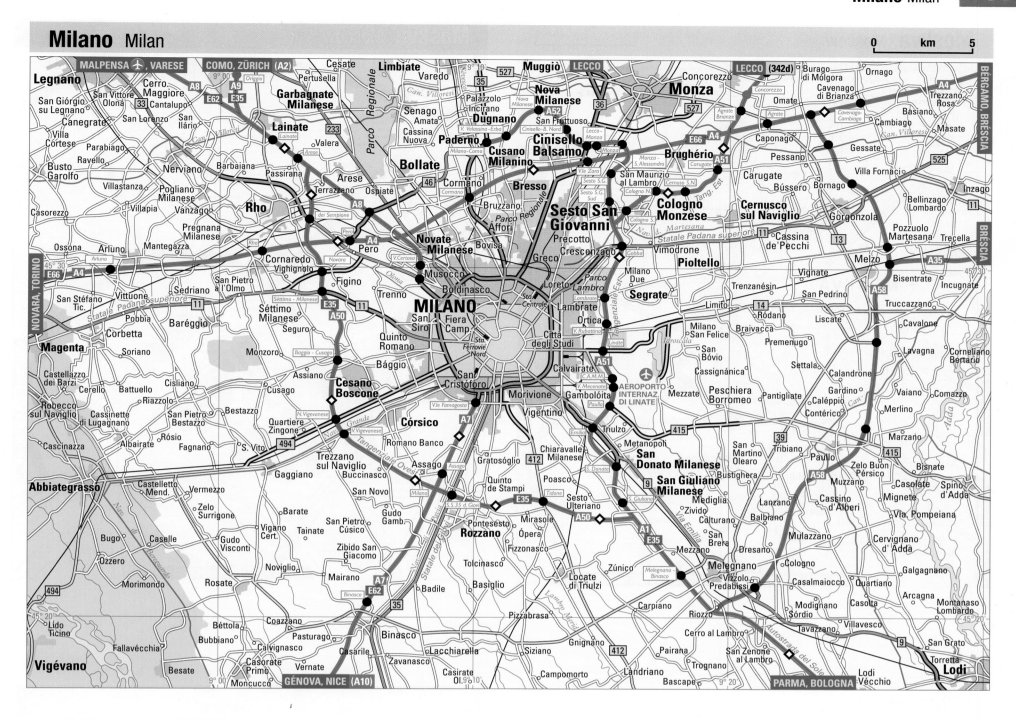

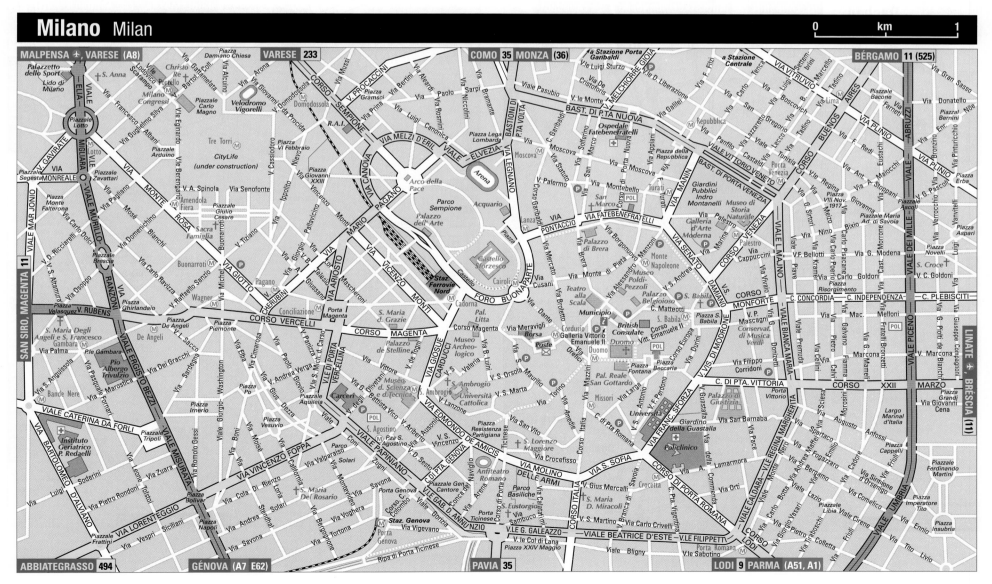

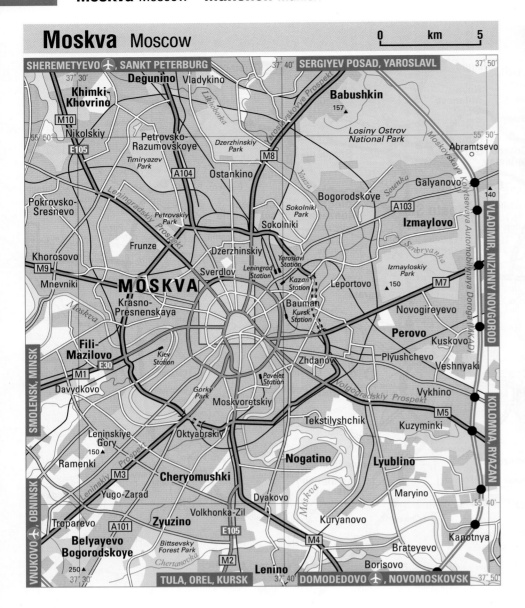

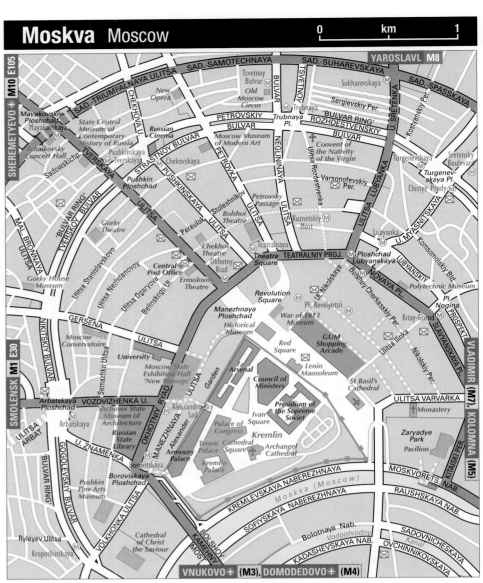

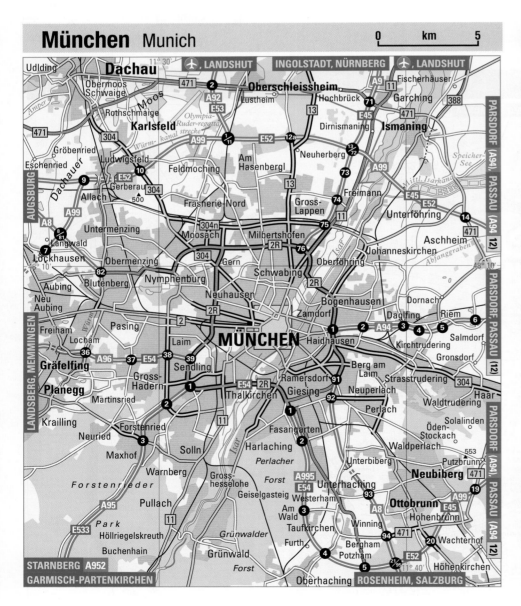

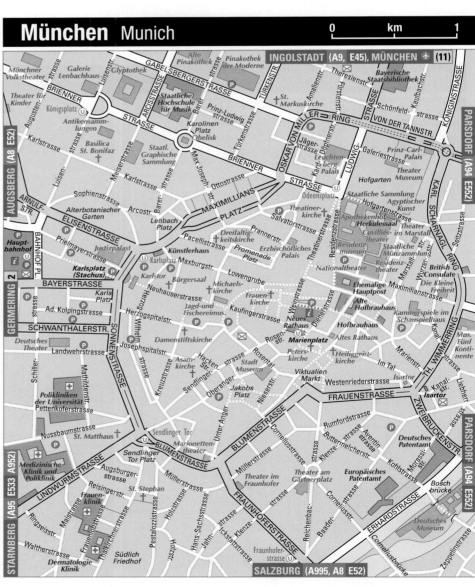

Nápoli Naples

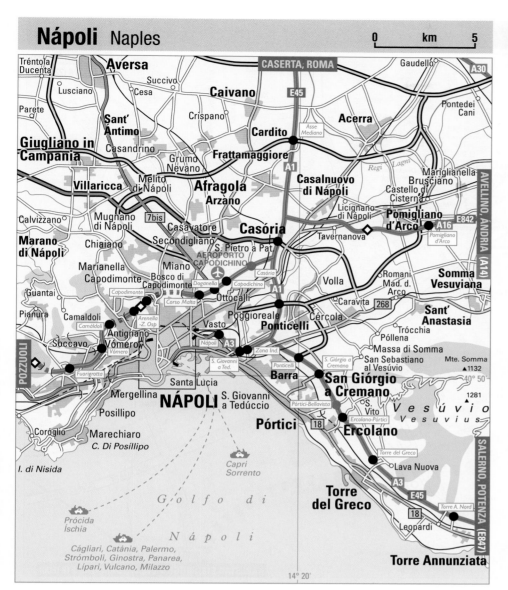

Nápoli Naples

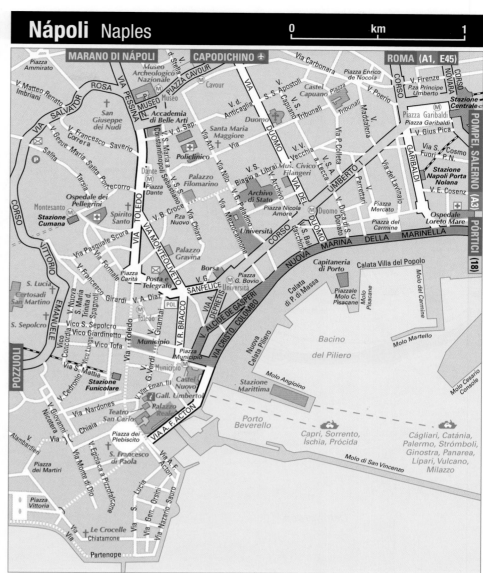

Oslo

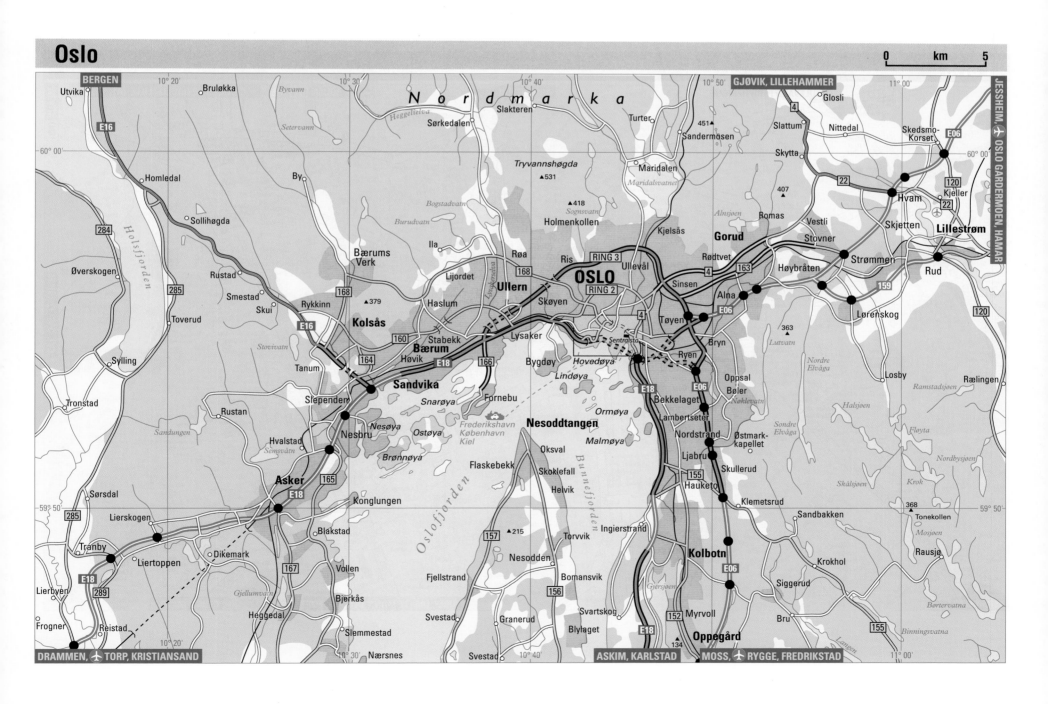

Oslo

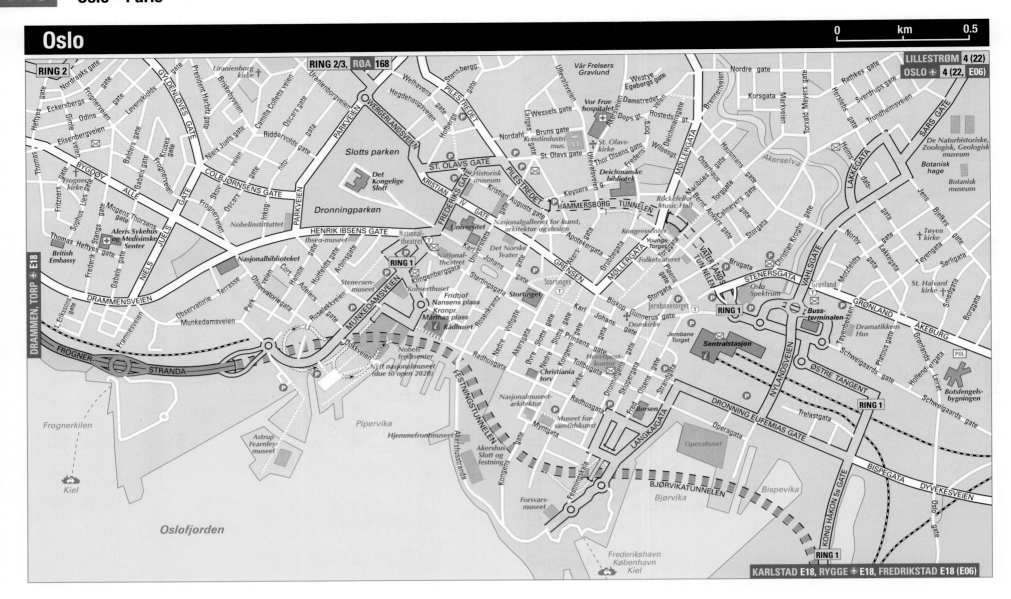

Paris

Paris

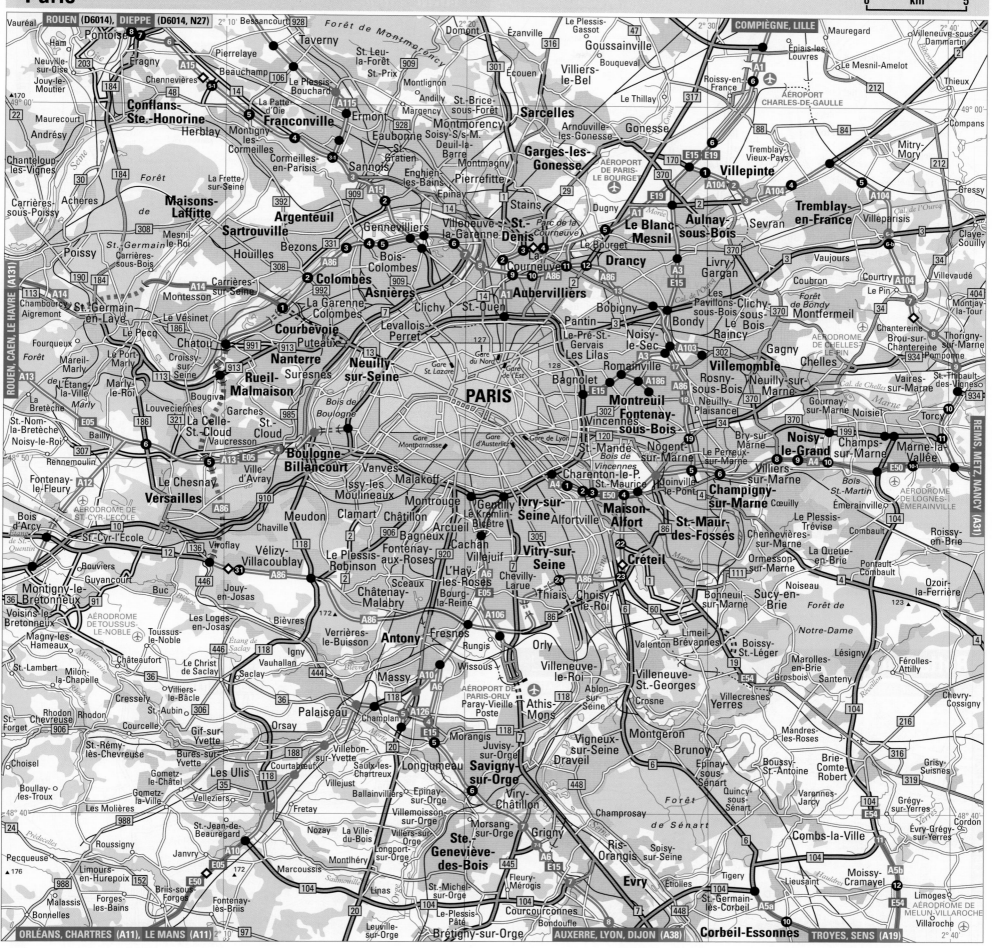

Praha Prague

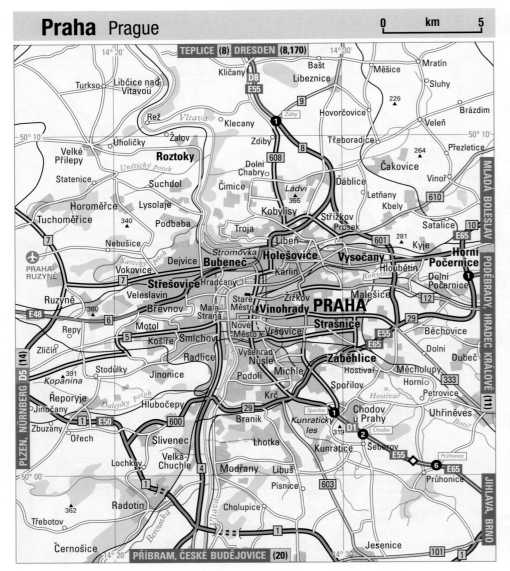

Praha Prague

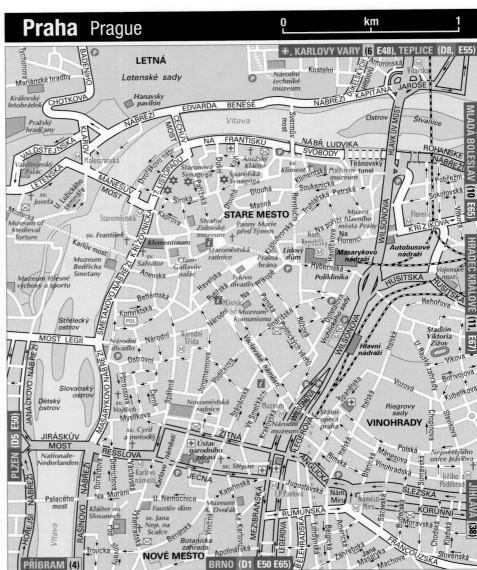

Rotterdam

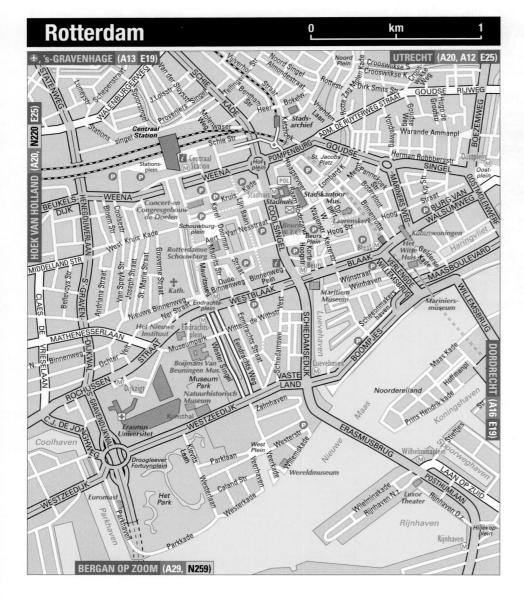

Sankt-Peterburg St. Petersburg

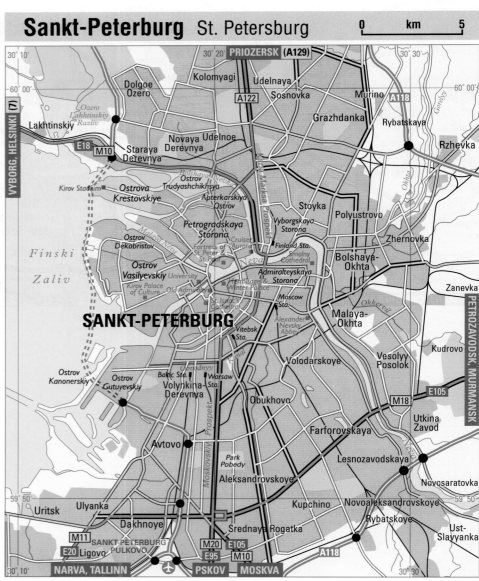

For **Rome** see page 143

Roma Rome

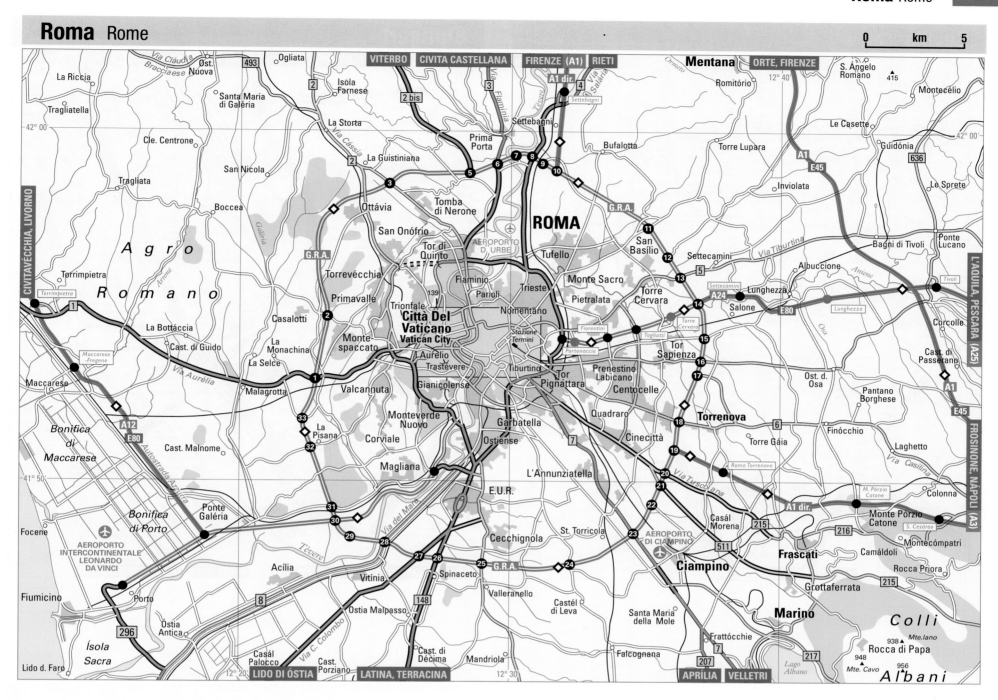

Roma Rome

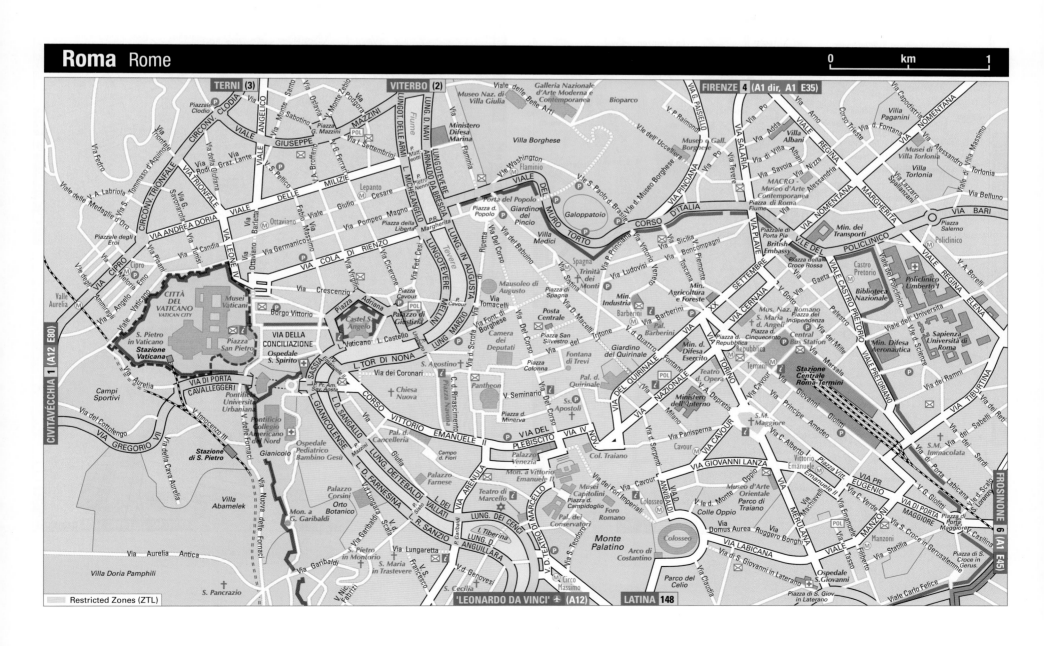

Sevilla Seville

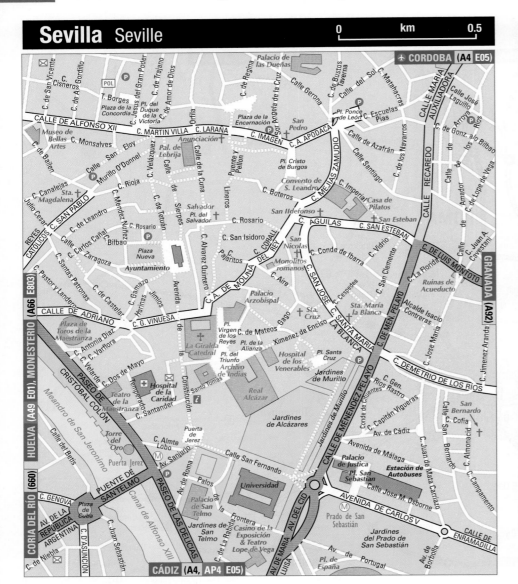

Stuttgart

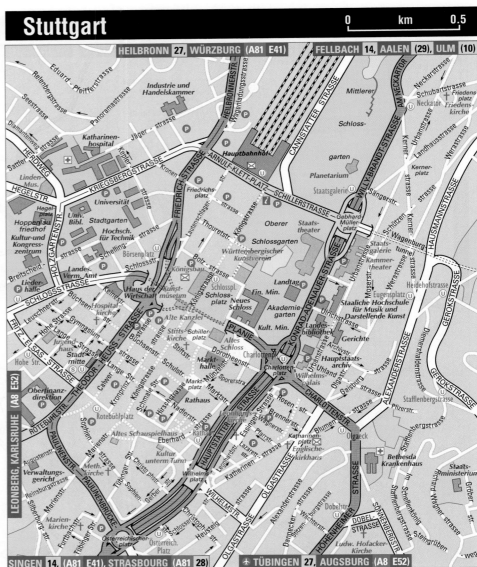

Strasbourg

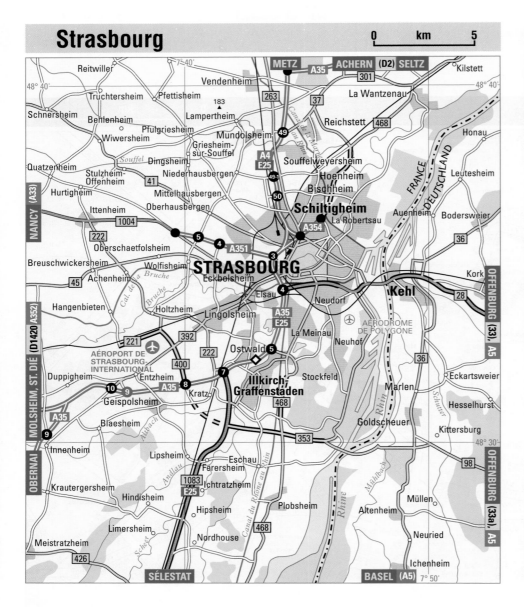

Strasbourg

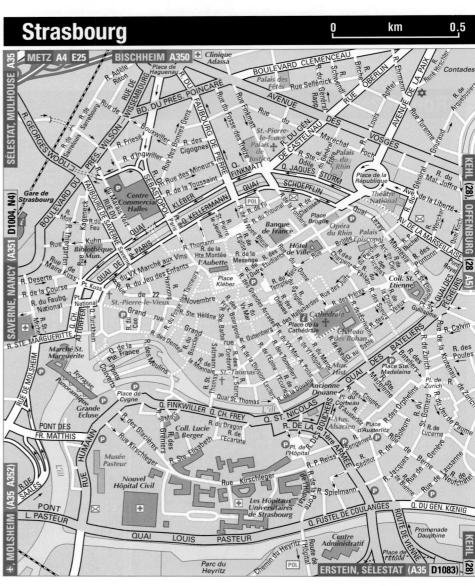

Stockholm

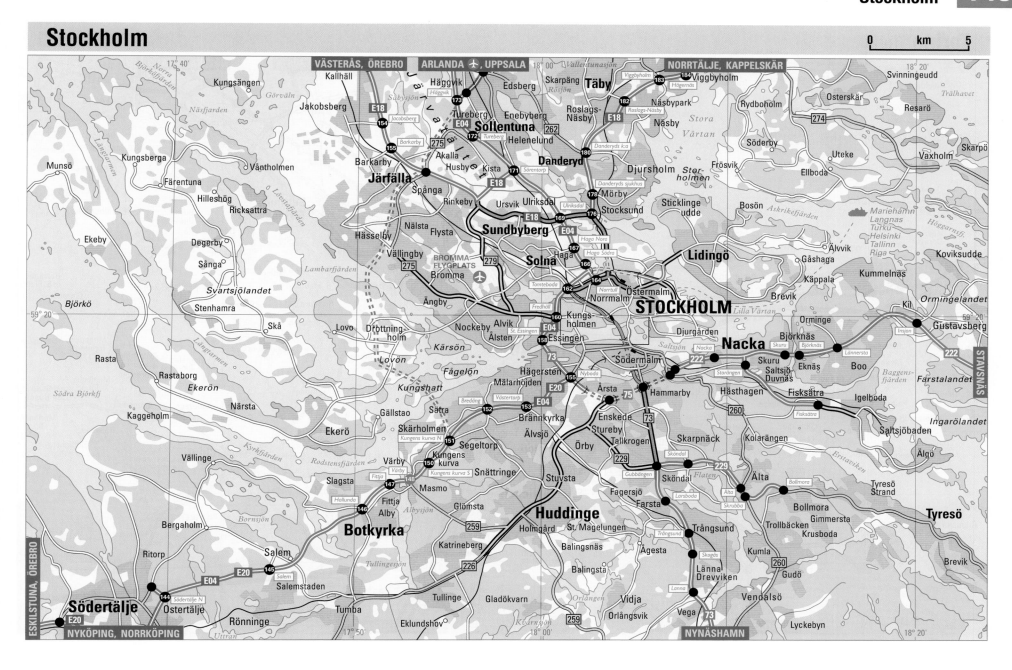

Stockholm

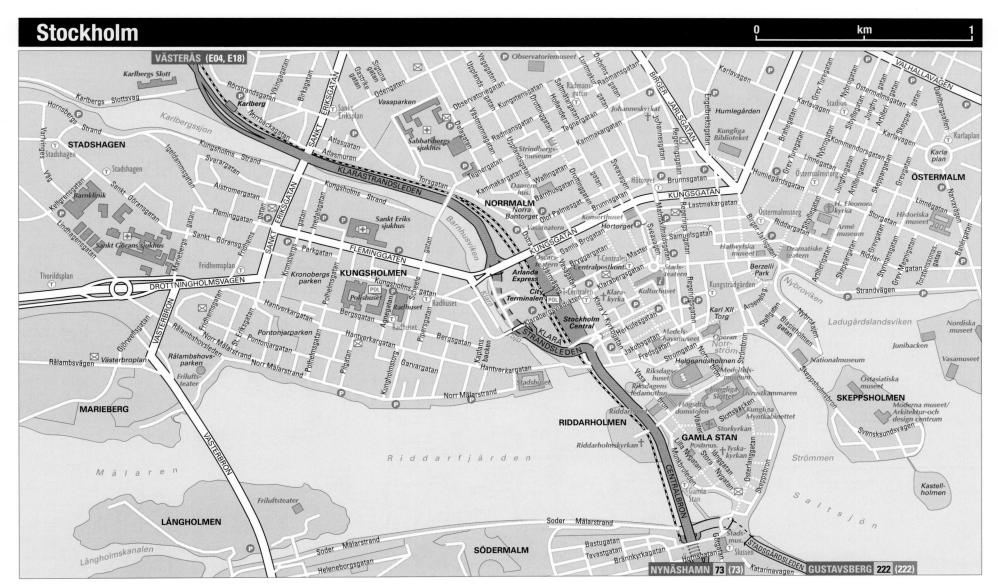

Torino Turin

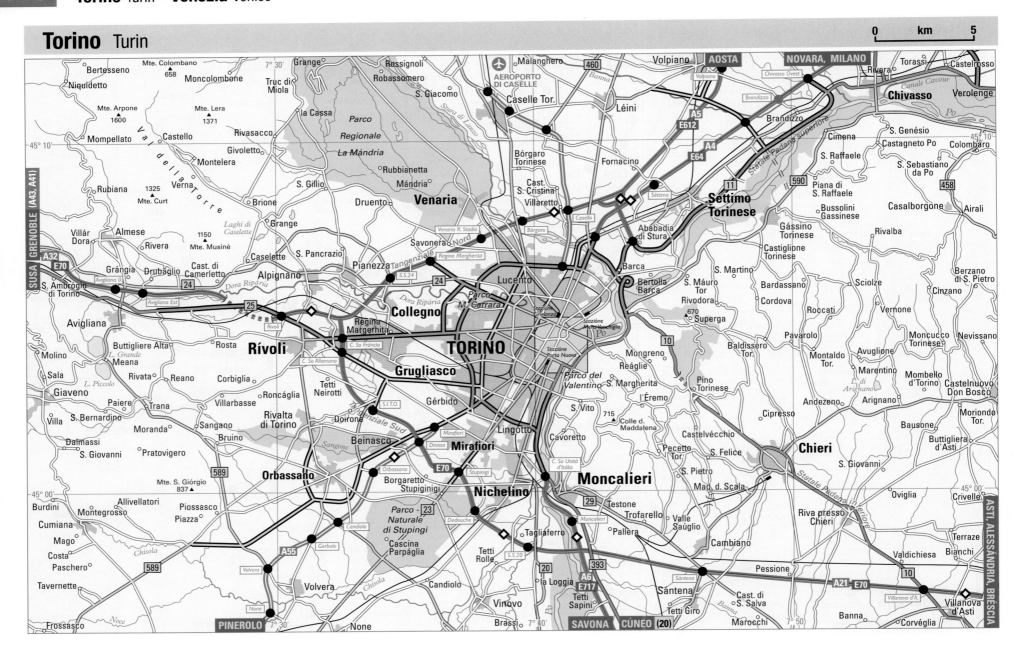

Venézia Venice

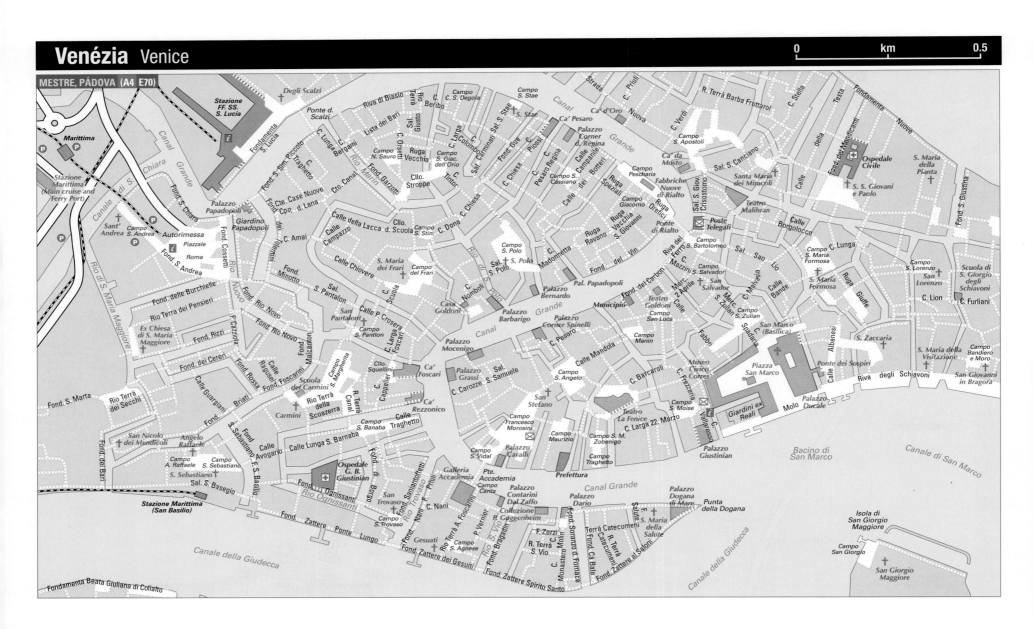

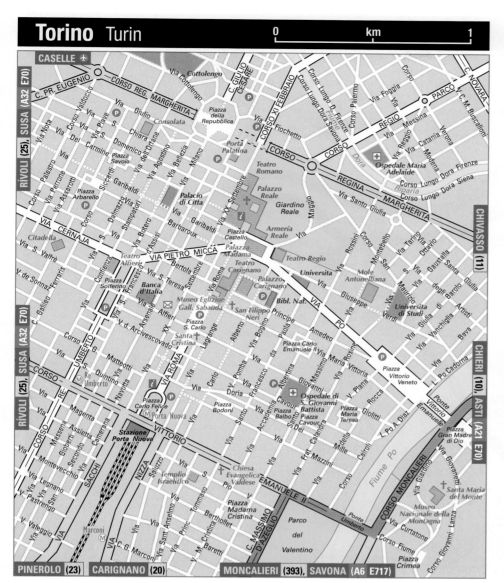

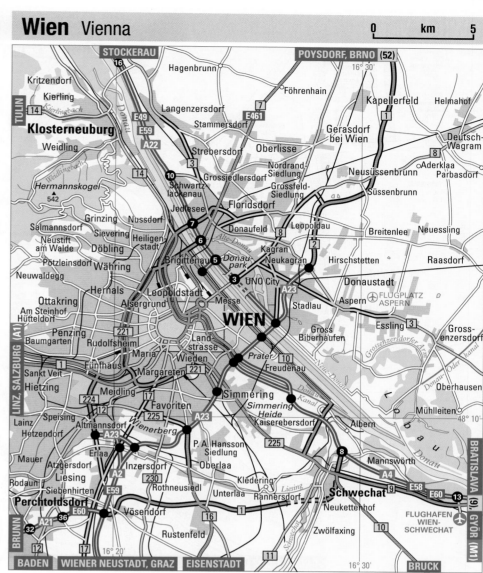

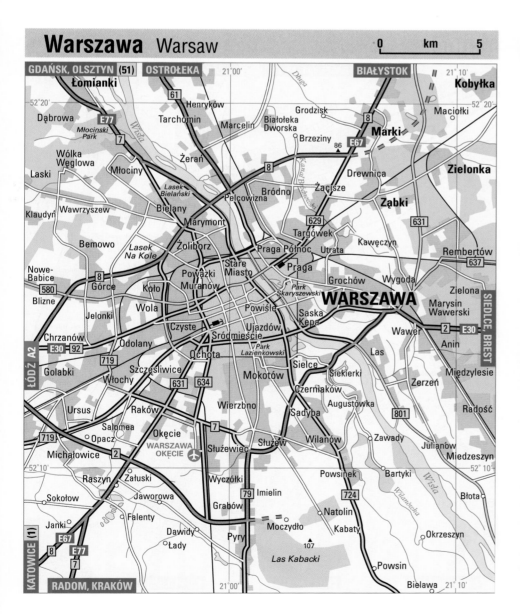

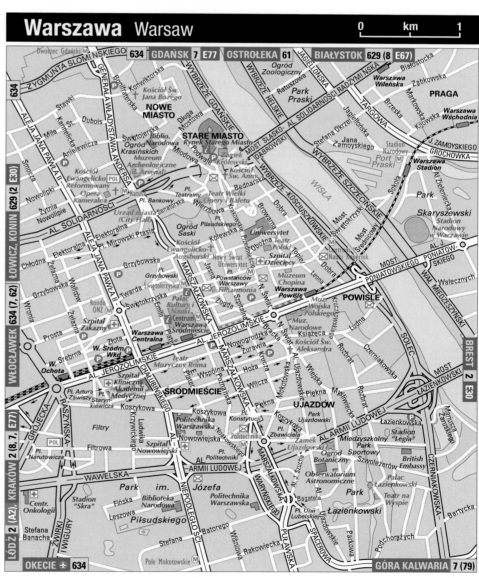

Wien Vienna

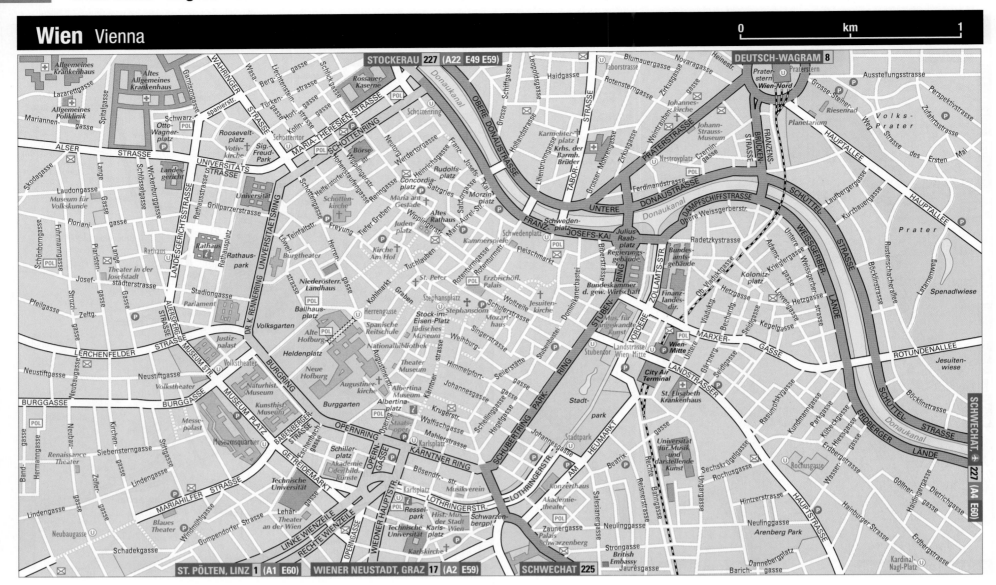

Zagreb

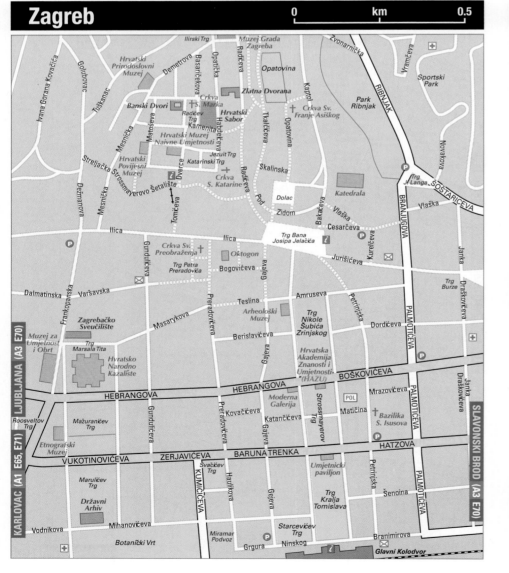

Zürich

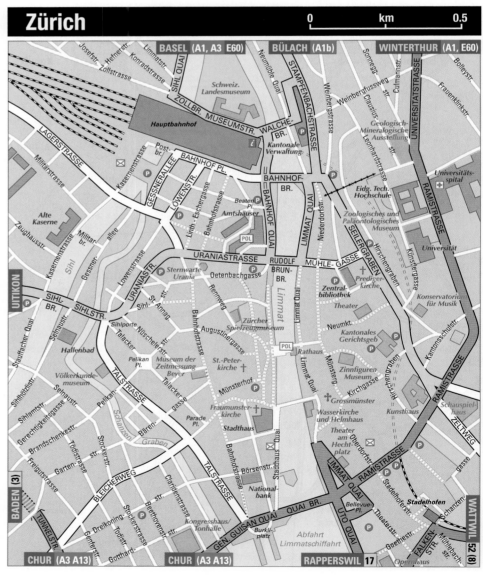

Index

Code	🇬🇧	🇫🇷	🇩🇪	🇮🇹
A	Austria	Autriche	Österreich	Austria
AL	Albania	Albanie	Albanien	Albania
AND	Andorra	Andorre	Andorra	Andorra
B	Belgium	Belgique	Belgien	Belgio
BG	Bulgaria	Bulgarie	Bulgarien	Bulgaria
BIH	Bosnia-Herzegovin	Bosnie-Herzegovine	Bosnien-Herzegowina	Bosnia-Herzogovina
BY	Belarus	Belarus	Weissrussland	Bielorussia
CH	Switzerland	Suisse	Schweiz	Svizzera
CY	Cyprus	Chypre	Zypern	Cipro
CZ	Czechia	République Tchèque	Tschechische Republik	Repubblica Ceca
D	Germany	Allemagne	Deutschland	Germania
DK	Denmark	Danemark	Dänemark	Danimarca
E	Spain	Espagne	Spanien	Spagna
EST	Estonia	Estonie	Estland	Estonia
F	France	France	Frankreich	Francia
FIN	Finland	Finlande	Finnland	Finlandia
FL	Liechtenstein	Liechtenstein	Liechtenstein	Liechtenstein
FO	Faeroe Islands	Îles Féroé	Färoër-Inseln	Isole Faroe
GB	United Kingdom	Royaume Uni	Grossbritannien und Nordirland	Regno Unito
GBZ	Gibraltar	Gibraltar	Gibraltar	Gibilterra
GR	Greece	Grèce	Greichenland	Grecia
H	Hungary	Hongrie	Ungarn	Ungheria
HR	Croatia	Croatie	Kroatien	Croazia
I	Italy	Italie	Italien	Italia
IRL	Ireland	Irlande	Irland	Irlanda
IS	Iceland	Islande	Island	Islanda
KOS	Kosovo	Kosovo	Kosovo	Kosovo
L	Luxembourg	Luxembourg	Luxemburg	Lussemburgo
LT	Lithuania	Lituanie	Litauen	Lituania
LV	Latvia	Lettonie	Lettland	Lettonia
M	Malta	Malte	Malta	Malta
MC	Monaco	Monaco	Monaco	Monaco
MD	Moldova	Moldavie	Moldawien	Moldavia
MK	Macedonia	Macédoine	Makedonien	Macedonia
MNE	Montenegro	Monténégro	Montenegro	Montenegro
N	Norway	Norvège	Norwegen	Norvegia
NL	Netherlands	Pays-Bas	Niederlande	Paesi Bassi
P	Portugal	Portugal	Portugal	Portogallo
PL	Poland	Pologne	Polen	Polonia
RO	Romania	Roumanie	Rumanien	Romania
RSM	San Marino	Saint-Marin	San Marino	San Marino
RUS	Russia	Russie	Russland	Russia
S	Sweden	Suède	Schweden	Svezia
SK	Slovakia	République Slovaque	Slowak Republik	Repubblica Slovacca
SLO	Slovenia	Slovénie	Slowenien	Slovenia
SRB	Serbia	Serbie	Serbien	Serbia
TR	Turkey	Turquie	Türkei	Turchia
UA	Ukraine	Ukraine	Ukraine	Ucraina

A

Aabenraa DK . . . 39 D2
Aabybro DK . . . 38 B2
Aach D . . . 71 A4
Aachen D . . . 50 C2
Aalborg DK . . . 38 B2
Aalen D . . . 61 B6
Aalestrup DK . . . 38 C2
Aalsmeer NL . . . 49 A5
Aalst B . . . 49 C5
Aalten NL . . . 50 B2
Aalter B . . . 49 B4
Äänekoski FIN . . . 3 E26
Aapajärvi FIN . . . 113 E16
Aapajärvi TR . . . 118 C5
Aarau CH . . . 70 A3
Aarberg CH . . . 70 A2
Aarburg CH . . . 70 A2
Aardenburg NL . . . 49 B4
Aars DK . . . 38 C2
Aarschot B . . . 49 C5
Aarup DK . . . 39 D3
Aba H . . . 74 A3
Abádanes E . . . 95 B4
Abades E . . . 94 B2
Abadin E . . . 86 A3
Abádszalók H . . . 75 A5
Abaliget H . . . 74 B3
Abana TR . . . 16 A7
A Baña E . . . 86 B2
Abanilla E . . . 101 A4
Abano Terme I . . . 72 C1
Abarán E . . . 101 A4
Abasár H . . . 65 C6
Abbadia San Salvatore
  I . . . 81 D5
Abbaue I . . . 45 B5
Abbehausen D . . . 43 B5
Abbekäs S . . . 41 D3
Abbeville F . . . 48 C2
Abbey IRL . . . 20 A3
Abbeydorney IRL . . . 20 B2
Abbeyfeale IRL . . . 20 B2
Abbeyleix IRL . . . 21 B4
Abbiategrasso I . . . 70 C3
Abborrträsk S . . . 115 B16
Abbots Bromley GB . . . 27 C4
Abbotsbury GB . . . 29 C5
Abda H . . . 64 C3
Abejar E . . . 89 C4
Abela P . . . 98 B2
Abelvær N . . . 114 C8
Abenberg D . . . 62 A1
Abenójar E . . . 100 A1
Abensberg D . . . 62 B2
Aberaeron GB . . . 28 A3
Aberchirder GB . . . 23 D6
Aberdare GB . . . 29 B4
Aberdaron GB . . . 26 C1
Aberdeen GB . . . 23 D6
Aberdulais GB . . . 28 B4
Aberdyfi GB . . . 26 C1
Aberfeldy GB . . . 25 B4
Aberffraw GB . . . 26 B1
Aberfoyle GB . . . 24 B3
Abergele GB . . . 26 B2
Abergynolwyn GB . . . 26 C2
Aberporth GB . . . 28 A3
Abersoch GB . . . 26 C1
Abertillery GB . . . 29 B4
Abertura E . . . 93 B5
Aberystwyth GB . . . 26 C1
Abetone I . . . 81 B4
Abfaltersbach A . . . 72 B2
Abide
  Çanakkale TR . . . 118 B1
  Kütahya TR . . . 118 D4
Abiego E . . . 90 A2
Abild DK . . . 39 E1
Abingdon-on-Thames
  GB . . . 31 C2
Abington GB . . . 25 C4
Abisko S . . . 112 D7
Abiul P . . . 92 B2
Abla E . . . 101 B3
Ablis F . . . 58 B2
A Bola E . . . 87 B3
Abondance F . . . 70 B1
Abony H . . . 75 A5
Aboyne GB . . . 23 D6
Abrantes P . . . 92 B2
Abreiro P . . . 87 C3
Abreschviller F . . . 60 B3
Abrest F . . . 68 B3
Abriès F . . . 79 B5
Abrud RO . . . 11 C7
Absdorf A . . . 64 B1
Abtenau A . . . 72 A3
Abtsgmünd D . . . 61 B5
Abusejo E . . . 93 A4
Aby
  Kronoberg S . . . 40 B4
  Östergötland S . . . 37 D3
Abyggeby S . . . 36 B4
Abytorp S . . . 37 C2
A Cañiza E . . . 87 B2
A Capela E . . . 86 A2
Acate I . . . 109 B3
Accadia I . . . 103 B8
Accéglio I . . . 79 B5
Accettura I . . . 104 C2
Acciaroli I . . . 106 A2

Accous F . . . 76 D2
Accrington GB . . . 26 B3
Accumoli I . . . 82 D2
Acedera E . . . 93 B5
Acehuche E . . . 93 B4
Acered E . . . 95 A5
Acerenza I . . . 104 C1
Acerno I . . . 103 C8
Acerra I . . . 103 C7
Aceuchal E . . . 93 C4
Acharacle GB . . . 24 B2
Acharnes GR . . . 117 D5
Achavanich GB . . . 23 C5
Achene B . . . 49 C6
Achenkirch A . . . 72 A1
Achensee A . . . 72 A1
Achenthal A . . . 72 A1
Achentrias GR . . . 117 H7
Achern D . . . 61 B4
Acheux-en-Amienois
  F . . . 48 C3
Achiltibuie GB . . . 22 D3
Achim D . . . 43 B6
Achladokambos GR . . . 117 E4
Achnasheen GB . . . 22 D3
Achnashellach GB . . . 22 D3
Achosnich GB . . . 24 B1
Aci Castello I . . . 109 B4
Aci Catena I . . . 109 B4
Acilia I . . . 102 B5
Acipayam TR . . . 119 E4
Acireale I . . . 109 B4
Acle GB . . . 30 B5
A Coruña E . . . 86 A2
Acquacadda I . . . 110 C1
Acqua Doria F . . . 102 B1
Acquanegra sul Chiese
  I . . . 81 C5
Acquapendente I . . . 81 D5
Acquasanta Terme I . . . 82 D2
Acquasparta I . . . 102 A5
Acquaviva I . . . 81 C5
Acquaviva delle Fonti
  I . . . 104 C2
Acquaviva Picena I . . . 82 D2
Acquigny F . . . 58 A2
Acqui Terme I . . . 80 B2
Acri I . . . 106 B3
Acs H . . . 64 C4
Acsa H . . . 65 C5
Acstesér H . . . 74 A2
Acy-en-Multien F . . . 59 A3
Ada SRB . . . 75 C5
Adak S . . . 115 B15
Adalsbruk N . . . 34 B3
Adamas GR . . . 117 F6
Adamsfjord N . . . 113 B15
Adamuz E . . . 100 A1
Adana TR . . . 16 C7
Adánd H . . . 74 B3
Adanero E . . . 94 B2
Adare IRL . . . 20 B3
Adaševci SRB . . . 85 A4
Adeanueva de Ebro E . . . 89 B5
Adelboden CH . . . 70 B2
Adelebsen D . . . 51 B5
Adélfia I . . . 104 B2
Adelmannsfelden D . . . 61 B6
Adelsheim D . . . 61 A5
Adelsö S . . . 37 C4
Ademuz E . . . 96 A1
Adenau D . . . 50 C2
Adendorf D . . . 44 B2
Adinkerke B . . . 48 B3
Adjud RO . . . 11 C9
Adliswil CH . . . 70 A3
Admont A . . . 63 C5
Adneram N . . . 33 C3
Adolfsström S . . . 115 A13
Adony H . . . 74 A3
Adorf
  Hessen D . . . 51 B4
  Sachsen D . . . 52 C2
Adra E . . . 100 C2
Adradas E . . . 89 C4
Adrall E . . . 91 A4
Adrano I . . . 109 B3
Adria I . . . 82 A1
Adrigole IRL . . . 20 C2
Adwick le Street GB . . . 27 B4
Adzaneta E . . . 96 A2
Aesch CH . . . 70 A2
A Estrada E . . . 86 B2
Afandou GR . . . 119 F3
Afarnes N . . . 114 E4
Affing D . . . 62 B1
Affoltern CH . . . 70 A3
Affric Lodge GB . . . 22 D3
Afjord N . . . 114 D7
Aflenz Kurort A . . . 73 A5
A Fonsagrada E . . . 86 A3
Afragóla I . . . 103 C7
Afritz A . . . 72 B3
Afyonkarahisar TR . . . 118 D5
Agasegyháza H . . . 75 B4
Agay F . . . 79 C5
Agazzano I . . . 80 B3
Agde F . . . 78 C2
Agdenes N . . . 114 D6
Agen F . . . 77 B3
Ager E . . . 90 B3
Agerbæk DK . . . 39 D1
Agerskov DK . . . 39 D2
Ageyevo RUS . . . 7 D14
Agger DK . . . 38 C1
Aggersund DK . . . 38 B2
Aggius I . . . 110 B2

Aggsbach Dorf A . . . 63 B6
Aggsbach Markt A . . . 63 B6
Aggtelek H . . . 65 B6
Aghalee GB . . . 19 B5
Aghia GR . . . 116 C4
Aghia Anna GR . . . 116 D5
Aghia Galini GR . . . 117 G6
Aghia Marina GR . . . 119 G1
Aghia Paraskevi GR . . . 118 C1
Aghia Pelagia GR . . . 117 F4
Aghia Triada GR . . . 117 E3
Aghiokambos GR . . . 116 C4
Aghios Efstratios
  GR . . . 116 C6
Aghios Kirikos GR . . . 119 E1
Aghios Matheos GR . . . 116 C1
Aghios Mironas GR . . . 117 G7
Aghios Nikolaos GR . . . 117 H7
Aghios Petros GR . . . 116 D2
Aghio Theodori GR . . . 117 E5
Agiči BIH . . . 83 B5
Agira I . . . 109 B3
Aglientu I . . . 110 A2
Agnières F . . . 79 B4
Agno CH . . . 70 C3
Agnone I . . . 103 B7
Agolada E . . . 86 B2
Agon Coutainville F . . . 57 A4
Agordo I . . . 72 B2
Agost E . . . 96 C2
Agramón E . . . 101 A4
Agramunt E . . . 91 B4
Agreda E . . . 89 C5
Agria GR . . . 116 C5
Agrigento I . . . 108 B2
Agrinio GR . . . 116 D3
Agrón E . . . 100 B2
Agrópoli I . . . 103 C7
Aguadulce
  Almería E . . . 101 C3
  Sevilla E . . . 100 B1
Agualada E . . . 86 A2
Agua Longa P . . . 87 C2
A Guarda E . . . 87 C2
Aguarón E . . . 89 C5
Aguas E . . . 90 A2
Aguas Belas P . . . 92 B2
Aguas de Busot E . . . 96 C2
Aguas de Moura P . . . 92 C2
Aguas Frias P . . . 87 C3
Aguas Santas P . . . 87 C2
Aguaviva E . . . 90 C2
Aguaviva de la Vega
  E . . . 89 C4
A Gudiña E . . . 87 B3
Agudo E . . . 94 D2
Águeda P . . . 92 A2
Aguessac F . . . 78 B2
Agugliano I . . . 82 C2
Aguiar P . . . 92 C3
Aguiar da Beira P . . . 87 D3
Aguilafuente E . . . 94 A2
Aguilar de Campóo E . . . 88 B2
Aguilar de la Frontera
  E . . . 100 B1
Aguilas E . . . 101 B4
Agunnaryd S . . . 40 C4
Ahat TR . . . 118 D4
Ahaus D . . . 50 A2
Aheim N . . . 114 E2
Ahigal E . . . 93 A4
Ahigal de Villarino E . . . 87 C4
Ahillones E . . . 99 A5
Ahlbeck
  Mecklenburg-
  Vorpommern D . . . 45 B6
  Mecklenburg-
  Vorpommern D . . . 45 B6
Ahlen D . . . 50 B3
Ahlhorn D . . . 43 C5
Ahmetbey TR . . . 118 A2
Ahmetler TR . . . 119 D4
Ahmetli TR . . . 119 D2
Ahoghill GB . . . 19 B5
Ahrensbök D . . . 44 A2
Ahrensburg D . . . 44 B2
Ahrenshoop D . . . 44 A4
Ahun F . . . 68 B2
Ähus S . . . 41 D4
Ahvenselkä FIN . . . 113 F17
Aibar E . . . 89 B5
Aich D . . . 62 B3
Aicha D . . . 63 B4
Aichach D . . . 62 B2
Aielo de Malferit E . . . 96 C2
Aigen im Mühlkreis A . . . 63 B4
Aigle CH . . . 70 B1
Aignan F . . . 76 C3
Aignay-le-Duc F . . . 59 C5
Aigre F . . . 67 C5
Aigrefeuille-d'Aunis F . . . 66 B4
Aigrefeuille-sur-Maine
  F . . . 66 A3
Aiguablava E . . . 91 B6
Aiguebelle F . . . 69 C6
Aigueperse F . . . 68 B3
Aigues-Mortes F . . . 78 C3
Aigues-Vives F . . . 78 C1
Aiguilles F . . . 79 B5
Aiguillon F . . . 77 B3
Aigurande F . . . 68 B1
Ailefroide F . . . 79 B5
Aillant-sur-Tholon F . . . 59 C4
Ailly-sur-Noye F . . . 58 A3
Ailly-sur-Somme F . . . 58 A3
Aimargues F . . . 78 C3

Aime F . . . 69 C6
Ainaži LV . . . 6 C8
Ainet A . . . 72 B2
Ainhoa F . . . 76 C1
Aiud-Iulia RO . . . 11 C7
Ainsa E . . . 90 A3
Airaines F . . . 48 D2
Aird GB . . . 24 B2
Aird Asaig Tairbeart
  GB . . . 22 D2
Airdrie GB . . . 25 C4
Aire-sur-l'Adour F . . . 76 C2
Aire-sur-la-Lys F . . . 48 C3
Airole I . . . 80 C1
Airolo CH . . . 70 B3
Airvault F . . . 67 B4
Aisey-sur-Seine F . . . 59 C5
Aïssey F . . . 69 A6
Aisy-sur-Armançon F . . . 59 C5
Aiterhofen D . . . 62 B3
Aith
  Orkney GB . . . 23 B6
  Shetland GB . . . 22 A7
Aitona E . . . 90 B3
Aitrach D . . . 61 C6
Aiud RO . . . 11 C7
Aix-en-Othe F . . . 59 B4
Aix-en-Provence F . . . 79 C4
Aixe-sur-Vienne F . . . 67 C6
Aix-les-Bains F . . . 69 C5
Aizenay F . . . 66 B3
Aizkraukle LV . . . 7 C8
Aizpute LV . . . 6 C6
Ajac F . . . 77 C5
Ajaccio F . . . 102 B1
Ajain F . . . 68 B1
Ajaureforsen S . . . 115 B12
Ajdovščina SLO . . . 72 C3
Ajka H . . . 74 A2
Ajo E . . . 89 A3
Ajofrin E . . . 94 C3
Ajuda P . . . 93 C3
Akanthou CY . . . 120 A2
Akarca TR . . . 118 D4
Akasztó H . . . 75 B4
Akçakoca TR . . . 118 A6
Akçaova TR . . . 119 D3
Akçay TR . . . 119 F4
Aken D . . . 52 B2
Åkerby S . . . 36 B4
Åkernes N . . . 33 D4
Åkers Styckebruk S . . . 37 C4
Akervik N . . . 115 B10
Akhisar TR . . . 118 D2
Akirkeby DK . . . 41 D4
Akköy TR . . . 119 E2
Akkrum NL . . . 42 B2
Akören TR . . . 119 E7
Akra N . . . 32 C3
Akranes IS . . . 111 C3
Akrehamn N . . . 33 C2
Akrotiri CY . . . 120 B1
Aksaray TR . . . 16 B7
Akşehir TR . . . 119 D6
Akseki TR . . . 119 E6
Aksla N . . . 32 A3
Aksu TR . . . 119 F5
Aktsyabrski BY . . . 7 E10
Akureyri IS . . . 111 B7
Akyazı TR . . . 118 B5
Al N . . . 32 B5
Ala I . . . 71 C6
Alacaatlı TR . . . 118 C3
Alaçam TR . . . 16 A7
Alaçatı TR . . . 119 D1
Ala di Stura I . . . 70 C2
Alaejos E . . . 88 C1
Alagna Valsésia I . . . 70 C2
Alagón E . . . 90 B1
Alaior E . . . 97 B4
Alájar E . . . 99 B4
Alakurtti RUS . . . 3 C29
Alalpardo E . . . 95 B3
Alameda E . . . 100 B1
Alameda de la Sagra
  E . . . 94 B3
Alamedilla E . . . 100 B2
Alamillo E . . . 100 A1
Alaminos E . . . 95 B4
Ala-Nampa FIN . . . 113 F15
Alanäs S . . . 115 C12
Alandroal P . . . 92 C3
Alange E . . . 93 C4
Alanis E . . . 99 A5
Alanno I . . . 103 A6
Alansbro S . . . 115 E14
Alanya TR . . . 119 F7
Alap H . . . 74 B3
Alaquàs E . . . 96 B2
Alar del Rey E . . . 88 B2
Alaró E . . . 97 B2
Alaşehir TR . . . 119 D3
Alássio I . . . 80 C2
Alatoz E . . . 96 C1
Alavus FIN . . . 3 E25
Alba
  E . . . 95 B5
  I . . . 80 B2
Alba Adriática I . . . 82 D2
Albacete E . . . 95 D5

Alba de Tormes E . . . 94 B1
Alba de Yeltes E . . . 93 A4
Albaida E . . . 96 C2
Albala del Caudillo E . . . 93 B4
Albaladejo E . . . 101 A3
Albalat E . . . 96 B2
Albalate de Cinca E . . . 90 B3
Albalate del Arzobispo
  E . . . 90 B2
Albalete de Zorita E . . . 95 B4
Albánchez E . . . 101 B3
Albánchez de Ubeda
  E . . . 100 B2
Albano Laziale I . . . 102 B5
Albares E . . . 95 B3
Albaracin E . . . 95 B5
Albaron F . . . 78 C3
Albatana E . . . 101 A4
Albatàrrec E . . . 90 B3
Albatera E . . . 101 A5
Albbruck D . . . 61 C4
Albedin E . . . 100 B1
Albelda de Iregua E . . . 89 B4
Albenga I . . . 80 B2
Albens F . . . 69 C5
Alberga
  Södermanland S . . . 37 C3
  Södermanland S . . . 37 D3
Albergaria-a-Nova P . . . 87 D2
Albergaria dos Doze
  P . . . 92 B2
Alberic E . . . 96 B2
Albernoa P . . . 98 B3
Alberobello I . . . 104 C3
Alberoni I . . . 72 C2
Albersdorf D . . . 43 A6
Albersloh D . . . 50 B3
Albert F . . . 48 C3
Albertirsa H . . . 75 A4
Albertville F . . . 69 C6
Albi F . . . 77 C5
Albidona I . . . 106 B3
Albillos E . . . 88 B3
Albinia I . . . 102 A4
Albino I . . . 71 C4
Albinshof D . . . 45 B5
Albires E . . . 88 B1
Albisola Marina I . . . 80 B2
Albocàsser E . . . 90 C3
Albolote E . . . 100 B2
Albondón E . . . 100 C2
Alborea E . . . 96 B1
Albox E . . . 101 B3
Albrechtice nad Vltavou
  CZ . . . 63 A5
Albstadt D . . . 61 B5
Albufeira P . . . 98 B2
Albuñol E . . . 100 C2
Albuñuelas E . . . 100 C2
Alburquerque E . . . 93 B3
Alby
  Öland S . . . 41 C6
  Västernorrland S . . . 115 E12
Alcácer do Sal P . . . 92 C2
Alcáçovas P . . . 92 C2
Alcadozo E . . . 101 A4
Alcafoces P . . . 93 B3
Alcains P . . . 92 B3
Alcalá de Guadaira E . . . 99 B5
Alcalá de Gurrea E . . . 90 A2
Alcalá de Henares E . . . 95 B3
Alcalá de la Selva E . . . 90 C2
Alcalá del Júcar E . . . 96 B1
Alcalá de los Gazules
  E . . . 99 C5
Alcalá del Río E . . . 99 B5
Alcalá del Valle E . . . 99 C5
Alcalá la Real E . . . 100 B2
Alcamo I . . . 108 B1
Alcampell E . . . 90 B3
Alcanadre E . . . 89 B4
Alcanar E . . . 90 C3
Alcanede P . . . 92 B2
Alcanena P . . . 92 B2
Alcántara E . . . 93 B4
Alcantarilla E . . . 101 B4
Alcañices E . . . 87 C4
Alcañiz E . . . 90 C2
Alcaracejos E . . . 100 A1
Alcara il Fusi I . . . 109 A3
Alcaraz E . . . 101 A3
Alcaria Ruiva P . . . 98 B3
Alcarraz E . . . 90 B3
Alcaudete E . . . 100 B1
Alcaudete de la Jara
  E . . . 94 C2
Alcázar de San Juan
  E . . . 95 C3
Alcazarén E . . . 88 C2
Alcester GB . . . 29 A6
Alcoba E . . . 94 C2
Alcobaça P . . . 92 B1
Alcobendas E . . . 94 B3
Alcocer E . . . 95 B4
Alcochete P . . . 92 C2
Alcoentre P . . . 92 B1

Alcolea
  Almería E . . . 100 C3
  Córdoba E . . . 100 B1
Alcolea de Calatrava
  E . . . 94 D2
Alcolea de Cinca E . . . 90 B3
Alcolea del Pinar E . . . 95 A4
Alcolea del Rio E . . . 99 B5
Alcolea de Tajo E . . . 93 C5
Alcollarin E . . . 93 B5
Alconchel E . . . 93 C3
Alconera E . . . 93 C4
Alcontar E . . . 101 B3
Alcora E . . . 96 A2
Alcorcón E . . . 94 B3
Alcorisa E . . . 90 C2
Alcossebre E . . . 90 C3
Alcoutim P . . . 98 B3
Alcover E . . . 91 B4
Alcoy E . . . 96 C2
Alcsútdoboz H . . . 74 A3
Alcubierre E . . . 90 B2
Alcubilla de Avellaneda
  E . . . 89 C3
Alcubilla de Nogales
  E . . . 88 B1
Alcubillas E . . . 100 A2
Alcublas E . . . 96 B2
Alcúdia E . . . 97 B3
Alcudia de Guadix E . . . 100 B2
Aldeacentenera E . . . 93 B5
Aldea del Cano E . . . 93 B4
Aldea del Fresno E . . . 94 B2
Aldea del Obispo E . . . 87 D4
Aldea del Rey E . . . 100 A2
Aldea de Trujillo E . . . 93 B5
Aldealcorvo E . . . 94 A3
Aldealuenga de Santa
  Maria E . . . 89 C3
Aldeamayor de San
  Martin E . . . 88 C2
Aldeanueva de
  Barbarroya E . . . 94 C1
Aldeanueva del Camino
  E . . . 93 A5
Aldeanueva del Codonal
  E . . . 94 A2
Aldeanueva de San
  Bartolomé E . . . 94 C1
Aldeaquemada E . . . 100 A2
Aldea Real E . . . 94 A2
Aldearrubia E . . . 94 A1
Aldeaseca de la Frontera
  E . . . 94 B1
Aldeasoña E . . . 88 C2
Aldeavieja E . . . 94 B2
Aldeburgh GB . . . 30 B5
Aldehuela E . . . 96 A1
Aldehuela de Calatañazor
  E . . . 89 C4
Aldeia da Serra P . . . 92 C3
Aldeia do Bispo P . . . 93 A4
Aldeia do Mato P . . . 92 B2
Aldeia Gavinha P . . . 92 B1
Aldenhoven D . . . 50 C2
Aldersbach D . . . 62 B4
Aldershot GB . . . 31 C3
Aldudes F . . . 76 C1
Aled S . . . 40 C2
Alegria E . . . 89 B4
Aleksandrovac
  Srbija SRB . . . 85 B6
  Srbija SRB . . . 85 C6
Aleksandrów Kujawski
  PL . . . 47 C4
Aleksandrów Łódzki
  PL . . . 55 B4
Aleksa Šantić SRB . . . 75 C4
Aleksin RUS . . . 7 D14
Alem S . . . 40 C6
Alençon F . . . 57 B6
Alenquer P . . . 92 B1
Alepu E . . . 91 A5
Aléria F . . . 102 A2
Alès F . . . 78 B3
Alessándria I . . . 80 B2
Alessándria della Rocca
  I . . . 108 B2
Alessano I . . . 107 B5
Alesund N . . . 114 E3
Alet-les-Bains F . . . 77 D5
Alexandria
  GB . . . 24 C3
  RO . . . 11 E8
Alexandroupoli GR . . . 116 B7
Alezio I . . . 107 A5
Alfacar E . . . 100 B2
Alfaiates P . . . 93 A4
Alfajarin E . . . 90 B2
Alfândega da Fé P . . . 87 C4
Alfarela de Jafes P . . . 87 C3
Alfarelos P . . . 92 A2
Alfarim P . . . 92 C1

Alfarnate E . . . 100 C1
Alfaro E . . . 89 B5
Alfarràs E . . . 90 B3
Alfaz del Pi E . . . 96 C2
Alfedena I . . . 103 B7
Alfeizarão P . . . 92 B1
Alfeld
  Bayern D . . . 62 A2
  Niedersachsen D . . . 51 B5
Alfena P . . . 87 C2
Alferce P . . . 98 B2
Alfés E . . . 90 B3
Alfhausen D . . . 43 C4
Alfonsine I . . . 81 B6
Alford
  Aberdeenshire GB . . . 23 D6
  Lincolnshire GB . . . 27 B6
Alforja E . . . 90 B3
Alfoz E . . . 86 A3
Alfreton GB . . . 27 B4
Alfta S . . . 36 A3
Alfundão P . . . 98 A2
Algaida E . . . 97 B2
Algar E . . . 99 C5
Algård N . . . 33 D2
Algarinejo E . . . 100 B1
Algarrobo E . . . 100 C1
Algatocin E . . . 99 C5
Algeciras E . . . 99 C5
Algemesí E . . . 96 B2
Algés P . . . 92 C1
Algeté E . . . 95 B3
Alghero I . . . 110 B1
Alginet E . . . 96 B2
Algodonales E . . . 99 C5
Algodor
  E . . . 94 C3
  P . . . 98 B3
Algora E . . . 95 B4
Algoso P . . . 87 C4
Algoz P . . . 98 B2
Älgsjö S . . . 115 C14
Alguaire E . . . 90 B3
Alguazas E . . . 101 A4
Algutsrum S . . . 41 C6
Algyö H . . . 75 B5
Alhama de Almería
  E . . . 101 C3
Alhama de Aragón E . . . 89 C5
Alhama de Granada
  E . . . 100 C2
Alhama de Murcia E . . . 101 B4
Alhambra E . . . 100 A2
Alhaurin de la Torre
  E . . . 100 C1
Alhaurin el Grande
  E . . . 100 C1
Alhendin E . . . 100 B2
Alhóndiga E . . . 95 B4
Ali I . . . 109 B4
Ália I . . . 108 B2
Aliaga TR . . . 118 D1
Aliaga E . . . 90 C2
Aliaguilla E . . . 96 B1
Alibunar SRB . . . 85 A5
Alicante E . . . 96 C2
Alicún de Ortega E . . . 100 B2
Alife I . . . 103 B7
Alija del Infantado E . . . 88 B1
Alijó P . . . 87 C3
Alimena I . . . 109 B3
Alingsås S . . . 40 B2
Alinyà E . . . 91 A4
Aliseda E . . . 93 B4
Ali Terme I . . . 109 A4
Aljaraque E . . . 99 B3
Aljezur P . . . 98 B2
Aljorra P . . . 87 D2
Aljubarrota P . . . 92 B2
Aljucen E . . . 93 B4
Aljustrel P . . . 98 B2
Alken B . . . 49 C6
Alkmaar NL . . . 42 C1
Alkoven A . . . 63 B5
Allaines F . . . 58 B2
Allaire F . . . 57 C3
Allanche F . . . 68 C2
Alland A . . . 64 B2
Allariz E . . . 87 B3
Allassac F . . . 67 C6
Allauch F . . . 79 C4
Alleen N . . . 33 D4
Allegre F . . . 68 C3
Allein I . . . 70 C2
Allemont F . . . 69 C6
Allendale Town GB . . . 25 D5
Allendorf D . . . 51 C4
Allensteig A . . . 63 B6
Allepuz E . . . 90 C2
Allersberg D . . . 62 A2
Allershausen D . . . 62 B2
Alles E . . . 88 A2
Allevard F . . . 69 C6
Allgunnen S . . . 40 B5
Allihies IRL . . . 20 C1
Allingåbro DK . . . 38 C3
Alló E . . . 89 B4
Alloa GB . . . 25 B4
Allogny F . . . 68 A2
Alloluokta S . . . 112 E8
Allones
  Eure et Loire F . . . 58 B2
  Maine-et-Loire F . . . 67 A5

Allons F . . . 76 B2
Allos F . . . 79 B5
Allstedt D . . . 52 B1
Alltwalis GB . . . 28 B3
Allumiere I . . . 102 A4
Almaceda P . . . 92 B3
Almacelles E . . . 90 B3
Almáchar E . . . 100 C1
Almada P . . . 92 C1
Almadén E . . . 100 A1
Almadén de la Plata
  E . . . 99 B4
Almadenejos E . . . 100 A1
Almagro E . . . 100 A2
Almajano E . . . 89 C4
Almansa E . . . 96 C1
Almansil P . . . 98 B2
Almanza E . . . 88 B1
Almaraz E . . . 93 B5
Almargen E . . . 100 C1
Almarza E . . . 89 C4
Almásfüzitö H . . . 64 C4
Almassora E . . . 96 A2
Almazán E . . . 89 C4
Almazul E . . . 89 C4
Alme D . . . 51 B4
Almedina E . . . 100 A3
Almedinilla E . . . 100 B1
Almeida
  E . . . 87 C4
  P . . . 93 A4
Almeirim P . . . 92 B2
Almelo NL . . . 42 C3
Almenar E . . . 90 B3
Almenara E . . . 96 B2
Almenar de Soria E . . . 89 C4
Almendra P . . . 87 C3
Almendral E . . . 93 C4
Almendral de la Cañada
  E . . . 94 B2
Almendralejo E . . . 93 C4
Almenno San Bartolomeo
  I . . . 71 C4
Almere NL . . . 42 C2
Almería E . . . 101 C3
Almerimar E . . . 101 C3
Almese I . . . 70 C2
Almexial P . . . 98 B3
Älmhult S . . . 40 C4
Almiropotamos GR . . . 117 D6
Almiros GR . . . 116 C4
Almodôvar P . . . 98 B2
Almodóvar del Campo
  E . . . 100 A1
Almodóvar del Pinar
  E . . . 95 C5
Almodóvar del Río E . . . 99 B5
Almofala P . . . 87 D3
Almogia E . . . 100 C1
Almoharin E . . . 93 B4
Almonacid de la Sierra
  E . . . 89 C5
Almonacid de Toledo
  E . . . 94 C3
Almonaster la Real E . . . 99 B4
Almonte E . . . 99 B4
Almoradí E . . . 101 A5
Almoraima E . . . 99 C5
Almorox E . . . 94 B2
Almoster P . . . 92 B2
Almsele S . . . 115 C14
Älmsta S . . . 36 C5
Almudévar E . . . 90 A2
Almuñécar E . . . 100 C2
Almunge S . . . 36 C5
Almuradiel E . . . 100 A2
Almussafes E . . . 96 B2
Almvik S . . . 40 B6
Alness GB . . . 23 D4
Alnmouth GB . . . 25 C6
Alnwick GB . . . 25 C6
Aloppe S . . . 36 C4
Álora E . . . 100 C1
Alosno E . . . 99 B3
Alozaina E . . . 100 C1
Alpbach A . . . 72 A1
Alpedrete de la Sierra
  E . . . 95 B3
Alpedrinha P . . . 92 A3
Alpen D . . . 50 B2
Alpera E . . . 96 C1
Alphen aan de Rijn
  NL . . . 49 A5
Alpiarça P . . . 92 B2
Alpignano I . . . 70 C2
Alpirsbach D . . . 61 B4
Alpu TR . . . 118 C5
Alpuente E . . . 96 B1
Alqueva P . . . 98 A3
Alquézar E . . . 90 A3
Als DK . . . 38 C3
Alsdorf D . . . 50 C2
Alselv DK . . . 39 D1
Alsfeld D . . . 51 C5
Alsike S . . . 36 C4
Alskog S . . . 37 E5
Alsleben D . . . 52 B1
Alsónémedi H . . . 75 A4
Alsótold H . . . 65 C5

Alsóújlak H 74 A1
Alstad N 112 E4
Alstätte D 50 A2
Alsterbro S 40 C5
Alstermo S 40 C5
Alston GB 25 D5
Alsvåg N 112 D4
Alsvik N 112 E3
Alta N 113 C12
Älta S 37 C5
Altamura I 104 C2
Altarejos E 95 C4
Altaussee A 63 C4
Altavilla Irpina I 103 B7
Altavilla Silentina I 103 C8
Altdöbern D 53 B4
Altdorf
CH 70 B3
D 62 B3
Altdorf bei Nürnberg
D 62 A2
Alte P 98 B2
Altea E 96 C2
Altedo I 81 B5
Altena D 50 B3
Altenau D 51 B6
Altenberg D 53 C3
Altenberge D 50 A3
Altenbruch D 43 B5
Altenburg D 52 C2
Altenfelden A 63 B4
Altengronau D 51 C5
Altenheim D 60 B3
Altenhundem D 50 B4
Altenkirchen
Mecklenburg-Vorpommern D 45 A5
Radom D 50 C3
Altenkunstadt D 52 C1
Altenmarkt
A 63 C5
D 62 B3
Altenmarkt im Pongall
A 72 A3
Altensteig D 61 B4
Altentreptow D 45 B5
Altenwalde D 43 B5
Alten-weddingen D 52 A1
Alter do Chão P 92 B3
Altfraunhofen D 62 B3
Altheim
A 63 B4
D 61 A5
Althofen A 73 B4
Altınoluk TR 118 C1
Altınova TR 118 C1
Altıntaş TR 118 C5
Altınyaka TR 119 F5
Altınyayla TR 119 E4
Altkirch F 60 C3
Altlandsberg D 45 C5
Altlewin D 45 C6
Altmannstein D 62 B2
Altmorschen D 51 B5
Altmunster A 63 C4
Altnaharra GB 23 C4
Alto Campoó E 88 A2
Altofonte I 108 A2
Altomonte I 106 B3
Alton
Hampshire GB 31 C3
Staffordshire GB 27 C4
Altopáscio I 81 C4
Altötting D 62 B3
Altreichenau D 63 B4
Alt Ruppin D 45 C4
Altshausen D 61 C5
Altstätten CH 71 A4
Altura E 96 B2
Altusried D 61 C6
Alūksne LV 7 C9
Alunda S 36 B5
Alustante E 95 B5
Alva GB 25 B4
Alvaiázere P 92 B2
Alvalade P 98 B2
Älvängen S 38 B5
Alvarenga P 87 D2
Alvares P 92 A2
Alvdal N 114 E7
Älvdalen S 34 A6
Alverca P 92 C1
Alversund N 32 B2
Alvesta S 40 C4
Alvignac F 77 B4
Alvignano I 103 B7
Ålvik N 32 B3
Alvik S 36 B1
Alvimare F 58 A1
Alviobeira P 92 B2
Alvito P 98 A3
Älvkarleby S 36 B4
Älvkarleöbruk S 36 B4
Alvor P 98 B2
Alvorge P 92 B2
Alvøy N 32 B2
Älvros S 115 E11
Alvsbacka S 35 C5
Älvsbyn S 3 D24
Älvsered S 40 B2
Alwernia PL 55 C4
Alwinton GB 25 C5
Alyth GB 25 B4
Alytus LT 6 D8
Alzénau D 51 C5
Alzey D 61 A4
Alzira E 96 B2
Alzonne F 77 C5
Amadora P 92 C1
Åmål S 35 C4
Amalfi I 103 C7
Amaliada GR 117 E3
Amance F 60 C2
Amancey F 69 A6
Amándola I 82 D2
Amantea I 106 B3
Amarante P 87 C2
Amareleja P 98 A3
Amares P 87 C2
Amaseno I 103 B6
Amasra TR 118 A7
Amasya TR 16 A8
Amatrice I 103 A6
Amay B 49 C6
Ambarnyy RUS 3 D30
Ambazac F 67 C6
Ambelonas GR 116 C4
Amberg D 62 A2
Ambérieu-en-Bugey
F 69 C5
Ambérieux-en-Dombes
F 69 B4
Ambert F 68 C3
Ambés F 76 A2
Ambjörby S 34 B5
Ambjörnarp S 40 B3
Amble GB 25 C6
Ambleside GB 26 A3
Ambleteuse F 48 C2
Amboise F 67 A5
Ambrières-les-Vallées
F 57 B5
Amden CH 71 A4
Amel B 50 C2
Amélia I 102 A5
Amélie-les-Bains-Palalda
F 91 A5
Amelinghausen D 44 B2
Amendoa P 92 B2
Amendoeira P 98 B3
Améndola I 104 B1
Amendolara I 106 B3
Amer E 91 A5
A Merca E 87 B3
Amerongen NL 49 A6
Amersfoort NL 49 A6
Amersham GB 31 C3
Amesbury GB 29 B6
Amfiklia GR 116 D4
Amfilochia GR 116 D3
Amfipoli GR 116 B5
Amfissa GR 116 D4
Amièira P 98 A3
Amieira P 92 B3
Amieiro P 92 A2
Amiens F 58 A3
Amindeo GR 116 B3
Åminne S 40 B3
Åmli N 33 D5
Amlwch GB 26 B1
Ammanford GB 28 B4
Ammarnäs S 115 B13
Åmmeberg S 37 D1
Amorbach D 61 A5
Amorebieta E 89 A4
Amorgos GR 117 F7
Amorosa P 87 C2
Amorosi I 103 B7
Åmot
Buskerud N 34 C1
Telemark N 33 C4
S 36 B3
Åmotfors S 34 C4
Åmotsdal N 33 C5
Amou F 76 C2
Ampezzo I 72 B2
Ampfing D 62 B3
Ampflwang A 63 B4
Amplepuis F 69 C4
Amposta E 90 C3
Ampthill GB 30 B3
Ampudia E 88 C2
Ampuero E 89 A3
Amriswil CH 71 A4
Åmsele S 115 C16
Amstelveen NL 49 A5
Amsterdam NL 42 C1
Amstetten A 63 B5
Amtzell D 61 C5
Amulree GB 25 B4
Amurrio E 89 A4
Amusco E 88 B2
Anacapri I 103 C7
Anadia P 92 A2
Anadon E 90 C1
Anafi GR 117 F7
Anagni I 102 B6
Anamur TR 16 C6
Ananyiv UA 11 C10
Anascaul IRL 20 B1
Ånäset S 3 D24
Åna-Sira N 33 D3
Anastażewo PL 47 C4
Anaya de Alba E 94 B1
Ança P 92 A2
Ancaster GB 27 C5
Ancede P 87 C2
Ancenis F 66 A3
Ancerville F 59 B6
Anchuras E 94 C2
Ancona I 82 C2
Ancora P 87 C2
Ancrum GB 25 C5
Ancy-le-Franc F 59 C5
Andalo I 71 B5
Åndalsnes N 114 E4
Andance F 69 C4
Andau A 64 C3
Andebu N 35 C2
Andeer CH 71 B4
Andelfingen CH 61 C4
Andelot-Blanchville F 59 B6
Andelot-en-Montagne
F 69 B5
Andenes N 112 C5
Andenne B 49 C6
Anderlues B 49 C5
Andermatt CH 70 B3
Andernach D 50 C3
Andernos-les-Bains F 76 B1
Anderslöv S 41 D3
Anderstorp S 40 B3
Andijk NL 42 C2
Andoain E 89 A4
Andocs H 74 B2
Andolsheim F 60 B3
Andorra E 90 C2
Andorra La Vella AND 91 A4
Andosilla E 89 B5
Andover GB 31 C2
Andratx E 97 B2
Andreapol RUS 7 C12
Andreas GB 26 A1
Andréspol PL 55 B4
Andrest F 76 C3
Andretta I 103 C8
Andrezieux-Bouthéon
F 69 C4
Ándria I 104 B2
Andrijevica MNE 85 D4
Andritsena GR 117 E3
Andros GR 117 E6
Andrychów PL 65 A5
Andselv N 112 C7
Andújar E 100 A1
Anduze F 78 B2
Åneby N 34 B2
Aneby S 40 B4
Añes E 89 A3
Anet F 58 B2
Anfo I 71 C5
Ang S 40 B4
Anga S 37 E5
Angaïs F 76 C2
Änge S 115 D11
Ånge S 115 E12
Angeja P 92 A2
Ängelholm S 41 C2
Angeli FIN 113 D14
Ängelsberg S 36 C3
Anger A 73 A5
Angera I 70 C3
Angermünde D 45 B6
Angern A 64 B2
Angers F 67 A4
Angerville F 58 B3
Anghiari I 82 C1
Angle GB 28 B2
Anglès E 91 B5
Anglés F 77 C5
Angles F 66 B3
Anglesola E 91 B4
Angles sur l'Anglin F 67 B5
Anglet F 76 C1
Anglisidhes CY 120 B2
Anglure F 59 B4
Angoulême F 67 C5
Angoulins F 66 B3
Angsö S 37 C3
Angueira P 87 C4
Angües E 90 A2
Anguiano E 89 B4
Anguillara Sabazia I 102 A5
Anguillara Véneta I 72 C1
Anhée B 49 C5
Anholt DK 38 C4
Aniane F 78 C2
Aniche F 49 C4
Ånimskog S 35 D4
Anina RO 10 D6
Anixi GR 116 C3
Anizy-le-Château F 59 A4
Anjalankoski FIN 3 F27
Anjan S 115 D9
Ankara TR 118 C7
Ankaran SLO 72 C3
Ankarsrum S 40 B6
Ankerlia N 112 C9
Anklam D 45 B5
Ankum D 43 C4
Anlaúftal A 72 A3
Anlezy F 68 B3
Ånn S 115 D9
Annaberg A 63 C6
Annaberg-Buchholz
D 52 C3
Annaberg im Lammertal
A 72 A3
Annaburg D 52 B3
Annahütte D 53 B3
Annalong GB 19 B6
Annan GB 25 D4
Anndalsvågen N 115 B9
Anneberg
Halland S 38 B5
Jönköping S 40 B4
Annecy F 69 C6
Annelund S 40 B3
Annemasse F 69 B6
Annenskiy Most RUS 7 A14
Annerstad S 40 C3
Annestown IRL 21 B4
Annevoie-Rouillon B 49 C5
Annonay F 69 C4
Annot F 79 C5
Annweiler D 60 A3
Ano Poroia GR 116 A5
Añora E 100 A1
Ano Siros GR 117 E6
Anould F 60 B2
Anquela del Ducado
E 95 B4
Anröchte D 51 B4
Ans DK 39 C2
Ansager DK 39 D1
Ansbach D 62 A1
Anse F 69 C4
Anseroeul B 49 C4
Ansfelden A 63 B5
Ansião P 92 B2
Ansó E 76 D2
Ansoain E 76 D1
Anstruther GB 25 B5
Antalya TR 119 F5
Antas E 101 B4
Antegnate I 71 C4
Antequera E 100 B1
Anterselva di Mezzo I 72 B2
Antibes F 79 C6
Antigüedad E 88 C2
Antillo I 109 B4
Antirio GR 117 D3
An t-Ob GB 22 D1
Antoing B 49 C4
Antonin PL 54 B2
Antrain F 57 B4
Antrim GB 19 B5
Antrodoco I 102 A6
Antronapiana I 70 B3
Anttis S 113 E11
Antuzede P 92 A2
Antwerp = Antwerpen
B 49 B5
Antwerpen = Antwerp
B 49 B5
Anversa d'Abruzzi I 103 B6
Anvin F 48 C3
Anzat-le-Luguet F 68 C3
Anzi I 104 C1
Ánzio I 102 B5
Anzola d'Emilia I 81 B5
Anzón E 89 C5
Aoiz E 76 D1
Aosta I 70 C2
Apalhão P 92 B3
Apátfalva H 75 B5
Apatin SRB 75 C4
Apatity RUS 3 C30
Apc H 65 C5
Apécchio I 82 C1
Apeldoorn NL 50 A1
Apen D 43 B4
Apenburg D 44 C3
Apensen D 43 B6
A Peroxa E 86 B3
Apiro I 82 C2
Apliki CY 120 B2
Apolda D 52 B1
Apolonia GR 117 F6
A Pontenova E 86 A3
Apostag H 75 B3
Äppelbo S 34 B6
Appennino I 82 D2
Appenzell CH 71 A4
Appiano I 71 B6
Appingedam NL 42 B3
Appleby-in-Westmorland
GB 26 A3
Applecross GB 22 D3
Appledore GB 28 B3
Appoigny F 59 C4
Apremont-la-Forêt F 60 B1
Aprica I 71 B5
Apricena I 103 B8
Aprigliano I 106 B3
Aprilia I 102 B5
Apt F 79 C4
Apúlia P 87 C2
Aquiléia I 72 C3
Aquilónia I 103 C8
Aquino I 103 B6
Ar S 37 E5
Arabayona E 94 A1
Arabba I 72 B1
Araç TR 16 A6
Aracena E 99 B4
Arachova GR 116 D4
Arad RO 75 B6
Aradac SRB 75 C5
Aradhippou CY 120 B2
Aragnouet F 76 D3
Aragona I 108 B2
Aramits F 76 C2
Aramon F 78 C3
Aranda de Duero E 88 C3
Aranda de Moncayo
E 89 C5
Arandjelovac SRB 85 B5
Aranjuez E 95 B3
Arantzazu E 89 B4
Aranzueque E 95 B3
Aras de Alpuente E 96 B1
Arauzo de Miel E 89 C3
Arazede P 92 A2
Arbas F 77 D3
Árbatax I 110 C2
Arbeca E 90 B3
Arberg D 62 A1
Arbesbach A 63 B5
Arboga S 37 C2
Arbois F 69 B5
Arbon CH 71 A4
Arboréa I 110 C1
Arbório I 70 C3
Årbostad N 112 D6
Arbrå S 36 A3
Arbroath GB 25 B5
Arbùcies E 91 B5
Arbuniel E 100 B2
Arbus I 110 C1
Arcachon F 76 B1
Arce I 103 B6
Arcen NL 50 B2
Arc-en-Barrois F 59 C5
Arces-Dilo F 59 B4
Arc-et-Senans F 69 A5
Arcévia I 82 C1
Arcey F 70 A1
Archanes GR 117 G7
Archangelos GR 119 F3
Archena E 101 A4
Archez E 100 C2
Archiac F 67 C4
Archidona E 100 B1
Archiestown GB 23 D5
Archivel E 101 A4
Arcidosso I 81 D5
Arcille I 81 D5
Arcis-sur-Aube F 59 B5
Arc-lès-Gray F 69 A5
Arco I 71 C5
Arcones E 94 A3
Arcos E 88 B3
Arcos de Jalón E 95 A4
Arcos de la Frontera
E 99 C5
Arcos de la Sierra E 95 B4
Arcos de las Salinas
E 96 B1
Arcos de Valdevez P 87 C2
Arcozelo P 92 A3
Arc-sur-Tille F 69 A5
Arcusa E 90 A3
Arcy-sur-Cure F 59 C4
Ardagh IRL 20 B2
Årdal N 33 C3
Ardala S 35 D5
Ardales E 100 C1
Årdalstangen N 32 A4
Ardara
I 110 B1
IRL 18 B3
Ardarroch GB 22 D3
Ardbeg GB 24 C1
Ardcharnich GB 22 D3
Ardchyle GB 24 B3
Ardee IRL 19 C5
Arden DK 38 C2
Ardentes F 68 B1
Ardenza I 81 C4
Ardersier GB 23 D4
Ardes F 68 C3
Ardessie GB 22 D3
Ardez CH 71 B5
Ardfert IRL 20 B2
Ardgay GB 23 D4
Ardglass GB 19 B6
Ardgroom IRL 20 C2
Ardhasig GB 22 D2
Ardino BG 116 A7
Ardisa E 90 A2
Ardkearagh IRL 20 C1
Ardlui GB 24 B3
Ardlussa GB 24 B2
Ardón E 88 B1
Ardooie B 49 C4
Ardore I 106 C3
Ardrahan IRL 20 A3
Ardre S 37 E5
Ardres F 48 C2
Ardrishaig GB 24 B2
Ardrossan GB 24 C3
Are N 33 C2
Åre S 115 D10
Areia Branca P 92 B1
Aremark N 35 C3
Arenales de San Gregorio
E 95 C3
Arenas E 100 C1
Arenas de Iguña E 88 A2
Arenas del Rey E 100 C2
Arenas de San Juan
E 95 C3
Arenas de San Pedro
E 94 B1
Arendal N 33 D5
Arendonk B 49 B6
Arengosse F 76 B2
Arentorp S 35 D4
Arenys de Mar E 91 B5
Arenys de Munt E 91 B5
Arenzano I 80 B2
Areo E 91 A4
Areopoli GR 117 F4
Ares E 86 A2
Arès F 76 B1
Ares del Maestrat E 90 C2
Aresvika N 114 D5
Arette F 76 C2
Aretxabaleta E 89 A4
Arevalillo E 93 A5
Arévalo E 94 A2
Arez P 92 B3
Arezzo I 81 C5
Arfeuilles F 68 B3
Argalasti GR 116 C5
Argallón E 99 A5
Argamasilla de Alba
E 95 C3
Argamasilla de Calatrava
E 100 A1
Arganda E 95 B3
Arganil P 92 A2
Argasion GR 117 E2
Argegno I 71 C4
Argelès-Gazost F 76 C2
Argelès-sur-Mer F 91 A6
Argenta I 81 B5
Argentan F 57 B5
Argentat F 77 A4
Argentera I 79 B5
Argenteuil F 58 B3
Argenthal D 50 D3
Argentiera I 110 B1
Argentona E 91 B5
Argenton-Château F 67 B4
Argenton-sur-Creuse
F 67 B6
Argentré F 57 B5
Argentré-du-Plessis
F 57 B4
Argent-sur-Sauldre F 68 A2
Argirades GR 116 C1
Argithani TR 119 D6
Argos GR 117 E4
Argos Orestiko GR 116 B3
Argostoli GR 117 D2
Argote E 89 B4
Arguedas E 89 B5
Argueil F 58 A2
Arholma S 36 C6
Århus DK 39 C3
Ariano Irpino I 103 B8
Ariano nel Polésine I 82 B1
Aribe E 76 D1
Aridea GR 116 B4
Arienzo I 103 B7
Arild S 41 C2
Arileod GB 24 B1
Arilje SRB 85 C5
Arinagour GB 24 B1
Ariño E 90 B2
Arinthod F 69 B5
Arisaig GB 24 B2
Arisgotas E 94 C3
Aritzo I 110 C2
Ariza E 89 C4
Årjäng S 35 C4
Arjeplog S 115 A14
Arjona E 100 B1
Arjonilla E 100 B1
Arkasa GR 119 G2
Arkelstorp S 41 C4
Arklow IRL 21 B5
Arkösund S 37 D3
Ärla S 37 C3
Arlanc F 68 C3
Arlanzón E 89 B3
Arlebosc F 78 A3
Arlena di Castro I 102 A4
Arles F 78 C3
Arles-sur-Tech F 91 A5
Arló H 65 B6
Arlon B 60 A1
Armação de Pera P 98 B2
Armadale
Highland GB 22 D3
West Lothian GB 25 C4
Armagh GB 19 B5
Armamar P 87 C3
Armenistis GR 117 E8
Armeno I 70 C3
Armenteros E 93 A5
Armentières F 48 C3
Armilla E 100 B2
Armiñón E 89 B4
Armoy GB 19 A5
Armuña de Tajuña E 95 B3
Armutlu
Bursa TR 118 B3
İzmir TR 119 D2
Arnac-Pompadour F 67 C6
Arnafjord N 32 A3
Arnage F 57 C6
Arnas F 69 B4
Ärnäs S 35 D5
Arnay-le-Duc F 69 A4
Arnborg DK 39 C2
Arnbruck D 62 A3
Arnea GR 116 B5
Arneberg
Hedmark N 34 A2
Hedmark N 34 B4
Arneburg D 44 C4
Arnedillo E 89 B4
Arnedo E 89 B4
Arneguy F 76 C1
Arnés E 90 C3
Árnes IS 111 A4
Årnes
Akershus N 34 B3
Troms N 112 C7
Arnfels A 73 B5
Arnhem NL 50 B1
Arnissa GR 116 B3
Arno S 37 D4
Arnold GB 27 B4
Arnoldstein A 72 B3
Arnsberg D 50 B4
Arnschwang D 62 A3
Arnsdorf D 53 B3
Årnset N 114 D6
Arnside GB 26 A3
Arnstadt D 51 C6
Arnstein D 51 D5
Arnstorf D 62 B3
Arnum DK 39 D1
Aroche E 99 B4
Arolla CH 70 B2
Arolsen D 51 B5
Arona I 70 C3
Äros N 35 C2
Arosa
CH 71 B4
P 87 C2
Ærøskøbing DK 39 E3
Ærøsund DK 39 D2
Arouca P 87 D2
Årøysund N 35 C2
Arpajon F 58 B3
Arpajon-sur-Cère F 77 B5
Arpino I 103 B6
Arquata del Tronto I 82 D2
Arques F 48 C3
Arques-la-Bataille F 58 A2
Arquillos E 100 A2
Arraia-Maeztu E 89 B4
Arraiolos P 92 C2
Arrancourt F 60 B2
Arras F 48 C3
Arrasate E 89 A4
Årre DK 39 D1
Arreau F 77 D3
Arredondo E 89 A3
Arrens-Marsous F 76 D2
Arriate E 99 C5
Arrifana P 98 B2
Arrigorriaga E 89 A4
Arriondas E 88 A1
Arroba de los Montes
E 94 C2
Arrochar GB 24 B3
Arromanches-les-Bains
F 57 A5
Arronches P 92 B3
Arroniz E 89 B4
Arrou F 58 B2
Arroya E 88 B2
Arroya de Cuéllar E 88 C2
Arroyal E 88 B2
Arroyo de la Luz E 93 B4
Arroyo del Ojanco E 100 A3
Arroyo de San Servan
E 93 C4
Arroyomolinos de León
E 99 A4
Arroyomolinos de
Montánchez E 93 B4
Arruda dos Vinhos P 92 C1
Arsac F 76 B2
Ars-en-Ré F 66 B3
Arsiè I 72 C1
Arsiero I 71 C6
Årslev DK 39 D3
Ársoli I 102 A6
Ars-sur-Moselle F 60 A2
Årsunda S 36 B3
Artà E 97 B3
Arta GR 116 C3
Artajona E 89 B5
Artegna I 72 B3
Arteixo E 86 A2
Artemare F 69 C5
Arten I 72 B1
Artena I 102 B5
Artenay F 58 B2
Artern D 52 B1
Artés E 91 B4
Artesa de Segre E 91 B4
Arth CH 70 A3
Arthez-de-Béarn F 76 C2
Arthon-en-Retz F 66 A3
Arthurstown IRL 21 B5
Artieda E 90 A2
Artix F 76 C2
Artotina GR 116 D4
Artsyz UA 11 C10
Artziniega E 89 A3
A Rúa E 87 B3
Arudy F 76 C2
Arundel GB 31 D3
Arveyres F 76 B2
Arvidsjaur S 115 B16
Arvieux F 79 B5
Arvika S 35 C4
Åryd
Blekinge S 41 C5
Kronoberg S 40 C4
Arzachena I 110 A2
Arzacq-Arraziguet F 76 C2
Árzana I 110 C2
Arzano F 56 C2
Aržano HR 84 C1
Arzberg D 52 C2
Arzignano I 71 C6
Arzila P 92 A2
Arzl im Pitztal A 71 A5
Arzúa E 86 B2
As B 49 B6
Aš CZ 52 C2
Ås N 35 C2
Åsa S 40 B2
Asaa DK 38 B3
Aşağıçiğil TR 119 D6
Ašanja SRB 85 B5
Åsarna S 115 E11
Åsarøy N 33 C3
Åsarp S 40 A3
Asasp F 76 C2
Åsbro S 37 C2
Åsby S 40 B2
Åsby S 40 B5
Asbygri IS 111 A9
Ascain F 76 C1
Ascea I 106 A2
Ascha D 62 A3
Aschach an der Donau
A 63 B5
Aschaffenburg D 51 D5
Aschbach Markt A 63 B5
Ascheberg
Nordrhein-Westfalen
D 50 B3
Schleswig-Holstein D 44 A2
Aschendorf D 43 B4
Aschersleben D 52 B1
Asciano I 81 C5
Ascó E 90 B3
Asco F 102 A2
Áscoli Piceno I 82 D2
Áscoli Satriano I 104 B1
Ascona CH 70 B3
Ascot GB 31 C3
Ascoux F 58 B3
Åse N 112 C4
Åseda S 40 B5
Åsele S 115 C14
Åsen
N 114 D8
S 34 A5
Asendorf D 43 C6
Asenovgrad BG 11 E8
Åsensbruk S 35 D4
Åseral N 33 D4
Asfeld F 59 A5
Åsgårdstrand N 35 C2
Ásgarður IS 111 B1
Asgate CY 120 B2
Ash
Kent GB 31 C5
Surrey GB 31 C3
Åshammar S 36 B3
Ashbourne
GB 27 B4
IRL 21 A5
Ashburton GB 28 C4
Ashby-de-la-Zouch
GB 27 C4
Ashchurch GB 29 B5
Åsheim N 114 F8
Ashford GB 31 C4
Ashington GB 25 C6
Ashley GB 26 C3
Ashmyany BY 7 D8
Ashton Under Lyne
GB 26 B3
Ashwell GB 30 B3
Asiago I 71 C6
Asipovichy BY 7 E10
Aska FIN 113 E15
Askam-in-Furness
GB 26 A2
Askeaton IRL 20 B3
Asker N 34 C2
Askersund S 37 D1
Åskilje S 115 C14
Askim N 35 C3
Askland N 33 D5
Äsköping S 37 C3
Askvoll N 32 A2
Åsljunga S 41 C3
Asnæs DK 39 D4
As Neves E 87 B2
As Nogaís E 86 B3
Ásola I 71 C5
Asolo I 72 C1
Asos GR 116 D2
Asotthalom H 75 B4
Aspach A 63 B4
Aspang Markt A 64 C2
Aspariegos E 88 C1
Asparn an der Zaya A 64 B2
Aspatria GB 26 A2
Aspberg S 35 C5
Aspe E 101 A5
Aspet F 77 C3
Äspö S 41 C5
As Pontes de García
Rodríguez E 86 A3
Aspres-sur-Buëch F 79 B4
Aspsele S 115 D15
Assafora P 92 C1
Asse B 49 C5
Assebakte N 113 C14
Assel D 43 B6
Asselborn L 50 C1
Assémini I 110 C1
Assen NL 42 C3
Assenede B 49 B4
Assens
Aarhus Amt. DK 38 C3
Fyns Amt. DK 39 D2
Assesse B 49 C6
Assisi I 82 C1
Åsskard N 114 D5
Assling D 62 C3
Asso I 71 C4
Asson F 76 C2
Ássoro I 109 B3
Assumar P 92 B3
Åsta N 34 A3
Astaffort F 77 B3
Astakos GR 116 D3
Asten NL 50 B1
Asti I 80 B2
Astipalea GR 119 F1
Astorga E 86 B4
Åstorp S 41 C2
Åsträsk S 115 C16
Astudillo E 88 B2
Asuni I 110 C1
Asványráró H 64 C3
Aszód H 65 C5
Aszófő H 74 B2
Atabey TR 119 E5
Atalaia P 92 B3
Atalandi GR 116 D4
Atalho P 92 C2
Átány H 65 C6
Atanzón E 95 B3
Ataquines E 94 A2
Atarfe E 100 B2
Atça TR 119 E3
Ateca E 89 C5
A Teixeira E 87 B3
Atella I 104 C1
Atessa I 103 A7
Ath B 49 C4
Athboy IRL 19 C5
Athea IRL 20 B2
Athenry IRL 20 A3
Athens = Athina GR 117 E5
Atherstone GB 27 C4
Athienou CY 120 A2
Athies F 59 A3
Athies-sous-Laon F 59 A4
Athina = Athens GR 117 E5
Athleague IRL 20 A3
Athlone IRL 21 A4
Athna CY 120 A2
Athy IRL 21 B5
Atienza E 95 A4
Atina I 103 B6
Atkár H 65 C5
Atlantı TR 119 D7
Atna N 114 F7
Åtorp S 35 C6
Åtrå N 32 C5
Ätran S 40 B2
Atri I 103 A6
Atripalda I 103 C7
Atsiki GR 116 C7
Attendorn D 50 B3
Attichy F 59 A4
Attigliano I 102 A5
Attigny F 59 A5
Attleborough GB 30 B5
Åtvidaberg S 37 D2
Atzendorf D 52 B1
Au
Steiermark A 63 C6
Vorarlberg A 71 A4
Bayern D 62 B2
Bayern D 62 C2
Aub D 61 A6
Aubagne F 79 C4
Aubange B 60 A1
Aubel B 50 C1
Aubenas F 78 B3
Aubenton F 59 A5
Auberive F 59 C6
Aubeterre-sur-Dronne
F 67 C5
Aubiet F 77 C3
Aubigné F 67 B4
Aubigny F 66 B3
Aubigny-au-Bac F 49 C4
Aubigny-en-Artois F 48 C3
Aubigny-sur-Nère F 68 A2
Aubin F 77 B5
Aubonne CH 69 B6
Aubrac F 78 B1
Aubusson F 68 C2
Auch F 77 C3
Auchencairn GB 25 D4
Auchinleck GB 24 C3
Auchterarder GB 25 B4
Auchtermuchty GB 25 B4
Auchtertyre GB 22 D3
Auchy-au-Bois F 48 C3
Audenge F 76 B1
Auderville F 57 A4
Audierne F 56 B1
Audincourt F 70 A1
Audlem GB 26 C3
Audruicq F 48 C3
Audun-le-Roman F 60 A1
Audun-le-Tiche F 60 A1
Aue
Nordrhein-Westfalen
D 50 B4
Sachsen D 52 C2
Auerbach
Bayern D 62 A2
Sachsen D 52 C2
Auffach A 72 A2
Augher GB 19 B4
Aughnacloy GB 19 B5
Aughrim IRL 21 B5
Augignac F 67 C5
Augsburg D 62 B1
Augusta I 109 B4
Augusten-borg DK 39 E2
Augustfehn D 43 B4
Augustów PL 6 E7
Aukrug D 44 A1
Auktsjaur S 115 B16
Auldearn GB 23 D5
Aulendorf D 61 C5
Auletta I 103 C8
Aulla I 81 B3
Aullène F 102 B2
Aulnay F 67 B4
Aulnoye-Aymeries F 49 C4
Ault F 48 C2
Aultbea GB 22 D3
Aulum DK 39 C1
Aulus-les-Bains F 77 D4
Auma D 52 C1
Aumale F 58 A2
Aumetz F 60 A1
Aumont-Aubrac F 78 B2
Aunay-en-Bazois F 68 A3
Aunay-sur-Odon F 57 A5
Aune N 115 C10
Auneau F 58 B2
Auneuil F 58 A2
Auning DK 39 C3
Aunsetra N 115 C9
Aups F 79 C5
Aura D 51 C5
Auray F 56 C3
Aurdal N 32 B6
Aure N 114 D5
Aurich D 43 B4
Aurignac F 77 C3
Aurillac F 77 B5
Auriol F 79 C4
Auritz-Burguette E 76 D1
Aurlandsvangen N 32 B4
Auronzo di Cadore I 72 B2
Auros F 76 B2
Auroux F 78 B2
Aurskog N 34 C3
Aursmoen N 34 C3
Ausónia I 103 B6
Ausservillgraton A 72 B2
Austad N 33 D4
Austbygda N 32 B5
Aústis I 110 B2
Austmarka N 34 B4
Austre Moland N 33 D5
Austre Vikebygd N 33 C2
Austrheim N 32 B1
Auterive F 77 C4
Autheuil-Authouillet
F 58 A2
Authon F 79 B5
Authon-du-Perche F 58 B1
Autol E 89 B5
Autreville F 60 B1
Autrey-lès-Gray F 69 A5
Autun F 69 B4
Auty-le-Châtel F 58 C3
Auvelais B 49 C5
Auvillar F 77 B3
Auxerre F 59 C4
Auxi-le-Château F 48 C3
Auxon F 59 B4
Auxonne F 69 A5
Auxy F 69 B4
Auzances F 68 B2
Auzon F 68 C3
Ağva TR 118 A4
Availles-Limouzine F 67 B5
Avaldsnes N 33 C2
Avallon F 68 A3
Avantas GR 116 B7
Avaviken S 115 B15
Avebury GB 29 B6
A Veiga E 87 B3
Aveiras de Cima P 92 B2
Aveiro P 92 A2
Avelgem B 49 C4
Avellino I 103 C7
Avenches CH 70 B2
A-Ver-o-Mar P 87 C2
Aversa I 103 C7
Avesnes-le-Comte F 48 C3
Avesnes-sur-Helpe F 49 C4
Avesta S 36 B3
Avetrana I 105 C3
Avezzano I 103 A6
Avià E 91 A4
Aviano I 72 B2
Aviemore GB 23 D5
Avigliana I 80 A1
Avigliano I 104 C1
Avignon F 78 C3
Ávila E 94 B2
Avilés E 88 A1
Avilley F 69 A6
Avintes P 87 C2
Avinyo E 91 B4
Àvio I 71 C5
Avioth F 59 A6
Avis P 92 B3
Avize F 59 B5
Avlonari GR 116 D6
Ávola I 109 C4
Avon F 58 B3
Avonmouth GB 29 B5
Avord F 68 A2
Avranches F 57 B4
Avril F 60 A1
Avrillé F 67 A4
Avtovac BIH 84 C3
Awans B 49 C6
Axams A 71 A6
Axat F 77 D5
Axbridge GB 29 B5
Axel NL 49 B4
Ax-les-Thermes F 77 D4
Axmarby S 36 B4
Axmarsbruk S 36 A4
Axminster GB 29 C4
Axvall S 35 D5
Ay F 59 A5
Aya E 89 A4
Ayamonte E 98 B3
Ayancık TR 16 A7
Ayaş TR 118 B7
Aydın TR 119 E2
Ayelo de Malferit E 96 C2
Ayer CH 70 B2
Ayerbe E 90 A2
Ayette F 48 C3
Ayia Napa CY 120 B2
Ayia Phyla CY 120 B2
Áyios Amvrósios
CY 120 A2
Áyios Seryios CY 120 A2
Áyios Theodhoros
CY 120 A3
Aykirikçi TR 118 C5
Aylesbury GB 31 C3
Ayllón E 89 C3
Aylsham GB 30 B5
Ayna E 101 A3
Ayódar E 96 B2
Ayora E 96 B1
Ayr GB 24 C3
Ayrancı TR 16 C6
Ayrancılar TR 119 D2
Ayron F 67 B5
Aysgarth GB 27 A4
Ayton GB 25 C5
Aytos BG 11 E9
Ayvacık TR 118 C1
Ayvalık TR 118 C1
Aywaille B 49 C6
Azaila E 90 B2
Azambuja P 92 B2
Azambujeira P 92 B2
Azanja SRB 85 B5
Azannes-et-Soumazannes
F 60 A1
Azanúy-Alins E 90 B3
Azaruja P 92 C3
Azay-le-Ferron F 67 B6
Azay-le-Rideau F 67 A5
Azcoitia E 89 A4
Azé F 69 B4
Azeiteiros P 92 B3
Azenhas do Mar P 92 C1
Azinhaga P 92 B2
Azinhal P 98 B3
Azinheira dos Bairros
P 98 A2
Aznalcázar E 99 B4
Aznalcóllar E 99 B4
Azóia P 92 B2
Azpeitia E 89 A4
Azuaga E 99 A5
Azuara E 90 B2
Azuqueca de Henares
E 95 B3
Azur F 76 C1
Azzano Décimo I 72 C2

B

Baad A 71 A5
Baamonde E 86 A3
Baar CH 70 A3
Bağarasi TR 119 E2
Baarle-Nassau B 49 B5
Baarn NL 49 A6
Babadağ TR 119 E3
Babadag RO 11 D10
Babaeski TR 118 A2
Babayevo RUS 7 B13
Babenhausen
Bayern D 61 B6
Hessen D 51 D4
Babiak PL 54 A3
Babice PL 55 C4
Babigoszcz PL 45 B6
Babimost PL 53 A5
Babina Greda HR 84 A3
Babócsa H 74 B2
Bábolma H 64 C3
Baborów PL 54 C2
Baboszewo PL 47 C6
Babót H 64 C3
Babruysk BY 7 E10
Babsk PL 55 B5
Bac GB 22 C2
Bač
MNE 85 D5
SRB 75 C4
Bacares E 101 B3
Bacău RO 11 C9
Baccarat F 60 B2
Bacharach D 50 C3
Bačina SRB 85 C6
Backa S 36 B2
Bačka Palanka SRB 75 C4
Backaryd S 41 C5
Bačka Topola SRB 75 C4
Backe S 115 D13
Bäckebo S 40 C6
Bäckefors S 35 D4
Bäckhammar S 35 C6
Bački Breg SRB 75 C3
Bački-Brestovac SRB 75 C4
Bački Monoštor SRB 75 C3
Bački Petrovac SRB 75 C4
Bački Sokolac SRB 75 C4
Backnang D 61 B5
Bačko Gradište SRB 75 C5
Bačko Novo Selo
SRB 75 C4
Bačko Petrovo Selo
SRB 75 C5
Bácoli I 103 C7
Bacqueville-en-Caux
F 58 A2
Bácsalmás H 75 B4
Bácsbokod H 75 B4
Bad Abbach D 62 B3
Badacsonytomaj H 74 B2
Bad Aibling D 62 C3
Badajoz E 93 C4
Badalona E 91 B5
Badalucco I 80 C1
Bad Aussee A 63 C4
Bad Bederkesa D 43 B5
Bad Bentheim D 50 A3
Bad Bergzabern D 60 A3
Bad Berka D 52 C1
Bad Berleburg D 51 B4
Bad Berneck D 52 C1
Bad Bevensen D 44 B2
Bad Bibra D 52 B1
Bad Birnbach D 62 B4
Bad Blankenburg D 52 C1
Bad Bleiberg A 72 B3
Bad Brambach D 52 C2
Bad Bramstedt D 44 B1
Bad Breisig D 50 C3
Bad Brückenau D 51 C5
Bad Buchau D 61 B5
Bad Camberg D 50 C4
Badderen N 113 C11
Bad Doberan D 44 A3
Bad Driburg D 51 B5
Bad Düben D 52 B2
Bad Dürkheim D 61 A4
Bad Dürrenberg D 52 B2
Bad Dürrheim D 61 B4
Bad Elster D 52 C2
Bad Ems D 50 C3
Baden
A 64 B2
CH 70 A3
Bádenas E 90 B1
Baden-Baden D 61 B4
Bad Endorf D 62 C3
Badenweiler D 60 C3
Baderna HR 72 C3
Bad Essen D 50 A4
Bad Fischau A 64 C2
Bad Frankenhausen
D 52 B1
Bad Freienwalde D 45 C6
Bad Friedrichshall D 61 A5
Bad Füssing D 63 B4
Bad Gandersheim D 51 B6
Bad Gastein A 72 A3
Bad Gleichenberg A 73 B5
Bad Goisern A 63 C4
Bad Gottleuba D 53 C3
Bad Grund D 51 B6
Bad Hall A 63 B5
Bad Harzburg D 51 B6
Bad Herrenalb D 61 B4
Bad Hersfeld D 51 C5
Bad Hofgastein A 72 A3
Bad Homburg D 51 C4
Bad Honnef D 50 C3
Bad Hönningen D 50 C3
Badia Calavena I 71 C6
Badia Polésine I 81 A5
Badia Pratáglia I 81 C5
Badia Tedalda I 82 C1
Bad Iburg D 50 A4
Bad Innerlaterns A 71 A4
Bad Ischl A 63 C4
Bad Karlshafen D 51 B5
Bad Kemmeriboden
CH 70 B2
Bądki PL 47 B4
Bad Kissingen D 51 C6
Bad Kleinen D 44 B3
Bad Kohlgrub D 62 C2
Bad König D 61 A5
Bad Königshofen D 51 C6
Bad Köstritz D 52 C2
Badkowo PL 47 C4
Bad Kreuzen A 63 B5

Bad Kreuznach D 60 A3
Bad Krozingen D 60 C2
Bad Laasphe D 51 C4
Bad Langensalza D ..51 B6
Bad Lausick D 52 B2
Bad Lauterberg D 51 B6
Bad Leonfelden A 63 B5
Bad Liebenwerda D ..52 B3
Bad Liebenzell D 61 B4
Bad Lippspringe D ..51 B4
Badljevina HR 74 C2
Bad Meinberg D 51 B4
Bad Mergentheim D ..61 A5
Bad Mitterndorf A 72 A3
Bad Münder D 51 A5
Bad Münstereifel D ..50 C2
Bad Muskau D 53 B4
Bad Nauheim D 51 C4
Bad Nenndorf D 43 C6
Bad Neuenahr-Ahrweiler
  D 50 C3
Bad Neustadt D 51 C6
Bad Oeynhausen D ..51 A4
Badolato I 106 C3
Badolatosa E 100 B1
Bad Oldesloe D 44 B2
Badonviller F 60 B2
Bad Orb D 51 C5
Badovinci SRB 85 B4
Bad Peterstal D 61 B4
Bad Pyrmont D 51 B5
Bad Radkersburg A ..73 B5
Bad Ragaz CH 71 B4
Bad Rappenau D 61 A5
Bad Reichenhall D ..62 C3
Bad Saarow-Pieskow
  D 53 A4
Bad Sachsa D 51 B6
Bad Säckingen D 70 A2
Bad Salzdetfurth D ..51 A6
Bad Salzig D 50 C3
Bad Salzuflen D 51 A4
Bad Salzungen D 51 C6
Bad Sankt Leonhard
  A 73 B4
Bad Sassendorf D 50 B4
Bad Schandau D 53 C4
Bad Schmiedeberg D 52 B2
Bad Schönborn D 61 A4
Bad Schussenried D ..61 B5
Bad Schwalbach D ..50 C4
Bad Schwartau D 44 B2
Bad Segeberg D 44 B2
Bad Soden D 51 C4
Bad Soden-Salmünster
  D 51 C5
Bad Sooden-Allendorf
  D 51 B5
Bad Sulza D 52 B1
Bad Sülze D 45 A4
Bad Tatzmannsdorf A 73 A6
Bad Tennstedt D 51 B6
Bad Tölz D 62 C2
Badules E 90 B1
Bad Urach D 61 B5
Bad Vellach A 73 B4
Bad Vilbel D 51 C4
Bad Vöslau A 64 C2
Bad Waldsee D 61 C5
Bad Wiessee D 62 C2
Bad Wildungen D 51 B5
Bad Wilsnack D 44 C3
Bad Windsheim D 61 A6
Bad Wörishofen D ..62 B1
Bad Wurzach D 61 C5
Bad Zwesten D 51 B5
Bad Zwischenahn D ..43 B5
Baells E 90 B3
Baena E 100 B1
Baesweiler D 50 C2
Baeza E 100 B2
Baflo NL 42 B3
Bafra TR 16 A7
Baga E 91 A4
Bagaladi I 106 C2
Bagenkop DK 39 E3
Baggetorp S 37 C3
Bagh á Chaisteil GB ..22 E1
Bagheria I 108 A2
Bagn N 32 B6
Bagnacavallo I 81 B5
Bagnà i 102 A1
Bagnara Cálabra I ..106 C2
Bagnasco I 80 B2
Bagnères-de-Bigorre
  F 76 C3
Bagnères-de-Luchon
  F 77 D3
Bagni del Másino I ..71 B4
Bagni di Lucca I 81 B4
Bagni di Rabbi I 71 B5
Bagni di Tívoli I 102 B5
Bagno di Romagna I ..81 C5
Bagnoles-de-l'Orne F 57 B5
Bagnoli dei Trigno I ..103 B7
Bagnoli di Sopra I ..72 C1
Bagnoli Irpino I 103 C8
Bagnolo Mella I 71 C5
Bagnols-en-Forêt F ..79 C5
Bagnols-sur-Cèze F ..78 B3
Bagnorégio I 102 A5
Bagolino I 71 C5
Bagrationovsk RUS ..47 A6
Bagrdan SRB 85 B6
Baguena E 95 A5
Bahabón de Esgueva
  E 88 C3
Bahillo E 88 B2
Báia delle Zágare I ..104 B2
Báia Domízia I 103 B6
Baia Mare RO 11 C7
Baiano I 103 C7
Baião P 87 C2
Baiersbronn D 61 B4
Baiersdorf D 62 A2
Baignes-Ste Radegonde
  F 67 C4
Baigneux-les-Juifs F ..59 C5
Baildon GB 27 B4
Bailén E 100 A2
Baile, F 100 A2
Bailieborough IRL 19 C5
Bailleul F 48 C3
Baillonville B 49 C6
Bailó E 90 A2
Bain-de-Bretagne F ..57 C4
Bains F 78 A2
Bains-les-Bains F 60 B2
Baindt GB 27 B4
Baio E 86 A2
Baiona E 87 B2
Bais F 57 B5
Baiuca P 92 A3
Baja H 75 B3
Bajánsenye H 73 B6
Bajina Bašta SRB 85 C4
Bajmok SRB 75 C4
Bajna H 65 C4
Bajovo Polje MNE 84 C3
Bajram Curri AL 105 A6
Bajša SRB 75 C4
Bajzë AL 105 A5
Bak H 74 B1
Bakar HR 73 C4
Bakewell GB 27 B4
Bakhmach UA 7 F12
Bakio E 89 A4
Bakka N 32 C4
Bakkafjörður IS 111 A11
Bakkagerði IS 111 B12
Bække DK 39 D2
Bakonybél H 74 A2
Bakonycsernye H 74 A3
Bakonyjákó H 74 A2
Bakonyszentkirály H .74 A2

Bakonyszombathely
  H 74 A2
Bakov nad Jizerou
  CZ 53 C4
Bąkowiec PL 55 B6
Baks H 75 B5
Baksa H 74 C3
Bakum D 43 C5
Bala GB 26 C2
Bâlâ TR 16 B6
Balaguer E 90 B3
Balassagyarmat H 65 B5
Balástya H 75 B5
Balatonakali H 74 B2
Balatonalmádi H 74 A3
Balatonboglár H 74 B2
Balatonbozsok H 74 B3
Balatonederics H 74 B2
Balatonfenyves H 74 B2
Balatonföldvár H 74 B2
Balatonfüred H 74 B2
Balatonfüzfö H 74 A3
Balatonkenese H 74 A3
Balatonkiliti H 74 B3
Balatonlelle H 74 B2
Balatonszabadi H 74 B3
Balatonszemes H 74 B2
Balatonszentgyörgy
  H 74 B2
Balazote E 101 A3
Balbeggio I 25 B4
Balbigny F 69 C4
Balboa E 86 B4
Balbriggan IRL 19 C5
Balçova TR 119 D2
Baldock GB 31 C3
Bale HR 82 A2
Baleira E 86 A3
Baleizao P 98 A3
Balen B 49 B6
Balerma E 100 C3
Balestrand N 32 A3
Balestrate I 108 A2
Balfour GB 23 B6
Bălgarevo B 11 E10
Bălgarovo I 41 C5
Bălgari BG 11 E9
Balıkesir TR 118 C2
Balıklıçeşme TR 118 B2
Bälinge S 36 C4
Bälinge D 61 B4
Balingsta S 36 C4
Balintore GB 23 D5
Balizac F 76 B2
Baljevac SRB 85 C5
Balk NL 42 C2
Balkbrug NL 42 C3
Balla IRL 18 C2
Ballachulish GB 24 B2
Ballaghaderreen IRL ..18 C3
Ballancourt-sur-Essonne
  F 58 B3
Ballantrae GB 24 C3
Ballao I 110 C2
Ballasalla GB 26 A1
Ballater GB 23 D5
Ballen DK 39 D3
Ballenstedt D 52 B1
Balleroy F 57 A5
Ballerup DK 41 D2
Ballesteros de Calatrava
  E 100 A2
Balli TR 118 B2
Ballina IRL 18 B2
Ballinalack IRL 19 C4
Ballinamore IRL 19 B4
Ballinascarty IRL 20 C3
Ballinasloe IRL 20 A3
Ballindine IRL 18 C3
Balling DK 38 C1
Ballingarry
  Limerick IRL 20 B3
  Tipperary IRL 21 B4
Ballingeary IRL 20 C2
Ballinhassig IRL 20 C3
Ballinluig GB 25 B4
Ballino I 71 C5
Ballinrobe IRL 18 C2
Ballinskelligs IRL 20 C1
Ballinspittle IRL 20 C3
Ballintra IRL 18 B3
Ballivor IRL 21 A5
Balloball GB 90 B3
Ballon
  F 58 B1
  IRL 21 B5
Ballószög H 75 B4
Ballsh AL 105 C5
Ballstad N 112 D2
Ballybay IRL 19 B5
Ballybofey IRL 19 B4
Ballybunion IRL 20 B2
Ballycanew IRL 21 B5
Ballycarry GB 19 B6
Ballycastle
  GB 19 A5
  IRL 18 B2
Ballyclare GB 19 B6
Ballyconneely IRL 18 C1
Ballycotton IRL 20 C3
Ballycroy IRL 18 B2
Ballydehob IRL 20 C2
Ballyferriter IRL 20 B1
Ballygawley GB 19 B4
Ballygowan GB 19 B6
Ballyhaunis IRL 18 C3
Ballyheige IRL 20 B2
Ballyjamesduff IRL 19 C4
Ballylanders IRL 20 B3
Ballylynan IRL 21 B4
Ballymahon IRL 21 A4
Ballymena GB 19 B5
Ballymoe IRL 18 C3
Ballymoney GB 19 A5
Ballymore IRL 21 A4
Ballymote IRL 18 B3
Ballynacorra IRL 20 C3
Ballynagore IRL 21 A4
Ballynahinch GB 19 B6
Ballynure GB 19 B6
Ballyragget IRL 21 B4
Ballysadare IRL 18 B3
Ballyshannon IRL 18 B3
Ballyvaughan IRL 20 A2
Ballyvourney IRL 20 C2
Ballywalter GB 19 B6
Balmaclellan GB 24 C3
Balmaseda E 89 A3
Balmazújváros H 75 A6
Balme I 70 C2
Balmedie GB 23 D6
Balmuccia I 70 C3
Balna-paligh GB 23 D4
Balotaszállás H 75 B4
Balsa E 87 C3
Balsareny E 91 B4
Balsorano-Nuovo I ..103 B6
Balta UA 11 B10
Baltanás E 88 C2
Baltar E 87 C3
Baltasound GB 22 A8
Bălti MD 11 C9
Baltimore IRL 20 D2
Baltinglass IRL 21 B5
Baltiysk RUS 47 A5
Baltów PL 55 B6
Balugães P 87 C2
Bælum DK 38 C3
Balve D 50 B3
Balvi LV 7 C9
Balvicar GB 24 B2
Balya TR 118 C2
Balzo I 82 D2
Bamberg D 62 A1
Bamburgh GB 25 C6
Banatska Palanka
  SRB 85 B6

Banatski Brestovac
  SRB 85 B5
Banatski Despotovac
  SRB 75 C5
Banatski Dvor SRB ..75 C5
Banatsko-Karlovac
  SRB 85 A6
Banatsko Arandjelovo
  SRB 75 B5
Banatsko-Novo Selo
  SRB 85 B5
Banaz TR 118 D4
Banbridge GB 19 B6
Banbury GB 30 B2
Banchory GB 23 D6
Bande
  B 49 C6
  E 87 B3
Bandholm DK 39 E4
Bandırma TR 118 B3
Bandol F 79 C4
Bandon IRL 20 C3
Bañeres E 96 C2
Banff GB 23 D6
Bangor
  F 66 A1
  Down GB 19 B6
  Gwynedd GB 26 B1
  IRL 18 B2
Bangsund N 114 C8
Banie PL 45 B6
Banja PL 85 C4
Banja Koviljača SRB ..85 B4
Banjaloka SLO 73 C4
Banja Luka BIH 84 B2
Banjani SRB 85 B4
Banja Vručica BIH 84 B2
Banje KOS 85 D5
Banjska KOS 85 D5
Banka SK 64 B3
Bankekind S 37 D2
Bankend GB 25 C4
Bankeryd S 40 B4
Bankfoot GB 25 B4
Bankso RO 116 A5
Bannalec F 56 C2
Bannes F 59 B4
Bannockburn GB 25 B4
Bañobárez E 87 D4
Bañon E 90 C1
Baños E 93 A5
Baños de Gigonza E ..99 C5
Baños de la Encina
  E 100 A2
Baños de Molgas E ..87 B3
Baños de Rio Tobia
  E 89 B4
Baños de Valdearados
  E 89 C3
Bánov CZ 64 B3
Banova Jaruga HR 74 C1
Bánovce nad Bebravou
  SK 64 B4
Banovići BIH 84 B3
Banovići Selo BIH 84 B3
Bánréve H 65 B6
Bansin D 45 B6
Banská Belá SK 65 B4
Banská Bystrica SK ..65 B5
Banská Štiavnica SK ..65 B4
Banstead GB 31 C3
Banteer IRL 20 B3
Bantheville F 59 A6
Bantry IRL 20 C2
Banyalbufar E 97 B2
Banyoles E 91 A5
Banyuls-sur-Mer F 91 A6
Bapaume F 48 C3
Bar
  MNE 105 A5
  UA 11 B9
Barabhas GB 22 C2
Baracaldo E 89 A4
Baracs H 74 B3
Baracska H 74 A3
Barahona E 89 C4
Barajas de Melo E 95 B4
Barakaldo E 89 A4
Baralla E 86 B3
Barañain E 76 D1
Baranavichy BY 7 E9
Báránd H 75 A6
Baranda SRB 85 B5
Baranello I 103 B7
Baranów Sandomierski
  PL 55 C6
Baraqueville F 77 B5
Barásoain E 89 B5
Barbacena P 92 C3
Barbadás E 87 B3
Barbadillo E 94 B1
Barbadillo de Herreros
  E 89 B3
Barbadillo del Mercado
  E 89 B3
Barbadillo del Pez E ..89 B3
Barban HR 82 A3
Barbarano Vicento I ..71 C6
Barbariga HR 82 B2
Barbaros TR 118 B2
Barbastro E 90 A3
Barbate E 99 C5
Barbatona E 95 A4
Barbâtre F 66 B2
Barbazan F 77 C3
Barbeitos E 86 A3
Barbentane F 78 C3
Barberino di Mugello
  I 81 B5
Barbezieux-St Hilaire
  F 67 C4
Barbonne-Fayel F 59 B4
Barbotan-les-Thermes
  F 76 C2
Barby D 52 B1
Bárcabo E 90 A3
Barca de Alva P 87 C4
Barcarrota E 93 C4
Barcellona-Pozzo di Gotto
  I 109 A4
Barcelona E 91 B5
Barcelonette F 79 B5
Barcelos P 87 C2
Bárcena del Monasterio
  E 86 A4
Barcena de Pie de
  Concha E 88 A2
Barchfeld D 51 C6
Barcin PL 46 C3
Barcino PL 46 A2
Bárcis I 72 B2
Barco P 92 A3
Barcones E 89 C4
Barcs H 74 C2
Barczewo PL 47 B6
Bardejov SK 10 B6
Bárdenas N 114 E4
Bardi I 81 B3
Bardney GB 27 B5
Bardo PL 54 C1
Bardolino I 71 C5
Bardonécchia I 79 A5
Bardoñóvo SK 65 B4
Barèges F 76 D3
Barenstein D 52 C3
Barentin F 58 A1
Barenton F 57 B5
Barevo BIH 84 B2
Barfleur F 57 A4
Barga I 81 B4
Bargas E 94 C2
Barge I 79 B6
Bargemon F 79 C5
Barghe I 71 C5
Bargoed GB 29 B4
Bargrennan GB 24 C3
Bargteheide D 44 B2
Barham GB 31 C5

Bari I 104 B2
Barič Draga HR 83 B4
Barie F 76 B2
Bari Sardo I 110 C2
Barisciano I 103 A6
Barjac F 78 B3
Barjols F 79 C4
Barjon F 59 C5
Bárkáber N 35 C2
Barkald N 114 F7
Barkowo
  Dolnoslaskie PL 54 B1
  Pomorskie PL 46 B3
Bârlad RO 11 C9
Barles F 79 B5
Barletta I 104 B2
Barlinek PL 45 C7
Barmouth GB 26 C1
Barmstedt D 43 B6
Barnard Castle GB 27 A4
Barnarp S 40 B4
Bärnau D 62 A3
Bärnbach A 73 A5
Barnenitz D 45 C4
Barnet GB 31 C3
Barnetby le Wold GB .27 B5
Barneveld NL 49 A6
Barneville-Carteret F ..57 A4
Barnoldswick GB 26 B3
Barnowko PL 45 C6
Barnsley GB 27 B4
Barnstädt D 52 B1
Barnstaple GB 28 B3
Barnstorf D 43 C5
Barntrup D 51 B5
Baron F 58 A3
Baronissi I 103 C7
Barösund FIN 36 B4
Barqueiro P 92 B2
Barquinha P 92 B2
Barr
  F 60 B3
  GB 24 C3
Barra
  P 92 A2
Barracas E 96 A2
Barraco E 94 B2
Barrado E 93 A5
Barranco do Velho P ..98 B3
Barrancos P 99 A4
Barranda E 101 A4
Barrax E 95 C4
Barrbaar I 62 B1
Barre-des-Cevennes
  F 78 B2
Barreiro P 92 C1
Barreiros E 86 A3
Barrême F 79 C5
Barret-le-Bas F 79 B4
Barrhead GB 24 C3
Barrhill GB 24 C3
Barrio de Nuesra Señora
  E 88 B1
Barrowford GB 26 B3
Barrow-in-Furness
  GB 26 A2
Barrow upon Humber
  GB 27 B5
Barruecopardo E 87 C4
Barruelo de Santullán
  E 88 B2
Barruera E 90 A3
Barry GB 29 B4
Bårse DK 39 D4
Barsinghausen D 51 A5
Barssel D 43 B4
Bartenheim F 60 C3
Barth D 45 A4
Bartholomä D 61 B5
Bartin TR 118 A7
Barton upon Humber
  GB 27 B5
Bartoszyce PL 47 A6
Bárúmini I 110 C1
Baruth D 52 A3
Barvaux B 49 C6
Barver D 43 C5
Barwałd PL 65 A5
Barwice PL 46 B2
Barysaw BY 7 D10
Barzana E 88 A1
Barzava RO 75 C6
Bárzio I 71 C4
Bas E 91 A5
Bašaïd SRB 75 C5
Basaluzzo I 80 B2
Basarabeasca MD 11 C10
Basauri E 89 A4
Baschi I 82 D1
Baschurch GB 26 C3
Basconcillos del Tozo
  E 88 B3
Bascones de Ojeda E 88 B2
Basécles B 49 C4
Basel CH 70 A2
Baselice I 103 B7
Basildon GB 31 C4
Basingstoke GB 31 C2
Baška
  CZ 65 A4
  HR 83 B3
Baška Voda HR 84 C1
Bäskskjö S 115 C14
Baslow GB 27 B4
Başmakçı TR 119 E5
Bąsobiory PL 46 B2
Bassacutena I 110 A2
Bassano del Grappa I 72 C1
Bassano Romano I ..102 A5
Bassecourt CH 70 A2
Bassella E 91 A4
Bassevuovdde N 113 E14
Bassou F 59 C4
Bassoues F 76 C3
Båstad S 40 C2
Bastardo I 82 D1
Bástelica F 102 A2
Bástelicaccia I 102 B1
Bastia
  F 102 A2
  I 82 C1
Bastogne B 50 C1
Baston GB 30 B3
Baśtraträsk S 115 C17
Bata H 74 B3
Batajnica SRB 85 B5
Batalha P 92 B2
Bátaszék H 74 B3
Batea E 90 B3
Batelov CZ 63 A6
Bath GB 29 B5
Bathgate GB 25 C4
Batida H 75 B5
Batignano I 81 D5
Batina HR 74 C3
Bátka SK 65 B6
Batković BIH 85 B4
Batlava KOS 85 D6
Batley GB 27 B4
Batnfjordsøra N 114 E4
Batočina SRB 85 B6
Bátonyterenye H 65 C5
Batrina HR 74 C2
Båtsfjord N 113 B18
Battaglia Terme I 72 C1
Bätterkinden CH 70 A2
Battice B 50 C1
Battipáglia I 103 C7
Battle GB 31 D4
Battonya H 75 B6
Batuša SRB 85 B6
Bátya H 75 B3
Bau I 110 C1
Baud F 56 C2
Baudour B 49 C4
Baugé F 67 A4
Baugy F 68 A2
Bauma CH 70 A3
Baume-les-Dames F ..60 A2
Baumholder D 60 A3

Baunatal D 51 B5
Baunei I 110 B2
Bauska LV 6 C8
Bautzen D 53 B4
Bavanište SRB 85 B5
Bavay F 49 C4
Bavilliers F 60 C2
Bavorov CZ 63 A5
Bawdsey GB 31 B5
Bawinkel D 43 C4
Bawtry GB 27 B4
Bayat TR 118 D5
Bayel F 59 B5
Bayeux F 57 A5
Bayındır TR 119 D2
Bayon F 60 B2
Bayonne F 76 C1
Bayons F 79 B5
Bayramiç TR 118 C1
Bayreuth D 52 D1
Bayrischzell D 62 C3
Baza E 101 B3
Bazas F 76 B2
Bazoches-les-Gallerandes
  F 58 B3
Bazoches-sur-Hoëne
  F 58 B1
Bazzano I 81 B5
Beaconsfield GB 31 C3
Beade E 87 B2
Beadnell GB 25 C6
Beaminster GB 29 C5
Bearsden GB 24 C3
Beas E 99 B4
Beasain E 89 A4
Beas de Segura E 100 A3
Beattock GB 25 C4
Beaubery F 69 B4
Beaucaire F 78 C3
Beaufort
  F 69 C6
  IRL 20 B2
Beaufort-en-Vallée F ..67 A4
Beaugency F 58 C2
Beaujeu
  Alpes-de-Haute-
  Provence F 79 B5
  Rhône F 69 B4
Beaulac F 76 B2
Beaulieu
  F 66 B3
  GB 31 D2
Beaulieu-sous-la-Roche
  F 66 B3
Beaulieu-sur-Dordogne
  F 77 B4
Beaulieu-sur-Mer F 80 C1
Beaulon F 68 B3
Beauly GB 23 D4
Beaumaris GB 26 B1
Beaumesnil F 58 A1
Beaumont
  B 49 C5
  F 77 B3
Beaumont-de-Lomagne
  F 77 C3
Beaumont-du-Gâtinais
  F 58 B3
Beaumont-en-Argonne
  F 59 A6
Beaumont-Hague F 57 A4
Beaumont-la-Ronce F 58 C1
Beaumont-le-Roger F 58 A1
Beaumont-sur-Oise F 58 A3
Beaumont-sur-Sarthe
  F 58 B1
Beaune F 69 A4
Beaune-la-Rolande F 58 B3
Beaupréau F 66 A3
Beaurainville F 48 C2
Beaurepaire F 69 C5
Beaurepaire-en-Bresse
  F 69 B5
Beaurières F 79 B4
Beauvais F 58 A3
Beauval F 48 C3
Beauville F 77 B3
Beauvoir-sur-Mer F 66 B2
Beauvoir-sur-Niort F ..67 B4
Beba Veche RO 75 B5
Bebertal D 52 A1
Bebington GB 26 B2
Bebra D 51 C5
Bebrina HR 84 A2
Beccles GB 30 B5
Becedas E 93 A5
Beceite E 90 C3
Bečej SRB 75 C5
Becerreá E 86 B3
Becerril de Campos E 88 B2
Bécherel F 57 B4
Bechhofen D 61 A6
Bechyně CZ 63 A5
Bečići MNE 105 A4
Becilla de Valderaduey
  E 88 B1
Beckfoot GB 25 D4
Beckingham GB 27 B5
Beckum D 50 B4
Beco P 92 B2
Bécon-les-Granits F ..66 A4
Bečov nad Teplou CZ 52 C2
Becsehely H 74 B1
Bedale GB 27 A4
Bedames E 89 A3
Bédar E 101 B4
Bédarieux F 78 C2
Bédarrides F 78 B3
Beddgelert GB 26 B1
Beddingstrand S 41 D3
Bédée F 57 B4
Bedegkér H 74 B3
Beden TR 119 F7
Bedford GB 30 B3
Bedlington GB 25 C6
Bedlno PL 55 A4
Bedmar E 100 B2
Bédoin F 79 B4
Bedónia I 81 B3
Bedretto CH 70 B3
Bedsted DK 38 C1
Bedum NL 42 B3
Bedwas GB 29 B4
Bedworth GB 30 B2
Będzin PL 55 C4
Beek en Donk NL 49 B6
Beelen D 50 B4
Beelitz D 52 A2
Beer GB 29 C5
Beerfelde D 53 A4
Beerfelden D 61 A4
Beernem B 49 B4
Beeskow D 53 A4
Beetsterzwaag NL 42 B3
Beetzendorf D 44 C3
Beflelay CH 70 A2
Begaljica SRB 85 B5
Bégard F 56 B2
Begejci SRB 75 C5
Begijar E 100 B2
Begijnendijk B 49 B5
Begndal N 34 B1
Begonte E 86 A3
Begues E 91 B5
Beguildy GB 26 C2
Begur E 91 B6
Beho B 50 C1
Behringen D 51 B6
Beilen NL 42 C3
Beilngries D 62 A2
Beine-Nauroy F 59 A5
Beinwil CH 70 A3
Beiseförth D 51 B5
Beith GB 24 C3
Beitostølen N 32 A5
Beiuş RO 11 D7

Beja P 98 A3
Béjar E 93 A5
Bekçiler TR 119 F4
Békés H 75 B6
Békéscsaba H 75 B6
Bekilli TR 119 D4
Bekkarfjord N 113 B16
Bela
  CZ 62 A3
  SK 65 A4
Bélâbre F 67 B6
Bela Crkva SRB 85 B6
Belalcázar E 93 C5
Bélánad Radbuzou
  CZ 62 A3
Belanovica SRB 85 B5
Belančica HR 74 C3
Belascoáin E 89 B5
Bélavár H 74 B2
Belazaima do Chão P 92 A2
Belbroughton GB 26 C3
Belcaire F 77 D4
Bełchatów PL 55 B4
Belchite E 90 B2
Belcoo GB 19 B4
Belecke D 51 B4
Beled H 74 A2
Belej HR 83 B3
Beleño E 88 A1
Bélesta F 77 D4
Belev RUS 7 E14
Belfast GB 19 B6
Belford GB 25 C6
Belgern D 52 B3
Belgioioso I 71 C4
Belgodère F 102 A2
Belgooly IRL 20 C3
Belgorod RUS 7 F14
Belgrade = Beograd
  SRB 85 B5
Beli Manastir HR 74 C3
Belin-Béliet F 76 B2
Belinchón E 95 B3
Belišće HR 74 C3
Bělkovice-Lašťany
  CZ 64 A3
Bella I 104 C1
Bellac F 67 B6
Bellágio I 71 C4
Bellananagh IRL 19 C4
Bellano I 71 B4
Bellária I 82 B1
Bellavary IRL 18 C2
Belleau F 59 A4
Belleek GB 18 B3
Bellegarde
  Gard F 78 C3
  Loiret F 58 C3
Bellegarde-en-Diois F 79 B4
Bellegarde-en-Marche
  F 68 C2
Bellegarde-sur-Valserine
  F 69 B5
Belle-Isle-en-Terre F ..56 B2
Bellême F 58 B1
Bellenaves F 68 B3
Bellentre F 70 C1
Belleu F 59 A4
Bellevesvre F 69 B5
Belleville F 69 B4
Belleville-sur-Vie F 66 B3
Bellevue-la-Montagne
  F 68 C3
Belley F 69 C5
Bellheim D 61 A4
Bellingham GB 25 C5
Bellingwolde NL 43 B4
Bellinzago Novarese
  I 70 C3
Bellinzona CH 70 B4
Bell-lloc d'Urgell E 90 B3
Bello E 95 B5
Bellpuig d'Urgell E 91 B4
Bellreguart E 96 C2
Bellsbank GB 24 C3
Belltall E 91 B4
Belluno I 72 B2
Bellver de Cerdanya
  E 91 A4
Bellvis E 90 B3
Bélmez E 93 C5
Belmez de la Moraleda
  E 100 B2
Belmonte
  Asturias E 86 A4
  Cuenca E 95 C4
Belmonte P 92 A3
Belmonte de San José
  E 90 C2
Belmonte de Tajo E ..95 B3
Belmont-sur-Rance F 78 C1
Belmullet IRL 18 B1
Belobresca RO 85 B6
Beloeil B 49 C4
Belogradchik BG 11 E7
Belokorovichi UA 11 A10
Belorado E 89 B3
Belotić SRB 85 B4
Bělotín CZ 64 A3
Belozërsk RUS 7 B14
Belp CH 70 B2
Belpasso I 109 B3
Belpech F 77 C4
Belper GB 27 B4
Belsay GB 25 C6
Belsh AL 105 C5
Belsk Duzy PL 55 B5
Beltra SK 64 A3
Beltinci SLO 73 B6
Belturbet IRL 19 B4
Belušić SRB 85 C6
Belvedere Marittimo
  I 106 B2
Belver de Cinca E 90 B3
Belver de los Montes
  E 88 C1
Belvès F 77 B3
Belvezet F 78 B2
Belvis de la Jara E 94 C2
Belvis de Monroy E ..93 B5
Belyy RUS 7 D12
Belz
  F 56 C2
  UA 11 A8
Belžec PL 11 A8
Belzig D 52 A2
Bembibre E 86 B4
Bembridge GB 31 D2
Bemmel NL 50 B1
Bemposta
  Bragança P 87 C4
  Santarém P 92 B2
Benabarre E 90 A3
Benacazón E 99 B4
Benaguasil E 96 B2
Benahadux E 101 C3
Benalmádena E 100 C1
Benalúa de Guadix E 100 B2
Benalúa de las Villas
  E 100 B2
Benalup E 99 C5
Benamargosa E 100 C1
Benamaurel E 101 B3
Benameji E 100 B1
Benamocarra E 100 C1
Benaocaz E 99 C5
Benaoján E 99 C5
Benarrabá E 99 C5
Benasque E 90 A3
Benátky nad Jizerou
  CZ 53 C4
Benavente
  E 88 B1
  P 92 C2
Benavides de Órbigo
  E 88 B1
Benavila P 92 B3

Bendorf D 50 C3
Benedikt SLO 73 B5
Benejama E 101 A5
Benejúzar E 101 A5
Benešov CZ 63 A5
Benestroff F 60 B2
Benet F 67 B4
Bene Vagienna I 80 B1
Bénévent-l'Abbaye F 67 B6
Benevento I 103 B7
Benfeld F 60 B3
Benfica P 92 B2
Bengtsfors S 35 C4
Bengtsheden S 36 B2
Beničanci HR 74 C3
Benicarló E 90 C3
Benicássim E 96 A3
Benidorm E 96 C2
Benifaió E 96 B2
Beniganim E 96 C2
Benington GB 27 B6
Benisa E 96 C3
Benkovac HR 83 B4
Benllech GB 26 B1
Benlloch E 90 C3
Benneckenstein D 51 B6
Bénodet F 56 C1
Benquerencia de la
  Serena E 93 C5
Bensafrim P 98 B2
Bensdorf D 44 C4
Benshausen D 51 C6
Bensheim D 61 A4
Bentley GB 31 C2
Bentwisch D 44 A4
Beočin SRB 75 C4
Beograd = Belgrade
  SRB 85 B5
Beragh GB 19 B4
Berane MNE 85 D4
Beranga E 89 A3
Berat AL 105 C5
Bérat F 77 C4
Beratzhausen D 62 A2
Bérbaltavár H 74 A1
Berbegal E 90 B2
Berbenno di Valtellina
  I 71 B4
Berberana E 89 B3
Berbesti RO 11 D7
Berceto I 81 B3
Berchem B 49 C4
Berching D 62 A2
Berchtesgaden D 62 C4
Bérchules E 100 C2
Bercianos de Aliste E 87 C4
Berck F 48 C2
Berclaire d'Urgell E ..90 B3
Berdoias E 86 A1
Berducedo E 86 A4
Berdún E 90 A2
Berdychiv UA 11 B10
Bere Alston GB 28 C3
Bereguardo I 70 C4
Berehommen N 33 C4
Berehove UA 11 B7
Berek BIH 84 A2
Beremend H 74 C3
Bere Regis GB 29 C5
Berestechko UA 11 A8
Berettyóújfalu H 10 C6
Berezhany UA 11 B8
Berezina UA 11 C11
Berezna UA 7 F11
Berg
  Baden-Württemberg
  D 61 B4
  Bayern D 62 B2
  Brandenburg D 45 C4
  Mecklenburg-
  Vorpommern D 45 A5
  Niedersachsen D 45 A5
  Niedersachsen D 44 A2
  NL 42 C1
  S 37 B5
Berga
  Brandenburg D 45 C4
  Sachsen-Anhalt D 51 B7
  Thüringen D 52 C2
  E 91 A4
  S 40 B6
Bergama TR 118 C2
Bérgamo I 71 C4
Bergara E 89 A4
Bergby S 36 B4
Berge
  Brandenburg D 45 C4
  Niedersachsen D 43 C4
  Telemark N 33 C5
  Telemark N 33 C5
  E 90 C2
Bergeijk NL 49 B6
Bergen
  Mecklenburg-
  Vorpommern D 45 A5
  Niedersachsen D 43 C6
  Niedersachsen D 44 C2
  NL 42 C1
  N 32 B2
Bergen op Zoom NL ..49 B5
Bergerac F 77 B3
Bergères-lès-Vertus F 59 B5
Bergheim D 50 C2
Berghem NL 50 B1
Bergisch Gladbach D 50 C3
Bergkamen D 50 B3
Bergkvara S 41 C6
Berglern D 62 B2
Bergnäset S ....115 ?
Bergneustadt D 50 B3
Bergs slussar S 37 D2
Bergshamra S 37 C5
Bergsjö S 115 F14
Bergtheim D 61 A6
Bergues F 48 B3
Bergum NL 42 B2
Bergün Bravuogn CH 71 B4
Bergwitz D 52 B2
Berhida H 74 A3
Beringel P 98 A3
Beringen B 49 B6
Berja E 100 C3
Berkåk N 114 E7
Berkeley GB 29 B5
Berkenthin D 44 B2
Berkhamsted GB 31 C3
Berkheim D 61 B5
Berkhof D 43 C6
Berković BIH 84 C3
Berkovitsa BG 11 E7
Berlanga E 93 C5
Berlanga de Duero E 89 C4
Berlevåg N 113 B17
Berlikum NL 42 B2
Berlin D 45 C5
Berlstedt D 52 B1
Bermeo E 89 A4
Bermillo de Sayago E 87 C4
Bern CH 70 B2
Bernalda I 104 C2
Bernardos E 94 A2
Bernartice
  Jihočeský CZ 63 A5
  Vychodočeský CZ ..53 C5
Bernau
  Baden-Württemberg
  D 61 C4
  Bayern D 62 C3
  Brandenburg D 45 C5
Bernaville F 48 C3
Bernay F 58 A1
Bernburg D 52 B1
Berndorf A 64 C2
Berne D 43 B5
Bernecebaráti H 65 B4
Bernhardsthal A 64 B2
Bernkastel-Kues D 60 A3
Bernolakovo SK 64 B3
Bernsdorf D 53 B4
Bernstadt D 53 B4
Bernstein A 73 A6
Bernués E 90 A2
Beromünster CH 70 A3
Berovo MK 116 A4

Berre-l'Etang F 79 C4
Berriedale GB 23 C5
Berriew GB 26 C2
Berrocal E 99 B4
Bersenbrück D 43 C4
Berthelming F 60 B2
Bertincourt F 48 C3
Bertinoro I 82 B1
Bertogne B 49 C6
Bertrix B 59 A6
Berufjörður IS 111 C11
Berville-sur-Mer F 58 A1
Berwick-upon-Tweed
  GB 25 C5
Berzasca RO 10 D6
Berzence H 74 B2
Berzocana E 93 B5
Besalú E 91 A5
Besançon F 69 A6
Besenfeld D 61 B4
Besenyötelek H 65 C6
Besenyszög H 75 A5
Beshenkovichi BY 7 D10
Besigheim D 61 B5
Bēšiny CZ 63 A4
Beška SRB 75 C5
Beşkonak TR 119 E6
Besle F 57 C4
Besnyö H 74 A3
Bessais-le-Fromental
  F 68 B2
Bessan F 78 C2
Besse-en-Chandesse
  F 68 C2
Bessèges F 78 B2
Bessé-sur-Braye F 58 C1
Bessines-sur-Gartempe
  F 67 B6
Best NL 49 B6
Bestorp S 37 D2
Betanzos E 86 A2
Betelu E 76 C1
Bétera E 96 B2
Beteta E 95 B5
Béthenville F 59 A5
Bethesda GB 26 B1
Béthune F 48 C3
Beton-Bazoches F 59 B4
Bettembourg L 60 A2
Bettna S 37 D3
Béttola I 80 B3
Bettona I 82 C1
Bettyhill GB 23 C4
Betws-y-Coed GB 26 B2
Betxi E 96 B2
Betzdorf D 50 C3
Beuil F 79 B5
Beulah GB 29 A4
Beuzeville F 58 A1
Bevagna I 82 D1
Bevensen D 44 B2
Beveren B 49 B5
Beverley GB 27 B5
Beverstedt D 43 B5
Beverungen D 51 B5
Beverwijk NL 42 C1
Bex CH 70 B2
Bexhill GB 31 D4
Beyazköy TR 118 A2
Beychevelle F 76 A2
Beydağ TR 119 D3
Beyeğaç TR 119 E3
Beykoz TR 118 A4
Beynat F 68 C1
Beyoğlu TR 118 A4
Beypazarı TR 118 B6
Beyşehir TR 119 E6
Bezas E 95 B5
Bezau A 71 A4
Bezdan SRB 75 C3
Bèze F 69 A5
Bezenet F 68 B2
Bezhetsk RUS 7 C14
Béziers F 78 C2
Bezzecca I 71 C5
Biadki PL 54 B2
Biała
  Łódzkie PL 55 B4
  Opolskie PL 54 C2
Białaczów PL 55 B5
Biała Podlaska PL 6 E7
Biała Rawska PL 55 B5
Białobłoty PL 54 A2
Białobrzegi PL 55 B5
Białogard PL 46 B1
Biały Bór PL 46 B2
Białystok PL 6 E7
Biancavilla I 109 B3
Bianco I 106 C3
Biandrate I 70 C3
Biar E 101 A5
Biarritz F 76 C1
Bias F 76 B1
Biasca CH 70 B3
Biatorbágy H 74 A3
Bibbiena I 81 C5
Bibbona I 81 C4
Biberach
  Baden-Württemberg
  D 61 B4
  Baden-Württemberg
  D 61 B5
Bibinje HR 83 B4
Bibione I 72 C3
Biblis D 61 A4
Bibury GB 29 B6
Biccari I 103 B8
Bicester GB 31 C2
Bichl D 62 C2
Bichlbach A 71 A5
Bicorp E 96 B2
Bicos P 98 B2
Bicske H 74 A3
Bidache F 76 C1
Bidart F 76 C1
Biddinghuizen NL 42 C2
Biddulph GB 26 B3
Bideford GB 28 B3
Bidford-on-Avon GB ..29 A6
Bidjovagge N 113 C11
Bie S 37 C3
Bieber D 51 C5
Biebersdorf D 53 A3
Biedenkopf D 51 C4
Biel E 90 A2
Biel/Bienne CH 70 A2
Bielany Wrocławskie
  PL 54 B1
Bielawa PL 54 C1
Bielawy PL 55 A4
Bielefeld D 51 A4
Biella I 70 C3
Bielsa E 90 A3
Bielsk PL 47 C5
Bielsko-Biała PL 65 A5
Bielsk Podlaski PL 6 E7
Bienenbüttel D 44 B2
Bieniów PL 53 B5
Bienservida E 101 A3
Bienvenida E 93 C4
Bierné F 57 C5
Biersted DK 38 B3
Bierun PL 55 C4
Bierutów PL 54 B2
Bierwart B 49 C6
Bierzwina PL 46 B1
Bierzwnik PL 46 B1
Biesenthal D 45 C5

Biesiekierz PL . 46 A2
Bietigheim-Bissingen
D . 61 B5
Bièvre B . 49 D6
Bieżuń PL . 47 C5
Biga TR . 118 B2
Bigadiç TR . 118 C3
Biganos F . 76 B2
Bigas P . 87 C2
Bigastro E . 101 A5
Bigbury GB . 28 C4
Biggar GB . 25 C4
Biggin Hill GB . 31 C4
Biggleswade GB . 30 B3
Bignasco CH . 70 B3
Biguglia F . 102 A2
Bihać BIH . 83 B4
Biharnagybajom H . 75 A6
Bijela MNE . 105 A4
Bijeljani BIH . 84 C3
Bijeljina BIH . 84 B4
Bijelo Polje MNE . 85 C4
Bijuesca E . 89 C5
Bij, HR . 83 B4
Bila Tserkva UA . 11 B11
Bilbao E . 89 A4
Bilcza PL . 55 C5
Bildudalur IS . 111 B2
Bileća BIH . 84 D3
Bilecik TR . 118 B4
Bilgoraj PL . 11 A7
Bilhorod-Dnistrovskyy
UA . 11 C11
Bilina CZ . 53 C3
Bilje HR . 74 C3
Billdal S . 38 B4
Billerbeck D . 50 B3
Billericay GB . 31 C4
Billesholm S . 41 C2
Billingborough GB . 30 B3
Billinge S . 41 D3
Billingham GB . 27 A4
Billinghay GB . 27 B5
Billingsfors S . 35 D4
Billingshurst GB . 31 C3
Billom F . 68 C3
Billsta S . 115 D15
Billund DK . 39 D2
Bilopillya UA . 7 F13
Bilsten D . 50 B4
Bilthoven NL . 49 A6
Bilto N . 112 C10
Bilzen B . 49 C6
Biña SK . 65 C4
Binaced I . 90 B3
Binasco I . 71 C4
Binbrook GB . 27 B5
Binche B . 49 C5
Bindlach D . 52 D1
Bindslev DK . 38 B3
Binefar E . 90 B3
Bingen D . 50 D3
Bingham GB . 27 C5
Bingley GB . 27 B4
Bingsjö S . 36 A2
Binic F . 56 B3
Binz D . 45 A5
Bioče MNE . 105 A5
Biograd na Moru HR . 83 C4
Bionaz I . 70 C2
Bioska SRB . 85 C4
Birda RO . 75 C6
Birdlip GB . 29 B5
Biri N . 34 B2
Birkeland N . 33 D5
Birkenfeld
Baden-Württemberg
D . 61 B4
Rheinland-Pfalz D . 60 A3
Birkenhead GB . 26 B2
Birkerød DK . 41 D2
Birkfeld A . 73 A5
Birkirkara M . 107 C5
Birmingham GB . 27 C4
Birr IRL . 21 A4
Birresborn D . 50 C2
Birstein D . 51 C5
Birżai LT . 6 C8
Birżebbuġia M . 107 C5
Biscaria I . 103 B8
Biscarrosse F . 76 B1
Biscarrosse Plage F . 76 B1
Biscarrués E . 90 A2
Biséglie I . 104 B2
Bischheim F . 60 B3
Bischofsheim D . 51 C5
Bischofshofen A . 72 A3
Bischofswerda D . 53 B4
Bischofswiesen D . 62 C3
Bischofszell CH . 71 A4
Bischwiller F . 60 B3
Bisenti I . 103 A6
Bishop Auckland GB . 27 A4
Bishop's Castle GB . 26 C2
Bishops Lydeard GB . 29 B4
Bishop's Stortford
GB . 31 C4
Bishop's Waltham
GB . 31 D2
Bisignano I . 106 B3
Bisingen D . 61 B4
Biskupice-Oławskie
PL . 54 B2
Biskupiec PL . 47 B5
Bismark D . 44 C3
Bismo N . 114 F5
Bispgården S . 115 D13
Bispingen D . 44 B1
Bissen L . 60 A2
Bissendorf D . 50 A4
Bisserup DK . 39 D4
Bistango I . 80 B2
Bistarac Donje BIH . 84 B3
Bistrica
BIH . 84 B2
MNE . 85 C4
SRB . 85 B5
Bistrica ob Sotli SLO . 73 B5
Bistrița RO . 11 C8
Bisztynek PL . 47 A6
Bitburg D . 50 D2
Bitche F . 60 A3
Bitetto I . 104 B2
Bitola MK . 116 A3
Bitonto I . 104 B2
Bitschwiller F . 60 C3
Bitterfeld D . 52 B2
Bitti I . 110 B2
Biville-sur-Mer F . 48 D2
Bivona I . 108 B2
Biwer L . 60 A2
Bizeljsko SLO . 73 B5
Bizovac HR . 74 C3
Bjåen N . 33 C4
Bjärnum S . 41 C3
Bjärred S . 41 D3
Bjästa S . 115 D15
Bjelland
Vest-Agder N . 33 D3
Vest-Agder N . 33 D4
Bjelovar HR . 74 C1
Bjerkreim N . 33 D3
Bjerkvik N . 112 D6
Bjerreby DK . 39 E3
Bjerregrav DK . 38 C2
Bjerringbro DK . 38 C2
Bjøberg N . 32 B5
Bjølànes N . 112 F3
Bjørbo S . 36 B1
Bjordal N . 32 A2
Bjørg IS . 111 B8
Bjørkåsen N . 112 D5
Björke
Gävleborg S . 36 B4

Björke continued
Östergötland S . 37 D2
Björkelangen N . 34 C3
Björketorp S . 40 B2
Björkholmen S . 112 F8
Björkliden S . 112 D7
Björklinge S . 36 B4
Björkö S . 36 C6
Björkö S . 38 B4
Björköby S . 40 B4
Björkvik S . 37 D3
Björn N . 115 A9
Björn S . 115 D15
Björneborg S . 35 C6
Björnerod S . 35 C3
Bjørnevatn N . 113 C18
Bjørnlunda S . 37 C4
Bjørnstad N . 113 C19
Björsäter S . 37 D3
Bjurberget S . 34 B4
Bjurholm S . 115 D16
Bjursås S . 36 B2
Bjurtjärn S . 35 C6
Bjuv S . 41 C2
Blace SRB . 85 C6
Blachownia PL . 54 C3
Blackburn GB . 26 B3
Blackpool GB . 26 B2
Blackstad S . 40 B6
Blackwater IRL . 21 B5
Blackwaterfoot GB . 24 C2
Blacy F . 59 B5
Bladåker S . 36 B5
Blaenau Ffestiniog
GB . 26 C2
Blaenavon GB . 29 B4
Blaengarw GB . 29 B4
Blagaj
BIH . 83 A5
BIH . 84 C2
Blagdon GB . 29 B5
Blagnac F . 77 C4
Blagoevgrad BG . 11 E7
Blaichach D . 61 C6
Blain F . 66 A3
Blainville-sur-l'Eau F . 60 B2
Blair Atholl GB . 25 B4
Blairgowrie GB . 25 B4
Blajan F . 77 C3
Blakeney GB . 29 B5
Blakstad N . 33 D5
Blâmont F . 60 B2
Blanca E . 101 A4
Blancos E . 87 C3
Blandford Forum GB . 29 C5
Blanes E . 91 B5
Blangy-sur-Bresle F . 58 A2
Blankaholm S . 40 B6
Blankenberge B . 49 B4
Blankenburg D . 51 B6
Blankenfelde D . 45 C5
Blankenhain D . 52 C1
Blankenheim D . 50 C2
Blanquefort F . 76 B2
Blansko CZ . 64 A2
Blanzac F . 67 C5
Blanzy F . 69 B4
Blaricum NL . 49 A6
Blarney IRL . 20 C3
Blascomillán E . 94 B1
Blascosancho E . 94 B2
Blatná CZ . 63 A4
Blatnica SK . 65 B4
Blatnice CZ . 64 B3
Blatníky BIH . 84 B2
Blato HR . 84 D1
Blato na Cetini HR . 84 C1
Blatten CH . 70 B2
Blattnicksele S . 115 B14
Blatzheim D . 50 C2
Blaubeuren D . 61 B5
Blaufelden D . 61 A5
Blaustein D . 61 B5
Blaydon GB . 25 D6
Blaye F . 76 A2
Blaye-les-Mines F . 77 B5
Blázquez E . 93 C5
Bleckede D . 44 B2
Blecua E . 90 A2
Bled SLO . 73 B4
Bleialf D . 73 B4
Bleicherode D . 51 B6
Bleik N . 112 C4
Bleikvassli N . 115 B10
Bléneau F . 59 C3
Blentarp S . 41 D3
Blera I . 102 A5
Blérancourt F . 59 A4
Bléré F . 67 A5
Blesle F . 68 C3
Blessington IRL . 21 A5
Blet F . 68 B2
Bletchley GB . 31 C3
Bletterans F . 69 B5
Blidö S . 37 C5
Blidsberg S . 40 B3
Blieskastel D . 60 A3
Bligny-sur-Ouche F . 69 A4
Blikstorp S . 35 D6
Blinisht AL . 105 B6
Blinja HR . 73 C6
Blitzingen CH . 70 B3
Bliżanówek PL . 54 B3
Bliżyn PL . 55 B5
Blois F . 58 C2
Blokhus DK . 38 B2
Blokzijl NL . 42 C2
Blomberg D . 51 B5
Blomskog S . 35 C4
Blomvåg N . 32 B1
Blönduós IS . 111 B5
Blonie PL . 55 A5
Blonville-sur-Mer F . 57 A6
Blötberget S . 36 B2
Blovice CZ . 63 A4
Bloxham GB . 31 B2
Blšany CZ . 52 C3
Bludov CZ . 64 A2
Blumberg D . 61 C4
Blyberg S . 36 A6
Blyth
Northumberland
GB . 25 C6
Nottinghamshire GB . 27 B4
Blyth Bridge GB . 25 C4
Blythburgh GB . 30 B5
Blythe Bridge GB . 26 B3
Bø
Nordland N . 112 D3
Telemark N . 33 C6
Boal E . 86 A4
Boan MNE . 85 D4
Boario Terme I . 71 C5
Boat of Garten GB . 23 D5
Boa Vista P . 92 B2
Boğazkale TR . 16 A7
Boğazlıyan TR . 16 B7
Boba H . 74 A2
Bobadilla
Logroño E . 89 B4
Málaga E . 100 B1
Bobadilla del Campo
E . 94 A1
Bobadilla del Monte
E . 94 B3
Bóbbio I . 80 B3
Bóbbio Péllice I . 79 B6
Bobigny F . 58 B3
Bobingen D . 62 B1
Böblingen D . 61 B5
Bobolice PL . 46 B2
Boboras E . 87 B2
Boboshevo BG . 16 D5
Bobowa PL . 11 B4
Bobrová CZ . 64 A2
Bobrovitsa UA . 11 A11
Bobrówko PL . 46 C1

Boca de Huérgano E . 88 B2
Bocairent E . 96 C2
Bočar SRB . 75 C5
Bocchigliero I . 106 B3
Boceguillas E . 89 C3
Bochnia PL . 55 D5
Bocholt
B . 49 B6
D . 50 B2
Bochov CZ . 52 C3
Bochum D . 50 B3
Bockara S . 40 B6
Bockenem D . 51 A6
Bockfliess A . 64 B2
Bockhorn D . 43 B5
Bočna SLO . 73 B4
Bocognano F . 102 A2
Boconád H . 65 C6
Bócsa H . 75 B4
Boda S . 36 A2
Böda S . 41 B7
Boda
Stockholm S . 36 B5
Värmland S . 35 C5
Västernorrland S . 115 E13
Bodafors S . 40 B4
Boda Glasbruk S . 40 C5
Bodajk H . 74 A3
Boddam
Aberdeenshire GB . 23 D7
Shetland GB . 22 B7
Boddin D . 44 B3
Bödefeld-Freiheit D . 51 B4
Boden S . 3 D24
Bodenmais D . 62 A4
Bodenteich D . 44 C2
Bodenwerder D . 51 B5
Bodiam GB . 31 C4
Bodinnick GB . 28 C3
Bodio CH . 70 B3
Bodjani SRB . 75 C4
Bodmin GB . 28 C3
Bodø N . 112 E3
Bodonal de la Sierra
E . 99 A4
Bodrum TR . 119 E2
Bodstedt D . 45 A4
Bodzanów PL . 47 C6
Bodzanów PL . 55 C6
Bodzechów PL . 55 C5
Bodzentyn PL . 55 C5
Boecillo E . 88 C2
Boëge F . 69 B6
Boën F . 68 C3
Bogács H . 65 C6
Bogadmindszent H . 74 C3
Bogajo E . 87 D4
Bogarra E . 101 A4
Bogarre E . 100 B2
Bogatić SRB . 85 B4
Bogatynia PL . 53 C5
Bogdaniec PL . 45 C7
Bogë AL . 105 A5
Boge S . 37 E5
Bgen
Nordland N . 112 D5
Nordland N . 112 E4
S . 34 B4
Bogense DK . 39 D3
Bogetići MNE . 84 D3
Bognanco Fonti I . 70 B3
Bognev N . 113 B11
Bognes N . 112 D5
Bogno CH . 70 B3
Bognor Regis GB . 31 D3
Bogoria PL . 55 C5
Bograngen S . 34 B4
Boguchwały PL . 47 B6
Bogumiłowice PL . 55 B4
Boguslav UA . 11 B11
Boguszów-Gorce PL . 53 C6
Bogutovac SRB . 85 C5
Bogyiszló H . 74 B3
Bohain-en-Vermandois
F . 49 D4
Böheimkirchen A . 64 B1
Bohinjska Bistrica
SLO . 72 B3
Böhlen D . 52 B2
Böhmenkirch D . 61 B5
Bohmte D . 43 C5
Bohonal de Ibor E . 93 B5
Böhönye H . 74 B2
Bohumín CZ . 64 A4
Boiro E . 86 B2
Bóixols E . 90 A3
Boizenburg D . 44 B2
Bojadła PL . 53 B5
Bojanie F . 70 C3
Bojano I . 103 B7
Bojanowo PL . 54 B1
Bøjden DK . 39 D3
Bojkovice CZ . 64 A3
Bojná SK . 64 B4
Bojnice SK . 65 B4
Boka SRB . 75 C5
Bököny H . 77 C6
Böklund DK . 43 A6
Bokod H . 74 A3
Boksitogorsk RUS . 7 B12
Bol HR . 83 C5

Bolaños de Calatrava
E . 100 A2
Bolayır TR . 118 B1
Bolbec F . 58 A1
Bölcske H . 75 B3
Bolderslev DK . 39 E2
Boldva H . 65 B6
Bolea E . 90 A2
Bolekhiv UA . 11 B7
Bolesławiec PL . 53 B5
Boleszkowice PL . 45 C6
Bolewice PL . 46 C2
Bólgheri I . 81 C4
Bolhrad UA . 11 D10
Boliden S . 3 D24
Bolimów PL . 55 A5
Boliqueime P . 98 B2
Boljevci SRB . 85 B5
Boljkovci SRB . 85 B5
Bolków PL . 53 C6
Bollebygd S . 40 B2
Bollène F . 78 B3
Bóllhag S . 95 B4
Bollstabruk S . 115 E14
Bollullos E . 99 B4
Bollullos par del Condado
E . 99 B4
Bologna I . 81 B5
Bologne F . 59 B6
Bolognetta I . 108 B2
Bolognola I . 82 D2
Bologoye RUS . 7 C13
Bolótana I . 110 B1
Bolsena I . 102 A4
Bolshaya Vradiyevka
UA . 11 C11
Bolsover GB . 27 B4
Bolstad S . 35 D4
Bolsward NL . 42 B2
Boltaña E . 90 A3
Boltenhagen D . 44 B3
Boltigen CH . 70 B2
Bolton GB . 26 B3
Bolu TR . 118 B6
Bolungarvik IS . 111 A2
Bolvadín TR . 118 D6
Bóly H . 74 C3
Bolzaneto I . 80 B2
Bolzano I . 71 B6
Bombarral P . 92 B1
Bömenzien D . 44 C3
Bomlitz D . 43 C6
Bømlo N . 33 C2
Bøn N . 34 B3

Bona F . 68 A3
Bonaduz CH . 71 B4
Bonanza E . 99 C4
Bonar E . 88 B1
Boñar E . 88 B1
Bonarbridge GB . 23 D4
Bonárcado I . 110 B1
Bonares E . 99 B4
Bonäs S . 36 A1
Bonassola I . 80 B3
Bonawe GB . 24 B2
Bondeno I . 81 B5
Bondorf D . 61 B4
Bondstorp S . 40 B3
Bönen D . 50 B3
Bones N . 112 D5
Bon-Encontre F . 77 B3
Bonefro I . 103 B7
Bo'ness GB . 25 B4
Bonete E . 101 A4
Bonifacio F . 102 B2
Bonigen CH . 70 B2
Bonin PL . 46 A2
Bonn D . 50 C3
Bonnánaro I . 110 B1
Bonnåsjøen N . 112 E4
Bonnat F . 68 B1
Bonndorf D . 61 C4
Bonnétable F . 58 B1
Bonnétage F . 70 A1
Bonneuil-les-Eaux F . 58 A3
Bonneuil-Matours F . 67 B5
Bonneval F . 58 B2
Bonneval-sur-Arc F . 70 C2
Bonneville F . 69 B6
Bonnières-sur-Seine
F . 58 A2
Bonnieux F . 79 C4
Bönnigheim D . 61 A5
Bonnyrigg GB . 25 C4
Bonny-sur-Loire F . 68 A2
Bono
E . 90 A3
I . 110 B2
Bonorva I . 110 B1
Bønsnes N . 34 B2
Bonyhád H . 74 B3
Boom B . 49 B5
Boos F . 58 A2
Boostedt D . 44 A2
Bootle
Cumbria GB . 26 A2
Merseyside GB . 26 B2
Bopfingen D . 61 B6
Boppard D . 50 C3
Boqueixón E . 86 B2
Bor
CZ . 62 A3
S . 40 B4
SRB . 11 D7
TR . 16 C7
Boran-sur-Oise F . 58 A3
Borås S . 40 B2
Borba P . 92 C3
Borobia I . 89 C5
Borča SRB . 85 B5
Borci BIH . 84 C3
Borculo NL . 50 A2
Bordány H . 75 B4
Bordeaux F . 76 B2
Bordeira P . 98 B2
Bordesholm D . 44 A2
Bordeyri IS . 111 B4
Bordighera I . 80 C1
Bording DK . 39 C2
Bordón E . 90 C2
Bore I . 81 B3
Borehamwood GB . 31 C3
Borek Strzeliński PL . 54 C2
Borek Wielkopolski
PL . 54 B2
Borello I . 82 B1
Borensberg S . 37 D2
Borgafjäll S . 115 C12
Borgarnes IS . 111 C4
Borgentreich D . 51 B5
Börger D . 43 C4
Borgerhout B . 49 B5
Borggård S . 37 D1
Borghetto di Vara I . 81 B3
Borghetto d'Arróscia
I . 80 B1
Borghetto Santo Spírito
I . 80 B2
Borgholm S . 41 C6
Borghorst D . 50 A3
Bórgia I . 106 C3
Borgloon B . 49 C6
Børglum DK . 38 B2
Borgo F . 102 A2
Borgo alla Collina I . 81 C5
Borgo a Mozzano I . 81 C4
Borgoforte I . 81 A4
Borgofranco d'Ivrea I . 70 C2
Borgomanero I . 70 C3
Borgomasino I . 70 C2
Borgonovo Val Tidone
I . 80 B3
Borgo Pace I . 82 C1
Borgorose I . 102 A6
Borgo San Dalmazzo
I . 80 B1
Borgo San Lorenzo I . 81 C5
Borgosésia I . 70 C3
Borgo Val di Taro I . 81 B3
Borgo Valsugana I . 71 B6
Borgo Vércelli I . 70 C3
Borgue GB . 24 D3
Borgund N . 32 A4
Borgvik S . 35 C4
Borisova RUS . 7 F14
Borja E . 89 C5
Bork D . 50 B3
Borken D . 50 B2
Borkenes N . 112 D5
Børkop DK . 39 D2
Borkow D . 44 B3
Borkowice PL . 55 B5
Borkowo PL . 47 C6
Borkum D . 42 B3
Borlänge S . 36 B2
Borlu TR . 118 D3
Bormes-les-Mimosas
F . 79 C5
Bórmio I . 71 B5
Bormujos E . 99 B4
Borna
D . 52 B2
NL . 50 A2
Borne Sulinowo PL . 46 B2
Bornheim D . 50 C2
Bornhöved D . 44 A2
Börnicke D . 45 C5
Bornos E . 99 C5
Borodino RUS . 7 D13
Borohrádek CZ . 53 C6
Boronów PL . 54 C3
Borota H . 75 B4
Boroughbridge GB . 27 A4
Borovany CZ . 63 B5
Borovichi RUS . 7 B12
Borovnica SLO . 73 C4
Borovo HR . 75 C4
Borovsk RUS . 7 D14
Borovy CZ . 63 A4
Borów PL . 54 C2
Borowa PL . 54 B2
Borowie PL . 55 B6
Borox E . 94 B3
Borrby S . 41 D4
Borre
DK . 41 E2
N . 35 C2
Borredà E . 91 A4
Borrenes E . 86 B4
Borriol E . 96 A2
Borris
DK . 39 D1
IRL . 21 B5
Borris-in-Ossory IRL . 21 A4
Borrisokane IRL . 20 B3

Borrisoleigh IRL . 21 B4
Borrowdale GB . 26 A2
Borrud N . 34 C4
Borsa RO . 11 C8
Borsdorf D . 52 B2
Børselv N . 113 B14
Borsfa H . 74 B1
Borský Mikuláš SK . 64 B3
Borsodivánka H . 65 C6
Borsodnádasd H . 65 B6
Börte N . 33 C4
Borth GB . 26 C1
Bort-les-Orgues F . 68 C2
Börtnan S . 115 E10
Børtnes N . 32 B6
Borup DK . 39 D4
Boryslav UA . 11 B7
Borysław UA . 11 A11
Boryszyn PL . 46 C1
Borzechów PL . 55 A5
Borzna UA . 7 F12
Borzonasca I . 80 B3
Borzyszkowy PL . 46 A3
Borzytuchom PL . 46 A3
Bosa I . 110 B1
Bosáca SK . 64 B3
Bosanci HR . 73 C5
Bosanska Dubica BIH . 74 C1
Bosanska Gradiška
BIH . 74 C2
Bosanska Kostajnica
BIH . 74 C1
Bosanska Krupa BIH . 83 B5
Bosanski Brod BIH . 84 A2
Bosanski Novi BIH . 83 A5
Bosanski Petrovac
BIH . 83 B5
Bosanski Šamac BIH . 84 A3
Bosansko Grahovo
BIH . 83 B5
Bosány SK . 64 B4
Bösárkány H . 64 C3
Bosau D . 44 A2
Bósca H . 75 B4
Boscastle GB . 28 C3
Bosco I . 80 B3
Bosco Chiesanuova I . 71 C6
Bösel D . 43 B4
Bösensell D . 43 B4
Bosham GB . 31 D3
Bösingfeld D . 51 A5
Bosjön S . 34 C5
Boskoop NL . 49 A5
Boskovice CZ . 64 A2
Bošnjaci HR . 84 A3
Bošnjane SRB . 85 C6
Bossàst E . 77 D3
Bossolasco I . 80 B2
Boštanj SLO . 73 B5
Boston GB . 27 C5
Bostrak N . 33 C5
Böszénfa H . 74 B2
Bot E . 90 B3
Botajica BIH . 84 B3
Bøte By DK . 44 A3
Bothel GB . 26 A2
Boticas P . 87 C3
Botilsäter S . 35 C5
Botngård N . 114 D6
Botoš SRB . 85 B5
Botoşani RO . 11 C9
Botricello I . 107 C3
Botsmark N . 3 D24
Bottendorf D . 51 B4
Botticino I . 71 C5
Bottnaryd S . 40 B3
Bottrop D . 50 B2
Botunje SRB . 85 B6
Bötzingen D . 60 B3
Bouaye F . 66 A3
Bouça P . 87 C3
Boucau F . 76 C1
Bouchain F . 49 C4
Bouchoir F . 58 A3
Boudreville F . 59 C5
Boudry CH . 70 B1
Bouesse F . 68 B1
Bouguenais F . 66 A3
Bouhy F . 68 A3
Bouillargues F . 78 C3
Bouillon B . 59 A6
Bouilly F . 59 B4
Bouin F . 66 B3
Boujailles F . 69 B6
Boulay-Moselle F . 60 A2
Boulazac F . 67 C5
Boule-d'Amont F . 91 A5
Bouligny F . 60 A1
Boulogne-sur-Gesse
F . 77 C3
Boulogne-sur-Mer F . 48 C2
Bouloire F . 58 C1
Boulzicourt F . 59 A5
Bourbon-Lancy F . 68 B3
Bourbon-l'Archambault
F . 68 B3
Bourbonne-les-Bains
F . 60 C1
Bourbourg F . 48 C3
Bourbriac F . 56 B2
Bourcefranc-le-Chapus
F . 66 C3
Bourdeaux F . 79 B4
Bourdeilles F . 67 C5
Bourg F . 76 A2
Bourg-Achard F . 58 A1
Bourganeuf F . 68 C1
Bourg-Argental F . 69 C4
Bourg-de-Péage F . 79 A4
Bourg-de-Thizy F . 69 B4
Bourg-de-Visa F . 77 B3
Bourg-en-Bresse F . 69 B5
Bourges F . 68 A2
Bourg-et-Comin F . 59 A4
Bourg-Lastic F . 68 C2
Bourg-Madame F . 91 A4
Bourgneuf-en-Retz F . 66 A3
Bourgogne F . 59 A5
Bourgoin-Jallieu F . 69 C5
Bourgueil F . 67 A5
Bourmont F . 60 B1
Bourne GB . 30 B3
Bournemouth GB . 29 C6
Bourneville F . 58 A1
Bournezeau F . 66 B3
Bourron-Marlotte F . 58 B3
Bourret F . 77 C4
Bourton-on-The-Water
GB . 29 B6
Boussac F . 68 B2
Boussens F . 77 C3
Boutersem B . 49 C5
Bouttencourt F . 48 D2
Bouvières F . 79 B4
Bouvron F . 66 A3
Bouxwiller F . 60 B3
Bouzas E . 87 B2
Bouzonville F . 60 A2
Bova I . 106 D2
Bovalino Marina I . 106 C3
Bovallstrand S . 35 D3
Bova Marina I . 106 D2
Bovec SLO . 72 B3
Bóveda E . 86 B3
Bóvegno I . 71 C5
Bovenau D . 44 A1
Bovenden D . 51 B5
Bøverdal N . 114 F5
Bøvlingbjerg DK . 38 C1
Bovolenta I . 72 C1
Bovolone I . 71 C6
Bowes GB . 27 A4
Bowmore GB . 24 C1

Bowness-on-Windermere
GB . 26 A3
Box GB . 29 B5
Boxberg
Baden-Württemberg
D . 61 A5
Sachsen D . 53 B4
Boxholm S . 37 D2
Boxmeer NL . 50 B1
Boxtel NL . 49 B6
Boyabat TR . 16 A7
Boyalıca TR . 118 B4
Boyle IRL . 18 C3
Boynton GB . 27 A5
Bozan TR . 118 C6
Bozava HR . 83 B3
Bozburun TR . 119 F3
Bozcaada TR . 118 C1
Bozdoğan TR . 119 E3
Bozel F . 70 C2
Bozouls F . 78 B1
Bozova TR . 119 E5
Bozüyük TR . 118 C5
Božice CZ . 64 B2
Bozkır TR . 119 E7
Bózzolo I . 81 A4
Bra I . 80 B1
Braás S . 40 B5
Brabrand DK . 39 C3
Bracadale GB . 22 D2
Bracciano I . 102 A5
Bracieux F . 67 A6
Bräcke S . 115 E12
Brackenheim D . 61 A5
Brackley GB . 31 B2
Bracklin IRL . 19 C5
Bracknell GB . 31 C3
Brackwede D . 51 B4
Braco GB . 25 B4
Brad RO . 11 C7
Bradford GB . 27 B4
Bradford on Avon GB . 29 B5
Bradina BIH . 84 C3
Brådland N . 33 D3
Brædstrup DK . 39 D2
Brae GB . 22 A7
Braemar GB . 23 D5
Braemore GB . 22 D3
Braga P . 87 C2
Bragança P . 87 C4
Brahestad FIN . 3 D26
Brăila RO . 11 D9
Braine F . 59 A4
Braine-le-Comte B . 49 C5
Braintree GB . 31 C4
Braives B . 49 C6
Brake D . 43 B5
Brakel
B . 49 C4
D . 51 B5
Bräkne-Hoby S . 41 C5
Brålanda S . 35 D4
Bralin PL . 54 B2
Brallo di Pregola I . 80 B3
Bramafan F . 79 C5
Bramberg am Wildkogel
A . 72 A2
Bramdrupdam DK . 39 D2
Bramming DK . 39 D1
Brampton GB . 25 D5
Bramsche D . 43 C4
Brancaleone Marina
I . 106 D3
Brancaster GB . 30 B4
Brand
Nieder Österreich A . 63 B6
Vorarlberg A . 71 A4
Brandbu N . 34 B2
Brande DK . 39 D2
Brande-Hornerkirchen
D . 43 B6
Brandenberg A . 72 A1
Brandenburg D . 45 C4
Brand-Erbisdorf D . 52 C3
Brandis D . 52 B2
Brandomil E . 86 A2
Brandon GB . 30 B4
Brandshagen D . 45 A5
Brandval N . 34 B4
Brandýs nad Labem
CZ . 53 C4
Branice CZ . 54 C2
Braničevo SRB . 85 B6
Braniewo PL . 47 A5
Branik SLO . 72 C3
Brankovina SRB . 85 B4
Branky CZ . 64 A3
Branne F . 76 B2
Brannenburg-Degerndorf
D . 62 C3
Brantôme F . 67 C5
Branzi I . 71 B4
Bras d'Asse F . 79 C5
Braskereidfoss N . 34 B3
Braslaw BY . 7 D9
Brașov RO . 11 D8
Brasparts F . 56 B1
Brassac F . 77 C5
Brassac-les-Mines F . 68 C3
Brasschaat B . 49 B5
Brastad S . 35 D3
Břasy CZ . 63 A4
Braszewice PL . 54 B3
Bratanj AL . 105 C5
Bratislava SK . 64 B3
Brattfors S . 35 C6
Brattvåg N . 114 E3
Bratunac BIH . 85 B4
Braubach D . 50 C3
Braunau A . 62 B4
Braunfels D . 51 C4
Braunlage D . 51 B6
Braunsbedra D . 52 B1
Braunschweig D . 51 A6
Bray IRL . 21 A5
Bray Dunes F . 48 B3
Bray-sur-Seine F . 59 B4
Bray-sur-Somme F . 48 D3
Brazatortas E . 100 A1
Brazey-en-Plaine F . 69 A5
Brbinj HR . 83 B4
Brčko BIH . 84 B3
Brdani SRB . 85 C5
Brdów PL . 47 C4
Brea de Tajo E . 95 B3
Brécey F . 57 B4
Brechen D . 50 C4
Brechin GB . 25 B5
Brecht B . 49 B5
Břeclav CZ . 64 B2
Brecon GB . 29 B4
Breda
E . 91 B5
NL . 49 B5
Bredaryd S . 40 B3
Bredbyn S . 115 D15
Breddin D . 44 C4
Bredebro DK . 39 E1
Bredelar D . 51 B4
Bredenfelde D . 45 B5
Bredsjö S . 36 C1
Bredstedt D . 43 A5
Bredsträsk S . 115 D15
Bredviken S . 115 A12
Bree B . 49 B6
Bregana HR . 73 C5
Breganze I . 72 C1
Bregenz A . 71 A4
Breginj SLO . 72 B3
Bregninge DK . 39 E3
Breguzzo I . 71 B5
Bréhal F . 57 B4
Brehna D . 52 B2
Breidenbach F . 60 A3
Breiðdalsvík IS . 111 C11
Breil-sur-Roya F . 80 C1
Breisach D . 60 B3
Breitenbach
CH . 70 A2

Breitenbach continued
D . 51 C5
Breitenberg D . 63 B4
Breitenfelde D . 44 B2
Breitengussbach D . 51 D6
Breivikbotn N . 113 B11
Brejning DK . 39 D2
Brekke N . 32 A2
Brekken N . 114 E8
Brekkestø N . 33 D5
Brekstad N . 114 D6
Breland N . 33 D4
Bremanger N . 114 F1
Bremen D . 43 B5
Bremerhaven D . 43 B5
Bremervörde D . 43 B6
Bremgarten CH . 70 A3
Bremsnes N . 114 D4
Brem-sur-Mer F . 66 B3
Brenderup DK . 39 D2
Brenes E . 99 B5
Brengova SLO . 73 B5
Brenna PL . 65 A4
Breno I . 71 C5
Brénod F . 69 B5
Brensbach D . 61 A4
Brentwood GB . 31 C4
Brescello I . 81 B4
Bréscia I . 71 C5
Breskens NL . 49 B4
Bresles F . 58 A3
Bresnica SRB . 85 C5
Bressana I . 80 B3
Bressanone I . 72 B1
Bressuire F . 67 B4
Brest
BY . 6 E7
F . 56 B1
HR . 72 C3
Brestač SRB . 85 B4
Brestanica SLO . 73 B5
Brestova HR . 82 A3
Brestovac HR . 74 C2
Brétigny-sur-Orge F . 58 B3
Bretten D . 61 A4
Bretteville-sur-Laize
F . 57 A5
Brettheim D . 61 A6
Breuil-Cervínia I . 70 C2
Breukelen NL . 49 A6
Brevik
N . 35 C1
Stockholm S . 37 C5
Västra Götaland S . 37 D1
Breza BIH . 84 B3
Brežice SLO . 73 C5
Breznica SLO . 73 B5
Breznica Našička HR . 74 C3
Březnice CZ . 63 A4
Brezno SK . 65 B5
Brezolles F . 58 B2
Březová nad Svitavou
CZ . 64 A2
Březovápod Bradlom
SK . 64 B3
Brezovica
SK . 65 A6
SLO . 73 B4
Brezovo Polje Selo
BIH . 84 B3
Brezovo BG . 11 E8
Briançon F . 79 B5
Brianconnet F . 79 C5
Briare F . 58 C3
Briatexte F . 77 C4
Briático I . 106 C2
Briaucourt F . 59 B6
Bribir HR . 73 C4
Bricquebec F . 57 A4
Bridgend
Argyll & Bute GB . 24 C1
Bridgend GB . 29 B4
Bridge of Cally GB . 25 B4
Bridge of Don GB . 23 D6
Bridge of Earn GB . 25 B4
Bridge of Orchy GB . 24 B3
Bridgnorth GB . 26 C3
Bridgwater GB . 29 B5
Bridlington GB . 27 A5
Bridport GB . 29 C5
Briec F . 56 B1
Brie-Comte-Robert F . 58 B3
Brienne-le-Château F . 59 B5
Brienon-sur-Armançon
F . 59 C4
Brienz CH . 70 B3
Brienza I . 104 C1
Briesen D . 45 C6
Brieskow Finkenheerd
D . 53 A4
Brietlingen D . 44 B2
Brieva de Cameros E . 89 B4
Briey F . 60 A1
Brig CH . 70 B3
Brigg GB . 27 B5
Brighouse GB . 27 B4
Brightlingsea GB . 31 C5
Brighton GB . 31 D3
Brignogan-Plage F . 56 B1
Brignoles F . 79 C5
Brigstock GB . 30 B3
Brihuega E . 95 B4
Brijuni HR . 82 B2
Brillon-en-Barrois F . 59 B6
Brilon D . 51 B4
Brimnes N . 32 B3
Brinches P . 98 A3
Bríndisi I . 105 C4
Brinje HR . 83 A4
Brinon-sur-Beuvron
F . 68 A3
Brinon-sur-Sauldre F . 68 A2
Brinyan GB . 23 B5
Brión E . 86 B2
Briones E . 89 B4
Brione F . 70 B3
Brionne F . 58 A1
Brioude F . 68 C3
Brioux-sur-Boutonne
F . 67 B4
Briouze F . 57 B5
Briscous F . 76 C1
Brisighella I . 81 B5
Brissac-Quincé F . 67 A4
Brissago CH . 70 B3
Bristol GB . 29 B5
Brive-la-Gaillarde F . 67 C6
Briviesca E . 89 B3
Brixham GB . 28 C4
Brixen im Thale A . 72 A2
Brixlegg A . 72 A1
Brka BIH . 84 B3
Brnaze HR . 83 C5
Brniště CZ . 53 C4
Brno CZ . 64 A2
Bro
S . 37 C4
Broadclyst GB . 29 C4
Broadford
GB . 22 D3
IRL . 20 B3
Broad Haven GB . 28 B2
Broadstairs GB . 31 C5
Broadstone GB . 29 C5
Broadway GB . 29 A6
Broager DK . 39 E2
Broaryd S . 40 B3
Broby S . 41 C4
Brobyværk DK . 39 D3
Broćanac BIH . 84 C2
Brocēni LV . 6 C7
Brock D . 50 A3
Brockel D . 43 B6
Brockenhurst GB . 31 D2
Brod
BIH . 84 D3
MK . 116 A3
Brodalen S . 35 D3
Brodarevo SRB . 85 C4
Broddbo S . 36 C3
Brodek u Přerova CZ . 64 A3
Broden-bach D . 50 C3
Brodick GB . 24 C2
Brodnica PL . 47 B5
Brodnica Graniczna
PL . 47 A4
Brody
Lubuskie PL . 53 B4
Lubuskie PL . 53 B5
Mazowieckie PL . 55 A5
UA . 11 A8
Broglie F . 58 B1
Brójce PL . 53 A5
Brokind S . 37 D2
Brolo I . 109 A3
Brome D . 44 C2
Bromley GB . 31 C4
Bromölla S . 41 C4
Bromont-Lamothe F . 68 C2
Brömsebro S . 41 C5
Bromsgrove GB . 29 A5
Bromyard GB . 29 A5
Bronchales E . 95 B5
Bronco E . 93 A4
Brønderslev DK . 38 B2
Broni I . 80 B3
Brønnøysund N . 114 B9
Brøns DK . 39 D1
Bronte I . 109 B3
Bronzani Mejdan BIH . 84 B1
Bronzolo I . 71 B6
Broons F . 57 B3
Broomhill GB . 25 C6
Broquies F . 78 B1
Brora GB . 23 C5
Brørup DK . 39 D2
Brösarp S . 41 D4
Brossac F . 67 C4
Brostrud N . 32 B5
Brotas P . 92 C2
Brötjärna S . 36 B2
Broto E . 90 A2
Brottby S . 37 C5
Brøttum N . 34 A2
Brou F . 58 B2
Brouage F . 66 C3
Brough GB . 26 A3
Broughshane GB . 19 B5
Broughton GB . 25 C4
Broughton-in-Furness
GB . 26 A2
Broumov CZ . 53 C6
Broût-Vernet F . 68 B3
Brouvelieures F . 60 B2
Brouwershaven NL . 49 B4
Brovary UA . 11 A11
Brovst DK . 38 B2
Brownhills GB . 27 C4
Brozas E . 93 B4
Brozzo I . 71 C5
Brtnice CZ . 63 A6
Brtonígla HR . 72 C3
Bruay-la-Buissière F . 48 C3
Bruchhausen-Vilsen
D . 43 C6
Bruchsal D . 61 A4
Bruck D . 62 A3
Brück D . 52 A2
Bruck an der
Grossglocknerstrasse
A . 72 A2
Bruck an der Leitha A . 64 B2
Bruck an der Mur A . 73 A5
Brückl A . 73 B4
Brue-Auriac F . 79 C4
Brüel D . 44 B3
Bruen CH . 70 B3
Bruère-Allichamps F . 68 B2
Bruff IRL . 20 B3
Bruflat N . 32 B6
Brugg CH . 70 A3
Brugge B . 49 B4
Brüggen D . 50 B2
Brühl D . 50 C2
Bruinisse NL . 49 B5
Brûlon F . 57 C5
Brumano I . 71 C4
Brumath F . 60 B3
Brummen NL . 50 A2
Brumov-Bylnice CZ . 64 A4
Brumunddal N . 34 B2
Brunau D . 44 C3
Brunehamel F . 59 A5
Brünen D . 50 B2
Brunete E . 94 B2
Brunflo S . 115 D11
Brunico I . 72 B1
Brunkeberg N . 33 C5
Brunn D . 45 B5
Brunnen CH . 70 B3
Brunsbüttel D . 43 B6
Brunssum NL . 50 C1
Bruntál CZ . 54 D2
Brus SRB . 85 C6
Brusand N . 33 D2
Brusasco I . 80 A2
Brusio CH . 71 B5
Brusno SK . 65 B5
Brusque F . 78 C1
Brussel = Bruxelles
B . 49 C5
Brusson I . 70 C2
Brüssow D . 45 B6
Brusy PL . 46 B3
Bruton GB . 29 B5
Bruvno HR . 83 B4
Bruvoll N . 34 B3
Bruxelles = Brussels
B . 49 C5
Bruyères F . 60 B2
Bruz F . 57 B4
Bruzaholm S . 40 B5
Brwinów PL . 55 A5
Bryansk RUS . 7 E13
Brynamman GB . 28 B4
Bryncrug GB . 26 C1
Bryne N . 33 D2
Brynmawr GB . 29 B4
Bryrup DK . 39 C2
Brzeće SRB . 85 C5
Brzeg PL . 54 C2
Brzeg Dolny PL . 54 B1
Brześć Kujawski PL . 47 C4
Brzesko PL . 55 D5
Brzeszcze PL . 55 D4
Brzezie PL . 46 B2
Brzeziny
Łódzkie PL . 55 B4
Wielkopolskie PL . 54 B3
Brzeźnica Nowa PL . 55 B4
Brzeźno PL . 46 B1
Brzotín SK . 65 B6
Brzozie Lubawskie
PL . 47 B5
Bua S . 40 B2
Buarcos P . 92 A2
Buavåg N . 33 C2
Bubbio I . 80 B2
Bubry F . 56 C2
Buca TR . 119 D2
Bucak TR . 119 E5
Bučany SK . 64 B3
Buccheri I . 109 B3
Buccino I . 103 C8
Bucelas P . 92 C1
Buch
Bayern D . 61 B6
Bayern D . 61 B6
Buchach UA . 11 B8
Bucharest = Bucureşti
RO . 11 D9
Buchbach D . 62 B3
Buchboden A . 71 A4
Buchen D . 61 A5
Büchen D . 44 B2
Buchenberg D . 61 C6

Buchères F . . . 59 B5
Buchholz D . . . 44 B1
Buchloe D . . . 62 B1
Buchlovice CZ . . . 64 A3
Buchlyvie GB . . . 24 B3
Buchoiz D . . . 44 B4
Buchs CH . . . 71 A4
Buchy F . . . 58 A2
Bückeburg D . . . 51 A5
Buckfastleigh GB . . . 28 C4
Buckhaven GB . . . 25 B4
Buckie GB . . . 23 D6
Buckingham GB . . . 31 B3
Buckley GB . . . 26 B2
Bückwitz D . . . 44 C4
Bučovice CZ . . . 64 A3
Bucsa H . . . 75 A6
Bucureşti = Bucharest
RO . . . 11 D9
Bucy-lès-Pierrepont
F . . . 59 A4
Buczek PL . . . 55 B4
Bud N . . . 114 E3
Budakalasz H . . . 65 C5
Budakeszi H . . . 75 A3
Budal N . . . 114 E7
Budaörs H . . . 75 A3
Budapest H . . . 75 A4
Búðardalur IS . . . 111 B4
Búdča SK . . . 65 B5
Buddusò I . . . 110 B2
Bude GB . . . 28 C3
Budeč CZ . . . 63 A6
Büdelsdorf D . . . 43 A6
Budens P . . . 98 B2
Budia E . . . 95 B4
Budimlić-Japra BIH . . . 83 B5
Büdingen D . . . 51 C5
Budišov CZ . . . 64 A3
Budleigh Salterton
GB . . . 29 C4
Budmerice SK . . . 64 B3
Budoni I . . . 110 B2
Búdrio I . . . 81 B5
Budva MNE . . . 105 A4
Budyně nad Ohří CZ . . . 53 C4
Budziszewice PL . . . 55 B4
Budzyń PL . . . 46 C2
Bue N . . . 33 D2
Bueña E . . . 95 B5
Buenache de Alarcón
E . . . 95 C4
Buenache de la Sierra
E . . . 95 B5
Buenaventura E . . . 94 B2
Buenavista de Valdavia
E . . . 88 B2
Buendia E . . . 95 B4
Bueu E . . . 87 B2
Buezo E . . . 89 B3
Bugac H . . . 75 B4
Bugarra E . . . 96 B2
Bugeat F . . . 68 C1
Bugojno BIH . . . 84 B2
Bugøyfjord N . . . 113 C18
Bugøynes N . . . 113 C18
Bugyi H . . . 75 A4
Buharkent TR . . . 119 E3
Bühl
Baden-Württemberg
D . . . 61 B4
Bayern D . . . 61 C6
Bühlertal D . . . 61 B4
Bühlertann D . . . 61 A5
Buia I . . . 72 B3
Builth Wells GB . . . 29 A4
Buin N . . . 32 C3
Buis-les-Baronnies F . . . 79 B4
Buitenpost NL . . . 42 B3
Buitrago del Lozoya
E . . . 94 B3
Bujalance E . . . 100 B1
Bujaraloz E . . . 90 B2
Buje HR . . . 72 C3
Bujedo E . . . 89 B3
Bük H . . . 74 A1
Buk PL . . . 46 C2
Bükkösd H . . . 74 B2
Bükkzsérc H . . . 65 C6
Bukovci SLO . . . 73 B5
Bukowiec PL . . . 53 A6
Bukowina Tatrzańska
PL . . . 65 A6
Bukownica PL . . . 54 B3
Bukowno PL . . . 55 C5
Bülach CH . . . 70 A3
Búland IS . . . 111 D7
Buldan TR . . . 119 D3
Bulgnéville F . . . 60 B1
Bulgurca TR . . . 119 D2
Bülkau D . . . 43 B5
Bulken N . . . 32 B3
Bulkowo PL . . . 47 C6
Bullas E . . . 101 A4
Bulle CH . . . 70 B2
Büllingen B . . . 50 C2
Büllest HR . . . 72 D2
Buna BIH . . . 84 C2
Bunahowen IRL . . . 18 B2
Bunbeg IRL . . . 18 A3
Bunclody IRL . . . 21 B5
Buncrana IRL . . . 19 A4
Bunde D . . . 43 B4
Bünde D . . . 51 A4
Bundoran IRL . . . 18 B3
Bunessan GB . . . 24 B1
Bungay GB . . . 30 B5
Bunge S . . . 37 E6
Bunić HR . . . 83 B4
Bunmahon IRL . . . 21 B4
Bunnyconnellan IRL . . . 18 B2
Buñol E . . . 96 B2
Buñuel E . . . 89 C5
Bunratty IRL . . . 20 B3
Bunsbeek B . . . 49 C5
Buñuel E . . . 89 C5
Bünyan TR . . . 16 B7
Bunyola E . . . 97 B2
Buonabitácolo I . . . 104 C1
Buonalbergo I . . . 103 B7
Buonconvento I . . . 81 C5
Buonvicino I . . . 106 B2
Burano I . . . 72 C2
Burbach D . . . 50 C4
Burcei I . . . 110 C2
Burdons-sur-Rognon
F . . . 59 B6
Burdur TR . . . 119 E5
Bureå S . . . 3 D24
Burela E . . . 86 A3
Büren D . . . 51 B4
Büren an der Aare
CH . . . 70 A2
Burford GB . . . 29 B6
Burg
Cottbus D . . . 53 B4
Magdeburg D . . . 52 A1
Schleswig-Holstein D . . . 43 A6
Burgas BG . . . 11 E9
Burgau
A . . . 73 A4
D . . . 61 B6
P . . . 98 B2
Burg auf Fehmarn D . . . 44 A3
Burgbernheim D . . . 61 A6
Burgdorf
CH . . . 70 A2
D . . . 44 C2
Bürgel D . . . 52 C1
Burgess Hill GB . . . 31 D3
Burghaslach D . . . 61 A6
Burghausen D . . . 62 B3
Burghead GB . . . 23 D5
Burgh le Marsh GB . . . 27 B6
Búrgio I . . . 108 B2
Burgkirchen D . . . 62 B3
Burgkunstadt D . . . 52 C1
Burglengenfeld D . . . 62 A3

Burgo P . . . 87 D2
Burgoberbach D . . . 61 A6
Burgohondo E . . . 94 B2
Burgos E . . . 88 B3
Burgsinn D . . . 51 C5
Burgstädt D . . . 52 C2
Burgstall D . . . 44 C3
Burg Stargard D . . . 45 B5
Burgsvik S . . . 37 E5
Burgui E . . . 76 D2
Burguillos E . . . 99 B5
Burguillos del Cerro
E . . . 93 C4
Burguillos de Toledo
E . . . 94 C3
Burhaniye TR . . . 118 C1
Burhave D . . . 43 B5
Burie F . . . 67 C4
Burjassot E . . . 96 B2
Burk D . . . 61 A6
Burkhardtsdorf D . . . 52 C2
Burladingen D . . . 61 B5
Burlage D . . . 43 B4
Burness GB . . . 23 B6
Burnham GB . . . 31 C3
Burnham Market GB . . . 30 B4
Burnham-on-Crouch
GB . . . 31 C4
Burnham-on-Sea GB . . . 29 B5
Burniston GB . . . 27 A5
Burnley GB . . . 26 B3
Burntisland GB . . . 25 B4
Buron F . . . 88 A1
Buronzo I . . . 70 C3
Burovac SRB . . . 85 B6
Burow D . . . 45 B5
Burravoe GB . . . 22 A7
Burrel AL . . . 105 B6
Burret F . . . 77 D4
Burriana E . . . 96 B2
Burry Port GB . . . 28 B3
Bürs A . . . 71 A4
Bursa TR . . . 118 B4
Burseryd S . . . 40 B3
Bürstadt D . . . 61 A4
Burton Agnes GB . . . 26 A3
Burton Bradstock GB . . . 29 C5
Burton Latimer GB . . . 30 B3
Burton upon Stather
GB . . . 27 B5
Burton upon Trent
GB . . . 27 C4
Burujón E . . . 94 C2
Burwell GB . . . 30 B4
Burwick GB . . . 23 C6
Bury GB . . . 26 B3
Buryn UA . . . 7 F12
Bury St Edmunds GB . . . 30 B4
Burzenin PL . . . 54 B3
Busachi I . . . 110 B1
Busalla I . . . 80 B3
Busana I . . . 81 B4
Busano I . . . 70 C2
Busca I . . . 80 B1
Busch D . . . 44 C3
Buševec HR . . . 73 C6
Bushat AL . . . 105 B5
Bushey GB . . . 31 C3
Bushmills GB . . . 19 A5
Bušince SK . . . 65 B5
Buskhyttan S . . . 37 D3
Busko-Zdrój PL . . . 55 C5
Busot E . . . 96 C2
Busovača BIH . . . 84 B2
Busquistar E . . . 100 C2
Bussang F . . . 60 C2
Busseto I . . . 81 B4
Bussière-Badil F . . . 67 C5
Bussière-Poitevine F . . . 67 B5
Bussolengo I . . . 71 C5
Bussoleno I . . . 70 C2
Bussum NL . . . 49 A6
Busto Arsízio I . . . 70 C3
Büsum D . . . 43 A5
Butera I . . . 109 B3
Butgenbach B . . . 50 C2
Butler's Bridge IRL . . . 19 B4
Butryny PL . . . 47 B6
Bütschwil CH . . . 70 A4
Buttermere GB . . . 26 A2
Buttevant IRL . . . 20 B3
Buttle S . . . 37 E5
Buttstädt D . . . 52 B1
Butzbach D . . . 51 C4
Bützfleth D . . . 43 B6
Bützow D . . . 44 B3
Buxières-les-Mines F . . . 68 B2
Buxtehude D . . . 43 B6
Buxton GB . . . 27 B4
Buxy F . . . 69 B4
Büyükçekmece TR . . . 118 A3
Büyükkariştiran TR . . . 118 A2
Büyükorhan TR . . . 118 C3
Buzançais F . . . 67 B6
Buzancy F . . . 59 A5
Buzău RO . . . 11 D9
Buzet HR . . . 72 C3
Buzsák H . . . 74 B2
Buzy F . . . 76 C2
By S . . . 36 B3
Byala BG . . . 11 E8
Byaroza BY . . . 6 E8
Byczyna PL . . . 54 B3
Bydalen S . . . 115 D10
Bydgoszcz PL . . . 47 B4
Bygdin N . . . 32 A5
Bygdsiljum S . . . 115 B5
Bygland N . . . 33 D4
Byglandsfjord N . . . 33 D4
Bykhaw BY . . . 7 E11
Bykle N . . . 33 C4
Bylderup-Bov DK . . . 39 E2
Byrkjedal N . . . 33 D3
Byrkjelo N . . . 114 F3
Byrum DK . . . 38 B3
Byšice CZ . . . 53 C4
Byske S . . . 3 D24
Býškovice CZ . . . 64 A3
Bysław PL . . . 46 B3
Bystré CZ . . . 64 A2
Bystřice CZ . . . 63 A5
Bystřice CZ . . . 65 A4
Bystřice nad Pernštejnem
CZ . . . 64 A2
Bystřice pod Hostýnem
CZ . . . 64 A3
Bystrzyca Kłodzka
PL . . . 54 C1
Bytča SK . . . 65 A4
Bytnica PL . . . 53 A5
Bytom PL . . . 54 C3
Bytom Odrzański PL . . . 53 B5
Bytów PL . . . 46 A3
Byxelkrok S . . . 41 B7
Bzenec CZ . . . 64 B3
Bzince SK . . . 64 B3

C
Çağa TR . . . 118 B7
Cabações P . . . 92 B2
Cabaj-Čápor SK . . . 64 B4
Cabana E . . . 86 A2
Cabanac-et-Villagrains
F . . . 76 B2
Cabañaquinta E . . . 88 A1
Cabanas P . . . 44 C2
Cabañas del Castillo
E . . . 93 B5
Cabañas de Yepes E . . . 95 C3
Cabanelas E . . . 87 B2
Cabanes E . . . 96 A3
Cabanillas E . . . 89 B5
Cabar HR . . . 73 C4
Cabasse F . . . 79 C5
Cabdella E . . . 91 A4
Cabeceiras de Basto
P . . . 87 C2
Cabeço de Vide P . . . 92 B3
Cabella Ligure I . . . 80 B3
Cabeza la Vaca E . . . 99 A4
Cabeza del Buey E . . . 93 C5
Cabezamesada E . . . 95 C3
Cabezarados E . . . 100 A1
Cabezarrubias del Puerto
E . . . 100 A1
Cabezas del Villar E . . . 94 B1
Cabezas Rubias E . . . 98 B3
Cabezón E . . . 88 C2
Cabezón de la Sal E . . . 88 A2
Cabezón de Liébana
E . . . 88 A2
Cabezuela E . . . 94 A3
Cabezuela del Valle E . . . 93 A5
Cabo de Gata E . . . 101 C4
Cabo de Palos E . . . 101 B5
Cabolafuente E . . . 95 A4
Cabourg F . . . 57 A5
Cabra
E . . . 100 B1
P . . . 92 A3
Cabra del Santo Cristo
E . . . 100 B2
Cábras I . . . 110 C1
Cabreiro P . . . 87 C2
Cabreiros E . . . 86 A3
Cabrejas E . . . 89 C4
Cabrela P . . . 92 C2
Cabrillas E . . . 87 D4
Cabuna HR . . . 74 C2
Cacabelos E . . . 86 B4
Čačak SRB . . . 85 C5
Cáccamo I . . . 108 B2
Caccuri I . . . 107 B3
Cacela P . . . 98 B3
Cacém P . . . 92 C1
Cáceres E . . . 93 B4
Cachafeiro E . . . 87 B2
Cachopo P . . . 98 B3
Cachtice SK . . . 64 B3
Cacin E . . . 100 B2
Čačinci HR . . . 74 C2
Cadafais P . . . 92 C1
Cadalen F . . . 77 C5
Cadalso E . . . 93 A4
Cadaqués E . . . 91 A6
Cadaval P . . . 92 B1
Cadavedo E . . . 86 A4
Čadavica BIH . . . 84 B1
Čadca SK . . . 65 A4
Cadéac F . . . 77 D3
Cadelbosco di Sopra
I . . . 81 B4
Cadenazzo CH . . . 70 B3
Cadenberge D . . . 43 B6
Cadenet F . . . 79 C4
Cadeuil F . . . 66 C4
Cádiar E . . . 100 C2
Cadillac F . . . 76 B2
Cádiz E . . . 99 C4
Čadjavica HR . . . 74 C2
Cadouin F . . . 77 B3
Cadours F . . . 77 C4
Cadrete E . . . 90 B2
Caen F . . . 57 A5
Caerleon GB . . . 29 B5
Caernarfon GB . . . 26 B1
Caerphilly GB . . . 29 B4
Caersws GB . . . 26 C2
Cafede P . . . 92 B3
Caggiano I . . . 104 C1
Cagli I . . . 82 C1
Cágliari I . . . 110 C2
Čaglin HR . . . 74 C2
Cagnano Varano I . . . 104 B1
Cagnes-sur-Mer F . . . 79 C6
Caher IRL . . . 21 B4
Caherciveen IRL . . . 20 C1
Caherdaniel IRL . . . 20 C1
Cahors F . . . 77 B4
Cahul MD . . . 11 D10
Caiazzo I . . . 103 B7
Caion E . . . 86 A2
Cairndow GB . . . 24 B3
Cairnryan GB . . . 24 D2
Cairo Montenotte I . . . 80 B2
Caister-on-Sea GB . . . 30 B5
Caistor GB . . . 27 B5
Caivano I . . . 103 C7
Cajarc F . . . 77 B4
Čajetina SRB . . . 85 C4
Čajniče BIH . . . 84 C4
Čakajovce SK . . . 64 B4
Čakmak TR . . . 118 C6
Čakovec HR . . . 73 B6
Cakran AL . . . 105 C5
Çal TR . . . 119 D4
Čala E . . . 99 B4
Calabritto I . . . 103 C8
Calaceite E . . . 90 C3
Calacuccia F . . . 102 A2
Cala d'Or E . . . 97 B3
Calaf E . . . 91 B4
Calafat RO . . . 11 D7
Calafell E . . . 91 B4
Cala Galdana E . . . 97 B3
Cala Gonone I . . . 110 B2
Calahonda
Granada E . . . 100 C2
Málaga E . . . 100 C1
Calahorra E . . . 89 B5
Calais F . . . 48 C2
Cala Llonga E . . . 97 C1
Calalzo di Cadore I . . . 72 B2
Cala Millor E . . . 97 B3
Calamocha E . . . 95 B5
Calamonte E . . . 93 C4
Cala Morell E . . . 97 A3
Calañas E . . . 99 B4
Calanda E . . . 90 C2
Calangiánus I . . . 110 B2
Călăraşi RO . . . 11 D9
Cala Ratjada E . . . 97 B3
Calascibetta I . . . 109 B3
Calasetta I . . . 110 C1
Calasparra E . . . 101 A4
Calatafimi I . . . 108 B1
Calatayud E . . . 89 C5
Calatorao E . . . 89 C5
Calau D . . . 53 B3
Calbe D . . . 52 B1
Calcena E . . . 89 C5
Calcinelli I . . . 82 C1
Calco I . . . 71 C4
Caldaro sulla strada del
Vino I . . . 71 B6
Caldas da Rainha P . . . 92 B1
Caldas de Boi E . . . 90 A3
Caldas de Malavella
E . . . 91 B5
Caldas de Reis E . . . 86 B2
Caldas de San Jorge
P . . . 87 D2
Caldas de Vizela P . . . 87 C2
Caldbeck GB . . . 26 A2
Caldearenas E . . . 90 A2
Caldelas P . . . 87 C2
Calders E . . . 91 B4
Caldes de Montbui E . . . 91 B5
Caldicot GB . . . 29 B5
Caldirola I . . . 80 B3
Caledon GB . . . 19 B5
Calella
Barcelona E . . . 91 B5
Girona E . . . 91 B6
Calenzana F . . . 102 A1
Calera de León E . . . 99 A4
Calera y Chozas E . . . 94 C2
Caleruega E . . . 89 C3
Caleruela E . . . 93 B5
Cales de Mallorca E . . . 97 B3
Calestano I . . . 81 B4
Calfsound GB . . . 23 B6
Calgary GB . . . 24 B1
Calimera I . . . 105 C4
Calitri I . . . 103 C8

Calizzano I . . . 80 B2
Callac F . . . 56 B2
Callan IRL . . . 21 B4
Callander GB . . . 24 B3
Callas F . . . 79 C5
Calliano
Piemonte I . . . 80 A2
Trentino Alto Adige I . . . 71 C6
Callosa de Ensarriá
E . . . 96 B2
Callosa de Segura E . . . 101 A5
Callús E . . . 91 B4
Čalma SRB . . . 85 A4
Calmbach D . . . 61 B4
Calne GB . . . 29 B6
Calolziocorte I . . . 71 C4
Calonge E . . . 91 B6
Čalovec E . . . 64 C3
Calpe E . . . 96 C3
Caltabellotta I . . . 108 B2
Caltagirone I . . . 109 B3
Caltanissetta I . . . 109 B3
Caltavuturo I . . . 108 B2
Çaltılıbük TR . . . 118 C3
Caltojar E . . . 89 C4
Caluire-et-Cuire F . . . 69 C4
Caluso I . . . 70 C2
Calvello I . . . 104 C1
Calvi F . . . 102 A1
Calviá E . . . 97 B2
Calvinet F . . . 77 B5
Calvisson F . . . 78 C3
Calvörde D . . . 44 C3
Calw D . . . 61 B4
Calzada de Calatrava
E . . . 100 A2
Calzada de Valdunciel
E . . . 94 A1
Calzadilla de los Barros
E . . . 93 C4
Cam GB . . . 29 B5
Camaiore I . . . 81 C4
Camarasa E . . . 90 B3
Camarena E . . . 94 B2
Camarès F . . . 78 C1
Camaret-sur-Aigues
F . . . 78 B3
Camaret-sur-Mer F . . . 56 B1
Camarillas E . . . 90 C2
Camariñas E . . . 86 A1
Camarma E . . . 95 B3
Camarzana de Tera E . . . 87 B4
Camas E . . . 99 B4
Camastra I . . . 108 B2
Cambados E . . . 86 B2
Cambarinho P . . . 92 A2
Camberley GB . . . 31 C3
Cambil E . . . 100 B2
Cambligeu F . . . 48 C3
Cambo-les-Bains F . . . 76 C1
Camborne GB . . . 28 C2
Cambrai F . . . 49 C4
Cambre E . . . 86 A2
Cambridge GB . . . 30 B4
Cambrils E . . . 90 B3
Cambs D . . . 44 B3
Camburg D . . . 52 B1
Camden GB . . . 31 C3
Cameleño E . . . 88 A2
Camelford GB . . . 28 C3
Çameli TR . . . 119 E4
Camelle E . . . 86 A1
Camerano I . . . 82 C2
Camerino I . . . 82 C2
Camerota I . . . 106 A2
Camigliatello Silano
I . . . 106 B3
Caminha P . . . 87 C2
Caminomorisco E . . . 93 A4
Caminreal E . . . 95 B5
Camisano Vicentino I . . . 72 C1
Çamlıdere TR . . . 118 B7
Cammarata I . . . 108 B2
Camogli I . . . 80 B3
Camors F . . . 56 C3
Camp IRL . . . 20 B2
Campagna I . . . 103 C8
Campagnano di Roma
I . . . 102 A5
Campagnático I . . . 81 D5
Campan F . . . 76 C3
Campana I . . . 107 B3
Campanario E . . . 93 C5
Campanillas E . . . 100 C1
Campano E . . . 99 C4
Campaspero E . . . 88 C2
Campbeltown GB . . . 24 C2
Campello E . . . 96 C2
Campelos P . . . 92 B1
Campi Bisénzio I . . . 81 C5
Campico López E . . . 101 B4
Campíglia Maríttima I . . . 81 C4
Campíglio de Altobuey
E . . . 95 C5
Campillo de Aragón
E . . . 95 A5
Campillo de Arenas
E . . . 100 B2
Campillo de Llerena
E . . . 93 C5
Campillos E . . . 100 B1
Câmpina RO . . . 11 D8
Campi Salentina I . . . 105 C4
Campli I . . . 82 D2
Campo E . . . 90 A3
Campobasso I . . . 103 B7
Campobello di Licata
I . . . 108 B2
Campobello di Mazara
I . . . 108 B1
Campo da Feira E . . . 86 A3
Campodársego I . . . 72 C1
Campo de Bacerros
E . . . 87 B3
Campo de Caso E . . . 88 A1
Campo de Criptana E . . . 95 C3
Campodónico I . . . 82 C1
Campofelice di Roccella
I . . . 108 B2
Campofiorito I . . . 108 B2
Campofórmido I . . . 72 B3
Campofranco I . . . 108 B2
Campofrío E . . . 99 B4
Campogalliano I . . . 81 B4
Campo Ligure I . . . 80 B2
Campolongo P . . . 92 C2
Campo Lugar E . . . 93 B5
Campo Maior P . . . 93 B3
Campomanes E . . . 88 A1
Campomarino I . . . 103 B8
Campo Molino I . . . 79 B6
Campomono F . . . 102 B1
Campo Real E . . . 95 B3
Campora San Giovanni
I . . . 106 B3
Camporeale I . . . 108 B2
Camporeggiano I . . . 82 C1
Camporrells E . . . 90 B3
Camporrobles E . . . 96 B1
Campos E . . . 97 B3
Camposa P . . . 87 C2
Camposampiero I . . . 72 C1
Camposanto I . . . 81 B5
Campospinoso I . . . 80 A3
Campotéjar E . . . 100 B2
Campotosto I . . . 103 A6
Campo Túres I . . . 72 B1
Camprodón E . . . 91 A5
Campsegret F . . . 77 B3
Camrose GB . . . 28 B2
Camuñas E . . . 95 C3
Çamyazı TR . . . 119 F7
Çan TR . . . 118 B2
Cana I . . . 81 D5
Cañada del Hoyo E . . . 95 C5
Cañadajuncosa E . . . 95 C4
Cañada Rosal E . . . 99 B5
Čanak HR . . . 83 B4
Çanakkale TR . . . 118 C1
Canale I . . . 80 B1

Canales continued
Castellón de la Plana
E . . . 96 B2
Canals E . . . 96 C2
Canal San Bovo I . . . 72 B1
Cañamares E . . . 95 B4
Cañamero E . . . 93 B5
Cañar E . . . 100 C2
Cañate la Real E . . . 99 C5
Cañaveral E . . . 93 B4
Cañaveral de León E . . . 99 A4
Cañaveras E . . . 95 B4
Cañaveruelas E . . . 95 B4
Canazei I . . . 72 B1
Cancale F . . . 57 B4
Cancellara I . . . 104 C1
Cancello ed Arnone
I . . . 103 B7
Cancon F . . . 77 B3
Canda E . . . 87 B4
Candamil E . . . 86 A3
Candanchu E . . . 76 D2
Çandarlı TR . . . 118 D1
Candas E . . . 88 A1
Candasnos E . . . 90 B3
Candé F . . . 66 A3
Candela I . . . 104 B1
Candelario E . . . 93 A5
Candeleda E . . . 93 A5
Cándia Lomellina I . . . 70 C3
Candide Casamazzagno
I . . . 72 B2
Candin E . . . 86 B4
Candosa P . . . 92 A3
Canela E . . . 98 B3
Canelli I . . . 80 B2
Canena E . . . 100 A2
Canencia E . . . 94 B3
Canero E . . . 86 A4
Canet F . . . 78 C2
Canet de Mar E . . . 91 B5
Canet d'en Berenguer
E . . . 96 B2
Cañete E . . . 95 B5
Cañete de las Torres
E . . . 100 B1
Canet-Plage F . . . 91 A6
Canfranc E . . . 76 D2
Cangas
Lugo E . . . 86 A3
Pontevedra E . . . 87 B2
Cangas de Narcea E . . . 86 A4
Cangas de Onís E . . . 88 A1
Canha P . . . 92 C2
Canhestros P . . . 98 A2
Canicatti I . . . 108 B2
Canicattini Bagni I . . . 109 B4
Caniçada P . . . 87 C2
Caniçal P . . . 95 B3
Canicosa de la Sierra
E . . . 89 C3
Caniles E . . . 101 B3
Canillas de Aceituno
E . . . 100 C1
Canino I . . . 102 A4
Canisy F . . . 57 A4
Cañizal E . . . 94 A1
Cañizo E . . . 88 C1
Canjáyar E . . . 101 C3
Çankırı TR . . . 16 A6
Cannai I . . . 110 C1
Cannara I . . . 82 C1
Cánnero Riviera I . . . 70 B3
Cannes F . . . 79 C6
Canneto
Sicilia I . . . 106 C1
Toscana I . . . 81 C4
Canneto sull'Oglio I . . . 71 C5
Cannich GB . . . 22 D4
Cannóbio I . . . 70 B3
Cannock GB . . . 26 C3
Canonbie GB . . . 25 C5
Canosa di Púglia I . . . 104 B2
Can Pastilla E . . . 97 B2
Cantalapiedra E . . . 94 A1
Cantalejo E . . . 94 B3
Cantalgallo E . . . 99 A4
Cantalice I . . . 102 A5
Cantalpino E . . . 94 A1
Cantalupo in Sabina
I . . . 102 A5
Cantanhede P . . . 92 A2
Cantavieja E . . . 90 C2
Čantavir SRB . . . 75 C4
Canterbury GB . . . 31 C5
Cantiano I . . . 82 C1
Cantillana E . . . 99 B5
Cantimpalos E . . . 94 B2
Cantiveros E . . . 94 B2
Cantoria E . . . 101 B3
Cantù I . . . 71 C4
Canvey GB . . . 31 C4
Cany-Barville F . . . 58 A1
Canyet de Mar E . . . 91 B5
Caol GB . . . 24 B2
Cáorle I . . . 72 C2
Caorso I . . . 81 A3
Cap Ferret F . . . 76 B1
Capáccio I . . . 103 C8
Capáci I . . . 108 A2
Capálbio I . . . 102 A4
Capánnori I . . . 81 C4
Capbreton F . . . 76 C1
Capdenac-Gare F . . . 77 B5
Capdepera E . . . 97 B3
Capel Curig GB . . . 26 B2
Capellades E . . . 91 B4
Capena I . . . 102 A5
Capendu F . . . 77 C5
Capestang F . . . 78 C2
Capestrano I . . . 103 A6
Capileira E . . . 100 C2
Capinha P . . . 92 A3
Ca' Pisani I . . . 82 B1
Capistrello I . . . 103 B6
Capizzi I . . . 109 B3
Čapljina BIH . . . 84 C2
Capo di Ponte I . . . 71 B5
Caposile I . . . 72 C2
Capoterra I . . . 110 C1
Cappamore IRL . . . 21 B4
Cappeln D . . . 43 C5
Cappoquin IRL . . . 21 B4
Capracotta I . . . 103 B7
Capránica I . . . 102 A5
Caprarola I . . . 102 A5
Capretta I . . . 82 D1
Capri I . . . 103 C7
Capriati a Volturno I . . . 103 B7
Caprino Veronese I . . . 71 C5
Captieux F . . . 76 B2
Cápua I . . . 103 B7
Capurso I . . . 104 C2
Caputh D . . . 45 C5
Carabaña E . . . 95 B3
Carabias E . . . 89 C3
Caracal RO . . . 11 D8
Caracenilla E . . . 95 B4
Caráglio I . . . 79 B6
Caraman F . . . 77 C4
Caramánico Terme I . . . 103 A7
Caranga E . . . 86 A4
Caransebeş RO . . . 11 D7
Carapelle I . . . 104 B1
Carasco I . . . 80 B3
Carate Brianza I . . . 71 C4
Caravaca de la Cruz
E . . . 101 A4
Caravággio I . . . 71 C4
Carbajal E . . . 100 C1
Carbajo E . . . 93 B3
Carballeda E . . . 87 B3
Carballeda de Avia E . . . 87 B2
Carballo E . . . 86 A2
Carbis Bay GB . . . 28 C2
Carbon-Blanc F . . . 76 B2
Carbonera de Frentes
E . . . 89 C4

Carboneras E . . . 101 C4
Carboneras de
Guadazón E . . . 95 C5
Carbonero el Mayor E . . . 94 B2
Carboneros E . . . 100 A2
Carbónia I . . . 110 C1
Carbonin I . . . 72 B2
Carbonne F . . . 77 C4
Carbost
Highland GB . . . 22 D2
Highland GB . . . 22 D2
Carcaboso E . . . 93 A4
Carcabuey E . . . 100 B1
Carcaixent E . . . 96 B2
Carcans F . . . 76 A1
Carcans-Plage F . . . 76 A1
Carção P . . . 87 C4
Carcar E . . . 89 B5
Cárcar E . . . 89 B5
Carcare I . . . 80 B2
Carcassonne F . . . 77 C5
Carcastillo E . . . 89 B5
Carcedo de Burgos E . . . 89 B3
Carcelén E . . . 96 B1
Carcès F . . . 79 C5
Carchelejo E . . . 100 B2
Cardak
Çanakkale TR . . . 118 B1
Denizli TR . . . 119 E4
Cardedeu E . . . 91 B5
Cardeña E . . . 100 A1
Cardenete E . . . 95 C5
Cardeñosa E . . . 94 B2
Cardeto I . . . 109 A4
Cardiff GB . . . 29 B4
Cardigan GB . . . 28 A3
Cardona E . . . 91 B4
Cardosos P . . . 92 B2
Carei RO . . . 11 C7
Carentan F . . . 57 A4
Carentoir F . . . 57 C3
Careri I . . . 106 C3
Carevdar HR . . . 74 B1
Cargèse F . . . 102 A1
Carhaix-Plouguer F . . . 56 B2
Caria P . . . 92 A3
Cariati I . . . 107 B3
Carignan F . . . 59 A6
Carignano I . . . 80 B1
Cariñena E . . . 90 B1
Carini I . . . 108 A2
Cariño E . . . 86 A3
Carínola I . . . 103 B7
Carisbrooke GB . . . 31 D2
Carlabhagh GB . . . 22 C2
Carlepont F . . . 59 A4
Carlet E . . . 96 B2
Carlingford IRL . . . 19 B5
Carlisle GB . . . 25 D5
Carloforte I . . . 110 C1
Carlópoli I . . . 106 B3
Carlow
D . . . 44 B2
IRL . . . 21 B5
Carlton GB . . . 27 C4
Carluke GB . . . 25 C4
Carmagnola I . . . 80 B1
Carmarthen GB . . . 28 B3
Carmaux F . . . 77 B5
Carmena E . . . 94 C2
Cármenes E . . . 88 B1
Carmine I . . . 80 B1
Carmona E . . . 99 B5
Carmónita I . . . 93 B4
Carmyllie GB . . . 25 B5
Carnac F . . . 56 C2
Carndonagh IRL . . . 19 A4
Carnew IRL . . . 21 B5
Carnforth GB . . . 26 A3
Cárnia I . . . 72 B3
Carnlough GB . . . 19 B6
Carno GB . . . 26 C2
Carnon Plage F . . . 78 C2
Carnota E . . . 86 B1
Carnoustie GB . . . 25 B5
Carnwath GB . . . 25 C4
Carolei I . . . 106 B3
Carolinensiel D . . . 43 B4
Carolles F . . . 57 B4
Carona I . . . 71 B4
Caronía I . . . 109 A3
Carovigno I . . . 104 C3
Carovilli I . . . 103 B7
Carpaneto Piacentino
I . . . 81 B3
Carpegna I . . . 82 C1
Carpenédolo I . . . 71 C5
Carpentras F . . . 79 B4
Carpi I . . . 81 B4
Carpignano Sésia I . . . 70 C3
Carpineti I . . . 81 B4
Carpineto Romano I . . . 102 B6
Cărpinis RO . . . 75 C5
Carpino I . . . 104 B1
Carpinone I . . . 103 B7
Carpio E . . . 94 A1
Carquefou F . . . 66 A3
Carqueiranne F . . . 79 C5
Carral E . . . 86 A2
Carranque E . . . 94 B3
Carrapichana P . . . 92 A3
Carrara I . . . 81 B4
Carraroe IRL . . . 20 A2
Carrascalejo E . . . 93 B5
Carrascosa del Campo
E . . . 95 B4
Carratraca E . . . 100 C1
Carrazeda de Ansiães
P . . . 87 C3
Carrazedo de Montenegro
P . . . 87 C3
Carrbridge GB . . . 23 D5
Carregal do Sal P . . . 92 A2
Carreña E . . . 88 A2
Carrick IRL . . . 18 B3
Carrickart IRL . . . 19 A4
Carrickfergus GB . . . 19 B6
Carrickmacross IRL . . . 19 C5
Carrick-on-Shannon
IRL . . . 18 C3
Carrick-on-Suir IRL . . . 21 B4
Carrigallen IRL . . . 19 C4
Carrión de Calatrava
E . . . 94 C3
Carrión de los Condes
E . . . 88 B2
Carrizo de la Ribera E . . . 88 B1
Carrizosa E . . . 100 A3
Carro F . . . 79 C4
Carrocera E . . . 88 B1
Carros F . . . 79 C6
Carrouges F . . . 57 B5
Carrù I . . . 80 B1
Carryduff GB . . . 19 B6
Carry-le-Rouet F . . . 79 C4
Carsóli I . . . 102 A6
Carsphairn GB . . . 24 C3
Cártama E . . . 100 C1
Cartaxo P . . . 92 B2
Cartaya E . . . 98 B3
Carteret F . . . 57 A4
Cartes E . . . 88 A2
Carviçães P . . . 87 C4
Carvin F . . . 48 C3
Carvoeira P . . . 92 B1
Carvoeiro P . . . 98 B2
Casa Branca
Portalegre P . . . 92 C3
Setúbal P . . . 98 A2
Casacalenda I . . . 103 B7
Casa Castalda I . . . 82 C1
Casáio E . . . 87 B4
Casa l'Abate I . . . 105 C4
Casalarreina E . . . 89 B4
Casalbordino I . . . 103 A7
Casalbuono I . . . 104 C1

Casalbuttano ed Uniti
I . . . 71 C4
Casàl di Principe I . . . 103 B7
Casalécchio di Reno
I . . . 81 B5
Casale Monferrato I . . . 70 C3
Casalina I . . . 82 D1
Casalmaggiore I . . . 81 B4
Casalnuovo Monterotaro
I . . . 103 B8
Casaloldo I . . . 71 C5
Casalpusterlengo I . . . 71 C4
Casamássima I . . . 104 C2
Casamicciola Terme
I . . . 103 C6
Casamozza F . . . 102 A2
Casarabonela E . . . 100 C1
Casarano I . . . 107 A5
Casar de Cáceres E . . . 93 B4
Casar de Palomero E . . . 93 A4
Casarejos E . . . 89 C3
Casares E . . . 99 C5
Casares de las Hurdes
E . . . 93 A4
Casariche E . . . 100 B1
Casarrubios del Monte
E . . . 94 B2
Casas de Don Pedro
E . . . 93 B5
Casas de Fernando
Alonso E . . . 95 C4
Casas de Haro E . . . 95 C4
Casas de Juan Gil E . . . 96 B1
Casas del Juan Núñez
E . . . 95 C5
Casas del Puerto E . . . 101 A4
Casas del Rio E . . . 96 B1
Casas de Millán E . . . 93 B4
Casas de Reina E . . . 99 A5
Casas de Ves E . . . 96 B1
Casas-Ibáñez E . . . 96 B1
Casasimarro E . . . 95 C4
Casas Nuevas E . . . 101 B4
Casasola E . . . 94 B2
Casasola de Arión E . . . 88 C1
Casasuertes E . . . 88 A2
Casatejada E . . . 93 B5
Casavieja E . . . 94 B2
Casazza I . . . 71 C4
Cascais P . . . 92 C1
Cascante E . . . 89 C5
Cascante del Rio E . . . 96 A1
Cáscia I . . . 82 D2
Casciana Terme I . . . 81 C4
Cáscina I . . . 81 C4
Cásola Valsénio I . . . 81 B5
Cásole d'Elsa I . . . 81 C5
Cásoli I . . . 103 A7
Casória I . . . 103 C7
Caspe E . . . 90 B2
Cassàgnas F . . . 78 B2
Cassàgnes-Bégonhès
F . . . 77 B5
Cassano allo Iónio I . . . 106 B3
Cassano d'Adda I . . . 71 C4
Cassano delle Murge
I . . . 104 C2
Cassano Magnago I . . . 70 C3
Cassano Spínola I . . . 80 B2
Cassel F . . . 48 C3
Cássine I . . . 80 B2
Cássino I . . . 103 B6
Cassis F . . . 79 C4
Cassolnovo I . . . 70 C3
Cassuéjouls F . . . 78 B1
Častá SK . . . 64 B3
Castagnaro I . . . 71 C6
Castagneto Carducci
I . . . 81 C4
Castagnola CH . . . 70 B3
Castalla E . . . 96 C2
Castañar de Ibor E . . . 93 B5
Castanheira de Pera
P . . . 92 A2
Castàno Primo I . . . 70 C3
Castasegna CH . . . 71 B4
Castéggio I . . . 80 A3
Casteição P . . . 87 D3
Castejón E . . . 89 B5
Castejón de Monegros
E . . . 90 B2
Castejón de Sos E . . . 90 A3
Castejón de Valdejasa
E . . . 90 B2
Castèl Baronia I . . . 103 B8
Castel Bolognese I . . . 81 B5
Casteldáccia I . . . 108 A2
Castel d'Aiano I . . . 81 B4
Castel d'Ario I . . . 71 C5
Castel de Cabra E . . . 90 C2
Casteldelfino I . . . 79 B6
Castel del Monte I . . . 103 A6
Castel del Piano I . . . 81 D5
Castel di Iúdica I . . . 109 B3
Castel di Sangro I . . . 103 B7
Castelfidardo I . . . 82 C2
Castelfiorentino I . . . 81 C5
Castelforte I . . . 103 B6
Castelfranco Emília I . . . 81 B5
Castelfranco in Miscano
I . . . 103 B8
Castelfranco Véneto
I . . . 72 C1
Castelfrentano I . . . 103 A7
Casteljaloux F . . . 76 B3
Castell'Arquato I . . . 81 B3
Castell'Azzara I . . . 81 D5
Castellbell i Villar E . . . 91 B4
Castelldefels E . . . 91 B4
Castell de Cabres E . . . 90 C3
Castell de Castells E . . . 96 C2
Castelldans E . . . 90 B3
Castellde Ferro E . . . 100 C2
Castellet E . . . 91 B4
Castellfollit de la Roca
E . . . 91 A5
Castellfollit de Riubregos
E . . . 91 B4

Castellfort E . . . 90 C2
Castellina in Chianti I . . . 81 C5
Castellina Maríttima I . . . 81 C4
Castellóde Farfaña E . . . 90 B3
Castellóde la Plana E . . . 96 B2
Castello d'Empúries
E . . . 91 A6
Castello di Fiemme I . . . 71 B6
Castellóli I . . . 91 B4
Castelló-Don de Rugat
E . . . 96 C2
Castellote E . . . 90 C2
Castello Tesino I . . . 72 B1
Castellterçol E . . . 91 B5
Castellúccio de'Sáuri
I . . . 103 B8
Castelluccio Inferiore
I . . . 106 A2
Castelmássa I . . . 81 A5
Castelmáuro I . . . 103 B7
Castelmoron-sur-Lot
F . . . 77 B3
Castelnaudary F . . . 77 C4
Castelnau-de-Médoc
F . . . 76 A2
Castelnau-de-Montmirail
F . . . 77 C4
Castelnau-Magnoac
F . . . 77 C3
Castelnau-Montratier
F . . . 77 B4
Castelnovo ne'Monti I . . . 81 B4
Castelnuovo Berardenga
I . . . 81 C5
Castelnuovo della Dáunia
I . . . 103 B8
Castelnuovo di
Garfagnana I . . . 81 B4
Castelnuovo di Val di
Cécina I . . . 81 C4
Castelnuovo Don Bosco
I . . . 80 A1
Castelnuovo Scrivia I . . . 80 B2
Castelo Branco
Bragança P . . . 87 C4
Castelo Branco P . . . 92 B3
Castelo de Paiva P . . . 87 C2
Castelo de Vide P . . . 92 B3
Castelo do Neiva P . . . 87 C2
Castelo Mendo P . . . 93 A4
Castelraimondo I . . . 82 C2
Castel San Gimignano
I . . . 81 C5
Castèl San Giovanni I . . . 80 A3
Castèl San Pietro Terme
I . . . 81 B5
Castelsantángelo I . . . 82 D2
Castèl Sant'Elia I . . . 102 A5
Castelsaraceno I . . . 106 A2
Castelsardo I . . . 110 B1
Castelsarrasin F . . . 77 B4
Castelserás E . . . 90 C2
Casteltérmini I . . . 108 B2
Castelvecchio Subéquo
I . . . 103 A6
Castelvetere in Val
Fortore I . . . 103 B8
Castelvetrano I . . . 108 B1
Castél Volturno I . . . 103 B6
Castendolo I . . . 71 C5
Castets F . . . 76 C1
Castiádas I . . . 110 C2
Castiglioncello I . . . 81 C4
Castíglione Chiavarese
I . . . 80 B3
Castiglione d'Adda I . . . 71 C4
Castiglione dei Pepoli
I . . . 81 B5
Castiglione del Lago
I . . . 81 C6
Castiglione della Pescáia
I . . . 81 D4
Castiglione delle Stiviere
I . . . 71 C5
Castiglione di Sicília
I . . . 109 B4
Castiglione d'Órcia I . . . 81 C5
Castiglione Messer
Marino I . . . 103 B7
Castiglione Messer
Raimondo I . . . 103 A6
Castiglion Fibocchi I . . . 81 C5
Castiglion Fiorentino
I . . . 81 C5
Castilblanco E . . . 94 C1
Castilblanco de los
Arroyos E . . . 99 B5
Castil de Peones E . . . 89 B3
Castilfrío de la Sierra
E . . . 89 C4
Castilgaleu E . . . 90 A3
Castiliscar E . . . 90 A1
Castilleja E . . . 99 B4
Castillejar E . . . 101 B3
Castillejo de Martin Viejo
E . . . 93 A4
Castillejo de Mesleón
E . . . 89 C3
Castillejo de Robledo
E . . . 89 C3
Castillo de Bayuela E . . . 94 B2
Castillo de Locubín
E . . . 100 B1
Castillón-la-Bataille F . . . 76 B2
Castillonès F . . . 77 B3
Castillon-Len-Couserans
F . . . 77 D4
Castillonroy E . . . 90 B3
Castilruiz E . . . 89 C4
Castione CH . . . 70 B3
Castions di Strada I . . . 72 C3
Castirla F . . . 102 A2
Castle Acre GB . . . 30 B4
Castlebar IRL . . . 18 C2
Castlebellingham IRL . . . 19 C5
Castleblaney IRL . . . 19 B5
Castlebridge IRL . . . 21 B5
Castle Cary GB . . . 29 B5
Castlecomer IRL . . . 21 B4
Castlederg GB . . . 19 B4
Castledermot IRL . . . 21 B5
Castle Douglas GB . . . 25 D4
Castleford GB . . . 27 B4
Castleisland IRL . . . 20 B2
Castlemaine IRL . . . 20 B2
Castlemartyr IRL . . . 20 C3
Castlepollard IRL . . . 19 C4
Castlerea IRL . . . 18 C3
Castleside GB . . . 25 D6
Castletown
Highland GB . . . 23 C5
Isle of Man GB . . . 26 A1
Castletown Bearhaven
IRL . . . 20 C2
Castletownroche IRL . . . 20 B3
Castlewellan GB . . . 19 B6
Castres F . . . 77 C5
Castricum NL . . . 42 C1
Castries F . . . 78 C2

Castril E . . . 101 B3
Castrillo de Duero E . . . 88 C3
Castrillo de la Vega E . . . 88 C3
Castrillo de Onielo E . . . 88 C2
Castro
E . . . 88 A2
I . . . 107 A5
Castrocabón E . . . 88 B1
Castro-Caldelas E . . . 87 B3
Castrocaro Terme I . . . 81 B5
Castrocontrigo E . . . 87 B4
Castro Daire P . . . 87 D3
Castro dei Volsci I . . . 103 B6
Castro del Rio E . . . 100 B1
Castrofilippo I . . . 108 B2

154 Cas–Cou

Castrogonzaio E . .88 B1
Castrojeriz E . .88 B2
Castro Laboreiro P . .87 B2
Castromonte E . .98 B3
Castromonte E . .88 C1
Castronuevo E . .88 C1
Castronuño E . .88 C1
Castrocontrigo E . .86 A3
Castroreale I . .109 A4
Castroserracin E . .88 C3
Castro-Urdiales E . .89 A3
Castroverde E . .86 A3
Castro Verde P . .98 B2
Castroverde de Campos
E . .88 C1
Castroverde de Cerrato
E . .88 C2
Castrovillari I . .106 B3
Castuera E . .93 C5
Catadau E . .96 B2
Catáeggio I . .71 B4
Catalca TR . .118 A3
Çatallar TR . .119 F5
Catalzeytin TR . .16 A7
Catánia I . .109 B4
Catanzaro I . .106 C3
Catanzaro Marina I . .106 C3
Catarroja E . .96 B2
Catarruchos P . .92 A2
Catcleugh GB . .25 C5
Catenanuova I . .109 B3
Caterham GB . .31 C3
Cati E . .90 C3
Čatići BIH . .84 B3
Catignano I . .103 A6
Catillon F . .49 C4
Catoira E . .86 B2
Cerese F . .79 C4
Catral E . .101 A5
Catterick GB . .27 A4
Cattólica I . .82 C1
Cattólica Eraclea I . .108 B2
Catton GB . .25 D5
Caudebec-en-Caux F . .58 A1
Caudete E . .101 A5
Caudete de las Fuentes
E . .96 B1
Caudiel E . .96 B2
Caudiès-de-Fenouillèdes
F . .77 D5
Caudry F . .49 C4
Caulkerbush GB . .25 D4
Caulnes F . .57 B3
Caulonia I . .106 C3
Caumont-l'Évente F . .57 A5
Caunes-Minervois F . .77 C5
Cauro F . .102 B1
Caussade F . .77 B4
Causse-de-la-Selle F . .78 C2
Cauterets F . .76 D2
Cava de' Tirreni I . .103 C7
Cavaglia I . .70 C3
Cavaillon F . .79 C4
Cavalaire-sur-Mer F . .79 C5
Cavaleiro P . .98 B2
Cavalese I . .71 B6
Cavallermaggiore I . .80 B1
Cavallini I . .72 C2
Cavan IRL . .19 C4
Cavàrzere I . .72 C2
Çavdarhisar TR . .118 C4
Çavdır TR . .119 E4
Cavernães P . .87 D3
Cavezzo I . .81 B5
Çavışnac F . .76 A2
Cavle HR . .73 C4
Cavo I . .81 D4
Cavour I . .80 B1
Cavtat HR . .84 D3
Cawdor GB . .23 D5
Çay TR . .118 D6
Çaycuma TR . .118 A7
Cayeux-sur-Mer F . .48 C2
Çayıralan TR . .16 B7
Çayırhan TR . .118 B6
Caylus F . .77 B4
Cayres F . .78 B2
Cazalilla E . .100 B2
Cazalla de la Sierra E . .99 B5
Cazals F . .77 B4
Cazaubon F . .76 C2
Cazaux F . .76 B1
Cazavet F . .77 C4
Cazin BIH . .83 B4
Čazis CH . .71 B4
Cazo E . .88 A1
Cazorla E . .100 B3
Cazouls-lès-Béziers
F . .78 C2
Cea
León E . .88 B1
Orense E . .86 B3
Ceánuri E . .89 A4
Ceauce F . .57 B5
Cebolla E . .94 C2
Čebovce SK . .65 B5
Çebreros E . .94 B2
Čečava BIH . .84 B2
Ceccano I . .103 B6
Cece H . .74 B3
Čečenovo PL . .47 A4
Čechtice CZ . .63 A6
Cechtin CZ . .64 A1
Cécina I . .81 C4
Ceclavin E . .93 B4
Cedégolo I . .71 B5
Cedeira E . .86 A2
Cedillo E . .92 B3
Cedillo del Condado
E . .94 B3
Cedrillas E . .90 C2
Cedynia PL . .45 C6
Cée E . .86 B1
Cefalù I . .109 A3
Céggia I . .72 C2
Céglied H . .75 A4
Ceglie Messápica I . .104 C3
Cehegín E . .101 A4
Ceilhes-et-Rocozels
F . .78 C2
Ceinos de Campos E . .88 B1
Ceira P . .92 A2
Čejč CZ . .64 B2
Cekcyn PL . .47 B4
Çela BIH . .83 B5
Čelákovice CZ . .53 C4
Celano I . .103 A6
Celanova E . .87 B3
Celbridge IRL . .21 A5
Čelebić BIH . .83 C5
Celenza Valfortore I . .103 B7
Čelić BIH . .84 B3
Čelinac BIH . .84 B2
Celje SLO . .73 B5
Cella E . .95 B5
Celldömölk H . .74 A2
Celle D . .44 C2
Celle Ligure I . .80 B2
Celles B . .49 C5
Celles-sur-Belle F . .67 B4
Cellino San Marco I . .105 C3
Celorico da Beira P . .92 A3
Celorico de Basto P . .87 C2
Çeltik TR . .118 C6
Çeltikçi TR . .119 E5
Cemaes GB . .26 B1
Cembra I . .71 B6
Čemerno BIH . .84 C3
Cenad RO . .75 B5
Cencenighe Agordino
I . .72 B1
Cenei RO . .75 C5
Ceneselli I . .81 A5
Cenicero E . .89 B4

Cenicientos E . .94 B2
Censeau F . .69 B6
Centa SRB . .85 A5
Centallo I . .80 B1
Centelles E . .91 B5
Cento I . .81 B5
Centúripe I . .109 B3
Cepeda la Mora E . .93 A5
Čepin HR . .74 C3
Čepinski Martinci HR . .74 C3
Cépet F . .77 C4
Cepovan SLO . .72 B3
Ceprano I . .103 B6
Čeralije HR . .74 C2
Cerami I . .109 B3
Cerano I . .70 C3
Cérans Foulletourte
F . .57 C6
Ceraso I . .106 A2
Cerbaia I . .81 C5
Cerbère F . .91 A6
Cercadillo E . .95 A4
Cercal
Lisboa P . .92 B1
Setúbal P . .98 B2
Čerčany CZ . .63 A5
Cerceda E . .94 B3
Cercedilla E . .94 B2
Cercemaggiore I . .103 B7
Cercs E . .91 A4
Cercy-la-Tour F . .68 B3
Cerda I . .108 B2
Cerdedo E . .86 B2
Cerdeira P . .93 A3
Cerdon F . .58 C3
Cereal I . .71 C6
Ceres
GB . .25 B5
I . .70 C2
Cerese I . .81 A4
Ceresole-Reale I . .70 C2
Cereste F . .79 C4
Céret F . .91 A5
Cerezo de Abajo E . .95 A3
Cerezo de Riotirón E . .89 B3
Cerfontaine B . .49 C5
Cergy F . .58 A3
Cerignola I . .104 B1
Cerilly F . .68 B2
Cerisiers F . .59 B4
Cerizay F . .67 B4
Çerkeş TR . .16 A6
Çerkezköy TR . .118 A3
Čerkije SLO . .73 B4
Cerknica SLO . .73 C4
Cerkno SLO . .72 B3
Čermë-Proshkë AL . .105 B5
Černa H . .74 C1
Černá Hora CZ . .64 A2
Cernavodă RO . .11 D10
Cernay F . .60 C3
Cerne Abbas GB . .29 C5
Cernóbbio I . .70 C4
Cernik HR . .74 C2
Černošin CZ . .62 A3
Cernovice CZ . .63 A5
Cérons F . .76 B2
Cerovlje HR . .73 C4
Cerovo SK . .65 B5
Cerqueto I . .82 D1
Cerralbo E . .87 C4
Cerreto d'Esi I . .82 C1
Cerreto Sannita I . .103 B7
Cerrigydrudion GB . .26 B2
Čerrik AL . .105 B5
Cerro Muriano E . .100 A1
Certaldo I . .81 C5
Certosa di Pésio I . .80 B1
Cerva E . .87 C3
Cervaro I . .103 B6
Cervatos de la Cueza
E . .88 B2
Červená Řečice CZ . .63 A6
Červená-Skala SK . .65 B6
Červená Voda CZ . .54 C1
Červený Kostelec CZ . .53 C6
Cervera E . .91 B4
Cervera de la Cañada
E . .95 C4
Cervera del Llano E . .95 C4
Cervera del Río Alhama
E . .89 B5
Cervera de Pisuerga
E . .88 B2
Cervéteri I . .102 B5
Cérvia I . .82 B1
Cerviáde les Garrigues
E . .90 B3
Cervignano del Friuli
I . .72 C3
Cervinara I . .103 B7
Cervione F . .102 A2
Cervo
E . .86 A3
I . .80 C2
Cervon F . .68 A3
Cesana Torinese I . .79 B5
Cesarica HR . .83 B4
Cesarò I . .109 B3
Cesena I . .82 B1
Cesenático I . .82 B1
Čēsis LV . .7 C8
Česká Belá CZ . .63 A6
Česká Kamenice CZ . .53 C4
Česká Lipa CZ . .53 C4
Česká Třebová CZ . .64 A2
České Budějovice CZ . .63 B5
České Velenice CZ . .63 B5
Český Brod CZ . .53 C4
Český Dub CZ . .53 C4
Český Krumlov CZ . .63 B5
Český Těšín CZ . .65 A4
Česlieva Bara SRB . .85 B6
Cessenon F . .78 C2
Cesson-Sévigné F . .57 B4
Cestas F . .76 B2
Čestobrodica SRB . .85 C5
Cesuras E . .86 A2
Cetina E . .89 C5
Cetin Grad HR . .73 C5
Cetinje MNE . .105 A4
Cetraro I . .106 B2
Ceuta E . .99 D5
Ceuti E . .101 A4
Ceva I . .80 B2
Cevico de la Torre E . .88 C2
Cévico Navero E . .88 C2
Cevins F . .69 C6
Čevo MNE . .105 A4
Cewice PL . .46 A3
Ceylan TR . .119 F4
Ceylanköy TR . .119 F4
Ceyrat F . .68 C3
Ceyzériat F . .69 B5
Cham
NL . .49 B5
Chabanais F . .67 C5
Chabeuil F . .79 B4
Chabielice PL . .55 B4
Chablis F . .59 C4
Chabons F . .69 C5
Chabówka PL . .65 A5
Chabreloche F . .68 C3
Chabris F . .67 A6
Chagford GB . .28 C4
Chagny F . .69 B4
Chaholín RUS . .7 B13
Chaillac F . .67 B6
Chaillé-les-Marais F . .66 B3
Chailles F . .58 C2
Chailley F . .59 B4
Chalabre F . .77 D5
Chalais F . .67 C5
Chalampé F . .60 C3
Chalamont F . .69 C5
Chalonnes-sur-Loire
F . .66 A4
Châlons-en-Champagne
F . .59 B5
Chalon-sur-Saône F . .69 B4
Chalupy PL . .47 A4
Châlus F . .67 C5

Challes-les-Eaux F . .69 C5
Chalmazel F . .68 C3
Chalmoux F . .68 B3
Chambon-sur-Voueize
F . .68 B2
Cham
CH . .70 A3
D . .62 A3
Chamberet F . .68 C1
Chambéry F . .69 C5
Chambilly F . .68 B4
Chambley F . .60 A1
Chambly F . .58 A3
Chambois F . .57 B6
Chambon-sur-Lac F . .68 C2
Chambord F . .58 C2
Chamborigaud F . .78 B2
Chamboulive F . .68 C1
Chamerau D . .62 A3
Chamonix-Mont Blanc
F . .70 C1
Chamoux-sur-Gelon
F . .69 C6
Champagnac-le-Vieux
F . .68 C2
Champagnole F . .69 B5
Champagny-Mouton
F . .67 B5
Champaubert F . .59 B4
Champdeniers-St Denis
F . .67 B4
Champdieu F . .68 C4
Champdôtre F . .69 A5
Champeix F . .68 C3
Champéry CH . .70 B1
Champigne F . .57 C5
Champignelles F . .59 C4
Champigny-sur-Veude
F . .67 A5
Champlitte-et-le-Prelot
F . .60 C1
Champoluc I . .70 C2
Champoly F . .68 C3
Champorcher I . .70 C2
Champrond-en-Gâtine
F . .58 B2
Champs-sur-Tarentaine
F . .68 C2
Champs-sur-Yonne F . .59 C4
Champtoceaux F . .66 A3
Chamrousse F . .69 C5
Chamusca P . .92 B2
Chanac F . .78 B2
Chanaleilles F . .78 B2
Chandler's Ford GB . .31 D2
Chandra CH . .117 G8
Chandrexa de Queixa
E . .87 B3
Chañe E . .88 C2
Changy F . .68 B4
Chania GR . .117 G6
Channes F . .59 C5
Chantada E . .86 B3
Chantelle F . .68 B3
Chantemerle F . .79 B5
Chantenay-St Imbert
F . .68 B3
Chanteuges F . .78 A2
Chantilly F . .58 A3
Chantonnay F . .66 B3
Chão de Codes P . .92 B2
Chapa E . .86 B2
Chapareillan F . .69 C5
Chapel en le Frith GB . .27 B4
Chapelle Royale F . .58 B2
Chapelle-St Laurent F . .67 B4
Charbonnat F . .68 B4
Chard GB . .29 C5
Charenton-du-Cher F . .68 B2
Charlbury GB . .31 C2
Charleroi B . .49 C5
Charlestown
GB . .28 C3
IRL . .18 C3
Charlestown of Aberlour
GB . .23 D5
Charleville IRL . .20 B3
Charleville-Mézières
F . .59 A5
Charlieu F . .68 B4
Charlottenberg S . .34 C4
Charlton Kings GB . .29 B5
Charly F . .59 B4
Charmes-sur-Rhône
F . .78 B3
Charmey CH . .70 B2
Charminster GB . .29 C5
Charmont-en-Beauce
F . .58 B3
Charny F . .59 C4
Charolles F . .69 B4
Chârost F . .68 B2
Charquemont F . .70 A1
Charrin F . .68 B3
Charroux F . .67 B5
Chartres F . .58 B2
Charzykow PL . .46 B3
Chasseneuil-sur-
Bonnieure F . .67 C5
Chassigny F . .59 C6
Château-Arnoux F . .79 B5
Châteaubernard F . .67 C4
Châteaubourg F . .57 B4
Châteaubriant F . .57 C4
Château-Chinon F . .68 A3
Château-d'Oex CH . .70 B2
Château-d'Olonne F . .66 B3
Château-du-Loir F . .58 C1
Châteaudun F . .58 B2
Châteaugiron F . .57 B4
Château-Gontier F . .57 C5
Château-Landon F . .58 B3
Château-la-Vallière F . .67 A5
Château-l'Évêque F . .67 C5
Châteaulin F . .56 B1
Châteaumeillant F . .68 B2
Châteauneuf
Nièvre F . .68 A3
Saône-et-Loire F . .69 B4
Châteauneuf-de-Randon
F . .78 B2
Châteauneuf-d'Ille-et-
Vilaine F . .57 B4
Châteauneuf-du-Faou
F . .56 B2
Châteauneuf-du-Pape
F . .78 B3
Châteauneuf-en-
Thymerais F . .58 B2
Châteauneuf la-Forêt
F . .67 C6
Châteauneuf-le-Rouge
F . .79 C4
Châteauneuf-sur-
Charente F . .67 C4
Châteauneuf-sur-Cher
F . .68 B2
Châteauneuf-sur-Loire
F . .58 C3
Châteauneuf-sur-Sarthe
F . .57 C5
Châteauponsac F . .67 B6
Château-Porcien F . .59 A5
Châteauredon F . .79 B5
Châteaurenard
Bouches du Rhône
F . .78 C3
Loiret F . .59 C4
Château-Renault F . .58 C1
Châteauroux F . .68 B1
Châteauroux-les-Alpes
F . .79 B5
Château-Salins F . .60 B2

Château-Thierry F . .59 A4
Châteauvillain F . .59 B5
Châtel F . .70 B1
Châtelaillon-Plage F . .66 B3
Châtelaudren F . .56 B3
Châtel-Censoir F . .68 A3
Châtelguyon F . .68 C3
Châtellerault F . .67 B5
Châtel-Montagne F . .68 B3
Châtel-St Denis CH . .70 B1
Châtel-sur-Moselle F . .60 B2
Châtelus-Malvaleix F . .68 B2
Châtenois F . .60 B1
Châtenois-les-Forges
F . .70 A1
Chatham GB . .31 C4
Châtillon I . .70 C2
Châtillon-Coligny F . .59 C3
Châtillon-en-Bazois
F . .68 A3
Châtillon-en-Diois F . .79 B4
Châtillon-sur-Indre F . .67 B6
Châtillon-sur-Loire F . .58 C3
Châtillon-sur-Marne
F . .59 A4
Châtillon-sur-Seine F . .59 C5
Châtres F . .59 B4
Chatteris GB . .30 B4
Chatton GB . .25 C6
Chauchina E . .100 B2
Chaudes-Aigues F . .78 B2
Chaudrey F . .59 B5
Chauffailles F . .69 B4
Chaulnes F . .58 A3
Chaument Gistoux B . .49 C5
Chaumergy F . .69 B5
Chaumont F . .59 B6
Chaumont-en-Vexin F . .58 A2
Chaumont-Porcien F . .59 A5
Chaumont-sur-Aire F . .59 B6
Chaumont-sur-Loire
F . .67 A6
Chaunay F . .67 B5
Chaussin F . .69 B5
Chauvigny F . .67 B5
Chavagnes-en-Paillers
F . .66 B3
Chavanges F . .59 B5
Chaves P . .87 C3
Chavignon F . .59 A4
Chazelles-sur-Lyon F . .69 C4
Chazey-Bons F . .69 C5
Cheadle
Greater Manchester
GB . .26 B3
Staffordshire GB . .27 C4
Cheb CZ . .52 C2
Chebsara RUS . .7 B15
Checa E . .95 B5
Checiny PL . .55 C5
Cheddar GB . .29 B5
Cheddleton GB . .26 B3
Chef-Boutonne F . .67 B4
Chekalin RUS . .7 D14
Chekhovo RUS . .47 A6
Cheles E . .93 C3
Chella E . .96 B2
Chelles F . .58 B3
Chelm PL . .11 A7
Chelmno
Kujawsko-Pomorskie
PL . .47 B4
Wielkopolskie PL . .46 C2
Chojnów PL . .53 B5
Cholet F . .66 A4
Chomérac F . .78 B3
Chomutov CZ . .52 C3
Chop UA . .11 B7
Chora GR . .117 E3
Chora Sfakion GR . .117 G6
Chorges F . .79 B5
Choristancó E . .86 A2
Chorley GB . .26 B3
Chornobyl = Chernobyl
UA . .7 F11
Chortkiv UA . .11 B8
Chorzów PL . .54 C3
Chorz2cno PL . .54 C3
Choszczno PL . .46 B1
Chotcza-Józefów PL . .55 B6
Chotěboř CZ . .63 A6
Chouilly F . .59 A5
Chouto P . .92 B2
Chouzy-sur-Cisse F . .67 A6
Chozas de Abajo E . .88 B1
Chrast CZ . .64 A1
Chrast CZ . .63 A4
Chrastava CZ . .53 C4
Chřibská CZ . .53 C4
Christchurch GB . .29 C6
Christiansfeld DK . .39 D2
Chroberz PL . .55 C5
Chropyně CZ . .64 A3
Chrudim CZ . .53 D5
Chrzanów PL . .55 C4
Chtelnica SK . .64 B3
Chudovo RUS . .7 B11
Chueca E . .94 C3
Chulmleigh GB . .28 C4
Chur CH . .71 B4
Churriana E . .100 C1
Churwalden CH . .71 B4
Chvalšiny CZ . .63 B5
Chwaszczyno PL . .47 A4
Chynava CZ . .53 C4
Chýnov CZ . .63 A5
Ciacova RO . .75 C6
Ciadîr-Lunga MD . .11 C10
Ciadoncha E . .88 B3
Cianciana I . .108 B2
Ciażen PL . .54 A2
Cibakhaza H . .75 B5
Cicagna I . .80 B3
Cicarlău RO . .11 C7
Cicciano I . .103 C7
Čičevac SRB . .85 C6
Ciciliano I . .102 B5
Cicognolo I . .71 C5
Cidadelhe P . .87 D3
Cide TR . .16 A6
Cidones E . .89 C4
Ciechanów
Dolnośląskie PL . .54 B1
Mazowieckie PL . .47 C6
Ciechocinek PL . .47 C4
Cielądz PL . .55 B5
Ciemnik PL . .46 B1
Ciempozuelos E . .95 B3
Ciepielów PL . .55 B6
Cierny Balog SK . .65 B5
Cierp-Gaud F . .77 D3
Cierpice PL . .47 C4
Ciervana E . .89 A3
Cierznie PL . .47 B4
Cieslé PL . .47 C6
Cieszyn PL . .65 A4
Cieutat F . .76 C3
Cieza E . .101 A4
Cifer SK . .64 B3
Ciftelier TR . .118 C6
Cifuentes E . .95 B4
Cigales E . .88 C2
Cigliano I . .70 C3
Cihanbeyli TR . .16 B6
Cilipi HR . .105 A4
Cillas E . .95 B5
Cilleros E . .93 A4
Cilleruelo de Arriba E . .88 C3
Cilleruelo de Bezana
E . .88 B3
Cimalmotto CH . .70 B3
Cimanes del Tejar E . .88 B1
Ciminna I . .108 B2
Cîmpia MD . .11 C10
Cimoláis I . .72 B2
Cîmpulung RO . .11 D8
Çınarcık TR . .118 B4
Cinctorres E . .90 C2
Cinderford GB . .29 B5
Cine TR . .119 E3
Cinéves CZ . .53 C5
Cinfães P . .87 C2
Cingia de' Botti I . .81 A4
Cíngoli I . .82 C2
Cinigiano I . .81 D5
Cinobaña SK . .65 B5
Cinq-Mars-la-Pile F . .67 A5
Cinquefondi I . .106 C3
Cintegabelle F . .77 C4
Cintruénigo E . .89 B5
Ciółkowo PL . .47 C5
Ciperez E . .87 C4
Cirat E . .96 A2
Cirella I . .106 B2
Cirencester GB . .29 B6
Cirey-sur-Vezouze F . .60 B2
Ciria E . .89 C5
Ciriè I . .70 C2
Cirigliano I . .104 C2
Cirò I . .107 B4
Cirò Marina I . .107 B4
Ciry-le-Noble F . .69 B4
Cislàu RO . .11 D9
Cismon del Grappa I . .72 C1

Chipping Campden
GB . .29 A6
Chipping Norton GB . .31 C2
Chipping Ongar GB . .31 C4
Chipping Sodbury
GB . .29 B5
Chirac F . .78 B2
Chirbury GB . .26 C2
Chiré CH . .53 C4
Chirivel E . .101 B3
Chirk GB . .26 C2
Chirnside GB . .25 C5
Chişinau = Khisinev
MD . .11 C10
Chişineu Criş RO . .10 C6
Chissey-en-Morvan F . .69 B4
Chiténois F . .70 A1
Chiusa I . .71 B6
Chiusa di Pésio I . .80 B1
Chiusaforte I . .72 B3
Chiusa Scláfani I . .108 B2
Chiusi I . .81 C5
Chiva E . .96 B2
Chivasso I . .70 C2
Chlewiska PL . .55 B5
Chludowo PL . .46 C2
Chlumec nad Cidlinou
CZ . .53 C5
Chlum u Třeboně CZ . .63 B5
Chmielnik PL . .55 C5
Chobienia PL . .54 B1
Chobienice PL . .53 A5
Choceň CZ . .54 C1
Choceň PL . .47 C5
Chochołow PL . .65 A5
Chociw PL . .55 B4
Chociwel PL . .46 B1
Choczewo PL . .46 A3
Chodaków PL . .55 A5
Chodecz PL . .47 C5
Chodov CZ . .52 C2
Chodzież PL . .46 C2
Chojna PL . .45 C6
Chojnice PL . .46 B3
Chojno
Kujawsko-Pomorskie
PL . .47 C5
Wielkopolskie PL . .46 C2
Chojnów PL . .53 B5

Cisneros E . .88 B2
Cissac-Médoc F . .66 C4
Cista CZ . .52 C3
Cisterna di Latina I . .102 B5
Cisternino I . .104 C3
Cistierna E . .88 B1
Citluk BIH . .84 C2
Citov CZ . .53 C4
Cittadella I . .72 C1
Cittàdella Pieve I . .81 D6
Cittàdi Castello I . .82 C1
Cittaducale I . .102 A5
Cittanova I . .106 C3
Città Sant'Angelo I . .103 A7
Ciudadela de Menorca
E . .97 B3
Ciudad Real E . .94 D3
Ciudad Rodrigo E . .93 A4
Ciutadilla E . .91 B4
Cividale del Friuli I . .72 B3
Cividate Camuno I . .71 C5
Civita I . .106 B3
Civita Castellana I . .102 A5
Civitanova Alta I . .82 C2
Civitanova Marche I . .82 C2
Civitavécchia I . .102 A4
Civitella di Romagna
I . .81 B5
Civitella di Tronto I . .82 D2
Civitella Roveto I . .103 B6
Civray F . .67 B5
Çivril TR . .119 D4
Cizur Mayor E . .76 D1
Clabhach GB . .24 B1
Clachan GB . .22 D2
Clachan na Luib GB . .22 D1
Clacton-on-Sea GB . .31 C5
Cladich GB . .24 B2
Claggan GB . .24 B2
Clairvaux-les-Lacs F . .69 B5
Clamecy F . .68 A3
Claonaig GB . .24 C2
Clarecastle IRL . .20 B3
Claregalway IRL . .20 A3
Claremorris IRL . .18 C2
Clarinbridge IRL . .20 A3
Clashmore
GB . .23 D4
IRL . .21 B4
Claudy GB . .19 B4
Clausthal-Zellerfeld D . .51 B6
Clay Cross GB . .27 B4
Claye-Souilly F . .58 B3
Cleadale GB . .24 B1
Cleanor GB . .26 A2
Cleator Moor GB . .26 A2
Clécy F . .57 B5
Cléder F . .56 B1
Cléguérec F . .56 B2
Clelles F . .79 B4
Clenze D . .44 C2
Cleobury Mortimer
GB . .29 A5
Clères F . .58 A2
Clermont F . .58 A3
Clermont-en-Argonne
F . .59 A6
Clermont-Ferrand F . .68 C3
Clermont-l'Hérault F . .78 C2
Clerval F . .69 A6
Clervaux L . .50 C2
Cléry-St André F . .58 C2
Cles I . .71 B6
Clevedon GB . .29 B5
Cleveleys GB . .26 B2
Cley GB . .30 B5
Clifden IRL . .18 C1
Clifford GB . .29 A4
Clisson F . .66 A3
Clitheroe GB . .26 B3
Clogh IRL . .21 B4
Cloghan
Donegal IRL . .19 B4
Offaly IRL . .21 A4
Clogheen IRL . .21 B4
Clogher GB . .19 B4
Cloghjordan IRL . .20 B3
Clohars-Carnoët F . .56 C2
Clonakilty IRL . .20 C3
Clonaslee IRL . .21 A4
Clonbur IRL . .18 C2
Clones IRL . .19 B4
Clonmany IRL . .19 A4
Clonmel IRL . .21 B4
Clonmellon IRL . .19 C4
Clonord IRL . .21 A4
Clonroche IRL . .21 B5
Cloone IRL . .19 C4
Cloppenburg D . .43 C5
Clough GB . .19 B6
Clova GB . .25 B4
Clovelly GB . .28 C3
Clowne GB . .27 B4
Cloyes-sur-le-Loir F . .58 C2
Cloyne IRL . .20 C3
Cluis F . .68 B1
Cluj-Napoca RO . .11 C7
Clun GB . .26 C2
Clunes GB . .24 B3
Cluny F . .69 B4
Clusone I . .71 C4
Clydach GB . .28 B4
Clydebank GB . .24 C3
Coachford IRL . .20 C3
Coagh GB . .19 B5
Coalisland GB . .19 B5
Coalville GB . .27 C4
Coaña E . .86 A4
Çobanlar TR . .118 D5
Cobeta E . .95 B4
Cobh IRL . .20 C3
Cobreces E . .88 A2
Coburg D . .52 C1
Coca E . .94 A2
Cocentaina E . .96 C2
Cochem D . .50 C3
Cockburnspath GB . .25 C5
Cockermouth GB . .26 A2
Codigoro I . .82 B1
Codó RO . .71 C4
Codos E . .89 C5
Codróipo I . .72 C2
Codrongianos I . .110 B1
Coelhoso P . .87 C4
Coesfeld D . .50 B3
Coevorden NL . .42 C3
Cofrentes E . .96 B1
Cogeces del Monte E . .88 C2
Coggeshall GB . .31 C4
Cognac F . .67 C4
Cognin F . .69 C5
Cogny F . .69 B4
Cogolin F . .79 C5
Cogollos de Guadix
E . .100 B2
Cogollos-Vega E . .100 B2
Cogolludo E . .95 B3
Coimbra P . .92 A2
Coín E . .100 C1
Coirós E . .86 A2
Čoka SRB . .75 C5
Col SLO . .73 C4
Colares P . .92 C1
Cölbe D . .51 C4
Cölbitz D . .52 A1
Colchester GB . .31 C4
Coldingham GB . .25 C5
Colditz D . .52 B2
Coldstream GB . .25 C5
Colebrooke GB . .28 C4
Colera E . .91 A6
Coleraine GB . .19 A5
Colfiorito I . .82 C1
Cólico I . .71 B4
Coligny F . .69 B5

Colindres E . .89 A3
Collado-Mediano E . .94 B2
Collado Villalba E . .94 B3
Collagna I . .81 B4
Collanzo E . .88 A1
Collat F . .78 C3
Coll de Nargó E . .91 A4
Colldecanco I . .81 B4
Colldimezzo I . .103 B7
Colle di Val d'Elsa I . .81 C5
Colleferro I . .102 B6
Colle Isarco I . .71 B6
Collelongo I . .103 B6
Collepasso I . .107 A5
Collepepe I . .82 D1
Collesalvetti I . .81 C4
Colle Sannita I . .103 B7
Collesano I . .108 B2
Colli a Volturno I . .103 B7
Collin GB . .25 C4
Collinée F . .56 B3
Collingham
Nottinghamshire
GB . .27 B5
West Yorkshire GB . .27 B4
Collinghorst D . .43 B4
Cóllio I . .71 C5
Collobrières F . .79 C5
Collon IRL . .19 C5
Collooney IRL . .18 B3
Colmar F . .60 B3
Colmars F . .79 B5
Colmenar E . .100 C1
Colmenar de la Sierra
E . .95 A3
Colmenar de Oreja E . .95 B3
Colmenar Viejo E . .94 B3
Colne GB . .26 B3
Colobraro I . .106 A3
Cologna Véneta I . .71 C6
Cologne = Köln D . .50 C2
Cologne F . .77 C3
Cologne al Serio I . .71 C4
Colombey-les-deux-
Églises F . .59 B5
Colombres E . .88 A2
Colomera E . .100 B2
Colomers E . .91 A5
Colomiers F . .77 C4
Colònia de Sant Jordi
E . .97 B3
Colorno I . .81 B4
Colos P . .98 B2
Cölpin D . .45 B5
Colpy GB . .23 D6
Colsterworth GB . .30 B3
Coltishall GB . .30 B5
Colunga E . .88 A1
Colwell GB . .25 C5
Colwyn Bay GB . .26 B2
Colyford GB . .29 C4
Comácchio I . .82 B1
Coma-ruga E . .91 B4
Combarros E . .86 B4
Combeaufontaine F . .60 C1
Comber GB . .19 B6
Combloux F . .70 C1
Combourg F . .57 B4
Combronde F . .68 C3
Comeglians I . .72 B2
Comillas E . .88 A2
Comines F . .49 C4
Cómiso I . .109 C3
Comloşu Mare RO . .75 C5
Commensacq F . .76 B2
Commentry F . .68 B2
Commerau D . .53 B4
Commercy F . .60 B1
Como I . .71 C4
Cómpeta E . .100 C2
Comps-sur-Artuby F . .79 C5
Comporta P . .92 C2
Comrat MD . .11 C10
Comrie GB . .24 B3
Comunanza I . .82 D2
Cona
Emília Romagna I . .81 B5
Véneto I . .72 C1
Concarneau F . .56 C2
Conceição P . .98 B2
Conches-en-Ouche F . .58 B1
Concordia Sagittaria
I . .72 C2
Concordia sulla Sécchia
I . .81 B4
Concots F . .77 B4
Condat F . .68 C2
Condé-en-Brie F . .59 B4
Condeixa P . .92 A2
Condé-sur-l'Escaut F . .49 C4
Condé-sur-Marne F . .59 B5
Condé-sur-Noireau F . .57 B5
Condino I . .71 C5
Condom F . .77 C3
Condove I . .70 C2
Condrieu F . .69 C4
Conegliano I . .72 C2
Conflans-sur-Lanterne
F . .60 C2
Confolens F . .67 B5
Conforto E . .86 A3
Cong IRL . .18 C2
Congleton GB . .26 B3
Congosto de Valdavia
E . .88 B2
Congostrina E . .95 A3
Conil de la Frontera
E . .99 C4
Coningsby GB . .27 B5
Conlie F . .57 B5
Conliège F . .69 B5
Conna IRL . .20 B3
Connah's Quay GB . .26 B2
Connantre F . .59 B4
Connaugh IRL . .20 B3
Connaux F . .78 B3
Connel GB . .24 B2
Connerré F . .58 B1
Cononbridge GB . .23 D4
Čonoplja SRB . .75 C4
Conques-sur-Orbiel F . .77 C5
Con001 UA . .11 A11
Conselice I . .81 B5
Consell E . .97 B2
Conselve I . .72 C1
Consenvoye F . .59 A6
Consett GB . .25 D6
Constância P . .92 B2
Constanţa RO . .11 D10
Constanti E . .91 B4
Constantina E . .99 B5
Consuegra E . .95 C3
Consuma I . .81 C5
Contarina I . .72 C2
Contay F . .48 D3
Conthey CH . .70 B2
Contigliano I . .102 A5
Contis-Plage F . .76 B1
Contrada I . .103 C7
Contres F . .67 A6
Contrexéville F . .60 B1
Conty F . .58 A3
Conversano I . .104 C3
Conwy GB . .26 B2
Cookstown GB . .19 B5

Coole F . .59 B5
Coolgreany IRL . .21 B5
Cooneen GB . .19 B4
Cootehill IRL . .19 B4
Cope E . .101 B4
Copenhagen =
København DK . .41 D2
Copertino I . .105 C4
Copparo I . .81 B5
Coppenbrugge D . .51 A5
Corabia RO . .11 E8
Córaci I . .106 B3
Coralići BIH . .83 B4
Corato I . .104 B2
Coray F . .56 B2
Corbeil-Essonnes F . .58 B3
Corbeny F . .59 A4
Corbera E . .96 B2
Corbigny F . .68 A3
Corbridge GB . .25 D5
Corby GB . .30 B3
Corconte E . .88 A3
Corcubión E . .86 B1
Corcumello I . .103 A6
Cordenons I . .72 C2
Cordes-sur-Ciel F . .77 B4
Córdoba E . .93 B4
Cordobilla de Lácara
E . .93 B4
Cordovado I . .72 C2
Corella E . .89 B5
Coreses E . .88 C1
Corfe Castle GB . .29 C5
Corga de Lobão P . .87 D2
Cori I . .102 B5
Coria E . .93 B4
Coria del Rio E . .99 B4
Corigliano Cálabro I . .106 B3
Corinaldo I . .82 C2
Corinth = Korinthos
GR . .117 E4
Cório I . .70 C2
Coripe E . .99 C5
Cork IRL . .20 C3
Corlay F . .56 B2
Corleone I . .108 B2
Corleto Monforte I . .103 C8
Corleto Perticara I . .104 C2
Çorlu TR . .118 A2
Cormainville F . .58 B2
Cormatin F . .69 B4
Cormeilles F . .57 A6
Cormery F . .67 A5
Cormòns I . .72 C3
Cormoz F . .69 B5
Cornago E . .89 B4
Cornberg D . .51 B5
Cornellana E . .86 A4
Cornesti MD . .11 C10
Corníglio I . .81 B4
Cornimont F . .60 C2
Corníolo I . .81 C5
Cornuda I . .72 C2
Cornudella de Montsant
E . .90 B3
Cornudilla E . .89 B3
Cornus F . .78 C2
Corovodë AL . .116 B2
Corpach GB . .24 B2
Corps F . .79 B4
Corps Nuds F . .57 C4
Corral de Almaguer E . .95 C3
Corral de Ayllón E . .89 C3
Corral de Calatrava
E . .100 A1
Corrales E . .88 C1
Corral-Rubio E . .101 A4
Corran GB . .24 B2
Corredoiras E . .86 A2
Corréggio I . .81 B4
Corré F . .60 C1
Corridónia I . .82 C2
Corris GB . .26 C2
Corrubedo E . .86 B1
Córsico I . .71 C4
Corsock GB . .25 C4
Corte F . .102 A2
Corteconceptión E . .99 B4
Corte de Peleas E . .93 C4
Cortegaça P . .87 D2
Cortegada E . .87 B2
Cortegana E . .99 B4
Cortemaggiore I . .81 B3
Cortemilia I . .80 B2
Corte Pinto P . .98 B3
Cortes E . .89 C5
Cortes de Aragón E . .90 C2
Cortes de Arenoso E . .96 A2
Cortes de Baza E . .101 B3
Cortes de la Frontera
E . .99 C5
Cortes de Pallás E . .96 B2
Cortijada E . .101 B3
Cortico P . .87 C3
Cortijo de Arriba E . .94 C2
Cortijos Nuevos E . .101 A3
Cortina d'Ampezzo I . .72 B2
Corton GB . .30 B5
Cortona I . .81 C6
Coruche P . .92 C2
Corullón E . .86 B4
Çorum TR . .16 A7
Corvara in Badia I . .72 B1
Corvera E . .101 B4
Corwen GB . .26 C2
Cosenza I . .106 B3
Cosham GB . .31 D2
Coslada E . .95 B3
Cosne-Cours-sur-Loire
F . .68 A2
Cosne-d'Allier F . .68 B2
Cospeito E . .86 A3
Cossato I . .70 C3
Cossaye F . .68 B3
Cossé-le-Vivien F . .57 C5
Cossonay CH . .69 B6
Costa da Caparica P . .92 C1
Costa de Santo André
P . .98 A2
Costalpino I . .81 C5
Costa Nova P . .92 A2
Costaros F . .78 B2
Costeşti RO . .11 D8
Costigliole d'Asti I . .80 B2
Costigliole Saluzzo
I . .80 B1
Coswig
Sachsen D . .52 B3
Sachsen-Anhalt D . .52 B2
Cotherstone GB . .27 A4
Cotronei I . .107 B3
Cottbus D . .53 B4
Cottenham GB . .30 B4
Cottingham GB . .27 B5
Coublanc F . .60 C1
Couches F . .69 B4
Couço P . .92 C2
Coucouron F . .78 B2
Coucy-le-Château-
Auffrique F . .59 A4
Couëron F . .66 A3
Couflens F . .77 D4
Couhé F . .67 B5
Couiza F . .77 D5
Coulags GB . .22 D3
Coulanges F . .68 B3
Coulanges-la-Vineuse
F . .59 C4
Coulanges-sur-Yonne
F . .68 A3
Couleuvre F . .68 B2
Coulmier-le-Sec F . .59 C5
Coulommiers F . .59 B4
Coulonges-sur-l'Autize
F . .67 B4
Coulport GB . .24 B3
Coupar Angus GB . .25 B4
Coupéville F . .59 B5
Couptrain F . .57 B5

Coura P 87 C2
Courcelles B 49 C5
Courcelles-Chaussy F 60 A2
Courchevel F 70 C1
Cour-Cheverny F 67 A6
Courçôme F 67 C5
Courçon F 66 B4
Cour-et-Buis F 69 C4
Courgenay CH 70 A2
Courmayeur F 70 C1
Courniou F 78 C1
Cournon d'Auvergne F 68 C3
Cournonterral F 78 C2
Courpière F 68 C3
Coursan F 78 C2
Courseulles-sur-Mer F 57 A5
Cours-la-Ville F 69 B4
Courson-les-Carrières F 59 C4
Courtalain F 58 B2
Courtenay F 59 B4
Courtomer F 58 B1
Courville
  Eure-et-Loire F 58 B2
  Marne F 59 A4
Coussac-Bonneval F 67 C6
Coutances F 57 A4
Couterne F 57 B5
Coutras F 76 A2
Couvet CH 70 B1
Couvin B 49 C5
Couzon F 68 B3
Covadonga E 88 A1
Covaleda E 89 C4
Covarrubias E 89 B3
Covas E 87 C2
Cove GB 22 D3
Coventry GB 30 B2
Coverack GB 28 C2
Covigliáio I 81 B5
Covilhã P 92 A3
Cowbridge GB 29 B4
Cowdenbeath GB 25 B4
Cowes GB 31 D2
Cox F 77 C4
Cozar E 100 A2
Cozes F 66 C4
Cozzano F 102 B2
Craco I 104 C2
Cracow = Kraków PL 55 C4
Craibstone GB 23 D6
Craighouse GB 24 C2
Craignure GB 24 B2
Crail GB 25 B5
Crailsheim D 61 A6
Craiova RO 11 D7
Cramlington GB 25 C6
Cranleigh GB 31 C3
Craon F 57 C5
Craonne F 59 A4
Craponne F 69 C4
Craponne-sur-Arzon F 68 C3
Crathie GB 23 D5
Crato P 92 B3
Craughwell IRL 20 A3
Craven Arms GB 26 C3
Crawford GB 25 C4
Crawinkel D 51 C6
Crawley GB 31 C3
Creag Ghoraidh GB 22 D1
Crécente E 87 B2
Crèches-sur-Saône F 69 B4
Crécy-en-Ponthieu F 48 C2
Crécy-la-Chapelle F 59 B3
Crécy-sur-Serre F 59 A4
Crediton GB 29 C4
Creeslough IRL 19 A4
Creetown GB 24 D3
Creeve IRL 19 B5
Creglingen D 61 A6
Creil F 58 A3
Creissels F 78 B2
Crema I 71 C4
Cremeaux F 68 C3
Crémenes E 88 B1
Crémieu F 69 C5
Cremlingen D 51 A6
Cremona I 81 A4
Creney F 59 B5
Črenšovci SLO 73 B6
Créon F 76 B2
Crepaja SRB 85 A5
Crépey F 60 B1
Crépy F 59 A4
Crépy-en-Valois F 59 A3
Cres HR 83 B3
Crescentino I 70 C3
Crespino I 81 B5
Crespos E 94 B2
Cressage GB 26 C3
Cressensac F 77 A4
Cressia F 69 B5
Crest F 79 B4
Cresta CH 71 B4
Créteil F 58 B3
Creully F 57 A5
Creussen D 62 A2
Creutzwald F 60 A2
Creuzburg D 51 B6
Crevalcore I 81 B5
Crèvecoeur-le-Grand F 58 A3
Crevillente E 101 A5
Crévola d'Ossola I 70 B3
Crewe GB 26 B3
Crewkerne GB 29 C5
Criales E 89 B3
Crianlarich GB 24 B3
Criccieth GB 26 C1
Cricklade GB 29 B6
Crieff GB 25 B4
Crikvenica HR 73 C4
Crillon F 58 A2
Crimmitschau D 52 C2
Crimond GB 23 D7
Crinitz D 53 B3
Cripán E 89 B4
Criquetot-l'Esneval F 57 A6
Crispiano I 104 C3
Crissolo I 79 B6
Cristóbal E 93 A5
Črivitz D 44 B3
Crna SLO 73 B4
Crna Bara
  Srbija SRB 85 B4
  Vojvodina SRB 75 C5
Crnac HR 74 C2
Crnča SRB 85 B4
Crni Lug
  BIH 83 B5
  HR 73 C4
Črni Vrh SLO 73 B4
Crnjelovo Donje BIH 85 B4
Črnomelj SLO 73 C5
Crockford GB 68 C2
Crocq F 68 C2
Croglin GB 25 D5
Crolly IRL 18 A3
Cromarty GB 23 D4
Cromer GB 30 B5
Cronat F 68 B3
Crookhaven IRL 20 C2
Crookstown IRL 20 C3
Croom IRL 20 B3
Cropalati I 106 B3
Crópani I 107 C3
Crosbost GB 22 C2
Crosby GB 26 B2
Crosia I 106 B3
Crossakiel IRL 19 C4
Cross-Hands GB 28 B3
Crosshaven IRL 20 C3
Crosshill GB 24 C3
Crossmolina IRL 18 B2
Crotone I 107 B4

Crottendorf D 52 C2
Crouy F 59 A4
Crowborough GB 31 C4
Crowland GB 30 B3
Crowthorne GB 31 C3
Croyde GB 28 B3
Croydon GB 31 C3
Crozon F 56 B1
Cruas F 78 B3
Cruceni RO 75 B6
Crúcoli I 107 B4
Cruden Bay GB 23 D7
Crudgington GB 26 C3
Cruis F 79 B4
Crumlin GB 19 B5
Cruseilles F 69 B6
Crusheen IRL 20 B3
Červenka SRB 75 C4
Červen Kamen SK 64 A4
Csabacsüd H 75 B5
Csabrendek H 74 A2
Csákánydoroszló H 74 B1
Csákvár H 74 A3
Csány H 65 C5
Csanádapáca H 75 B5
Csanádpalota H 75 B5
Csány H 75 B5
Csapod H 74 A1
Császár H 74 A3
Császártöltés H 75 B4
Csávoly H 75 B4
Csemő H 75 A4
Csengőd H 75 B4
Csépa H 75 B5
Cserepreg H 74 A1
Cserkeszölö H 75 B5
Csernely H 65 B6
Csesztreg H 74 B1
Csökmő H 75 A6
Csökonyavisonta H 74 B2
Csolyospálos H 75 B4
Csongrád H 75 B5
Csopak H 74 B2
Csorna H 64 C3
Csorvás H 75 B5
Csurgo H 74 B2
Cuacos de Yuste E 93 A5
Cualedro E 87 C3
Cuanca de Campos E 88 B1
Cuba P 98 A3
Cubel E 95 A5
Cubelles E 91 B4
Cubillos E 89 C4
Cubillos del Sil E 86 B4
Cubjac F 67 C5
Cubo de la Solana E 89 C4
Çuçak TR 16 A6
Cuckfield GB 31 C3
Cucuron F 79 C4
Cudillero E 86 A4
Cuéllar E 88 C2
Cuenca E 95 B4
Cuers F 79 C5
Cuerva E 94 C2
Cuevas de Agreda E 89 C5
Cuevas Bajas E 100 B1
Cuevas del Almanzora E 101 B4
Cuevas del Becerro E 99 C5
Cuevas del Campo E 100 B3
Cuevas del Valle E 94 B1
Cuevas de San Clemente E 89 B3
Cuevas de San Marcos E 100 B1
Cuges-les-Pins F 79 C4
Cúglieri I 110 B1
Cugnaux F 77 C4
Cuijk NL 50 B1
Cuinzier F 69 B4
Cuiseaux F 69 B5
Cuisery F 69 B5
Culan F 68 B2
Culemborg NL 49 B6
Cúllar E 101 B3
Cullaville GB 19 B5
Cullera E 96 B2
Cullivoe GB 22 A7
Cully CH 70 B1
Culoz F 69 C5
Cults GB 23 D6
Cumbernauld GB 25 C4
Cumbres de San Bartolomé E 99 A4
Cumbres Mayores E 99 A4
Çumiana I 80 B1
Čumić SRB 85 B5
Cumnock GB 24 C3
Çumra TR 16 C6
Cúneo I 80 B1
Cunlhat F 68 C3
Cunski HR 83 B3
Cuntis E 86 B2
Cuorgnè I 70 C2
Cupar GB 25 B4
Cupello I 103 A7
Cupra Maríttima I 82 C2
Cupramontana I 82 C2
Čuprija SRB 85 C6
Curinga I 106 C3
Currelos P 86 B3
Currie GB 25 C4
Curtea de Argeş RO 11 D8
Curtici RO 75 B6
Curtis E 86 A2
Curtis Santa Eulalia E 86 A2
Čurug SRB 75 C5
Cusano Mutri I 103 B7
Cushendall GB 19 A5
Cusset F 68 B3
Cussy-les-Forges F 68 A4
Custines F 60 B2
Cutanda E 90 C1
Cutro I 107 B3
Cutrofiano I 107 A5
Cuvilly F 58 A3
Cuxhaven D 43 B5
Cvikov CZ 53 C4
Cwmbran GB 29 B4
Cybinka PL 53 A4
Czaczcz PL 54 A1
Czajków PL 54 B3
Czarlin PL 47 A4
Czarna
  Łódzkie PL 55 B4
  Podkarpackie PL 55 C6
Czarna Białostocka PL 6 D8
Czarna-Dąbrówka PL 46 A3
Czarna Woda PL 47 B4
Czarnca PL 55 C4
Czarne PL 46 B2
Czarnków PL 46 C2
Czarnowo PL 47 B4
Czarnozyly PL 54 B3
Czarny Bór PL 53 C6
Czarny Dunajec PL 65 A5
Czarny Las PL 54 B2
Czchów PL 65 A6
Czechowice-Dziedzice PL 65 A4
Czempiń PL 54 A1
Czermno PL 55 B5
Czerniejewo PL 46 C3
Czernikowo PL 47 C4
Czersk PL 46 B3
Czerwieńsk PL 53 A5
Czerwionka-Leszczyny PL 54 C3
Częstochowa PL 55 C4
Czeszewo PL 46 C3
Człopa PL 46 B2
Człuchów PL 46 B3
Czołpino PL 46 A2

D

Dağ TR 119 E5
Daaden D 50 C3
Dabas H 75 A4
Dąbie H 54 A3
Dąbki PL 46 A2
Dabo F 60 B3
Dabrowa PL 46 C3
Dąbrowa Górnicza PL 55 C4
Dąbrowa Tarnowska PL 55 C5
Dąbrowice PL 55 A4
Dabrowno PL 47 B6
Dachau D 62 B2
Dačice CZ 63 A6
Daday TR 16 A6
Dagali N 32 B5
Dägebüll D 39 E1
Dagmersellen CH 70 A2
Dahlen D 52 B2
Dahlenburg D 44 B2
Dahme D 52 B3
Dahn D 60 A3
Dähre D 44 C2
Daikanvik S 115 B13
Dail bho Dheas GB 22 C2
Dailly GB 24 C3
Daimiel E 95 C3
Daingean IRL 21 A4
Đakovica KOS 10 E6
Đakovo HR 74 C3
Dal
  Akershus N 34 B3
  Telemark N 32 C5
Dalaas A 71 A5
Dalabrog GB 22 D1
Dala-Floda S 36 B1
Dala-Husby S 36 B2
Dala-Järna S 36 B1
Dalaman TR 119 F3
Dalarö S 37 C5
Dalbeattie GB 25 D4
Dalby
  DK 39 D3
  Skåne S 41 D3
  Uppsala S 37 C4
  Värmland S 34 B4
Dale
  Pembrokeshire GB 28 B2
  Shetland GB 22 A7
  Hordaland N 32 B2
  Sogn og Fjordane N 32 A2
Dalen
  Akershus N 34 C3
  Telemark N 33 C5
Daleszyce PL 55 C5
Dalhalvaig GB 23 C5
Dalheim L 60 A2
Dalhem S 37 E5
Dálias E 100 C3
Dalj HR 75 C3
Dalkeith GB 25 C4
Dalkey IRL 21 A5
Dalmally GB 24 B3
Dalmellington GB 24 C3
Dalmose DK 39 D4
Daløy N 32 A1
Dalry
  Dumfries & Galloway GB 24 C3
  North Ayrshire GB 24 C3
Dalrymple GB 24 C3
Dalseter N 32 A6
Dalsjöfors S 40 B3
Dalskog S 35 D4
Dals Långed S 35 D4
Dals Rostock S 35 D4
Dalston GB 25 D5
Dalstorp S 40 B3
Dalton-in-Furness GB 26 A2
Daluis F 79 B5
Dalum
  D 43 C4
  S 40 B3
Dalvík IS 111 B7
Dalwhinnie GB 24 B3
Dalyan TR 119 F3
Damasi GR 116 C4
Damasławek PL 46 C3
Damazan F 76 B3
Dambaslar TR 118 A2
Damville F 58 B2
Damvillers F 59 A6
Damwoude NL 42 B2
Danasjö S 115 B13
Danbury GB 31 C4
Dångebo S 40 C5
Dangé-St Romain F 67 B5
Dangeul F 58 B1
Danilovgrad MNE 105 A5
Danischenhagen D 44 A2
Daniszyn PL 54 B2
Danjoutin F 60 C2
Dannas S 40 B3
Dannemarie F 60 C3
Dannemora S 36 B4
Dannenberg D 44 B3
Dánszentmiklós H 75 A4
Dány H 75 A4
Daoulas F 56 B1
Darabani RO 11 B9
Darány H 74 C2
Darda HR 74 C3
Dardesheim D 51 B6
Darfeld D 50 A3
Darfo I 71 C5
Dargin PL 46 A2
Dargun D 45 B4
Darlington GB 27 A4
Darłowo PL 46 A2
Darmstadt D 61 A4
Darney F 60 B2
Daroca E 95 A5
Darque P 87 C2
Darragh IRL 20 B2
Dartford GB 31 C4
Dartington GB 28 C4
Dartmouth GB 29 C4
Darton GB 27 B4
Daruvar HR 74 C2
Darvas H 75 A6
Darvel GB 24 C3
Darwen GB 26 B3
Dassel D 51 B5
Dassow D 44 B2
Datça TR 119 F2
Datteln D 50 B3
Dattenfeld D 50 C3
Daugard D 39 D2
Daumeray F 57 C5
Daun D 50 C2
Daventry GB 30 B2
Davor HR 74 A3
Davos CH 71 B4
Davutlar TR 119 E2
Davyd Haradok BY 7 E9
Dawlish GB 29 C4
Dax F 76 C1
Dazkırı TR 119 E4
Deal GB 31 C5
Deauville F 57 A6
Deba E 89 A4
Debar MK 116 A2
Debe Wielkie PL 55 A6
Dębica PL 55 C6

Dębnica Kaszubska PL 46 A3
Dębno PL 45 C6
Debołęka PL 54 B3
Debrc SRB 85 B4
Debrecen H 10 C6
Debrznica PL 53 A5
Debrzno PL 46 B3
Debstedt D 43 B5
Decazeville F 77 B5
Dechtice SK 64 B3
Decima I 102 B5
Decimomannu I 110 C1
Děčín CZ 53 C4
Decize F 68 B3
De Cocksdorp NL 42 B1
Decollatura I 106 B3
Decs H 74 B3
Dedaj AL 105 A5
Deddington GB 31 C2
Dedeler TR 118 B5
Dedelow D 45 B5
Dedemli TR 119 E7
Dedemsvaart NL 42 C3
Dédestapolcsány H 65 B6
Dedovichi RUS 7 C10
Deeping St Nicholas GB 30 B3
Deftera CY 120 A2
Dég H 74 B3
Degaña E 86 B4
Degeberga S 41 D4
Degerby FIN 37 B7
Degerfors S 37 C1
Degerhamn S 41 C6
Degernes N 35 C3
Deggendorf D 62 B3
Deggingen D 61 B5
Dego I 80 B2
Degolados P 93 B3
Dehesa de Guadix E 100 B3
Dehesas Viejas E 100 B2
Deia E 97 B2
Deining D 62 A2
Deinze B 49 C4
Déiva Marina I 80 B3
Dej RO 11 C7
Deje S 35 C5
De Koog NL 42 B1
Delabole GB 28 C3
Delary S 40 C4
Delbrück D 51 B4
Delden NL 50 A2
Deleitosa E 93 B5
Delekovec HR 74 B1
Delémont CH 70 A2
Delft NL 49 A5
Delfzijl NL 42 B3
Délia I 108 B2
Delianuova I 106 C2
Deliblato SRB 85 B6
Delice TR 16 B6
Deliceto I 103 B8
Delitzsch D 52 B2
Dellach A 72 B3
Delle F 70 A2
Delme F 60 A2
Delmenhorst D 43 B5
Delnice HR 73 C4
Delsbo S 115 B13
Delvin IRL 19 C4
Delvinë AL 116 C2
Demandice SK 65 B4
Demen D 44 B3
Demidov RUS 7 D11
Demigny F 69 B4
Demir Kapija MK 116 A4
Demirci TR 118 C3
Demirtaş TR 118 B4
Demmin D 45 B5
Demonte I 80 B1
Demyansk RUS 7 C12
Denain F 49 C4
Denbigh GB 26 B2
Den Burg NL 42 B1
Dender-monde B 49 B5
Denekamp NL 42 C3
Den Ham NL 42 C3
Den Helder NL 42 C1
Denholm GB 25 C5
Denia E 96 C3
Denizli TR 119 E4
Denkendorf D 62 B2
Denklingen D 50 C3
Denny GB 25 B4
Den Oever NL 42 C2
Denta RO 75 C6
Déols F 68 B1
De Panne B 48 B3
Derbent TR 119 D3
Derby GB 27 C4
Dereköy TR 118 A2
Derenberg D 51 B6
Derinkuyu TR 16 B7
Dermbach D 51 C6
Dermulo I 71 B6
Deronje SRB 75 C4
Derrygonnelly GB 19 B4
Derrylin GB 19 B4
Derry/Londonderry GB 19 B4
Dersingham GB 30 B4
Deruta I 82 D1
Dervaig GB 24 B1
Derval F 57 C4
Derveni GR 117 D4
Dervock GB 19 A5
Desana I 70 C3
Descartes F 67 B5
Desenzano del Garda I 71 C5
Deset N 34 A3
Deševa BIH 84 C3
Desfina GR 116 D4
Désio I 71 C4
Deski SLO 73 B6
Desná CZ 53 C5
Despetovac SRB 85 B6
Despotovo SRB 75 C4
Dessau D 52 B2
Deštná CZ 63 A5
Destriana E 87 B4
Désulo I 110 B2
Desvres F 48 C2
Deszk H 75 B5
Deta RO 75 C6
Detmold D 51 B4
Dětřichov CZ 64 A3
Dettelbach D 61 A6
Dettingen
  Baden-Württemberg D 61 B5
  Baden-Württemberg D 61 C5
Dettwiller F 60 B3
Detva SK 65 B5
Deurne NL 50 B1
Deutsch Wagram A 64 B2
Deutschkreutz A 64 C2
Deutschlandsberg A 73 B5
Deva RO 11 D7
Dévaványa H 75 A5
Devecikonağı TR 118 C4
Devecser H 74 A2
Develi TR 16 B7
Devene BG 11 E7
Deventer NL 50 A2
Devesa E 87 A3
Devil's Bridge GB 26 C1
Devin BG 116 A6
Devínska Nová Ves SK 64 B3
Devizes GB 29 B6
Devonport GB 28 C3
Devrek TR 118 A6
Devrekâni TR 16 A6
Đevrske HR 83 C4

De Wijk NL 42 C3
Dewsbury GB 27 B4
Deza E 89 C4
Dežanovac HR 74 C2
Dezzo I 71 C5
Dhali CY 120 A2
Dherinia CY 120 A2
Dhërmi AL 105 C5
Diamante I 106 B2
Dianalund DK 39 D4
Diano d'Alba I 80 B2
Diano Marina I 80 C2
Dicomano I 81 C5
Didcot GB 31 C2
Didim TR 119 E2
Didymoticho GR 118 A1
Die F 79 B4
Diebling F 60 A2
Diedorf D 62 B1
Diego del Carpio E 93 A5
Diekirch L 60 A2
Diélette F 57 A4
Diemelstadt D 51 B5
Diémoz F 69 C5
Dienten am Hochkönig A 72 A2
Diepenbeck B 49 C6
Diepholz D 43 C5
Dieppe F 58 A2
Dierberg D 45 B4
Dierdorf D 50 C3
Dieren NL 50 A2
Dierhagen D 44 A4
Diesdorf D 44 C2
Diessen D 62 C2
Diest B 49 C6
Dietenheim D 61 B6
Dietfurt D 62 A2
Dietikon CH 70 A3
Dietzenbach D 51 C4
Dieue-sur-Meuse F 59 A6
Dieulefit F 79 B4
Dieulouard F 60 B2
Dieuze F 60 B2
Diever NL 42 C3
Diez D 50 C4
Diezma E 100 B2
Differdange L 60 A1
Digermulen N 112 D4
Dignac F 67 C5
Dignano I 72 B2
Digne-les-Bains F 79 B5
Digny F 58 B2
Digoin F 68 B3
Dijon F 69 A5
Dikanäs S 115 B13
Dikili TR 118 C1
Diksmuide B 48 B3
Dilar E 100 B2
Dillenburg D 50 C4
Dillingen
  Bayern D 61 B6
  Saarland D 60 A2
Dilsen B 50 B1
Dimaro I 71 B5
Dimitrovgrad BG 11 E8
Dimitsana GR 117 E4
Dinami I 106 C3
Dinan F 57 B3
Dinant B 49 C5
Dinar TR 119 D5
Dinard F 57 B3
Dingden D 50 B2
Dingelstädt D 51 B6
Dingle
  IRL 20 B1
  S 35 D3
Dingolfing D 62 B3
Dingtuna S 37 C3
Dingwall GB 23 D4
Dinkelsbühl D 61 A6
Dinkelscherben D 62 B1
Dinklage D 43 C5
Dinslaken D 50 B2
Dinxperlo NL 50 B2
Diö S 40 C4
Diósgyör H 65 B6
Diósjeno H 65 C5
Diou F 68 B3
Dippen GB 24 C2
Dipperz D 51 C5
Dippoldiswalde D 53 C3
Dirdal N 33 D3
Dirksland NL 49 B5
Dirlewang D 61 C6
Dischingen D 61 B6
Diso I 107 A5
Diss GB 30 B5
Dissen D 50 A4
Distington GB 26 A2
Ditzingen D 61 B5
Ditzum D 43 B4
Divača SLO 72 C3
Dives-sur-Mer F 57 A5
Divín SK 65 B5
Divišov CZ 63 A5
Divonne les Bains F 69 B6
Dixmont F 59 B4
Dizy-le-Gros F 59 A5
Djúpivogur IS 111 C11
Djupvasshytta N 114 F6
Djura S 36 B1
Djurås S 36 B2
Djurmo S 36 B2
Djursdala S 40 B5
Dlouhá Loučka CZ 64 A3
Długowola PL 55 B6
Dmitriyev Lgovskiy RUS 7 E13
Dmitrov RUS 7 C14
Dmitrovsk-Orlovskiy RUS 7 E13
Dno RUS 7 C10
Doade E 86 B3
Doğanhisar TR 119 D6
Dobanovci SRB 85 B5
Dobbertin D 44 B4
Dobbiaco I 72 B2
Dobczyce PL 65 A6
Dobele LV 6 C7
Döbeln D 52 B3
Doberlug-Kirchhain D 52 B3
Dobern D 53 B4
Dobersberg A 63 B6
Dobiegniew PL 46 C1
Dobieszyn PL 55 B6
Doboj BIH 84 B3
Dobošnica BIH 84 B3
Doboz H 75 B6
Dobra
  Wielkopolskie PL 54 A3
  Zachodnio-Pomorskie PL 45 B7
Dobra
  Kujawsko-Pomorskie PL 47 C4
  Mazowieckie PL 55 A6
Dobrá Niva SK 65 B5
Dobřany CZ 63 A4
Dobre
  Kujawsko-Pomorskie PL 47 C4
  Mazowieckie PL 55 A6
Dobre Miasto PL 47 B6
Dobri H 74 B1
Dobrich BG 11 E9
Dobri Do SRB 85 D6
Dobrinishte BG 116 A5
Dobříš CZ 63 A5
Dobro E 89 B3
Dobrodzień PL 54 C3
Dobromierz PL 54 C1

Dobrovnik SLO 73 B6
Dobruška CZ 53 C6
Dobrzany PL 46 B1
Dobrzeń Wielki PL 54 B2
Dobrzyca
  Wielkopolskie PL 46 B2
  Wielkopolskie PL 54 B2
Dobrzyń nad Wisłą PL 47 C5
Dobšiná SK 65 B6
Dobwalls GB 28 C3
Dochamps B 49 C6
Docking GB 30 B4
Docksta S 115 D15
Doddington GB 25 C5
Döderhult S 40 B6
Doesburg NL 50 A2
Doetinchem NL 50 B2
Dogliani I 80 B1
Dogueno P 98 B3
Doische B 49 C5
Dois Portos P 92 B1
Dojč SK 64 B3
Dokka N 34 B2
Dokkedal DK 38 C3
Dokkum NL 42 B2
Dokležovje SLO 73 B6
Doksy CZ 53 C4
Dokuz TR 119 D7
Dolancourt F 59 B5
Dolceácqua I 80 C1
Dol-de-Bretagne F 57 B4
Dole F 69 A5
Dølemo N 33 D5
Dolenja vas SLO 73 C4
Dolenjske Toplice SLO 73 C5
Dolfor GB 26 C2
Dolgarrog GB 26 B2
Dolgellau GB 26 C2
Dolianá GR 116 C2
Dolianova I 110 C2
Dolice PL 45 B7
Doljani HR 83 B5
Döllach im Mölltal A 72 B2
Dollar GB 25 B4
Dollnstein D 62 B2
Dollot F 59 B4
Döllstädt D 51 B6
Dolná Strehová SK 65 B5
Dolné Saliby SK 64 B3
Dolni Benešov CZ 64 A4
Dolni Bousov CZ 53 C5
Dolní Kounice CZ 64 A2
Dolní Kralovice CZ 63 A6
Dolní Újezd CZ 64 A2
Dolní Žandov CZ 52 C2
Dolný Kubín SK 65 A5
Dolo I 72 C2
Dolores E 101 A5
Dolovo SRB 85 B5
Dölsach A 72 B2
Dolsk PL 54 A2
Dolwyddelan GB 26 B2
Domaljevac BIH 84 A3
Domanic TR 118 C4
Domaniža SK 65 A4
Domanovići BIH 84 C3
Domašov CZ 64 A3
Domaszék H 75 B4
Domaszków PL 54 C1
Domaszowice PL 54 B2
Domat-Ems CH 71 B4
Domažlice CZ 62 A3
Dombås N 114 E6
Dombasle-sur-Meurthe F 60 B2
Dombegyház H 75 B6
Dombóvár H 74 B3
Domène F 69 C5
Domérat F 68 B2
Domfessel F 60 B3
Domfront F 57 B5
Domfront-en-Champagne F 57 B6
Domingão P 92 B2
Domingo Pérez
  Granada E 100 B2
  Toledo E 94 C2
Dömitz D 44 B3
Dommartin-le-Franc F 59 B5
Domme F 77 B4
Dommitzsch D 52 B2
Domodóssola I 70 B3
Domokos GR 116 C3
Domoszló H 65 C6
Dompaire F 60 B2
Dompierre-du-Chemin F 57 B5
Dompierre-sur-Besbre F 68 B3
Dompierre-sur-Mer F 66 B3
Dömsöd H 75 A4
Domsure F 69 B5
Dómus de María I 110 D1
Domusnóvas I 110 C1
Domvena GR 117 D4
Domžale SLO 73 B4
Don Benito E 93 C5
Donabate IRL 21 A5
Donaghadee GB 19 B6
Don Álvaro E 93 C4
Doña Mencía E 100 B1
Donaueschingen D 61 C4
Donaustauf D 62 B3
Donauwörth D 62 B1
Doncaster GB 27 B4
Donegal IRL 18 B3
Donestebe-Santesteban E 76 C1
Donges F 66 A2
Dongo I 71 B4
Donington GB 30 B3
Doniños E 86 A2
Donja Bebrina HR 84 A3
Donja Brela HR 84 C1
Donja Dubica BIH 84 A3
Donja Dubrava HR 74 B1
Donja Kupčina HR 73 C5
Donja Šatornja SRB 85 B5
Donja Stubica HR 73 C5
Donje Brišnik BIH 84 C2
Donji Andrijevci HR 74 C3
Donji Kazanci BIH 83 C5
Donji Koričáni BIH 84 B2
Donji Lapac HR 83 B4
Donji Malovan BIH 84 C2
Donji Miholjac HR 74 C3
Donji Mosti HR 74 B1
Donji Poloj HR 73 C5
Donji Rujani BIH 83 C5
Donji Srb HR 83 B5
Donji Svilaj BIH 84 A3
Donji Tovarnik SRB 85 B4
Donji Vakuf BIH 84 B2
Donnalucata I 109 C3
Donnemarie-Dontilly F 59 B4
Donnersbach A 73 A4
Donnersbachwald A 73 A4
Donnerskirchen A 64 C2
Donorático I 81 C4
Donostia-San Sebastián E 76 C1
Donovaly SK 65 B5
Donzenac F 67 C6
Donzère F 78 B3
Donzy F 68 A3
Doonbeg IRL 20 B2
Doorn NL 49 A6
Dorchester GB 29 C5

Dørdal N 33 D6
Dordrecht NL 49 B5
Dörentrup D 50 A3
Dores GB 23 D4
Dorfen D 62 B3
Dorfgastein A 72 A3
Dorf Mecklenburg D 44 B3
Dorgali I 110 B2
Dorking GB 31 C3
Dormagen D 50 B2
Dormans F 59 A4
Dornava SLO 73 B5
Dornbirn A 71 A4
Dornburg D 52 B1
Dorndorf D 51 C6
Dornecy F 68 A3
Dornes F 68 B3
Dornhan D 61 B4
Dornie GB 22 D3
Dornoch GB 23 D4
Dornstetten D 61 B4
Dornum D 43 B4
Dorog H 65 C4
Dorogobuzh RUS 7 D12
Dorohoi RO 11 C9
Dorotea S 115 C13
Dorotowo PL 47 B6
Dörpen D 43 C4
Dorsten D 50 B2
Dortan F 69 B5
Dortmund D 50 B3
Doruchów PL 54 B3
Dorum D 43 B5
Dörzbach D 61 A5
Dos Aguas E 96 B2
Dosbarrios E 95 C3
Dösemealtı TR 119 F5
Dos Hermanas E 99 B5
Dospat BG 116 A6
Dos-Torres E 100 A1
Dottignies B 49 C4
Döttingen CH 70 A3
Douai F 49 C4
Douarnenez F 56 B1
Douchy F 59 C4
Douchy-les-Mines F 49 C4
Doucier F 69 B5
Doudeville F 58 A1
Doué-la-Fontaine F 67 A4
Douglas
  Isle of Man GB 26 A1
  South Lanarkshire GB 25 C4
Doulaincourt-Saucourt F 59 B6
Doulevant-le-Château F 59 B5
Doullens F 48 C3
Dounby GB 23 B5
Doune GB 24 B3
Dounreay GB 23 C5
Dourgne F 77 C5
Dournazac F 67 C5
Douro Calvo P 87 D3
Douvaine F 69 B6
Douvres-la-Délivrande F 57 A5
Douzy F 59 A6
Dover GB 31 C5
Dovje SLO 72 B3
Dovre N 114 F6
Downham Market GB 30 B4
Downhill GB 19 A5
Downpatrick GB 19 B6
Dowra IRL 18 B3
Doxato GR 116 B6
Doyet F 68 B2
Dozule F 57 A5
Drača SRB 85 B5
Dračevo BIH 84 D3
Drachten NL 42 B3
Draga SLO 73 C4
Drăgăşani RO 11 D8
Dragatuš SLO 73 C5
Dragichyn BY 7 E8
Draginja SRB 85 B4
Dragobi AL 105 A5
Dragocvet SRB 85 C6
Dragolovci BIH 84 B2
Dragoni I 103 B7
Dragør DK 41 D2
Dragotina HR 73 C6
Dragozetići HR 82 A3
Draguignan F 79 C5
Drahnsdorf D 52 B3
Drahovce SK 64 B3
Drama GR 116 B6
Drammen N 35 C2
Drangedal N 33 C6
Drangsnes IS 111 B4
Dransfeld D 51 B5
Dranske D 45 A5
Draperstown GB 19 B5
Drassburg A 64 C2
Drávaszabolcs H 74 C3
Dravograd SLO 73 B5
Drawsko Pomorskie PL 46 B1
Drayton GB 30 B5
Draženov CZ 62 A3
Draževac SRB 85 B5
Dražice HR 73 C4
Drebkau D 53 B4
Dreieich D 51 C4
Dreisen D 61 A4
Drenovci HR 84 A3
Drensteinfurt D 50 B3
Dreux F 58 B2
Dřevohostice CZ 64 A3
Drezdenko PL 46 C1
Dřiteň CZ 63 A5
Driffield GB 27 A5
Drimnin GB 24 B2
Drimoleague IRL 20 C2
Dringenberg D 51 B5
Drinić BIH 83 B5
Drinjača BIH 85 B4
Drinovci BIH 84 C2
Driopida GR 117 E6
Drivstua N 114 E7
Drlače SRB 85 B4
Drnholec CZ 64 B2
Drniš HR 83 C5
Drnje HR 74 B1
Drnovice CZ 64 A2
Dro I 71 C5
Drøbak N 35 C2
Drochia MD 11 B10
Drochtersen D 43 B6
Drogheda IRL 19 C5
Drohobych UA 11 B8
Droitwich Spa GB 29 A5
Dromahair IRL 18 B3
Dromara GB 19 B5
Dromcolliher IRL 20 B3
Dromore
  Down GB 19 B5
  Tyrone GB 19 B4
Dromore West IRL 18 B3
Dronero I 79 B6
Dronfield GB 27 B4
Drongan GB 24 C3
Dronninglund DK 38 B3
Dronten NL 42 C2

Drösendorf A 63 B6
Drösing A 64 B2
Drottningholm S 37 C4
Droué F 58 B2
Drulingen F 60 B3
Drumbeg GB 22 C3
Drumcliff IRL 18 B3
Drumkeeran IRL 18 B3
Drummore GB 24 D3
Drumnadrochit GB 23 D4
Drumquin GB 19 B4
Drumshanbo IRL 18 B3
Drumsna IRL 19 C4
Drunen NL 49 B6
Druskininkai LT 6 D7
Druya BY 7 D9
Družetići SRB 85 B5
Drvar BIH 83 B5
Drvenik HR 84 C2
Drwalew PL 55 B6
Drymen GB 24 B3
Drynoch GB 22 D2
Drzewica PL 55 B5
Dualchi I 110 B1
Duas Igrejas P 87 C4
Dub SRB 85 C4
Dubá CZ 53 C4
Dubăsari MD 11 C10
Dübendorf CH 70 A3
Dubi CZ 53 C3
Dubica HR 74 C1
Dublin IRL 21 A5
Dubna RUS 7 C14
Dubňany CZ 64 B2
Dubnica nad Váhom SK 64 B4
Dubník SK 65 C4
Dubno UA 11 A8
Dubodiel SK 64 B4
Dubona SRB 85 B5
Dubovac SRB 85 B6
Dubovic BIH 83 B5
Dubranec HR 73 C5
Dubrava HR 74 C1
Dubrave BIH 84 B3
Dubravica
  HR 73 C5
  SRB 85 B5
Dubrovnik HR 84 D3
Dubrovytsya UA 7 F9
Ducey F 57 B4
Duchcov CZ 53 C3
Ducherow D 45 B5
Dučina SRB 85 B5
Duclair F 58 A1
Dudar H 74 A2
Duddington GB 30 B3
Dudelange L 60 A2
Dudeldorf D 51 B6
Dudeştii Vechi RO 75 B5
Dudley GB 26 C3
Dueñas E 88 C2
Duesund N 32 B2
Dueville I 72 C1
Duffield GB 27 C4
Dufftown GB 23 D5
Duga Poljana SRB 85 C5
Duga Resa HR 73 C5
Dugi Rat HR 83 C5
Dugny-sur-Meuse F 59 A6
Dugopolje HR 83 C5
Dugo Selo HR 73 C6
Duino I 72 C3
Duisburg D 50 B2
Dukat AL 105 C5
Dukovany CZ 64 A2
Duleek IRL 19 C5
Dülken D 50 B2
Dülmen D 50 B3
Dulovo BG 11 E9
Dulpetorpet N 34 B4
Dulverton GB 29 B4
Dumbarton GB 24 C3
Dümerek TR 118 C6
Dumfries GB 25 C4
Dumlupinar TR 118 C4
Dümpelfeld D 50 C2
Dunaalmás H 65 C4
Dunabogdány H 65 C5
Dunafalva H 74 B3
Dunaföldvár H 74 B3
Dunaharaszti H 75 A4
Dunajská Streda SK 64 B3
Dunakeszi H 75 A4
Dunakömlöd H 74 B3
Dunapataj H 75 B3
Dunaszekcsö H 74 B3
Dunaszentgyorgy H 74 B3
Dunatetétlen H 75 B4
Dunaújváros H 74 B3
Dunavecse H 75 B3
Dunbar GB 25 B5
Dunbeath GB 23 C5
Dunblane GB 24 B3
Dunboyne IRL 21 A5
Dundalk IRL 19 B5
Dundee GB 25 B5
Dunfanaghy IRL 19 A4
Dunfermline GB 25 B4
Dungannon GB 19 B5
Dungarvan IRL 21 B4
Dungiven GB 19 B5
Dunglow IRL 18 B3
Dunkeld GB 25 B4
Dunkerque = Dunkirk GB 48 B3
Dunkineely IRL 18 B3
Dunkirk = Dunkerque GB 48 B3
Dun Laoghaire IRL 21 A5
Dunlavin IRL 21 A5
Dunleer IRL 19 C5
Dun-le-Palestel F 67 B6
Dunlop GB 24 C3
Dunloy GB 19 A5
Dunmanway IRL 20 C2
Dunmore IRL 18 C3
Dunmore East IRL 21 B5
Dunmurry GB 19 B5
Dunnet GB 23 C5
Dunningen D 61 B4
Dunoon GB 24 C3
Dunscore GB 25 C4
Dunshaughlin IRL 21 A5
Dunstable GB 31 C3
Dunster GB 29 B4
Dun-sur-Auron F 68 B2
Dun-sur-Meuse F 59 A6
Dunure GB 24 C3
Dunvegan GB 22 D2
Duplek SLO 73 B5
Dupnitsa BG 11 E7
Durağan TR 16 A7
Durak TR 118 C3
Durana E 89 B4
Durance F 76 B3
Durango E 89 A4
Durankulak BG 11 E10
Duras F 76 B3
Durban-Corbières F 78 D1
Durbheim D 61 B4
Durbuy B 49 C6

Dúrcal E....100 C2
Đurđevovac HR....74 C3
Đurđevac HR....74 B2
Đurđevik BIH....84 B3
Düren D....50 C2
Đurinci SRB....85 B5
Đurlach D....61 B4
Đurmanec HR....73 B5
Đuness GB....22 C4
Đurnkrut A....64 B2
Dürröhren CH....71 B4
Dürrboden CH....70 B3
Dürres AL....105 B5
Durrow IRL....21 B4
Durrus IRL....20 C2
Dursunbey TR....118 C3
Durtal F....57 C5
Đurup DK....38 C1
Đurusu TR....118 A3
Dusina BIH....84 C2
Dusnok H....75 B3
Dusocin PL....47 B4
Düsseldorf D....50 B2
Dusslingen D....61 B5
Duszniki PL....46 C2
Duszniki-Zdrój PL....54 C1
Dutovlje SLO....72 C3
Duvebo S....40 A4
Duved S....115 D9
Düzağac TR....118 D5
Düzce TR....118 B6
Dvärsätt S....115 D11
Dvor HR....83 A5
Dvorce CZ....64 A3
Dvorníky SK....64 B3
Dvory nad Žitavou
    SK....64 C4
Dvůr Králové nad Labem
    CZ....53 C5
Dyatkovo RUS....7 E13
Dybvad DK....38 B3
Dyce GB....23 D6
Dygowo PL....46 A1
Dykehead GB....25 B4
Dymchurch GB....31 C5
Dymer UA....11 A11
Dyrnes N....114 D4
Dywity PL....47 B6
Džanići BIH....84 C2
Dziadowa Kłoda PL....54 B2
Działdowo PL....47 B6
Działoszyce PL....55 C5
Działoszyn PL....54 B3
Dziemiany PL....46 A3
Dzierzążnia PL....47 C6
Dzierzgoń PL....47 B5
Dzierzgowo PL....47 B6
Dzierżoniów PL....54 C1
Dzisna BY....7 D10
Dziwnów PL....45 A6
Dzyarzhynsk BY....7 E9
Dzyatlava BY....7 E8

E

Ea E....89 A4
Eaglesfield GB....25 C4
Ealing GB....31 C3
Eardisley GB....29 A5
Earls Barton GB....30 B3
Earl Shilton GB....30 B2
Earlston GB....25 C5
Easington GB....27 B6
Easky IRL....18 B3
Eastbourne GB....31 D4
East Calder GB....25 C4
East Dereham GB....30 B4
Easter Skeld GB....22 A7
East Grinstead GB....31 C4
East Ilsley GB....31 C2
East Kilbride GB....24 C3
Eastleigh GB....31 D2
East Linton GB....25 C5
East Markham GB....27 B5
Easton GB....29 C5
East Wittering GB....31 D3
Eaton Socon GB....30 B3
Eaux-Bonnes F....76 D2
Eauze F....76 C3
Ebberup DK....39 D2
Ebbs A....62 C2
Ebbw Vale GB....29 B4
Ebeleben D....51 B6
Ebeltoft DK....39 C3
Ebene Reichenau A....72 B3
Eben im Pongau A....72 A3
Ebensee A....63 C4
Ebersfeld D....51 C6
Eberbach D....61 A6
Ebergötzen D....51 B6
Ebermann-Stadt D....62 A2
Ebern D....51 C6
Eberndorf A....73 B4
Ebersbach D....53 B4
Ebersberg D....62 B2
Ebersdorf
    Bayern D....52 C1
    Niedersachsen D....43 B6
Eberstein A....73 B4
Eberswalde D....45 C5
Ebnat-Kappel CH....71 A4
Éboli I....103 C8
Ebrach D....51 D6
Ebreichsdorf A....64 C2
Ebreuil F....68 B3
Ebstorf D....44 B2
Ecclefechan GB....25 C4
Eccleshall GB....26 C3
Eceabat TR....118 B1
Echallens CH....69 B6
Echauri E....76 D1
Echinos GR....116 A7
Échiré F....67 B4
Échirolles F....69 C5
Echourgnac F....76 A3
Echt NL....50 B1
Echte D....51 B6
Echternach L....60 A2
Écija E....99 B5
Ečka SRB....75 C5
Eckartsberga D....52 B1
Eckelshausen D....51 C4
Eckental D....62 A2
Eckernförde D....44 A1
Eckerö FIN....36 B6
Eckington GB....27 B4
Éclaron F....59 B5
Écommoy F....58 C1
Écouché F....57 B5
Ecoust-St Mein F....48 C3
Ecséd H....65 C5
Ecsegfalva H....75 A5
Ecueillé F....67 A6
Ed S....35 D3
Eda S....34 C4
Eda glasbruk S....34 C4
Edam NL....42 C2
Edane S....35 C4
Edderton GB....23 D4
Ede NL....49 A6
Edebäck S....34 B5
Edelény H....65 B6
Edelschrott A....73 A5
Edemissen D....44 C2
Edenbridge GB....31 C4
Edenderry IRL....21 A4
Edenkoben D....61 A4
Edesheim D....61 A4
Edessa GR....116 B4
Edewecht D....43 B4
Edgeworthstown IRL....19 C4
Edinburgh GB....25 C4
Edinet MD....11 B9
Edirne TR....118 A1
Edland N....33 C4
Edolo I....71 B5

Edøy N....114 D5
Edremit TR....118 C2
Edsbro S....36 C5
Edsbruk S....40 A6
Edsbyn S....36 A2
Edsele S....115 D13
Edsleskog S....35 C4
Edsvalla S....35 C5
Eekloo B....49 B4
Eemshaven NL....42 B3
Eerbeek NL....50 A2
Eersel NL....49 B6
Eferding A....63 B5
Effiat F....68 B3
Effeltrich D....62 A2
Effeltel N....35 C1
Egeln D....52 B1
Eger H....65 C6
Egerbakta H....65 C6
Egernsund DK....39 E2
Egersund N....33 D3
Egerszólát H....65 C6
Egervár H....74 B1
Egg
    A....71 A4
    D....61 B6
Eggby S....35 D5
Eggedal N....32 B6
Eggenburg A....64 B1
Eggenfelden D....62 B3
Eggesin D....45 B6
Eggum N....112 D2
Eghezée B....49 C5
Egiertowo PL....47 A4
Egilsstaðir IS....111 B11
Egina GR....117 E5
Eginio GR....116 B4
Egio GR....117 D4
Egletons F....68 C2
Egling D....62 C2
Eglinton GB....19 A4
Eglisau CH....61 C4
Égliseneuve-d'Entraigues
    F....68 C2
Eglofs D....61 C5
Egmond aan Zee NL....42 C1
Egna I....71 B6
Egosthena GR....117 D5
Egremont GB....26 A2
Egtved DK....39 D2
Éguilles F....79 C4
Éguilly-sous-Bois F....59 B5
Eguzon-Chantôme F....67 B6
Egyek H....65 C6
Egyházasrádóc H....74 A1
Ehekirchen D....62 B2
Ehingen D....61 B5
Ehra-Lessien D....44 C2
Ehrang D....60 A2
Ehrenfriedersdorf D....52 C2
Ehrenhain D....52 C2
Ehrenhausen A....73 B5
Ehringshausen D....51 C4
Ehrwald A....71 A5
Eibar E....89 A4
Eibelstadt D....61 A6
Eibenstock D....52 C2
Eibergen NL....50 A2
Eibiswald A....73 B5
Eichenbarleben D....52 A1
Eichendorf D....62 B3
Eichstätt D....62 B2
Eickelborn D....50 B4
Eide
    Hordaland N....32 B3
    Møre og Romsdal
    N....114 E4
Eidet N....112 C7
Eidfjord N....32 B4
Eidsberg N....35 C3
Eidsbugarden N....32 A5
Eidsdal N....114 E4
Eidsfoss N....35 C2
Eidskog N....34 B4
Eidsvåg
    Hordaland N....32 B3
    Møre og Romsdal
    N....114 E5
Eidsvoll N....34 B3
Eikefjord N....114 F2
Eikelandsosen N....32 B2
Eiken N....33 D4
Eikesdal N....114 E5
Eikstrand N....35 C1
Eilenburg D....52 B2
Eilsleben D....52 A1
Eina N....34 B2
Einbeck D....51 B5
Eindhoven NL....49 B6
Einsiedeln CH....70 A3
Einville-au-Jard F....60 B2
Eisenach D....51 C6
Eisenberg
    Rheinland-Pfalz D....61 A4
    Thüringen D....52 C1
Eisenerz A....73 A4
Eisenhüttenstadt D....53 A4
Eisenkappel A....73 B4
Eisenstadt A....64 C2
Eisentratten A....72 B3
Eisfeld D....51 C6
Eisleben D....52 B1
Eislingen D....61 B5
Eitensheim D....62 B2
Eiterfeld D....51 C5
Eitorf D....50 C3
Eivindvik N....32 B2
Eivissa = Ibiza E....97 C1
Eixo P....92 A2
Ejby DK....39 D2
Ejea de los Caballeros
    E....90 A1
Ejstrupholm DK....39 D2
Ejulve E....90 C2
Eke B....49 C4
Ekeby
    Gotland S....37 E5
    Skåne S....41 D2
    Uppsala S....36 B5
Ekeby-Almby S....37 C2
Ekenäs S....35 D5
Ekenässjön S....40 B5
Ekerö S....37 C4
Eket S....41 C3
Eketorp S....41 C6
Ekevik S....40 A6
Ekkerøy N....113 B19
Ekshärad S....34 B5
Eksingedal N....32 B3
Eksjö S....40 B4
Ekträsk S....115 C16
El Alamo
    Madrid E....94 B3
    Sevilla E....99 B4
El Algar E....101 B5
El Almendro E....98 B3
El Alquián E....101 C3
Élancourt F....58 B2
El Arahal E....99 B5
El Arenal E....94 B1
El Arguellite E....101 A3
Elassona GR....116 C4
El Astillero E....88 A3
Elati GR....116 C3
Zelazno PL....54 C1
El Ballestero E....101 A4
El Barco de Ávila E....93 A5
Elbasan AL....105 B6
El Berrón E....88 A1
El Berrueco E....95 B3
Elbeuf F....58 A2
Elbingerode D....51 B6
Elbląg PL....47 A5
El Bodón E....93 A4
El Bonillo E....95 D4
El Bosque E....99 C5
El Bullaque E....94 C2
Elburg NL....42 C2
El Burgo E....100 C1
El Burgo de Ebro E....90 B2
El Burgo de Osma E....89 C3

El Burgo Ranero E....88 B1
El Buste E....89 C5
El Cabaco E....93 A4
El Callejo E....89 A3
El Campillo E....99 B4
El Campillo de la Jara
    E....94 C1
El Cañavate E....95 C4
El Carpio E....100 B1
El Carpio de Tajo E....94 C2
El Casar E....95 B3
El Casar de Escalona
    E....94 B2
El Castillo de las Guardas
    E....99 B4
El Centenillo E....100 A2
El Cerro E....93 A5
El Cerro de Andévalo
    E....99 B4
El Comenar E....99 C5
El Coronil E....99 B5
El Crucero E....86 A4
El Cubo de Tierra del Vino
    E....88 C1
El Cuervo E....99 C4
Elda E....101 A5
Eldena D....44 B3
Eldingen D....44 C2
Elefsina GR....117 D5
El Ejido E....101 C3
Elek H....75 B6
Elemir SRB....75 C5
El Escorial E....94 B2
El Espinar E....94 B2
El Frago E....90 A2
El Franco E....86 A4
El Frasno E....89 C5
Elgå N....114 F8
El Garrobo E....99 B4
El Gastor E....99 C5
Elgin GB....23 D5
Elgoibar E....89 A4
Elgol GB....22 D2
El Gordo E....93 B5
El Grado E....90 A3
El Granado E....98 B3
El Grao de Castelló E....96 B3
El Grau E....96 C2
Elgshøa N....34 A4
El Higuera E....100 B1
El Hijate E....101 B3
El Hontanar E....96 A2
El Hoyo E....100 A2
Elie GB....25 B5
Elizondo E....76 C1
Elk PL....6 E7
Ellenberg D....61 A6
Ellennesse D....26 C3
Ellezelles B....49 C4
Ellingen D....62 A1
Ellmau D....72 A2
Ellon GB....23 D6
Ellös S....35 D3
Ellrich D....51 B6
Ellwangen D....61 B6
Elm
    CH....71 B4
    D....43 B6
Elmadağ TR....16 B6
El Madroño E....99 B4
El Maillo E....93 A4
Elmalı TR....119 F4
El Masnou E....91 B5
El Mirón E....93 A5
El Molar E....95 B3
El Molinillo E....94 C2
El Morell E....91 B4
Elmshorn D....43 B6
Elmstein D....60 A3
El Muyo E....89 C3
Elne F....91 A5
Elnesvågen N....114 E4
El Olmo E....88 C3
El Palo E....100 C1
El Pardo E....94 B3
El Payo E....93 A4
El Pedernoso E....95 C4
El Pedroso E....99 B5
El Peral E....95 C5
El Perelló
    Tarragona E....90 C3
    Valencia E....96 B2
Elphin GB....22 C3
El Picazo E....95 C4
El Pinell de Bray E....90 B3
El Piñero E....88 C1
El Pla de Santa Maria
    E....91 B4
El Pobo E....90 C2
El Pobo de Dueñas E....95 B5
El Pont d'Armentera
    E....91 B4
El Port de la Selva E....91 A6
El Port de Llançà E....91 A6
El Port de Sagunt E....96 B2
El Prat de Llobregat
    E....91 B5
El Provencio E....95 C4
El Puente E....89 A3
El Puente del Arzobispo
    E....94 C1
El Puerto E....86 A4
El Puerto de Santa María
    E....99 C4
El Real de la Jara E....99 B4
El Real de San Vincente
    E....94 B2
El Robledo E....94 C2
El Rocio E....99 B4
El Rompido E....99 B3
El Ronquillo E....99 B4
El Royo E....89 C4
El Rubio E....100 B1
El Saler E....96 B2
El Saler E....101 A4
El Salobral E....101 A4
El Saucejo E....99 B5
Els Castells E....91 A4
Elsdorf D....50 C2
Elsenfeld D....61 A5
Elsfleth D....43 B5
Elspeet NL....50 A1
Elst NL....50 A1
Elstead GB....31 C3
Elster D....52 B2
Elsterberg D....52 C2
Elsterwerda D....52 B3
Elstra D....53 B4
El Temple E....90 B2
El Tiemblo E....94 B2
Eltmann D....51 D6
El Toboso E....95 C4
El Tormillo E....90 B2
El Torno E....93 A5
Eltville D....50 C4
El Valle de las Casas
    E....88 B1
Elvas P....93 C3
Elvebakken N....113 C12
El Vellón E....95 B3
Elven F....56 C3
El Vendrell E....91 B4
Elverum N....34 B3
El Villar de Arnedo E....89 B4
Elvington GB....27 B5
El Viso E....100 A1
El Viso del Alcor E....99 B5
Ely GB....30 B4
Elzach D....61 B4
Elze D....51 A5

Emådalen S....36 A1
Embleton GB....25 C6
Embonas GR....119 F2
Embrun F....79 B5
Emden D....43 B4
Emecik TR....119 F2
Emet TR....118 C4
Emirdağ TR....118 C6
Emlichheim D....42 C3
Emmaboda S....40 C5
Emmaljunga S....41 C3
Emmeloord NL....42 C2
Emmen
    CH....70 A3
    NL....42 C3
Emmendingen D....60 B3
Emmer-Compascuum
    NL....43 C4
Emmerich D....50 B2
Emmern D....51 A5
Emöd H....65 C6
Émpoli I....81 C4
Emsbüren D....43 C4
Emsdetten D....50 A3
Emsfors S....40 B6
Emskirchen D....62 A1
Emstek D....43 C5
Emsworth GB....31 D3
Emyvale IRL....19 B5
Enafors S....115 D9
Enänger S....115 F14
Encamp AND....91 A4
Encarnação P....92 C1
Encinas de Abajo E....94 B1
Encinas de Esgueva
    E....88 C2
Encinasola E....99 A4
Encinas Reales E....100 B1
Encio E....89 B3
Enciso E....89 B4
Enden N....114 F7
Endingen D....60 B3
Endrinal E....93 A5
Endröd H....75 B5
Enebakk N....34 C3
Eneryda S....40 C4
Enese H....64 C3
Enez TR....116 B8
Enfield IRL....21 A5
Eng A....72 A1
Engelberg CH....70 B3
Engelhartszell A....63 B4
Engelskirchen D....50 C3
Engen D....61 C4
Enger N....34 B2
Engerdal N....114 F8
Engerneset N....34 A4
Enge-sande D....39 E1
Engesvang DK....39 C2
Enghien B....49 C5
Engstingen D....61 B5
Engter D....43 C5
Enguera E....96 C2
Enguidanos E....95 C5
Enkenbach D....60 A3
Enkhuizen NL....42 C2
Enklinge FIN....36 B7
Enköping S....37 C4
Enna I....109 B3
Ennezat F....68 C3
Enningdal N....35 D3
Ennis IRL....20 B3
Enniscorthy IRL....21 B5
Enniskean IRL....20 C3
Enniskillen GB....19 B4
Ennistimon IRL....20 B2
Enns A....63 B5
Eno FIN....3 E29
Enontekiö FIN....113 D12
Ens NL....42 C2
Enschede NL....50 A2
Ensdorf D....62 A2
Ensisheim F....60 C3
Enstaberga S....37 D3
Enstone GB....31 C2
Entlebuch CH....70 A3
Entrácque I....80 B1
Entradas P....98 B2
Entrains-sur-Nohain
    F....68 A3
Entrambasaguas E....88 A3
Entrambasmestas E....88 A3
Entraygues-sur-Truyère
    F....77 B5
Entre-os-Rios P....87 C2
Entrevaux F....79 C5
Entrín Bajo E....93 C4
Entroncamento P....92 B2
Entzheim F....60 B3
Envermeu F....58 A2
Enviken S....36 B2
Enying H....74 B3
Enzingerboden A....72 A2
Enzklösterle D....61 B4
Épagny F....59 A4
Epaignes F....58 A1
Epalinges CH....70 B1
Epannes F....67 B4
Epanomi GR....116 B4
Epe
    D....50 A3
    NL....42 C2
Épernay F....59 A4
Épernon F....58 B2
Epfig F....60 B3
Epierre F....69 C6
Épila E....90 B1
Épinac F....69 B4
Épinal F....60 B2
Episcopia I....106 A3
Episkopi CY....120 B1
Epitalio GR....117 E3
Epoisses F....69 A4
Eppenbrunn D....60 A3
Eppendorf D....52 C3
Epping GB....31 C4
Eppingen D....61 A5
Epsom GB....31 C3
Epworth GB....27 B5
Eraclea I....72 C2
Eraclea Mare I....72 C2
Erba I....71 C4
Erbach
    Baden-Württemberg
    D....61 B5
    Hessen D....61 A4
Erbalunga F....102 A2
Erbendorf D....62 A3
Érchie I....105 C3
Ercolano I....103 C7
Ercsi H....74 A3
Érd H....74 A3
Erdek TR....118 B2
Erdemli TR....16 C7
Erdevik SRB....85 A4
Erding D....62 B2
Erdut HR....75 C4
Erdweg D....62 B2
Ereğli
    Konya TR....16 C7
    Zonguldak TR....118 A6
Erenkaya TR....119 E7
Eresfjord N....114 E5
Eresos GR....116 C7
Eretria GR....116 D5
Erfde D....43 A6
Erfjord N....33 C3
Erftstadt D....50 C2
Erfurt D....52 C1
Ergli LV....8 D4
Ergoldsbach D....62 B3
Eriboll GB....22 C4
Érice I....108 A1
Ericeira P....92 C1
Eridurt HR....75 C4
Eriksberg S....115 B12
Eriksmåle S....40 C5
Eringsboda S....40 C5
Eriswil CH....70 A2
Erithres GR....117 D5

Erkelenz D....50 B2
Erkner D....45 C5
Erkrath D....50 B2
Erla E....90 A2
Erlangen D....62 A2
Erli I....80 B2
Erlsbach A....72 B2
Ermelo NL....49 A6
Ermenak TR....16 C6
Ermenonville F....58 A3
Ermezinde P....87 C2
Ermidas P....98 A2
Ermioni GR....117 E5
Ermoupoli GR....117 E6
Ermsleben D....52 B1
Erndtebrück D....50 C4
Ernée F....57 B5
Ernestinovo HR....74 C3
Ernstbrunn A....64 B2
Erolzheim D....61 B6
Erquelinnes B....49 C5
Erquy F....56 B3
Erra P....92 C2
Erratzu E....76 C1
Errindlev DK....44 A3
Erro E....76 D1
Ersa F....102 A2
Érsekcsanád H....75 B3
Érsekë AL....116 B2
Érsekvadkert H....65 C5
Erstein F....60 B3
Ertebølle DK....38 C2
Ertingen D....61 B5
Ervedal
    Coimbra P....92 A2
    Portalegre P....92 B3
Ervenik HR....83 B4
Ervidel P....98 B2
Ervy-le-Châtel F....59 B4
Erwitte D....51 B4
Erxleben D....52 A1
Erzsébet H....74 B3
Esbjerg DK....39 D1
Esbly F....58 B3
Escacena del Campo
    E....99 B4
Escalada E....88 B3
Escalante E....89 A3
Escalaplano I....110 C2
Escalona E....94 B2
Escalona del Prado E....94 A2
Escalonilla E....94 C2
Escalos de Baixo P....92 B3
Escalos de Cima P....92 B3
Escamilla E....95 B4
Es Caná E....97 C1
Escanaulea E....100 B1
Escatrón E....90 B2
Eschach D....61 C5
Eschau D....61 A5
Eschede D....44 C2
Eschenau D....62 A2
Eschenbach D....62 A2
Eschenlohe D....62 C2
Eschershausen D....51 B5
Esch-sur-Alzette L....60 A1
Esch-sur-Sûre L....60 A1
Eschwege D....51 B6
Eschweiler D....50 C2
Escombreras E....101 B5
Escos F....76 C1
Escource F....76 B1
Escragnolles F....79 C5
Escrick GB....27 B4
Escurial E....93 B5
Escurial de la Sierra
    E....93 A5
Esens D....43 B4
Esgos E....87 B3
Esher GB....31 C3
Eskdalemuir GB....25 C4
Eskifjörður IS....111 B12
Eskilhem S....37 E5
Eskilsäter S....35 D5
Eskilstrup DK....39 E4
Eskilstuna S....37 C3
Eskipazar TR....118 B7
Eskişehir TR....118 C5
Eslava E....89 B5
Eslida E....96 B2
Eslohe D....50 B4
Eslöv S....41 D3
Esme TR....119 D3
Es Mercadal E....97 B4
Es Migjorn Gran E....97 B4
Espa N....34 B3
Espalion F....78 B1
Esparragalejo E....93 C4
Esparragosa del Caudillo
    E....93 C5
Esparragossa de la
    Serena E....93 C5
Esparreguera E....91 B4
Esparron F....79 C4
Espe N....32 B3
Espedal N....33 D3
Espejo
    Alava E....89 B3
    Córdoba E....100 B1
Espeland N....32 B2
Espelkamp D....43 C5
Espeluche F....78 B3
Espelúy E....100 B2
Espera E....99 C5
Esperança P....93 B3
Esperstedt D....52 B1
Espéria I....103 B6
Espevær N....33 C2
Espiel E....99 A5
Espinama E....88 A2
Espinasses F....79 B5
Espinelves E....91 B5
Espinhal P....92 A2
Espinho P....87 C2
Espinilla E....88 A2
Espinosa de Cerrato
    E....88 C3
Espinosa de los Monteros
    E....88 A3
Espinoso del Rey E....94 C2
Espírito Santo P....98 B3
Esplantas F....78 B2
Espluga de Francolí
    E....91 B4
Esplús E....90 B3
Espolla E....91 A5
Espoo FIN....6 A8
Esporles E....97 B2
Es Port d'Alcúdia E....97 B3
Esposende P....87 C2
Es Pujols E....97 C1
Esquedas E....90 A2
Esquivias E....94 B3
Essay F....57 B6
Essen
    B....49 B5
    Niedersachsen D....43 C4
    Nordrhein-Westfalen
    D....50 B3
Essenbach D....62 B3
Essertaux F....58 A3
Essí E....76 C1
Esslingen D....61 B5
Essoyes F....59 B5
Estables F....79 B6
Estadilla E....90 A3
Estagel F....78 D1
Estaing F....77 B5
Estaires F....48 C3
Estang F....76 C2
Estárreja P....92 A2
Estartit E....91 A6
Estavayer-le-Lac CH....70 B1
Este I....72 C1

Esteiro E....86 A2
Estela P....87 C2
Estella E....89 B4
Estellencs E....97 B2
Estepa E....100 B1
Estépar E....88 B3
Estepona E....99 C5
Esternay F....59 B4
Esterri d'Aneu E....91 A4
Esterwegen D....43 C4
Estissac F....59 B4
Estivadoira E....87 C2
Estivareilles F....68 B2
Estivella E....96 B2
Estói P....98 B3
Estopiñán E....90 B3
Estoril P....92 C1
Estoublon F....79 C5
Estrée-Blanche F....48 C3
Estrées-St Denis F....58 A3
Estreito P....92 B3
Estremera E....95 B3
Estremoz P....92 C3
Esyres F....67 A5
Esztergom H....65 C4
Etables-sur-Mer F....56 B3
Etalans F....69 A6
Etalle B....60 A1
Etampes F....58 B3
Étang-sur-Arroux F....69 B4
Étaples F....48 C2
Etauliers F....67 C4
Etel TR....118 C1
Etne N....34 B1
Etne N....33 C2
Etoges F....59 B4
Etoliko GR....116 D3
Eton GB....31 C3
Étréaupont F....59 A4
Étréchy F....58 B3
Étrépagny F....58 A2
Étretat F....57 A6
Étroeungt F....49 C4
Etroubles I....70 C2
Ettal D....62 C2
Ettelbruck L....60 A2
Etten NL....49 B5
Ettenheim D....60 B3
Ettington GB....29 A6
Ettlingen D....61 B4
Ettringen D....62 B1
Etuz F....69 A5
Etxarri-Aranatz E....89 B4
Etyek H....74 A3
Eu F....48 C2
Euerdorf D....51 C6
Eulate E....89 B4
Euratsfeld A....63 B5
Europoort NL....49 B5
Eutin D....44 A2
Evanger N....32 B3
Évaux-les-Bains F....68 B2
Evciler
    Afyon TR....119 D4
    Çanakkale TR....118 C1
Evenhus N....114 D7
Everöd S....41 D4
Eversberg D....50 B4
Everswinkel D....50 B3
Evertsberg S....34 A5
Évian-les-Bains F....69 B6
Evisa F....102 A1
Evje N....33 D4
Evolène CH....70 B2
Évora P....92 C3
Evoramonte P....92 C3
Évran F....57 B4
Évrecy F....57 A5
Evrenseki TR....119 E4
Évreux F....58 A2
Évron F....57 B5
Évry F....58 B3
Ewell GB....31 C3
Ewersbach D....50 C4
Excideuil F....67 C6
Exeter GB....29 C4
Exmes F....57 B6
Exminster GB....29 C4
Exmouth GB....29 C4
Eydehamn N....33 D5
Eye
    Peterborough GB....30 B3
    Suffolk GB....30 B5
Eyemouth GB....25 C5
Eyguians F....79 B4
Eyguières F....79 C4
Eygurande F....68 C2
Eymet F....77 B3
Eymoutiers F....68 C1
Eynsham GB....31 C2
Eyrarbakki IS....111 D4
Eystrup D....43 C6
Ezaro E....86 B1
Ezcaray E....89 B4
Ezcároz E....76 D1
Ezine TR....118 C1
Ezmoriz P....87 D2

F

Fabara E....90 B3
Fábbrico I....81 B4
Fåberg N....34 A2
Fabero E....86 B4
Fábiánsebestyén H....75 B5
Fåborg DK....39 D3
Fabrègues F....78 C2
Fabriano I....82 C1
Fabrizia I....106 C3
Facha P....87 C2
Facinas E....99 C5
Fačkov SK....65 A4
Fadagosa P....92 B3
Fadd H....74 B3
Faédis I....72 B3
Faenza I....81 B5
Fafe P....87 C2
Fagagna I....72 B3
Fågelberget S....115 C11
Fågelfors S....40 B5
Fågelmara S....41 C5
Fågelsta S....37 D2
Fagerås S....35 C4
Fagerheim N....32 B4
Fagerhøy N....34 A1
Fagerhult S....40 B5
Fagerlund N....34 B2
Fagernes
    Oppland N....32 B6
    Troms N....112 C8
Fagersanna S....35 D6
Fagersta S....36 C2
Fagerström S....35 D4
Fåglavik S....35 D4
Fagnano Castello I....106 B3
Fagnières F....59 B5
Fagurhólsmýri IS....111 D5
Fai della Paganella I....71 B6
Faido CH....70 B3
Fairford GB....29 B6
Fairlie GB....24 C3
Fakenham GB....30 B4
Fåker S....115 D11
Fakse DK....39 D5
Fakse Ladeplads DK....41 D2
Falaise F....57 B5
Falcade I....72 B1
Falcarragh IRL....18 A3
Falces E....89 B5
Fălciu RO....11 C10
Falconara I....109 B3
Falconara Maríttima I....82 C2
Falcone I....109 A3
Faldingworth GB....27 B5

Falerum S....37 D3
Fălești MD....11 C9
Fernancaballero E....94 C3
Falkenberg
    Bayern D....62 A3
    Bayern D....62 B3
    Brandenburg D....52 B3
    S....40 C2
Falkensee D....45 C5
Falkenstein
    Bayern D....62 A3
    Sachsen D....52 C2
Falkirk GB....25 B4
Falkland GB....25 B4
Falköping S....35 D5
Fall D....62 C2
Falla S....37 D2
Fallingbostel D....43 C6
Falmouth GB....28 C2
Falset E....90 B3
Fălticeni RO....11 C8
Falun S....36 B2
Famagusta CY....120 A2
Fammestad N....32 B2
Fana N....32 B2
Fanano I....81 B4
Fanari GR....116 C3
Fangel DK....39 D3
Fano I....82 C2
Fântânele RO....75 B6
Fão P....87 C2
Fara in Sabina I....102 A5
Faramontanos de Tábara
    E....88 C1
Fara Novarese I....70 C3
Farasdues E....90 A1
Fårbo S....40 B6
Fareham GB....31 D2
Färentuna S....37 C4
Färgelanda S....35 D3
Färila S....115 F12
Faringdon GB....31 C2
Faringe S....36 B5
Farini I....80 B3
Fariza E....87 C4
Farkadona GR....116 C4
Farkasfa H....73 B6
Farlete E....90 B2
Fårlöv S....41 C4
Farnes H....75 A4
Farná SK....65 C4
Färnäs S....36 B1
Farnborough GB....31 C3
Farnese I....102 A4
Farnham GB....31 C3
Farnroda D....51 C6
Faro P....98 B3
Fårö S....37 E6
Fårösund S....37 E6
Farra d'Alpago I....72 B2
Farranfore IRL....20 B2
Farsala GR....116 C4
Farsø DK....38 C2
Farsund N....33 D3
Farum DK....41 D2
Fårup DK....38 C2
Fasana I....103 C8
Fasano I....104 C3
Fáskrúðsfjörður
    IS....111 C11
Fassberg D....44 C2
Fastiv UA....11 A10
Fastnäs S....34 B5
Fatesh RUS....7 E13
Fátima P....92 B2
Fatmomakke S....115 B12
Fättjaur S....115 B12
Faucogney-et-la-Mer
    F....60 C2
Fauguerolles F....76 B3
Faulenrost D....45 B4
Faulquemont F....60 A2
Fauquembergues F....48 C3
Fauske N....112 E4
Fauville-en-Caux F....58 A1
Fauvillers B....60 A1
Fåvang N....34 A2
Favara
    E....96 B2
    I....108 B2
Faverges F....69 C6
Faverney F....60 C2
Faversham GB....31 C4
Favignana I....108 B1
Fay-aux-Loges F....58 C3
Fayence F....79 C5
Fayet F....78 C1
Fayl-Billot F....60 C1
Fayón E....90 B3
Fearn GB....23 D5
Fécamp F....58 A1
Feda N....33 D3
Fedje N....32 B1
Feering GB....31 C4
Fegen S....40 B3
Fegyvernek H....75 A5
Fehrbellin D....45 C4
Fehring A....73 B5
Feichten A....71 A5
Feiring N....34 B3
Feke TR....16 C7
Feketić SRB....75 C4
Felanitx E....97 B3
Feld am See A....72 B3
Feldbach A....73 B5
Feldberg D....45 B5
Feldkirch A....71 A4
Feldkirchen in Kärnten
    A....73 B4
Feldkirchen-Westerham
    D....62 C2
Felgueiras P....87 C2
Felitto I....103 C8
Félix E....101 C3
Felixstowe GB....31 C5
Felizzano I....80 B2
Felletin F....68 C2
Fellingsbro S....37 C2
Felnac RO....75 B6
Felnémet H....65 C6
Felpéc H....74 A2
Fels am Wagram A....64 B1
Felsberg D....51 B5
Felsönyék H....74 B3
Felsöszentiván H....75 B4
Felsöszentmárton H....74 C2
Felsözsolca H....65 B6
Felsted DK....39 E2
Feltre I....72 B1
Femsjö S....40 C3
Fenagh IRL....19 B4
Fene E....86 A2
Fenestrelle I....79 A5
Fénétrange F....60 B3
Feneu F....57 C5
Fengersfors S....35 D4
Fenwick GB....24 C3
Feolin Ferry GB....24 C1
Ferbane IRL....21 A4
Ferdinandovac HR....74 B2
Ferdinandshof D....45 B5
Fère-Champenoise F....59 B4
Fère-en-Tardenois F....59 A4
Ferentillo I....102 A5
Ferentino I....102 B6
Feres GR....116 B8
Feria E....93 C4
Feričanci HR....74 C2
Ferizli TR....118 B5
Ferla I....109 B3
Ferlach A....73 B4
Ferleiten A....72 A2
Fermil P....87 C3
Fermo I....82 C2
Fermoselle E....87 C4

Fermoy IRL....20 B3
Fernancaballero E....94 C3
Fernán Núñez E....100 B1
Fernán Peréz E....101 C3
Fernão Ferro P....92 C1
Fernay-Voltaire F....69 B6
Ferndown GB....29 C6
Ferness GB....23 D5
Fernhurst GB....31 C3
Ferns IRL....21 B5
Ferpécle CH....70 B2
Ferrals-les-Corbières
    F....78 C1
Ferrandina I....104 C2
Ferrara I....81 B5
Ferrara di Monte Baldo
    I....71 C5
Ferreira E....86 A3
Ferreira do Alentejo
    P....98 A2
Ferreira do Zêzere P....92 B2
Ferreras de Abajo E....87 C4
Ferreras de Arriba E....87 C4
Ferreries E....97 B4
Ferreruela E....90 B1
Ferreruela de Tábara
    E....87 C4
Ferret CH....70 B2
Ferrette F....70 A2
Ferriere I....80 B3
Ferrière-la-Grande F....49 C4
Ferrières
    Hautes-Pyrénées F....76 C2
    Loiret F....58 B3
    Oise F....58 A3
Ferrières-sur-Sichon
    F....68 B3
Ferrol E....86 A2
Ferryhill GB....27 A4
Fertöendréd H....64 C2
Festøy N....114 E3
Festvåg N....112 E3
Fetești RO....11 D9
Fethard
    Tipperary IRL....21 B4
    Wexford IRL....21 B5
Fethiye TR....119 F4
Fetsund N....34 C3
Fettercairn GB....25 B5
Feucht D....62 A2
Feuchtwangen D....61 A6
Feudingen D....50 C4
Feuges F....59 B5
Feuquières F....58 A2
Feurs F....69 C4
Feytiat F....67 C6
Feyzin F....69 C4
Ffestiniog GB....26 C2
Fiamignano I....102 A6
Fiano I....70 C2
Ficarazzi I....108 A2
Ficarolo I....81 B5
Fichtelberg D....52 C1
Ficulle I....82 D1
Fidenza I....81 B4
Fidjeland N....33 D3
Fieberbrunn A....72 A2
Fier AL....105 C5
Fiera di Primiero I....72 B1
Fierzë AL....105 A6
Fiesch CH....70 B3
Fiesso Umbertiano I....81 B5
Figari F....102 B2
Figeac F....77 B5
Figeholm S....40 B6
Figgjo S....33 D2
Figline Valdarno I....81 C5
Figols E....90 A3
Figueira da Foz P....92 A2
Figueira de Castelo
    Rodrigo P....87 D4
Figueira dos Caveleiros
    P....98 A2
Figueiredo P....92 B3
Figueiredo de Alva P....87 D3
Figueiródos Vinhos
    P....92 B2
Figueres E....91 A5
Figueroles E....96 A2
Figueruela de Arriba
    E....87 C4
Filadélfia I....106 C3
Fil'akovo SK....65 B5
Filderstadt D....61 B5
Filey GB....27 A5
Filiași RO....11 D7
Filiates GR....116 C2
Filiatra GR....117 E3
Filipstad S....35 C6
Filisur CH....71 B4
Fillan N....114 D5
Filotio GR....117 F7
Filottrano I....82 C2
Filskov DK....39 D2
Filton GB....29 B5
Filtvet N....35 C2
Filzmoos A....72 A3
Finale Emília I....81 B5
Finale Ligure I....80 B2
Fiñana E....101 B3
Finby FIN....36 B7
Finchampstead GB....31 C3
Finchingfield GB....31 C4
Findhorn GB....23 D5
Findochty GB....23 D6
Finike TR....119 F5
Finkenberg A....72 A1
Finnasand N....33 C2
Finnbodarne S....35 C5
Finneidfjord N....115 A10
Finnerödja S....37 D1
Finnskog N....34 B4
Finnsnes N....112 C7
Fintorp S....35 C4
Finócchio I....102 B5
Finsjö S....40 B6
Finsland N....33 D4
Finspång S....37 D2
Finsterwalde D....53 B3
Finsterwolde NL....43 B4
Finstown GB....23 B5
Fintona GB....19 B4
Fionnphort GB....24 B1
Fiorenzuola d'Arda I....81 B3
Firenze = Florence I....81 C5
Firenzuola I....81 B5
Firmi F....77 B5
Firminy F....69 C4
Firmo I....106 B3
Fischamend Markt A....64 B2
Fischbach
    A....73 A5
    D....60 A3
Fischbeck D....44 C4
Fischen D....71 A5
Fishbourne GB....31 D2
Fishguard GB....28 A3
Fiskardo GR....116 D2
Fiskebäckskil S....35 D3
Fiskebøl N....112 D3
Fismes F....59 A4
Fisterra E....86 B1
Fitero E....89 B5
Fitjar N....32 C2
Fiuggi I....102 B6
Fiumata I....102 A6
Fiumefreddo Brúzio
    I....106 B3
Fiumefreddo di Sicilia
    I....109 B4
Fiumicino I....102 B5
Fivemiletown GB....19 B4
Fivizzano I....81 B4
Fjälkinge S....41 C4
Fjällåsen S....112 E9
Fjällbacka S....35 D3
Fjæra N....32 C3
Fjärdhundra S....36 C3
Fjellerup DK....38 C3
Fjerritslev DK....38 B2
Fjordgard N....112 C6

Fjugesta S 37 C1
Flå N 32 B6
Flåbygd N 33 C5
Flaga E 91 A5
Flace F 79 C5
Fladungen D 51 C6
Flaine F 70 B1
Flåm N 32 B4
Flamatt CH. 70 B2
Flamborough GB 27 A5
Flammersfeld D 50 C3
Flassans-sur-Issole F 79 C5
Flatdal N 33 C5
Flatebø N 32 B3
Flateby N 34 C3
Flateland N 33 C4
Flateyri IS 111 A2
Flatøydegard N 32 B6
Flatråker N 32 C2
Flattach A 72 B3
Flatvarp S 37 E3
Flauenskjold DK 38 B3
Flavigny-sur-Moselle F 60 B2
Flavy-le-Martel F 59 A4
Flawil CH. 71 A4
Flayosc F 79 C5
Flechtingen D 44 C3
Fleckeby D. 44 A1
Fleet GB 31 C3
Fleetmark D. 44 C3
Fleetwood GB 26 B2
Flehingen D 61 A4
Flekke N. 32 A2
Flekkefjord N. 33 D3
Flen S 37 C3
Flensburg D 39 E2
Fleringe S 37 E5
Flerohopp S. 40 C5
Flers F 57 B5
Flesberg N 32 C6
Fleurance F 77 C3
Fleuré F 67 B5
Fleurier CH 69 B6
Fleurus B 49 C5
Fleury
 Hérault F 78 C2
 Yonne F 59 C4
Fleury-les-Aubrais F 58 C2
Fleury-sur-Andelle F 58 A2
Fleury-sur-Orne F 57 A5
Flieden D 51 C5
Flimby GB 26 A2
Flims CH 71 B4
Flines-lèz-Raches F 49 C4
Flint GB 26 B2
Flirey F 60 B1
Flirsch A. 71 A5
Flisa N 34 B4
Flisby S 40 B4
Fliseryd S 40 B6
Flix E 90 B3
Flixecourt F 48 C3
Flize F 59 A5
Flobecq B 49 C4
Floby S 35 D5
Floda S 40 B2
Flodden GB 25 C5
Flogny-la-Chapelle F 59 C4
Flöha D 52 C3
Flonheim D 61 A4
Florac F 78 B2
Floreffe B 49 C5
Florence = Firenze I 81 C5
Florennes B 49 C5
Florensac F 78 C2
Florentin F 77 C5
Florenville B 59 A6
Flores de Ávila E 94 B1
Floresta I 109 B3
Florești MD 11 C10
Florídia I. 109 C4
Florina GR 116 B3
Florø N 114 F2
Flörsheim D. 51 C4
Floss D 62 A3
Fluberg N. 34 B2
Flúðir IS 111 C5
Flühli CH 70 B3
Fluminimaggiore I 110 C1
Flums CH 71 A4
Flumet F 69 C6
Flyeryd S 41 C5
Flygsfors S 40 C5
Foča BIH 84 C3
Fockbek D 43 A6
Focșani RO 11 D9
Foel GB 26 C2
Foeni RO 75 C5
Fogdö S 37 C3
Fóggia I 104 B1
Föglö FIN 36 B7
Fohnsdorf A. 73 A4
Foiano della Chiana I 81 C5
Foix F 77 D4
Fojnica
 BIH. 84 C2
 BIH. 84 C3
Fokino RUS 7 E13
Fokstua N 114 E6
Foldereid N. 114 C9
Földes H 75 A6
Folegandros GR 117 F6
Folelli I 102 A2
Folgaria I 71 C6
Folgosinho P. 92 A3
Folgoso de la Ribera E 86 B4
Folgoso do Courel E. 86 B3
Foligno I. 82 D1
Folkärna S 36 B3
Folkestad N. 114 E3
Folkestone GB 31 C5
Follafoss N 114 D8
Folldal N 114 E6
Follebu N. 34 A2
Follina I 72 C2
Föllinge S 115 D11
Follónica I 81 D4
Fölsbyn S 35 C4
Foncebadón E 86 B4
Foncine-le-Bas F 69 B6
Fondevila E 87 C2
Fondi I 103 B6
Fondo I 71 B6
Fonelas E 100 B2
Fonfría
 Teruel E 90 C1
 Zamora E 87 C4
Fonnes N 32 B1
Fonni I 110 B2
Fontaine F 59 B5
Fontainebleau F 58 B3
Fontaine de Vaucluse F. 79 C4
Fontaine-Française F 69 A5
Fontaine-le-Dun F 58 A1
Fontan F 80 B1
Fontanarejo E 94 C2
Fontäne I 80 B1
Fontanélice E 81 B5
Fontanières F 68 B2
Fontanosas E 100 A1
Fonteblanda E 81 D5
Fontenay-le-Comte F 66 B4
Fontenay-Trésigny F 58 B3
Fontevrault-l'Abbaye F 67 A5
Fontiveros E 94 B2
Fontoy F 60 A1
Fontpédrouse F 91 A5
Fontstown IRL 21 A5
Fonyód H 74 B2
Fonz E 90 A3
Fonzaso I 72 B1
Fóppolo I 71 B4
Föra S 41 B6

Forbach
 D 61 B4
 F 60 A2
Forcall E 90 C2
Forcalquier F 79 C4
Forcarei E 86 B2
Forchheim D. 62 A2
Forchtenau A. 64 C2
Forchtenberg D. 61 A5
Ford GB 24 B2
Førde
 Hordaland N 33 C2
 Sogn og Fjordane N 32 A2
Førdesfjorden N 33 C2
Fordham GB 30 B4
Fordingbridge GB 29 C6
Fordon PL 47 B4
Fordongiánus I 110 C1
Forenza I 104 C1
Foresta di Búrgos I 110 B1
Forfar GB 25 B5
Forges-les-Eaux F 58 A2
Foria I 106 A2
Forio I 103 C6
Forjães P 87 C2
Førland N. 33 D4
Forlì I. 81 B6
Forlimpópoli I 82 B1
Formazza I 70 B3
Formby GB 26 B2
Formerie F 58 A2
Fórmia I 103 B6
Formigine I 81 B4
Formigliana I 70 C3
Formiguères F 91 A5
Formalutx E 97 B2
Fórnaca S 37 D2
Fornelli I 110 B1
Fornells E 97 A4
Fornelos de Montes
 E 87 B2
Fornes E 100 C2
Forneset N. 112 C8
Forni Avoltri I 72 B2
Forni di Sopra I 72 B2
Forni di Sotto I 72 B2
Forno
 Piemonte I 70 C3
 Piemonte I 79 A6
Forno Alpi-Gráie I 70 C2
Forno di Zoldo I. 72 B2
Fornos de Algodres P 92 A3
Fornovo di Taro I. 81 B4
Foros do Arrão P. 92 B2
Forráskút H 75 B4
Forres GB 23 D5
Forríolo E. 87 B3
Fors S 36 B3
Forsand N 33 D3
Forsbacka S 36 B3
Forserum S 40 B4
Forshaga S 35 C5
Forsheda S 40 B3
Forsinain GB 23 C5
Førslev DK 39 D4
Förslöv S 41 C2
Forsmark
 Uppsala S 36 B5
 Västerbotten S 115 B12
Forsmo S 115 D14
Forsnäs S 115 A15
Forsnes N 114 D5
Forssa FIN 3 F25
Forssjöbruk S 37 D3
Forst D 53 B4
Forsvik S 37 D1
Fortanete E 90 C2
Fort Augustus GB 24 B4
Fortezza I 72 B1
Forth GB 25 C4
Fort-Mahon-Plage F 48 C2
Fortrie GB 23 D6
Fortrose GB 23 D4
Fortun N. 32 A4
Fortuna E 101 A4
Fortuneswell GB 29 C5
Fort William GB 24 B2
Fosdinovo I 81 B4
Foss N 32 B6
Fossacésia I 103 A7
Fossano I 80 B1
Fossato di Vico I 82 C1
Fossbakken N 112 D6
Fosse-la-Ville B 49 C5
Fossombrone I 82 C1
Fos-sur-Mer F 78 C3
Fot H 65 C5
Fouchères F 59 B5
Fouesnant F 56 C1
Foug F 60 B1
Fougères F 57 B4
Fougerolles F 60 C2
Foulain F 59 B6
Fountainhall GB 25 C5
Fouras F 66 C3
Fourchambault F 68 A3
Fourmies F 49 C5
Fourna GR 116 C3
Fournels F 78 B2
Fourni GR 119 E1
Fournols F 68 C3
Fourques F 91 A5
Fourquevaux F 77 C4
Fours F 68 B3
Fowey GB 28 C3
Foxdale GB 26 A1
Foxford IRL 18 C2
Foyers GB 23 D4
Foynes IRL 20 B2
Foz
 E 86 A3
Foza I 72 C1
Foz do Arelho P 92 B1
Foz do Giraldo P 92 B3
Frabosa Soprana I 80 B1
Frades de la Sierra E 93 A5
Fraga E 90 B3
Fragagnano I 104 C3
Frailes E 100 B2
Fraire B 49 C5
Fraize F 60 B2
Framlingham GB 30 B5
Frammersbach D 51 C5
Framnes N. 35 C2
França P 87 C4
Francaltroff F 60 B2
Francavilla al Mare I 103 A7
Francavilla di Sicília I 109 B4
Francavilla Fontana I 104 C3
Francavilla in Sinni I 106 A3
Francescas F 77 B3
Franco P 87 C3
Francofonte I 109 B3
Francos E 89 C3
Frändefors S 35 D4
Frangy F 69 B5
Frankenau D 51 B4
Frankenberg
 Hessen D 51 B4
 Sachsen D 52 C3
Frankenburg A. 63 B4
Frankenfels A. 63 C6
Frankenmarkt A. 63 C4
Frankenthal D 61 A4
Frankfurt
 Brandenburg D 45 C6
 Hessen D 51 C4
Frankowo PL 47 A6
Fränsta S 115 E13
Franzburg D 45 A4
Frascati I 102 B5
Frasdorf D 62 C3

Fraserburgh GB 23 D6
Frashër AL 116 B2
Frasne F. 69 B6
Frasnes-lez-Anvaing B 49 C4
Frasseto F 102 B2
Frastanz A 71 A4
Fratel P. 92 B3
Fratta Todina I 82 D1
Frauenau D 63 B4
Frauenfeld CH. 70 A3
Frauenkirchen A 64 C2
Frauenstein D 52 C3
Frauental A 73 B5
Frayssinet F 77 B4
Frayssinet-le-Gélat F 77 B3
Frechas P. 87 C3
Frechen D 50 C2
Frechilla E 88 B2
Freckenhorst D 50 B3
Fredeburg D 50 B4
Fredelsloh D 51 B5
Fredeng N 34 B2
Fredensborg DK 41 D2
Fredericia DK 39 D2
Frederiks DK 39 C2
Frederikshavn DK. 38 B3
Frederikssund DK. 39 D5
Frederiksværk DK 39 D5
Fredrika S 115 C15
Fredriksberg S 34 B6
Fredriksdal S. 40 B4
Fredrikstad N 35 C2
Fregenal de la Sierra
 E 99 A4
Fregene I 102 B5
Freiberg D 52 C3
Freiburg
 Baden-Württemberg D 60 C3
 Niedersachsen D. 43 B6
Freienhagen D. 51 B5
Freienhufen D 53 B3
Freienstein D. 51 C5
Freihung D. 62 A2
Freilassing D 62 C3
Freisen D 60 A3
Freising D 62 B2
Freistadt A 63 B5
Freital D 52 B3
Freixedas P 93 A3
Freixo de Espada à Cinta P 87 C4
Fréjus F 79 C5
Fremdingen D 61 B6
Frenštát pod Radhoštěm CZ. 64 A4
Freren D 43 C4
Freshford IRL 21 B4
Freshwater GB 31 D2
Fresnay-sur-Sarthe F 57 B6
Fresneda de la Sierra
 E 95 B4
Fresneda de la Sierra Tirón E 89 B3
Fresnedillas E 94 B2
Fresnes-en-Woevre F 60 A1
Fresnes-St Mamès F 69 A5
Fresno Alhandiga E 94 B1
Fresno de la Ribera E 88 C1
Fresno de la Vega E 88 B1
Fresno de Sayago E 87 C5
Fresnoy-Folny F 58 A2
Fresnoy-le-Grand F 59 A4
Fressenville F 48 C2
Fresvik N 32 A3
Fréteval F 58 C2
Fretigney F 69 A5
Freudenberg
 Baden-Württemberg D 61 A5
 Nordrhein-Westfalen D 50 C3
Freudenstadt D 61 B4
Freux B 59 A6
Frévent F 48 C3
Freyburg D 52 B1
Freyenstein D 44 B4
Freyming-Merlebach F 60 A2
Freystadt D 62 A2
Freyung D 63 B4
Frias de Albarracin E 95 B5
Fribourg CH. 70 B2
Frick CH. 70 A3
Fridafors S 41 C4
Fridaythorpe GB 27 A5
Friedberg
 Bayern D 62 B1
 Hessen D 51 C4
Friedeburg D 43 B4
Friedewald D 51 C5
Friedland
 Brandenburg D 53 A4
 Mecklenburg-Vorpommern D 45 B5
 Niedersachsen D. 51 B5
Friedrichroda D 51 C6
Friedrichsbrunn D 52 B1
Friedrichshafen D 61 C5
Friedrichstadt D 43 A6
Friedrichswalde D. 45 B5
Friesach A 73 B4
Friesack D 44 C4
Friesenheim D 60 B3
Friesoythe D 43 B4
Friggesund S 115 F12
Frigiliana E 100 C2
Frihetsli N 112 D8
Frillesås S 40 B2
Frinnaryd S 40 B4
Frinton-on-Sea GB 31 C5
Friockheim GB 25 B5
Friol E 86 A3
Fristad S 40 B2
Fritsla S. 40 B2
Fritzlar D 51 B5
Frizington GB. 26 A2
Frödinge S 40 B6
Froges F 69 C5
Frohburg D 52 B2
Frohnhausen D 50 C4
Frohnleiten A 73 A5
Froissy F 58 A3
Frombork PL 47 A5
Frome GB 29 B5
Frómista E 88 B2
Fröndenberg D 50 B3
Fronsac F 76 B2
Front I 70 C2
Fronteira P 92 B3
Frontenay-Rohan-Rohan F 67 B4
Frontenhausen D 62 B3
Frontignan F 78 C2
Fronton F 77 C4
Fröseke S 40 C5
Frosinone I 103 B6
Frosolone I 103 B7
Frosta N 114 D7
Frøstrup DK 38 B1
Frosunda S 37 C5
Frøyset N 32 B2
Frövi S 37 C2
Fruges F 48 C3
Frutigen CH 70 B2
Frýdek-Místek CZ 65 A4
Frýdlant CZ 53 C5
Frýdlant nad Ostravicí CZ. 65 A4
Frygnowo PL 47 B6
Fryšták CZ 64 A3
Fucécchio I 81 C4
Fuencaliente
 Ciudad Real E 94 C2
 Ciudad Real E 100 A1
Fuencemillán E 95 B3
Fuendejalón E 89 C5
Fuengirola E 100 C1

Fuenlabrada E 94 B3
Fuenlabrada de los Montes E 94 C2
Fuensalida E 94 B2
Fuensanta E 101 B4
Fuensanta de Martos E 100 B2
Fuente-Álamo E 101 A4
Fuente-Álamo de Murcia E 101 B4
Fuentealbilla E 96 B1
Fuentecén E 88 C3
Fuente de Cantos E 99 A4
Fuente del Arco E 99 A5
Fuente del Conde E 100 B1
Fuente del Maestre E 93 C4
Fuente de Santa Cruz E 94 A2
Fuente el Fresno E 94 C3
Fuente el Saz de Jarama E 95 B3
Fuente el Sol E 94 A2
Fuenteguinaldo E 93 A4
Fuentelapeña E 88 C1
Fuentelcésped E 89 C3
Fuentelespino de Haro E 95 C4
Fuentelespino de Moya E 96 B1
Fuentenovilla E 95 B3
Fuente Obejuna E 99 A5
Fuente Palmera E 99 B5
Fuentepelayo E 94 A2
Fuentepinilla E 89 C4
Fuenterrobles E 96 B1
Fuentes E 95 C4
Fuentesauco E 88 C2
Fuentesaúco E 94 A1
Fuentes de Andalucía E 99 B5
Fuentes de Ebro E 90 B2
Fuentes de Jiloca E 89 C5
Fuentes de la Alcarria E 95 B4
Fuentes de León E 99 A4
Fuentes de Nava E 88 B2
Fuentes de Oñoro E 93 A4
Fuentes de Ropel E 88 B1
Fuentespalda E 90 C3
Fuentespina E 88 C3
Fuente-Tójar E 100 B1
Fuente Vaqueros E 100 B2
Fuentidueña E 88 C3
Fuentidueña de Tajo E 95 B3
Fuerte del Rey E 100 B2
Fügen A 72 A1
Fuglebjerg DK 39 D4
Fuglevik N 35 C2
Fuhrberg D 44 C1
Fulda D 51 C5
Fulgatore I 108 B1
Fully CH. 70 B2
Fülöpszállás H 75 B4
Fulpmes A 71 A6
Fulunäs S 34 A5
Fumay F 49 D5
Fumel F 77 B3
Funäsdalen S 115 E9
Fundão P 92 A3
Funzie GB 22 A8
Furadouro P 87 D2
Fure N 32 A2
Furingstad S 37 D3
Furnari I 109 B3
Fürstenau D 43 C4
Furtei I 110 C1
Fürstenberg D 45 B5
Fürstenfeld A. 73 A6
Fürstenfeldbruck D 62 B2
Fürstenstein D 63 B4
Fürstenwalde D. 45 C6
Fürstenwerder D. 45 B5
Fürstenzell D 63 B4
Furta H 75 A6
Fürth
 Bayern D 62 A1
 Hessen D 61 A4
Furth im Wald D 62 A3
Furtwangen D 61 B4
Furuby S 40 C5
Furudal S 36 A2
Furuflaten N 112 C9
Furulund S 41 D3
Furusjö S 40 B3
Fusa N 32 B2
Fuscaldo I 106 B3
Fusch an der Grossglocknerstrasse A 72 A2
Fushë Arrëz AL 105 A6
Fushë-Krujë AL 105 B5
Fusina I 72 C2
Fusio CH 70 B3
Füssen D 71 A5
Fustiñana E 89 B5
Futog SRB 75 C4
Futrikelv N 112 C8
Füzesabony H 65 C6
Füzesgyarmat H 75 A6
Fužine HR 73 C4
Fylling S 40 C2
Fynshav DK 39 E2
Fyresdal N 33 C5

G

Gaaldorf A 73 A4
Gabaldón E 95 C5
Gabarret F 76 C2
Gabčíkovo SK 64 C3
Gabin PL 47 C5
Gabrovo BG 11 E8
Gaby I 70 C2
Gacé F 57 B6
Gacko BIH 84 C3
Gäddede S 115 C11
Gadebusch D 44 B3
Gadmen CH 70 B3
Gádor E 101 B3
Gádoros H 75 B5
Gael F 57 B3
Găesti RO 11 D8
Gaeta I 103 B6
Gafanhoeira P 92 C2
Gaflenz A 63 C5
Gagarin RUS 7 D13
Gaggenau D 61 B4
Gagliano Castelferrato I 109 B3
Gagliano del Capo I 107 B5
Gagnef S 36 B2
Gaibanella I 81 B5
Gaildorf D 61 B5
Gaillac F 77 C4
Gaillefontaine F 58 A2
Gaillon F 58 A2
Gainsborough GB 27 B5
Gairloch GB 22 D3
Gairlochy GB 24 B3
Gáiro I 110 C2
Gaj
 HR 74 C2
 SRB 85 B6
Gaja-la-Selve F 77 C4
Gajanejos E 95 B4
Gajary SK 64 B3
Gaj Oławski PL 54 B2
Galápagos E 95 B3
Galapagar E 94 B2
Galaroza E 99 B4
Galashiels GB 25 C5
Galatás GR 117 E5
Galați RO 11 D10
Galatina I 107 A5

Galatista GR 116 B5
Galátone I 107 A5
Galaxidi GR 117 D4
Galdakao E 89 A4
Galeata I. 81 C5
Galende E 87 B4
Galera E 101 B3
Galéria F 102 A1
Galgamácsa H 65 C5
Galgate GB 26 B3
Galgon F 76 B2
Galinduste E 93 A5
Galinoporni CY 120 A3
Galisteo E 93 B4
Galizes P 92 A3
Galków PL 55 B4
Gallarate I 70 C3
Gallardon F 58 B2
Gallegos de Argañán E 93 A4
Gallegos del Solmirón E 93 A5
Galleguillos de Campos E 88 B1
Galleno I 81 C4
Galliate I 70 C3
Gállio I 72 C1
Gallneukirchen A 63 B5
Gallo I 82 C1
Gallocanta E 95 B5
Gällö S 115 E12
Gällstad S 40 B3
Gallur E 90 B1
Galmisdale GB 24 B1
Galmpton GB 29 C4
Galston GB 24 C3
Galta N 33 C2
Galtelli I 110 B2
Galten DK 39 C2
Galtür A 71 B5
Galve de Sorbe E 95 A3
Galveias P 92 B2
Gálvez E 94 C2
Galway IRL 20 A2
Gamaches F 48 C2
Gámbara I 71 C5
Gambárie I 106 C2
Gambassi Terme I. 81 C4
Gambatesa I 103 B7
Gambolò I 70 C3
Gaming A. 63 C6
Gamla Uppsala S 36 C4
Gamleby S 40 B6
Gammelgarn S 37 E5
Gammelstad S 3 D25
Gammertingen D. 61 B5
Gams CH. 71 A4
Gamvik
 Finnmark N 113 A17
 Finnmark N 113 B11
Gan F 76 C2
Ganda di Martello I 71 B5
Gandarela P. 87 C2
Ganddal N 33 D2
Ganderkesee D 43 B5
Gandesa E 90 B3
Gandía E 96 C2
Gandino I 71 C4
Gandrup DK 38 B3
Gänghester S 40 B3
Gangi I 109 B3
Gångkofen D 62 B3
Gannat F 68 B3
Gannay-sur-Loire F 68 B3
Gänserdorf A 64 B2
Ganzlin D 44 B4
Gap F 79 B5
Gara H 75 B4
Garaballa E 96 B1
Garaguso I 104 C1
Garbayuela E 94 C1
Garbsen D 43 C6
Garching D 62 B3
Garciaz E 93 B5
Garcihernández E 94 B1
Garcillán E 94 B2
Garcisobaco E 99 C5
Garda I 71 C5
Gardanne F 79 C4
Gärdås S 34 B5
Gårdby S 41 C6
Gardeja PL 47 B4
Gardelegen D 44 C3
Gardermoen N 34 B3
Gardiki GR 116 D3
Garding D 43 A5
Gardone Riviera I 71 C5
Gardone Val Trómpia I 71 C5
Gärdserum S 37 D3
Gardouch F 77 C4
Gårdsjö S 37 D1
Gards Köpinge S 41 D4
Garein F 76 B2
Garelochhead GB 24 B3
Garéoult F 79 C5
Garešnica HR 74 C1
Garéssio I 80 B2
Garforth GB 27 B4
Gargaliani GR 117 E3
Gargaligas E 93 B5
Gargaliano del Capo I 107 B5
Garganta la Olla E 93 A5
Gargantiel E 100 A1
Gargellen A 71 B4
Gargilesse-Dampierre F 67 B6
Gargnano I 71 C5
Gargnäs S 115 B14
Gárgoles de Abajo E 95 B4
Gargrave GB 26 B3
Garin F 77 D3
Garlasco I 70 C3
Garlieston GB 24 D3
Garlin F 76 C2
Garlitos E 94 D1
Garmisch-Partenkirchen D 71 A6
Garnat-sur-Engièvre F 68 B3
Garpenberg S 36 B3
Garphyttan S 37 C1
Garray E 89 C4
Garrafe de Torio E 88 B1
Garrel D 43 C5
Garriguella E 91 A6
Garrison GB 18 B3
Garrovillas E 93 B4
Garrucha E 101 B4
Gars-am-Kamp A 63 B6
Garsås S 36 B1
Garsdale Head GB 26 A3
Gärsnäs S 41 D4
Garstang GB 26 B3
Gartow D 44 B3
Gartz D. 45 B6
Gærum DK 38 B3
Garvagh GB 19 B5
Garváo P 98 B2
Garve GB 23 D4
Garwolin PL 55 B6
Garz D 45 A5
Garzyn PL 54 B1
Gasawa PL 46 C3
Gåsborn S 34 C6
Gaschurn A 71 B5
Gascueña E 95 B4
Gasny F 58 A2
Gasocin PL 47 C6

Gata
 E 93 A4
 HR 83 C5
Gata de Gorgos E 96 C3
Gatchina RUS 7 B11
Gatehouse of Fleet GB. 24 D3
Gátér H. 75 B4
Gateshead GB 25 D6
Gátova E 96 B2
Gattendorf A 64 B2
Gatteo a Mare I 82 B1
Gattinara I 70 C3
Gattorna I 80 B3
Gaucín E 99 C5
Gaulstad N. 114 D9
Gaupne N. 32 A4
Gautefall N 33 C5
Gauting D 62 B2
Gauto S 115 A13
Gava E 91 B5
Gavardo I 71 C5
Gavarnie F 76 D2
Gávavencsellő H 65 B6
Gavião P 92 B3
Gaviño P 92 B3
Gävle S 36 B4
Gavoi I 110 B2
Gavorrano I 81 D4
Gavray F 57 B4
Gavrio GR 117 E6
Gazipaşa TR 119 F7
Gazoldo degli Ippoliti I 71 C5
Gazzuolo I 81 A4
Gbelce SK 65 C4
Gdańsk PL 47 A4
Gdinj HR 84 C1
Gdov RUS 7 B9
Gdów PL 65 A6
Gdynia PL 47 A4
Gea de Albarracin E 95 B5
Geary GB 22 D2
Géaudot F 59 B5
Geaune F 76 C2
Gebesee D 51 B6
Gebze TR 118 B4
Géderlak H 75 B3
Gedern D 51 C5
Gedinne B 49 D5
Gediz TR 118 D4
Gèdre F 76 D3
Gedser DK 44 A3
Gedsted DK 38 C2
Geel B 49 B5
Geesthacht D 44 B2
Geertruidenberg NL 49 B5
Geetbets B 49 C6
Gefell D 52 C1
Gehrden D 51 A5
Gehren D 52 C1
Geilenkirchen D 50 C2
Geilo N 32 B5
Geinsheim D 61 A4
Geisa D 51 C5
Geiselhöring D 62 B3
Geiselwind D 61 A6
Geisenfeld D 62 B2
Geisenhausen D 62 B3
Geisenheim D 50 D4
Geising D 53 C3
Geisingen D 61 C4
Geislingen D 61 B5
Geistthal A 73 A5
Geithain D 52 B2
Geithus N 34 C1
Gela I 109 B3
Geldermalsen NL 49 B6
Geldern D 50 B2
Geldrop NL 49 B6
Geleen NL 50 C1
Gelembe TR 118 C2
Gelendost TR 119 D6
Gelida E 91 B4
Gelnhausen D 51 C5
Gelnica SK 65 B6
Gelse H 74 B1
Gelsenkirchen D 50 B3
Gelsted DK 39 D2
Geltendorf D 62 B2
Gelterkinden CH 70 A2
Gelting D 39 D2
Gelu RO 75 B6
Gelves E 99 B4
Gembloux B 49 C5
Gemeaux F 69 A5
Gémenos F 79 C4
Gemerská Poloma SK 65 B6
Gemerská Ves SK 65 B6
Gemert NL 50 B1
Gemla S 40 C4
Gemlik TR 118 B4
Gemmenich D 50 C1
Gemona del Friuli I 72 B3
Gémozac F 66 C4
Gemund D 50 C2
Gemünden
 Bayern D 51 C5
 Hessen D 51 C4
 Rheinland-Pfalz D 60 A3
Genappe B 49 C5
Génave E 101 A3
Genazzano I 102 B5
Gençay F 67 B5
Gencsapáti H 74 A1
Gendringen NL 50 B2
Genelard F 68 B4
Genemuiden NL 42 C3
Generalski Stol HR 73 C5
Genevad S 40 C3
Genève = Geneva CH 69 B6
Genevrières F 60 C1
Gengenbach D 61 B4
Genillé F 67 A6
Genk B 49 C6
Genlis F 69 A5
Gennep NL 50 B1
Genner DK 39 D2
Gennes F 67 A4
Genoa = Génova I 80 B1
Génova = Genoa I 80 B1
Genowefa PL 54 A3
Gensingen D 61 A4
Gent = Ghent B 49 B4
Genthin D 44 C4
Gentioux F 68 C1
Genzano di Lucánia I 104 C1
Genzano di Roma I 102 B5
Georgenthal D 51 C6
Georgsmarienhütte D 50 A4
Gera D 52 C2
Geraardsbergen B 49 C4
Gerabronn D 61 A5
Geraci Sículo I 109 B3
Geras A 63 B6
Gérardmer F 60 B2
Geras A 63 B6
Gerbéviller F 60 B2
Gerbini I 109 B3
Gerbstedt D 52 B1
Gerchsheim D 61 A5
Gerði IS 111 D6
Gerede TR 118 B7
Gerei I 110 C2
Geretsried D 62 C2
Gérgal E 101 B3
Gergy F 69 B4
Gerindote E 94 C2
Gerjen H 74 B3
Gerlos A 72 A2
Germay F 59 B6
Germencik TR 119 E2
Germering D 62 B2
Germersheim D 61 A4
Gernika-Lumo E 89 A4
Gernrode D 52 B1
Gernsbach D 61 B4
Gernsheim D 61 A4
Gerola Alta I 71 B4
Geroldsgrün D 52 C1
Gerolsbach D 62 B2
Gerolstein D 50 C2
Gerolzhofen D 61 A6
Gerovo HR 73 C4
Gerpinnes B 49 C5
Gerrards Cross GB 31 C3
Gerri de la Sal E 91 A4
Gersfeld D 51 C5
Gersheim D 60 A3
Gerstetten D 61 B6
Gerstungen D 51 C6
Gerswalde D 45 B5
Gerzat F 68 C3
Gerze TR 16 A7
Gerzen D 62 B3
Gescher D 50 B3
Geseke D 51 B4
Geslau D 61 A6
Gespunsart F 59 A5
Gesté F 66 A3
Gestorf D 51 A5
Gesualda I 103 C8
Gesunda S 36 B1
Geta FIN 36 B6
Getafe E 94 B3
Getinge S 40 C2
Getxo E 89 A4
Gevelsberg D 50 B3
Gevgelija MK 116 A4
Gevora del Caudillo E 93 C4
Gevrey-Chambertin F 69 A4
Gex F 69 B6
Gey D 50 C2
Geyikli TR 118 C1
Geysir IS 111 C5
Geyve TR 118 B5
Gföhl A 63 B6
Ghedi I 71 C5
Ghent = Gent B 49 B4
Gheorgheni RO 11 C8
Ghigo I 79 B6
Ghilarza I 110 B1
Ghisonaccia F 102 A2
Ghisoni F 102 A2
Gialtra GR 116 D4
Gianitsa GR 116 B4
Giardinetto Vécchio I 103 B8
Giardini Naxos I 109 B4
Giarratana I 109 B3
Giarre I 109 B4
Giat F 68 C2
Giaveno I 80 A1
Giazza I 71 C6
Giba I 110 C1
Gibellina Nuova I 108 B1
Gibostad N 112 C7
Gibraléon E 99 B4
Gibraltar GBZ 99 C5
Gic H 74 A2
Gideå S 115 D16
Gideåkroken S 115 C14
Gidle PL 55 C4
Giebelstadt D 61 A5
Gieboldehausen D 51 B6
Gielniow PL 55 B5
Gielow D 45 B4
Gien F 58 C3
Giengen D 61 B6
Giens F 79 C5
Giera RO 75 C5
Gieselwerder D 51 B5
Giessen D 51 C4
Gieten NL 42 B3
Giethoorn NL 42 C3
Giffaumont-Champaubert F 59 B5
Gifford GB 25 C5
Gifhorn D 44 C2
Gige H 74 B2
Giglio Porto I 102 A3
Gignac F 78 C2
Gijón = Xixón E 88 A1
Gilena E 100 B1
Gilford GB 19 B5
Gillberga S 35 C4
Gilleleje DK 41 C2
Gilley F 69 A6
Gilley-sur-Loire F 68 B3
Gillingham
 Dorset GB 29 B5
 Medway GB 31 C4
Gilocourt F 59 A3
Gilserberg D 51 C5
Gilten D 43 C6
Gilze NL 49 B5
Gimåt S 115 D15
Gimo S 36 B5
Gimont F 77 C3
Ginasservis F 79 C4
Gingelom B 49 C6
Gingst D 45 A5
Ginosa I 104 C2
Ginzling A 72 A1
Giões P 98 B3
Gióia dei Marsi I 103 B6
Gióia del Colle I 104 C2
Gióia Sannitica I 103 B7
Gióia Táuro I 106 C2
Gioiosa Iónica I 106 C3
Gioiosa Marea I 109 A3
Giosla E 90 B3
Giovinazzo I 104 B2
Girifalco I 106 B3
Giromagny F 60 C2
Girona E 91 A5
Gironcourt-sur-Vraine F 60 B1
Gironella E 91 A4
Gironville-sous-les-Côtes F 60 B1
Girvan GB 24 C3
Gislaved S 40 B3
Gislev DK 39 D3
Gisors F 58 A2
Gissi I 103 A7
Gistad S 37 D2
Gistel B 48 B3
Gistrup DK 38 C3
Giswil CH 70 B3
Githio GR 117 F4
Giugliano in Campania I 103 C7
Giulianova I 103 A6
Giulvăz RO 75 C5
Giurgiu RO 11 E8
Give DK 39 D2
Givet F 49 C5
Givors F 69 C4
Givry
 B 49 C5
 F 69 B4
Givry-en-Argonne F 59 B6
Givskud DK 39 D2
Giżałki PL 54 A2
Giżycko PL 6 D6
Gizzeria I 106 B3
Gizzeria Lido I 106 B3
Gjedved DK 39 D2
Gjegjan AL 105 B6
Gjendesheim N 32 A5
Gjerde N 32 B3
Gjerlev DK 38 C3
Gjermundshamn N 32 B2
Gjerrild DK 39 C3
Gjerstad N 33 D6
Gjesås N 34 B4

Gjesvær N 113 A14
Gjirokastër AL 116 B2
Gjøfjell N 35 C2
Gjøl DK 38 B2
Gjøra N 114 E6
Gjøvik N 34 B2
Gladbach D 50 C2
Gladbeck D 50 B2
Gladenbach D 51 C4
Gladstad N 114 B8
Glamis GB 25 B5
Glamoč BIH 84 B1
Glamsbjerg DK 39 D3
Gland CH 69 B6
Glandorf D 50 A3
Glanegg A 73 B4
Glanshammar S 37 C2
Glarus CH 70 A4
Glasgow GB 24 C3
Glashütte
 Bayern D 62 C2
 Sachsen D 53 C3
Glastonbury GB 29 B5
Glatzau A 73 B5
Glauchau D 52 C2
Glava S 35 C4
Glavatičevo BIH 84 C3
Glavičice BIH 85 B4
Glavnik KOS 85 C5
Gledica SRB 85 C5
Glein
 A 73 A4
 N 115 A9
Gleinstätten A 73 B5
Gleisdorf A 73 A5
Glenamoy IRL 18 B2
Glenarm GB 19 B6
Glenavy GB 19 B5
Glenbarr GB 24 C2
Glenbeigh IRL 20 C2
Glenbrittle GB 22 D2
Glencoe GB 24 B2
Glencolumbkille IRL 18 B3
Glendalough IRL 21 A5
Glenealy IRL 21 B5
Glenelg GB 22 D3
Glenfinnan GB 24 B2
Glengarriff IRL 20 C2
Glenluce GB 24 D3
Glennamaddy IRL 18 C3
Glenrothes GB 25 B4
Glenties IRL 18 B3
Glesborg DK 38 C3
Glesien D 52 B2
Glesné CH 45 A4
Gletsch CH 70 B3
Glewitz D 45 A4
Glifada GR 117 E5
Glimåkra S 41 C4
Glin IRL 20 B2
Glina HR 73 C6
Glinde D 44 B2
Glinojeck PL 47 C6
Glinsk IRL 20 A2
Gliwice PL 54 C3
Glödnitz A 73 B4
Gloggnitz A 64 C1
Głogoczów PL 65 A5
Glogonj SRB 85 B5
Glogovac SRB 85 B6
Głogów PL 53 B6
Głogówek PL 54 C2
Glomel F 56 B2
Glomfjord N 112 F2
Glommen S 40 C2
Glommersträsk S 115 B16
Glonn D 62 C2
Glorenza I 71 B5
Gloria P 92 B2
Glosa GR 116 C5
Glossop GB 27 B4
Gloucester GB 29 B5
Głowaczów PL 55 B6
Głowno PL 55 A4
Glöwen D 44 C4
Głozan SRB 75 C4
Głubczyce PL 54 C2
Głuchołazy PL 54 C2
Głuchów PL 55 B5
Głuchowo PL 54 A1
Glücksburg D 39 E2
Glückstadt D 43 B6
Glumina BIH 85 B4
Glumsø DK 39 D4
Glušci SRB 85 B4
Glusk BY 7 E10
Głuszyca PL 53 C6
Glyngøre DK 38 C1
Glyn Neath GB 29 B4
Gmünd
 Kärnten A 72 B3
 Nieder Österreich A 63 B5
Gmund D 62 C2
Gmunden A 63 C4
Gnarp S 115 E14
Gnarrenburg D 43 B6
Gnesau A 72 B3
Gnesta S 37 C4
Gniechowice PL 54 B1
Gniew PL 47 B4
Gniewkowo PL 47 C4
Gniezno PL 46 C3
Gnoien D 45 B4
Gnojnice BIH 84 C2
Gnojno PL 55 C5
Gnosall GB 26 C3
Gnosjö S 40 B3
Göbel TR 118 B3
Göçbeyli TR 118 C2
Goch D 50 B2
Gochsheim D 51 C6
Göd H 65 C5
Godalming GB 31 C3
Godby FIN 36 B6
Goðdalir IS 111 B6
Godech BG 11 E7
Godegård S 37 D2
Godelheim D 51 B5
Goderville F 58 A1
Godiasco I 80 B3
Godič SLO 73 B4
Godkowo PL 47 A5
Godmanchester GB 30 B3
Gödöllő H 65 C5
Gödre H 74 B2
Godshill GB 31 D2
Godzikowice PL 54 C2
Godziszewo PL 47 A4
Goes NL 49 B4
Goetzenbrück F 60 B3
Göggingen D 61 B6
Göhren D 45 A5
Goirle NL 49 B5
Góis P 92 A2
Góito I 71 C5
Goizueta E 76 C1
Gojna Gora SRB 85 C5
Gójsk PL 47 C5
Gökçedag TR 118 C3
Gökçen TR 119 D2
Gökçeören TR 119 D3
Gökçeyazı TR 118 C2
Göktepe TR 119 E3
Gol N 32 B6
Gola
 HR 74 B2

Goldbeck D 44 C3
Goldberg D 44 B4
Goldelund D 43 A6
Goldenstedt D 43 C5
Gołębiowo PL 47 A4
Golegã P 92 B2
Goleniów PL 45 B6
Golfo Aranci I 110 E4
Gölhisar TR 119 E4
Golina PL 54 A3
Gölle H 74 B3
Göllersdorf A 64 B2
Golling an der Salzach A 63 C4
Gölmarmara TR 118 D2
Golnice PL 53 B5
Golnik SLO 73 B4
Gölova TR 119 F5
Gölpazarı TR 118 B5
Gols A 64 C2
Golspie GB 23 D5
Golssen D 52 B3
Golubac SRB 85 B6
Golub-Dobrzyń PL 47 B5
Golubinci SRB 85 B5
Goluchow HR 105 A5
Goluchów PL 54 B2
Golzow D 52 A2
Gomagoi I 71 B5
Gómara E 89 C4
Gomaringen D 61 B5
Gömbe TR 119 F4
Gömeç TR 118 C1
Gomel = Homyel BY 7 E11
Gomes Aires P 98 B2
Gómezserracin E 88 C2
Gommern D 52 A1
Gomulin PL 55 B4
Gonäs S 36 B2
Goncelin F 69 C5
Gończyce PL 55 B6
Gondomar
  P 87 B2
  E 87 C2
Gondrecourt-le-Château F 60 B1
Gondrin F 76 C3
Gönen
  Balıkesir TR 118 B2
  Isparta TR 119 E5
Gonfaron F 79 C5
Goñi E 76 D1
Goni
  GR 116 C4
  I 110 C2
Gonnesa I 110 C1
Gonnosfanádiga I 110 C1
Gönyü H 64 C3
Gonzaga I 81 B4
Goodrich GB 29 B5
Goodwick GB 28 A2
Gooik B 49 C5
Goole GB 27 B5
Goor NL 50 A2
Göpfritz an der Wild A 63 B6
Goppenstein CH 70 B2
Göppingen D 61 B5
Gor E 100 B3
Góra
  Dolnośląskie PL 54 B1
  Mazowieckie PL 47 C6
Gorafe E 100 B2
Góra Kalwaria PL 55 B6
Gorawino PL 46 B1
Goražde BIH 84 C3
Gördalen S 34 A4
Gordaliza del Pino E 88 B1
Gördes TR 118 D3
Gerding DK 39 D1
Górdola CH 70 B3
Gordon GB 25 C5
Gordoncillo E 88 B1
Gorebridge GB 25 C4
Gorenja Vas SLO 73 B4
Gorenje Jelenje HR 73 C4
Gorey
  GB 57 A3
  IRL 21 B5
Gorgonzola I 71 C4
Gorica HR 83 B4
Gorican HR 74 B1
Gorinchem NL 49 B5
Goring GB 31 C2
Goritsy RUS 7 C14
Göritz D 45 B5
Gorizia I 72 C3
Górki PL 47 C5
Gorleben D 44 B3
Gorleston-on-sea GB 30 B6
Garley DK 39 D4
Görlitz D 53 B4
Gorliz E 89 A4
Görmin D 45 B5
Górna Grupa PL 47 B4
Gorna Oryahovitsa BG 11 E8
Gornja Gorevnica SRB 85 C5
Gornja Klina KOS 85 D5
Gornja Ploča HR 83 B4
Gornja Radgona SLO 73 B5
Gornja Sabanta SRB 85 C6
Gornja Trešnjevica SRB 85 B5
Gornja Tuzla BIH 84 B3
Gornje Polje MNE 84 D3
Gornje Ratkovo BIH 84 B1
Gornji Grad SLO 73 B4
Gornji Humac HR 83 C5
Gornji Jasenjani BIH 84 C2
Gornji Kamengrad BIH 83 B5
Gornji Kneginec HR 74 B1
Gornji Kokoti MNE 105 A5
Gornji Kosinj HR 83 B4
Gornji Milanovac SRB 85 B5
Gornji Podgradci BIH 84 A2
Gornji Ravno BIH 84 C2
Gornji Sjenicak HR 73 C5
Gornji Vakuf BIH 84 C2
Görömböly H 65 B6
Górowo Iławeckie PL 47 A6
Gorran Haven GB 28 C3
Gorredijk NL 42 B3
Gorron F 57 B5
Gorseinon GB 28 B3
Gort IRL 20 A3
Gortin GB 19 B4
Görzke D 52 A2
Gorzkowice PL 55 B4
Górzno
  Kujawsko-Pomorskie PL 47 B5
  Zachodnio-Pomorskie PL 45 C7
Gorzów Śląski PL 54 B3
Gorzów Wielkopolski PL 45 C7
Górzyca PL 45 C6
Gorzyce PL 53 B4
Gorzyń PL 46 C1
Gorzyno PL 46 A3
Gosaldo I 72 B1
Gosau A 63 C4
Gosberton GB 30 B3
Gościcino PL 47 A4
Goślcin PL 54 C2
Gościm PL 46 C1
Gościno PL 46 A1
Gosdorf A 73 B5
Gosforth GB 26 A2
Goslar D 51 B6
Goslice PL 47 C5
Gospić HR 83 B4
Gosport GB 31 D2

Gössäter S 35 D5
Gossau CH 71 A4
Goss Ilsede D 51 A6
Gössnitz D 52 C2
Gössweinstein D 62 A2
Gostimë AL 105 C6
Gostkow PL 55 B4
Gostomia PL 46 B2
Gostycyn PL 46 B3
Gostyń PL 54 B2
Gostynin PL 47 C5
Goszczyn PL 55 B5
Göta S 35 D4
Göteborg = Gothenburg S 38 B4
Götene S 35 D5
Gotha D 51 C6
Gothem S 37 E5
Gothenburg = Göteborg S 38 B4
Gotse Delchev BG 116 A5
Gottersdorf D 62 B3
Göttingen D 51 B5
Gottne S 115 D15
Götzis A 71 A4
Gouarec F 56 B2
Gouda NL 49 A5
Goudhurst GB 31 C4
Goumenissa GR 116 B4
Goura GR 117 E4
Gourdon F 77 B4
Gourgançon F 59 B5
Gourin F 56 B2
Gournay-en-Bray F 58 A2
Gourock GB 24 C3
Gouveia P 92 A3
Gouvy B 50 C1
Gouzeacourt F 49 C4
Gouzon F 68 B2
Govedari HR 84 D1
Govérnolo I 81 A4
Gowarczów PL 55 B5
Gowerton GB 28 B3
Gowidlino PL 46 A3
Gowran IRL 21 B4
Goyatz D 53 A4
Göynük
  TR 118 B5
  Antalya TR 119 F5
Gozdnica PL 53 B5
Gozdowo PL 47 C5
Gozee B 49 C5
Graal-Müritz D 44 A4
Grab BIH 84 D3
Grabenstätt D 62 C3
Grabhair GB 22 C2
Gräbo S 38 B5
Grabovac
  HR 84 C1
  SRB 85 B5
Grabovci SRB 85 B4
Grabow D 44 B3
Grabów nad Pilicą PL 55 B6
Grabów nad Prosną PL 54 B3
Grabowno PL 46 B3
Grabs CH 71 A4
Gračac HR 83 B4
Gračanica
  BIH 84 B3
  KOS 85 D6
Graçay F 68 A1
Gracen AL 105 B5
Grad SLO 73 B6
Gradac
  BIH 84 D3
  BIH 84 C2
  MNE 85 C4
  SRB 85 C5
Gradec HR 74 C1
Gradefes E 88 B1
Grades A 73 B4
Gradil P 92 C1
Gradina
  HR 74 C2
  MNE 85 C4
Gradisca d'Isonzo I 72 C3
Gradište HR 74 C3
Grado
  E 86 A4
  I 72 C3
Grafenau D 63 B4
Gräfenberg D 62 A2
Gräfenhainichen D 52 B2
Grafenschlag A 63 B6
Grafenstein A 73 B4
Gräfenthal D 52 C1
Grafentonna D 51 B6
Gräfenwöhr D 62 A2
Grafing D 62 B2
Grafling D 62 B3
Gräfsnäs S 40 B2
Gragnano I 103 C7
Grahovo
  MNE 84 D3
  SLO 72 B3
Graiguenamanagh IRL 21 B5
Grain GB 31 C4
Grainau D 71 A6
Graja de Iniesta E 95 C5
Grajera E 89 C3
Gram DK 39 D2
Gramais A 71 A5
Gramat F 77 B4
Gramatneusiedl A 64 B2
Grambow D 45 B6
Grammichele I 109 B3
Gramsh AL 116 B2
Gramzow D 45 B6
Gran N 34 B2
Granada E 100 B2
Granard IRL 19 C4
Grañas E 86 A3
Granátula de Calatrava E 100 A2
Grancey-le-Château F 59 C6
Grandas de Salime E 86 A4
Grandcamp-Maisy F 57 A4
Grand-Champ F 56 C3
Grand Couronne F 58 A2
Grand-Fougeray F 57 C4
Grândola P 98 A2
Grandpré F 59 A5
Grandrieu F 78 B2
Grandson CH 70 B1
Grandvillars F 70 A1
Grandvilliers F 58 A2
Grañén E 90 B2
Grangärde S 36 B1
Grange IRL 18 B3
Grangemouth GB 25 B4
Grange-over-Sands GB 26 A3
Grängesberg S 36 B1
Granges-de-Crouhens F 77 D3
Granges-sur-Vologne F 60 B2
Gräningen D 44 C4
Granitola-Torretta I 108 B1
Granja
  Évora P 98 A3
  Porto P 87 C2
Granja de Moreruela E 88 C1
Granja de Torrehermosa E 93 C4
Gränna S 40 B4
Grannäs
  Västerbotten S 115 B13
  Västerbotten S 115 B14
Granö S 115 C16
Granollers E 91 B5
Granowiec PL 54 B2

Granowo PL 54 A1
Gransee D 45 B5
Gransherad N 33 C6
Grantham GB 27 C5
Grantown-on-Spey GB 23 D5
Grantshouse GB 25 C5
Granville F 57 B4
Granvin N 32 B3
Grærup Strand DK 39 D1
Gräsås S 40 C2
Grasbakken N 113 B17
Grasberg D 43 B6
Grasmere GB 26 A2
Gräsmyr S 115 D16
Grasö S 36 B5
Grassano I 104 C2
Grassau D 62 C3
Grasse F 79 C6
Grassington GB 27 A4
Gråsten DK 39 E2
Grästorp S 35 D4
Gratkorn A 73 A5
Gratwein A 73 A5
Graulhet F 77 C4
Graus E 90 A3
Grávalos E 89 B5
Gravberget N 34 B4
Grave NL 50 B1
Gravedona I 71 B4
Gravelines F 48 B3
Gravellona Toce I 70 C3
Gravendal S 36 B1
Gravens DK 39 D2
Gravesend GB 31 C4
Graveson F 78 C3
Gravina in Púglia I 104 C2
Gray F 69 A5
Grayrigg GB 26 A3
Grays GB 31 C4
Grayshott GB 31 C3
Grayvoron RUS 7 F13
Graz A 73 A5
Grazalema E 99 C5
Grążawy PL 47 B5
Grazzano Visconti I 80 B3
Greåker N 35 C3
Great Dunmow GB 31 C4
Great Malvern GB 29 A5
Great Torrington GB 28 C3
Great Waltham GB 31 C4
Great Yarmouth GB 30 B5
Grebbestad S 35 D3
Grebenstein D 51 B5
Grebocice PL 53 B6
Grębocin PL 47 B4
Greding D 62 A2
Gredstedbro DK 39 D1
Greencastle IRL 19 A4
Greenhead GB 25 D5
Greenisland GB 19 B6
Greenlaw GB 25 C5
Greenock GB 24 C3
Greenway GB 28 B3
Greenwich GB 31 C4
Grefrath D 50 B2
Greifenburg A 72 B3
Greiffenberg D 45 B5
Greifswald D 45 A5
Grein A 63 B5
Greipstad N 33 D4
Greiz D 52 C2
Grenaa DK 39 C3
Grenade F 77 C4
Grenade-sur-l'Adour F 76 C2
Grenchen CH 70 A2
Grendi N 33 D4
Grenivík IS 111 B7
Grenoble F 69 C5
Grésy-sur-Isère F 69 C6
Gréoux-les-Bains F 79 C4
Gresenhorst D 44 A4
Gressoney-la-Trinité I 70 C2
Gressoney-St-Jean I 70 C2
Gressthal D 51 C6
Gressvik N 35 C2
Gresten A 63 C6
Gretna GB 25 D4
Greussen D 51 B6
Greve in Chianti I 81 C5
Greven
  Mecklenburg-Vorpommern D 44 B2
  Nordrhein-Westfalen D 50 A3
Grevena GR 116 B3
Grevenbroich D 50 B2
Grevenbrück D 50 B4
Grevenmacher L 60 A2
Grevesmühlen D 44 B3
Grevestrand DK 41 D2
Grevie S 41 C2
Greystoke GB 26 A3
Greystones IRL 21 A5
Grez-Doiceau B 49 C5
Grèzec F 77 B4
Grez-en-Bouère F 57 C5
Grezzana I 71 C6
Grgar SLO 72 B3
Grgurevci SRB 85 A4
Gries A 71 A6
Griesbach D 63 B4
Gries in Sellrain A 71 A6
Grieskirchen A 63 B4
Griffen A 73 B4
Grignan F 78 B3
Grignano I 72 C3
Grignols F 76 B2
Grignon F 69 C6
Grijota E 88 B2
Grijpskerk NL 42 B3
Grillby S 37 C4
Grimaud F 79 C5
Grimbergen B 49 C5
Grimma D 52 B2
Grimmen D 45 A5
Grimmialp CH 70 B2
Grimsås S 40 B3
Grimsby GB 27 B5
Grímsey IS 111 A8
Grimslöv S 40 C4
Grimstad N 33 D5
Grimstorp S 40 B4
Grindavík IS 111 D3
Grindelwald CH 70 B2
Grindheim N 33 D3
Grindsted DK 39 D1
Griñón E 94 B3
Gripenberg S 40 B4
Gripsholm S 37 C4
Grisolles F 77 C4
Grisslehamn S 36 B5
Gritley GB 23 C6
Grizebeck GB 26 A2
Gröbming A 72 A3
Grocka SRB 85 B5
Gröditz D 52 B3
Gródki PL 47 B6
Grodków PL 54 C2
Grodzisk Mazowiecki PL 55 A5
Grodzisk Wielkoposki PL 54 A1
Groenlo NL 50 A2
Groesbeek NL 50 B1
Grohote HR 83 C5
Groitzsch D 52 B2
Grójec PL 55 B5
Grom PL 47 B6
Gromiljca BIH 84 C3
Grömitz D 44 A2
Gromnik PL 65 A6

Gromo I 71 C4
Gronau
  Niedersachsen D 51 A5
  Nordrhein-Westfalen D 50 A3
Grønbjerg DK 39 C1
Grönenbach D 61 C6
Grong N 114 C9
Grönhögen S 41 C6
Groningen NL 42 B3
Grønnestrand DK 38 B2
Grono CH 71 B4
Grönskåra S 40 B5
Grootegast NL 42 B3
Gropello Cairoli I 70 C3
Grorud N 34 C2
Grósio I 71 B5
Grošnica SRB 85 C5
Grossalmerode D 51 B5
Grossarl A 72 A3
Gross Beeren D 45 C5
Gross Berkel D 51 A5
Grossbodungen D 51 B6
Gross-botwar D 61 B5
Grossburgwedel D 44 C1
Grosschönau D 53 C4
Gross-Dölln D 45 B5
Grossbrode D 44 A3
Grossenhain D 52 B3
Grossenkneten D 43 C5
Grossenlüder D 51 C5
Grossensee D 44 B2
Grossenzersdorf A 64 B2
Grosseto I 81 D5
Gross-Gerau D 61 A4
Grossgerungs A 63 B5
Grossglobnitz A 63 B6
Grosshabersdorf D 62 A1
Grossharras A 64 B2
Grosshartmansdorf D 52 C3
Grosshöchstetten CH 70 B2
Gross Kreutz D 45 C4
Grosskrut A 64 B2
Gross Lafferde D 51 A6
Gross Leuthen D 53 A4
Grosslohra D 51 B6
Gross Muckrow D 53 A4
Gross Oesingen D 44 C2
Grossostheim D 61 A5
Grosspertholz A 63 B5
Grosspetersdorf A 73 A6
Grosspostwitz D 53 B4
Grossraming A 63 C5
Grossräschen D 53 B4
Gross Reken D 50 B3
Grossrinderfeld D 61 A5
Grossröhrsdorf D 53 B4
Gross Sarau D 44 B2
Gross Särchen D 53 B4
Grossschirma D 52 C3
Gross Schönebeck D 45 C5
Grossschweinbarth A 64 B2
Grosssiegharts A 63 B6
Grosssölk A 72 A3
Gross Umstadt D 61 A4
Grosswarasdorf A 74 A1
Gross Warnow D 44 B3
Gross-Weikersdorf A 64 B1
Gross-Welle D 44 B4
Grosswilfersdorf A 73 A5
Gross Wokern D 44 B4
Grostenquin F 60 B2
Grosuplje SLO 73 C4
Grótli N 114 E4
Grottáglie I 104 C3
Grottammare I 82 D2
Grotte di Castro I 81 D5
Grotteria I 106 C3
Gróttole I 104 C2
Grou NL 42 B2
Grov N 112 D6
Grova N 33 C5
Grove E 86 B2
Grube D 44 A3
Grubišno Polje HR 74 C2
Gruda HR 105 A4
Grude BIH 84 C2
Grudusk PL 47 B6
Grudziądz PL 47 B4
Grue N 34 B4
Gruissan F 78 C2
Grullos E 86 A4
Grumo Áppula I 104 B2
Grums S 35 C5
Grünau im Almtal A 63 C4
Grünberg D 51 C4
Grünburg A 63 C5
Grundarfjörður IS 111 C2
Grundforsen S 34 A4
Grundlsee A 63 C4
Grundsund S 35 D3
Grunewald D 53 B3
Grungedal N 33 C4
Grunow D 53 A4
Grünstadt D 61 A4
Gruvberget S 36 A3
Gruyères CH 70 B2
Gruža SRB 85 C5
Grybów PL 65 A6
Grycksbo S 36 B2
Gryfice PL 45 B7
Gryfino PL 45 B6
Gryfów Śląski PL 53 B5
Grymyr N 34 B2
Gryt S 37 D3
Grytgöl S 37 D2
Grythyttan S 37 C1
Grytnäs S 36 B3
Grzmiąca PL 46 B2
Grzybno PL 45 B6
Grzywna PL 47 B4

Guadahortuna E 100 B2
Guadalajara E 95 B3
Guadalaviar E 95 B5
Guadalcanal E 99 A5
Guadalcázar E 100 B1
Guadalix de la Sierra E 94 B3
Guadálmez E 100 A1
Guadalupe E 93 B5
Guadamur E 94 C2
Guadarrama E 94 B2
Guadiaro E 99 C5
Guadix E 100 B2
Guagnano I 105 C3
Guagno F 102 A1
Guajar-Faragüit E 100 C2
Gualchos E 100 C2
Gualdo Tadino I 82 C1
Gualtieri I 81 B4
Guarcino I 103 B6
Guarda P 92 A3
Guardamar del Segura E 96 C2
Guardão P 92 A2
Guardavalle I 106 C3
Guardea I 102 A5
Guárdia I 106 B2
Guardiagrele I 103 A7
Guardiarégia I 103 B7
Guárdia Sanframondi I 103 B7
Guardias Viejas E 100 C3
Guardiola de Berguedá E 91 A4
Guareña E 93 C4
Guaro E 100 C1
Guarromán E 100 A2
Guasila I 110 C2
Guastalla I 81 B4
Gubbhögen S 115 C12
Gúbbio I 82 C1
Gubin PL 53 B4
Guča SRB 85 C5
Gudå N 114 D8
Gudavac BIH 83 B5
Guddal N 32 A2
Güderup DK 39 E2
Gudhem S 35 D5
Gudhjem DK 41 D4
Gudovac HR 74 C1
Gudow D 44 B2
Güdül TR 118 B7
Gudvangen N 32 B3
Guebwiller F 60 C3
Guéjar-Sierra E 100 B2
Guémené-Penfao F 57 C4
Guémené-sur-Scorff F 56 B2
Güenes E 89 A3
Guer F 57 C3
Guérande F 66 A2
Guéret F 68 B1
Guérigny F 68 A3
Guesa E 76 D1
Gueugnon F 68 B4
Guglionesi I 103 B7
Guia P 98 B2
Guichen F 57 C4
Guidizzolo I 71 C5
Guidónia-Montecélio I 102 B5
Guiglia I 81 B4
Guignes F 58 B3
Guijo de Coria E 93 A4
Guijo de Santa Bábera E 93 A5
Guijuelo E 93 A5
Guildford GB 31 C3
Guillaumes F 79 B5
Guillena E 99 B4
Guillestre F 79 B5
Guillos F 76 B2
Guilsfield GB 26 C2
Guilvinec F 56 C1
Guimarães P 87 C2
Guincho P 92 C1
Guînes F 48 C2
Guingamp F 56 B2
Guipavas F 56 B1
Guisborough GB 27 A4
Guiscard F 59 A4
Guiscriff F 56 B2
Guisona E 91 B4
Guitiriz E 86 A3
Guîtres F 76 A2
Gujan-Mestras F 76 B1
Gulbene LV 7 C9
Gulçayır TR 118 C6
Guldborg DK 39 E4
Gullabo S 40 C6
Gullane GB 25 B5
Gullbrå N 32 B3
Gullbrandstorp S 40 C2
Gullerásen S 36 A2
Gullhaug N 35 C2
Gullringen S 40 B5
Gullspång S 35 D6
Gulsvik N 34 B1
Gumiel de Hizán E 88 C3
Gummersbach D 50 B3
Gümüldür TR 119 D1
Gümüşhaciköy TR 16 A7
Gümüşova TR 118 B5
Gundelfingen D 61 B6
Gundel-fingen D 60 B3
Gundelsheim D 61 A5
Gunderschoffen F 60 B3
Gundertshausen A 62 B3
Gundinci HR 74 C3
Gündoğmuş TR 119 F7
Güney
  Burdur TR 119 E4
  Denizli TR 119 D4
Gunja HR 84 B3
Günlüce TR 119 F3
Gunnarn S 115 B14
Gunnarskog S 34 C4
Gunnarsnäs S 35 D4
Gunnebo S 40 B6
Gunnislake GB 28 C3
Günselsdorf A 64 C2
Guntersblum D 61 A4
Guntersdorf A 64 B2
Guntin E 86 B3
Günyüzü TR 118 C6
Günzburg D 61 B6
Gunzenhausen D 62 A1
Güre
  Balıkesir TR 118 C1
  Uşak TR 118 D4
Gurk A 73 B4
Gurrea de Gállego E 90 A2
Gürsu TR 118 B4
Gušće HR 74 C1
Gusev RUS 6 D7
Gúspini I 110 C1
Gusselby S 37 C2
Güssing A 73 A6
Gusswerk A 63 C6
Gustav Adolf S 34 B5
Gustavsfors S 35 C4
Güsten D 52 B1
Gusterath D 60 A2
Gustow D 45 A5
Gusum S 37 D3
Gúttaring A 73 B4
Guttannen CH 70 B3
Guttau D 53 B4
Güttingen CH 61 C5
Gützkow D 45 B5
Guzów PL 55 A5
Gvardeysk RUS 6 D6
Gvarv N 33 C6
Gvozd MNE 85 D4
Gvozdansko HR 83 A5
Gwda Wielka PL 46 B2
Gwennap GB 28 C2
Gy F 69 A5
Gyál H 75 A4
Gyarmat H 74 A2
Gyékényes H 74 B2
Gyé-sur-Seine F 59 B5
Gylling DK 39 D3
Gyoma H 75 B5
Gyömöre H 74 A2
Gyömrő H 75 A4
Gyón H 75 A4
Gyöngyfa H 74 C2
Gyöngyös H 65 C5
Gyöngyöspata H 65 C5
Gyönk H 74 B3
Győr H 64 C3
Györszemere H 74 A2
Gypsera CH 70 B2
Gysinge S 36 B3
Gyttorp S 37 C1
Gyula H 75 B6
Gyulafirátót H 74 A2
Gyulaj H 74 B3

H

Haacht B 49 C5
Haag
  Nieder Österreich A 63 B5
  Ober Österreich A 63 B4
Haaksbergen NL 50 A2
Haamstede NL 49 B4
Haan D 50 B3
Haapajärvi FIN 3 E26
Haapsalu EST 6 B7
Haarlem NL 42 C1
Habas F 76 C2
Habay B 60 A1
Habo S 40 B4
Håbol S 35 D4
Habry CZ 63 A6
Habsheim F 60 C3
Hachenburg D 50 C3
Hacibektaş TR 16 B7
Hacılar TR 16 B7
Hacketstown IRL 21 B5
Hackthorpe GB 26 A3
Hadamar D 50 C4
Hädanberg S 115 D15
Haddington GB 25 C5
Hadersdorf am Kamp A 63 B6
Haderslev DK 39 D2
Haderup DK 39 C1
Hadim TR 119 F7
Hadleigh
  Essex GB 31 C4
  Suffolk GB 30 B4
Hadlow GB 31 C4
Hadmersleben D 52 A1
Hadsten DK 39 C3
Hadsund DK 38 C3
Hadyach UA 7 F13
Hadžići BIH 84 C3
Hafnarfjörður IS 111 C4
Hafnir IS 111 D3
Hafslo N 32 A4
Haganj HR 74 C1
Hagby S 40 C6
Hage D 43 B4
Hægebostad N 33 D4
Hægeland N 33 D4
Hagen
  Niedersachsen D 43 B5
  Nordrhein-Westfalen D 50 B3
Hagenbach D 61 A4
Hagenow D 44 B3
Hagetmau F 76 C2
Hagfors S 34 B5
Häggenås S 115 D11
Hagondange F 60 A2
Håcksvik S 40 B3
Haguenau F 60 B3
Hahnbach D 62 A2
Hahnslätten D 50 C4
Hahót H 74 B1
Haiger D 50 C4
Haigerloch D 61 B4
Hailsham GB 31 D4
Hainburg A 64 B3
Hainfeld A 63 B6
Hainichen D 52 C3
Hajdúböszörmény H 10 C6
Hajdúdorog H 10 C6
Hajdúnánás H 10 C6
Hajdúszoboszló H 75 A6
Hajnáčka SK 65 B5
Hajnówka PL 6 E7
Hajós H 75 B4
Håkafot S 115 C11
Hakkas S 113 F10
Halaszi H 64 C3
Halberstadt D 52 B1
Halberton GB 29 C4
Hald Ege DK 38 C2
Haldem D 43 C5
Halden N 35 C3
Haldensleben D 52 A1
Halenbeck D 44 B4
Halesowen GB 26 C3
Halesworth GB 30 B5
Halfing D 62 C3
Halhjem N 32 B2
Halifax GB 27 B4
Häljelöt S 37 D3
Halkirk GB 23 C5
Hall S 37 E5
Hälla S 115 D14
Hällabrottet S 37 C2
Hallabro S 41 C5
Hallaryd S 40 C4
Hällaryd S 41 C4
Hällberga S 37 C3
Hällbybrunn S 37 C3
Halle
  Nordrhein-Westfalen D 51 A4
  Sachsen-Anhalt D 52 B1
  B 49 C5
Hälleberga S 40 C5
Hällefors S 37 C1
Halleforsnäs S 37 C3
Hällekis S 35 D5
Hallen S 115 D11
Hällevadsholm S 35 D3
Hällevik S 41 C4
Hälleviksstrand S 35 D3
Hallingby N 34 B2
Hallingeberg S 40 B6
Hallingen N 32 B6
Hall in Tirol A 71 A6
Hällnäs
  S 115 A15
  S 115 C16
Hallormsstaður IS 111 B11
Hallsberg S 37 C2
Hallschlag D 50 C2
Hallstahammar S 37 C3
Hallstatt A 63 C4
Hallstavik S 36 B5
Halltorp S 40 C6
Halluin F 49 C4
Halmstad S 40 C2
Hals DK 38 B3
Halsa N 114 E5
Halstead GB 31 C4
Haltdalen N 114 E8
Haltern D 50 B3
Halver D 50 B3
Halvrimmen DK 38 B2
Ham F 59 A4
Hamar N 34 B3
Hamarhaug N 32 B2
Hamarøy N 112 E4
Hambergen D 43 B5
Hambergsund S 35 D3
Hambledon GB 31 D2
Hambuhren D 43 C6
Hamburg D 44 B1
Hamdibey TR 118 C2
Hamdorf D 43 A6
Hämeenlinna FIN 3 F26
Hameln = Hameln D 51 A5
Hamersleben D 52 A1
Hamidiye TR 118 B4
Hamilton GB 24 C3
Hamina FIN 3 F27
Hamlagrø N 32 B3
Hamm D 50 B3

Hammar S 37 D1
Hammarland FIN 36 B6
Hammarö S 35 C5
Hammarstrand S 115 D13
Hamme B 49 B5
Hammel DK 39 C2
Hammelburg D 51 C5
Hammelspring D 45 B5
Hammenhög S 41 D4
Hammerdal S 115 D12
Hammerfest N 113 B12
Hammershøj DK 38 C2
Hammerum DK 39 C2
Hamminkeln D 50 B2
Hamnavoe GB 22 A7
Hamneidet N 112 C9
Hamningberg N 113 B19
Hamoir B 49 C6
Hamont B 49 B6
Hámor H 65 B6
Hamra
  Gävleborg S 115 F12
  Gotland S 37 F5
Hamrångefjärden S 36 B4
Hamstreet GB 31 C4
Hamsund N 112 D4
Han
  49 C5
  MNE 84 D3
Haut-Fays B 49 C6
Hautmont F 49 C4
Hautrage B 49 C4
Hauzenberg D 63 B4
Hanau D 51 C4
Händelöp S 40 B6
Handlová SK 65 B4
Hanerau-Hademarschen D 43 A6
Hånger S 40 B3
Hanhimaa FIN 113 E14
Hani i Hotit AL 105 A5
Hankamäki FIN 3 E27
Hankasalmi FIN 3 E26
Hankensbüttel D 44 C2
Han Knežica BIH 83 A5
Hanko FIN 6 B7
Hannover D 43 C6
Hannut B 49 C6
Han Pijesak BIH 84 B3
Hansnes N 112 C8
Hanstedt D 44 B1
Hanstholm DK 38 B1
Hantsavichy BY 7 E9
Hanušovce CZ 54 C1
Haparanda S 3 D26
Haradok BY 7 D10
Harads S 3 C24
Häradsbäck S 40 C4
Häradsbygden S 36 B2
Harbo S 36 B4
Harboør DK 38 C1
Harburg
  Bayern D 62 B1
  Hamburg D 44 B1
Hårby DK 39 D3
Harc H 74 B3
Hardegarijp NL 42 B2
Hardegsen D 51 B5
Hardelot Plage F 48 C2
Hardenberg NL 42 C3
Hardheim D 61 A5
Hardinxveld NL 49 B5
Hardt D 61 B4
Hareid N 114 E3
Haren
  D 43 C4
  NL 42 B3
Harestua N 34 B2
Harfleur F 57 A6
Harg S 36 B5
Hargicourt F 49 D4
Hargnies F 49 D5
Hargshamn S 36 B5
Härja S 40 A3
Härkeberga S 37 C4
Harkebrügge D 43 B4
Harlech GB 26 C1
Harleston GB 30 B5
Harlingen NL 42 B2
Harlösa S 41 D3
Harlow GB 31 C4
Harmancık TR 118 C4
Harmånger S 115 F14
Härnevi S 36 C4
Härnösand S 115 E14
Haro E 89 B4
Haroldswick GB 22 A8
Háromfa H 74 B2
Haroué F 60 B2
Harpenden GB 31 C3
Harplinge S 40 C2
Harpstedt D 43 C5
Harrogate GB 27 B4
Harrow GB 31 C3
Härryda S 40 B2
Harsefeld D 43 B6
Harsewinkel D 50 B4
Hârşova RO 11 D9
Harstad N 112 D5
Harsum D 51 A5
Harsvik N 114 C7
Hartberg A 73 A5
Hartburn GB 25 C6
Hartennes F 59 A4
Hartha D 52 B2
Hartland GB 28 C3
Hartlepool GB 27 A4
Hartmanice CZ 63 A4
Hartmannsdorf A 73 A5
Harvassdal N 115 B11
Harwell GB 31 C2
Harwich GB 31 C5
Harzgerode D 52 B1
Häselgehr A 71 A5
Haselünne D 43 C4
Haskovo BG 11 F8
Hasköy TR 118 A1
Haslach D 61 B4
Hasle DK 41 D4
Haslemere GB 31 C3
Haslev DK 39 D4
Hasloch D 61 A5
Hasparren F 76 C1
Hassela S 115 E13
Hasselfelde D 51 B6
Hasselfors S 37 C1
Hasselt
  B 49 C6
  NL 42 C3
Hassfurt D 51 C6
Hassleben D 45 B5
Hässleholm S 41 C3
Hasslö S 41 C5
Hassloch D 61 A4
Hästbo S 36 B3
Hastersboda FIN 36 B7
Hästholmen S 37 D1
Hastière-Lavaux B 49 C5
Hastigrow GB 23 C5
Hastings GB 31 D4
Hästveda S 41 C3
Hasvik N 113 B11
Hatfield
  Hertfordshire GB 31 C3
  South Yorkshire GB 27 B5
Hatherleigh GB 28 C3
Hathersage GB 27 B4
Hatlestrand N 32 B2
Hattem NL 42 C3
Hatten
  D 43 B5
  F 60 B3
Hattfjelldal N 115 B10
Hatting DK 39 D2
Hattingen D 50 B3
Hattstadt F 60 B3
Hattstedt D 43 A6
Hatvan H 65 C5
Hatvik N 32 B2

Hau D 50 B2
Haudainville F 59 A6
Hauganes IS 111 B7
Haugastøl N 32 B4
Hauge N 33 D3
Haugesund N 33 C2
Haughom N 33 D3
Haugsdal N 32 B2
Haugsdorf A 64 B2
Haukedal N 32 A3
Haukeland N 32 B2
Haukeligrend N 33 C4
Haukeliseter N 32 C4
Haukipudas FIN 3 D26
Haulerwijk NL 42 B3
Haunersdorf D 62 B3
Hausach D 61 B4
Hausham D 62 C2
Hausmannstätten A 73 B5
Hausvik N 33 D3
Hautajärvi FIN 3 C28
Hautefort F 67 C6
Hauteville-Lompnès F 69 C5
Havant GB 31 D3
Håvberget S 36 B1
Havdhem S 37 E5
Havdrup DK 39 D5
Havelange B 49 C6
Havelberg D 44 C4
Havelte NL 42 C3
Haverfordwest GB 28 B2
Haverhill GB 30 B4
Havering GB 31 C4
Håverud S 35 D4
Havířov CZ 65 A4
Havixbeck D 50 B3
Havlíčkův Brod CZ 63 A6
Havndal DK 38 C3
Havneby DK 39 D1
Havnebyen DK 39 D4
Havnsø DK 39 D4
Havøysund N 113 A13
Havran TR 118 C2
Havrebjerg DK 39 D4
Havsa TR 118 A1
Havstenssund S 35 D3
Havza TR 16 A7
Hawarden GB 26 B2
Hawes GB 26 A3
Hawick GB 25 C5
Hawkhurst GB 31 C4
Hawkinge GB 31 C5
Haxey GB 27 B5
Hayange F 60 A2
Haydarlı TR 119 E5
Haydon Bridge GB 25 D5
Hayle GB 28 C2
Haymana TR 118 C7
Hay-on-Wye GB 29 A4
Hayrabolu TR 118 A2
Haysyn UA 11 B10
Hayvoron UA 11 B10
Haywards Heath GB 31 D3
Hazebrouck F 48 C3
Hazlov CZ 52 C2
Heacham GB 30 B4
Headcorn GB 31 C4
Headford IRL 20 A2
Heanor GB 27 B4
Héas F 76 D3
Heathfield GB 31 D4
Hebden Bridge GB 26 B3
Heberg S 40 C2
Hechingen D 61 B4
Hechlingen D 62 B1
Hecho E 76 D2
Hechtel B 49 B6
Hechthausen D 43 B6
Heckelberg D 45 C5
Heckington GB 27 C5
Hecklingen D 52 B1
Hed S 37 C2
Hedalen N 34 B1
Hedared S 40 B2
Heddal N 33 C6
Hédé F 57 B4
Hedekas S 35 D3
Hedemora S 36 B2
Hedensted DK 39 D2
Hedersleben D 52 B1
Hedesunda S 36 B4
Hedge End GB 31 D2
Hedon GB 27 B5
Heede D 43 C4
Heek D 50 A3
Heemstede NL 42 C1
Heerde NL 42 C3
Heerenveen NL 42 C2
Heerhugowaard NL 42 C1
Heerlen NL 50 C1
Heeze NL 49 B6
Hegge N 32 A6
Heggenes N 32 A6
Hegra N 114 D8
Hegyeshalom H 64 C3
Hegyközség H 74 A1
Heia N 114 C9
Heide D 43 A6
Heidelberg D 61 A4
Heiden D 50 B2
Heidenau D 53 C3
Heidenheim D 61 B6
Heidenreichstein A 63 B6
Heikendorf D 44 A2
Heilam GB 22 C4
Heilbad Heiligenstadt D 51 B6
Heilbronn D 61 A5
Heiligenblut A 72 A2
Heiligendamm D 44 A3
Heiligendorf D 44 C2
Heiligengrabe D 44 B4
Heiligenhafen D 44 A2
Heiligenhaus D 50 B2
Heiligenkreuz A 73 B6
Heiligenstadt D 62 A2
Heiligenstedten D 43 B6
Heilitz-le-Maurupt F 59 B5
Heilsbronn D 62 A1
Heim N 114 D5
Heimburg D 51 B6
Heimdal N 114 D7
Heinerscheid L 50 C2
Heinersdorf D 45 C6
Heining D 63 B4
Heiningen D 61 B5
Heinola FIN 3 F26
Heinsberg D 50 B2
Heist-op-den-Berg B 49 B5
Hejde S 37 E5
Hejls DK 39 D2
Hejnice CZ 53 C5
Hel PL 47 A4
Helchteren B 49 B6
Heldburg D 51 C6
Heldrungen D 52 B1
Helechosa E 94 C2
Helensburgh GB 24 B3
Helfenberg A 63 B5
Helgen N 33 C6
Helgeroa N 35 C1
Hella
  IS 111 D5
  N 32 A3
Helland N 112 E4
Hellebæk DK 41 C2
Hellendoorn NL 42 C3
Hellenthal D 50 C2
Hellesøy N 32 B1
Hellesylt N 114 E3
Hellevoetsluis NL 49 B5
Helligskogen N 112 C9

Hellín E 101 A4
Hellissandur IS 111 C2
Hellnar IS 111 C2
Hellum DK 38 B3
Hellví S 37 E5
Hellvik N 33 D2
Helmdon NL 49 B6
Helmsdale GB 23 C5
Helmsley GB 27 A4
Helmstedt D 51 A6
Hel'pa SK 65 B5
Helsa D 51 B5
Helsby GB 26 B3
Helsingborg S 41 C2
Helsinge DK 41 C2
Helsingør DK 41 C2
Helsinki FIN 6 A8
Helston GB 28 C2
Hemau D 62 A2
Hemavan S 115 D12
Hemel Hempstead
  GB 31 C3
Hemer D 50 B3
Héming F 60 B2
Hemmet DK 39 D1
Hemmingstedt D 43 A6
Hemmoor D 43 B6
Hemnes N 35 C3
Hemnesberget N . . . 115 A10
Hemse S 37 E5
Hemsedal N 32 B5
Hemslingen D 43 B6
Hemsworth GB 27 B4
Hen N 34 B2
Henån S 35 D3
Hendaye F 76 C1
Hendek TR 118 B5
Hendungen D 51 C6
Henfield GB 31 D3
Hengelo
  Gelderland NL 50 A2
  Overijssel NL 50 A2
Hengoed GB 29 B4
Hénin-Beaumont F . . . 48 C3
Henley-on-Thames
  GB 31 C3
Hennan S 115 E12
Henneberg D 51 C6
Hennebont F 56 C2
Henne Strand DK 39 D1
Hennigsdorf D 45 C5
Hennset N 114 D5
Hennstedt
  Schleswig-Holstein
    D 43 A6
  Schleswig-Holstein D . 43 A6
Henrichemont F 68 A2
Henryków PL 54 C2
Henrykowo PL 47 A6
Hensås N 32 A5
Henstedt-Ulzburg D . . 44 B1
Heppenheim D 61 A4
Herad
  Buskerud N 32 B6
  Vest-Agder N 33 D3
Heradsbygd N 34 B3
Heraklion = Iraklio
  GR 117 G7
Herálec CZ 64 A2
Herand N 32 B3
Herault F 58 C2
Herbault F 58 A2
Herbern D 50 B3
Herbertstown IRL . . . 20 B3
Herbeumont B 59 A6
Herbignac F 66 A2
Herbisse F 59 B5
Herbitzheim F 60 A3
Herbolzheim D 60 B3
Herborn D 50 C4
Herbrechtingen D 61 B6
Herby PL 54 C3
Herceg-Novi MNE . . . 105 A4
Hercegovac HR 74 C2
Hercegovačka Goleša
  SRB 85 C4
Hercegszántó H 75 C3
Herchen D 50 C3
Heréd H 65 C5
Hereford GB 29 A5
Herefoss N 33 D5
Hereke TR 118 B4
Herencia E 95 C3
Herend H 74 A2
Herent B 49 C5
Herentals B 49 B5
Herépian F 78 C2
Herford D 51 A4
Herfølge DK 41 D2
Herguijuela E 93 B5
Héric F 66 A3
Héricourt F 60 C2
Héricourt-en-Caux F . . 69 A4
Hérimoncourt F 70 A1
Heringsdorf D 44 A3
Herisau CH 71 A4
Hérisson F 68 B2
Herk-de-Stad B 49 C6
Herlufmagle DK 39 D4
Hermagor A 72 B3
Hermannsburg D 44 C2
Hermansverk N 32 A3
Heřmanův Městec
  CZ 53 D5
Herment F 68 C2
Hermeskeil D 60 A2
Hermisende E 87 C4
Hermonville F 59 A4
Hermsdorf D 52 C1
Hernani E 76 C1
Hernansancho E 94 B2
Herne D 50 B3
Herne Bay GB 31 C5
Hernes N 34 B3
Herning DK 39 C1
Herøya N 35 C1
Herramélluri E 89 B3
Herräng S 36 B5
Herre N 33 C6
Herrenberg D 61 B4
Herrera E 100 B1
Herrera de Alcántara
  E 92 B3
Herrera del Duque E . . 94 C1
Herrera de los Navarros
  E 90 B1
Herrera de Pisuerga
  E 88 B2
Herreros del Suso E . . 94 B1
Herrestad S 35 D3
Herrhamra S 37 D4
Herritslev DK 44 A3
Herrljunga S 40 A3
Herrnhut D 53 B4
Herrsching D 62 B2
Hersbruck D 62 A2
Hersby S 37 C5
Herscheid D 50 B3
Herselt B 49 B5
Herso GR 116 A4
Herstal B 49 C6
Herstmonceux GB . . . 31 D4
Herten D 50 B3
Hertford GB 31 C3
Hervás E 93 A5
Hervik N 33 C2
Herxheim D 61 A4
Herzberg
  Brandenburg D 45 C4
  Brandenburg D 52 B3
  Niedersachsen D . . . 51 B5
Herzebrock D 50 B4
Herzfelde D 45 C5
Herzlake D 43 C4
Herzogenaurach D . . . 62 A1
Herzogenbuchsee CH . 70 A2
Herzogenburg A 63 B6
Herzsprung D 44 B4
Hesby N 33 C2
Hesdin F 48 C3

Hesel D 43 B4
Heskestad N 33 D3
Hessdalen N 114 E8
Hesselager DK 39 D3
Hessen N 113 C18
Hessisch Lichtenau
  D 51 B5
Hessisch-Oldendorf
  D 51 A5
Hestra S 40 B3
Heswall GB 26 B2
Hetlevik N 32 B2
Hettange-Grande F . . 60 A2
Hetton-le-Hole GB . . . 25 D6
Hettstedt D 52 B1
Heuchin F 48 C3
Heudicourt-sous-les-
  Côtes F 60 B1
Heukelum NL 49 B5
Heusden NL 49 B5
Heusenstamm D 51 C4
Heustreu D 51 C6
Heves H 65 C6
Héviz H 74 B2
Hexham GB 25 D5
Heysham GB 26 A3
Heytesbury GB 29 B5
Hidas H 74 B3
Hieflau A 63 C5
Hiendelaencina E 95 A4
Hiersac F 67 C5
High Bentham GB . . . 26 A3
Highclere GB 31 C2
High Hesket GB 25 D5
Highley GB 26 C3
High Wycombe GB . . . 31 C3
Higuera de Arjona E . . 100 B2
Higuera de Calatrava
  E 100 B1
Higuera de la Serena
  E 93 C5
Higuera de la Sierra
  E 99 B4
Higuera de Vargas E . 93 C4
Higuera la Real E . . . 99 A4
Higuers de Llerena E . 93 C4
Higueruela E 96 C1
Híjar E 90 B2
Hilchenbach D 50 B4
Hildburghausen D . . . 51 C6
Hilden D 50 B2
Hilders D 51 C5
Hildesheim D 51 A5
Hilgay GB 30 B4
Hillared S 40 B3
Hille D 51 A4
Hillegom NL 49 A5
Hillerød DK 41 D2
Hillerstorp S 40 B3
Hillesheim D 50 C2
Hillestad N 35 C2
Hillmersdorf D 52 B3
Hillsborough GB 19 B5
Hillswick GB 22 A7
Hilpoltstein D 62 A2
Hiltpoltstein D 62 A2
Hilvarenbeek NL 49 B6
Hilversum NL 49 A6
Himarë AL 116 B1
Himbergen D 44 B2
Himeshaza H 74 B3
Himmelberg A 73 B4
Himmelpforten D 43 B6
Himod H 74 A2
Hinckley GB 30 B2
Hindås S 40 B2
Hindelang D 71 A6
Hinderavåg N 33 C2
Hindhead GB 31 C3
Hinjosa del Valle E . . . 93 C4
Hinnerup DK 39 C3
Hinneryd S 40 C3
Hinojal E 93 B4
Hinojos E 99 B4
Hinojosa de Calatrava
  E 100 A1
Hinojosa del Duque E . 93 C5
Hinojosas de Calatrava
  E 100 A1
Hinterhornbach A . . . 71 A5
Hinterriss A 71 A6
Hintersee
  A 63 C4
  D 45 B6
Hinterstoder A 63 C5
Hintertux A 72 A1
Hinterweidenthal D . . 60 A3
Hinwil CH 70 A3
Hios GR 116 D8
Hippolytushoef NL . . . 42 C1
Hirschaid D 62 A1
Hirschau D 62 A3
Hirschberg D 52 C1
Hirschhorn D 61 A4
Hirsingue F 60 C3
Hîrşova RO 11 D9
Hirtshals DK 38 B2
Hirzenhain D 51 C5
Hisarcık TR 118 C4
Hishult S 41 C3
Hitchin GB 31 C3
Hitra N 114 D5
Hittarp S 41 C2
Hittisau A 71 A4
Hittun N 32 A1
Hitzacker D 44 B3
Hjallerup DK 38 B3
Hjällstad S 34 B5
Hjältevad S 40 B5
Hjärnarp S 41 C2
Hjärtdal N 33 C5
Hjellestad N 32 B2
Hjelmeland N 33 C3
Hjelset N 114 E4
Hjerkinn N 114 E6
Hjerm DK 38 C1
Hjerpsted DK 39 D1
Hjerting DK 39 D1
Hjo S 35 D6
Hjordkær DK 39 D2
Hjørring DK 38 B2
Hjorted S 40 B6
Hjortkvarn S 37 D2
Hjortnäs S 36 B1
Hjortsberga S 40 C4
Hjukse N 33 C6
Hjuksebø N 33 C6
Hjulsjö S 36 C1
Hliník nad Hronom
  SK 65 B4
Hlinsko CZ 64 A1
Hlío IS 111 A10
Hlohovec SK 64 B3
Hluboká nad Vltavou
  CZ 63 A5
Hlučín CZ 64 A4
Hlukhiv UA 7 F12
Hlyboka BY 11 B8
Hlybokaye BY 7 D9
Hniezdne SK 65 A6
Hnilec SK 65 B6
Hnúšťa SK 65 B5
Hobol H 74 B2
Hobro DK 38 C2
Hobscheid L 60 A1
Hocalar TR 119 D4
Hochdonn D 43 A6
Hochdorf CH 70 A3
Hochfelden F 60 B3
Hochspeyer D 60 A3
Höchst im Odenwald
  D 61 A5
Höckendorf D 52 C3
Hockenheim D 61 A4
Hoddesdon GB 31 C3
Hodkovice CZ 53 C5
Hódmezővásárhely
  H 75 B5
Hodnet GB 26 C3

Hodonín CZ 64 B3
Hodslavice CZ 64 A4
Hoedekenskerke NL . . 49 B4
Hoegaarden B 49 C5
Hoek van Holland NL . 49 B5
Hoenderlo NL 50 A1
Hof
  D 52 C1
  N 35 C2
Hofbieber D 51 C5
Hoff GB 26 A3
Hofgeismar D 51 B5
Hofheim
  Bayern D 51 C6
  Hessen D 51 C4
Hofkirchen im Mühlkreis
  A 63 B4
Höfn IS 111 C10
Hofors S 36 B3
Hofsós IS 111 B6
Hofstad N 114 C7
Höganäs S 41 C2
Högbo S 36 B3
Hogdal S 35 C3
Høgebru N 32 A4
Högfors S 36 C2
Högklint S 37 E5
Högsäter S 35 D4
Högsby S 40 B6
Högsjö S 37 C2
Hogstad S 37 D2
Hőgyész H 74 B3
Hohenau A 64 B2
Hohenberg A 63 C6
Hohenbucko D 52 B3
Hohenburg D 62 A2
Hohendorf D 45 A4
Hohenems A 71 A4
Hohenhameln D 51 A6
Hohenhausen D 51 A4
Hohenkirchen D 43 B4
Hohenlinden D 62 B2
Hohenlockstedt D 43 B6
Hohenmölsen D 52 B2
Hohennauen D 44 C4
Hohen Neuendorf D . . 45 C5
Hohentauern A 73 A4
Hohentengen D 70 A3
Hohenwepel D 51 B5
Hohenwestedt D 43 A6
Hohenzieritz D 45 B5
Hohn D 44 A1
Hohne D 44 C2
Hohnstorf D 44 B2
Højer DK 39 E1
Højslev Stby DK 38 C2
Hok S 40 B5
Hökerum S 40 B3
Hökhuvud S 36 B5
Hokksund N 34 C1
Hökön S 40 C4
Hol N 32 B5
Hola Pristan UA 11 C12
Hólar IS 111 B6
Holašovice CZ 63 B5
Holbæk
  Aarhus Amt. DK . . . 38 C3
  Vestsjællands Amt.
    DK 39 D4
Holbeach GB 30 B4
Holdenstedt D 44 C2
Holdhus N 32 B2
Holdorf D 43 C5
Holeby DK 44 A3
Holen N 32 B6
Hølervasseter N 32 B6
Holešov CZ 64 A3
Holguera E 93 B4
Holíč SK 64 B3
Holice
  CZ 53 C5
  SK 64 C3
Höljes S 34 B4
Hollabrunn A 64 B2
Hollandstoun GB 23 B6
Høllen N 33 D4
Hollfeld D 52 D1
Hollókő H 65 C5
Hollstadt D 51 C6
Hollum NL 42 B2
Höllviksnäs S 41 D2
Holm
  N 114 B9
Hólmavík IS 111 B4
Holmbukt N 113 B10
Holmedal S 35 C3
Holmegil N 35 C3
Holmen N 34 B2
Holme-on-Spalding-Moor
  GB 27 B5
Holmes Chapel GB . . . 26 B3
Holmestrand N 35 C2
Holmfirth GB 27 B4
Holmfoss N 113 C19
Holmsbu N 35 C2
Holmsjö S 41 C5
Holmsund S 3 E24
Holmsveden S 36 B3
Holmudden S 37 E6
Holsbybrunn S 40 B5
Holseter N 32 A1
Holsljunga S 40 B2
Holstebro DK 39 C1
Holsted DK 39 D1
Holsworthy GB 28 C3
Holt
  Norfolk GB 30 B5
  Wrexham GB 26 B3
Holten NL 50 A2
Holtwick D 50 A3
Holum N 33 D4
Holwerd NL 42 B2
Holycross IRL 21 B4
Holyhead GB 26 B1
Holýšov CZ 62 A3
Holywell GB 26 B2
Holywood GB 19 B6
Holzdorf D 52 B3
Holzhausen D 51 A4
Holzheim D 61 B6
Holzkirchen D 62 C2
Holzminden D 51 B5
Holzthaleben D 51 B6
Homberg
  Hessen D 51 B5
  Hessen D 51 C5
Homburg D 60 A3
Homécourt F 60 A1
Hommelstø N 115 B9
Hommersåk N 33 D2
Homokmegy H 75 B4
Homokszentgyörgy
  H 74 B2
Homrogd H 65 B6
Homyel = Gomel BY . . 7 E11
Hondarribia E 76 C1
Hondón de los Frailes
  E 101 A5
Hondschoote F 48 C3
Hönebach D 51 C5
Hønefoss N 34 B2
Honfleur F 57 A6
Høng DK 39 D4
Honiton GB 29 C4
Hønning DK 39 D1
Honningsvåg N 113 A14
Hönö S 38 B4
Honrubia E 95 C4
Hontalbilla E 88 C2
Hontheim D 50 C2
Hontianske-Nemce
  SK 65 B4
Hontoria de la Cantera
  E 88 B3
Hontoria del Pinar E . . 89 C3

Hontoria de Valdearados
  E 89 C3
Hoofddorp NL 49 A5
Hoogerheide NL 49 B5
Hoogeveen NL 42 C3
Hoogezand-Sappemeer
  NL 42 B3
Hoogkarspel NL 42 C2
Hoogkerk NL 42 B3
Hoogstede D 42 C3
Hoogstraten B 49 B5
Hook GB 31 C3
Hooksiel D 43 B5
Höör S 41 D3
Hoorn NL 42 C2
Hope GB 26 B2
Hopen N 112 E4
Hope under Dinmore
  GB 29 A5
Hopfgarten A 72 B2
Hopfgarten in Defereggen
  A 72 B2
Hopseidet N 113 B16
Hopsten D 43 C4
Hoptrup DK 39 D2
Hora Svatého Šebestiána
  CZ 52 C3
Horažďovice CZ 63 A4
Horb am Neckar D . . . 61 B4
Horbelev DK 39 E5
Hørby DK 38 B3
Hörby S 41 D3
Horcajada de la Torre
  E 95 B4
Horcajo de los Montes
  E 94 C2
Horcajo de Santiago
  E 95 C3
Horcajo-Medianero E . 93 A5
Horche E 95 B3
Horda S 40 B4
Hordabø N 32 B1
Hordalia N 32 C3
Hordvik N 32 B2
Hořesedly CZ 52 C3
Horezu RO 11 D7
Horgen CH 70 A3
Horgoš SRB 75 B4
Hořice CZ 53 C5
Horjul SLO 73 B4
Horka D 53 B4
Hörken S 36 B1
Horki BY 7 D11
Hörle S 40 B4
Horn
  A 63 B6
  D 51 B4
  N 34 B2
  S 40 B5
Horná E 101 A4
Hornachos E 93 C4
Hornachuelos E 99 B5
Horná Marikova SK . . 64 A4
Hornanes N 32 C2
Horná Štředa SK 64 B3
Horná Strubna SK . . . 65 B4
Horná Súča SK 64 B3
Hornbæk
  Aarhus Amt. DK . . . 38 C2
  Frederiksværk DK . . 41 C2
Hornberg D 61 B4
Hornburg D 51 A6
Horncastle GB 27 B5
Horndal S 36 B3
Horndean GB 31 D2
Horne
  Fyns Amt. DK 39 D3
  Ribe Amt. DK 39 D1
Hörnebo S 35 D6
Horneburg D 43 B6
Hornindal N 114 F3
Hørning DK 39 C3
Hörningsholm S 37 C4
Horní Bečva CZ 64 A4
Horní Benešov CZ . . . 64 A3
Horní Cerekev CZ . . . 63 A6
Horní Jiřetín CZ 52 C3
Horní Lomná CZ 65 A4
Horní Maršov CZ 53 C5
Horní Planá CZ 63 B5
Horní Slavkov CZ 52 C2
Horní Vltavice CZ 63 A4
Hornnes N 33 D4
Horno D 53 B4
Hornos E 101 A3
Hornoy-le-Bourg F . . . 58 A2
Hornsea GB 27 B5
Hornsjø N 34 A2
Hornslet DK 39 C3
Hornstein A 64 C2
Hörnum D 39 E1
Horný Tisovnik SK . . . 65 B5
Horodenka UA 11 B8
Horodnya UA 7 F11
Horodok
  Khmelnytskyy UA . . 11 B9
  Lviv UA 11 B8
Horodyshche UA 11 B11
Horokhiv UA 11 A8
Horovice CZ 63 A4
Horred S 40 B2
Hörröd S 41 D4
Hörsching A 63 B5
Horsens DK 39 D2
Horsham GB 31 C3
Hørsholm DK 41 D2
Horslunde DK 39 E4
Horšovský Týn CZ . . . 62 A3
Horst NL 50 B2
Horstel D 50 A3
Horsten D 43 B4
Horstmar D 50 A3
Hort H 65 C5
Horta P 87 C4
Horten N 35 C2
Hortezuela E 89 C4
Hortiguela E 89 B3
Hortobágy H 75 A6
Horton in Ribblesdale
  GB 26 A3
Hørve DK 39 D4
Horwich GB 26 B3
Hosanger N 32 B2
Hösbach D 51 C5
Hosena D 53 B4
Hosenfeld D 51 C5
Hosingen L 50 C2
Hospental CH 70 B3
Hospital IRL 20 B3
Hossegor F 76 C1
Hosszúhetény H 74 B3
Hostal de Ipiés E 90 A2
Hoštálková CZ 64 A3
Hostalric E 91 B5
Hostens F 76 B2
Hostěradice CZ 64 B2
Hostinné CZ 53 C5
Hostomice CZ 63 A5
Hostouň CZ 62 A3
Hotagen S 115 D13
Hoting S 115 C13
Hotolisht AL 116 A2
Hotton B 49 C6
Houdain F 48 C3
Houdan F 58 B2
Houdelaincourt F 59 B6
Houeillès F 76 B3
Houffalize B 50 C1
Houghton-le-Spring
  GB 25 D6
Houlberg DK 39 C2
Houlgate F 57 A5
Hourtin F 66 C3
Hourtin-Plage F 66 C3
Houthalen B 49 B6
Houyet B 49 C5
Hov
  DK 39 D3

Hov continued
  N 34 B2
Hova S 35 D6
Høvåg N 33 D5
Hovborg DK 39 D1
Hovda N 32 B6
Hovden N 33 C4
Hove GB 31 D3
Hovedgård DK 39 D2
Hovelhof D 51 B4
Hoven DK 39 D1
Hovet N 32 B5
Hovingham GB 27 A5
Hovmantorp S 40 C5
Hovsta S 37 C2
Howden GB 27 B5
Howe D 44 B2
Höxter D 51 B5
Hoya D 43 C6
Hoya de Santa Maria
  E 99 B4
Hoya-Gonzalo E 95 D5
Høyanger N 32 A3
Hoyerswerda D 53 B4
Høyjord N 35 C2
Hoylake GB 26 B2
Hoylandet N 114 C9
Hoym D 52 B1
Høymyr N 32 C6
Hoyocasero E 94 B2
Hoyo de Manzanares
  E 94 B3
Hoyo de Pinares E . . . 94 B2
Hoyos E 93 A4
Hoyos del Espino E . . 93 A5
Hrabušice SK 65 B6
Hradec Králové CZ . . . 53 C5
Hradec nad Moravicí
  CZ 64 A3
Hrádek CZ 64 B2
Hrádek nad Nisou CZ . 53 C4
Hradište SK 65 B4
Hrafnagil IS 111 B7
Hrafnseyri IS 111 B2
Hranice
  Severomoravsky
    CZ 64 A3
  Západočeský CZ . . . 52 C2
Hranovnica SK 65 B6
Hrasnica BIH 84 C3
Hrastnik SLO 73 B5
Hrebenne UA 11 A7
Hřensko CZ 53 C4
Hriňová SK 65 B5
Hrisoupoli GR 116 B6
Hrochov CZ 64 A2
Hrochův Tynec CZ . . . 53 D5
Hrodna BY 6 E7
Hrodzyanka BY 7 E10
Hronov CZ 53 C6
Hronský Beňadik SK . . 65 B4
Hrotovice CZ 64 A2
Hrtkovci SRB 85 B4
Hrun IS 111 A5
Hrvaćani BIH 84 B2
Hrvace HR 83 C5
Hrymayliv UA 11 B9
Huben A 72 B2
Hückel-hoven D 50 B2
Hückeswagen D 50 B3
Hucknall GB 27 B4
Hucqueliers F 48 C2
Huddersfield GB 27 B4
Huddinge S 37 C4
Huddunge S 36 B3
Hude D 43 B5
Huélamo E 95 B5
Huelgoat F 56 B2
Huelma E 100 B2
Huelva E 99 B4
Huéneja E 100 B3
Huércal-Overa E 101 B4
Huerta de Abajo E . . . 89 B3
Huerta del Rey E 89 C3
Huerta de
  Valdecarabanos E . . 95 C3
Huertahernando E . . . 95 B4
Huesa E 100 B2
Huesca E 90 A2
Huéscar E 101 B3
Huete E 95 B4
Huétor Tájar E 100 B1
Hüfingen D 61 C4
Hufthamar N 32 B2
Hugh Town GB 28 D1
Huglfing D 62 C2
Huissen NL 50 B1
Huittinen FIN 3 F25
Huizen NL 49 A6
Hulin CZ 64 A3
Hüls D 50 B2
Hulsig DK 38 B3
Hulst NL 49 B5
Hult S 40 B5
Hulta S 40 A6
Hulteby S 35 C6
Hultsfred S 40 B5
Humanes E 95 B3
Humberston GB 27 B5
Humble DK 39 E3
Humenné SK 10 B6
Humilladero E 100 B1
Humlebæk DK 41 D2
Humlum DK 38 C1
Hummelsta S 37 C3
Humpolec CZ 63 A6
Humshaugh GB 25 C5
Hundåla N 115 B9
Hundested DK 39 D4
Hundorp N 32 A6
Hundvåg N 33 C2
Hundvin N 32 B2
Hunedoara RO 11 D7
Hünfeld D 51 C5
Hungen D 51 C4
Hungerford GB 31 C2
Hunndalen N 34 B2
Hunnebostrand S 35 D3
Hunstanton GB 30 B4
Huntingdon GB 30 B3
Huntley GB 29 B5
Huntly GB 23 D6
Hünxe D 50 B2
Hurbanovo SK 64 C4
Hurdal N 34 B3
Hurezani RO 11 D7
Hurlford GB 24 C3
Hurstbourne Tarrant
  GB 31 C2
Hurstpierpoint GB . . . 31 D3
Hürth D 50 C2
Hurum N 32 A5
Húsafell IS 111 C4
Húsavík IS 111 A8
Husbands Bosworth
  GB 30 B2
Husby
  D 39 E2
  DK 39 C1
Husey IS 111 B11
Húsi RO 11 C10
Husina BIH 84 B3
Husinec CZ 63 A4
Husinish GB 22 D1
Huskvarna S 40 B4
Hustad N 114 E4
Hüsten D 50 B4
Hustopeče CZ 64 B2
Hustopeče nad Bečvou
  CZ 64 A3

Husum
  D 43 A6
  S 115 D16
Huta PL 46 C2
Hutovo BIH 84 D2
Hüttenberg A 73 B4
Hüttlingen D 61 B6
Huttoft GB 27 B6
Hutton Cranswick GB . 27 B5
Hüttschlag A 72 A3
Huttwil CH 70 A2
Huy B 49 C6
Hüyük TR 119 E6
Hval N 34 B2
Hvåle N 32 B6
Hvaler N 35 C3
Hvalpsund DK 38 C2
Hvammstangi IS 111 B5
Hvammur IS 111 B6
Hvanneyri IS 111 C4
Hvar HR 83 C5
Hvarnes N 35 C1
Hveragerði IS 111 D4
Hvide Sande DK 39 D1
Hvittingfoss N 35 C2
Hvolsvöllur IS 111 D5
Hybe SK 65 A5
Hyen N 114 F2
Hyères F 79 C5
Hyères Plage F 79 C5
Hylestad N 33 C4
Hylke DK 39 D2
Hyllestad N 32 A2
Hyllstofta S 41 C3
Hyltebruk S 40 B3
Hynish GB 24 B1
Hynnekleiv N 33 D5
Hythe
  Hampshire GB 31 D2
  Kent GB 31 C5
Hyvinkää FIN 3 F26

I
Iam RO 85 A4
Iaşi RO 11 C9
Iasmos GR 116 A7
Ibahernando E 93 B5
Iballë AL 105 A5
Ibarranguelua E 89 A4
Ibbenbüren D 50 A3
Ibeas de Juarros E . . . 89 B3
Ibestad N 112 D6
Ibi E 96 C2
Ibiza = Eivissa E 97 C1
Ibradı TR 119 E6
Ibriktepe TR 118 A1
Ibros E 100 A2
Ichenhausen D 61 B6
Ichnya UA 11 A12
Ichtegem B 49 B4
Ichtershausen D 51 C6
Idanha-a-Novo P 93 B3
Idar-Oberstein D 60 A3
Idd N 35 C3
Idiazábal E 89 B4
Idivuoma S 113 D10
Idkerberget S 36 B2
Idön S 36 B5
Idre S 115 E9
Idrija SLO 73 B4
Idritsa RUS 7 C10
Idstein D 50 C4
Iecca Mare RO 75 C5
Ielsi I 103 B7
Ieper = Ypres B 48 C3
Ierapetra GR 117 G7
Ierissos GR 116 B5
Ifjord N 113 B16
Ig SLO 73 C4
Igal H 74 B2
Igea E 89 B4
Igea Marina I 82 B1
Igelfors S 37 D2
Igersheim D 61 A5
Iggesund S 115 F14
Iglesias E 89 B3
Igls A 71 A6
Igny-Comblizy F 59 A4
Igorre E 89 A4
Igoumenitsa GR 116 C2
Igries E 90 A2
Igualada E 91 B4
Iguerande F 68 B4
Iharosberény H 74 B2
Ihl'any SK 65 A6
Ihlienworth D 43 B5
Ihringen D 60 B3
Ihtiman BG 11 E7
Iisalmi FIN 3 E27
IJmuiden NL 42 C1
IJsselmuiden NL 42 C2
IJzendijke NL 49 B4
Ikast DK 39 C2
Ikervár H 74 A1
Ilandža SRB 75 C5
Ilanz CH 71 B4
Ilava SK 64 B4
Iława PL 47 B5
Il Castagno I 81 C4
Ilche E 90 B3
Ilchester GB 29 C5
Ilfeld D 51 B6
Ilfracombe GB 28 B3
Ilgaz TR 16 A6
Ilgın TR 119 D6
Ilhavo P 92 A2
Ilica TR 118 C2
Ilidža BIH 84 C3
Ilijaš BIH 84 C3
Ilirska Bistrica SLO . . 73 C4
Ilkeston GB 27 C4
Ilkley GB 27 B4
Illana E 95 B4
Illano E 86 A4
Illar E 101 C3
Illas E 88 A1
Illats F 76 B2
Ille-sur-Têt F 91 A5
Illertissen D 61 B6
Illescas E 94 B3
Illfurth F 60 C3
Illichivsk UA 11 C11
Illiers-Combray F 58 B2
Illkirch-Graffenstaden
  F 60 B3
Illmensee D 61 C5
Illmitz A 64 C2
Illora E 100 B2
Illueca E 89 C5
Ilmajoki FIN 3 E25
Ilmenau D 51 C6
Ilminster GB 29 C5
Ilok HR 75 C4
Ilomantsi FIN 3 E28
Ilova HR 74 C2
Iłowa PL 53 B5
Iłów-Osada PL 47 C6
Ilsenburg D 51 B6
Ilshofen D 61 A5
Ilz A 73 A5
Iłża PL 55 B6
Imamoğlu TR 16 C7
Imatra FIN 3 F28
Imielin PL 55 C4
Imingen N 32 B5
Immeln S 41 C4

Immenhausen D 51 B5
Immenstadt D 61 C6
Immingham GB 27 B5
Imola I 81 B5
Imon E 95 A4
Imotski HR 84 C2
Impéria I 80 C2
Imphy F 68 B3
İmroz TR 116 B7
Imsland N 33 C2
Imst A 71 A5
Inagh IRL 20 B2
Inari FIN 113 D15
Inca E 97 B2
Inchnadamph GB 22 C4
Incinillas E 89 B3
Indal S 115 E14
Indjija SRB 85 A5
Indre Arna N 32 B2
Indre Billefjord N 113 B14
Indre Brenna N 113 B14
Iğneada TR 118 A2
Inebolu TR 16 A6
İnecik TR 118 B2
İnegöl TR 118 B4
Inerthal CH 70 A3
Infiesto E 88 A1
Ingatorp S 40 B5
Ingedal N 35 C3
Ingelheim D 50 D4
Ingelmunster B 49 C4
Ingelstad S 40 C4
Ingleton GB 26 A3
Ingolfsland N 32 C5
Ingolstadt D 62 B2
Ingrandes
  Maine-et-Loire F . . . 66 A4
  Vienne F 67 B5
Ingwiller F 60 B3
Inhisar TR 118 B5
Inhulec UA 11 C12
Iniesta E 95 C5
Inishannon IRL 20 C3
Inishcrone IRL 18 B2
Inke H 74 B2
Inndyr N 112 E3
Innellan GB 24 C3
Innerleithen GB 25 C4
Innermessan GB 24 D3
Innertkirchen CH 70 B3
Innervillgraten A 72 B2
Innsbruck A 71 A6
Innset N 112 D7
Innvik N 114 F3
Inol IRL 18 B2
Inowłódz PL 55 B5
Inowrocław PL 47 C4
Ins CH 70 A2
Insch GB 23 D6
Insjön S 36 B1
Ińsko PL 46 B1
Instow GB 28 B3
Intepe TR 118 B1
Interlaken CH 70 B2
Intragna CH 70 B3
Introbio I 71 C4
Inveran
  GB 23 D4
  IRL 20 A2
Inveraray GB 24 B2
Inverbervie GB 25 B5
Invergarry GB 22 D4
Invergordon GB 23 D4
Invergowrie GB 25 B4
Inverkeilor GB 25 B5
Inverkeithing GB 25 B4
Invermoriston GB 22 D4
Inverness GB 23 D4
Inveruno I 70 C3
Inverurie GB 23 D6
Ioannina GR 116 C2
Iolanda di Savoia I . . . 81 B5
Ion Corvin RO 11 D9
Ióppolo I 106 C2
Ios GR 117 F7
Ipati GR 116 D4
İpsala TR 118 B1
Ipswich GB 30 B5
Iraklia GR 116 A4
Iraklio = Heraklion
  GR 117 G7
Irdning A 73 A4
Iregszemcse H 74 B3
Irgoli I 110 B2
İrig SRB 85 A4
Ironbridge GB 26 C3
Irpin UA 11 A11
Irrel D 60 A2
Irsina I 104 C2
Irsta S 37 C3
Irthlingborough GB . . . 30 B3
Iruela E 100 A2
Irún E 76 C1
Irurita E 76 C1
Irurzun E 76 D1
Irvine GB 24 C3
Irvinestown GB 19 B4
Isaba E 76 D2
Isabela E 100 A2
Isafjörður IS 111 A3
Isane N 114 F2
Isaszeg H 75 A4
İşbister GB 22 A7
İscar E 88 C2
Iscehisar TR 118 D5
Ischgl A 71 A5
Íschia I 103 C6
Íschia di Castro I 102 A4
Ischitella I 104 B1
Isdes F 58 C3
Ise N 35 C3
Iselle I 70 B3
Iseltwald CH 70 B2
Isen D 62 B3
Isenbüttel D 44 C2
Iseo I 71 C5
Iserlohn D 50 B3
Isérnia I 103 B7
Isfjorden N 114 E4
Ishëm AL 105 B5
Isigny-sur-Mer F 57 A4
Işıklı TR 119 D4
Isili I 110 C2
Iskar BG 11 E8
Iskilip TR 16 A7
Isla Canela E 98 B3
Isla Cristina E 98 B3
Islares E 89 A3
Isleham GB 30 B4
Isle of Whithorn GB . . 24 E3
Ismaning D 62 B2
Ismnal? — Isna P 92 B3
Isnestoften N 113 B11
Isny D 61 C6
Isoba E 88 A1
Isokylä
  FIN 113 F16
  S 113 E11
Isola F 79 B6
Isola d'Asti I 80 B2
Isola del Gran Sasso
  d'Itália I 103 A6
Isola delle Fémmine
  I 108 A2
Isola del Liri I 103 B6
Isola di Capo Rizzuto
  I 107 C4
Isona E 91 A4
Isópnac F 67 C5
Isorella I 71 C5
Isparta TR 119 E5
Isperih BG 11 E9
İspica I 109 C3
Isselburg D 50 B2
Issigeac F 77 B3
Issogne I 70 C2
Issoire F 68 C3
Issoncourt F 59 B6
Issoudun F 68 B1
Issum D 50 B2
Is-sur-Tille F 69 A5
Issy-l'Évêque F 68 B4

Istán E 100 C1
İstanbul TR 118 A3
Istebna PL 65 A4
Istia d'Ombrone I 81 D5
Istiea GR 116 D5
Istok KOS 85 D5
Istres F 78 C3
Istvándi H 74 B2
Itea GR 116 D4
Itháki GR 117 D2
Itoiz E 76 D1
Itrabo E 100 C2
Itri I 103 B6
Ittireddu I 110 B1
Ittiri I 110 B1
Itzehoe D 43 B6
Ivalo FIN 113 D16
Ivanava BY 7 E8
Ivančice CZ 64 A2
Ivančna Gorica SLO . . 73 C4
Iváncsa H 74 A3
Ivanec HR 73 B6
Ivanić Grad HR 73 C6
Ivanjica SRB 85 C5
Ivanka SK 64 B3
Ivankovo HR 74 C3
Ivano-Frankivsk UA . . 11 B8
Ivanovice na Hané
  CZ 64 A3
Ivanska HR 74 C2
Ivatsevichy BY 7 E8
Ivaylovgrad BG 116 A8
Iveland N 33 D4
Ivoz Ramet B 49 C6
Ivrea I 70 C2
Ivrindi TR 118 C2
Ivry-en-Montagne F . . 69 A4
Ivry-la-Bataille F 58 B2
Ivybridge GB 28 C4
Iwaniska PL 55 C6
Iwiny PL 53 B5
Iwuy F 49 C4
Ixworth GB 30 B4
Izarra E 89 B4
Izbica Kujawska PL . . 47 C4
Izbište SRB 85 A6
Izeda P 87 C4
Izegem B 49 C4
Izernore F 69 B5
Izmail UA 11 D10
İzmir TR 119 D2
İzmit = Kocaeli TR . . . 118 B4
Iznájar E 100 B1
Iznalloz E 100 B2
İznik TR 118 B4
Izola SLO 72 C3
Izsák H 75 B4
Izsófalva H 65 B6
Izyaslav UA 11 A9

J
Jabalquinto E 100 A2
Jablanac HR 83 B3
Jablanica BIH 84 C2
Jablonec nad Jizerou
  CZ 53 C5
Jablonec nad Nisou
  CZ 53 C5
Jablonica SK 64 B3
Jablonka PL 65 A5
Jabłonna PL 55 A5
Jablonné nad Orlicí
  CZ 54 C1
Jablonné Podještědí
  CZ 53 C4
Jablonov nad Turňou
  SK 65 B6
Jabłonowo Pomorskie
  PL 47 B5
Jablůnka CZ 64 A3
Jabłonków CZ 65 A4
Jabugo E 99 B4
Jabuka
  Srbija SRB 85 C5
  Vojvodina SRB 85 B5
Jabukovac HR 73 C6
Jaca E 90 A2
Jáchymov CZ 52 C2
Jacobidrebber D 43 C5
Jade D 43 B5
Jäderfors S 36 B3
Jädraås S 36 B3
Jadraque E 95 B4
Jaén E 100 B2
Jagare BIH 84 B2
Jagel D 43 A6
Jagenbach A 63 B6
Jagodina SRB 85 C6
Jagodnjak HR 74 C3
Jagodzin PL 53 B5
Jagstheim D 61 A6
Jagstzell D 61 A6
Jahodna SK 64 B3
Jajce BIH 84 B2
Ják H 74 A1
Jakabszállás H 75 B4
Jäkkvik S 115 A14
Jakobsnes N 113 C19
Jakšić HR 74 C2
Jakubany SK 65 A6
Jalance E 96 B1
Jalasjärvi FIN 3 E25
Jalhay B 50 C1
Jaligny-sur-Besbre F . 68 B3
Jallais F 66 A4
Jalón E 96 C2
Jâlons F 59 B5
Jamena SRB 85 B4
Jamilena E 100 B2
Jämjö S 41 C5
Jamnička Kiselica
  HR 73 C5
Jamno PL 46 A2
Jamoigne B 59 A6
Jämsä FIN 3 E26
Jämshög S 41 C4
Janakkala FIN 3 F26
Jandelsbrunn D 63 B4
Jänickendorf D 52 A3
Janikowo PL 47 C4
Janja BIH 85 B4
Janki
  Łódzkie PL 55 B4
  Mazowieckie PL . . . 55 A5
Jankov CZ 63 A5
Jankowo Dolne PL . . . 46 C3
Jánoshalma H 75 B4
Jánosháza H 74 A2
Jánoshida H 75 A4
Jánossomorja H 64 C3
Janovice nad Uhlavou
  CZ 63 A4
Janów PL 55 C4
Janowiec Wielkopolski
  PL 46 C3
Janowo PL 47 B6
Janville F 58 B2
Janzé F 57 C4
Jarabá SK 65 B5
Jaraczewo PL 54 B2
Jarafuel E 96 B1
Jaraicejo E 93 B5
Jaraíz de la Vera E . . . 93 A5
Jarak SRB 85 B4
Jarandilla de la Vera
  E 93 A5
Jaray E 89 C4

Järbo S 36 B3
Jard-sur-Mer F 66 B3
Jaren N 34 B2
Jargeau F 58 C3
Jarkovac SRB 75 C5
Järlåsa S 36 C4
Jarmen D 45 B5
Järna S 37 C4
Jarnac F 67 C4
Järnäs S 115 D16
Järnforsen S 40 B5
Jarny F 60 A1
Jarocin PL 54 B2
Jaroměř CZ 53 C5
Jaroměřice nad Rokytnou
CZ 64 A1
Jaroslav CZ 53 C6
Jaroslavice CZ 64 B2
Jarosław PL 11 A7
Jaroslawiec PL 46 A2
Jarošov nad Nežarkou
CZ 63 A6
Järpås S 35 D4
Järpen S 115 D10
Jarrow GB 25 D6
Järso FIN 36 B6
Järvenpää FIN 7 A8
Jarvorník CZ 54 C1
Järvsö S 115 F13
Jarzé F 67 A4
Jaša Tomic SRB 75 C5
Jasenak HR 73 C5
Jasenica BIH 83 B5
Jasenice HR 83 B4
Jasenovac HR 74 C1
Jasenovo
Srbija SRB 85 C4
Vojvodina SRB 85 B6
Jasień PL 53 B5
Jasienica PL 53 B4
Jasika SRB 85 C6
Jasło PL 10 B6
Jásova SK 65 C4
Jasseron F 69 B5
Jastarnia PL 47 A4
Jastrebarsko HR 73 C5
Jastrowie PL 46 B2
Jastrzębia-Góra PL 47 A4
Jastrzębie Zdrój PL 54 D3
Jászals-Lószentgyörgy
H 75 A5
Jászapáti H 75 A5
Jászárokszállás H 65 C5
Jászberény H 75 A4
Jászdózsa H 65 C6
Jászfényszaru H 75 A4
Jászjakóhalma H 75 A5
Jászkarajenö H 75 A5
Jászkisér H 75 A5
Jászladány H 75 A5
Jászszentlászló H 75 B4
Jásztelek H 75 A5
Játar E 100 C2
Jättendal S 115 F14
Jatznick D 45 B5
Jaun CH 70 B2
Jausiers F 79 B5
Jávea E 96 C3
Jävenitz D 44 C3
Javerlhac F 67 C5
Javier E 90 A1
Javorani BIH 84 B2
Javorina SK 65 A6
Javron F 57 B5
Jawor PL 53 B6
Jaworzno PL 55 C4
Jaworzyna Śl. PL 54 C1
Jayena E 100 C2
Jażow PL 53 B4
Jebel RO 75 C6
Jebjerg DK 38 C2
Jedburgh GB 25 C5
Jedlinsk PL 55 B6
Jedlnia PL 55 B6
Jedlnia Letnisko PL 55 B6
Jedovnice CZ 64 A2
Jędrychow PL 47 B5
Jędrzejów PL 55 C5
Jedwabno PL 47 B6
Jeesiö FIN 113 E15
Jegłownik PL 47 A5
Jegun F 77 C3
Jēkabpils LV 7 C8
Jektevik N 32 C2
Jektvik N 112 F2
Jelakci SRB 85 C5
Jelcz-Laskowice PL 54 B2
Jelenec SK 64 B4
Jelenia Góra PL 53 C5
Jelgava LV 6 C7
Jelka SK 64 B3
Jelling DK 39 D2
Jels DK 39 D2
Jelsa
HR 83 C5
N 33 C3
Jelšava SK 65 B6
Jemgum D 43 B4
Jemnice CZ 63 A6
Jena D 52 C1
Jenaz CH 71 B4
Jenbach A 72 A1
Jenikow PL 45 B7
Jennersdorf A 73 B6
Jenny S 40 B6
Jerchel D 44 C3
Jeres del Marquesado
E 100 B2
Jerez de la Frontera
E 99 C4
Jerez de los Caballeros
E 99 A4
Jerica E 96 B2
Jerichow D 44 C4
Jerka PL 54 A1
Jermenovci SRB 75 C6
Jerslev DK 38 B3
Jerte E 93 A5
Jerup DK 38 B3
Jerxheim D 51 A6
Jerzmanowice PL 55 C4
Jerzu I 110 C2
Jerzwałd PL 47 B5
Jesberg D 51 C5
Jesenice
Středočeský CZ 52 C3
Středočeský CZ 53 D4
SLO 73 B4
Jeseník CZ 54 C2
Jesenké SK 65 B6
Jesi I 82 C2
Jésolo I 72 C2
Jessen D 52 B2
Jessenitz D 44 B3
Jessheim N 34 B3
Jessnitz D 52 B2
Jesteburg D 44 B1
Jeumont F 49 C5
Jeven-stedt D 43 A6
Jever D 43 B4
Jevíčko CZ 64 A2
Jevišovice CZ 64 B1
Jevnaker N 34 B2
Jezerane HR 83 A4
Jezero
BIH 84 B2
HR 83 A4
Jeziorany PL 47 B6
Jezów PL 55 B4
Jičín CZ 53 C5
Jičiněves CZ 53 C5
Jihlava CZ 63 A6
Jijona E 96 C2
Jilemnice CZ 53 C5
Jilové CZ 53 C4
Jilovéu Prahy CZ 63 A5
Jimbolia RO 75 C5
Jimena E 100 B2
Jimena de la Frontera
E 99 C5
Jimera de Libar E 99 C5
Jimramov CZ 64 A2
Jince CZ 63 A4
Jindřichovice CZ 52 C2
Jindřichův Hradec
CZ 63 A6
Jirkov CZ 52 C3
Jistebnice CZ 63 A5
Joachimsthal D 45 C5
João da Loura P 92 C2
Jobbágyi H 65 C5
Jochberg A 72 A2
Jockfall S 113 F11
Jódar E 100 B2
Jodoigne B 49 C5
Joensuu FIN 3 E28
Joesjö S 115 B11
Joeuf F 60 A1
Jõgeva EST 7 B9
Johanngeorgenstadt
D 52 C2
Johannishus S 41 C5
Johanniskirchen D 62 B3
Johansfors S 40 C5
John o'Groats GB 23 C5
Johnshaven GB 25 B5
Johnstone GB 24 C3
Johnstown IRL 21 B4
Jõhvi EST 7 B9
Joigny F 59 C4
Joinville F 59 B6
Jokkmokk S 112 F8
Jöllenbeck D 51 A4
Jomala FIN 36 B6
Jönåker S 37 D3
Jonava LT 6 D8
Jonchery-sur-Vesle F 59 A4
Jondal N 32 B3
Jondalen N 33 C6
Joniškis LT 6 C7
Jönköping S 40 B4
Jonkowo PL 47 B6
Jønnbu N 33 C6
Jonsberg S 37 D3
Jonsered S 38 B5
Jonstorp S 41 C2
Jonzac F 67 C4
Jorba E 91 B4
Jordanów PL 65 A5
Jordanowo PL 46 C1
Jordanów Ślaski PL 54 C1
Jordbro S 37 C5
Jordbrua N 115 A11
Jördenstorf D 45 B4
Jordet N 34 A4
Jordøse DK 39 D3
Jork D 43 B6
Jörlanda S 38 B4
Jormlien S 115 C10
Jormvattnet S 115 C11
Jörn S 115 B17
Jørpeland N 33 C3
Jorquera E 96 B1
Jošan HR 83 B4
Jošanička Banja SRB 85 C5
Jošavka BIH 84 B2
Josipdol HR 73 C5
Josipovac HR 74 C3
Jössefors S 35 C4
Josselin F 56 C3
Jøssund N 114 C7
Jostedal N 114 F4
Jósvafő H 65 B6
Jou P 87 C3
Jouarre F 59 B4
Joué-lès-Tours F 67 A5
Joué-sur-Erdre F 66 A3
Joure NL 42 C2
Joutseno FIN 3 F28
Joutsijärvi FIN 113 F16
Joux-la-Ville F 59 C4
Jouy F 58 B2
Jouy-le-Châtel F 59 B4
Jouy-le-Potier F 58 C2
Joyeuse F 78 B3
Joze F 68 C3
Józefów PL 55 A6
Juankoski FIN 3 E28
Juan-les-Pins F 79 C6
Juban AL 105 A5
Jübek D 43 A6
Jubera E 89 B4
Jubrique E 99 C5
Jüchsen D 51 C6
Judaberg N 33 C2
Judenburg A 73 A4
Juelsminde DK 39 D3
Jugon-les-Lacs F 56 B3
Juillac F 67 C6
Juillan F 76 C3
Juist D 43 B4
Jukkasjärvi S 112 E9
Jule N 115 C10
Julianadorp NL 42 C1
Julianstown IRL 19 C5
Jülich D 50 C2
Jullouville F 57 B4
Jumeaux F 68 C3
Jumièges F 58 A1
Jumilhac-le-Grand F 67 C6
Jumilla E 101 A4
Juncosa E 90 B3
Juneda E 90 B3
Jung S 35 D5
Jungingen D 61 B5
Junglingster L 60 A2
Juniville F 59 A5
Junosuando S 113 E11
Junqueira P 87 C3
Junsele S 115 D13
Juoksengi S 113 F12
Juoksenki FIN 113 F12
Juprelle B 49 C6
Jurata PL 47 A4
Jurbarkas LT 6 D7
Jurjevo HR 83 B3
Jūrmala LV 6 C7
Juromenha P 93 C3
Jursla S 37 D3
Jussac F 77 B5
Jussey F 60 C1
Jussy F 59 A4
Juta H 74 B2
Jüterbog D 52 B3
Juuka FIN 3 E28
Juvigny-le-Terte F 57 B4
Juvigny-sous-Andaine
F 57 B5
Juzennecourt F 59 B5
Jyderup DK 39 D4
Jyväskylä FIN 3 E26

K

Kaamanen FIN 113 C16
Kaamasmukka FIN 113 C15
Kaaresuvanto FIN 113 D11
Kaarssen D 44 B3
Kaatscheuvel NL 49 B6
Kaba H 75 A6
Kåbdalis S 115 A17
Kačarevo SRB 85 B5
Kačikol KOS 85 D6
Kács H 65 C6
Kadan CZ 52 C3
Kadarkút H 74 B2
Kadınhanı TR 119 D7
Kaduy RUS 7 B14
Kåfalla S 37 C2
Kåfjord N 113 C12
Kåfjordbotn N 112 C9
Kågeröd S 41 D3
Kahl D 51 C5
Kahla D 52 C1
Kainach bei Voitsberg
A 73 A5
Kaindorf A 73 A5
Kainulasjärvi S 113 F11
Kairala FIN 113 E16
Kaisepakte S 112 D8
Kaisersesch D 50 C3
Kaiserslautern D 60 A3
Kaisheim D 62 B1
Kajaani FIN 3 D27
Kajárpéc H 74 A2
Kajdacs H 74 B3
Kakanj BIH 84 B3
Kakasd H 74 B3
Kaklik TR 119 E4
Kakolewo PL 54 B1
Kál H 65 C6
Kalače MNE 85 D5
Kalajoki FIN 3 D25
Kalak N 113 B16
Kalamata GR 117 E4
Kalambaka GR 116 C3
Kalamria GR 116 B4
Kalandra GR 116 C5
Kälarne S 115 E13
Kalavrita GR 117 D4
Kalbe D 44 C3
Kalce SLO 73 C4
Káld H 74 A2
Kale
Antalya TR 119 F4
Denizli TR 119 E3
Kalecik TR 16 A6
Kalefeld D 51 B6
Kalenić SRB 85 C5
Kalesija BIH 84 B3
Kalety PL 54 C3
Kalevala RUS 3 D29
Kalhovd N 32 B5
Kali HR 83 B4
Kalimnos GR 119 F2
Kaliningrad RUS 47 A6
Kalinkavichy BY 7 E10
Kalinovac HR 74 B2
Kalinovik BIH 84 C3
Kalinovo SK 65 B5
Kalirachi GR 116 B6
Kaliska
Pomorskie PL 47 A4
Pomorskie PL 47 B4
Kalisko PL 55 B4
Kalisz PL 54 B3
Kalisz Pomorski PL 46 B1
Kalix S 3 D25
Kaljord N 112 D4
Kalkan TR 119 F4
Kalkar D 50 B2
Kalkım TR 118 C2
Kall
D 50 C2
S 115 D10
Källby S 35 D5
Kållered S 38 B5
Kållerstad S 40 B3
Kallinge S 41 C5
Kallmeti i Madh AL 105 B5
Kallmünz D 62 A2
Kallo FIN 113 E13
Kallsedet S 115 D9
Källvik S 37 D4
Kalmar S 40 C6
Kalmthout B 49 B5
Kalná SK 65 B4
Kalocsa H 75 B3
Kalokhorio CY 120 B2
Kalo Nero GR 117 E3
Kaloni GR 116 C8
Káloz H 74 B3
Kals A 72 A2
Kalsdorf A 73 B5
Kaltbrunn CH 70 A4
Kaltenbach A 72 A1
Kaltenkirchen D 44 B1
Kaltennordheim D 51 C6
Kaluga RUS 7 D14
Kalundborg DK 39 D4
Kalush UA 11 B8
Kałuszyn PL 55 A6
Kalv S 40 B3
Kalvåg N 114 F1
Kalvehave DK 41 D2
Kalwang A 73 A4
Kalwaria-Zebrzydowska
PL 65 A5
Kalyazin RUS 7 C14
Kam H 74 A1
Kaman TR 16 B6
Kamares GR 117 F6
Kambos CY 120 A1
Kamen D 50 B3
Kamenice CZ 64 A1
Kamenice nad Lipou
CZ 63 A6
Kameničná SK 64 C4
Kamenný Most SK 65 C4
Kamenny Ujezd CZ 63 B5
Kamenska HR 74 C2
Kamensko HR 84 C1
Kamenz D 53 B4
Kamičak BIH 84 B1
Kamień PL 55 B5
Kamieniec Zabk PL 54 C1
Kamienka SK 65 A6
Kamień Krajeński PL 46 B3
Kamienna Góra PL 53 C6
Kamień Pomorski PL 45 B6
Kamieńsk PL 55 B4
Kaminka UA 11 B12
Kamiros Skala GR 119 F2
Kamnik SLO 73 B4
Kampen NL 42 C2
Kampinos PL 55 A5
Kamp-Lintfort D 50 B2
Kampor HR 83 B3
Kamyanets-Podil's'kyy
UA 11 B9
Kamyanka-Buz'ka UA 11 A8
Kamýk nad Vltavou
CZ 63 A5
Kanal SLO 72 B3
Kanalia GR 116 C4
Kandalaksha RUS 3 C30
Kandanos GR 117 G5
Kandel D 61 A4
Kandern D 60 C3
Kandersteg CH 70 B2
Kandila GR 117 E4
Kandıra TR 118 A5
Kandyty PL 47 A6
Kanfanar HR 82 A2
Kangasala FIN 3 F26
Kangos S 113 E11
Kangosjärvi FIN 113 E12
Kaninë AL 105 C5
Kaniów PL 53 B4
Kanjiža SRB 75 B5
Kankaanpää FIN 3 F25
Kannus FIN 3 E25
Kanturk IRL 20 B3
Kaonik SRB 85 C6
Kapaklı TR 118 A2
Kapellen
A 63 C6
B 49 B5
Kapellskär S 37 C6
Kapfenberg A 73 A5
Kapfenstein A 73 B5
Kaplice CZ 63 B5
Kapljuh BIH 83 B5
Kápolna H 65 C6
Kápolnásnyék H 74 A3
Kaposfő H 74 B2
Kaposfüred H 74 B2
Kaposszekcsö H 74 B3
Kaposvár H 74 B2
Kapp N 34 B2
Kappel D 60 B3
Kappeln D 44 A1
Kappelshamn S 37 E5
Kappl A 71 A5
Kappstad S 35 C5
Kaprun A 72 A2
Kaptol HR 74 C2
Kapuvár H 64 C3
Karaadilli TR 119 D5
Karabiğa TR 118 B2
Karabük TR 118 A7
Karaburun TR 118 D1
Karacabey TR 118 B3
Karacaköy TR 118 A3
Karacaören TR 119 D5
Karacasu TR 119 E3
Karachev RUS 7 E13
Karácsond H 65 C6
Karád H 74 B2
Karahallı TR 119 D4
Karaisali TR 16 C7
Karaman
Balıkesir TR 118 C3
Karaman TR 16 C6
Karamanlı TR 119 E4
Karamürsel TR 118 B4
Karan SRB 85 C4
Karancslapujto H 65 B5
Karaova TR 119 E2
Karapınar TR 16 C6
Karasjok N 113 C14
Karasu TR 118 A5
Karataş
Adana TR 16 C7
Manisa TR 119 D3
Karatoprak TR 119 E2
Karavostasi CY 120 A1
Karbenning S 36 B3
Kårberg S 37 D1
Kårböle S 115 F12
Karbunara AL 105 C5
Karby
D 44 A1
DK 38 C1
Kårby S 40 B6
Karby S 37 C5
Karcag H 75 A5
Karczew PL 55 A6
Karczów PL 54 C2
Karczowiska PL 53 B6
Kardamena GR 119 F2
Kardamila GR 116 D8
Kardamili GR 117 F4
Kardašova Rečice CZ 63 A5
Kardis S 113 F12
Karditsa GR 116 C3
Kärdla EST 6 B7
Kardoskút H 75 B5
Kardzhali BG 15 C10
Karesuando S 113 D11
Kargı TR 16 A7
Kargowa PL 53 A5
Karigasniemi FIN 113 C14
Karise DK 41 D2
Karistos GR 117 D6
Karkkila FIN 6 A8
Karlholmsbruk S 36 B4
Karlino PL 46 A1
Karl Liebknecht RUS 7 F13
Karlobag HR 83 B4
Karlovac HR 73 C5
Karlovasi GR 119 E1
Karlovčic SRB 85 B5
Karlovice CZ 54 C2
Karlovo BG 11 E8
Karlovy Vary CZ 52 C2
Karłowice PL 54 C2
Karlsborg S 37 D1
Karlshamn S 41 C4
Karlshöfen D 43 B6
Karlshus N 35 C2
Karlskoga S 37 C1
Karlskrona S 41 C5
Karlsrud N 32 B5
Karlsruhe D 61 A4
Karlstad S 35 C5
Karlstadt D 51 D5
Karlstetten A 63 B6
Karlstift A 63 B5
Karlstorp S 40 B5
Karmacs H 74 B2
Karmin PL 54 B2
Kärna S 38 B4
Karnobat BG 11 E9
Karojba HR 72 C3
Karow D 44 B4
Karpacz PL 53 C5
Karpathos GR 119 G2
Karpenisi GR 116 D3
Karpuzlu TR 119 E2
Kärrbo S 37 C3
Karrebaeksminde DK 39 D4
Karshult S 40 B3
Karsin PL 46 B3
Kårsta S 37 C5
Karstädt D 44 B3
Kartal TR 118 B4
Kartitsch A 72 B2
Kartuzy PL 47 A4
Karup DK 39 C2
Karviná CZ 65 A4
Kås DK 38 B2
Kaş TR 119 F4
Kasaba TR 119 F4
Kašava CZ 64 A3
Kåseberga S 41 D4
Kasejovice CZ 63 A4
Kasfjord N 112 D5
Kashin RUS 7 C14
Kašina HR 73 C6
Kasina-Wielka PL 65 A6
Kaskinen FIN 3 E24
Kašperské Hory CZ 63 A4
Kassandrino GR 116 B5
Kassel D 51 B5
Kassiopi GR 116 C1
Kastamonu TR 16 A6
Kastav HR 73 C4
Kasteli GR 117 G5
Kastellaun D 50 C3
Kastelli GR 117 G7
Kaštel-Stari HR 83 C5
Kaštel Zegarski HR 83 B4
Kasterlee B 49 B5
Kastl D 62 A2
Kastlösa S 41 C6
Kastorf D 44 B2
Kastoria GR 116 B3
Kastorio GR 117 E4
Kastraki GR 117 F7
Kastrosikia GR 116 C2
Kastsyukovichy BY 7 E12
Kaszaper H 75 B5
Katakolo GR 117 E3
Katapola GR 117 F7
Katastari GR 117 E2
Katerbow D 45 C4
Katerini GR 116 B4
Kathikas CY 120 B1
Kätkesuando S 113 D12
Katlenburg-Lindau D 51 B6
Kato Achaia GR 117 D3
Káto Pyrgos CY 120 A1
Katouna GR 116 D3
Katovice CZ 63 A4
Katowice PL 55 C4
Katrineberg S 36 A3
Katrineholm S 37 D3
Kattarp S 41 C2
Kattavia GR 119 G2
Katthammarsvik S 37 E5
Kattilstorp S 40 A3
Katwijk NL 49 A5
Katymár H 75 B4
Kąty Wrocławskie
PL 54 B1
Katzenelnbogen D 50 C3
Katzhütte D 52 C1
Kaub D 50 C3
Kaufbeuren D 62 C1
Kauhajoki FIN 3 E25
Kauhava FIN 3 E25
Kaukonen FIN 113 E13
Kaulsdorf D 52 C1
Kaunas LT 6 D7
Kaunisvaara S 113 E12
Kaupanger N 32 A4
Kautokeino N 113 C12
Kautzen A 63 B6
Kavadarci MK 116 A4
Kavajë AL 105 B5
Kavakköy TR 118 B1
Kavaklı TR 118 A2
Kavaklıdere TR 119 E3
Kavala GR 116 B6
Kavarna BG 11 E10
Kävlinge S 41 D3
Kawcze PL 46 A2
Kaxås S 115 D10
Kaxholmen S 40 B4
Kaymakçı TR 119 D3
Kaymaz TR 118 C6
Kaynarca TR 118 A5
Käyrämö FIN 113 F15
Kayseri TR 16 B7
Kaysersberg F 60 B3
Kazanlak BG 11 E8
Kazár H 65 B5
Kazimierza Wielka PL 55 C5
Kazincbarcika H 65 B6
Kaźmierz PL 46 C2
Kcynia PL 46 B3
Kdyně CZ 62 A4
Kea GR 117 E6
Keadew IRL 18 B3
Keady GB 19 B5
Kecel H 75 B4
Keçiborlu TR 119 E5
Kecskemét H 75 B4
Kėdainiai LT 6 D7
Kędzierzyn-Koźle PL 54 C3
Keel IRL 18 C1
Keenagh IRL 19 C4
Keerbergen B 49 B5
Kefalos GR 119 F1
Kefken TR 118 A5
Keflavík IS 111 C3
Kegworth GB 27 C4
Kehl D 60 B3
Kehrigk D 53 A3
Keighley GB 27 B4
Keila EST 6 B8
Keillmore GB 24 C2
Keiss GB 23 C5
Keith GB 23 D6
Kelberg D 50 C2
Kelbra D 51 B7
Kelč CZ 64 A3
Kelchsau A 72 A2
Këlcyrë AL 116 B2
Keld GB 26 A3
Kelebia H 75 B4
Kelekçi TR 119 E4
Kelemér H 65 B6
Keles TR 118 C4
Kelheim D 62 B2
Kell D 60 A2
Kellas GB 23 D5
Kellinghusen D 43 B6
Kelloselkä FIN 113 F17
Kells
GB 19 B5
IRL 19 C5
Kelmis B 50 C2
Kelokedhara CY 120 B1
Kelottijärvi FIN 113 D11
Kelsall GB 26 B3
Kelso GB 25 C5
Kelsterbach D 51 C4
Keltneyburn GB 24 B3
Kelujärvi FIN 113 E16
Kemaliye TR 119 D3
Kemalpaşa TR 119 D2
Kematen A 71 A6
Kemberg D 52 B2
Kemer
Antalya TR 119 F5
Burdur TR 119 E5
Muğla TR 119 F4
Kemerkaya TR 118 D6
Kemeten A 73 A6
Kemi FIN 3 D26
Kemijärvi FIN 113 F16
Kemnath D 62 A2
Kemnay GB 23 D6
Kemnitz
Brandenburg D 52 A2
Mecklenburg-Vorpommern D 45 A5
Kempen D 50 B2
Kempsey GB 29 A5
Kempten D 61 C6
Kemptthal CH 70 A3
Kendal GB 26 A3
Kenderes H 75 A5
Kengyel H 75 A5
Kenilworth GB 30 B2
Kenmare IRL 20 C2
Kenmore GB 25 B4
Kennacraig GB 24 C2
Kenyeri H 74 A2
Kenzingen D 60 B3
Kepez TR 118 B1
Kępice PL 46 A2
Kępno PL 54 B3
Kepsut TR 118 C3
Keramoti GR 116 B6
Keräntöjärvi S 113 E12
Keratea GR 117 E5
Kerava FIN 7 A8
Kerecsend H 65 C6
Kerekegyhaza H 75 B4
Kerepestarcsa H 75 A4
Keri GR 117 E2
Kérien F 56 B2
Kerkafalva H 74 B1
Kerken D 50 B2
Kerkrade NL 50 C2
Kerkyra GR 116 C1
Kerlouan F 56 B1
Kernascléden F 56 B2
Kernhof A 63 C6
Kerns CH 70 B3
Kerpen D 50 C2
Kerrysdale GB 22 D3
Kerta H 74 A2
Kerteminde DK 39 D3
Kerzers CH 70 B2
Keşan TR 118 B1
Kesgrave GB 30 B5
Kesh GB 19 B4
Keskin TR 16 B6
Kesselfall A 72 A2
Kestenga RUS 3 D29
Keswick GB 26 A2
Keszthely H 74 B2
Kétegyháza H 75 B6
Kéthely H 74 B2
Kętrzyn PL 6 D6
Kettering GB 30 B3
Kettlewell GB 26 A3
Kęty PL 65 A5
Ketzin D 45 C4
Keula D 51 B6
Keuruu FIN 3 E26
Kevelaer D 50 B2
Kevermes H 75 B6
Kevi SRB 75 C4
Keyingham GB 27 B5
Keynsham GB 29 B5
Kežmarok SK 65 A6
Kherson UA 11 C12
Khimki RUS 7 D14
Khisinev = Chişinău
MD 11 C10
Khmelnik UA 11 B9
Khmelnytskyy UA 11 B9
Khodoriv UA 11 B8
Kholm RUS 7 C11
Khorol UA 11 B12
Khotyn UA 11 B9
Khoyniki BY 7 F10
Khust UA 11 B7
Khvoynaya RUS 7 B13
Kiato GR 117 D4
Kibæk DK 39 C1
Kiberg N 113 B19
Kicasalih TR 118 A1
Kičevo MK 116 A2
Kidderminster GB 26 C3
Kidlington GB 31 C2
Kidsgrove GB 26 B3
Kidwelly GB 28 B3
Kiefersfelden D 62 C3
Kiel D 44 A2
Kielce PL 55 C5
Kiełczygłów PL 54 B4
Kielder GB 25 C5
Kiełpino PL 47 A4
Kielpiny PL 47 B5
Kierinki FIN 113 E14
Kiernozia PL 55 A4
Kierspe D 50 B3
Kietrz PL 54 C3
Kietz D 45 C6
Kiev = Kyyiv UA 11 A11
Kiezmark PL 47 A4
Kiffisia GR 117 D5
Kifino Selo BIH 84 C3
Kihlanki
FIN 113 E12
S 113 E12
Kiistala FIN 113 E14
Kije PL 55 C5
Kijevo HR 83 C5
Kikallen N 32 B2
Kikinda SRB 75 C5
Kil
N 33 D6
Örebro S 37 C2
Värmland S 35 C5
Kila S 35 C4
Kilafors S 36 A3
Kilbaha IRL 20 B2
Kilbeggan IRL 21 A4
Kilberry GB 24 C2
Kilbirnie GB 24 C3
Kilboghamn N 112 F2
Kilbotn N 112 D5
Kilb Rabenstein A 63 B6
Kilchattan GB 24 C2
Kilchoan GB 24 B1
Kilcock IRL 21 A5
Kilconnell IRL 20 A3
Kilcormac IRL 21 A4
Kilcreggan GB 24 C3
Kilcullen IRL 21 A5
Kilcurry IRL 19 B5
Kildare IRL 21 A5
Kildinstroy RUS 3 B30
Kildonan GB 23 C5
Kildorrery IRL 20 B3
Kilegrend N 33 C5
Kilen N 33 C5
Kilgarvan IRL 20 C2
Kiliya UA 11 D10
Kilkee IRL 20 B2
Kilkeel GB 19 B5
Kilkelly IRL 18 C3
Kilkenny IRL 21 B4
Kilkieran IRL 20 A2
Kilkinlea IRL 20 B2
Kilkis GR 116 A4
Kill IRL 21 B4
Killadysert IRL 20 B2
Killala IRL 18 B2
Killaloe IRL 20 B3
Killarney IRL 20 B2
Killashandra IRL 19 B4
Killashee IRL 19 C4
Killearn GB 24 B3
Killeberg S 40 C4
Killeigh IRL 21 A4
Killenaule IRL 21 B4
Killimor IRL 20 A3
Killin GB 24 B3
Killinaboy IRL 20 B2
Killinge S 112 E9
Killinick IRL 21 B5
Killorglin IRL 20 B2
Killucan IRL 21 A4
Killybegs IRL 18 B3
Killyleagh GB 19 B6
Kilmacrenan IRL 19 A4
Kilmacthomas IRL 21 B4
Kilmaine IRL 18 C2
Kilmallock IRL 20 B3
Kilmarnock GB 24 C3
Kilmartin GB 24 B2
Kilmaurs GB 24 C3
Kilmeadan IRL 21 B4
Kilmeedy IRL 20 B3
Kilmelford GB 24 B2
Kilmore Quay IRL 21 B5
Kilmuir GB 23 D4
Kilnaleck IRL 19 C4
Kilninver GB 24 B2
Kilpisjärvi FIN 112 C9
Kilrea GB 19 B5
Kilrush IRL 20 B2
Kilsmo S 37 C2
Kilsyth GB 24 C3
Kiltoom IRL 20 A3
Kilwinning GB 24 C3
Kimasozero RUS 3 D29
Kimi GR 116 D6
Kimolos GR 117 F6
Kimovsk RUS 7 D14
Kimratshofen D 61 C6
Kimry RUS 7 C14
Kimstad S 37 D2
Kinbrace GB 23 C5
Kincardine GB 25 B4
Kincraig GB 23 D5
Kindberg A 73 A5
Kindelbruck D 52 B1
Kingarrow IRL 18 B3
Kingisepp RUS 7 B10
Kingsbridge GB 28 C4
Kingsclere GB 31 C2
Kingscourt IRL 19 C5
King's Lynn GB 30 B4
Kingsteignton GB 29 C4
Kingston
Greater London GB 31 C3
Moray GB 23 D5
Kingston Bagpuize
GB 31 C2
Kingston upon Hull
GB 27 B5
Kingswear GB 29 C4
Kingswood GB 29 B5
Kington GB 29 A4
Kingussie GB 23 D4
Kınık
Antalya TR 119 F4
İzmir TR 118 C2
Kinloch
Highland GB 22 C4
Highland GB 22 D2
Kinlochbervie GB 22 C3
Kinlochewe GB 22 D3
Kinlochleven GB 24 B3
Kinlochmoidart GB 24 B2
Kinloch Rannoch GB 24 B3
Kinloss GB 23 D5
Kinlough IRL 18 B3
Kinn N 34 B2
Kinna S 40 B2
Kinnared S 40 B3
Kinnarp S 40 A3
Kinnegad IRL 21 A4
Kinne-Kleva S 35 D5
Kinnitty IRL 21 A4
Kinrooi B 50 B1
Kinross GB 25 B4
Kinsale IRL 20 C3
Kinsarvik N 32 B3
Kintarvie GB 22 C2
Kintore GB 23 D6
Kinvarra IRL 20 A3
Kioni GR 116 D2
Kiparissia GR 117 E3
Kipfenburg D 62 B2
Kippen GB 24 B3
Kiraz TR 119 D3
Kirazlı TR 118 B1
Kirberg D 50 C4
Kirchbach in Steiermark
A 73 B5
Kirchberg
CH 70 A2
Baden-Württemberg
D 61 A5
Rheinland-Pfalz D 60 A3
Kirchberg am Wechsel
A 64 C1
Kirchberg an der Pielach
A 63 B6
Kirchberg in Tirol A 72 A2
Kirchbichl A 72 A2
Kirchdorf
Bayern D 63 B4
Mecklenburg-Vorpommern D 44 B3
Niedersachsen D 43 C5
Kirchdorf an der Krems
A 63 C5
Kirchdorf in Tirol A 72 A2
Kirchenlamitz D 52 C1
Kirchenthumbach D 62 A2
Kirchhain D 51 C4
Kirchheim
Baden-Württemberg
D 61 B5
Bayern D 61 B6
Hessen D 51 C5
Kirchheimbolanden D 61 A4
Kirchhundem D 50 B4
Kirchlintein D 43 C6
Kirchschlag A 73 A6
Kirchweidach D 62 B3
Kirchzarten D 60 C3
Kircubbin GB 19 B6
Kireç TR 118 C3
Kırıkkale TR 16 B6
Kirillov RUS 7 B15
Kirishi RUS 7 B12
Kırka TR 118 C5
Kırkağaç TR 118 C2
Kirkbean GB 25 D4
Kirkbride GB 25 D4
Kirkby GB 26 B3
Kirkby Lonsdale GB 26 A3
Kirkby Malzeard GB 27 A4
Kirkbymoorside GB 27 A5
Kirkby Stephen GB 26 A3
Kirkcaldy GB 25 B4
Kirkcolm GB 24 D2
Kirkconnel GB 24 C3
Kirkcowan GB 24 D3
Kirkcudbright GB 24 D3
Kirkehamn N 33 D3
Kirke Hyllinge DK 39 D4
Kirkenær N 34 B4
Kirkenes N 113 C19
Kirkham GB 26 B3
Kirkintilloch GB 24 C3
Kirkjubæjarklaustur
IS 111 D7
Kirkkonummi FIN 6 A8
Kırklareli TR 118 A2
Kirkmichael GB 25 B4
Kirk Michael GB 26 A1
Kirkoswald GB 24 C3
Kirkpatrick Fleming
GB 25 C4
Kirkton of Glenisla
GB 25 B4
Kirkwall GB 23 C6
Kirkwhelpington GB 25 C6
Kirn D 60 A3
Kiro AL 105 A5
Kirov RUS 7 D13
Kirovohrad UA 11 B12
Kirovsk RUS 3 C30
Kirriemuir GB 25 B5
Kırşehir TR 16 B7
Kirton GB 30 B3
Kirton in Lindsey GB 27 B5
Kirtorf D 51 C5
Kiruna S 112 E9
Kisa S 40 B5
Kisač SRB 75 C4
Kisbér H 74 A3
Kiseljak BIH 84 C3
Kisielice PL 47 B5
Kisköre H 75 A5
Kiskőrös H 75 B4
Kiskunfélegyháza H 75 B4
Kiskunhalas H 75 B4
Kiskunlacháza H 75 A3
Kiskunmajsa H 75 B4
Kisláng H 74 B3
Kisslegg D 61 C5
Kissolt H 75 B4
Kissónerga CY 120 B1
Kist D 61 A5
Kistanje HR 83 C4
Kistelek H 75 B4
Kisterenye H 65 B5
Kisújszállás H 75 A5
Kisvárda H 11 B7
Kisvejke H 74 B3
Kiszkowo PL 46 C3
Kiszombor H 75 B5
Kitee FIN 3 E29
Kithnos GR 117 E6
Kiti CY 120 B2
Kitkiöjärvi S 113 E12
Kitkiöjoki S 113 E12
Kittelfjäll S 115 B12
Kittendorf D 45 B4
Kittilä FIN 113 E13
Kittlitz D 53 B4
Kittsee A 64 B3
Kitzbühel A 72 A2
Kitzingen D 61 A6
Kiuruvesi FIN 3 E27
Kivertsi UA 11 A8
Kividhes CY 120 B1
Kivik S 41 D4
Kivotos GR 116 B3
Kiwity PL 47 A6
Kıyıköy TR 118 A3
Kızılcabölük TR 119 E4
Kızılcadağ TR 119 E4
Kızılcahamam TR 16 A6
Kızılırmak TR 16 A6
Kızılkaya TR 119 E5
Kızılkuyu TR 118 D6
Kızılören
Afyon TR 119 D5
Konya TR 119 E7
Kjeldebotn N 112 D5
Kjellerup DK 39 C2
Kjellmyra N 34 B4
Kjøllefjord N 113 B16
Kjopmannskjaer N 35 C2
Kjøpsvik N 112 D5
Kl'ačno SK 65 B4
Kladanj BIH 84 B3
Kläden D 44 C3
Klädesholmen S 38 B4
Kladnica SRB 85 C5
Kladnice HR 83 C5
Kladno CZ 53 C4
Kladruby CZ 62 A3
Klagenfurt A 73 B4
Klågerup S 41 D3
Klagstorp S 41 D3
Klaipėda LT 6 D6
Klaistow D 52 A2
Klaksvík FO 2 E10
Klana HR 73 C4
Klanac HR 83 B4
Klanjec HR 73 B5
Klardorf D 62 A3
Klarup DK 38 B3
Klašnice BIH 84 B2
Klässbol S 35 C4
Klášterec nad Ohří
CZ 52 C3
Kláštor pod Znievom
SK 65 B4
Klatovy CZ 63 A4
Klaus an der Pyhrnbahn
A 63 C5
Klazienaveen NL 42 C3
Kłecko PL 46 C3
Kleczew PL 47 C4
Klein Plasten D 45 B4
Klein Sankt Paul A 73 B4
Kleinsölk A 72 A3
Kleinzell A 64 C1
Klejtrup DK 38 C2
Klek SRB 75 C5
Klemensker DK 41 D4
Klenak SRB 85 B4
Klenci pod Cerchovem
CZ 62 A3
Klenica PL 53 B5
Klenje SRB 85 B4
Klenoec MK 116 A2
Klenovec SK 65 B5
Klenovica HR 83 A3
Klenovnik HR 73 B6
Kleppe N 33 D2
Kleppestø N 32 B2
Kleptow D 45 B5
Kletnya RUS 7 E12
Kleve D 50 B2
Klevshult S 40 B4
Klewki PL 47 B6
Kličevac SRB 85 B6
Kliening A 73 B4
Klietz D 44 C4
Klikuszowa PL 65 A5
Klimkovice CZ 64 A4
Klimontów PL 55 C6
Klimovichi BY 7 E11
Klimpfjäll S 115 B11
Klin RUS 7 C14
Klina KOS 85 D5
Klinča Sela HR 73 C5
Klingenbach A 64 C2
Klingenberg D 61 A5
Klingenmunster D 61 A4
Klingenthal D 52 C2
Klinken D 44 B3
Klintehamn S 37 E5
Klintsy RUS 7 E12
Kliny PL 55 B5
Kliplev DK 39 E2
Klippan S 41 C3
Klis HR 83 C5
Klitmøller DK 38 B1
Klitten S 34 A6
Klixbüll D 39 E1
Kljajićevo SRB 75 C4
Ključ BIH 83 B5
Klobouky CZ 64 B2
Kłobuck PL 54 C3
Klockestrand S 115 E14
Kłodawa
Lubuskie PL 45 C7
Wielkopolskie PL 54 A3
Kłodzko PL 54 C1
Kløfta N 34 B3
Klokkarvik N 32 B2
Klokkerholm DK 38 B3
Klokočov SK 65 A4
Kłomnice PL 55 C4
Klonowa PL 54 B3
Kloosterzande NL 49 B5
Kłopot PL 53 A4
Klos AL 116 A2
Kloštar Ivanić HR 73 C6
Kloster
D 45 A5
DK 39 C1
Klösterle A 71 A5
Klostermansfeld D 52 B1
Klosterneuburg A 64 B2
Klosters CH 71 B4
Kloten CH 70 A3
Klötze D 44 C3
Klövsjö S 115 E11
Kluczbork PL 54 C3
Kluczewo PL 46 B2
Kluisbergen B 49 C4
Klundert NL 49 B5
Klutz D 44 B3
Klwów PL 55 B5
Klyetsk BY 7 E9
Knaben N 33 D3
Knaften S 115 C15
Knapstad N 35 C3
Knäred S 40 C3
Knaresborough GB 27 A4
Knarvik N 32 B2
Knebel DK 39 C3
Knebworth GB 31 C3
Knesebeck D 44 C2
Knesselare B 49 B4
Knežak SLO 73 C4
Kneževi Vinogradi
HR 74 C3
Kneževo HR 74 C3
Knić SRB 85 C5
Knighton GB 29 A4
Knin HR 83 B5
Knislinge S 41 C4
Knittelfeld A 73 A4
Knivsta S 37 C4
Knock IRL 18 C3
Knocktopher IRL 21 B4
Knokke-Heist B 49 B4
Knowle GB 30 B2
Knurów PL 54 C3
Knutby S 36 C5
Knutsford GB 26 B3
Kobarid SLO 72 B3
København = Copenhagen DK 41 D2
Kobenz A 73 A4
Kobersdorf A 64 C2
Kobiernice PL 65 A5
Kobierzyce PL 54 C1
Kobilje SLO 73 B6
Kobiór PL 54 C3
Koblenz
CH 61 C4
D 50 C3
Kobryn BY 6 E8
Kobylanka PL 45 B6
Kobylin PL 54 B2
Kobyłka PL 55 A6
Kobylniki PL 47 C6
Kocaali TR 118 A5
Kocaaliler TR 119 E5
Kocaeli = İzmit TR 118 B4
Kočani MK 11 F7
Koçarlı TR 119 E2
Koceljevo SRB 85 B4
Kočerin BIH 84 C2
Kočevje SLO 73 C4
Kočevska Reka SLO 73 C4
Kochel am see D 62 C2
Kocs H 64 C4
Kocsér H 75 A4
Kocsola H 74 B3
Koczala PL 46 B3
Kodal N 35 C2
Kode S 38 B4
Kodersdorf D 53 B4
Kodrab PL 55 B4
Koekelare B 48 B3
Kofçaz TR 118 A2
Köflach A 73 A5
Køge DK 41 D2
Kohlberg D 62 A3
Kohtla-Järve EST 7 B9
Köinge S 40 B2
Kojetín CZ 64 A3
Kökar FIN 36 C7
Kokava SK 65 B5
Kokkinotrimithia CY 120 A2
Kokkola FIN 3 E25
Kokori BIH 84 B2
Kokoski PL 47 A4
Koksijde B 48 B3
Kola
BIH 84 B2
RUS 3 B30
Köla S 34 C4
Kołacin PL 55 B4
Kolari FIN 113 E12
Kolárovo SK 64 C3
Kolašin MNE 85 D4
Kolbäck S 37 C3
Kolbacz PL 45 B6
Kolbeinsstaðir IS 111 C3
Kolbermoor D 62 C3
Kołbiel PL 55 A6
Kolbnitz A 72 B3
Kolbotn N 34 C2
Kolbu N 34 B2
Kolby Kås DK 39 D3
Kolczewo PL 45 B6
Kolczyglowy PL 46 A3

Kolding DK 39 D2
Kölesd H 74 B3
Kolgrov N 32 A1
Kolín CZ 53 C5
Kolind DK 39 C3
Kolinec CZ 63 A4
Koljane HR 83 C5
Kølkær DK 39 C2
Kölleda D 52 B1
Kollum NL 42 B3
Köln = Cologne D 50 C2
Koło PL 54 A3
Kołobrzeg PL 46 A1
Kolochau D 52 B3
Kolomyya UA 11 B8
Kolonje AL 105 C5
Kolonowskie PL 54 C3
Koloveč CZ 62 A4
Kolpino RUS 7 B11
Kolpny RUS 7 E14
Kolrep D 44 B4
Kölsillre S 115 E12
Kolsko PL 53 B5
Kolsva S 37 C2
Kolta SK 65 B4
Kolunič BIH 83 B5
Koluszki PL 55 B4
Kolut SRB 75 C3
Kolvereid N 114 C8
Kølvrå DK 39 C2
Komagvær N 113 B19
Koman AL 105 A5
Komarica BIH 84 B2
Komárno SK 64 C4
Komárom H 64 C4
Komatou Yialou CY 120 A3
Komboti GR 116 C3
Komen SLO 72 C3
Komin HR 84 C2
Komiža HR 83 C5
Komjáti H 65 B6
Komjatice SK 64 B4
Komletinci HR 75 C3
Komló H 74 B3
Kömlo H 65 C6
Komoča SK 64 C4
Komorane KOS 85 D5
Komorniki PL 54 A1
Komorzno PL 54 B3
Komotini GR 116 A7
Konak SRB 75 C5
Konakovo RUS 7 C14
Konary PL 55 B6
Konarzyny PL 46 B3
Kondias GR 116 C7
Kondorfa H 73 B6
Kondoros H 75 B5
Kondrovo RUS 7 D13
Køng DK 39 D4
Konga S 40 C5
Köngäs FIN 113 E13
Kongerslev DK 38 C3
Kongsberg N 35 C1
Kongshamn N 33 D5
Kongsmark DK 39 D1
Kongsmoen N 115 C9
Kongsvik N 112 D5
Kongsvinger N 34 B4
Konice CZ 64 A2
Konie PL 55 B5
Koniecpol PL 55 C4
Königsberg D 51 C6
Königsbronn D 61 B6
Königsbrück D 53 B3
Königsbrunn D 62 B1
Konigsdorf D 62 C2
Königsee D 52 C1
Königshorst D 45 C4
Königslutter D 51 A6
Königssee D 62 C3
Königstein
Hessen D 51 C4
Sachsen D 53 C4
Königstetten A 64 B2
Königswartha D 53 B4
Konigswiesen A 63 B5
Königswinter D 50 C3
Königs Wusterhausen
D 52 A3
Konin PL 54 A3
Konispol AL 116 C2
Konitsa GR 116 B2
Köniz CH 70 B2
Konjevići BIH 85 B4
Konjevrate HR 83 C5
Konjic BIH 84 C2
Konjščina HR 73 B6
Könnern D 52 B1
Konnerud N 35 C2
Konopiska PL 54 C3
Konotop
PL 53 B5
UA 7 F12
Końskie PL 55 B5
Konsmo N 33 D4
Konstancin-Jeziorna
PL 55 A6
Konstantynów Łódźki
PL 55 B4
Konstanz D 61 C5
Kontich B 49 B5
Kontiolahti FIN 3 E28
Konya TR 119 E7
Konz D 60 A2
Kópasker IS 111 A9
Kópavogur IS 111 C4
Kopčany SK 64 B3
Koper SLO 72 C3
Kopervik N 33 C2
Kópháza H 64 C2
Kopice PL 54 C2
Kopidlno CZ 53 C5
Köping S 37 C2
Köpingebro S 41 D3
Köpingsvik S 41 C6
Koplik AL 105 A5
Köpmanholmen S 115 D15
Koppang N 34 A3
Koppangen N 112 C9
Kopparberg S 36 C1
Koppelo FIN 113 D16
Koppom S 35 C4
Koprivlen BG 116 A5
Koprivna BIH 84 B3
Koprivnica HR 74 B1
Kopřivnice CZ 64 A4
Köprübaşı TR 118 D3
Koprzywnica PL 55 C6
Kopstal L 60 A2
Kopychyntsi UA 11 B8
Kopytkowo PL 47 B4
Korbach D 51 B4
Körbecke D 50 B4
Korçë AL 116 B2
Korčula HR 84 D2
Korczyców PL 53 A4
Korenevo RUS 7 F13
Korenita SRB 85 B4
Korets UA 11 A9
Korfantów PL 54 C2
Körfez TR 118 B4
Korgen N 115 A10
Korinth DK 39 D3
Korinthos = Corinth
GR 117 E4
Korita
BIH 83 B5
HR 84 D2
Korithi GR 117 E2
Korkuteli TR 119 E5
Körmend H 74 A1
Korne PL 46 A3
Korneuburg A 64 B2
Kornevo RUS 47 A6
Kórnik PL 54 A2
Kornsjø N 35 D3
Környe H 74 A3
Koromačno HR 82 B3
Koroni GR 117 F3
Koronos GR 117 E7
Koronowo PL 46 B3
Körösladány H 75 B6
Köröstarcsa H 75 B6
Korosten UA 11 A10
Korostyshev UA 11 A10
Korpilombolo S 113 F12
Korsberga
Jönköping S 40 B5
Skaraborg S 35 D6
Korshavn N 35 C2
Korskrogen S 115 F12
Korsnäs S 36 B2
Korsør DK 39 D4
Korsun Shevchenkovskiy
UA 11 B11
Kortrijk B 49 C4
Korucu TR 118 C2
Koryčany CZ 64 A3
Koryukovka UA 7 F12
Korzeńsko PL 54 B1
Korzybie PL 46 A2
Kos GR 119 F2
Kosakowo PL 47 A4
Kosanica MNE 85 C4
Kosaya Gora RUS 7 D14
Kösching D 62 B2
Kościan PL 54 A1
Kościelec PL 54 A3
Kościerzyna PL 46 A3
Koserow D 45 A5
Košetice CZ 63 A6
Košice SK 10 B6
Kosjerić SRB 85 C4
Koška HR 74 C3
Koskullskulle S 112 E9
Kosovska Mitrovica
KOS 85 D5
Kosta S 40 C5
Kostajnica HR 74 C1
Kostajnik SRB 85 B4
Kostanica MNE 105 A5
Kostanjevica SLO 73 C5
Kostelec nad Černými
Lesy CZ 53 D4
Kostelec na Hané CZ 64 A3
Kostice CZ 53 C3
Kostkowo PL 47 A4
Kostojevići SRB 85 B4
Kostolac SRB 85 B6
Kostomłoty PL 54 B1
Kostopil UA 11 A9
Kostów PL 54 B3
Kostrzyn
Lubuskie PL 45 C6
Wielkopolskie PL 46 C3
Koszalin PL 46 A2
Koszęcin PL 54 C3
Köszeg H 74 A1
Koszwaly PL 47 A4
Koszyce PL 55 C5
Kot SLO 73 C5
Kotala FIN 113 E17
Kotë AL 105 C5
Kötelek H 75 A5
Köthen D 52 B1
Kotka FIN 7 A9
Kotomierz PL 47 B4
Kotor MNE 105 A4
Kotoriba HR 74 B1
Kotorsko BIH 84 B3
Kotor Varoš BIH 84 B2
Kotovsk UA 11 C10
Kotraža SRB 85 C5
Kotronas GR 117 F4
Kötschach A 72 B2
Kötzting D 62 A3
Koudum NL 42 C2
Kouřim CZ 53 C4
Kout na Šumave CZ 62 A4
Kouvola FIN 3 F27
Kovačevac SRB 85 B5
Kovačica SRB 85 A5
Kovdor RUS 3 C29
Kovel' UA 11 A8
Kovilj SRB 75 C5
Kovin SRB 85 B5
Kovren MNE 85 C4
Kowal PL 47 C5
Kowalewo Pomorskie
PL 47 B4
Kowalów PL 45 C6
Kowary PL 53 C5
Köyceğiz TR 119 F3
Kozan TR 16 C7
Kozani GR 116 B3
Kozarac
BIH 84 B1
HR 73 C5
Kozárovce SK 65 B4
Kozelets UA 11 A11
Kozelsk RUS 7 D13
Kozica HR 84 C2
Koziegłowy PL 55 C4
Kozienice PL 55 B6
Kozina SLO 72 C3
Kozje SLO 73 B5
Kozlu TR 118 A6
Kozluk BIH 85 B4
Koźmin PL 54 B2
Koźminek PL 54 B3
Kozolupy CZ 63 A4
Kożuchów PL 53 B5
Kožuhe BIH 84 B3
Kozyatyn UA 11 B10
Kozyürük TR 118 A1
Krackow D 45 B6
Kraddsele S 115 B13
Krąg PL 46 A2
Kragenæs DK 39 E4
Kragerø N 33 D6
Krągi PL 46 B2
Kragujevac SRB 85 B5
Kraiburg D 62 B3
Krajenka PL 46 B2
Krajišnik SRB 75 C5
Krajková CZ 52 C2
Krajné SK 64 B3
Krajnik Dolny PL 45 B6
Krakača BIH 83 A4
Kräklingbo S 37 E5
Kraków = Cracow PL 55 C4
Krakow am See D 44 B4
Králíky CZ 54 C1
Kraljevica HR 73 C4
Kraljevo SRB 85 C5
Kral'ovany SK 65 A5
Král'ov Brod SK 64 B3
Kralovice CZ 52 D3
Kralupy nad Vltavou
CZ 53 C4
Králův Dvůr CZ 63 A5
Kramfors S 115 E14
Kramsach A 72 A1
Kramsk PL 54 A3
Kråmvik N 32 C5
Kranenburg D 50 B2
Krania GR 116 C3
Krania Elasonas GR 116 C4
Kranichfeld D 52 C1
Kranidi GR 117 E5
Kranj SLO 73 B4
Kranjska Gora SLO 72 B3
Krapanj HR 83 C4
Krapina HR 73 B5
Krapje HR 74 C1
Krapkowice PL 54 C2
Kraselov CZ 63 A4
Krašić HR 73 C5
Krāslava LV 7 D9
Kraslice CZ 52 C2
Krasna PL 55 B5
Krasna Lipa CZ 53 C4
Kraśnik PL 11 A7
Krašnja SLO 73 B4
Krásno SK 65 A4
Krásnohorské Podhradie
SK 65 B6
Krasno Polje HR 83 B4
Krasnozavodsk RUS 7 C15
Krasnystaw PL 11 A7
Krasnyy RUS 7 D11
Krasnyy Kholm RUS 7 B14
Krasocin PL 55 C5
Kraszewice PL 54 B3
Kraszkowice PL 54 B3
Kratigos GR 118 C1
Kraubath A 73 A4
Krausnick D 53 A3
Krautheim D 61 A5
Kravaře CZ 53 C4
Kraváre CZ 64 A4
Kravarsko HR 73 C6
Kraznějov CZ 63 A4
Krčedin SRB 75 C5
Kŭrdzhali BG 116 A7
Krefeld D 50 B2
Kregme DK 39 D5
Krembz D 44 B3
Kremenchuk UA 11 B12
Kremenets UA 11 A8
Kremmen D 45 C5
Kremna SRB 85 C4
Kremnica SK 65 B4
Krempe D 43 B6
Krems A 63 B6
Kremsbrücke A 72 B3
Kremsmünster A 63 B5
Křemže CZ 63 B5
Křenov CZ 64 A2
Krepa PL 54 B3
Krępa Krajeńska PL 46 B2
Krepsko PL 46 B2
Kreševo BIH 84 C3
Kressbronn D 61 C5
Krestena GR 117 E3
Kretinga LT 6 D6
Krettsy RUS 7 B12
Kreuth D 62 C2
Kreuzau D 50 C2
Kreuzlingen CH 61 C5
Kreuztal D 50 C3
Krewelin D 45 C5
Krezluk BIH 84 B2
Krieglach A 73 A5
Kriegsfeld D 60 A3
Kriens CH 70 A3
Krimml A 72 A2
Krimpen aan de IJssel
NL 49 B5
Křinec CZ 53 C5
Kristdala S 40 B6
Kristiansand N 33 D5
Kristianstad S 41 C4
Kristiansund N 114 D4
Kristiinankaupunki
FIN 3 E24
Kristinefors S 34 B4
Kristinehamn S 35 C6
Kriváň SK 65 B5
Křivokát CZ 53 C3
Krivoy Rog = Kryvyy Rih
UA 11 C12
Kriź HR 74 C1
Křižanov CZ 64 A2
Križevci HR 74 B1
Krk HR 83 A3
Krka SLO 73 C4
Krnjača SRB 85 B5
Krnjak HR 73 C5
Krnjeuša BIH 83 B5
Krnjevo SRB 85 B6
Krnov CZ 54 C2
Krobia PL 54 B1
Kroczyce PL 55 C4
Krøderen N 34 B1
Krokees GR 117 F4
Krokek S 37 D3
Krokom S 115 D11
Krokowa PL 47 A4
Krokstad-elva N 34 C1
Kroksund N 35 C3
Krolevets UA 7 F12
Kroměříž CZ 64 A3
Krommenie NL 42 C1
Krompachy SK 65 B6
Kromy RUS 7 E13
Kronach D 52 C1
Kronshagen D 44 A2
Kronshtadt RUS 7 B10
Kröpelin D 44 A3
Kropp D 43 A6
Kroppenstedt D 52 B1
Kropstädt D 52 B2
Krościenko nad
Dunajcem PL 65 A6
Kröslin D 45 A5
Krośnice PL 54 B2
Krośniewice PL 55 A4
Krosno PL 10 B6
Krosno Odrzańskie
PL 53 A5
Krostitz D 52 B2
Krotoszyn PL 54 B2
Krottendorf A 73 A5
Krouna CZ 64 A2
Krowiarki PL 54 C3
Krrabë AL 105 B5
Kršan HR 73 C4
Krško SLO 73 C5
Krstac MNE 84 C3
Krstur SRB 75 B5
Křtiny CZ 64 A2
Kruft D 50 C3
Kruishoutem B 49 C4
Krujë AL 105 B5
Krulyewshchyna BY 7 D9
Krumbach
A 73 A6
D 61 B6
Krumovgrad BG 116 A7
Krün D 71 A6
Krupá CZ 53 C3
Krupa na Vrbasu BIH 84 B2
Krupanj SRB 85 B4
Krupina SK 65 B5
Krupka CZ 53 C3
Krupki BY 7 D10
Kruså DK 39 E2
Kruščica BIH 84 B2
Kruševac SRB 85 C6
Kruševo MK 116 A3
Kruszwica PL 47 C4
Kruszyn PL 47 C5
Krute MNE 105 A5
Krychaw BY 7 E11
Krynica PL 65 A6
Krynica Morska PL 47 A5
Kryvyy Rih = Krivoy Rog
UA 11 C12
Krzęcin PL 46 B1
Krzelów PL 54 B1
Krzepice PL 54 C3
Krzepielów PL 53 B6
Krzeszowice PL 55 C4
Krzeszyce PL 45 C7
Krzynowlaga Mała
PL 47 B6
Krzywiń PL 54 B1
Krzyżanowice PL 54 D3
Krzyżowa PL 65 A5
Krzyż Wielkopolski
PL 46 C2
Ksiaz Wielkopolski
PL 55 C5
Książ Wielkopolski
PL 54 A2
Ktębowiec PL 46 B2
Kübekháza H 75 B5
Küblis CH 71 B4
Kuç AL 105 C5
Kuchary PL 54 B2
Kuchl A 63 C4
Kucice PL 47 C6
Kuciste HR 84 D2
Kućište KOS 85 D5
Kuçovë AL 105 C5
Küçükbahçe TR 118 D1
Küçükköy TR 118 C1
Küçükkuyu TR 118 C1
Kucura SRB 75 C4
Kuczbork-Osada PL 47 B6
Kuddby S 37 D3
Kudowa-Zdrój PL 53 C6
Kufstein A 62 C3
Kuggeboda S 41 C5
Kuggörana S 115 F14
Kühbach D 62 B2
Kuhmo FIN 3 D28
Kuhmoinen FIN 3 F26
Kuhnsdorf A 73 B4
Kuhstedt D 43 B5
Kuinre NL 42 C2
Kuivastu EST 6 B7
Kukës AL 10 E6
Kuklin PL 47 B6
Kukljica HR 83 B4
Kukujevci SRB 85 A4
Kula
Srbija SRB 85 B6
Vojvodina SRB 75 C4
TR 119 D3
Kuldīga LV 6 C6
Kulen Vakuf BIH 83 B5
Kulina BIH 84 B3
Kullstedt D 51 B6
Kulmain D 62 A2
Kulmbach D 52 C1
Kulu TR 16 B6
Kumafşarı TR 119 E4
Kumane SRB 75 C5
Kumanovo MK 10 E6
Kumbağ TR 118 B2
Kumdanlı TR 119 D5
Kumkale TR 118 C1
Kumla S 37 C2
Kumlakyrkby S 36 C3
Kumlinge FIN 36 B7
Kumluca TR 119 F5
Kumrovec HR 73 B5
Kunadacs H 75 B4
Kunágota H 75 B6
Kunbaja H 75 B4
Kunda EST 7 B9
Kundl A 72 A1
Kunes N 113 B15
Kunfehértó H 75 B4
Kungälv S 38 B4
Kungsängen S 37 C4
Kungsäter S 40 B2
Kungsbacka S 38 B5
Kungsgården S 36 B3
Kungshamn S 35 D3
Kungs-Husby S 37 C4
Kungsör S 37 C3
Kunhegyes H 75 A5
Kunmadaras H 75 A5
Kunovice CZ 64 A3
Kunów PL 55 C6
Kunowo
Wielkopolskie PL 54 B2
Zachodnio-Pomorskie
PL 45 B6
Kunštát CZ 64 A2
Kunszállás H 75 B4
Kunszentmárton H 75 B5
Kunszentmiklós H 75 A4
Kunžak CZ 63 A6
Künzelsau D 61 A5
Kuolayarvi RUS 113 F18
Kuopio FIN 3 E27
Kuosku FIN 113 E17
Kup
H 74 A2
PL 54 C2
Kupa H 65 B6
Kupari HR 84 D3
Kupci SRB 85 C6
Kupferzell D 61 A5
Kupinec HR 73 C5
Kupinečki Kraljevac
HR 73 C5
Kupinovo SRB 85 B5
Kupirovo HR 83 B5
Kupjak HR 73 C4
Kuppenheim D 61 B4
Kupres BIH 84 C2
Küps D 52 C1
Kurbnesh AL 105 B6
Kurd H 74 B3
Küre TR 16 A6
Kuressaare EST 6 B7
Kurikka FIN 3 E25
Kuřim CZ 64 A2
Kuřivody CZ 53 C4
Kurki PL 47 B6
Kurort Oberwiesenthal
D 52 C2
Kurort Schmalkalden
D 51 C6
Kurort Stolberg D 51 B6
Kurort Wippra D 52 B1
Kurów PL 11 A7
Kurowice PL 55 B4
Kurravaara S 112 E9
Kursk RUS 7 F14
Kursu FIN 113 F17
Kuršumlija SRB 85 C6
Kuršumlijska Banja
SRB 85 C6
Kurşunlu
Bursa TR 118 B4
Çankırı TR 16 A6
Kurtakko FIN 113 E13
Kürten D 50 B3
Kurucaşile TR 16 A6
Kurzelów PL 55 C4
Kusadak SRB 85 B5
Kuşadası TR 119 E2
Kusel D 60 A3
Kusey D 44 C3
Küsnacht CH 70 A3
Kütahya TR 118 C4
Kutenholz D 43 B6
Kutina HR 74 C1
Kutjevo HR 74 C2
Kutná Hora CZ 53 D5
Kutno PL 55 A4
Kuttara FIN 113 D15
Küttingen CH 70 A3
Kúty SK 64 B3
Kuusamo FIN 3 D28
Kuusankoski FIN 3 F27
Kuvshinovo RUS 7 C13
Kuyucak TR 119 E3
Kuzmin SRB 85 A4
Kuźnia Raciborska
PL 54 C3
Kuźnica Czarnkowska
PL 46 C2
Kuźnica Żelichowska
PL 46 C2
Kvaløysletta N 112 C7
Kvalsund N 113 B12
Kvam
Nord-Trøndelag N 114 C8
Oppland N 114 F6
Kvamsøy N 32 A3
Kvænangsbotn N 113 C11
Kvanndal N 32 B3
Kvänum S 35 D5
Kværndrup DK 39 D3
Kvås N 33 D4
Kvasice CZ 64 A3
Kvelde N 35 C1
Kvenna N 114 E5
Kvernaland N 33 D2
Kvibille S 40 C2
Kvicksund S 37 C3
Kvidinge S 41 C3
Kvikkjokk S 112 F6
Kvikne N 114 E7
Kvilda CZ 63 A4
Kville S 35 D3
Kvillsfors S 40 B5
Kvinesdal N 33 D3
Kvinlog N 33 D3
Kvinnherad N 32 C3
Kvissel DK 38 B3
Kvissleby S 115 E14
Kviteseid N 33 C5
Kvitsøy N 33 C2
Kwakowo PL 46 A3
Kwidzyn PL 47 B4
Kwilcz PL 46 C2
Kyjov CZ 64 B3
Kyleakin GB 22 D3
Kyle of Lochalsh GB 22 D3
Kylerhea GB 22 D3
Kylestrome GB 22 C3
Kyllburg D 50 C2
Kyllini GR 117 E3
Kynšperk nad Ohří
CZ 52 C2
Kyperounda CY 120 B1
Kyrenia CY 120 A2
Kyritz D 44 C4
Kyrkesund S 38 A4
Kyrkhult S 41 C4
Kyrksæterøra N 114 D6
Kysucké Nové Mesto
SK 65 A4
Kythira GR 117 F4
Kythréa CY 120 A2
Kyustendil BG 11 E7
Kyyiv = Kiev UA 11 A11
Kyyjärvi FIN 3 E26

L

Laa an der Thaya A 64 B2
La Adrada E 94 B2
Laage D 44 B4
La Alameda E 100 A2
La Alberca E 93 A4
La Alberca de Záncara
E 95 C4
La Albergueria de
Argañán E 93 A4
La Albuera E 93 C4
La Aldea del Portillo del
Busto E 89 B3
La Algaba E 99 B4
La Aliseda de Tormes
E 93 A5
La Almarcha E 95 C4
La Almolda E 90 B2
La Almunia de Doña
Godina E 89 C5
Laanila FIN 113 D16
La Antillas E 98 B3
La Arena E 86 A4
Laatzen D 51 A5
La Aulaga E 99 B4
La Balme-de-Sillingy
F 69 C6
La Bañeza E 88 B1
La Barca de la Florida
E 99 C5
La Barre-de-Monts F 66 B2
La Barre-en-Ouche F 58 B1
La Barrosa E 99 C4
La Barthe-de-Neste F 77 C3
La Bassée F 48 C3
La Bastide-de-Sèrou
F 77 C4
La Bastide-des-Jourdans
F 79 C4
Labastide-Murat F 77 B4
La Bastide-Puylaurent
F 78 B2
Labastide-Rouairoux
F 77 C5
Labastide-St Pierre F 77 C4
La Bathie F 69 C6
Lábatlan H 65 C4
La Baule-Escoublac
F 66 A2
La Bazoche-Gouet F 58 B1
La Bégude-de-Mazenc
F 78 B3
Labenne F 76 C1
La Bernerie-en-Retz F 66 A2
Labin HR 82 A3
La Bisbal d'Empordà
E 91 B6
Łabiszyn PL 46 C3
Lablachère F 78 B3
Lábod H 74 B2
Laboe D 44 A2
La Boissière F 57 A6
Labouheyre F 76 B2
La Bourboule F 68 C2
La Bóveda de Toro E 88 C1
Łabowa PL 65 A6
La Brède F 76 B2
La Bresse F 60 B2
La Bridoire F 69 C5
La Brillanne F 79 C4
Labrit F 76 B2
Labros E 95 A5
La Bruffière F 66 A3
Labruguière F 77 C5
Labrujo P 87 C2
L'Absie F 67 B4
La Bussière F 58 C3
Laç AL 105 B5
La Caillère F 66 B4
Lacalahorra E 100 B2
La Caletta
Cágliari I 110 C1
Núoro I 110 B2
La Calmette F 78 C3
La Calzada de Oropesa
E 93 B5
La Campana E 99 B5
La Cañada E 94 B2
Lacanau F 76 B1
Lacanau-Océan F 76 A1
Lacanche F 69 A4
La Canourgue F 78 B2
La Capelle F 49 D4
Lacapelle-Marival F 77 B4
Laćarak SRB 85 A4
La Cardanchosa E 99 A5
La Caridad E 86 A4
La Carlota E 100 B1
La Carolina E 100 A2
Lacaune F 78 C1
La Cava E 90 C3
La Cavalerie F 78 B2
Laceby GB 27 B5
Lacedónia I 103 B8
La Celle-en-Moravan
F 69 A4
La Celle-St Avant F 67 A5
La Cerca E 89 B3
Láces I 71 B5
La Chaise-Dieu F 68 C3
La Chaize-Giraud F 66 B3
La Chaize-le-Vicomte
F 66 B3
La Chambre F 69 C6
Lachania GR 119 G2
La Chapelaude F 68 B2
La Chapelle-d'Angillon
F 68 A2
La Chapelle-en-
Aalgaudémar F 79 B5
La Chapelle-en-Vercors
F 79 B4
La Chapelle-Glain F 57 C4
La Chapelle-la-Reine
F 58 B3
La Chapelle-Laurent
F 68 C3
La Chapelle-St Luc F 59 B5
La Chapelle-sur-Erdre
F 66 A3
La Chapelle-Vicomtesse
F 58 C2
La Charce F 79 B4
La Charité-sur-Loire
F 68 A3
La Chartre-sur-le-Loir
F 58 C1
La Châtaigneraie F 67 B4
La Châtre F 68 B1
La Chaussée-sur-Marne
F 59 B5
La Chaux-de-Fonds
CH 70 A1
Lachen CH 70 A3
Lachendorf D 44 C2
La Cheppe F 59 A5
La Chèze F 56 B3
Lachowice PL 65 A5
La Ciotat F 79 C4
Łąck PL 47 C5
Läckeby S 40 C6
Läckö S 35 D5
La Clayette F 69 B4
La Clusaz F 69 C6
Lacock GB 29 B5
La Codosera E 93 B3
La Concha E 88 A3
La Condamine-Châtelard
F 79 B5
Láconi I 110 C2
La Contienda E 99 A4
La Coquille F 67 C5
La Coronada E 93 C5
La Côte-St André F 69 C5
La Cotinière F 66 C3
La Courtine F 68 C2
Lacq F 76 C2
La Crau F 79 C5
La Crèche F 67 B4
La Croix F 67 A5
Lacroix-Barrez F 77 B5
Lacroix-St Ouen F 58 A3
Lacroix-sur-Meuse F 60 B1
La Croix-Valmer F 79 C5
La Cumbre E 93 B5
Łącznik PL 54 C2
Lad H 74 B2
Ladbergen D 50 A3
Lądek-Zdrój PL 54 C1
Ladelund D 39 E2
Ladendorf A 64 B2
Ladignac-le-Long F 67 C6
Ladíspoli I 102 B5
Ladoeiro P 93 B3
Ladon F 58 C3
La Douze F 77 A3
Ladushkin RUS 47 A6
Ladybank GB 25 B4
Laer D 50 A3
La Espina E 86 A4
La Estrella E 94 C1
La Farga de Moles E 91 A4
La Fatarella E 90 B3
La Felipa E 95 C5
La Fère F 59 A4
La Ferrière
Indre-et-Loire F 58 C1
Vendée F 66 B3
La Ferrière-en-Parthenay
F 67 B4
La-Ferté-Alais F 58 B3
La Ferté-Bernard F 58 B1
La Ferté-Frênel F 58 B1
La Ferté-Gaucher F 59 B4
La Ferté-Imbault F 68 A1
La Ferté-Macé F 57 B5
La Ferté-Milon F 59 A4
La Ferté-sous-Jouarre
F 59 B4
La Ferté-St-Aubin F 58 C2
La Ferté-St-Cyr F 58 C2
La Ferté-Vidame F 58 B1
La Ferté Villeneuil F 58 C2
La Feuillie F 58 A2
Lafkos GR 116 C5
La Flèche F 57 C5
La Flotte F 66 B3
Lafnitz A 73 A6
La Font de la Figuera
E 101 A5
La Fouillade F 77 B5
Lafrançaise F 77 B4
La Fregeneda E 87 D4
La Fresneda E 90 C3
La Fuencubierta E 99 B6
La Fuente de San Esteban
E 87 D4
La Fulioala E 91 B4
La Gacilly F 57 C3
La Galera E 90 C3
Lagan S 40 C3
Laganadi I 109 A4
Lagarde F 77 C4
La Garde-Freinet F 79 C5
Lagares
Coimbra P 92 A3
Porto P 87 C2
La Garnache F 66 B3
Lagaro I 81 B5
La Garriga E 91 B5
La Garrovilla E 93 C4
Lagartera E 93 B5
La Gaubretière F 66 B3
Lågbol S 36 B5
Lage D 51 B4
Lägerdorf D 43 B6
Lagg GB 24 C2
Laggan GB 22 D4
Laggartorp S 35 C6
Łagiewniki PL 54 C1
La Gineta E 95 C4
Láglio I 71 C4
Lagnieu F 69 C5
Lagny-sur-Marne F 58 B3
Lago
Calabria I 106 B3
Veneto I 72 C2
Lagôa P 98 B2
Lagoaça P 87 C4
Lagonegro I 106 A2
Lagos
GR 116 A7
P 98 B2
Lagosanto I 82 B1
Łagów
Lubuskie PL 46 C1
Świętokrzyskie PL 55 C6
La Granadella
Alicante E 96 C3
Lleida E 90 B3
La Grand-Combe F 78 B3
La Grande-Croix F 69 C4
La Grande-Motte F 78 C3
La Granja d'Escarp E 90 B3
La Granjuela E 93 C5
Lagrasse F 77 C5
La Grave F 79 A5
La Gravelle F 57 B4
Laguardia E 89 B4
La Guardia E 95 C3
La Guardia de Jaén
E 100 B2
Laguarres E 90 A3
Laguenne F 68 C1
Laguépie F 77 B4
La Guerche-de-Bretagne
F 57 C4
La Guerche-sur-l'Aubois
F 68 B2
La Guérinière F 66 B2
Laguiole F 78 B1
Laguna de Duera E 88 C2
Laguna del Marquesado
E 95 B5
Laguna de Negrillos
E 88 B1
Lagundo I 71 B6
Lagunilla E 93 A4
La Haba E 93 C5
Laharie F 76 B2
La Haye-du-Puits F 57 A4
La Haye-Pesnel F 57 B4
Lahden D 43 C4
La Herlière F 48 C3
La Hermida E 88 A2
La Herrera E 95 D4
Laheycourt F 59 B6
La Higuera E 101 A4
La Hiniesta E 88 C1
Lahnstein D 50 C3
Laholm S 40 C3
La Horcajada E 93 A5
La Horra E 88 C3
Lahr D 60 B3
Lahti FIN 3 F26
La Hulpe B 49 C5
La Hutte F 57 B6
Laichingen D 61 B5
L'Aigle F 58 B1
La Iglesuela E 94 B2
La Iglesuela del Cid E 90 C2
Laignes F 59 C5
Laiguéglia I 80 C2
L'Aiguillon-sur-Mer F 66 B3
Laimbach am Ostrong
A 63 B6
Laina E 95 A4
Lainio S 113 E11
Lairg GB 23 C4
La Iruela E 100 B3
Laissac F 78 B1
Laisvall S 115 A14
Láives I 71 B6
La Javie F 79 B5
Lajkovac SRB 85 B5
La Jonchère-St Maurice
F 67 B6
La Jonquera E 91 A5
Lajoskomárom H 74 B3
Lajosmizse H 75 A4
Lak H 65 B6
Lakenheath GB 30 B4
Laki BG 116 A6
Lakitelek H 75 B5
Lakki GR 117 G5
Lakolk DK 39 D1
Łąkorz PL 47 B5
Lakšárska Nová Ves
SK 64 B3
Lakselv N 113 B13
Laksfors N 115 B10
Laktaši BIH 84 B2
La Lantejuela E 99 B5
Lalapaşa TR 118 A1
L'Albagès E 90 B3
Lalbenque F 77 B4
L'Alcudia E 96 B2
L'Aldea E 90 C3
Lalëz AL 105 B5
Lalín E 86 B2
Lalinde F 77 B3
La Línea de la
Concepción E 99 C5
Lalizolle F 68 B3
La Llacuna E 91 B4
Lalley F 79 B4
Lalling D 62 B4
Lalm N 114 F6
La Londe-les-Maures
F 79 C5
La Loupe F 58 B2
La Louvière B 49 C5
L'Alpe-d'Huez F 79 A5
La Luisiana E 99 B5
Laluque F 76 C1
Lam D 62 A4
La Machine F 68 B3
la Maddalena I 110 A2
Lama dei Peligni I 103 A7
Lamadrid E 88 A2
Lamagistére F 77 B3
La Mailleraye-sur-Seine
F 58 A1
La Malène F 78 B2
Lama Mocogno I 81 B4
La Mamola E 100 C2
La Manresana dels Prats
E 91 B4
Lamarche F 60 B1
Lamarche-sur-Saône
F 69 A5
Lamargelle F 69 A4
Lamarosa P 92 B2
Lamarque F 76 A2
Lamas P 92 A2
La Masadera E 90 B2
Lamas de Moaro P 87 B2
Lamastre F 78 B3
La Mata E 94 C2
La Mata de Ledesma
E 94 A1
La Mata de Monteagudo
E 88 B1
Lambach A 63 B4
Lamballe F 56 B3
Lamberhurst GB 31 C4
Lambesc F 79 C4
Lambia GR 117 E3
Lambley GB 25 D5
Lambourn GB 31 C2
Lamego P 87 C3
La Meilleraye-de-Bretagne
F 66 A3
La Ménitré F 67 A4
L'Ametlla de Mar E 90 C3
Lamia GR 116 D4
Lammhult S 40 B4
La Mojonera E 101 C3
La Mole F 79 C5
La Molina E 91 A4
La Monnerie-le-Montel
F 68 C3
La Morera E 93 C4
La Mothe-Achard F 66 B3
Lamothe-Cassel F 77 B4
Lamothe-Montravel F 76 B3
La Mothe-St Héray F 67 B4
Lamotte-Beuvron F 58 C3
La Motte-Chalançon
F 79 B4
La Motte-du-Caire F 79 B5
La Motte-Servolex F 69 C5
Lampertheim D 61 A4
Lampeter GB 28 A3
L'Ampolla E 90 C3
Lamprechtshausen A 62 C3
Lamsfeld D 53 B4
Lamspringe D 51 B6
Lamstedt D 43 B6
La Mudarra E 88 C2
La Muela E 90 B1
La Mure F 79 B4
Lamure-sur-Azergues
F 69 B4
Lana I 71 B6
Lanaja E 90 B2
Lanarce F 78 B2
Lanark GB 25 C4
La Nava E 99 B4
La Nava de Ricomalillo
E 94 C2
La Nava de Santiago
E 93 B4
Lancaster GB 26 A3
Lanchester GB 25 D6
Lanciano I 103 A7
Lancing GB 31 D3
Lançon-Provence F 79 C4
Lancova Vas SLO 73 B5
Landau
Bayern D 62 B3
Rheinland-Pfalz D 61 A4
Landeck A 71 A5
Landen B 49 C6
Landerneau F 56 B1
Landeryd S 40 B3
Landesbergen D 43 C6
Landete E 96 B1
Landévant F 56 C2
Landévennec F 56 B1
Landeyjahöfn IS 111 D5
Landivisiau F 56 B1
Landivy F 57 B4
Landl A 62 C3
Landön S 115 D11
Landos F 78 B2
Landouzy-le-Ville F 59 A5
Landquart CH 71 B4
Landrecies F 49 C4
Landreville F 59 B5
Landriano I 71 C4
Landsberg D 62 B1
Lands-berg D 52 B2
Landsbro S 40 B4
Landscheid D 50 D2
Landshut D 62 B3
Landskrona S 41 D2
Landstuhl D 60 A3
Lanesborough IRL 19 C4
Lanester F 56 C2
Lanestosa E 89 A3
La Neuve-Lyre F 58 B1
La Neuveville CH 70 A2
Langå DK 39 C2
Langada GR 116 D8
Langadas GR 116 B5
Langa de Duero E 89 C3
Langadia GR 117 E4
Langangen N 35 C1
Långared S 40 A2
Långaröd S 41 D3
Långaryd S 40 B3
Långås S 40 C2
Långasjö S 40 C5
Langau A 63 B6
Langeac F 78 A2
Langeais F 67 A5
Langedijk NL 42 C1
Langeln D 51 B6
Langelsheim D 51 B6
Langemark-Poelkapelle
B 48 C3
Langen
Hessen D 51 D4
Niedersachsen D 43 B5
Langenau D 61 B6
Langenberg D 50 B4
Langenbruck CH 70 A2
Langenburg D 61 A5
Längenfeld A 71 A5
Langenfeld D 50 B2
Langenhorn D 43 A5
Langenlois A 63 B6
Langenlonsheim D 60 A3
Langennaudorf D 52 B3
Langenneufnach D 62 B1
Langenthal CH 70 A2
Langenzenn D 62 A1
Langeoog D 43 B4
Langeskov DK 39 D3
Langesund N 35 C1
Langewiesen D 51 C6
Långflon S 34 A4
Langförden D 43 C5
Langhagen D 44 B4
Länghem S 40 B3
Langhirano I 81 B4
Langholm GB 25 C5
Langholt IS 111 D7
Långlöt S 41 C6
Langnau CH 70 B2
Langø DK 39 E4
Langogne F 78 B2
Langon F 76 B2
Langquaid D 62 B3
Långrådna S 37 D3
Langreo E 88 A1
Langres F 59 C6
Långsele S 115 D14
Långserud S 35 C4
Langset N 34 B3
Långshyttan S 36 B3
Langstrand N 113 B12
Långträsk S 115 B17
Langueux F 56 B3
Languidic F 56 C2
Längvik S 37 C5
Langwarden D 43 B5
Langwathby GB 26 A3
Langwedel D 43 C6
Langweid D 62 B1
Langwies CH 71 B4
Lanheses P 87 C2
Lanięta PL 47 C5
Lanildut F 56 B1
Lanjarón E 100 C2
Lanmeur F 56 B2
Lanna
Jönköping S 40 B3
Örebro S 37 C1
Lännaholm S 36 C4
Lannavaara S 113 D10
Lannéanou F 56 B2
Lannemezan F 77 C3
Lanneuville-sur-Meuse
F 59 A6
Lannilis F 56 B1
Lannion F 56 B2
La Nocle-Maulaix F 68 B3
Lanouaille F 67 C6
Lansjärv S 113 F11
Lanškroun CZ 64 A2
Lanslebourg-Mont-Cenis
F 70 C1
Lanta F 77 C4
Lantadilla E 88 B2
Lanton F 76 B1
Lantosque F 79 C6
La Nuez de Arriba E 88 B3
Lanusei I 110 C2
Lanúvio I 102 B5
Lanvollon F 56 B3
Lánycsók H 74 B3
Lanz D 44 B3
Lanza E 86 A2
Lanzada E 86 B2
Lanzahita E 94 B2
Lanžhot CZ 64 B2
Lanzo Torinese I 70 C2
Laole SRB 85 B6
Laon F 59 A4
Laons F 58 B2
La Paca E 101 B4
La Pacaudière F 68 B3
Lapalisse F 68 B3
La Palma d'Ebre E 90 B3
La Palma del Condado
E 99 B4
La Palme F 78 D2
La Palmyre F 66 C3
La Parra E 93 C4
Łapczyna Wola PL 55 C4
La Pedraja de Portillo
E 88 C2
La Peraleja E 95 B4
La Petit-Pierre F 60 B3
Lapeyrade F 76 B2
Lapeyrouse F 68 B2
Lapford GB 28 C4
La Pinilla E 101 B4
Lapithos CY 120 A2
La Plagne F 70 C1
La Plaza E 86 A4
Laplje Selo KOS 85 D6
Laplume F 77 B3
La Pobla de Lillet E 91 A4
La Pobla de Vallbona
E 96 B2
La Pobla Llarga E 96 B2
La Pola de Gordón E 88 B1
la Porta F 102 A2
La Pouëze F 66 A4
Lapoutroie F 60 B3
La Póveda de Soria
E 89 B4
Lapovo SRB 85 B6
Läppe S 37 C2
Lappeenranta FIN 3 F28
Lappoluobbal N 113 C12
La Preste F 91 A5
La Primaube F 77 B5
Lapseki TR 118 B1
Lapua FIN 3 E25
La Puebla de Almoradie
E 95 C3
La Puebla de Cazalla
E 99 B5
La Puebla de los Infantes
E 99 B5
La Puebla del Río E 99 B4
La Puebla de Montalbán
E 94 C2
La Puebla de Roda E 90 A3
La Puebla de Valdavia
E 88 B2
La Puebla de Valverde
E 96 A2
La Pueblanueva E 94 C2
La Puerta de Segura
E 101 A3
La Punt CH 71 B4
L'Áquila I 103 A6
La Quintana E 100 B1
La Quintera E 99 B5

La Rábita
Granada E 100 C2
Jaén E 100 B1
Laracha E 86 A2
Laragh IRL 21 A5
Laragne-Montéglin F 79 B4
La Rambla E 100 B1
l'Arboç E 91 B4
L'Arbresle F 69 C4
Lärbro S 37 E5
Larceveau F 76 C1
Larche
Alpes-de-Haute-Provence F 79 B5
Corrèze F 77 A4
Lårdal N 33 C5
Lærdalsøyri N 32 A4
Lardosa P 92 B3
La Reale I 110 A1
Laredo E 89 A3
La Redondela E 98 B3
La Réole F 76 B2
Largentière F 78 B3
L'Argentière-la-Bessée F 79 B5
Largs GB 24 C3
Lari I 81 C4
La Riera E 86 A4
La Riera de Gaià E 91 B4
La Rinconada E 99 B4
Lariño E 86 B1
Larino I 103 B7
Larisa GR 116 C4
La Rivière-Thibouville F 58 A1
Larkhall GB 25 C4
Larkollen N 35 C2
Larmor-Plage F 56 C2
Larnaca CY 120 B2
Larne GB 19 B6
La Robla E 88 B1
La Roca de la Sierra E 93 B4
La Roche CH 70 B2
La Rochebeaucourtet-Argentine F 67 C5
La Roche-Bernard F 66 A2
La Roche-Canillac F 68 C1
La Roche-Chalais F 67 C5
La Roche Derrien F 56 B2
La Roche-des-Arnauds F 79 B4
La Roche-en-Ardenne B 49 C6
La Roche-en-Brénil F 69 A4
La Rochefoucauld F 67 C5
La Roche-Guyon F 58 A2
La Rochelle F 66 B3
La Roche-Posay F 67 B5
La Roche-sur-Foron F 69 B6
La Roche-sur-Yon F 66 B3
Larochette L 60 A2
La Rochette F 79 B4
La Roda
Albacete E 95 C4
Oviedo E 86 A4
La Roda de Andalucía E 100 B1
Laroquebrou F 77 B5
La Roquebrussanne F 79 C4
Laroque d'Olmes F 77 D4
La Roque-Gageac F 77 B4
La Roque-Ste Marguerite F 78 B2
Laroque-Timbaut F 77 B3
Larouco E 87 B3
Larraga E 89 B5
Larrau F 76 C2
Larrazet F 77 C4
Larsnes N 114 E2
La Rubia E 89 C4
Laruns F 76 C2
Larva E 100 B2
Larvik N 35 C2
La Sagrada E 87 D4
La Salceda E 94 A3
Lasalle F 78 B2
La Salle F 79 B5
la Salute di Livenza I 72 C2
La Salvetat-Peyralés F 77 B5
La Salvetat-sur-Agout F 78 C1
Las Arenas E 88 A2
La Sarraz CH 69 B6
Lasarte E 89 A4
Låsby DK 39 C2
Las Cabezadas E 95 A3
Las Cabezas de San Juan E 99 C5
Las Correderas E 100 A2
Las Cuevas de Cañart E 90 C2
La Seca E 88 C2
La Selva del Camp E 91 B4
La Senia E 90 C3
La Serra E 91 B4
La Seu d'Urgell E 91 A4
La Seyne-sur-Mer F 79 C4
Las Gabias E 100 B2
Las Herencias E 94 C2
Las Herrerias E 98 B3
Łasin PL 47 B5
Lask PL 55 B4
Laska PL 46 B3
Łaskarzow PL 55 B6
Laško SLO 73 B5
Laskowice PL 47 B4
Las Labores E 95 C3
Las Mesas E 95 C4
Las Minas E 101 A4
Las Navas E 100 B1
Las Navas de la Concepción E 99 B5
Las Navas del Marqués E 94 B2
Las Navillas E 94 C2
Las Negras E 101 C4
La Solana E 95 D3
La Souterraine F 67 B6
Las Pajanosas E 99 B4
Laspaules E 90 A3
Las Pedroñas E 95 C4
La Spézia I 81 B3
Las Planes d'Hostoles E 91 A5
Laspuña E 90 A3
Las Rozas
Cantabria E 88 B2
Madrid E 94 B3
Lassan D 45 B5
Lassay-les-Châteaux F 57 B5
Lasseube F 76 C2
Lassigny F 58 A3
La Storta I 102 B5
Lastovo HR 84 D1
Lastras de Cuéllar E 88 C2
Lästringe S 37 D4
Lastrup D 43 C4
Lastva BIH 84 D3
Las Uces E 87 C4
La Suze-sur-Sarthe F 57 C6
Las Veguillas E 94 B1
Las Ventas con Peña Aguilera E 94 C2
Las Ventas de San Julián E 93 A5
Las Villes E 96 A3
Latasa E 76 D1
Látera I 102 A4
Laterza I 104 C2
La Teste F 76 B1
Lathen D 43 C4
Latheron GB 23 C5
La Thuile I 70 C1
Latiano I 105 C3
Latina I 102 B5
Latisana I 72 C3
Látky SK 65 B5
La Toba E 95 B5
La Toledana E 94 C2
La Torre de Cabdella E 90 A3
La Torre de Esteban Hambrán E 94 B2
La Torre del l'Espanyol E 90 B3
La Torresaviñán E 95 B4
La Tour d'Aigues F 79 C4
La Tour de Peilz CH 70 B1
La Tour-du-Pin F 69 C5
Latowicz PL 55 A6
La Tranche-sur-Mer F 66 B3
La Tremblade F 66 C3
La Trimouille F 67 B6
La Trinité F 56 C2
La Trinité-Porhoët F 56 B3
Latrónico I 106 A3
Latronquière F 77 B5
Latterbach CH 70 B2
La Turballe F 66 A2
Laubach D 51 C4
Laubert F 78 B2
Laucha D 52 B1
Lauchhammer D 53 B3
Lauchheim D 61 B6
Lauda-Königshofen D 61 A5
Laudal N 33 D4
Lauder GB 25 C5
Lauenau D 51 A5
Lauenburg D 44 B2
Lauf D 62 A2
Laufach D 51 C5
Laufen
CH 70 A2
D 62 C3
Lauffen D 61 A5
Laugar IS 111 B8
Laugarás IS 111 C5
Laugarbakki IS 111 B5
Laugarvatn IS 111 C5
Laugharne GB 28 B3
Lauingen D 61 B6
Laujar de Andarax E 100 C3
Laukaa FIN 3 E26
Lauker S 115 B16
Laukvik N 112 E3
La Uña E 88 A1
Launceston GB 28 C3
La Unión E 101 B5
Launois-sur-Vence F 59 A5
Laupheim D 61 B5
Lauragh IRL 20 C2
Laureana di Borrello I 106 C3
Laurencekirk GB 25 B5
Laurencetown IRL 20 A3
Laurenzana I 104 C1
Lauria I 106 A2
Laurière F 67 B6
Laurieston GB 24 D3
Laurino I 103 C8
Lausanne CH 69 B6
Laussonne F 78 B3
Lauta D 53 B4
Lautenthal D 51 B6
Lauterach A 71 A4
Lauterbach D 51 C5
Lauterbrunnen CH 70 B2
Lauterecken D 60 A3
Lauterhofen D 62 A2
Lautrec F 77 C5
Lauvsnes N 114 C7
Lauvvlk N 33 D3
Lauzerte F 77 B4
Lauzès F 77 B4
Lauzun F 77 B3
Lavagna I 80 B3
Laval F 57 B5
La Vall d'Uixó E 96 B2
Lavamünd A 73 B4
Lavara GR 118 A1
Lavardac F 76 B3
Lavaris P 92 A2
Lavarone I 71 C6
Lavau F 59 C3
Lavaur F 77 C4
La Vecilla de Curueño E 88 B1
La Vega
Asturias E 88 A1
Asturias E 88 A1
Cantabria E 88 A2
Lavelanet F 77 D4
La Velilla E 94 A3
La Velles E 94 A1
Lavello I 104 B1
Lavelsloh D 43 C5
Lavenham GB 30 B4
Laveno I 70 C3
La Ventosa E 95 B4
Lavezzola I 81 B5
Laviano I 103 C8
La Victoria E 100 B1
La Vid E 89 C3
Lavik N 32 A2
La Vilavella E 96 B2
La Vilella Baixa E 90 B3
La Villa de Don Fadrique E 95 C3
Lavilledieu F 78 B3
La Villedieu F 67 B4
La Ville Dieu-du-Temple F 77 B4
Lavinio-Lido di Enea I 102 B5
Lav ìs I 71 B6
Lavit F 77 C3
Lavoncourt F 60 C1
Lavos P 92 A2
La Voulte-sur-Rhône F 78 B3
Lavoûte-Chilhac F 68 C3
Lavradio P 92 C1
Lavre P 92 C2
Lavrio GR 117 E6
La Wantzenau F 60 B3
Lawers GB 24 B3
Ławy PL 45 C6
Laxå S 37 D1
Laxamýri IS 111 B8
Laxe E 86 A2
Laxey GB 26 A1
Laxford Bridge GB 22 C3
Laxhall S 35 D5
Laxsjö S 115 D11
Laxtjarn S 34 B6
Laxvik S 40 C2
Laxviken S 115 D11
La Yesa E 96 B2
Laza E 87 B3
Lazarevac SRB 85 B5
Lazarev Krst MNE 105 A5
Lazarevo SRB 75 C5
Lazise I 71 C5
Łaziska Grn. PL 54 C3
Lazkao E 89 A4
Lázně Bělohrad CZ 53 C5
Lázně Bohdaneč CZ 53 C5
Lázně Kynžvart CZ 52 C2
Lazonby GB 26 A3
La Zubia E 100 B2
Łazy PL 46 A2
Lazzaro I 109 B4
Lea GB 27 B5
Leadburn GB 25 C4
Leadhills GB 25 C4
Leap IRL 20 C2
Leatherhead GB 31 C3
Łeba PL 46 A3
Lebach D 60 A2
Le Barp F 76 B2
Le Bar-sur-Loup F 79 C5
Le Béage F 78 B3
Le Beausset F 79 C4
Lebedyn UA 7 F13
Lebekke B 49 B5
Lébény H 64 C3
Le Bessat F 69 C4
Le Blanc F 67 B6
Le Bleymard F 78 B2
Łebno PL 47 A4
Leboreiro E 87 B3
Lębork PL 46 A3
Le Boullay-Mivoye F 58 B2
Le Boulou F 91 A5
Le Bourg F 77 B4
Le Bourg-d'Oisans F 79 A5
Le Bourget-du-Lac F 69 C5
Le Bourgneuf-la-Forêt F 57 B5
Le Bousquet d'Orb F 78 C2
Le Brassus CH 69 B6
Le Breuil F 68 B3
Le Breuil-en-Auge F 57 A6
Lebrija E 99 C4
Lebring A 73 B5
Le Brusquet F 79 B5
Le Bry CH 70 B2
Le Bugue F 77 B3
Le Buisson F 77 B3
Lebus D 45 C6
Lebusa D 52 B3
Leca da Palmeira P 87 C2
Le Caloy F 76 C2
Le Cap d'Agde F 78 C2
Le Cateau Cambrésis F 49 C4
Le Caylar F 78 C2
Le Cayrol F 78 B1
Lecce I 105 C4
Lecco I 71 C4
Lécera E 90 B2
Lećevica HR 83 C5
Lech A 71 A5
Le Chambon-Feugerolles F 69 C4
Le Chambon-sur-Lignon F 78 A3
Le Château d'Oléron F 66 C3
Le Châtelard F 69 C6
Le Châtelet F 68 B2
Le Chatelet-en-Brie F 58 B3
Lechbruck D 62 C1
Lechena GR 117 E3
Le Chesne F 59 A5
Le Cheylard F 78 B3
Lechlade GB 29 B6
Lechovice CZ 64 B2
Leciñena E 90 B2
Leck D 39 E1
Le Collet-de-Deze F 78 B2
Le Conquet F 56 B1
Le Creusot F 69 B4
Le Croisic F 66 A2
Le Crotoy F 48 C2
Lectoure F 77 C3
Łęczyca
Łódzkie PL 55 A4
Zachodnio-Pomorskie PL 45 B7
Ledaña E 95 C5
Ledbury GB 29 A5
Lede B 49 C4
Ledečnad Sazavou CZ 63 A6
Ledenice CZ 63 B5
Le Deschaux F 69 B5
Ledesma E 87 C4
Lédignan F 78 C3
Lédigos E 88 B2
Ledmore GB 22 C4
Lednice CZ 64 B2
Lednicke-Rovné SK 64 A4
Le Donjon F 68 B3
Le Dorat F 67 B6
Lędyczek PL 46 B2
Lędziny PL 55 C4
Leeds GB 27 B4
Leek
GB 26 B3
NL 42 B3
Leenaun IRL 18 C2
Leens NL 42 B3
Leer D 43 B4
Leerdam NL 49 B6
Leerhafe D 43 B4
Leese D 43 C6
Leeuwarden NL 42 B2
Leezen D 44 B2
Le Faou F 56 B1
Le Faoüet F 56 B2
Lefka CY 120 A1
Lefkada GR 116 D2
Lefkimis GR 116 C2
Lefkoniko CY 120 A2
Le Folgoet F 56 B1
Le Fossat F 77 C4
Le Fousseret F 77 C4
Le Fugeret F 79 B5
Leganés E 94 B3
Legau D 61 C6
Le Gault-Soigny F 59 B4
Legbąd PL 46 B3
Legé F 66 B3
Lège-Cap-Ferret F 76 B1
Legionowo PL 55 A5
Léglise B 60 A1
Legnago I 71 C6
Legnano I 70 C3
Legnaro I 72 C1
Legnica PL 53 B6
Łęgowo PL 47 A4
Legrad HR 74 B1
Le Grand-Bornand F 69 C6
Le-Grand-Bourg F 67 B6
Le Grand-Lucé F 58 C1
Le Grand-Pressigny F 67 B5
Le Grand-Quevilly F 58 A2
Le Grau-du-Roi F 78 C3
Léguevin F 77 C4
Legutiano E 89 B4
Le Havre F 57 A6
Lehesten D 52 C1
Lehnice SK 64 B3
Lehnin D 52 A2
Le Hohwald F 60 B3
Le Houga F 76 C2
Lehrberg D 61 A6
Lehre D 51 A6
Lehrte D 44 C1
Lehsen D 44 B3
Leibnitz A 73 B5
Leicester GB 30 B2
Leiden NL 49 A5
Leidschendam NL 49 A5
Leigh GB 26 B3
Leighlinbridge IRL 21 B5
Leighton Buzzard GB 31 C3
Leignon B 49 C6
Leikanger N 114 E2
Leimen D 61 A4
Leinefelde D 51 B6
Leinesfjord N 112 E4
Leintwardine GB 29 A5
Leipojärvi S 112 E10
Leipzig D 52 B2
Leira
Nordland N 115 A10
Oppland N 32 B6
Leiråmoen N 112 F3
Leiria P 92 B2
Leirvik
Hordaland N 32 C2
Sogn og Fjordane N 32 A2
Leisach A 72 B2
Leisnig D 52 B2
Leiston GB 30 B5
Leitholm GB 25 C5
Leitrim IRL 18 C3
Leitza E 76 C1
Leitzkau D 52 A1
Lejkowo PL 46 A2
Lekani GR 116 A6
Łękawa PL 55 B4
Łękawica PL 65 A5
Lekbibaj AL 105 A5
Lekeitio E 89 A4
Lekenik HR 73 C6
Lekeryd S 40 B4
Leknes N 112 D2
Łęknica PL 53 B4
Leksand S 36 B1
Leksvik N 114 D7
Lekunberri E 76 C1
Lekvattnet S 34 B4
Le Lardin-St Lazare F 67 C6
Le Lauzet-Ubaye F 79 B5
Le Lavandou F 79 C5
Le Lion-d'Angers F 57 C5
Lelkowo PL 47 A6
Le Locle CH 70 A1
Le Loroux-Bottereau F 66 A3
Le Louroux-Béconnais F 66 A4
Lelów PL 55 C4
Le Luc F 79 C5
Le Lude F 57 C6
Lelystad NL 42 C2
Lem
Ringkøbing DK 39 C1
Viborg Amt. DK 38 C1
Le Malzieu-Ville F 78 B2
Le Mans F 57 B6
Le Mas-d'Azil F 77 C4
Le Massegros F 78 B2
Le Mayet-de-Montagne F 68 B3
Le May-sur-Evre F 66 A4
Lembach F 60 A3
Lemberg F 60 A3
Lembèye F 76 C2
Lemelerveld NL 42 C3
Le Mêle-sur-Sarthe F 58 B1
Le Ménil F 60 B2
Le Merlerault F 57 B6
Le Mesnil-sur-Oger F 59 B5
Lemförde D 43 C5
Lemgo D 51 A4
Le Miroir F 69 B5
Lemland FIN 36 B7
Lemmer NL 42 C2
Le Molay-Littry F 57 A5
Le Monastier-sur-Gazeille F 78 B2
Le Monêtier-les-Bains F 79 B5
Le Mont-Dore F 68 C2
Le Montet F 68 B3
Le Mont-St Michel F 57 B4
Lempdes F 68 C3
Le Muret F 76 B2
Le Muy F 79 C5
Lemvig DK 38 C1
Lemwerder D 43 B5
Lena N 34 B2
Lenart SLO 73 B5
Lenartovce SK 65 B6
Lenauheim RO 75 C5
Lencloître F 67 B5
Lend A 72 A3
Lendalfoot GB 24 C3
Lendava SLO 73 B6
Lendery RUS 3 E29
Lendinara I 81 A5
Lendorf A 72 B3
Lendum DK 38 B3
Le Neubourg F 58 A1
Lengefeld D 52 C3
Lengerich
Niedersachsen D 43 C4
Nordrhein-Westfalen D 50 A3
Lenggries D 62 C2
Lengyeltóti H 74 B2
Lenhovda S 40 C5
Lenk CH 70 B2
Lennartsfors S 35 C3
Lennestadt D 50 B4
Lennoxtown GB 24 C3
Leno I 71 C5
Lénola I 103 B6
Le Nouvion-en-Thiérache F 49 C4
Lens
B 49 C4
F 48 C3
Lensahn D 44 A2
Lens Lestang F 69 C5
Lensvik N 114 D6
Lentellais E 87 B3
Lentföhrden D 44 B1
Lenti H 74 B1
Lentini I 109 B3
Lenungshammar S 35 C4
Lenzburg CH 70 A3
Lenzen D 44 B3
Lenzerheide CH 71 B4
Leoben A 73 A5
Leogang A 72 A2
Leominster GB 29 A5
León E 88 B1
Léon F 76 C1
Leonberg D 61 B5
Léoncel F 79 B4
Leonding A 63 B5
Leonessa I 102 A5
Leonforte I 109 B3
Leonidio GR 117 E4
Leopoldsburg B 49 B6
Leopoldsdorf im Marchfeld A 64 B2
Leopoldshagen D 45 B5
Leova MD 11 C10
Le Palais F 66 A1
Le Parcq F 48 C3
Lepe E 98 B3
Le Péage-de-Roussillon F 69 C4
Le Pellerin F 66 A3
Lepenac
MNE 85 D4
SRB 85 C6
Lepenou GR 116 D3
Le Perthus F 91 A5
Le Pertuis F 78 A3
Le Petit-Bornand F 69 C6
Lephin GB 22 D2
L'Épine F 79 B4
Le Poët F 79 B4
Lepoglava HR 73 B6
Le Poirè-sur-Vie F 66 B3
Le Pont CH 69 B6
Le Pont-de-Montvert F 78 B2
Le Porge F 76 B1
Le Porge-Océan F 76 B1
Le Portel F 48 C2
Le Pouldu F 56 C2
Le Pouliguen F 66 A2
Leppäjärvi FIN 113 D12
Leppävirta FIN 3 E27
Leppin D 44 C3
le Prese I 71 B5
Lepsény H 74 B3
Le Puy-en-Velay F 78 A2
Le Puy-Ste Réparade F 79 C4
Le Quesnoy F 49 C4
Léquile I 105 C4
Le Rayol F 79 C5
Lercara Friddi I 108 B2
Lerdal S 35 D3
Leré F 68 A2
Lérici I 81 B3
Lerin E 89 B5
Lerma E 88 B3
Lerm-et-Musset F 76 B2
Lermoos A 71 A5
Le Roeulx B 49 C5
Le Rouget F 77 B5
Lérouville F 60 B1
Le Rozier F 78 B2
Lerum S 40 B2
Le Russey F 70 A1
Lervik N 35 C2
Lerwick GB 22 A7
Lés E 77 D3
Les Abrets F 69 C5
Les Aix-d'Angillon F 68 A2
Lešak KOS 85 C5
Lesaka E 76 C1
Les Ancizes-Comps F 68 C2
Les Andelys F 58 A2
Les Arcs
Savoie F 70 C1
Var F 79 C5
Les-Aubiers F 67 B4
Les Baux-de-Provence F 78 C3
Les Bézards F 58 C3
Les Bois CH 70 A1
Les Bordes F 58 C3
Les Borges Blanques E 90 B3
Les Borges del Camp E 91 B4
Les Brunettes F 68 B3
Lesbury GB 25 C6
Les Cabannes F 77 D4
L'Escala E 91 A6
Lescar F 76 C2
L'Escarène F 80 C1
Lesce SLO 73 B4
Lescheraines F 69 C6
Lesconil F 56 C1
Les Contamines-Montjoie F 70 C1
les Coves de Vinroma E 90 C3
Les Déserts F 69 C5
Les Deux-Alpes F 79 B5
Les Diablerets CH 70 B2
Lesdins F 59 A4
Les Echelles F 69 C5
Le Sel-de-Bretagne F 57 C4
Le Sentier CH 69 B6
Les Escaldes AND 91 A4
Les Essarts F 66 B3
Les Estables F 78 B3
Les Eyzies-de-Tayac F 77 B4
Les Gets F 70 B1
Les Grandes-Ventes F 58 A2
Les Haudères CH 70 B2
Les Herbiers F 66 B3
Les Hôpitaux-Neufs F 69 B6
Lesično SLO 73 B5
Lésina I 103 B8
Lesjaskog N 114 E5
Lesjöfors S 34 C6
Leskovac SRB 10 E6
Leskova Dolina SLO 73 C4
Leskovec
CZ 64 A3
SLO 73 C5
Leskovice CZ 63 A6
Leskovik AL 116 B2
Leslie GB 25 B4
Les Lucs-sur-Boulogne F 66 B3
Les Mages F 78 B3
Lesmahagow GB 25 C4
Les Mazures F 59 A5
Les Mées F 79 B4
Lesmont F 59 B5
Les Mureaux F 58 B2
Leśna PL 53 B5
Lesneven F 56 B1
Leśnica PL 54 C3
Lešnica SRB 85 B4
Leśniów Wielkoplski PL 53 B5
Lesnoye RUS 7 B13
Les Omergues F 79 B4
Les Ormes-sur-Voulzie F 59 B4
Les Orres F 79 B5
Le Souquet F 76 C1
Lesparre-Médoc F 66 C4
l'Espérance F 59 A4
l'Esperou F 78 B2
Les Pieux F 57 A4
Lesponne F 76 C3
Les Ponts-de-Cé F 67 A4
Les Ponts-de-Martel CH 70 B1
Les Praz F 70 C1
L'Espunyola E 91 A4
Les Riceys F 59 C5
Les Roches F 69 C4
Les Rosaires F 56 B3
Les Rosiers F 67 A4
Les Rousses F 69 B6
Les Sables-d'Olonne F 66 B3
Lessach A 72 A3
Lessay F 57 A4
Lessebo S 40 C5
Les Settons F 68 A4
Lessines B 49 C4
L'Estany E 91 B5
Les Ternes F 78 A1
Lesterps F 67 B5
Les Thilliers en-Vexin F 58 A2
Les Touches F 66 A3
Les Trois Moûtiers F 67 A5
Les Vans F 78 B3
Les Verrières CH 69 B6
Les Vignes F 78 B2
Leswalt GB 24 D2
Leszno
Mazowieckie PL 55 A5
Wielkopolskie PL 54 B1
Leszno Górne PL 53 B5
Letchworth GB 31 C3
Le Teil F 78 B3
Le Teilleul F 57 B5
Le Temple-de-Bretagne F 66 A3
Letenye H 74 B1
Le Theil F 58 B1
Le Thillot F 60 C2
Letino I 103 B7
Letohrad CZ 54 C1
Le Touquet-Paris-Plage F 48 C2
Le Touvet F 69 C5
Letovice CZ 64 A2
Le Translay F 48 D2
Le Tréport F 48 C2
Letschin D 45 C6
Letterfrack IRL 18 C2
Letterkenny IRL 19 B4
Lettermacaward IRL 18 B3
Lettoch GB 23 D5
Letur E 101 A3
Letux E 90 B2
Letzlingen D 44 C3
Leucate F 78 D2
Leuchars GB 25 B5
Leuglay F 59 C5
Leuk CH 70 B2
Leukerbad CH 70 B2
Leumrabhagh GB 22 C2
Leuna D 52 B2
Leusden NL 49 A6
Leutenberg D 52 C1
Leuterschach D 61 C6
Leutershausen D 61 A6
Leutkirch D 61 C6
Leuven B 49 C5
Leuze-en-Hainaut B 49 C4
Le Val F 79 C5
Le Val-André F 56 B3
Le Val-d'Ajol F 60 C2
Levan AL 105 C5
Levanger N 114 D8
Levanjska Varoš HR 74 C3
Lévanto I 80 B3
Levaré F 57 B5
Levata I 71 C5
Leveld N 32 B5
Leven
East Yorkshire GB 27 B5
Fife GB 25 B5
Leverano I 105 C3
Le Verdon-sur-Mer F 66 C3
Leverkusen D 50 B2
Levern D 43 C5
Le Vernet F 79 B5
Levet F 68 B2
Levice SK 65 B4
Lévico Terme I 71 B6
Levie F 102 B2
Levier F 69 B6
Le Vigan F 78 C2
Lévignen F 59 A3
le Ville I 82 C1
Levinovac HR 74 C2
Le Vivier-sur-Mer F 57 B4
Levoča SK 65 A6
Levroux F 67 B6
Lewes GB 31 D4
Lewin Brzeski PL 54 C2
Lewisham GB 31 C3
Leyburn GB 27 A4
Leyland GB 26 B3
Leysdown-on-Sea GB 31 C4
Leysin CH 70 B2
Lezajsk PL 11 A7
Lézardrieux F 56 B2
Lézat-sur-Léze F 77 C4
Lezay F 67 B4
Lezhë AL 105 B5
Lézignan-Corbières F 78 C1
Lezignan-la-Cèbe F 78 C2
Ležimir SRB 75 C4
Lézinnes F 59 C5
Lezoux F 68 C3
Lezuza E 95 D4
Lgov RUS 7 F13
Lhenice CZ 63 B5
Lherm F 77 C4
Lhommaizé F 67 B5
L'Hospitalet F 91 A4
L'Hospitalet de l'Infant E 90 C3
L'Hospitalet de Llobregat E 91 B5
L'Hospitalet-du-Larzac F 78 C2
Lhuître F 59 B5
Liancourt F 58 A3
Liart F 59 A5
Liatorp S 40 C4
Liatrie GB 22 D4
Libáň CZ 53 C5
Libceves CZ 53 C3
Liběchov CZ 53 C4
Liber E 86 B3
Liberec CZ 53 C5
Libiąż PL 55 C4
Libina CZ 64 A3
Libochovice CZ 53 C4
Libofshë AL 105 C5
Libohovë AL 116 B2
Libourne F 76 B2
Libramont B 59 A6
Librazhd AL 116 A2
Librilla E 101 B4
Libros E 96 A1
Licata I 108 B2
Licciana Nardi I 81 B4
Licenza I 102 A5
Liceros E 89 C3
Lich D 51 C4
Lichères-près-Aigremont F 59 C4
Lichfield GB 27 C4
Lichtenau
A 63 B6
D 51 B4
Lichtenberg D 52 C1
Lichtenfels D 52 C1
Lichtensteig CH 71 A4
Lichtenstein D 52 C2
Lichtenvoorde NL 50 B2
Lichtervelde B 49 B4
Lička Jesenica HR 83 A4
Lickershamn S 37 E5
Lički Osik HR 83 B4
Ličko Lešce HR 83 B4
Licodía Eubéa I 109 B3
Licques F 48 C2
Lida BY 7 E8
Lidar N 32 A6
Lidečko CZ 64 A4
Liden S 115 E13
Lidhult S 40 C3
Lidköping S 35 D5
Lido I 72 C2
Lido Azzurro I 104 C3
Lido degli Estensi I 82 B1
Lido degli Scacchi I 82 B1
Lido della Nazioni I 82 B1
Lido di Camaiore I 81 C4
Lido di Casalbordino I 103 A7
Lido di Castél Fusano I 102 B5
Lido di Cincinnato I 102 B5
Lido di Classe I 82 B1
Lido di Fermo I 82 C2
Lido di Fondi I 103 B6
Lido di Jésolo I 72 C2
Lido di Lícola I 103 C7
Lido di Metaponto I 104 C2
Lido di Óstia I 102 B5
Lido di Policoro I 106 A3
Lido di Pomposa I 82 B1
Lido di Savio I 82 B1
Lido di Scanzano I 104 C2
Lido di Siponto I 104 B1
Lido di Squillace I 106 C3
Lido di Volano I 82 B1
Lido Riccio I 103 A7
Lidoriki GR 116 D4
Lido Silvana I 104 C3
Lidsjöberg S 115 C12
Lidzbark PL 47 B5
Lidzbark Warmiński PL 47 A6
Liebenau
A 63 B5
D 43 C6
Liebenwalde D 45 C5
Lieberose D 53 B4
Liebling RO 75 C6
Lieboch A 73 B5
Liège B 49 C6
Lieksa FIN 3 E29
Lienen D 50 A3
Lienz A 72 B2
Liepāja LV 6 C6
Lier B 49 B5
Lierbyen N 34 C2
Liernais F 69 A4
Liesing A 72 B2
Liestal CH 70 A2
Liétor E 101 A4
Lieurac F 77 D4
Lieurey F 58 A1
Liévin F 48 C3
Liezen A 73 A4
Liffol-le-Grand F 60 B1
Lifford IRL 19 B4
Liffré F 57 B4
Ligardes F 77 B3
Lignano Sabbiadoro I 72 C3
Ligne F 66 A3
Lignières F 68 B2
Ligny-en-Barrois F 59 B6
Ligny-le-Châtel F 59 C4
Ligoła Polska PL 54 B2
Ligourio GR 117 E5
Ligowo PL 47 C5
Ligueil F 67 A5
Lijeva Rijeka MNE 85 D4
Likavka SK 65 A5
Likenäs S 34 B5
Likhoslavl RUS 7 C13
Lild Strand DK 38 B1
L'Île-Bouchard F 67 A5
l'Île-Rousse F 102 A1
Lilienfeld A 63 B6
Lilienthal D 43 B5
Lilla Edet S 35 D4
Lilla Tjärby S 40 C3
Lille
B 49 B5
F 49 C4
Lillebonne F 58 A1
Lillehammer N 34 A2
Lillerød DK 41 D2
Lillers F 48 C3
Lillesand N 33 D5
Lillestrøm N 34 C3
Lillhärdal S 115 F11
Lillkyrka S 37 C4
Lillo E 95 C3
Lillögda S 115 C14
Lima S 34 B5
Limanowa PL 65 A6
Limassol CY 120 B2
Limavady GB 19 A5
Limbach-Oberfrohna D 52 C2
Limbaži LV 6 C8
Limbourg B 50 C1
Limburg D 50 C4
Lime DK 39 C3
Limedsforsen S 34 B5
Limenaria GR 116 B6
Limenas Chersonisou GR 117 G7
Limerick IRL 20 B3
Limes I 71 C5
Limésy F 58 A1
Limmared S 40 B3
Limni GR 116 D5
Limoges F 67 C6
Limogne-en-Quercy F 77 B4
Limoise F 68 B3
Limone Piemonte I 80 B1
Limone sul Garda I 71 C5
Limons F 68 C3
Limours F 58 B3
Limoux F 77 C5
Linares E 100 A2
Linares de Mora E 90 C2
Linares de Riofrio E 93 A5
Linaria GR 116 D6
Linas de Broto E 90 A2
Lincoln GB 27 B5
Lind DK 39 C1
Lindås N 32 B2
Lindau D 71 A4
Lindberget N 34 A3
Lindelse DK 39 E3
Lindenberg D 53 A4
Lindenberg im Allgäu D 61 C5
Lindern D 43 C4
Linderöd S 41 D3
Lindesberg S 37 C2
Lindesnäs S 36 B1
Lindesnes N 33 E4
Lindholmen S 37 C5
Lindknud DK 39 D2
Lindlar D 50 B3
Lindö S 37 D3
Lindome S 38 B5
Lindos GR 119 F3
Lindoso P 87 C2
Lindow D 45 C4
Lindsdal S 40 C6
Lindshammar S 40 B5
Lindstedt D 44 C3
Lindved DK 39 D2
Líně CZ 63 A4
Lingbo S 36 A3
Lingen D 43 C4
Linghed S 36 B2
Linghem S 37 D2
Linguaglossa I 109 B4
Linia PL 46 A3
Linie PL 45 B6
Liniewo PL 47 A4
Linkenheim D 61 A4
Linköping S 37 D2
Linksness GB 23 C5
Linlithgow GB 25 C4
Linneryd S 40 C5
Linnes Hammarby S 36 C4
Linnich D 50 C2
Linsell S 115 E10
Linslade GB 31 C3
Linthal CH 70 B4
Linyola E 90 B3
Linz
A 63 B5
D 50 C3
Liomseter N 32 A6
Lionárisso CY 120 A3
Lioni I 103 C8
Lion-sur-Mer F 57 A5
Lipany SK 65 A6
Lipar SRB 75 C4
Lípari I 106 C1
Lipcani MD 11 B9
Liperi FIN 3 E28
Liphook GB 31 C3
Lipiany PL 45 B6
Lipik HR 74 C2
Lipka PL 46 B3
Lipki Wielkie PL 46 C1
Lipnica PL 46 B3
Lipnica Murowana PL 65 A6
Lipnik PL 55 C6
Lipník nad Bečvou CZ 64 A3
Lipno
Kujawsko-Pomorskie PL 47 C5
Łódzkie PL 54 B3
Liposthey F 76 B2
Lipovac HR 84 A4
Lipovec CZ 64 A2
Lipovets UA 11 B10
Lipovljani HR 74 C1
Lipowina PL 47 A5
Lippborg D 50 B4
Lippó H 74 C3
Lippoldsberg D 51 B5
Lippstadt D 51 B4
Lipsko PL 55 B6
Liptál CZ 64 A3
Liptovská-Lúžna SK 65 B5
Liptovská Osada SK 65 B5
Liptovská-Teplička SK 65 B6
Liptovský Hrádok SK 65 A5
Liptovský Milkuláš SK 65 A5
Lipusz PL 46 A3
Lipůvka CZ 64 A2
Liré F 66 A3
Lis AL 105 B6
Lisa SRB 85 C5
Lisac BIH 84 B2
Lisbellaw GB 19 B4
Lisboa = Lisbon P 92 C1
Lisbon = Lisboa P 92 C1
Lisburn GB 19 B5
Liscannor IRL 20 B2
Lisdoonvarna IRL 20 A2
Lisewo PL 47 B4
Lisia Góra PL 55 C6
Lisięcice PL 54 C2
Lisieux F 57 A6
Lisjö S 37 C3
Liskeard GB 28 C3
L'Isle CH 69 B6
L'Isle-Adam F 58 A3
L'Isle-de-Noé F 77 C3
L'Isle-en-Dodon F 77 C3
L'Isle-Jourdain
Gers F 77 C4
Vienne F 67 B5
L'Isle-sur-la-Sorgue F 79 C4
L'Isle-sur-le Doubs F 69 A6
L'Isle-sur-Serein F 59 C5
Lisle-sur-Tarn F 77 C4
Lismore IRL 21 B4
Lisnaskea GB 19 B4
Lišov CZ 63 A5
Lisów
Lubuskie PL 45 C6
Lisów *continued*
Śląskie PL 54 C3
Lisse NL 49 A5
Lissycasey IRL 20 B2
List D 39 D1
Listerby S 41 C5
Listowel IRL 20 B2
Listrac-Médoc F 76 A2
Liszki PL 55 C4
Liszkowo PL 46 B3
Lit S 115 D11
Litava SK 65 B5
Litcham GB 30 B4
Lit-et-Mixe F 76 B1
Litija SLO 73 B4
Litke H 65 B5
Litlabø N 32 C2
Litochoro GR 116 B4
Litoměřice CZ 53 C4
Litomyšl CZ 64 A2
Litovel CZ 64 A3
Litschau A 63 B6
Littlehampton GB 31 D3
Littleport GB 30 B4
Littleton IRL 21 B4
Little Walsingham GB 30 B4
Litvinov CZ 52 C3
Livadero GR 116 B3
Livadhia CY 120 B2
Livadi GR 116 B4
Livadia GR 116 D4
Livarot F 57 B6
Liveras CY 120 A1
Livernon F 77 B4
Liverovici MNE 85 D4
Liverpool GB 26 B3
Livigno I 71 B5
Livingston GB 25 C4
Livno BIH 84 C1
Livold SLO 73 C4
Livorno I 81 C4
Livorno Ferraris I 70 C3
Livron-sur-Drôme F 78 B3
Livry-Louvercy F 59 A5
Lixheim F 60 B3
Lixouri GR 117 D2
Lizard GB 28 D2
Lizy-sur-Ourcq F 59 A4
Lizzano I 104 C3
Lizzano in Belvedere I 81 B4
Lješane KOS 85 D5
Ljig SRB 85 B5
Ljørdalen N 34 A4
Ljosland N 33 D4
Ljubija BIH 83 B5
Ljubinje BIH 84 D3
Ljubljana SLO 73 B4
Ljubno ob Savinji SLO 73 B4
Ljubovija SRB 85 B4
Ljubuški BIH 84 C2
Ljugarn S 37 E5
Ljung S 40 B3
Ljunga S 37 D3
Ljungaverk S 115 E13
Ljungby S 40 C3
Ljungbyhed S 41 C3
Ljungbyholm S 40 C6
Ljungdalen S 115 E9
Ljungsarp S 40 B3
Ljungsbro S 37 D2
Ljungskile S 35 D3
Ljusdal S 115 F13
Ljusfallshammar S 37 D2
Ljusne S 36 A4
Ljusterö S 37 C5
Ljutomer SLO 73 B6
Lladurs E 91 A4
Llafranc E 91 B6
Llagostera E 91 B5
Llanaelhaiarn GB 26 C1
Llanarth GB 28 A3
Llanbedr GB 26 C1
Llanbedrog GB 26 C1
Llanberis GB 26 B1
Llanbister GB 29 A4
Llanbrynmair GB 26 C2
Llançà E 91 A6
Llandeilo GB 28 B4
Llandissilio GB 28 B3
Llandovery GB 28 B4
Llandrillo GB 26 C2
Llandrindod Wells GB 29 A4
Llandudec F 56 B1
Llandudno GB 26 B2
Llandysul GB 28 A3
Llanelli GB 28 B3
Llanerchymedd GB 26 B1
Llanes E 88 A2
Llanfair Caereinion GB 26 C2
Llanfairfechan GB 26 B2
Llanfyllin GB 26 C2
Llangadog GB 28 B4
Llangefni GB 26 B1
Llangollen GB 26 C2
Llangrannog GB 28 A3
Llangurig GB 26 C2
Llanidloes GB 26 C2
Llanilar GB 28 A3
Llanrhystud GB 28 A3
Llanrwst GB 26 B2
Llansannan GB 26 B2
Llansawel GB 28 A3
Llanstephan GB 28 B3
Llanteno E 89 A3
Llanthony GB 29 B4
Llantrisant GB 29 B4
Llantwit-Major GB 29 B4
Llanuwchllyn GB 26 C2
Llanwddyn GB 26 C2
Llanwrda GB 28 B4
Llanwrtyd Wells GB 29 A4
Llanybydder GB 28 A3
Llanymynech GB 26 C2
Llavorsi E 91 A4
Lleida E 90 B3
Llera E 93 C4
Llerena E 99 A4
Lles E 91 A4
Llessui E 91 A4
Llinars E 91 A4
Lliria E 96 B2
Llivia E 91 A4
Llodio E 89 A4
Lloret de Mar E 91 B5
Llosa de Ranes E 96 B2
Lloseta E 97 B2
Llucena del Cid E 96 A2
Llucmajor E 97 B2
Llutxent E 96 C2
Llwyngwril GB 26 C1
Llyswen GB 29 A4
Lnáře CZ 63 A4
Lniano PL 47 B4
Loanhead GB 25 C4
Loano I 80 B2
Loarre E 90 A2
Löbau D 53 B4
Löbejün D 52 B1
Löberöd S 41 D3
Łobez PL 46 B1
Löbnitz D 45 A4
Lobón E 93 C4
Loburg D 52 A2
Łobżenica PL 46 B3
Locana I 70 C2
Locarno CH 70 B3
Loccum D 43 C6
Loče SLO 73 B5
Lochailort GB 24 B2
Lochaline GB 24 B2
Lochans GB 24 D2
Locharbriggs GB 25 C4
Lochau A 71 A4
Loch Baghasdail GB 22 D1
Lochcarron GB 22 D3
Lochearnhead GB 24 B3
Lochem NL 50 A2
Loches F 67 A5

Lochgelly GB 25 B4
Lochgilphead GB 24 B2
Lochgoilhead GB 24 B3
Lochinver GB 22 C3
Loch nam Madadh GB 22 D1
Lochranza GB 24 C2
Ločika SRB 85 C6
Lockenhaus A 73 A6
Lockerbie GB 25 C4
Löcknitz D 45 B6
Locmaria F 66 A1
Locmariaquer F 56 C3
Locmine F 56 C3
Locorotondo I 104 C3
Locquirec F 56 B2
Locri I 106 C3
Locronan F 56 B1
Loctudy F 56 C1
Lodares de Osma E 89 C4
Lodé I 110 B2
Lodeinoye Pole RUS 7 A12
Lodève F 78 C2
Lodi I 71 C4
Løding N 112 E3
Lodosa E 89 B4
Lödöse S 38 A5
Łódź PL 55 B4
Loeches E 95 B3
Løfallstrand N 32 B3
Lofer A 62 C3
Lofsdalen S 115 E10
Loftahammar S 40 B6
Lofthus N 32 B3
Loftus GB 27 A5
Loga N 33 D3
Logatec SLO 73 C4
Løgdeå S 115 D16
Lograto I 71 C5
Logroño E 89 B4
Logrosán E 93 B5
Løgstør DK 38 C2
Løgumkloster DK 39 D1
Lohals DK 39 D3
Lohiniva FIN 113 E14
Lohja FIN 6 A8
Löhlbach D 51 B4
Lohmen Mecklenburg-Vorpommern D 44 B4
Sachsen D 53 C4
Löhnberg D 50 C4
Lohne D 43 C5
Löhne D 51 A4
Lohr D 51 D5
Lohra D 51 C4
Lohsa D 53 B4
Loiano I 81 B5
Loimaa FIN 3 F25
Loiri I 110 B2
Loitz D 45 B5
Loivos P 87 C3
Loivos do Monte P 87 C3
Loja E 100 B1
Lojanice SRB 85 B4
Lojsta S 37 E5
Løjt Kirkeby DK 39 D2
Lok SK 65 A5
Lokca SK 65 A5
Løken N 34 C3
Lokeren B 49 B4
Loket CZ 52 C2
Lokhvitsa UA 11 A12
Lokka FIN 113 E16
Løkken DK 38 B2
N 114 D6
Loknya RUS 7 C11
Lökosháza H 75 B6
Lokot RUS 7 E13
Lokve SRB 75 C6
Lollar D 51 C4
L'Olleria E 96 C2
Lölling-Graben A 73 B4
Lom BG 11 E7
N 114 F5
SK 65 B5
Lombez F 77 C3
Lomello I 80 A2
Łomianki PL 55 A5
Lomma S 41 D3
Lommaryd S 40 B4
Lommatzsch D 52 B3
Lommel B 49 B6
Lommersum D 50 C2
Lomnice nad Lužnici CZ 63 A5
Lomnice CZ 53 C5
Lomnice nad Popelkou CZ 53 C5
Lompolo FIN 113 D13
Łomża PL 6 E7
Lönashult S 40 C4
Lønborg DK 39 D1
Londerzeel B 49 B5
Londinières F 58 A2
London GB 31 C3
Lonevåg N 32 B2
Longa GR 117 F3
Longare I 72 C1
Longares E 90 B1
Longarone I 72 B2
Longastrino I 81 B6
Long Bennington GB 27 C5
Longbenton GB 25 C6
Longchamp-sur-Aujon F 59 B5
Longchaumois F 69 B6
Long Eaton GB 27 C4
Longeau F 59 C6
Longecourt-en-Plaine F 69 A5
Long Melford GB 30 B4
Longny-au-Perche F 58 B1
Longobucco I 106 B3
Long Preston GB 26 A3
Longré F 67 B4
Longridge GB 26 B3
Longroiva P 87 D3
Long Sutton GB 30 B4
Longtown Cumbria GB 25 C5
Herefordshire GB 29 B5
Longué F 67 A4
Longueau F 58 A3
Longuyon F 60 A1
Longvic F 69 A5
Longvilly B 50 C1
Longwy F 60 A1
Lonigo I 71 C6
Löningen D 43 C4
Lonja HR 74 C1
Lönsboda S 41 C4
Lønset N 114 E6
Lons-le-Saunier F 69 B5
Lønstrup DK 38 B2
Looe GB 28 C3
Loone-Plage F 48 B3
Loon op Zand NL 49 B6
Loosdorf A 63 B6
Lo Pagán E 101 B5
Lopar HR 83 B3
Lopare BIH 84 B3
Lopera E 100 B1
Lopigna F 102 A1
Loppersum D 43 B4
Łopuszna PL 65 A6
Łopuszno PL 55 B5
Lor F 59 A5

Lora N 114 E5
Lora de Estepa E 100 B1
Lora del Río E 99 B5
Loranca del Campo E 95 B4
Lorbé E 86 A2
Lörby S 41 C4
Lorca E 101 B4
Lorch D 50 C3
Lørenfallet N 34 B3
Lørenskog N 34 C2
Loreo I 82 A1
Loreto I 82 C2
Lorgues F 79 C5
Lorica I 106 B3
Lorient F 56 C2
Loriga P 92 A3
Loriol-sur-Drôme F 78 B3
Lormes F 68 A3
Loro Ciuffenna I 81 C5
Lorquí E 101 A4
Lorrez-le-Bocage F 59 B3
Lorris F 58 C3
Lorup D 43 C4
Łoś PL 55 B5
Losacino E 87 C4
Los Alcázares E 101 B5
Los Arcos E 89 B4
Losar de la Vera E 93 A5
Los Barrios de Luna E 88 B1
Los Barrios E 99 C5
Los Caños de Meca E 99 C4
Los Cerricos E 101 B3
Los Corrales E 100 B1
Los Corrales de Buelna E 88 A2
Los Dolores E 101 B4
Losenstein A 63 C5
Los Gallardos E 101 B4
Losheim Nordrhein-Westfalen D 50 C2
Saarland D 60 A2
Los Hinojosos E 95 C4
Los Isidros E 96 B1
Los Molinos E 94 B2
Los Morales E 99 B5
Los Navalmorales E 94 C2
Los Navalucillos E 94 C2
Losne F 69 A5
Los Nietos E 101 B5
Løsning DK 39 D2
Los Palacios y Villafranca E 99 B5
Los Pozuelos de Calatrava E 100 A1
Los Rábanos E 89 C4
Los Santos E 99 A4
Los Santos de la Humosa E 95 B3
Los Santos de Maimona E 93 C4
Lossburg D 61 B4
Losse F 76 B2
Losser NL 50 A3
Lossiemouth GB 23 D5
Lössnitz D 52 C2
Loštice CZ 64 A2
Los Tijos E 88 A2
Lostwithiel GB 28 C3
Los Villares E 100 B2
Los Yébenes E 94 C3
Løten N 34 B3
Lotorp S 37 D2
Lottefors S 36 A3
Löttorp S 41 B7
Lotyń PL 46 B2
Lotzorai I 110 C2
Louargat F 56 B2
Loudéac F 56 B3
Loudun F 67 A4
Loué F 57 C5
Loughborough GB 27 C4
Loughbrickland GB 19 B5
Loughrea IRL 20 A3
Louhans F 69 B5
Louisburgh IRL 18 C2
Loukhi RUS 3 C10
Loulay F 67 B4
Loulé P 98 B2
Louny CZ 52 C3
Lourdes F 76 C2
Lourenzá E 86 A3
Loures P 92 C1
Loures-Barousse F 77 C3
Louriçal P 92 A2
Lourinhã P 92 B1
Lourmarin F 79 C4
Loury F 58 C3
Lousã Bragança P 87 C3
Castelo Branco P 92 B3
Lousada P 87 C2
Louth GB 27 B5
Loutra Edipsou GR 116 D5
Loutraki GR 117 E4
Loutropoli Thermis GR 118 C1
Louverné F 57 B5
Louvie-Juzon F 76 C2
Louviers F 58 A2
Louvigné-du-Désert F 57 B4
Louvois F 59 A5
Louvroil F 49 C4
Lova S 37 D5
Lovasberény H 74 A3
Lövåsen S 34 C5
Lovászpatona H 74 A2
Lövberga S 115 D12
Lovech BG 11 E8
Lövenich D 50 B2
Lövere I 71 C5
Lövestad S 41 D3
Loviisa FIN 3 F27
Lovikka S 113 E11
Lovinobaña SK 65 B4
Loviste HR 84 C2
Lovke HR 73 C4
Lovnäs S 34 A4
Lövö H 74 A1
Lovosice CZ 53 C4
Lovozero RUS 3 C31
Lovran HR 73 C4
Lovreć HR 84 C1
Lovrenc na Pohorju SLO 73 B5
Lovrin RO 75 C5
Lövstabruk S 36 B4
Löwenberg D 45 C5
Löwenstein D 61 A5
Lowestoft GB 30 B5
Lowick GB 25 C6
Łowicz PL 55 A4
Loxstedt D 43 B5
Loyew BY 7 F11
Lož SLO 73 C4
Loza E 63 A4
Lozarevo BG 11 E9
Lozničko Polje SRB 85 B4
Loznica SRB 85 B4
Lozorno SK 64 B3
Lozovik SRB 85 B6
Lozoya E 94 B3
Lozoyuela E 94 B3
Lozzo di Cadore I 72 B2
Luanco E 88 A1
Luarca E 86 A4
Lubaczów PL 11 A7
Lubań PL 53 B5
Lubanie PL 47 C4
Lubanów PL 55 B4
Lubars D 44 C4
Lubasz PL 46 C2
Lubawa PL 47 B5
Lubawka PL 53 C6

Lübbecke D 51 A4
Lübben D 53 B3
Lübbenau D 53 B3
Lubczyna PL 45 B6
Lübeck D 44 B2
Lubenec CZ 52 C3
Lubersac F 67 C6
Lübesse D 44 B3
Lubia E 89 C4
Lubian E 87 B4
Lubiatowo PL 45 B7
Lubichowo PL 47 B4
Lubicz Dolny PL 47 B4
Lubień PL 65 A5
Lubienia PL 55 B6
Lubień Kujawski PL 47 C5
Lubieszewo PL 46 B1
Lubin Dolnośląskie PL 53 B6
Zachodnio-Pomorskie PL 45 B6
Lublin PL 11 A7
Lubliniec PL 54 C3
Lubmin D 45 A5
Lubniewice PL 46 C1
Lubny UA 11 A12
Lubochnia PL 55 B5
Lubomierz Dolnośląskie PL 53 B5
Małopolskie PL 65 A6
Lubomino PL 47 A6
Luboń PL 54 A1
L'ubotín SK 65 A6
Lubowidz PL 47 B5
Łubowo Wielkopolskie PL 46 C3
Zachodnio-Pomorskie PL 46 B2
Lubraniec PL 47 C4
Lubrin E 101 B3
Lubrza PL 54 C2
Lubsko PL 53 B4
Lübtheen D 44 B3
Lubuczewo PL 46 A3
Luby CZ 52 C2
Lübz D 44 B4
Lucainena de las Torres E 101 B3
Lucan IRL 21 A5
Lučani SRB 85 C5
Lúcar E 101 B3
Lucay-le-Mâle F 67 A6
Lucca I 81 C4
Lucciana F 102 A2
Lucé F 58 B2
Luče SLO 73 B4
Lucena Córdoba E 100 B1
Huelva E 99 B4
Lucenay-les-Aix F 68 B3
Lucenay-l'Evêque F 69 A4
Luc-en-Diois F 78 B4
Lučenec SK 65 B5
Luceni E 90 B1
Lucens CH 70 B1
Lucera I 103 B8
Luciana E 94 D2
Lucignano I 81 C5
Lucija SLO 72 C3
Lucka D 52 B2
Luckau D 53 B3
Luckenwalde D 52 A3
Lückstedt D 44 C3
Lucko HR 73 C5
Luco dei Marsi I 103 B6
Luçon F 66 B3
Luc-sur-Mer F 57 A5
Ludanice SK 64 B4
Ludbreg HR 74 B1
Lüdenscheid D 50 B3
Lüderitz D 44 C3
Lüdersdorf D 44 B2
Ludgershall GB 29 C6
Lüdinghausen D 50 B3
Ludlow GB 29 A5
Ludomy PL 46 C2
Ludvika S 36 B2
Ludweiler Warndt D 60 A2
Ludwigsburg D 61 B5
Ludwigsfelde D 52 A3
Ludwigshafen D 61 A4
Ludwigslust D 44 B3
Ludwigsstadt D 52 C1
Ludza LV 7 C9
Luesia E 90 A1
Luftkurort Arendsee D 44 C3
Lug BIH 84 D3
HR 74 B3
Luga RUS 7 B10
Lugagnano Val d'Arda I 81 B3
Lugano CH 70 B3
Lugau D 52 C2
Lugnas S 35 D5
Lügnola I 102 A5
Lugny F 69 B4
Lugo Bragança P 87 C3
I 81 B5
Lugoj RO 10 B6
Lugones E 88 A1
Lugros E 100 B2
Luhačovice CZ 64 A3
Luhe D 62 A3
Luino I 70 C3
Luintra E 87 B3
Lújar E 100 C2
Luka nad Jihlavou CZ 63 A6
Lukavac BIH 84 B3
Lukavika BIH 84 B3
Lukovë AL 116 C1
Lukovica SLO 73 B4
Lukovit BG 11 E8
Lukovo KOS 85 B5
HR 83 B3
SRB 85 C6
Lukovo Šugorje HR 83 B4
Łukowice Brzeskie PL 54 C2
Luksefjell N 33 C6
Łukta PL 47 B6
Lula I 110 B2
Luleå S 3 D25
Lüleburgaz TR 118 A2
Lumbarda HR 84 D2
Lumbier E 90 A1
Lumbrales E 87 D4
Lumbreras E 89 B4
Lumbres F 48 C3
Lummelunda S 37 E5
Lummen B 49 C6
Lumparland FIN 36 B7
Lumpiaque E 90 B1
Lumsås DK 39 D4
Lumsden GB 23 D6
Lumsheden S 36 B3
Lun HR 83 B3
Luna E 90 A2
Lunamatrona I 110 C1
Lunano I 82 C1
Lunas F 78 C2
Lund Skåne S 41 D3
Västra Götaland S 35 C4
Lundamo N 114 D7
Lunde Sogn og Fjordane N 32 A3
Sogn og Fjordane N 32 A3
Telemark N 33 C6
S 115 E14
Lundebyvollen N 34 B4
Lunden D 43 A6
Lunderskov DK 39 D2

Lundsberg S 35 C6
Lüneburg D 44 B2
Lunel F 78 C3
Lünen D 50 B3
Lunéville F 60 B2
Lungern CH 70 B3
Lungro I 106 B3
Luninyets BY 7 E9
Lünne D 43 C4
Lunner N 34 B2
Lunteren NL 49 A6
Lunz am See A 63 C6
Luogosanto I 110 A2
Łupawa PL 46 A3
Lupión E 100 A2
Lupoglav HR 73 C4
Luppa D 52 B2
Lupsa RO 11 C8
Luque E 100 B1
Lurago d'Erba I 71 C4
Lúras I 110 B2
Lurcy-Lévis F 68 B2
Lure F 60 C2
Lurgan GB 19 B5
Luri F 102 A2
Lury-sur-Arnon F 68 A2
Lušci Palanka BIH 83 B5
Lusévera I 72 B3
Lusignan F 67 B5
Lusigny-sur-Barse F 59 B5
Lusnić BIH 84 C1
Luso P 92 A2
Lusówko PL 46 C2
Luspebryggan S 112 E8
Luss GB 24 B3
Lussac F 76 B2
Lussac-les-Châteaux F 67 B5
Lussac-les-Eglises F 67 B6
Lussan F 78 B3
Lüssow D 44 B3
Lustenau A 71 A4
Luštěnice CZ 53 C4
Luster N 32 A4
Lutago I 72 B1
Lutherstadt Wittenberg D 52 B2
Lütjenburg D 44 A2
Lutnes N 34 A4
Lutocin PL 47 C5
Lutomiersk PL 55 B4
Luton GB 31 C3
Lutry CH 70 B1
PL 47 A6
Lutter am Barenberge D 51 B6
Lutterworth GB 30 B2
Lututów PL 54 B3
Lützow D 44 B3
Luusua FIN 113 F16
Luvos S 112 F7
Luxembourg L 60 A2
Luxeuil-les-Bains F 60 C2
Luxey F 76 B2
Luz Évora P 92 C3
Faro P 98 B2
Faro P 98 B3
Luzarches F 58 A3
Luže CZ 64 A2
Luzech F 77 B4
Luzern CH 70 A3
Luzino PL 47 A4
Luz-St Sauveur F 76 D2
Luzy F 68 B3
Luzzi I 106 B3
L'viv UA 11 B8
Lwówek PL 46 C2
Lwówek Śląski PL 53 B5
Lyakhavichy BY 7 E9
Lybster GB 23 C5
Lychen D 45 B5
Lychkova RUS 7 C12
Lyckeby S 41 C5
Lycksele S 115 C15
Lydd GB 31 D4
Lydford GB 28 C3
Lydney GB 29 B5
Lyepyel' BY 7 D10
Lygna N 34 B2
Lykkja N 32 B5
Lykling N 33 C2
Lyme Regis GB 29 C5
Lymington GB 31 D2
Lympne GB 31 C5
Lyndhurst GB 31 D2
Lyneham GB 29 B6
Lyness GB 23 C5
Lyngdal Buskerud N 32 C6
Vest-Agder N 33 D4
Lyngør N 33 D6
Lyngsa DK 38 B3
Lyngseidet N 112 C9
Lyngsnes N 114 C8
Lynmouth GB 28 B4
Lynton GB 28 B4
Lyntupy BY 7 D9
Lyon F 69 C4
Lyozna BY 7 D11
Lyrestad S 35 D6
Lysá nad Labem CZ 53 C4
Lysá pod Makytou SK 64 A4
Lysebotn N 33 C3
Lysekil S 35 D3
Lysice CZ 64 A2
Lysomice PL 47 B4
Lysøysund N 114 D6
Lytham St Anne's GB 26 B2
Lyuban RUS 7 B11
Lyubertsy RUS 7 D14
Lyubimets BG 118 A3
Lyubytino RUS 7 B12
Lyudinovo RUS 7 E13

M

Maaninkavaara FIN 113 F17
Maarheeze NL 49 B6
Maaseik B 50 B1
Maasmechelen B 50 C1
Maassluis NL 49 B5
Maastricht NL 50 C1
Mablethorpe GB 27 B6
Mably F 68 B4
Macael E 101 B3
Maçanet de Cabrenys E 91 A5
Mação P 92 B2
Macau F 76 A2
Maccagno-Agra I 70 B3
Maccarese I 102 B5
Macchiagódena I 103 B7
Macclesfield GB 26 B3
Macduff GB 23 D6
Maceda E 87 B3
Macedo de Cavaleiros P 87 C4
Maceira Guarda P 92 A3
Leiria P 92 B2
Macelj HR 73 B5
Macerata I 82 C2
Macerata Féltria I 82 C1
Machault F 59 A5
Machecoul F 66 B3
Mchowo PL 47 B6
Machrihanish GB 24 C2
Machynlleth GB 26 C2
Macieira P 92 A2
Maciejowice PL 55 B6
Macinaggio F 102 A2
Mackenrode D 51 B6
Mačkovci SLO 73 B6
Macomer I 110 B1

Macon B 49 C5
Mâcon F 69 B4
Macotera E 94 B1
Macroom IRL 20 C3
Macugnaga I 70 C2
Madan BG 116 A6
Madängsholm S 35 D5
Madaras H 75 B4
Maddaloni I 103 B7
Madeley GB 26 C3
Maderuelo E 89 C3
Madetkoski FIN 113 E15
Madley GB 29 A5
Madocsa H 75 B3
Madona LV 7 C9
Madrid E 94 B3
Madridejos E 95 C3
Madrigal de las Altas Torres E 94 A1
Madrigal de la Vera E 93 A5
Madrigalejo E 93 B5
Madrigalejo de Monte E 88 B3
Madriguera E 89 C3
Madrigueras E 95 C5
Madroñera E 93 B5
Maël-Carhaix F 56 B2
Maella E 90 B3
Maello E 94 B2
Maesteg D 39 C4
Maestre de Campiglio I 71 B5
Mafra P 92 C1
Magacela E 93 C5
Magallón E 89 C5
Magaluf E 97 B2
Magán E 94 C3
Magaña E 89 C4
Magasa I 71 C5
Magaz E 88 C2
Magdeburg D 52 A1
Magenta I 70 C3
Magescq F 76 C1
Maghera GB 19 B5
Magherafelt GB 19 B5
Maghull GB 26 B3
Magilligan GB 19 A5
Magione I 82 C1
Magioto P 92 C1
Maglaj BIH 84 B3
Maglehem S 41 D4
Magliano de'Marsi I 103 A6
Magliano in Toscana I 102 A4
Magliano Sabina I 102 A5
Maglić SRB 75 C4
Máglie I 107 A5
Maglód H 75 A4
Magnac-Bourg F 67 C6
Magnac-Laval F 67 B6
Magnières F 60 B2
Magnor N 34 C4
Magnuszew PL 55 B6
Magny-Cours F 68 B3
Magny-en-Vexin F 58 A2
Magocs H 74 B3
Maguilla E 93 C5
Maguiresbridge GB 19 B4
Magyarbóly H 74 C3
Magyarkeszi H 74 B3
Magyarszék H 74 B3
Mahala MNE 105 A5
Mahide E 87 C4
Mahilyow BY 7 E11
Mahmudiye TR 118 C5
Mahora E 95 C5
Mahovo HR 73 C6
Mähring D 62 A3
Maia E 76 C1
P 87 C2
Maiaelrayo E 95 A3
Maials E 90 B3
Maîche F 70 A1
Maida I 106 C3
Maiden Bradley GB 29 B5
Maidenhead GB 31 C3
Maiden Newton GB 29 C5
Maidstone GB 31 C4
Maienfeld CH 71 A4
Maignelay Montigny F 58 A3
Maijanen FIN 113 E14
Maillezais F 66 B4
Mailly-le-Camp F 59 B5
Mailly-le-Château F 59 C4
Mainar E 90 B1
Mainbernheim D 61 A6
Mainburg D 62 B2
Mainhardt D 61 A5
Maintal D 51 C4
Maintenon F 58 B2
Mainvilliers F 58 B2
Mainz D 50 C4
Maiorca P 92 A2
Mairena de Aljarafe E 99 B5
Mairena del Alcor E 99 B5
Maisach D 62 B2
Maishofen A 72 A2
Maison-Rouge F 59 B4
Maisse F 58 B3
Maizières-lès-Vic F 60 B2
Maja HR 73 C6
Majadahonda E 94 B3
Majadas E 93 B5
Majavatn N 115 B10
Majs H 74 C3
Majšperk SLO 73 B5
Makarska HR 84 C2
Makkum NL 42 B2
Maklár H 65 C6
Makó H 75 B5
Makoszyce PL 54 C2
Makov SK 64 A4
Makovac KOS 85 C6
Mąkowarsko PL 46 B3
Maków Podhalański PL 65 A5
Makrakomi GR 116 D4
Maksniemi FIN 3 D26
Malå S 115 B15
Mala Bosna SRB 75 B4
Malacky SK 64 B3
Maladzyechna BY 7 D9
Málaga E 100 C1
Malagón E 94 C3
Malaguilla E 95 B3
Malahide IRL 21 A5
Mala Kladuša BIH 73 C5
Mala Krsna SRB 85 B6
Malalbergo I 81 B5
Malanów PL 54 B3
Mala Plana SRB 85 C6
Mala Subotica HR 74 B1
Malaucène F 79 B4
Malaunay F 58 A2
Mala Vyska UA 11 B11
Malax FIN 3 E25
Malborghetto I 72 B3
Malbork PL 47 A5
Malborn D 60 A2
Malbuisson F 69 B6
Malcesine I 71 C5
Malchin D 45 B4
Malching D 63 B4
Malchow D 44 B4
Malcocinado E 99 A5
Malczyce PL 54 B1
Maldegem B 49 B4
Maldon GB 31 C4
Małdyty PL 47 B5
Malè I 71 B5
Malemort F 67 C6
Malente D 44 A2
Målerås S 40 C5
Males GR 117 G7
Malesherbes F 58 B3
Malesina GR 116 D5
Malestroit F 56 C3

Maletto I 109 B3
Malexander S 40 A5
Malgrat de Mar E 91 B5
Malhadas P 87 C4
Malia CY 120 B1
GR 117 G7
Malicorne-sur-Sarthe F 57 C5
Malijai F 79 B5
Maliljoš SRB 75 C5
Malilla S 40 B5
Malin IRL 19 A4
Málinec SK 65 B5
Malines = Mechelen B 49 B5
Malingsbo S 36 C2
Maliniec PL 54 A3
Malinska HR 83 A3
Maliq AL 116 B2
Maljevac HR 73 C5
Malki PL 47 B5
Malko Tarnovo BG 11 E9
Mallaig GB 22 D3
Mallaranny IRL 18 C2
Mallemort F 79 C4
Mallén E 89 C5
Malléon F 77 C4
Mallersdorf-Pfaffenberg D 62 B3
Málles Venosta I 71 B5
Malliß D 44 B3
Mallnitz A 72 A3
Mallow IRL 20 B3
Mallwyd GB 26 C2
Malm N 114 C8
Malmbäck S 40 B4
Malmberget S 112 E9
Malmby S 37 C4
Malmesbury GB 29 B5
Malmköping S 37 C3
Malmö S 41 D3
Malmön S 35 D3
Malmslätt S 37 D2
Malnate I 70 C3
Malo I 71 C6
Maloarkhangelsk RUS 7 E14
Małogoszcz PL 55 C5
Maloja CH 71 B4
Małomice PL 53 B5
Maloyaroslavets RUS 7 D14
Malpartida de la Serena E 93 C5
Malpartida de Plasencia E 93 B4
Malpas E 90 A3
GB 26 B3
Malpica de Bergantiños E 86 A2
Malpica de Tajo E 94 C2
Malsch D 61 B4
Malšice CZ 63 A5
Malta A 72 B3
Maltby GB 27 B4
Malung S 34 B5
Malungsfors S 34 B5
Maluszów PL 45 C7
Malva E 88 C1
Malvaglia CH 70 B3
Malveira P 92 C1
Malvik N 114 D7
Malyn UA 11 A10
Mamarrosa P 92 A2
Mamer L 60 A2
Mamers F 58 B1
Mamirolle F 69 A6
Mammendorf D 62 B2
Mámmola I 106 C3
Mamoiada I 110 B2
Mamonovo RUS 47 A5
Mamuras AL 105 B5
Maña SK 64 B4
Manacor E 97 B3
Manavgat TR 119 F6
Mancera de Abajo E 94 B1
Mancha Real E 100 B2
Manchester GB 26 B3
Manching D 62 B2
Manchita E 93 C4
Manciano I 102 A4
Manciet F 76 C3
Mandal N 33 D4
Mandanici I 109 B4
Mándas I 110 C2
Mandatoriccio I 107 B3
Mandayona E 95 B4
Mandelieu-la-Napoule F 79 C5
Mandello del Lário I 71 C4
Mandelsloh D 43 C6
Manderfeld B 50 C2
Manderscheid D 50 C2
Mandino Selo BIH 84 C2
Mandoudi GR 116 D5
Mandraki GR 119 F2
Mandúria I 104 C3
Mane Alpes-de-Haute-Provence F 79 C4
Haute-Garonne F 77 C3
Manérbio I 71 C5
Mañeru E 89 B5
Manětin CZ 52 C3
Manfredónia I 104 B1
Mangalia RO 11 E10
Manganeses de la Lampreana E 88 C1
Manganeses de la Polvorosa E 88 B1
Mangen N 34 C3
Manger N 32 B2
Mangotsfield GB 29 B5
Mangualde P 92 A3
Maniago I 72 B2
Manilva E 99 C5
Manisa TR 118 D2
Manises E 96 B2
Månkarbo S 36 B4
Manlleu E 91 A5
Manna DK 38 B2
Männedorf CH 70 A3
Mannersdorf am Leithagebirge A 64 C2
Mannheim D 61 A4
Manningtree GB 31 C5
Mano F 76 B2
Manoppello I 103 A7
Manorbier GB 28 B3
Manorhamilton IRL 18 B3
Manosque F 79 C4
Manowo PL 46 A2
Manresa E 91 B4
Månsarp S 40 B4
Månsås S 35 D5
Manschnow D 45 C6
Mansfeld D 52 B1
Mansfield GB 27 B4
Mansilla de Burgos E 88 B3
Mansilla de las Mulas E 88 B1
Manskog S 35 C4
Mansle F 67 C5
Manso F 102 A1
Manteigas P 92 A3
Mantel D 62 A3
Manthelan F 67 A5
Mantes-la-Jolie F 58 B2
Mantes-la-Ville F 58 B2
Manthelan F 67 A5
Mantiel E 95 B4
Mantorp S 37 D2
Mántova I 71 C5

Mänttä FIN 3 E26
Manuel E 96 B2
Manyas TR 118 B2
Manzanal de Arriba E 87 B4
Manzanares E 95 C3
Manzanares el Real E 94 B3
Manzaneda León E 87 B4
Orense E 87 B3
Manzanedo E 88 B3
Manzaneque E 94 C3
Manzanera E 96 A2
Manzanilla E 99 B4
Manziana I 102 A5
Manziat F 69 B4
Mao E 97 B4
Maoča BIH 84 B3
Maqueda E 94 B2
Mara E 89 C5
Maramarereğlisi TR 118 B2
Maraña E 88 A1
Maranchón E 95 A4
Maranello I 81 B4
Marano I 103 C7
Marano Lagunare I 72 C3
Marans F 66 B3
Maratea I 106 B2
Marateca P 92 C2
Marathokambos GR 119 E1
Marathónas GR 117 D5
Marathóvouno CY 120 A2
Mararkraz E 88 C3

Marbach Baden-Württemberg D 61 B5
Hessen D 51 C5
F 60 B2
Marbäck S 40 B3
Marbella E 100 C1
Marboz F 69 B5
Marburg D 51 C4
Marcali H 74 B2
Marčana HR 82 B2
Marcaria I 71 C5
Marcelová SK 64 C4
Marcenat F 68 C2
March GB 30 B4
Marchamalo E 95 B3
Marchaux F 69 A6
Marche-en-Famenne B 49 C6
Marchegg A 64 B2
Marchena E 99 B5
Marchenoir F 58 C2
Marcheprime F 76 B2
Marciac F 76 C3
Marciana Marina I 81 D4
Marcianise I 103 B7
Marcigny F 68 B4
Marcilla E 89 B5
Marcillac-la-Croisille F 68 C2
Marcillac-Vallon F 77 B5
Marcillat-en-Combraille F 68 B2
Marcille-sur-Seine F 59 B4
Marcilloles F 69 C5
Marcilly-le-Hayer F 59 B4
Marcinkowice PL 46 B2
Marciszów PL 53 C6
Marck F 48 C2
Marckolsheim F 60 B3
Marco de Canevezes P 87 C2
Mårdsele S 115 C16
Mårdsjö S 115 D12
Mareham le Fen GB 27 B5
Marek S 40 B5
Marennes F 66 C3
Maresquel F 48 C2
Mareuil F 67 C5
Mareuil-en-Brie F 59 B4
Mareuil-sur-Arnon F 68 B2
Mareuil-sur-Lay F 66 B3
Mareuil-sur-Ourcq F 59 A4
Margam GB 29 B4
Margariti GR 116 C2
Margaux F 76 A2
Margerie-Hancourt F 59 B5
Margès F 79 A4
Margherita di Savóia I 104 B2
Margita SRB 75 C6
Margone I 70 C2
Margonin PL 46 C3
Margut F 59 A6
María E 101 B4
Mariager DK 38 C3
Mariana E 95 B4
Maria Neustift A 63 C5
Mariannelund S 40 B5
Marianópoli I 108 B2
Mariánské Lázně CZ 52 D2
Mariapfarr A 72 A3
Maria Saal A 73 B4
Mariazell A 63 C6
Maribo DK 39 E4
Maribor SLO 73 B5
Marieberg S 37 C2
Mariefred S 37 C4
Mariehamn FIN 36 B6
Marielund S 36 B4
Marienbaum D 50 B2
Marienberg D 52 C3
Marienheide D 50 B3
Mariental D 51 A6
Mariestad S 35 D5
Marieux F 48 C3
Marigliano I 103 C7
Marignane F 79 C4
Marigny Jura F 69 B5
Manche F 57 A4
Marigny-le-Châtel F 59 B4
Marija Bistrica HR 73 B6
Marijampole LT 6 D7
Marín E 87 B2
Marina HR 83 C5
Marina del Cantone I 103 C7
Marina di Acquappesa I 106 B2
Marina di Alberese I 81 D5
Marina di Amendolara I 106 B3
Marina di Campo I 81 D4
Marina di Carrara I 81 B4
Marina di Castagneto-Donorático I 81 C4
Marina di Cécina I 81 C4
Marina di Gáiro I 110 C2
Marina di Ginosa I 104 C2
Marina di Gioiosa Iónica I 106 C3
Marina di Grosseto I 81 D4
Marina di Léuca I 107 B5
Marina di Massa I 81 B4
Marina di Nováglie I 107 B5
Marina di Pisa I 81 C4
Marina di Ragusa I 109 C3
Marina di Ravenna I 82 B1
Marina di Torre Grande I 110 C1
Marinaleda E 100 B1
Marine de Sisco F 102 A2
Marinella I 108 B1
Marinella di Sarzana I 81 B4
Marineo I 108 B2
Marines F 58 A2
Maringues F 68 C3
Marinha das Ondas P 92 A2
Marinha Grande P 92 B2

Marjaliza E 94 C3
Markabygd N 114 D8
Markaryd S 40 C3
Markdorf D 61 C5
Markelo NL 50 A2
Market Deeping GB 30 B3
Market Drayton GB 26 C3
Market Harborough GB 30 B3
Markethill GB 19 B5
Market Rasen GB 27 B5
Market Warsop GB 27 B4
Market Weighton GB 27 B5
Markgröningen D 61 B5
Markhausen D 43 C4
Marki PL 55 A6
Markina-Xemein E 89 A4
Markinch GB 25 B4
Märkische Buchholz D 53 A3
Markitta S 113 E10
Markkleeberg D 52 B2
Marklohe D 43 C6
Markneukirchen D 52 C2
Markopoulo GR 117 E5
Markovac SRB 85 B6
Markowice PL 54 C3
Markranstädt D 52 B2
Marksuhl D 51 C6
Markt Allhau A 73 A6
Markt Bibart D 61 A6
Marktbreit D 61 A6
Markt Erlbach D 62 A1
Markt-heidenfeld D 61 A5
Markt Indersdorf D 62 B2
Marktl D 62 B3
Marktleuthen D 52 C1
Marktoberdorf D 62 C1
Marktredwitz D 52 C2
Markt Rettenbach D 61 C6
Markt Schwaben D 62 B2
Markt-Übelbach A 73 A5
Markušica HR 74 C3
Markušovce SK 65 B6
Marl D 50 B3
Marlborough Devon GB 28 C4
Wiltshire GB 29 B6
Marle F 59 A4
Marlieux F 69 B5
Marlow GB 31 C3
D 45 A4
Marma S 36 B4
Marmagne F 69 A4
Marmande F 76 B3
Marmara TR 118 B2
Marmaris TR 119 F3
Marmelete P 98 B2
Marmolejo E 100 A1
Marmoutier F 60 B3
Marnay F 69 A5
Marne D 43 B6
Marnheim D 61 A4
Marnitz D 44 B3
Maroldsweisach D 51 C6
Marolles-les-Braults F 58 B1
Maromme F 58 A2
Marónia GR 116 B7
Maroslele H 75 B5
Maróstica I 72 C1
Marotta I 82 C2
Marpisa GR 117 E7
Marquion F 49 C4
Marquise F 48 C2
Marradi I 81 B5
Marrasjärvi FIN 113 F14
Marraskoski FIN 113 F14
Marratxí E 97 B2
Marrúbiu I 110 C1
Marrum NL 42 B2
Marrupe E 94 B2
Marsac F 77 C5
Marsac-en-Livradois F 68 C3
Marságlia I 80 B3
Marsala I 108 B1
Marsberg D 51 B4
Marsciano I 82 D1
Marseillan F 78 C2
Marseille = Marseilles F 79 C4
Marseille en Beauvaisis F 58 A2
Marseilles = Marseille F 79 C4
Mársico Nuovo I 104 C1
Marske-by-the-Sea GB 27 A4
Mars-la-Tours F 60 A1
Marsliden S 115 B12
Marson F 59 B5
Märsta S 37 C4
Marstal DK 39 E3
Marstrand S 38 B4
Marta I 102 A4
Martano I 107 A5
Martel F 77 B4
Martelange B 60 A1
Martfeld D 43 C6
Martfű H 75 A5
Martham GB 30 B5
Marthon F 67 C5
Martiago E 93 A4
Martigné-Briand F 67 A4
Martigné-Ferchaud F 57 C4
Martigné-sur-Mayenne F 57 B5
Martigny CH 70 B2
Martigny-les-Bains F 60 B1
Martigues F 79 C4
Martim-Longo P 98 B3
Martin SK 65 A4
Martín E 96 A1
Martina CH 71 B5
Martina Franca I 104 C3
Martinamor E 94 B1
Martín de la Jara E 100 B1
Martinengo I 71 C4
Martin Muñoz de las Posadas E 94 A2
Martinniemi FIN 3 D26
Martinšćica HR 83 B3
Martinshöhe D 60 A3
Martinsicuro I 82 D2
Martinszell D 61 C6
Mártis I 110 B1
Martofte DK 39 D3
Martonvásár H 74 A3
Martorell E 91 B4
Martos E 100 B2
Martres Tolosane F 77 C4
Martti FIN 113 E17
Marugán E 94 B2
Marúggio I 104 C3
Marvão P 93 B3
Marvejols F 78 B2
Marville F 59 A6
Marykirk GB 25 B5
Marypark GB 23 D5
Marytavy GB 28 C3
Marzabotto I 81 B5
Marzahne D 44 C4
Marzamemi I 109 C4
Marzocca I 82 C2
Mas-Cabardès F 77 C5
Mascali I 109 B4
Mascalucía I 109 B4
Mascarenhas P 87 C3
Mascioni I 103 A6
Mas de Barberáns E 90 C3
Mas de las Matas E 90 C2
Masegoso E 101 A3

Masegoso de Tajuña E 95 B4
Masera I 70 B3
Masevaux F 60 C2
Masfjorden N 32 B2
Masham GB 27 A4
Masi N 113 C12
Maside E 87 B2
Maslacq F 76 C2
Maslinica HR 83 C5
Maslovare BIH 84 B2
Masone I 80 B2
Massa I 81 B4
Massa Fiscáglia I 81 B6
Massafra I 104 C3
Massa Lombarda I 81 B5
Massa Lubrense I 103 C7
Massamagrell E 96 B2
Massa Maríttima I 81 C4
Massa Martana I 82 D1
Massanassa E 96 B2
Massarosa I 81 C4
Massat F 77 D4
Massay F 68 A1
Massbach D 51 C6
Masseret F 67 C6
Masseube F 77 C3
Massiac F 68 C3
Massignac F 67 C5
Massing D 62 B3
Massmechelen B 50 C1
Masterud N 34 B4
Mästocka S 40 C3
Masty BY 6 E8
Masúa I 110 C1
Masueco E 87 C4
Masugnsbyn S 113 E11
Mašun SLO 73 C4
Maszewo
Lubuskie PL 53 A4
Zachodnio-Pomorskie PL 45 B7
Mata de Alcántara E 93 B4
Matala GR 117 H6
Matalebreras E 89 C4
Matallana de Torio E 88 B1
Matamala E 89 C4
Mataporquera E 88 B2
Matapozuelos E 88 C2
Mataró E 91 B5
Matarocco I 108 B1
Mataruge MNE 85 C4
Mataruška Banja SRB 85 C5
Matélica I 82 C2
Matera I 104 C2
Mateševo MNE 85 D4
Mátészalka H 11 C7
Matet E 96 B2
Matfors S 115 E14
Matha F 67 C4
Mathay F 70 A1
Matignon F 57 B3
Matilla de los Caños del Rio E 94 B1
Matlock GB 27 B4
Matosinhos P 87 C2
Matour F 69 B4
Mátrafüred H 65 C5
Mátraterenye H 65 B5
Matre
Hordaland N 32 B2
Hordaland N 32 C2
Matrei am Brenner A 71 A6
Matrei in Osttirol A 72 A2
Matrice I 103 B7
Matsdal S 115 B12
Mattarello I 71 B6
Mattersburg A 64 C2
Mattighofen A 62 B4
Mattinata I 104 B2
Mattos P 92 B2
Mattsee A 62 C4
Mattsmyra S 36 A2
Matulji HR 73 C4
Maubert-Fontaine F 59 A5
Maubeuge F 49 C4
Maubourguet F 76 C3
Mauchline GB 24 C3
Maud GB 23 D6
Mauer-kirchen A 62 B4
Mauern D 62 B2
Mauguio F 78 C3
Maulbronn D 61 B4
Maule F 58 B2
Mauléon F 67 B4
Mauléon-Barousse F 77 D3
Mauléon-Licharre F 76 C2
Maulévrier F 67 A4
Maum IRL 18 C2
Maurach A 72 A1
Maure-de-Bretagne F 57 C4
Maureilhan F 78 C2
Mauriac F 68 C2
Mauron F 57 B3
Maurs F 77 B5
Maury F 77 D5
Maussane-les-Alpilles F 78 C3
Mautern A 63 B6
Mauterndorf A 72 A3
Mautern im Steiermark A 73 A4
Mauthausen A 63 B5
Mauthen A 72 B2
Mauvezin F 77 C3
Mauzé-sur-le-Mignon F 67 B4
Maxent F 57 C3
Maxey-sur-Vaise F 60 B1
Maxial P 92 B1
Maxieira P 92 B2
Maxwellheugh GB 25 C5
Mayalde E 88 C1
Maybole GB 24 C3
Mayen D 50 C3
Mayenne F 57 B5
Mayet F 58 C1
Mayorga E 88 B1
Mayres F 78 B3
Mayrhofen A 72 A1
Mazagón E 99 B4
Mazaleón E 90 B3
Mazamet F 77 C5
Mazan F 79 B4
Mazara del Vallo I 108 B1
Mazarambroz E 94 C2
Mazarete E 95 B4
Mazaricos E 86 B2
Mazarrón E 101 B4
Mažeikiai LT 6 C7
Mazères F 77 C4
Mazères-sur-Salat F 77 C3
Mazières-en-Gâtine F 67 B4
Mazin HR 83 B4
Mazuelo E 88 B3
Mazyr BY 7 E10
Mazzarino I 109 B3
Mazzarrà Sant'Andrea I 109 A4
Mazzo di Valtellina I 71 B5
Mdzewo PL 47 C6
Mealabost GB 22 C2
Mealhada P 92 A2
Méan B 49 C6
Meana Sardo I 110 C2
Meaulne F 68 B2
Meaux F 59 B3
Mebonden N 114 D8
Mecerreyes E 89 B3
Mechelen B 49 B5
Mechernich D 50 C2
Mechnica PL 54 C3
Mechowo PL 45 B7
Mechterstädt D 51 C6
Mecidiye TR 118 B1
Mecikal PL 46 B3
Mecina-Bombarón E 100 C2
Mecitözü TR 16 A7
Meckenbeuren D 61 C5
Meckenheim
Rheinland-Pfalz D 50 C3
Rheinland-Pfalz D 61 A4
Meckesheim D 61 A4
Mecseknádasd H 74 B3
Meda
I 71 C4
P 87 D3
Medak HR 83 B4
Mede I 80 A2
Medebach D 51 B4
Medelim P 93 A3
Medemblik NL 42 C2
Medena Selista BIH 84 B1
Medesano I 81 B4
Medevi S 37 D1
Medgidia RO 11 D10
Medgyesháza H 75 B6
Medhamn S 35 C5
Mediaș RO 11 C8
Medicina I 81 B5
Medinaceli E 95 A4
Medina de las Torres E 93 C4
Medina del Campo E 88 C2
Medina de Pomar E 89 B3
Medina de Rioseco E 88 C1
Medina Sidonia E 99 C5
Medinilla E 93 A5
Medja SRB 75 C5
Medjedja BIH 85 C4
Medulin HR 82 B2
Meduno I 72 B2
Medveda SRB 85 B6
Medvedja SRB 85 C6
Medvedov SK 64 C3
Medvide HR 83 B4
Medvode SLO 73 B4
Medzev SK 65 B6
Medžitlija MK 116 B3
Meerane D 52 C2
Meerle B 49 B5
Meersburg D 61 C5
Meeuwen B 49 B6
Megalo Horio GR 119 F2
Megalopoli GR 117 E4
Megara GR 117 D5
Megève F 69 C6
Meggenhofen A 63 B4
Megra RUS 7 A14
Mehamn N 113 A16
Mehedeby S 36 B4
Méhkerék H 75 B6
Mehun-sur-Yèvre F 68 A2
Meigle GB 25 B4
Meijel NL 50 B1
Meilen CH 70 A3
Meilhan F 76 C2
Meimôa P 93 A3
Meina I 70 C3
Meine D 44 C2
Meinersen D 44 C2
Meinerzhagen D 50 B3
Meiningen D 51 C6
Meira E 86 A3
Meiringen CH 70 B3
Meisenheim D 60 A3
Meissen D 52 B3
Meitingen D 62 B1
Meix-devant-Virton B 60 A1
Męka PL 54 B3
Meka Gruda BIH 84 C3
Mel I 72 B2
Melbu N 112 D3
Melč CZ 64 A3
Meldal N 114 D6
Méldola I 82 B1
Meldorf D 43 A6
Melegnano I 71 C4
Melenci SRB 75 C5
Melendugno I 105 C4
Melfi I 104 C1
Melfjordbotn N 112 F2
Melgaço P 87 B2
Melgar de Arriba E 88 B1
Melgar de Fernamental E 88 B2
Melgar de Yuso E 88 B2
Melhus N 114 D7
Meliana E 96 B2
Melide
CH 70 C3
E 86 B2
Melides P 98 A2
Meligales GR 117 E3
Melilli I 109 B4
Melinovac HR 83 B4
Melisenda I 110 C2
Melisey F 60 C2
Mélito di Porto Salvo I 109 B4
Melk A 63 B6
Melksham GB 29 B5
Mellanström S 115 B15
Mellbystrand S 40 C2
Melle
B 49 B4
D 50 A4
F 67 B4
Mellendorf D 43 C6
Mellerud S 35 D4
Mellieha M 107 C5
Mellösa S 37 C3
Mellrichstadt D 51 C6
Mělník CZ 53 C4
Melón E 87 B2
Melrose GB 25 C5
Mels CH 71 A4
Melsungen D 51 B5
Meltaus FIN 113 F14
Meltham GB 27 B4
Melton Mowbray GB 30 B3
Meltosjärvi FIN 113 F13
Melun F 58 B3
Melvaig GB 22 D3
Melvich GB 23 C5
Mélykút H 75 B4
Melzo I 71 C4
Memaliaj AL 116 B1
Membrilla E 95 D3
Membrio E 93 B3
Memer F 77 B4
Memmelsdorf D 51 D6
Memmingen D 61 C6
Memoria P 92 B2
Mena UA 7 F12
Menággio I 71 B4
Menai Bridge GB 26 B1
Menasalbas E 94 C2
Menat F 68 B2
Mendavia E 89 B4
Mendaza E 89 B4
Mende F 78 B2
Menden D 50 B3
Menderes TR 119 D2
Mendig D 50 C3
Mendiga P 92 B2
Mendrisio CH 70 C3
Ménéac F 56 B3
Menemen TR 118 D2
Menen B 49 C4
Menesjärvi FIN 113 D15
Menetou-Salon F 68 A2
Menfi I 108 B1
Ménfőcsanak H 64 C3
Mengamuñoz E 94 B2
Mengen
D 61 B5
TR 118 B7
Mengeš SLO 73 B4
Mengíbar E 100 B2
Mengkofen D 62 B3
Menou F 68 A3
Mens F 79 B4
Menslage D 43 C4
Mensträsk S 115 B16
Mentana I 102 A5
Menton F 80 C1
Méntrida E 94 B2
Méobecq F 67 B6
Méounes-les-Montrieux F 79 C4
Meppel NL 42 C3
Meppen D 43 C4
Mequinenza E 90 B3
Mer F 58 C2
Mera
Coruña E 86 A2
Coruña E 86 A3
Meråker N 114 D8
Merano I 71 B6
Merate I 71 C4
Mercadillo E 89 A3
Mercatale I 82 C1
Mercatino Conca I 82 C1
Mercato San Severino I 103 C7
Mercato Saraceno I 82 C1
Merching D 62 B1
Merchtem B 49 C5
Merdrignac F 56 B3
Merdžanići BIH 84 C2
Meré E 88 A2
Mere GB 29 B5
Meréville F 58 B3
Merfeld D 50 B3
Méribel F 69 C6
Méribel Motraret F 69 C6
Meriç TR 118 A1
Mérida E 93 C4
Mérignac F 76 B2
Měřín CZ 64 A1
Mering D 62 B1
Merkendorf D 62 A1
Merklin CZ 63 A4
Merksplas B 49 B5
Merlånna S 37 C3
Merlimont Plage F 48 C2
Mern DK 39 D5
Mernye H 74 B2
Mersch L 60 A2
Merseburg D 52 B1
Mers-les-Bains F 48 C2
Merthyr Tydfil GB 29 B4
Mertingen D 62 B1
Mértola P 98 B3
Méru F 58 A3
Merufe P 87 B2
Mervans F 69 B5
Merville F 48 C3
Méry-sur-Seine F 59 B4
Merzen D 43 C4
Merzifon TR 16 A7
Merzig D 60 A2
Mesagne I 105 C3
Mesão Frio P 87 C3
Mesas de Ibor E 93 B5
Meschede D 50 B4
Meschers-sur-Gironde F 66 C4
Meshchovsk RUS 7 D13
Meslay-du-Maine F 57 C5
Mesna N 34 A2
Mesnalien N 34 A2
Mesocco CH 71 B4
Mésola I 82 B1
Mesologi GR 116 D3
Mesopotamo GR 116 C2
Mesoraca I 107 B3
Messac F 57 C4
Messancy B 60 A1
Messdorf D 44 C3
Messei F 57 B5
Messejana P 98 B2
Messelt N 34 A3
Messina I 109 A4
Messingen D 43 C4
Messini GR 117 E4
Messkirch D 61 C5
Messlingen S 115 E9
Messtetten D 61 B4
Mesta GR 117 D7
Mestanza E 100 A1
Městec Králové CZ 53 C5
Mestlin D 44 B3
Město Albrechtice CZ 54 C2
Město Libavá CZ 64 A3
Město Touškov CZ 63 A4
Mestre I 72 C2
Mesvres F 69 B4
Mesztegnyő H 74 B2
Meta I 103 C7
Metajna HR 83 B4
Metelen D 50 A3
Methana GR 117 E5
Methlick GB 23 D6
Methven GB 25 B4
Methwold GB 30 B4
Metković HR 84 C2
Metlika SLO 73 C5
Metnitz A 73 B4
Metslawier NL 42 B3
Metsovo GR 116 C3
Metten D 62 B3
Mettendorf D 50 D2
Mettet B 49 C5
Mettingen D 50 A3
Mettlach D 60 A2
Mettlen CH 70 B2
Mettmann D 50 B2
Metz F 60 A2
Metzervisse F 60 A2
Metzingen D 61 B5
Meulan F 58 A2
Meung-sur-Loire F 58 C2
Meuselwitz D 52 B2
Meuzac F 67 C6
Mevagissey GB 28 C3
Mexborough GB 27 B4
Meximieux F 69 C5
Mey GB 23 C5
Meyenburg D 44 B4
Meyerhöfen D 43 C5
Meylan F 69 C5
Meymac F 68 C2
Meyrargues F 79 C4
Meyrueis F 78 B2
Meyssac F 77 A4
Meysse F 78 B3
Meyzieu F 69 C4
Mèze F 78 C2
Mézériat F 69 B5
Mežica SLO 73 B4
Mézidon-Canon F 57 A5
Mézières-en-Brenne F 67 B6
Mézières-sur-Issoire F 67 B5
Mézilhac F 78 B3
Mézilles F 59 C4
Mézin F 76 B3
Mezöberény H 75 B6
Mezőcsát H 65 C6
Mezőfalva H 74 B3
Mezőhegyes H 75 B5
Mezőkeresztes H 65 C6
Mezőkomárom H 74 B3
Mezőkövácsháza H 75 B5
Mezőkövesd H 65 C6
Mezőörs H 74 A2
Mézos F 76 B1
Mezőszilas H 74 B3
Mezőtúr H 75 A5
Mezquita de Jarque E 90 C2
Mezzano
Emilia Romagna I 81 B6
Trentino Alto Adige I 72 B1
Mezzojuso I 108 B2
Mezzoldo I 71 B4
Mezzolombardo I 71 B6
Mgarr M 107 C5
Mglin RUS 7 E12
Miajadas E 93 B5
Miały PL 46 C2
Mianowice PL 46 A3
Miasteczko Krajeńskie PL 46 B3
Miasteczko Śl. PL 54 C3
Miastko PL 46 A2
Michalovce SK 10 B6
Michałowice PL 55 C4
Michelau D 61 A6
Michelbach D 61 A6
Micheldorf A 63 C5
Michelhausen A 64 B1
Michelsneukirchen D 62 A3
Michelstadt D 61 A5
Michendorf D 45 C5
Mickleover GB 27 C4
Midbea GB 23 B6
Middelburg NL 49 B4
Middelfart DK 39 D2
Middelharnis NL 49 B5
Middelkerke B 48 B3
Middelstum NL 42 B3
Middlesbrough GB 27 A4
Middleton Cheney GB 30 B2
Middleton-in-Teesdale GB 26 A3
Middletown GB 19 B5
Middlewich GB 26 B3
Middlezoy GB 29 B5
Midhurst GB 31 D3
Midleton IRL 20 C3
Midlum D 43 B5
Midsomer Norton GB 29 B5
Midtgulen N 114 F2
Midtskogberget N 34 A4
Midwolda NL 43 B4
Mid Yell GB 22 A7
Miechów PL 55 C5
Miedes de Aragón E 89 C5
Miedes de Atienza E 95 A3
Międzybodzie Bielskie PL 65 A5
Międzybórz PL 54 B2
Międzychód PL 46 C1
Międzylesie PL 54 C1
Międzyrzec Podlaski PL 6 F7
Międzyrzecz PL 46 C1
Międzywodzie PL 45 A6
Międzyzdroje PL 45 B6
Miejska Górka PL 54 B1
Miélan F 76 C3
Mielec PL 55 C6
Mielęcin PL 45 B6
Mielno
Warmińsko-Mazurskie PL 47 B6
Zachodnio-Pomorskie PL 46 A2
Miengo E 88 A3
Mieraslompolo FIN 113 C16
Miercurea Ciuc RO 11 C8
Mieres
Asturias E 88 A1
Girona E 91 A5
Mieroszów PL 53 C6
Mierzyn PL 55 B4
Miesau D 60 A3
Miesbach D 62 C2
Mieścisko PL 46 C3
Mieste D 44 C3
Miesterhorst D 44 C3
Mieszków PL 54 A2
Mieszkowice PL 45 C6
Mietków PL 54 C1
Migennes F 59 C4
Miggiano I 107 B5
Migliánico I 103 A7
Migliarino I 81 B5
Migliónico I 104 C2
Mignano Monte Lungo I 103 B6
Migné F 67 B6
Miguel Esteban E 95 C3
Miguelturra E 94 D3
Mihajlovac SRB 85 B5
Mihald H 74 B2
Mihalgazi TR 118 B5
Mihaliççık TR 118 C6
Mihályi H 74 A2
Mihla D 51 B6
Mihohnić HR 83 A3
Miholjsko HR 73 C5
Mihovljan HR 73 B5
Mijares E 94 B2
Mijas E 100 C1
Mijoska MNE 85 D4
Mike H 74 B2
Mikhnevo RUS 7 D14
Mikines GR 117 E4
Mikkeli FIN 3 F27
Mikkelvik N 112 B8
Mikleuš HR 74 C2
Mikołajki Pomorskie PL 47 B5
Mikołów PL 54 C3
Mikonos GR 117 E7
Mikorzyn PL 54 B3
Mikro Derio GR 116 A8
Mikstat PL 54 B2
Mikulášovice CZ 53 C4
Mikulov CZ 64 B2
Mikulovice CZ 54 C2
Milagro E 89 B5
Miłakowo PL 47 A6
Milan = Milano I 71 C4
Miland N 32 C5
Milano = Milan I 71 C4
Milano Marittima I 82 B1
Milas TR 119 E2
Milazzo I 109 A4
Mildenhall GB 30 B4
Milejewo PL 47 A5
Milelín CZ 53 C5
Miletić SRB 75 C4
Miletićevo SRB 75 C6
Mileto I 106 C3
Milevsko CZ 63 A5
Milford IRL 19 A4
Milford Haven GB 28 B2
Milford on Sea GB 31 D2
Milhão P 87 C4
Milići BIH 84 B4
Miličín CZ 63 A5
Milicz PL 54 B2
Milín CZ 63 A5
Militello in Val di Catánia I 109 B3
Miljevina BIH 84 C3
Milkowice PL 53 B6
Millançay F 68 A1
Millares E 96 B2
Millas F 91 A5
Millau F 78 B2
Millesimo I 80 B2
Millevaches F 68 C2
Millom GB 26 A2
Millport GB 24 C3
Millstatt A 72 B3
Millstreet
Cork IRL 20 B2
Waterford IRL 21 B4
Milltown
Galway IRL 18 C3
Kerry IRL 20 B1
Milltown Malbay IRL 20 B2
Milly-la-Forêt F 58 B3
Milmarcos E 95 A5
Milmersdorf D 45 B5
Milna HR 83 C5
Milnthorpe GB 26 A3
Miločaj SRB 85 C5
Milogórze PL 47 A6
Miłomłyn PL 47 B5
Milos GR 117 F6
Miloševo SRB 85 B6
Miłosław PL 54 A2
Milot AL 105 B5
Milówka PL 65 A5
Miltach D 62 A3
Miltenberg D 61 A5
Milton Keynes GB 31 B3
Miltzow D 45 A5
Milutovac SRB 85 C6
Milverton GB 29 B4
Milzyn PL 47 C4
Mimice HR 84 C1
Mimizan F 76 B1
Mimizan-Plage F 76 B1
Mimoň CZ 53 C4
Mina de Juliana P 98 B2
Mina de São Domingos P 98 B3
Minas de Riotinto E 99 B4
Minateda E 101 A4
Minaya E 95 C4
Minde P 92 B2
Mindelheim D 61 B6
Mindelstetten D 62 B2
Minden D 51 A4
Mindszent H 75 B5
Minehead GB 29 B4
Mineo I 109 B3
Minerbe I 71 C6
Minérbio I 81 B5
Minervino Murge I 104 B2
Minglanilla E 95 C5
Mingorria E 94 B2
Minnesund N 34 B3
Miño E 86 A2
Miño de San Esteban E 89 C3
Minsen D 43 B4
Minsk BY 7 E9
Mińsk Mazowiecki PL 55 A6
Minsterley GB 26 C3
Mintlaw GB 23 D6
Minturno I 103 B6
Mionica
BIH 84 B3
SRB 85 B5
Mios F 76 B2
Mira
E 96 B1
I 72 C2
P 92 A2
Mirabel E 93 B4
Mirabel-aux-Baronnies F 79 B4
Mirabella Eclano I 103 B8
Mirabella Imbáccari I 109 B3
Mirabello I 81 B5
Miradoux F 77 B3
Miraflores de la Sierra E 94 B3
Miralrio E 95 B4
Miramar P 87 C2
Miramare I 82 B1
Miramas F 78 C3
Mirambeau F 67 C4
Miramont-de-Guyenne F 77 B3
Miranda de Arga E 89 B5
Miranda de Ebro E 89 B4
Miranda do Corvo P 92 A2
Miranda do Douro P 87 C4
Mirande F 77 C3
Mirandela P 87 C3
Mirandilla E 93 C4
Mirándola I 81 B5
Miranje HR 83 B4
Mirano I 72 C2
Miras AL 116 B2
Miravet E 90 B3
Miré F 57 C5
Mirebeau F 67 B5
Mirebeau-sur-Bèze F 69 A5
Mirecourt F 60 B2
Mirepoix F 77 C4
Mires GR 117 G6
Miribel F 69 C4
Miričina BIH 84 B3
Mirina GR 116 C7
Mirna SLO 73 C5
Miroslav CZ 64 B2
Mirosławice PL 54 C1
Mirosławiec PL 46 B2
Mirošov CZ 63 A4
Mirotice CZ 63 A5
Mirovice CZ 63 A5
Mirow D 45 B4
Mirsk PL 53 C5
Mirzec PL 55 B6
Misi FIN 113 F15
Misilmeri I 108 A2
Miske H 75 B4
Miskolc H 65 B6
Mislinja SLO 73 B5
Missanello I 104 C2
Missillac F 66 A2
Mistelbach
A 64 B2
D 52 D1
Misten N 112 E3
Misterbianco I 109 B4
Misterhult S 40 B6
Mistretta I 109 B3
Misurina I 72 B2
Mitchelstown IRL 20 B3
Mithimna GR 116 C8
Mithoni GR 117 F3
Mitilini GR 118 C1
Mitilinii GR 119 E1
Mittelberg
Tirol A 71 B5
Vorarlberg A 71 B5
Mittenwald D 71 A6
Mittenwalde D 52 A3
Mitterback A 63 C6
Mitterdorf im Mürztal A 73 A5
Mitter-Kleinarl A 72 A3
Mittersheim F 60 B2
Mittersill A 72 A2
Mitterskirchen D 62 B3
Mitterteich D 62 A3
Mitton F 76 B2
Mittweida D 52 C2
Mitwitz D 52 C1
Mizhhir'ya UA 11 B7
Mjällby S 41 C4
Mjåvatn N 33 D5
Mjöbäck S 40 B2
Mjölby S 37 D2
Mjølfjell N 32 B3
Mjøndalen N 35 C2
Mjørlund N 34 B2
Mladá Boleslav CZ 53 C4
Mladá Vožice CZ 63 A5
Mladé Buky CZ 53 C5
Mladenovac SRB 85 B5
Mladenovo SRB 75 C4
Mladikovine BIH 84 B2
Mława PL 47 B6
Mlinište BIH 84 B1
Młodzieszyn PL 55 A5
Młogoszyn PL 55 A4
Młynary PL 47 A5
Mnichóvice CZ 63 A5
Mnichovo Hradiště CZ 53 C4
Mniów PL 55 B5
Mnisek nad Hnilcom SK 65 B6
Mníšek pod Brdy CZ 63 A5
Mniszek PL 55 B5
Mniszków PL 55 B5
Mo
Hedmark N 34 B3
Hordaland N 32 B2
Møre og Romsdal N 114 E5
Telemark N 33 C4
Gävleborg S 36 A3
Västra Götaland S 35 D3
Moaña E 87 B2
Moate IRL 21 A4
Mocejón E 94 C3
Močenok SK 64 B3
Mochales E 95 A4
Mochowo PL 47 C5
Mochy PL 53 A6
Mockern D 52 A1
Mockfjärd S 36 B1
Möckmühl D 61 A5
Mockrehna D 52 B2
Moclin E 100 B2
Mocsa H 64 C4
Mőcsény H 74 B3
Modane F 70 C1
Modbury GB 28 C4
Módena I 81 B4
Módica I 109 C3
Modigliana I 81 B5
Modlin PL 47 C6
Mödling A 64 B2
Modliszewice PL 55 B5
Modliszewko PL 46 C3
Modogno I 104 B2
Modra SK 64 B3
Modran BIH 84 B2
Modriča BIH 84 B3
Möðrudalur IS 111 B10
Modrý Kamen SK 65 B5
Moëlan-sur-Mer F 56 C2
Moelfre GB 26 B1
Moelv N 34 B2
Moen N 112 C7
Moena I 72 B1
Moerbeke B 49 B4
Moers D 50 B2
Móes P 87 D3
Moffat GB 25 C4
Mogadouro P 87 C4
Mogata S 37 D3
Móggio Udinese I 72 B3
Mogielnica PL 55 B5
Mogilany PL 65 A5
Mogilno PL 46 C3
Mogliano I 82 C2
Mogliano Véneto I 72 C2
Mogor E 87 B2
Mógoro I 110 C1
Moguer E 99 B4
Mohács H 74 C3
Moheda S 40 B4
Mohedas E 93 A4
Mohedas de la Jara E 93 B5
Mohelnice CZ 64 A2
Mohill IRL 19 C4
Möhlin CH 70 A2
Moholm S 35 D6
Mohorn D 52 B3
Mohyliv-Podil's'kyy UA 11 B9
Moi N 33 D3
Moià E 91 B5
Móie I 82 C2
Moimenta da Beira P 87 D3
Mo i Rana N 115 A11
Moirans F 69 C5
Moirans-en-Montagne F 69 B5
Moisaküla EST 7 B8
Moisdon-la-Rivière F 57 C4
Moissac F 77 B4
Moita
Coimbra P 92 A2
Guarda P 93 A3
Santarém P 92 B2
Setúbal P 92 C1
Moita dos Ferreiros P 92 B1
Moixent E 101 A5
Mojacar E 101 B4
Mojados E 88 C2
Mojkovac MNE 85 D4
Mojmírovce SK 64 B4
Mojtin SK 65 B4
Möklinta S 36 B3
Mokošica HR 84 D3
Mokra Gora SRB 85 C4
Mokronog SLO 73 C5
Mokro Polje HR 83 B5
Mokrzyska PL 55 C5
Møkster N 32 B2
Mol
B 49 B6
SRB 75 C5
Mola di Bari I 104 B3
Molai GR 117 F4
Molare I 80 B2
Molaretto I 70 C2
Molas F 77 C3
Molassano I 80 B2
Molbergen D 43 C4
Mold GB 26 B2
Molde N 114 E4
Møldrup DK 38 C2
Moledo do Minho P 87 C2
Molfetta I 104 B2
Molfsee D 44 A2
Moliden S 115 D15
Molières F 77 B4
Molina de Aragón E 95 B5
Molina de Segura E 101 A4
Molinar E 89 A3
Molinaseca E 86 B4
Molinella I 81 B5
Molinet F 68 B3
Molinicos E 101 A3
Molini di Tures I 72 B1
Molinos de Duero E 89 C4
Molins de Rei E 91 B5
Moliterno I 104 C1
Molkom S 35 C5
Möllbrücke A 72 B3
Mölle S 41 C2
Molledo E 88 A2
Möllenbeck D 45 B5
Mollerussa E 90 B3
Mollet de Perelada E 91 A5
Mollina E 100 B1
Mölln D 44 B2
Molló E 91 A5
Mollösund S 38 A4
Mölltorp S 37 D1
Mölnbo S 37 C4
Mölndal S 38 B5
Mölnlycke S 38 B5
Molompize F 68 C3
Moloy F 69 A4
Molsheim F 60 B3
Moltzow D 45 B4
Molve HR 74 B2
Molveno I 71 B5
Molvizar E 100 C2
Molzbichl A 72 B3
Mombaróccio I 82 C1
Mombeltrán E 94 B1
Mombris D 51 C5
Mombuey E 87 B4
Momchilgrad BG 116 A7
Mommark DK 39 E3
Momo I 70 C3
Monaghan IRL 19 B5
Monar Lodge GB 22 D4
Monasterace Marina I 106 C3
Monasterevin IRL 21 A4
Monasterio de Rodilla E 89 B3
Monastir I 110 C2
Monbahus F 77 B3
Monbazillac F 77 B3
Moncada E 96 B2
Moncalieri I 80 A1
Moncalvo I 80 A2
Monção P 87 B2
Moncarapacho P 98 B3
Moncel-sur-Seille F 60 B2
Monchegorsk RUS 3 C30
Mönchengladbach = Munchen-Gladbach D 50 B2
Mónchio della Corti I 81 B4
Monchique P 98 B2
Monclar-de-Quercy F 77 C4
Moncofa E 96 B2
Moncontour F 56 B3
Moncoutant F 67 B4
Monda E 100 C1
Mondariz E 87 B2
Mondavio I 82 C1
Mondéjar E 95 B3
Mondello I 108 A2
Mondim de Basto P 87 C3
Mondolfo I 82 C2
Mondoñedo E 86 A3
Mondorf-les-Bains L 60 A2
Mondoubleau F 58 C1
Mondovì I 80 B1
Mondragon F 78 B3
Mondragone I 103 B6
Mondsee A 63 C4
Monéglia I 80 B3
Monegrillo E 90 B2
Monein F 76 C2
Monemvasia GR 117 F5
Mónesi I 80 B1
Monesiglio I 80 B2
Monesterio E 99 A4
Monestier-de-Clermont F 79 B4
Monestiés F 77 B5
Monéteau F 59 C4
Moneygall IRL 21 B4
Moneymore GB 19 B5
Monfalcone I 72 C3
Monfero E 86 A2
Monflanquin F 77 B3
Monflorite E 90 A2
Monforte P 92 B3
Monforte da Beira
E 92 B3
P 92 B3
Monforte d'Alba I 80 B1
Monforte del Cid E 96 C2
Monforte de Lemos E 86 B3
Monforte de Moyuela E 90 B1
Monghidoro I 81 B5
Mongiana I 106 C3
Monguelfo I 72 B2
Monheim D 62 B1
Moniaive GB 25 C4
Monifieth GB 25 B5
Monikie GB 25 B5
Monistrol-d'Allier F 78 B2
Monistrol de Montserrat E 91 B4
Monistrol-sur-Loire F 68 C4
Mönkebude D 45 B5
Monkton GB 24 C3
Monmouth GB 29 B5
Monnaie F 67 A5
Monnerville F 58 B3
Monnickendam NL 42 C2
Monolithos GR 119 F2
Monópoli I 104 C3
Monor H 75 A4
Monóvar E 101 A5
Monpazier F 77 B3
Monreal
D 50 C3
E 76 D1
Monreal del Campo E 95 B5
Monreale I 108 A2
Monroy E 93 B4
Monroyo E 90 C2
Mons B 49 C4
Monsaraz P 92 C3
Monschau D 50 C2
Monségur F 76 B3
Monsélice I 72 C1
Mønshaug N 32 B3
Monster NL 49 A5
Mönsterås S 40 B6
Monsummano Terme I 81 C4
Montabaur D 50 C3
Montafia I 80 B2
Montagnac F 78 C2
Montagnana I 71 C6
Montaigu F 66 B3
Montaigu-de-Quercy F 77 B4
Montaiguët-en-Forez F 68 B3
Montaigut F 68 B2
Montaigut-sur-Save F 77 C4
Montainville F 58 B2
Montalbán E 90 C2
Montalbán de Córdoba E 100 B1
Montalbano Elicona I 109 A4
Montalbano Iónico I 104 C2
Montalbo E 95 C4
Montalcino I 81 C5
Montaldo di Cósola I 80 B3
Montalegre P 87 C3
Montalieu-Vercieu F 69 C5
Montalivet-les-Bains F 66 C3
Montallegro I 108 B2
Montalto delle Marche I 82 D2
Montalto di Castro I 102 A4
Montalto Pavese I 80 B3
Montalto Uffugo I 106 B3
Montalvão P 92 B3
Montamarta E 88 C1
Montana BG 11 E7
Montana-Vermala CH 70 B2
Montánchez E 93 B4
Montanejos E 96 A2
Montano Antilia I 106 A2
Montans F 77 C4
Montargil P 92 B2
Montargis F 58 C3
Montastruc-la-Conseillère F 77 C4
Montauban F 77 B4
Montauban-de-Bretagne F 57 B3
Montbard F 59 C5
Montbarrey F 69 A5
Montbazens F 77 B5
Montbazon F 67 A5
Montbéliard F 70 A1
Montbenoit F 69 B6
Montbeugny F 68 B3
Montblanc E 91 B4
Montbozon F 69 A6
Montbrison F 68 C4
Montbron F 67 C5
Montbrun-les-Bains F 79 B4
Montceau-les-Mines F 69 B4
Montcenis F 69 B4
Montchanin F 69 B4
Montcornet F 59 A5
Montcuq F 77 B4
Montdardier F 78 C2
Mont-de-Marsan F 76 C2
Montdidier F 58 A3
Monteagudo E 101 A4
Monteagudo de las Vicarias E 89 C4
Montealegre E 88 C2
Montealegre del Castillo E 101 A4
Montebello Iónico I 109 B4
Montebello Vicentino I 71 C6
Montebelluna I 72 C2
Montebourg F 57 A4
Montebruno I 80 B3
Monte-Carlo MC 80 C1
Montecarotto I 82 C2
Montecassiano I 82 C2
Montecastrilli I 102 A5
Montecatini Terme I 81 C4
Montécchio I 82 C1
Montécchio Emilia I 81 B4
Montécchio Maggiore I 71 C6
Montech F 77 C4
Montechiaro d'Asti I 80 A2
Monte Clara P 92 B3
Monte Clérigo P 98 B2
Montecórice I 103 C7
Montecorvino Rovella I 103 C7
Monte da Pedra P 92 B3
Monte de Goula P 92 B3
Montederramo E 87 B3
Montedoro I 108 B2
Monte do Trigo P 92 C3
Montefalco I 82 D1
Montefalcone di Val Fortore I 103 B8
Montefalcone nel Sánnio I 103 B7
Montefano I 82 C2
Montefiascone I 102 A5
Montefiorino I 81 B4
Montefortino I 82 D2
Montefranco I 102 A5
Montefrío E 100 B2
Montegiordano Marina I 106 A3
Montegiórgio I 82 C2
Monte Gordo P 98 B3
Montegranaro I 82 C2
Montehermoso E 93 A4
Montejicar E 100 B2
Montejo de la Sierra E 95 A3
Montejo de Tiermes E 89 C3
Monte Juntos P 92 C3
Montel-de-Gelat F 68 C2
Monteleone di Púglia I 103 B8
Monteleone di Spoleto I 102 A5
Monteleone d'Orvieto I 81 D6
Montelepre I 108 A2
Montelibretti I 102 A5
Montelier F 79 B4
Montélimar F 78 B3
Montella
E 91 A4
I 103 C8
Montellano E 99 B5
Montelupo Fiorentino I 81 C5
Montemaggiore Belsito I 108 B2
Montemagno I 80 B2
Montemayor E 100 B1
Montemayor de Pinilla E 88 C2
Montemésola I 104 C3
Montemilleto I 103 B7
Montemilone I 104 B1
Montemolín E 99 A4
Montemónaco I 82 D2
Montemor-o-Novo P 92 C2
Montemor-o-Velho P 92 A2
Montemurro I 104 C1
Montendre F 67 C4
Montenegro de Cameros E 89 B4
Montenero di Bisáccia I 103 B7
Monteneuf F 57 C3
Monteparano I 104 C3
Montepescali I 81 D5
Montepiano I 81 B5
Monte Porzio I 82 C2
Montepulciano I 81 C5
Monte Real P 92 B2
Montereale I 103 A6
Montereale Valcellina I 72 B2
Montereau-Faut-Yonne F 59 B3
Monte Redondo P 92 B2
Monterénzio I 81 B5
Monte Romano I 102 A4
Monteroni d'Arbia I 81 C5
Monteroni di Lecce I 105 C4
Monterosso al Mare I 80 B3
Monterosso Almo I 109 B3
Monterosso Grana I 79 B6
Monterotondo I 102 A5
Monterotondo Maríttimo I 81 C4
Monterrey E 87 C3
Monterroso E 86 B3
Monterrubio de la Serena E 93 C5
Monterubbiano I 82 C2
Montesa E 96 C2
Montesalgueiro E 86 A2
Monte San Giovanni Campano I 103 B6
Montesano sulla Marcellana I 104 C1
Monte San Savino I 81 C5
Monte Sant'Angelo I 104 B1
Montesárchio I 103 B7
Montescaglioso I 104 C2
Montesclaros E 94 B2
Montesilvano I 103 A7
Montespértoli I 81 C5
Montesquieu-Volvestre F 77 C4
Montesquiou F 77 C3
Montestruc-sur-Gers F 77 C3
Montes Velhos P 98 B2
Montevarchi I 81 C5
Montévéglio I 81 B5
Monte Vilar P 92 B1
Montfaucon F 66 A3
Montfaucon-d'Argonne F 59 A6
Montfaucon-en-Velay F 69 C4
Montferrat
Isère F 69 C5
Var F 79 C5
Montfort-en-Chalosse F 76 C2
Montfort-l'Amaury F 58 B2
Montfort-le-Gesnois F 58 B1
Montfort-sur-Meu F 57 B4
Montfort-sur-Risle F 58 A1
Montgai E 90 B3
Montgaillard F 76 C3
Montgenèvre F 79 B5
Montgiscard F 77 C4
Montgomery GB 26 C2
Montguyon F 67 C4
Monthermé F 59 A5
Monthey CH 70 B1
Monthois F 59 A5
Monthureux-sur-Saône F 60 B1
Monti I 110 B2
Monticelli d'Ongina I 81 A3
Montichiari I 71 C5
Monticiano I 81 C5
Montiel E 100 A3
Montier-en-Der F 59 B5
Montieri I 81 C5
Montiglio I 80 A2
Montignac F 77 A4
Montigny-le-Roi F 60 C1
Montigny-lès-Metz F 60 A2
Montigny-sur-Aube F 59 C5
Montijo
E 93 C4
P 92 C2
Montilla E 100 B1
Montillana E 100 B2
Montilly F 68 B3
Montivilliers F 57 A6
Montjaux F 78 B1
Montjean-sur-Loire F 66 A4
Montlhéry F 58 B3
Montlieu-la-Garde F 67 C4
Mont-Louis F 91 A5
Montlouis-sur-Loire F 67 A5
Montluçon F 68 B2
Montluel F 69 C5
Montmarault F 68 B2
Montmartin-sur-Mer F 57 B4
Montmédy F 59 A6
Montmélian F 69 C6
Montmeyan F 79 C5
Montmeyran F 78 B3
Montmirail
Marne F 59 B4
Sarthe F 58 B1
Montmirat F 69 C5
Montmirat F 78 C3
Montmirey-le-Château F 69 A5

Montmoreau-St Cybard F 67 C5
Montmorency F 58 B3
Montmorillon F 67 B5
Montmort-Lucy F 59 B4
Montoir-de-Bretagne F 66 A2
Montoire-sur-le-Loir F 58 C1
Montoito P 92 C3
Montolieu F 77 C5
Montório al Vomano I 103 A6
Montoro E 100 A1
Montpellier F 78 C2
Montpezat-de-Quercy F 77 B4
Montpezat-sous-Bouzon F 78 B3
Montpon-Ménestérol F 76 A3
Montpont-en-Bresse F 69 B5
Montréal
Aude F 77 C5
Gers F 76 C3
Montredon-Labessonnié F 77 C5
Montréjeau F 77 C3
Montrésor F 67 A6
Montresta I 110 B1
Montret F 69 B5
Montreuil
Pas de Calais F 48 C2
Seine St Denis F 58 B3
Montreuil-aux-Lions F 59 A4
Montreuil-Bellay F 67 A4
Montreux CH 70 B1
Montrevault F 66 A3
Montrevel-en-Bresse F 69 B5
Montrichard F 67 A6
Montricoux F 77 B4
Mont-roig del Camp E 90 B3
Montrond-les-Bains F 69 C4
Montrose GB 25 B5
Montroy E 96 B2
Montsalvy F 77 B5
Montsauche-les-Settons F 68 A4
Montseny E 91 B5
Montsoreau F 67 A5
Mont-sous-Vaudrey F 69 B5
Monts-sur-Guesnes F 67 B5
Mont-St Aignan F 58 A2
Mont-St Vincent F 69 B4
Montsûrs F 57 B5
Montuenga E 94 A2
Montuïri E 97 B3
Monturque E 100 B1
Monza I 71 C4
Monzón E 90 B3
Monzón de Campos E 88 B2
Moorbad Lobenstein D 52 C1
Moordorf D 43 B4
Moorslede B 49 C4
Moos D 61 C4
Moosburg D 62 B2
Moosburg im Kärnten A 73 B4
Mór H 74 A3
Mora E 94 C3
Móra P 92 C2
Mora S 36 A1
Moraby S 36 B2
Mòra d'Ebre E 90 B3
Mora de Rubielos E 96 A2
Moradillo de Roa E 88 C3
Morąg PL 47 B5
Mórahalom H 75 B4
Moraime E 86 A1
Morais P 87 C4
Mòra la Nova E 90 B3
Moral de Calatrava E 100 A2
Moraleda de Zafayona E 100 B2
Moraleja E 93 A4
Moraleja del Vino E 88 C1
Morales del Vino E 88 C1
Morales de Toro E 88 C1
Morales de Valverde E 88 C1
Moralina E 87 C4
Morano Cálabro I 106 B3
Mörarp S 41 C2
Morasverdes E 93 A4
Morata de Jalón E 89 C5
Morata de Jiloca E 89 C5
Morata de Tajuña E 95 B3
Moratalla E 101 A4
Moravče SLO 73 B4
Moravec CZ 64 A2
Moraviţa RO 75 C6
Morávka CZ 65 A4
Moravská Třebová CZ 64 A2
Moravské Budějovice CZ 64 A1
Moravské Lieskové SK 64 B3
Moravske Toplice SLO 73 B6
Moravský-Beroun CZ 64 A3
Moravský Krumlov CZ 64 A2
Moravský Svätý Ján SK 64 B3
Morawica PL 55 C5
Morawin PL 54 B3
Morbach D 60 A3
Morbegno I 71 B4
Morbier F 69 B6
Mörbisch am See A 64 C2
Mörbylånga S 41 C6
Morcenx F 76 B2
Morciano di Romagna I 82 C1
Morcone I 103 B7
Morcuera E 89 C3
Mordelles F 57 B4
Mordoğan TR 119 D1
Moréac F 56 C3
Morebattle GB 25 C5
Morecambe GB 26 A3
Moreda
Granada E 100 B2
Oviedo E 88 A1
Morée F 58 C2
Moreles de Rey E 88 B1
Morella E 90 C2
Moreruela de los Infanzones E 88 C1
Morés E 89 C5
Móres I 110 B1
Morestel F 69 C5
Moretonhampstead GB 28 C4
Moreton-in-Marsh GB 29 B6
Moret-sur-Loing F 58 B3
Moretta I 80 B1
Moreuil F 58 A3
Morez F 69 B6
Mörfelden D 51 D4
Morgat F 56 B1
Morges CH 69 B6
Morgex I 70 C2
Morgongåva S 36 C3
Morhange F 60 B2
Morhet B 49 D6
Mori I 71 C5
Morialmé B 49 C5
Morianes P 98 B3
Moriani Plage F 102 A2
Mórichida H 74 A2
Moriles E 100 B1
Morille E 94 B1
Moringen D 51 B5
Morjärv S 3 C25
Morkarla S 36 B4
Mørke DK 39 C3
Mørkøv DK 39 D4
Morkovice-Slížany CZ 64 A3
Morlaàs F 76 C2
Morlaix F 56 B2
Morley F 59 B6
Mörlunda S 40 B5
Mormanno I 106 B2
Mormant F 59 B3
Mornant F 69 C4
Mornay-Berry F 68 A2
Morokovo MNE 85 D4
Morón de Almazán E 89 C4
Morón de la Frontera E 99 B5
Morović SRB 85 A4
Morozzo I 80 B1
Morpeth GB 25 C6
Morphou CY 120 A1
Mörrum S 41 C4
Morsbach D 50 C3
Mörsch D 61 B4
Mörsil S 115 D10
Morsum D 39 E1
Mørsvikbotn N 112 E4
Mortagne-au-Perche F 58 B1
Mortagne-sur-Gironde F 66 C4
Mortagne-sur-Sèvre F 66 B4
Mortágua P 92 A2
Mortain F 57 B5
Mortara I 70 C3
Morteau F 69 A6
Mortegliano I 72 C3
Mortelle I 109 A4
Mortemart F 67 B5
Mortimer's Cross GB 29 A5
Mortrée F 57 B6
Mörtschach A 72 B2
Mortsel B 49 B5
Morud DK 39 D3
Morwenstow GB 28 C3
Moryń PL 45 C6
Morzeszczyn PL 47 B4
Morzewo PL 47 B5
Morzine F 70 B1
Mosalsk RUS 7 D13
Mosbach D 61 A5
Mosbjerg DK 38 B3
Mosby N 33 D4
Mosca P 87 C4
Moscavide P 92 C1
Moščenica HR 73 C6
Mošćenice HR 73 C4
Moščenicka Draga HR 73 C4
Mosciano Sant'Ángelo I 82 D2
Mościsko PL 54 C1
Moscow = Moskva RUS 7 D14
Mosina PL 54 A1
Mosjøen N 115 B10
Moskog N 32 A3
Moskorzew PL 55 C4
Moskosel S 115 B16
Moskuvarra FIN 113 E15
Moskva = Moscow RUS 7 D14
Moslavina Podravska HR 74 C2
Moşniţa Nouă RO 75 C6
Moso in Passíria I 71 B6
Mosonmagyaróvár H 64 C3
Mošorin SRB 75 C5
Mošovce SK 65 B4
Mosqueruela E 90 C2
Moss N 35 C2
Mossfellsbær IS 111 C4
Mössingen D 61 B5
Møsstrand N 32 C5
Most CZ 52 C3
Mosta M 107 C5
Mostar BIH 84 C2
Mosterhamn N 33 C2
Mostki PL 53 A5
Most na Soči SLO 72 B3
Móstoles E 94 B3
Mostová SK 64 B3
Mostowo PL 46 A2
Mostuéjouls F 78 B2
Mosty PL 45 B6
Mostys'ka UA 11 B7
Mosvik N 114 D7
Mota del Cuervo E 95 C4
Mota del Marqués E 88 C1
Motala S 37 D2
Motherwell GB 25 C4
Möthlow D 45 C4
Motilla del Palancar E 95 C5
Motnik SLO 73 B4
Motovun HR 72 C3
Motril E 100 C2
Motta I 71 C6
Motta di Livenza I 72 C2
Motta Montecorvino I 103 B8
Motta Visconti I 70 C3
Mottisfont GB 31 C2
Móttola I 104 C3
Mou DK 38 C3
Mouchard F 69 B5
Moudon CH 70 B1
Moudros GR 116 C7
Mougins F 79 C5
Mouilleron en-Pareds F 66 B4
Mouliherne F 67 A5
Moulinet F 80 C1
Moulins F 68 B3
Moulins-Engilbert F 68 B3
Moulins-la-Marche F 58 B1
Moulismes F 67 B5
Moult F 57 A5
Mountain Ash GB 29 B4
Mountbellew IRL 20 A3
Mountfield GB 19 B4
Mountmellick IRL 21 A4
Mountrath IRL 21 A4
Mountsorrel GB 30 B2
Moura P 98 A3
Mourão P 92 C3
Mourenx F 76 C2
Mouriés F 78 C3
Mourmelon-le-Grand F 59 A5
Mouronho P 92 A2
Mouscron B 49 C4
Mousehole GB 28 C2
Moussac F 78 C3
Moussey F 60 B2
Mousteru F 56 B2
Moustey F 76 B2
Moustiers-Ste Marie F 79 C5
Mouthe F 69 B6
Mouthier-Haute-Pierre F 69 A6
Mouthoumet F 77 D5
Moutier CH 70 A2
Moûtiers F 69 C6
Moutiers-les-Mauxfaits F 66 B3
Mouy F 58 A3
Mouzaki GR 116 C3
Mouzon F 59 A6
Møvik N 32 B2
Moville IRL 19 A4
Moy
Highland GB 23 D4
Tyrone GB 19 B5
Moycullen IRL 20 A2
Moyenmoutier F 60 B2
Moyenvic F 60 B2
Moylough IRL 18 C3
Mózar E 88 C1
Mozhaysk RUS 7 D14
Mozirje SLO 73 B4
Mözs H 74 B3
Mozzanica I 71 C4
Mramorak SRB 85 B5
Mrčajevci SRB 85 C5
Mrkonjić Grad BIH 84 B2
Mrkopalj HR 73 C4
Mrmoš SRB 85 C6
Mrocza PL 46 B3
Mroczeń PL 54 B2
Mroczno PL 47 B5
Mrozy PL 55 A6
Mrzezyno PL 45 A7
Mšec CZ 53 C3
Mšeno CZ 53 C4
Mstów PL 55 C4
Mstsislaw BY 7 D11
Mszana Dolna PL 65 A6
Mszczonów PL 55 B5
Mtsensk RUS 7 E14
Muć HR 83 C5
Múccia I 82 C2
Much D 50 C3
Mücheln D 52 B1
Much Marcle GB 29 B5
Muchów PL 53 B6
Much Wenlock GB 26 C3
Mucientes E 88 C2
Muckross IRL 20 B2
Mucur TR 16 B7
Muda P 98 B2
Mudanya TR 118 B3
Mudau D 61 A5
Müden D 44 C2
Mudersbach D 50 C3
Mudurnu TR 118 B6
Muel E 90 B1
Muelas del Pan E 88 C1
Muess D 44 B3
Muff IRL 19 A4
Mugardos E 86 A2
Muge P 92 B2
Mügeln
Sachsen D 52 B3
Sachsen-Anhalt D 52 B3
Múggia I 72 C3
Mugnano I 82 C1
Mugron F 76 C2
Mugueimes E 87 C3
Muhi H 65 C6
Mühlacker D 61 B4
Mühlbach am Hochkönig A 72 A3
Mühlberg
Brandenburg D 52 B3
Thüringen D 51 C6
Mühldorf
A 72 B3
D 62 B3
Muhleberg CH 70 B2
Mühleim D 61 B4
Muhlen-Eichsen D 44 B3
Mühlhausen
Bayern D 62 A1
Thüringen D 51 B6
Mühltroff D 52 C1
Muhos FIN 3 D27
Muhr A 72 A3
Muine Bheag IRL 21 B5
Muirkirk GB 24 C3
Muir of Ord GB 23 D4
Muirteira P 92 B1
Mukacheve UA 11 B7
Muker GB 26 A3
Mula E 101 A4
Muğla TR 119 E3
Mulben GB 23 D5
Mulegns CH 71 B4
Mules I 71 B6
Mülheim D 50 B2
Mulhouse F 60 C3
Muljava SLO 73 C4
Mullanys Cross IRL 18 B3
Müllheim D 60 C3
Mullhyttan S 37 C1
Mullinavat IRL 21 B4
Mullingar IRL 21 A4
Mullion GB 28 C2
Müllrose D 53 A4
Mullsjö S 40 B3
Mulseryd S 40 B3
Munaðarnes IS 111 A4
Munana E 94 B1
Muñás E 86 A4
Münchberg D 52 C1
Müncheberg D 45 C6
München = Munich D 62 B2
Munchen-Gladbach = Mönchengladbach D 50 B2
Münchhausen D 51 C4
Mundaka E 89 A4
Münden D 51 B5
Munderfing A 63 B4
Munderkingen D 61 B5
Mundesley GB 30 B5
Munera E 95 C4
Mungia E 89 A4
Munich = München D 62 B2
Muñico E 94 B1
Muniesa E 90 B2
Munka-Ljungby S 41 C2
Munkebo DK 39 D3
Munkedal S 35 D3
Munkflohögen S 115 D11
Munkfors S 34 C5
Munktorp S 37 C3
Münnerstadt D 51 C6
Muñopepe E 94 B2
Muñotello E 94 B1
Münsingen
CH 70 B2
D 61 B5
Munsö S 37 C4
Münster
CH 70 B3
Hessen D 61 A4
Munster D 44 C2
Münster D 50 B3
Munster F 60 B3
Muntibar E 89 A4
Münzkirchen A 63 B4
Muodoslompolo S 113 E12
Muonio FIN 113 E12
Muotathal CH 70 B3
Muradiye TR 118 D2
Murakeresztúr H 74 B1
Murán SK 65 B6
Murano I 72 C2
Muras E 86 A3
Murat F 78 A1
Muratlı TR 118 A2
Murato F 102 A2
Murat-sur-Vèbre F 78 C1
Murau A 73 A4
Muravera I 110 C2
Murazzano I 80 B2
Murça P 87 C3
Murchante E 89 B5
Murchin D 45 B5
Murcia E 101 B4
Murczyn PL 46 C3
Mur-de-Barrez F 77 B5
Mur-de-Bretagne F 56 B2
Mur-de-Sologne F 67 A6
Mureck A 73 B5
Mürefte TR 118 B2
Muret F 77 C4
Murg CH 71 A4
Murguia E 89 B4
Muri CH 70 A3
Murias de Paredes E 86 B4
Muriedas E 88 A3
Muriel Viejo E 89 C4
Murillo de Rio Leza E 89 B4
Murillo el Fruto E 89 B5
Murino MNE 85 D4
Muriqan AL 105 A5
Murlaggan GB 22 E3
Murmansk RUS 3 B30
Murmashi RUS 3 B30
Murnau D 62 C2
Muro
E 97 B3
F 102 A1
Muro de Alcoy E 96 C2
Murol F 68 C2
Muro Lucano I 103 C8
Muron F 66 B4
Muros E 86 B1
Muros de Nalón E 86 A4
Murowana Goślina PL 46 C3
Mürren CH 70 B2
Murrhardt D 61 B5
Murska Sobota SLO 73 B6
Mursko Središce HR 73 B6
Murtas E 100 C2
Murten CH 70 B2
Murter HR 83 C4
Murtiçi TR 119 F6
Murtosa P 87 D2
Murvica HR 83 B4
Murviel-lès-Béziers F 78 C2
Mürzsteg A 63 C6
Murzynowo PL 46 C1
Mürzzuschlag A 63 C6
Musculdy F 76 C2
Mushqeta AL 105 B5
Muskö S 37 C5
Mušov CZ 64 B2
Musselburgh GB 25 C4
Musselkanaal NL 43 C4
Mussidan F 77 A3
Mussomeli I 108 B2
Musson B 60 A1
Mussy-sur-Seine F 59 C5
Mustafakemalpaşa TR 118 B3
Muszaki PL 47 B6
Muszyna PL 65 A6
Mut TR 16 C6
Muta SLO 73 B5
Muthill GB 25 B4
Mutné SK 65 A5
Mutriku E 89 A4
Muttalip TR 118 C5
Mutterbergalm A 71 A6
Muxía E 86 A1
Muxilka-Ugarte E 89 A4
Muzillac F 66 A2
Mužla SK 65 C4
Muzzano del Turgnano I 72 C3
Mybster GB 23 C5
Myckelgensjö S 115 D14
Myennes F 68 A2
Myjava SK 64 B3
Myking N 32 B2
Mykland N 33 D5
Mykolayiv = Nikolayev UA 11 C12
Myra N 33 D6
Myrdal N 32 B4
Myre
Nordland N 112 C4
Nordland N 112 D4
Myresjö S 40 B4
Myrhorod UA 11 B12
Mýri IS 111 B8
Myrtou CY 120 A2
Mysen N 35 C3
Mysłakowice PL 53 C5
Myślenice PL 65 A5
Myślibórz PL 45 C6
Mysłowice PL 55 C4
Myszków PL 55 C4
Mytishchi RUS 7 D14
Mýtna SK 65 B5
Mýtne Ludany SK 65 B4
Mýto CZ 63 A4

N

Nå N 32 B3
Naaldwijk NL 49 B5
Naantali FIN 6 A6
Naas IRL 21 A5
Nabais P 92 A3
Nabbelund S 41 B7
Nabburg D 62 A3
Načeradec CZ 63 A5
Náchod CZ 53 C6
Nacław PL 46 A2
Nadarzyce PL 46 B2
Nadarzyn PL 55 A5
Nádasd H 74 B1
Nădlac RO 75 B5
Nádudvar H 75 A6
Nadvirna UA 11 B8
Näfels CH 70 A4
Nafpaktos GR 116 D3
Nafplio GR 117 E4
Nagel D 52 D1
Nagele NL 42 C2
Naggen S 115 E13
Nagłowice PL 55 C5
Nagold D 61 B4
Nagore E 76 D1
Nagyatád H 74 B2
Nagybajom H 74 B2
Nagybaracska H 74 B3
Nagybátony H 65 C5
Nagyberény H 74 B3
Nagybörzsöny H 65 C4
Nagycenk H 64 C2
Nagydorog H 74 B3
Nagyfüged H 65 C6
Nagyhersány H 74 C3
Nagyigmánd H 64 C4
Nagyiván H 75 A5
Nagykanizsa H 74 B1
Nagykáta H 75 A4
Nagykonyi H 74 B3
Nagykörös H 75 A4
Nagykörü H 75 A5
Nagylóc H 65 B5
Nagymágocs H 75 B5
Nagymányok H 74 B3
Nagymaros H 65 C4
Nagyoroszi H 65 B5
Nagyrábé H 75 A6
Nagyréde H 65 C5
Nagyszékely H 74 B3
Nagyszénás H 75 B5
Nagyszokoly H 74 B3
Nagytöke H 75 B5
Nagyvázsony H 74 B2
Nagyvenyim H 74 B3
Naharros E 95 B4
Nahe D 44 B2
Naidăş RO 85 B6
Naila D 52 C1
Nailloux F 77 C4
Nailsworth GB 29 B5
Naintré F 67 B5
Nairn GB 23 D5
Najac F 77 B4
Nájera E 89 B4
Nak H 74 B3
Nakksjø N 33 C6
Nakło nad Notecią PL 46 B3
Nakskov DK 39 E4
Nalda E 89 B4
Nälden S 115 D11
Nálepkovo SK 65 B6
Nalliers F 66 B3
Nallıhan TR 118 B6
Nalzen F 77 D4
Nalžouské Hory CZ 63 A4
Namdalseid N 114 C8
Náměšť nad Oslavou CZ 64 A2
Námestovo SK 65 A5
Namnå N 34 B4
Namsos N 114 C8
Namsskogan N 115 C10
Namur B 49 C5
Namysłów PL 54 B2
Nançay F 68 A2
Nanclares de la Oca E 89 B4
Nancy F 60 B2
Nangis F 59 B4
Nannestad N 34 B3
Nant F 78 B2
Nanterre F 58 B3
Nantes F 66 A3
Nanteuil-le-Haudouin F 58 A3
Nantiat F 67 B6
Nantua F 69 B5
Nantwich GB 26 B3
Naoussa
Cyclades GR 117 E7
Imathia GR 116 B4
Napajedla CZ 64 A3
Napiwoda PL 47 B6
Naples = Nápoli I 103 C7
Nápoli = Naples I 103 C7
Nar S 37 E5
Nara N 32 A1
Naraval E 86 A4
Narberth GB 28 B3
Nærbø N 33 D2
Narbonne F 78 C1
Narbonne-Plage F 78 C2
Narbuvollen N 114 E8
Narcao I 110 C1
Nardò I 107 A5
Narken S 113 F11
Narmo N 34 B3
Narni I 102 A5
Naro I 108 B2
Naro Fominsk RUS 7 D14
Narón E 86 A2
Narros del Castillo E 94 B1
Narta HR 74 C1
Naruszewo PL 47 C6
Narva EST 7 B10
Narvik N 112 D6
Narzole I 80 B1
Näs FIN 36 B7
Nås S 36 B1
Näs S 37 E5
Näsåker S 115 D13
Năsăud RO 11 C8
Nasavrky CZ 64 A1
Nasbinals F 78 B2
Næsbjerg DK 39 D1
Näshull S 40 B5
Našice HR 74 C3
Nasielsk PL 47 C6
Naso I 109 A3
Nassau D 50 C3
Nassenfels D 62 B2
Nassenheide D 45 C5
Nassereith A 71 A5
Nässjö S 40 B4
Nastätten D 50 C3
Næstved DK 39 D4
Näsum S 41 C4
Näsviken S 115 D12
Natalinci SRB 85 B5
Naters CH 70 B3
Nater-Stetten D 62 B2
Nattavaara S 112 F9
Natters A 71 A6
Nattheim D 61 B6
Nättraby S 41 C5
Naturno I 71 B5
Naucelle F 77 B5
Nauders A 71 B5
Nauen D 45 C4
Naul IRL 19 C5
Naumburg D 52 B1
Naundorf D 52 C3
Naunhof D 52 B2
Naustdal N 32 A2
Nautijaur S 112 F8
Nautsi RUS 113 D18
Nava E 88 A1
Navacerrada E 94 B2
Navaconcejo E 93 A5
Nava de Arévalo E 94 B2
Nava de la Asunción E 94 A2
Nava del Rey E 88 C1
Navafriá E 94 A3
Navahermosa E 94 C2
Navahrudak BY 7 E8
Naval E 90 A3
Navalacruz E 94 B2
Navalcán E 94 B1
Navalcarnero E 94 B2
Navaleno E 89 C3
Navalmanzano E 94 A2
Navalmoral E 94 B2
Navalmoral de la Mata E 93 B5
Naválón E 96 C2
Navalonguilla E 93 A5
Navalperal de Pinares E 94 B2
Navalpino E 94 C2
Navaltalgordo E 94 B2
Navaltoril E 94 C2
Navaluenga E 94 B2
Navalvillar de Pela E 93 B5
Navan IRL 19 C5
Navaperal de Tormes E 93 A5
Navapolatsk BY 7 D10
Navarclés E 91 B4
Navarredonda de Gredos E 93 A5
Navarrenx F 76 C2
Navarrés E 96 B2
Navarrete E 89 B4
Navarrevisca E 94 B2
Navás E 91 B4
Navascués E 76 D1
Navas del Madroño E 93 B4
Navas del Rey E 94 B2
Navas del Sepillar E 100 B1
Navas de Oro E 94 A2
Navas de San Juan E 100 A2
Navasfrias E 93 A4
Nave I 71 C5
Nave de Haver P 93 A4
Nävekvarn S 37 D3
Navelli I 103 A6
Navenby GB 27 B5
Näverkärret S 37 C2
Naverstad S 35 D3
Navés E 91 B4
Navezuelas E 93 B5
Navia E 86 A4
Navia de Suarna E 86 B4
Navilly F 69 B5
Navlya RUS 7 E13
Năvodari RO 11 D10
Naxos GR 117 E7
Nay F 76 C2
Nazaré P 92 B1
Nazarje SLO 73 B4
Nazilli TR 119 E3
Nazza D 51 B6
Ndroq AL 105 B5
Nea Anchialos GR 116 C4
Nea Epidavros GR 117 E5
Nea Flippias GR 116 C2
Nea Kalikratia GR 116 B5
Nea Makri GR 117 D5
Nea Moudania GR 116 B5
Neap GB 22 A7
Nea Peramos GR 116 B6
Neapoli
Kozani GR 116 B3
Kriti GR 117 G7
Lakonia GR 117 F5
Nea Stira GR 117 D6
Neath GB 28 B4
Nea Visa GR 118 A1
Nea Zichni GR 116 A5
Nebljusi HR 83 B4
Neblo SLO 72 B3
Nebolchy RUS 7 B12
Nebra D 52 B1
Nebreda E 88 C3
Nechanice CZ 53 C5
Neckargemünd D 61 A4
Neckarsulm D 61 A5
Neda E 86 A2
Neded SK 64 B3
Nedelišće HR 73 B6
Nederweert NL 50 B1
Nedreberg N 34 B3
Nedre Gärdsjö S 36 B2
Nedre Soppero S 113 D10
Nedstrand N 33 C2
Nedvědice CZ 64 A2
Nędza PL 54 C3
Neede NL 50 A2
Needham Market GB 30 B5
Needingworth GB 30 B3
Neermoor D 43 B4
Neeroeteren B 50 B1
Neerpelt B 49 B6
Neesen D 51 A4
Neetze D 44 B2
Nefyn GB 26 C1
Negbina SRB 85 C4
Negotin SRB 11 D7
Negotino MK 116 A4
Negrar I 71 C5
Negredo E 95 A4
Negreira E 86 B2
Nègrepelisse F 77 B4
Negru Vodă RO 11 E10
Negueira de Muñiz E 86 A4
Neheim D 50 B3
Neila E 89 B4
Néive I 80 B2
Nejdek CZ 52 C2
Nekla PL 46 C3
Neksø DK 41 D5
Nelas P 92 A3
Nelaug N 33 D5
Nelidovo RUS 7 C12
Nelim FIN 113 D17
Nellingen D 61 B5
Nelson GB 26 B3
Neman RUS 6 D7
Nemea GR 117 E4
Nemesgörzsöny H 74 A2
Nemeskér H 74 A1
Nemesnádudvar H 75 B4
Nemesszalók H 74 A2
Németkér H 74 B3
Nemours F 58 B3
Nemška Loka SLO 73 C5
Nemšová SK 64 B4
Nenagh IRL 20 B3
Nenince SK 65 B5
Nenita GR 117 D8
Nenzing A 71 A4
Neochori GR 116 C3
Neo Chori GR 116 D3
Neon Petritsi GR 116 A5
Nepi I 102 A5
Nepomuk CZ 63 A4
Nérac F 77 B3
Neratovice CZ 53 C4
Nerchau D 52 B2
Néré F 67 C4
Neresheim D 61 B6
Nereto I 82 D2
Nerezine HR 82 B3
Nerežišća HR 83 C5
Neringa LT 6 D6
Néris-les Bains F 68 B2
Nerito I 103 A6
Nerja E 100 C2
Néronde F 69 C4
Nérondes F 68 B2
Nerpio E 101 A3
Nersingen D 61 B6
Nerva E 99 B4
Nervesa della Battáglia I 72 C2
Nervi I 80 B3
Nes
N 114 D6
Buskerud N 34 B1
Hedmark N 34 B2
NL 42 B2
Nesbyen N 32 B6
Neset N 114 F7
Nesflaten N 33 C3
Nesjahverfi IS 111 C10
Neskaupstaður IS 111 B12
Nesland N 33 C4
Neslandsvatn N 33 D6
Nesle F 59 A3
Nesna N 115 A10
Nesoddtangen N 34 C2
Nesovice CZ 64 A3
Nesselwang D 61 C6
Nesslau CH 71 A4
Nessmersiel D 43 B4
Nesso I 71 C4
Nesterov UA 11 A7
Nestorio GR 116 B3
Nesttun N 32 B2
Nesvady SK 64 C4
Nesvatnstemmen N 33 D5
Nether Stowey GB 29 B4
Netland N 33 D3
Netolice CZ 63 A5
Netphen D 50 C4
Netstal CH 70 A4
Nettancourt F 59 B5
Nettetal D 50 B2
Nettlingen D 51 A6
Nettuno I 102 B5
Neualbenreuth D 52 D2
Neubeckum D 50 B4
Neubrandenburg D 45 B5
Neubruchhausen D 43 C5
Neubukow D 44 A3
Neuburg D 62 B2
Neuchâtel CH 70 B1
Neu Darchau D 44 B2
Neudau A 73 A6
Neudietendorf D 51 C6
Neudorf D 61 A4
Neuenbürg D 61 B4
Neuenburg D 43 B4
Neuendorf D 45 A5
Neuenhagen D 45 C5
Neuenhaus D 42 C3
Neuenkirchen
Niedersachsen D 43 B6
Niedersachsen D 43 C5
Nordrhein-Westfalen D 50 A3
Nordrhein-Westfalen D 50 C3
Neuenrade D 50 B3
Neuenwalde D 43 B5
Neuerburg D 50 C2
Neufahrn
Bayern D 62 B2
Bayern D 62 B3
Neuf-Brisach F 60 B3
Neufchâteau
B 60 A1
F 60 B1
Neufchâtel-en-Bray F 58 A2
Neufchâtel-sur-Aisne F 59 A5
Neuflize F 59 A5
Neugersdorf D 53 C4
Neuhardenberg D 45 C6
Neuharlingersiel D 43 B4
Neuhaus
Bayern D 62 A2
Bayern D 63 B4
Niedersachsen D 43 B6
Niedersachsen D 44 B2
Niedersachsen D 51 B5
Neuhaus a Rennweg D 52 C1
Neuhausen
CH 61 C4
D 52 C3
Neuhausen ob Eck D 61 C4
Neuhof
Bayern D 62 A1
Hessen D 51 C5
Neuhofen an der Krems A 63 B5
Neuillé-Pont-Pierre F 67 A5
Neuilly-en-Thelle F 58 A3
Neuilly-le-Réal F 68 B3
Neuilly-l'Évêque F 60 C1
Neuilly-St Front F 59 A4
Neu-Isenburg D 51 C4
Neukalen D 45 B4
Neu Kaliss D 44 B3
Neukirch D 53 B4
Neukirchen
A 62 B4
Hessen D 51 C5
Schleswig-Holstein D 39 E1
Neukirchen am Grossvenediger A 72 A2
Neukirchen bei Heiligen Blut D 62 A3
Neukloster D 44 B3
Neulengbach A 64 B1
Neulise F 68 C4
Neu Lübbenau D 53 A3
Neum BIH 84 D2
Neumagen D 60 A2
Neumarkt D 62 A2
Neumarkt am Wallersee A 63 C4
Neumarkt im Hausruckkreis A 63 B4
Neumarkt im Mühlkreis A 63 B5
Neumarkt im Steiermark A 73 A4
Neumarkt Sankt Veit D 62 B3
Neumünster D 44 A1
Neunburg vorm Wald D 62 A3
Neung-sur-Beuvron F 68 A1
Neunkirch
Luzern CH 70 A3
Schaffhausen CH 61 C4
Neunkirchen
A 64 C2
Nordrhein-Westfalen D 50 C3
Saarland D 60 A3
Neunkirchen am Brand D 62 A2
Neuötting D 62 B3
Neupetershain D 53 B4
Neuravensburg D 61 C5
Neureut D 61 A4
Neuruppin D 45 C4
Neusäss D 62 B1
Neusiedl A 64 C2
Neuss D 50 B2
Neussargues-Moissac F 68 C2
Neustadt
Bayern D 62 A1
Bayern D 62 A3
Bayern D 62 B2
Brandenburg D 44 C4
Hessen D 51 C5
Niedersachsen D 43 C6
Rheinland-Pfalz D 61 A4
Sachsen D 53 B4
Schleswig-Holstein D 44 A2
Thüringen D 52 C1
Thüringen D 52 C1
Neustadt-Glewe D 44 B3
Neustift im Stubaital A 71 A6
Neustrelitz D 45 B5
Neutal A 73 A6
Neutrebbin D 45 C6
Neu-Ulm D 61 B6
Neuves-Maisons F 60 B2
Neuvic
Corrèze F 68 C2
Dordogne F 77 A3
Neuville-aux-Bois F 58 B3
Neuville-de-Poitou F 67 B5
Neuville-les-Dames F 69 B5
Neuville-sur-Saône F 69 C4
Neuvy-le-Roi F 58 C1
Neuvy-Santour F 59 B4
Neuvy-St Sépulchre F 68 B1
Neuvy-sur-Barangeon F 68 A2
Neuwied D 50 C3
Neuzelle D 53 A4
Névache F 79 A5
Neveklov CZ 63 A5
Nevel RUS 7 D10
Neverfjord N 113 B12
Nevers F 68 B3
Nevesinje BIH 84 C3
Névez F 56 C2
Nevlunghavn N 35 D1
Nevşehir TR 16 B7
New Abbey GB 25 D4
New Aberdour GB 23 D6
New Alresford GB 31 C2
Newark-on-Trent GB 27 B5
Newbiggin-by-the-Sea GB 25 C6
Newbliss IRL 19 B4
Newborough GB 26 B1
Newbridge IRL 21 A5
Newbridge on Wye GB 29 A4
Newburgh
Aberdeenshire GB 23 D6
Fife GB 25 B4
Newbury GB 31 C2
Newby Bridge GB 26 A3
Newcastle GB 19 B6
Newcastle Emlyn GB 28 A3
Newcastleton GB 25 C5
Newcastle-under-Lyme GB 26 B3
Newcastle upon Tyne GB 25 D6
Newcastle West IRL 20 B2
Newchurch GB 29 A4
New Costessey GB 30 B5
New Cumnock GB 24 C3
Newent GB 29 B5
New Galloway GB 24 C3
Newham GB 31 C4
Newhaven GB 31 D4
Newington GB 31 C5
Newinn IRL 21 B4
Newlyn GB 28 C2
Newmachar GB 23 D6
Newmarket
Suffolk GB 30 B4
Western Isles GB 22 C2
IRL 20 B3
Newmarket-on-Fergus IRL 20 B3
New Mills GB 27 B4
New Milton GB 31 D2
New Pitsligo GB 23 D6
Newport
Isle of Wight GB 31 D2
Newport GB 29 B5
Pembrokeshire GB 28 A3
Telford & Wrekin GB 26 C3
Mayo IRL 18 C2
Tipperary IRL 20 B3
Newport-on-Tay GB 25 B5
Newport Pagnell GB 30 B3
Newquay GB 28 C2
New Quay GB 28 A3
New Radnor GB 29 A4
New Romney GB 31 D4
New Ross IRL 21 B5
Newry GB 19 B5
New Scone GB 25 B4
Newton Abbot GB 29 C4
Newton Arlosh GB 25 D4
Newton Aycliffe GB 27 A4
Newton Ferrers GB 28 C3
Newtonhill GB 23 D6
Newtonmore GB 23 D4
Newton Stewart GB 24 D3
Newtown
Herefordshire GB 29 A5
Powys GB 26 C2
Newtownabbey GB 19 B6
Newtownards GB 19 B6
Newtownbutler GB 19 B4
Newtown Cunningham IRL 19 B4
Newtownhamilton GB 19 B5
Newtownmountkennedy IRL 21 A5
Newtown St Boswells GB 25 C5
Newtown Sands IRL 20 B2
Newtownshandrum IRL 20 B3
Newtownstewart GB 19 B4
Nexon F 67 C6
Neyland GB 28 B3
Nibbiano I 80 B3
Nibe DK 38 C2
Nicaj-Shalë AL 105 A5
Nicastro I 106 C3
Niccone I 82 C1
Nice F 80 C1
Nickelsdorf A 64 C3
Nicolosi I 109 B4
Nicosia
CY 120 A2
I 109 B3
Nicótera I 106 C2
Nidda D 51 C5
Niğde TR 16 C7
Nidzica PL 47 B6
Niebla E 99 B4
Nieborów PL 55 A5
Niebüll D 39 E1
Niechanowo PL 46 C3
Niechorze PL 45 A7
Niedalino PL 46 A2
Niederaula D 51 C5
Niederbipp CH 70 A2
Niederbronn-les-Bains F 60 B3
Niederfischbach D 50 C3
Niedergörsdorf D 52 B2
Niederkrüchten D 50 B2
Niederndorf A 62 C3
Nieder-Olm D 61 A4
Niedersachswerfen D 51 B6
Niederstetten D 61 A5
Niederurnen CH 70 A4
Niederwölz A 73 A4
Niedoradz PL 53 B5
Niedzica PL 65 A6
Niegosławice PL 53 B5
Nieheim D 51 B5
Niemcza PL 54 C1
Niemegk D 52 A2
Niemodlin PL 54 C2
Nienburg
Niedersachsen D 43 C6
Sachsen-Anhalt D 52 B1
Niepołomice PL 55 C5
Nierstein D 61 A4
Niesky D 53 B4
Niestronno PL 46 C3
Nieświń PL 55 B5
Nieszawa PL 47 C4
Nieul-le-Dolent F 66 B3
Nieul-sur-Mer F 66 B3
Nieuw-Amsterdam NL 42 C3
Nieuw-Buinen NL 42 C3
Nieuwegein NL 49 A6
Nieuwe Niedorp NL 42 C1
Nieuwe-Pekela NL 42 B3
Nieuwerkerken B 49 C6
Nieuwe-schans NL 43 B4
Nieuwolda NL 42 B3
Nieuwpoort B 48 B3
Nieuw-Weerdinge NL 42 C3
Nigrita GR 116 B5
Nigüelas E 100 C2
Níjar E 101 C3
Nijemci HR 75 C4
Nijkerk NL 49 A6
Nijlen B 49 B5
Nijmegen NL 50 B1
Nijverdal NL 42 C3
Nikel RUS 113 C19
Nikinci SRB 85 B4
Nikiti GR 116 B5
Nikitsch A 74 A1
Nikkaluokta S 112 E8
Nikla H 74 B2
Niklasdorf A 73 A5
Nikolayev = Mykolayiv UA 11 C12
Nikšić MNE 84 D3
Nilivaara S 113 E10
Nîmes F 78 C3
Nimis I 72 B3
Nimtofte DK 39 C3
Nin HR 83 B4
Nindorf D 43 A6
Ninemilehouse IRL 21 B4
Ninove B 49 C5
Niort F 67 B4
Niš SRB 10 E6
Nisa P 92 B3
Niscemi I 109 B3
Nissafors S 40 B3
Nissan-lez-Ensérune F 78 C2
Nissedal N 33 C5
Nissumby DK 38 C1
Nisterud N 33 C6
Niton GB 31 D2
Nitra SK 64 B4
Nitrianske-Pravno SK 65 B4
Nitrianske Rudno SK 65 B4
Nitry F 59 C4
Nittedal N 34 B2
Nittenau D 62 A3
Nittendorf D 62 A2
Nivala FIN 3 E26
Nivelles B 49 C5
Nivenskoye RUS 47 A6
Nivnice CZ 64 B3
Nizhyn UA 11 A11
Nižná SK 65 A5
Nižná Boca SK 65 B5
Nižne Repaše SK 65 A6
Nizza Monferrato I 80 B2
Njarðvík IS 111 D3
Njegůsevo SRB 75 C4
Njivice HR 73 C4
Njurundabommen S 115 E14
Njutånger S 115 F14
Noailles F 58 A3
Noain E 76 D1
Noale I 72 C2
Noalejo E 100 B2
Noblejas E 95 C3
Noceda E 86 B4
Nocera Inferiore I 103 C7
Nocera Terinese I 106 B3
Nocera Umbra I 82 C1
Noceto I 81 B4
Noci I 104 C3
Nociglia I 107 A5
Nodeland N 33 D4
Nödinge S 38 B5
Nods F 69 A6
Noé F 77 C4
Noépoli I 106 A3
Noeux-les-Mines F 48 C3
Noez E 94 C2
Nogales E 93 C4
Nogara I 71 C6
Nogarejas E 87 B4
Nogaro F 76 C2
Nogent F 59 B6
Nogent l'Artaud F 59 B4
Nogent-le-Roi F 58 B2
Nogent-le-Rotrou F 58 B1
Nogent-sur-Seine F 59 B4
Nogent-sur-Vernisson F 58 C3
Nogersund S 41 C4
Noguera E 95 B5
Noguerones E 100 B1

Nohfelden D	60 A3
Nohn D	50 C2
Noia E	86 B2
Noicáttaro I	104 B2
Noirétable F	68 C3
Noirmoutier-en-l'Île F	66 A2
Noja E	89 A3
Nojewo PL	46 C2
Nokia FIN	3 F25
Nol S	38 B5
Nola I	103 C7
Nolay F	69 B4
Noli I	80 B2
Nolnyra E	94 B2
Nombela E	94 B2
Nomeny F	60 B2
Nomexy F	60 B2
Nonancourt F	58 B2
Nonant-le-Pin F	57 B6
Nonaspe E	90 B3
None I	80 B1
Nontron F	67 C5
Nonza F	102 A2
Noordeinde NL	42 B3
Noordwijk NL	49 A5
Noordwijkerhout N	49 A5
Noordwolde NL	42 C3
Noppikoski S	36 A1
Nora E	37 C2
Nørager DK	38 C2
Norberg S	36 B3
Norboda S	36 B5
Nórcia I	82 D2
Nordagutu N	33 C6
Nordanås S	115 C15
Nordausques F	48 C3
Nordborg DK	39 D2
Nordby	
Aarhus Amt. DK	39 D3
Ribe Amt. DK	39 D1
Norddeich D	43 B4
Norddorf D	43 A5
Norden D	43 B4
Nordenham D	43 B5
Norderhov N	34 B2
Norderney D	43 B4
Norderstapel D	43 A6
Norderstedt D	44 B1
Nordfjord N	113 B19
Nordfjordeid N	114 F3
Nordfold N	112 E4
Nordhalben D	52 C1
Nordhausen D	51 B6
Nordheim vor der Rhön	
D	51 C6
Nordholz D	43 B5
Nordhorn D	43 C4
Nordingrå S	115 E15
Nordkjosbotn N	112 C8
Nordli N	115 C10
Nördlingen D	61 B6
Nordmaling S	115 D16
Nordmark S	34 C6
Nordmela N	112 C4
Nordre Osen N	34 A3
Nordsinni N	34 B1
Nordstedalsæter N	114 F4
Nordstemmen D	51 A5
Nordvågen N	113 B15
Nordwalde D	50 A3
Noreña E	88 A1
Noresund N	34 B1
Norg NL	42 B3
Norheimsund N	32 B3
Norie S	41 C4
Norma I	102 B5
Nornäs S	34 A5
Norråker S	115 C12
Norrala S	36 A3
Norra Vi S	40 B5
Norrbron S	36 A3
Norrsholm S	37 C2
Norsjö S	115 C16
Nörten-Hardenberg D	51 B5
Northallerton GB	27 A4
Northampton GB	30 B3
North Berwick GB	25 B5
North Charlton GB	25 C6
Northeim D	51 B6
Northfleet GB	31 C4
North Frodingham	
GB	27 B5
North Kessock GB	23 D4
Northleach GB	29 B6
North Molton GB	28 B4
North Petherton GB	29 B4
Northpunds GB	22 B7
North Somercotes	
GB	27 B6
North Tawton GB	28 C4
North Thoresby GB	27 B5
North Walsham GB	30 B5
Northwich GB	26 B3
Norton GB	27 A5
Nortorf D	44 A1
Nort-sur-Erdre F	66 A3
Nörvenich D	50 C2
Norwich GB	30 B5
Norwick GB	22 B5
Nøsen N	32 B5
Nosivka UA	11 A11
Nossa Senhora do Cabo	
P	92 C1
Nossebro S	35 D4
Nössemark S	35 C3
Nossen D	52 B3
Notaresco I	103 A6
Noto I	109 C4
Notodden N	33 C6
Nottingham GB	27 C4
Nottuln D	50 B3
Nouan-le-Fuzelier F	68 A2
Nouans-les-Fontaines	
F	67 A6
Nougaroulet F	77 C3
Nouvion F	48 C2
Nouzonville F	59 A5
Nova H	74 B1
Nová Baňa SK	65 B4
Nová Bystrica SK	65 A5
Nová Bystřice CZ	63 A6
Novaféltria I	82 C1
Nova Gorica SLO	72 C3
Nova Gradiška HR	74 C2
Nováky SK	65 B4
Novalaise F	69 C5
Novales E	90 A2
Nova Levante I	71 B6
Novalja HR	83 B3
Nová Odesa UA	11 C11
Nová Paka CZ	53 C5
Nova Pazova SRB	85 B5
Nová Pec CZ	63 B4
Novara I	70 C3
Novara di Sicília I	109 A4
Novate Mezzola I	71 B4
Nova Topola BIH	84 A2
Nova Varoš SRB	85 C4
Novaya Ladoga RUS	7 A12

Nova Zagora BG	11 E8
Nové Hrady CZ	63 B5
Novelda E	101 A5
Novellara I	81 B4
Nové Město SK	64 B3
Nové Město nad Metují	
CZ	53 C6
Nové Město na Moravě	
CZ	64 A2
Nové Město pod Smrkem	
CZ	53 C5
Nové Mitrovice CZ	63 A4
Noventa di Piave I	72 C2
Noventa Vicentina I	71 C6
Novés E	94 B2
Noves F	78 C3
Nové Sady SK	64 B3
Nevés de Segre E	91 A4
Nové Strašeci CZ	53 C3
Nové Zámky SK	64 C4
Novgorod RUS	7 B11
Novhorod-Siverskyy	
UA	7 F12
Novi Bečej SRB	75 C5
Novi di Módena I	81 B4
Novigrad	
Istarska HR	72 C3
Zadarsko-Kninska	
HR	83 B4
Novigrad Podravski	
HR	74 B1
Novi Kneževac SRB	75 B5
Novi Lígure I	80 B2
Noville B	50 C1
Novi Marof HR	73 B6
Novion-Porcien F	59 A5
Novi Pazar	
BG	11 E9
SRB	85 C5
Novi Sad SRB	75 C4
Novi Slankamen SRB	75 C5
Novi Travnik BIH	84 B2
Novi Vinodolski HR	83 A3
Novo Brdo KOS	85 D6
Novohrad-Volynskyy	
UA	11 A9
Novo Mesto SLO	73 C5
Novo Miloševo SRB	75 C5
Novomirgorod UA	11 B11
Novorzhev RUS	7 C10
Novoselë AL	105 C5
Novo Selo	
BIH	84 A2
KOS	85 C5
SRB	85 C5
Novoselytsya UA	11 B9
Novosil RUS	7 E14
Novosokolniki RUS	7 C10
Novoukrayinka UA	11 B11
Novoveská Huta SK	65 B6
Novovolynsk UA	11 A8
Novozybkov RUS	7 E11
Novska HR	74 C1
Nový Bor CZ	53 C4
Nový Bydžov CZ	53 C5
Nový-Chevrières F	59 A5
Nový Dwór Mazowiecki	
PL	47 C6
Nový-Hrozenkov CZ	64 A4
Nový Jičín CZ	64 A4
Nový Knín CZ	63 A5
Nowa Buh UA	11 C12
Nowa Cerekwia PL	54 C2
Nowa Karczma PL	47 A4
Nowa Kościoł PL	53 B5
Nowa Ruda PL	54 C1
Nowa Słupia PL	55 C6
Nowa Sól PL	53 B5
Nowa Wieś PL	47 B5
Nowa-Wieś Wielka	
PL	47 C4
Nowe Brzesko PL	55 C5
Nowe Grudze PL	55 A4
Nowe Miasteczko PL	53 B5
Nowe Miasto	
Mazowieckie PL	47 C6
Mazowieckie PL	55 B5
Nowe Miasto Lubawskie	
PL	47 B5
Nowe Miasto nad Warta	
PL	54 A2
Nowe Skalmierzyce	
PL	54 B3
Nowe Warpno PL	45 B6
Nowica PL	47 A5
Nowogard PL	45 B7
Nowogród Bobrzanski	
PL	53 B5
Nowogrodziec PL	53 B5
Nowosolna PL	55 B4
Nowy Dwór Gdański	
PL	47 A5
Nowy Korczyn PL	55 C5
Nowy Sącz PL	65 A6
Nowy Staw PL	47 A5
Nowy Targ PL	65 A6
Nowy Tomyśl PL	46 C2
Nowy Wiśnicz PL	55 D5
Noyalo F	56 C3
Noyal-Pontivy F	56 B3
Noyant F	67 A5
Noyelles-sur-Mer F	48 C2
Noyen-sur-Sarthe F	57 C5
Noyers F	59 C4
Noyers-sur-Cher F	67 A6
Noyers-sur-Jabron F	79 B4
Noyon F	59 A3
Nozay F	66 A3
Nuaillé F	66 A4
Nuaillé-d'Aunis F	66 B4
Nuars F	68 A3
Nubledo E	95 C3
Nueno E	90 A2
Nuestra Señora Sa Verge	
des Pilar E	97 C1
Nueva E	88 A2
Nueva Carteya E	100 B1
Nuevalos E	95 A5
Nuits F	69 A4
Nuits-St Georges F	69 A4
Nule I	110 B2
Nules E	96 B2
Nulvi I	110 B1
Numana I	82 C2
Numansdorp NL	49 B5
Nümbrecht D	50 C3
Nunchritz D	52 B3
Nuneaton GB	30 B2
Nunnanen FIN	113 D13
Nunspeet NL	42 C2
Nuorgam FIN	113 B16
Núoro I	110 B2
Nurallao I	110 C2
Nuremberg = Nürnberg	
Nurmes FIN	3 E28
Nürnberg = Nuremberg	
D	62 A2
Nurri I	110 C2
Nürtingen D	61 B5
Nus I	70 C2
Nusnäs S	36 B1
Nusplingen D	61 B4
Nuštar HR	74 C3
Nyåker S	115 D16
Nyáregyháza H	75 A4
Nyarlőrinc H	75 B4
Nyasvizh BY	7 E9
Nybble S	35 C6
Nybergsund N	34 A4
Nybøl DK	39 D2
Nyborg DK	39 D3
Nybro S	40 C5
Nybster GB	23 C5
Nyby DK	39 E5
Nye S	40 B5
Nyékládháza H	65 C6
Nyergesújfalu H	65 C4
Nyhammar S	36 B1

Nyhyttan S	37 C1
Nyirád H	74 A2
Nyírbátor H	11 C7
Nyíregyháza H	10 C6
Nyker DK	41 D4
Nykil S	37 D2
Nykirke N	34 B2
Nykøbing	
Falster DK	39 E4
Vestsjællands Amt.	
DK	39 D4
Nykøbing Mors DK	38 C1
Nyköping S	37 D4
Nykroppa S	35 C6
Nykvarn S	37 C4
Nykyrke S	37 D1
Nyland S	115 D14
Nylars DK	41 D4
Nymburk CZ	53 C5
Nynäshamn S	37 D4
Nyon CH	69 B6
Nyons F	79 B4
Nýřany CZ	63 A4
Nýrsko CZ	63 A4
Nysa PL	54 C2
Nysäter S	35 C4
Nyseter N	114 E5
Nyskoga S	34 B4
Nysted DK	44 A3
Nystrand N	35 C1
Nyúl H	64 C3
Nyvoll N	113 B12

O

Oadby GB	30 B2
Oakengates GB	26 C3
Oakham GB	30 B3
Oanes N	33 D3
Obalj BIH	84 C3
Oban GB	24 B2
Obbola S	115 D18
O Barco E	86 B4
Obdach A	73 A4
Obejo E	100 A1
Oberammergau D	62 C2
Oberasbach D	62 A1
Oberau D	62 C2
Oberaudorf D	62 C3
Oberbruck F	60 C2
Oberdiessbach CH	70 B2
Oberdorf CH	70 A2
Oberdrauburg A	72 B2
Oberelsbach D	51 C6
Obere Stanz A	73 A5
Ober Grafendorf A	63 B6
Obergünzburg D	61 C6
Obergurgl A	71 B6
Oberhaslach F	60 B3
Oberhausen D	50 B2
Oberhof D	51 C6
Oberkirch D	61 B4
Oberkirchen D	51 B4
Oberkochen D	61 B6
Obermassfeld-	
Grimmenthal D	51 C6
Ober-Morlen D	51 C4
Obermünchen D	62 B2
Obernai F	60 B3
Obernberg A	63 B4
Obernburg D	61 A5
Oberndorf D	61 B4
Oberndorf bei Salzburg	
A	62 C3
Obernkirchen D	51 A5
Oberort A	73 A5
Oberpullendorf A	74 A1
Oberriet CH	71 A4
Oberröblingen D	52 B1
Oberrot D	61 A5
Oberstaufen D	61 C6
Oberstdorf D	61 C6
Obertauern A	72 A3
Obertilliach A	72 B2
Obertraubling D	62 B3
Obertrubach D	62 A2
Obertrum A	62 C4
Oberursel D	51 C4
Obervellach A	72 B3
Oberviechtach D	62 A3
Oberwart A	73 A6
Oberwesel D	50 C3
Oberwinter D	50 C3
Oberwölzstadt A	73 A4
Oberzell D	63 B4
Obice PL	55 C5
Óbidos P	92 B1
Obing D	62 C3
Objat F	67 C6
Objazda PL	46 A3
Oblarn A	73 A4
Obninsk RUS	7 D14
O Bolo E	87 B3
Oborniki PL	46 C2
Oborniki Śląskie PL	54 B1
Obornjača SRB	75 C5
Oboyan RUS	7 F14
Obrenovac SRB	85 B5
Obrež	
Srbija SRB	85 C6
Vojvodina SRB	85 B4
Obrigheim D	61 A5
Obrov SLO	73 C4
Obrovac	
HR	83 B4
SRB	75 C4
Obrovac Sinjski HR	83 C5
Obruk TR	16 B6
Obrzycko PL	46 C2
Obudovac BIH	84 B3
Ocaña E	95 C3
O Carballiño E	87 B2
Occhiobello I	81 B5
Occimiano I	80 A2
Očevlja BIH	84 B3
Ochagavía E	76 D1
Ochakiv UA	11 C11
Ochiltree GB	24 C3
Ochla PL	53 B5
Ochotnica-Dolna PL	65 A6
Ochotnica-Górna PL	65 A6
Ochsenfurt D	61 A6
Ochsenhausen D	61 B5
Ochtendung D	50 C3
Ochtrup D	50 A3
Ocieka PL	55 C6
Ockelbo S	36 B3
Öckerö S	38 B4
Očová SK	65 B5
Ócsa H	75 A4
Öcseny H	74 B3
Öcsöd H	75 A5
Octeville F	57 A4
Ocypel PL	47 B4
Öd S	41 C2
Odda N	32 B3
Odder DK	39 D3
Ödeborg S	35 D3
Odeceixe P	98 B2
Odeleite P	98 B3
Odemira P	98 B2
Ödemiş TR	119 D2
Odensbacken S	37 C2
Odense DK	39 D3
Odensjö	
Jönköpings S	40 B4
Kronoberg S	40 C4
Oderberg D	45 C6
Oderzo I	72 C2
Odesa = Odessa UA	11 C11
Ödeshög S	37 D1
Odessa = Odesa UA	11 C11
Odiáxere P	98 B2
Ódie GB	23 B6
Odintsovo RUS	7 D14

Odivelas P	98 A2
Odolanów PL	54 B2
Odón E	95 B5
Odorheiu Secuiesc	
RO	11 C8
Odoyevo RUS	7 E14
Odrowaz PL	55 B5
Ódry CZ	64 A3
Odrzywół PL	55 B5
Øksted DK	39 D2
Odžaci SRB	75 C4
Odžak BIH	84 A3
Oebisfelde D	44 C2
Oederan D	52 C3
Oeding D	50 B2
Oegstgeest NL	49 A5
Oelde D	50 B4
Oelsnitz D	52 C2
Oer-Erkenschwick D	50 B3
Oerlinghausen D	51 B4
Oettingen D	62 B1
Oetz A	71 A5
Oeventrop D	50 B4
Offanengo I	71 C4
Offenbach D	51 C4
Offenburg D	60 B3
Offida I	82 D2
Offingen D	61 B6
Offranville F	58 A2
Ofte N	33 C5
Ofterschwang D	71 A5
Oggiono I	71 C4
Ogíhares E	100 B2
Ogliastro Cilento I	103 C8
Ogliastro Marina I	103 C7
Ogmore-by-Sea GB	29 B4
Ogna N	33 D2
Ogre LV	6 C8
Ogrodzieniec PL	55 C4
Ogulin HR	73 C5
Ogur IS	111 A3
Ohanes E	101 B3
Ohey B	49 C6
Ohlstadt D	62 C2
Ohrdorf D	44 C2
Ohrdruf D	51 C6
Ohrid MK	116 A2
Öhringen D	61 A5
Oia E	87 B2
Oiã P	87 B2
Oiartzun E	76 C1
Oilgate IRL	21 B5
Oimbra E	87 C3
Oiselay-et-Grachoux	
F	69 A5
Oisemont F	48 D2
Oisterwijk NL	49 B6
Öja S	37 E5
Öje S	34 B5
Ojén E	100 C1
Ojrzeń PL	47 C6
Ojuelos Altos E	99 A5
Okalewo PL	47 B5
Okány H	75 B6
Okehampton GB	28 C3
Okhtyrka UA	7 F13
Oklaj HR	83 C5
Øknesham N	112 D4
Okoč SK	64 C3
Okoličné SK	65 A5
Okonek PL	46 B2
Okonin PL	47 B4
Okříšky CZ	64 A1
Oksa PL	55 C5
Oksbøl DK	39 D1
Oksby DK	39 D1
Øksfjord N	113 B11
Øksna N	34 B3
Okučani HR	74 C2
Okulovka RUS	7 B12
Ólafsfjörður IS	111 A7
Ólafsvík IS	111 C2
Olagüe E	76 D1
Oland N	33 D5
Olargues F	78 C1
Oława PL	54 C2
Olazagutia E	89 B4
Olbernhau D	52 C3
Ólbia I	110 B2
Olching D	62 B2
Oldbury GB	29 B5
Oldcastle IRL	19 C4
Old Deer GB	23 D6
Oldebroek NL	42 C2
Oldeboorn NL	42 B2
Olden N	114 F3
Oldenbrok D	43 B5
Oldenburg	
Niedersachsen D	43 B5
Schleswig-Holstein D	44 A2
Oldenzaal NL	50 A2
Olderdalen N	112 C9
Olderfjord N	113 B14
Oldersum D	43 B4
Oldervik N	112 C7
Oldham GB	26 B3
Oldisleben D	52 B1
Oldmeldrum GB	23 D6
Olea E	88 B2
Oleby S	34 B5
Olechów PL	55 B6
Oledo P	92 B3
Oléggio I	70 C3
Oleiros	
Coruña E	86 A2
Coruña E	86 B1
P	92 B3
Oleksandriya	
Kirovohrad UA	11 B12
Rivne UA	11 A9
Oleksandrovka UA	11 B12
Ølen N	33 C2
Olen B	49 B5
Olenegorsk RUS	3 B30
Olenino RUS	7 C12
Olesa de Montserrat	
E	91 B4
Oleśnica PL	54 B2
Oleśnice CZ	64 A2
Olesno PL	54 C3
Oletta F	102 A2
Olette F	91 A5
Olevsk UA	11 A9
Olfen D	50 B3
Olgiate Comasco I	70 C3
Olginate I	71 C4
Ølgod DK	39 D1
Olgrinmore GB	23 C5
Olhão P	98 B3
Olhava FIN	3 D26
Oliana E	91 A4
Olias del Rey E	94 C3
Oliena I	110 B2
Oliete E	90 B2
Olimbos GR	119 G2
Olite E	89 B5
Ólive E	96 C2
Oliva de la Frontera E	99 A4
Oliva de Mérida E	93 C4
Oliva de Plasencia E	93 A4
Olivadi I	106 C3
Olival P	92 B2
Olivar E	100 C2
Olivares de Duero E	88 C2
Olivares de Júcar E	95 C4
Oliveira de Azeméis	
P	87 D2
Oliveira de Frades P	87 D2
Oliveira do Conde P	92 A3
Oliveira do Douro P	87 C2
Oliveira do Hospital P	92 A3
Olivenza E	93 C3
Olivet F	58 C2
Olivone CH	70 B3
Öljehult S	41 C5
Olkusz PL	55 C4
Ollerton GB	27 B4
Ollerup DK	39 D3
Olliergues F	68 C3
Olmbrotorp S	37 C2

Ölme S	35 C5
Olmedilla de Alarcón	
E	95 C4
Olmedillo de Roa E	88 C3
Olmedo	
E	88 C2
I	110 B1
Olmeto F	102 B1
Olmillos de Castro E	87 C4
Olmos de Ojeda E	88 B2
Olney GB	30 B3
Ołobok PL	54 B3
Olocau del Rey E	90 C2
Olofström S	41 C4
Olonets RUS	7 A12
Olonne-sur-Mer F	66 B3
Olonzac F	78 C1
Oloron-Ste Marie F	76 C2
Olost E	91 B5
Olovo BIH	84 B3
Olpe D	50 B3
Olsberg D	51 B4
Olsene B	49 C4
Olserud S	35 C5
Olshammar S	37 D1
Olszanica PL	53 B5
Olsztyn	
Śląskie PL	55 C4
Warmińsko-Mazurskie	
PL	47 B6
Olsztynek PL	47 B6
Olszyna PL	53 B5
Oltedal N	33 D3
Olten CH	70 A2
Olteniţa RO	11 D9
Olula del Rio E	101 B3
Olva N	32 B2
Olvega E	89 C5
Olvera E	99 C5
Olympia GR	117 E3
Olzai I	110 B2
Omagh GB	19 B4
Omalos GR	117 G5
Omegna I	70 C3
Omiš HR	83 C5
Omišalj HR	73 C4
Ommen NL	42 C3
Omodhos CY	120 B1
Omoljica SRB	85 B5
On B	49 C6
Onano I	81 D5
O Näsberg S	34 B5
Oñati E	89 A4
Onda E	96 B2
Ondara E	96 C2
Ondarroa E	89 A4
Onesse-et-Laharie F	76 B1
Oneşti RO	11 C9
Onhaye B	49 C5
Onich GB	24 B2
Onil E	96 C2
Onis E	88 A2
Önnestad S	41 C4
Onsala S	38 B5
Ontinyent E	96 C2
Ontur E	101 A4
Onzain F	58 C2
Onzonilla E	88 B1
Oostburg NL	49 B4
Oostende B	48 B3
Oosterend NL	42 B2
Oosterhout NL	49 B5
Oosterwolde NL	42 C3
Oosterzele B	49 C4
Oosthuizen NL	42 C2
Oostkamp B	49 B4
Oostmalle B	49 B5
Oost-Vlieland NL	42 B2
Oostvoorne NL	49 B5
Ootmarsum NL	42 C3
Opalenica PL	46 C2
O Páramo E	86 B3
Opařany CZ	63 A5
Oparić SRB	85 C6
Opatija HR	73 C4
Opatów	
Śląskie PL	54 C3
Świętokrzyskie PL	55 C6
Wielkopolskie PL	54 B3
Opatowiec PL	55 C5
Opava CZ	64 A3
O Pedrouzo E	86 B2
Opeinde NL	42 B3
Oper Thalkirchdorf D	61 C6
Opglabbeek B	49 B6
Opicina I	72 C3
O Pino E	86 B2
Oplotnica SLO	73 B5
Opmeer NL	42 C1
Opochka RUS	7 C10
Opočno CZ	53 C6
Opoczno PL	55 B5
Opole PL	54 C2
Oporów PL	55 A4
O Porriño E	87 B2
Opovo SRB	85 A5
Oppach D	53 B4
Oppdal N	114 E6
Oppeby	
Östergötland S	40 A5
Södermanland S	37 D3
Oppedal N	32 A2
Oppegård N	34 C2
Oppenau D	61 B4
Oppenberg A	73 A4
Oppenheim D	61 A4
Oppido Lucano I	104 C1
Óppido Mamertina I	106 C2
Opponitz A	63 C5
Oppstad N	34 B3
Oprtalj HR	72 C3
Opsaheden S	34 B5
Opusztaszer H	75 B5
Opuzen HR	84 C2
Ora	
CY	120 B2
I	71 B6
Orada P	92 C3
Oradea RO	10 C6
Oradour-sur-Glane F	67 C6
Oradour-sur-Vayres	
F	67 C5
Oragonja SLO	72 C3
Orah BIH	84 D3
Orahova BIH	84 B2
Orahovica HR	74 C2
Orahovo BIH	74 C2
Oraison F	79 C4
Orajärvi FIN	113 F13
Orange F	78 B3
Orani I	110 B2
Oranienbaum D	52 B2
Oranienburg D	45 C5
Oranmore IRL	20 A3
Orašac SRB	85 B5
Orašje BIH	84 A3
Oravská Lesná SK	65 A5
Oravská Polhora SK	65 A5
Oravské Veselé SK	65 A5
Oravsky-Podzámok	
SK	65 A5
Orba E	96 C2
Orbacém P	87 C2
Ørbæk DK	39 D3
Orbassano I	80 A1
Orbe CH	70 B1
Orbetello I	81 D4
Orbetello Scalo I	81 D4
Orbigny F	67 A6
Ørby DK	39 D3
Ørbyhus S	36 B4
Orce E	101 B3
Orcera E	101 A3

Orchete E	96 C2
Orchies F	49 C4
Orchowo PL	47 C4
Ordal E	91 B4
Ordes E	86 A2
Ordhead GB	23 D6
Ordino AND	91 A4
Ordizia E	89 A4
Ore S	36 A2
Orea E	95 B5
Orebić HR	84 D2
Örebro S	37 C2
Orehoved DK	39 E4
Orellana E	93 B5
Orellana la Vieja E	93 B5
Ören TR	119 E2
Örencik TR	118 C4
Orestiada GR	118 A1
Organyà E	91 A4
Orgaz E	94 C3
Orgelet F	69 B5
Orgères-en-Beauce F	58 B2
Orgibet F	77 D3
Orgnac-l'Aven F	78 B3
Orgon F	79 C4
Orgósolo I	110 B2
Orhaneli TR	118 C3
Orhangazi TR	118 B4
Orhei MD	11 C10
Orhomenos GR	116 D4
Oria E	101 B3
Oria I	104 C3
Origny-Ste Benoite F	59 A4
Orihuela E	101 A5
Orihuela del Tremedal	
E	95 B5
Orikum AL	105 C5
Oriola P	92 C3
Oriolo I	106 A3
Oriovac HR	74 C2
Orissaare EST	6 B7
Oristano I	110 C1
Öriszentpéter H	73 B6
Ørje N	35 C3
Orjiva E	100 C2
Orkanger N	114 D6
Örkelljunga S	41 C3
Örkény H	75 A4
Orlamünde D	52 C1
Orlane KOS	85 D6
Orléans F	58 C2
Orlová CZ	65 A4
Orlovat SRB	75 C5
Ormea I	80 B1
Ormelet N	35 C2
Ormemyr N	33 C6
Ormilia GR	116 B5
Ormos GR	117 E6
Ormož SLO	73 B6
Ormskirk GB	26 B3
Ornans F	69 A6
Ornäs S	36 B2
Ørnes N	112 F2
Ørnhøj DK	39 C1
Ornö S	37 C5
Örnsköldsvik S	115 D15
Orolik HR	75 C4
Orom SRB	75 C4
Oron-la-Ville CH	70 B1
Oronsko PL	55 B5
Oropa I	70 C2
Oropesa	
Castellón de la Plana	
E	96 A3
Toledo E	93 B5
O Rosal E	87 C2
Orosei I	110 B2
Orosháza H	75 B5
Oroslavje HR	73 C5
Oroszlány H	74 A3
Oroszlo H	74 B3
Orotelli I	110 B2
Orozko E	89 A4
Orphir GB	23 C5
Orpington GB	31 C4
Orreaga-Roncesvalles	
E	76 C1
Orrefors S	40 C5
Orrliden S	115 D11
Orsa S	36 A1
Orsara di Púglia I	103 B8
Orsay F	58 B3
Orscholz D	60 A2
Orsennes F	67 B6
Orserum S	40 A4
Orsha BY	7 D11
Orsières CH	70 B2
Ørslev DK	39 D4
Örslösa S	35 D4
Orsogna I	103 A7
Orsomarso I	106 B2
Ørsta N	114 E3
Ørsted DK	38 C3
Örsundsbro S	37 C4
Ortaca TR	119 F3
Ortakent TR	119 E2
Ortaklar TR	119 E2
Ortaköy TR	16 B7
Orta Nova I	104 B1
Orte I	102 A5
Ortenburg D	63 B4
Orth F	64 B2
Orthez F	76 C2
Ortigueira E	86 A3
Ortilla E	90 A2
Ortisei I	72 B1
Ortnevik N	32 A3
Orton GB	26 A3
Ortona I	103 A7
Ortrand D	53 B3
Orubica HR	74 C2
Ørum DK	38 C2
Orune I	110 B2
Orusco E	95 B3
Orvalho P	92 A3
Orvault F	66 A3
Ørvella N	33 C6
Orvieto I	81 D5
Orvinio I	102 A5
Orwell GB	30 B3
Oryakhovo BG	11 E7
Oryakhovo RUS	7 B30
Orzesze PL	54 C3
Orzinuovi I	71 C4
Orzivécchi I	71 C4
Os	
Hedmark N	34 B3
Hedmark N	114 E8
Osann-Monzel D	60 A2
Osanica SRB	85 B6

Osiek	
Kujawsko-Pomorskie	
PL	47 B5
Kujawsko-Pomorskie	
Pomorskie PL	47 B4
Świętokrzyskie PL	55 C6
Osiek nad Notecią PL	46 B3
Osielsko PL	47 B4
Osijek HR	74 C3
Osilnica SLO	73 C4
Osilo I	110 B1
Ósimo I	82 C2
Osinja BIH	84 B2
Osintorf BY	7 D11
Osipaonica SRB	85 B6
Osjaków PL	55 B4
Oskamull GB	24 B1
Oskarshamn S	40 B6
Oskarström S	40 C2
Øsløs DK	38 B1
Osmancık TR	16 A7
Osmaneli TR	118 B4
Osmanville F	57 A4
Ösmo S	37 D4
Osmolin PL	55 A4
Osnabrück D	50 A4
Ośno Lubuskie PL	45 C6
Osoblaha CZ	54 C2
Osor	
HR	83 B3
E	91 B5
Osorno E	88 B2
Øsoyra N	32 A2
Øsøyro N	32 B2
Ospakseyri IS	111 B4
Os Peares E	86 B3
Ospedaletti I	80 C1
Ospitaletto I	71 C5
Oss NL	49 B6
Ossa de Montiel E	95 D4
Ossi I	110 B1
Ossjøen N	32 B5
Ostanå S	41 C4
Ostanvik S	36 A2
Ostashkov RUS	7 C12
Østavall S	115 E12
Ostbevern D	50 A3
Østborg N	115 C10
Østby N	34 A4
Osted DK	39 D4
Ostenfeld D	43 A6
Oster UA	11 A11
Øster Assels DK	38 C1
Osterburg D	44 C3
Osterburken D	61 A5
Øster Hornum DK	38 C2
Øster Hurup DK	38 C3
Østerild DK	38 B1
Øster Jølby DK	38 C1
Österlövsta S	36 B4
Øster-marie DK	41 D5
Ostermiething A	62 C3
Osterode am Harz D	51 B6
Østersiel D	43 A5
Østersund S	115 D11
Øster Tørslev DK	38 C3
Österväla S	36 B4
Östervallskog S	35 C3
Østervrå DK	38 B3
Ostffyassonyfa H	74 A2
Osthammar S	36 B5
Ostheim vor der Rhön	
D	51 C6
Osthofen D	61 A4
Ostiano I	71 C5
Ostíglia I	81 A4
Ostiz E	76 D1
Östmark S	34 B4
Östnor S	36 A1
Ostojićevo SRB	75 C5
Ostra I	82 C2
Östra Amtervik S	35 C5
Östraby S	41 D3
Ostrach D	61 C5
Östra Husby S	37 D3
Östra Ljungby S	41 C3
Östra Ryd S	37 D3
Østre Halsen N	35 C2
Ostrhauderfehn D	43 B4
Ostritz D	53 B4
Ostróda PL	47 B5
Ostrov	
CZ	52 C2
RUS	7 C10
Ostrov nad Oslavou	
CZ	64 A1
Ostrówek PL	55 B4
Ostrowiec PL	46 A2
Ostrowiec-Świętokrzyski	
PL	55 C6
Ostrowite PL	47 B5
Ostrów Mazowiecka	
PL	6 E6
Ostrowo PL	47 C4
Ostrów Wielkopolski	
PL	54 B2
Ostrożany PL	6 E7
Ostrzeszów PL	54 B2
Ostseebad Kühlungsborn	
D	44 A3
Ostuni I	104 C3
Osuna E	99 B5
Osvětimany CZ	64 A3
Oswestry GB	26 C2
Oświęcim PL	55 C4
Oszczów PL	11 A8
Oszkó H	74 B1
Oteiza E	89 B5
Otelec RO	75 C6
Oteo E	89 A3
Oterbekk N	35 C2
Oteren N	112 C8
Oterma FIN	3 D27
Otero de Herreros E	94 B2
Otero de O Bodas E	87 C4
Othem S	37 E5
Otley GB	27 B4
Otmuchów PL	54 C2
Otočac HR	83 B4
Otok	
Splitsko-Dalmatinska	
HR	83 C5
Vukovarsko-Srijemska	
HR	74 C3
Otoka BIH	83 B5
Otranto I	107 A5
Otrkovice CZ	64 A3
Otricoli I	102 A5
Otrokovice CZ	64 A3
Otta N	114 F6
Ottana I	110 B2
Ottaviano I	103 C7
Ottenby S	41 C6
Ottendorf-Okrilla D	53 B3
Ottenhöfen D	61 B4
Ottensheim A	63 B5
Ottenstein D	51 B5
Otterbäcken S	35 D6

Otterberg D	60 A3
Otterburn GB	25 C5
Otter Ferry GB	24 B2
Otterndorf D	43 B5
Ottersberg D	43 B6
Ottersweier D	61 B4
Otterup DK	39 D3
Ottery St Mary GB	29 C4
Ottignies B	49 C5
Ottmarsheim F	60 C3
Ottobeuren D	61 C6
Öttömös H	75 B4
Ottone I	80 B3
Ottsjö S	115 D10
Ottweiler D	60 A3
Ötvöskónyi H	74 B2
Otwock PL	55 A6
Ouanne F	59 C4
Ouarville F	58 B2
Oucques F	58 C2
Oud-Beijerland NL	49 B5
Ouddorp NL	49 B4
Oudemirdum NL	42 C2
Oudenaarde NL	49 C4
Oudenbosch NL	49 B5
Oudenburg B	48 B3
Oude-Pekela NL	43 B4
Oudewater NL	49 A5
Oud Gastel NL	49 B5
Oudon F	66 A3
Oue DK	38 C2
Oughterard IRL	20 A2
Ouguela P	93 B3
Ouistreham F	57 A5
Oulainen FIN	3 D26
Oulchy-le-Château F	59 A4
Oullins F	69 C4
Oulmes F	67 B4
Oulton GB	30 B5
Oulton Broad GB	30 B5
Oulu FIN	3 D26
Oulx I	79 A5
Oundle GB	30 B3
Ouranopoli GR	116 B6
Ourém P	92 B2
Ourense E	87 B3
Ourique P	98 B2
Ourol E	86 A3
Ouroux-en-Morvan F	68 A3
Ousdale GB	23 C5
Oust F	77 D4
Outakoski FIN	113 C15
Outeiro P	92 A2
Outeiro de Rei E	86 A3
Outes E	86 B2
Outokumpu FIN	3 E28
Outreau F	48 C2
Outwell GB	30 B4
Ouzouer-le-Marché F	58 C2
Ouzouer-sur-Loire F	58 C3
Ovada I	80 B2
Ovar P	87 D2
Ovelgönne D	43 B5
Overath D	50 C3
Overbister GB	23 B6
Øverbygd N	112 D8
Overdinkel NL	50 A3
Overenhörna S	37 C4
Overhalla N	114 C9
Overijse B	49 C5
Øverland DK	39 D2
Överlida S	38 B2
Øvermo N	36 B7
Overpelt B	49 B6
Overton GB	26 C3
Övertorneå S	3 C25
Överum S	40 B6
Ovídiopol UA	11 C11
Oviedo E	88 A1
Oviglio I	80 B2
Ovindoli I	103 A6
Ovodda I	110 B2

Ölme S	35 C5
Oteren N	
Otero de Herreros E	94 B2
Ohey E	

P

Paal B	49 B6
Pabianice PL	55 B4
Pacanów PL	55 C6
Paceco I	108 B1
Pachino I	109 C4
Pačir SRB	75 C4
Pack A	73 A5
Paços de Ferreira P	87 C2
Pacov CZ	63 A6
Pacsa H	74 B1
Pacy-sur-Eure F	58 B2
Paczków PL	54 C2
Padany RUS	3 E30
Padej SRB	75 C5
Padene HR	83 B5
Paderborn D	51 B4
Paderne P	98 B2
Padina SRB	85 A5
Padinska Skela SRB	85 B5
Padova I	72 C1
Padragkút H	74 A2
Padria I	110 B1
Padrón E	86 B2
Padru I	110 B2
Padstow GB	28 C3
Padul E	100 B2
Padula I	104 C1
Paesana I	79 B6
Paese I	72 C2
Pag HR	83 B4
Pagani I	103 C7
Pagánica I	103 A6
Pagánico I	81 D5
Paglieta I	103 A7
Pagny-sur-Moselle F	60 B2

Páhi H 75 B4
Pahkakumpu FIN . . 113 F17
Pahl D 62 C2
Paide EST 7 B8
Paignton GB . . . 29 C4
Pailhès F 77 C4
Paimboeuf F . . . 66 A2
Paimpol F 56 B2
Paimpont F 56 B2
Painswick GB . . . 29 B5
Painten D 62 B2
Paisley GB 24 C3
Pajala S 113 E12
Pajares E 88 A1
Pajares de los Oteros
E 88 B1
Pajęczno PL . . . 54 B3
Páka H 74 B1
Pakość PL 47 C4
Pakosławice PL . . 54 C2
Pakoštane HR . . . 83 C4
Pakrac HR 74 C2
Paks H 74 B3
Palacios de la Sierra
E 89 C3
Palaciòs de la Valduerna
E 88 B1
Palacios del Sil E . 86 B4
Palacios de Sanabria
E 87 B4
Palaciosrubios E . . 94 A1
Palafrugell E . . . 91 B6
Palagiano I 104 C3
Palagonia I 109 B3
Paláia I 81 C4
Palaiseau F 58 B3
Palaj AL 105 A5
Palamas GR . . . 116 C4
Palamòs E 91 B6
Palanga LT 6 D6
Palanzano I 81 B4
Palárikovo SK . . . 64 B4
Palas de Rei E . . . 86 B3
Palata I 103 B7
Palatna KOS . . . 85 C6
Palau I 110 A2
Palavas-les-Flots F . 78 C2
Palazuelos de la Sierra
E 89 B3
Palazzo Adriano I . 108 B2
Palazzo del Pero I . 81 C5
Palazzolo Acréide I . 109 B3
Palazzolo sull Oglio I . 71 C4
Palazzo San Gervásio
I 104 C1
Palazzuolo sul Senio
I 81 B5
Paldiski EST 6 B7
Pale BIH 84 C3
Palekastro GR . . . 117 G8
Palena I 103 B7
Palencia E 88 B2
Paleochora GR . . 117 G5
Paleometokho CY . 120 A2
Palermo I 108 A2
Paleros GR . . . 116 D2
Palestrina I . . . 102 B5
Pálfa H 74 B3
Palfau A 63 C5
Palhaça P 92 A2
Palheiros da Tocha P . 92 A2
Palheiros de Quiaios
P 92 A2
Paliano I 102 B5
Palić SRB 75 B4
Palidoro I 102 B5
Palinuro I 106 A2
Paliouri GR . . . 116 C5
Paliseul B 59 A6
Pallanza I 70 C3
Pallares E 99 A4
Palluelo de Monegros
E 90 B2
Pallerols E 91 A4
Palling D 62 A3
Palluau F 66 B3
Palma P 92 C2
Palma Campánia I . 103 C7
Palma del Río E . . 99 B5
Palma de Mallorca E . 97 B3
Palma di Montechiaro
I 108 B2
Palmádula I . . . 110 B1
Palmanova I . . . 72 C3
Palma Nova E . . . 97 B2
Palmela P 92 C2
Palmerola E . . . 91 A5
Palmi I 106 C2
Pálmonostora H . . 75 B4
Palo del Colle I . . 104 B2
Palojärvi FIN . . . 113 D12
Palojoensuu FIN . 113 D12
Palomares E . . . 101 B4
Palomares del Campo
E 95 C4
Palomas E 93 C4
Palombara Sabina I . 102 A5
Palos de la Frontera
E 99 B4
Palotaboszok H . . 74 B3
Palotás H 65 C5
Pals E 91 B6
Pålsboda S 37 C2
Paluzza I 72 B3
Pamhagen A . . . 64 C2
Pamiers F 77 C4
Pamietowo PL . . . 46 B3
Pampaneira E . . . 100 C2
Pamparato I . . . 80 B1
Pampilhosa
 Aveiro P 92 A2
 Coimbra P . . . 92 A3
Pamplega E . . . 88 B3
Pamplona E . . . 76 D1
Pampow D 44 B3
Pamukçu TR . . . 118 C2
Pamukkale TR . . 119 E4
Pamukova TR . . 118 B5
Panagyurishte BG . 11 E8
Pancalieri I 80 B1
Pančevo SRB . . . 85 B5
Pancey F 59 B6
Pancorvo E 89 B3
Pancrudo E 90 C1
Pandino I 71 C4
Pandrup DK 38 B2
Panenský-Týnec CZ . 53 C4
Panes E 88 A2
Panevėžys LT . . . 6 D8
Pangbourne GB . . 31 C2
Panissières F . . . 69 C4
Panki PL 54 C3
Pannes F 58 B3
Panningen NL . . . 50 B1
Pannonhalma H . . 74 A2
Pano Lefkara CY . 120 B2
Pano Panayia CY . 120 B1
Panormos GR . . 117 E7
Panschwitz-Kuckau
D 53 B4
Pansdorf D 44 B2
Pantano de Cijara E . 94 C2
Pantelleria I . . . 108 C1
Pantin F 86 A2
Pantoja E 94 B3
Pánuco I 87 B3
Páola I 106 B3
Paola I 107 C5
Pápa H 74 A2
Papasídero I . . . 106 B2
Pápateszér H . . . 74 A2
Papenburg D . . . 43 B4
Paprotnia PL . . . 55 A5
Parábita I 107 A5
Paracín SRB . . . 85 C6
Parád H 65 C6

Parada
 Bragança P . . . 87 C4
 Viseu P 92 A2
Paradas E 99 B5
Paradela E 86 B3
Paradinas de San Juan
E 94 A1
Paradiso di Cevadale
I 71 B5
Paradyż PL 55 B5
Parainen FIN . . . 6 A7
Parakhino Paddubye
RUS 7 B12
Parakka S 113 E10
Paralimni CY . . . 120 A2
Parallo Astros GR . 117 E4
Paramé F 57 B4
Paramithia GR . . 116 C2
Páramo E 86 A4
Páramo del Sil E . . 86 B4
Parandaça P . . . 87 C3
Paravadella E . . . 86 A3
Paray-le-Monial F . 68 B4
Parceiros P 92 B2
Parcey F 69 A5
Parchim D 44 B3
Parcice PL 54 B3
Pardilla E 88 C3
Pardubice CZ . . . 53 C5
Paredes
 E 95 A4
 P 87 C2
Paredes de Coura P . 87 C2
Paredes de Nava E . 88 B2
Paredes de Siguenza
E 95 A4
Pareja E 95 B4
Parennes F 57 B5
Parenti I 106 B3
Parentis-en-Born F . 76 B1
Parey D 44 C3
Parfino RUS 7 C11
Parga GR 116 C2
Pargny-sur-Saulx F . 59 B5
Pari-Gagné F . . . 69 B4
Parigné-l'Évêque F . 58 C1
Parikkala FIN . . . 3 F28
Paris F 58 B3
Parisot F 77 B4
Parkalompolo S . . 113 E11
Parkano FIN . . . 3 E25
Parkstein D . . . 62 A3
Parlavà E 91 A6
Parma I 81 B4
Parndorf A 64 C2
Párnica SK 65 A5
Parnu EST 6 B8
Parolis E 101 A3
Paros GR 117 E7
Parrillas E 94 B1
Parsberg D 62 A2
Parstein D 45 C6
Partakko FIN . . 113 C16
Parthenay F . . . 67 B4
Partinico I 108 A2
Partizani SRB . . . 85 B5
Partizánske SK . . 65 B4
Partney GB 27 B6
Páryd S 40 C5
Parysów PL 55 B6
Parzymiechy PL . . 54 B3
Pașcani RO 11 C9
Pasewalk D 45 B6
Pašina Voda MNE . 85 C4
Påskallavik S . . . 40 B6
Pasłęk PL 47 A5
Pašman HR 83 C4
Passage East IRL . 21 B5
Passage West IRL . 20 C3
Passail A 73 A5
Passais F 57 B5
Passau D 63 B4
Passignano sul
 Trasimeno I . . . 82 C1
Passo di Tréia I . . 82 C2
Passopisciaro I . . 109 B4
Passow D 45 B6
Passy F 70 C1
Pastavy BY 7 D9
Pastena I 103 B7
Pastrana E 95 B4
Pastrengo I 71 C5
Pasym PL 47 B6
Pásztó H 65 C5
Pata SK 64 B3
Patay F 58 B2
Pateley Bridge GB . 27 A4
Paterek PL 46 B3
Paterna E 96 B2
Paterna del Campo E . 99 B4
Paterna del Madera
E 101 A3
Paterna de Rivera E . 99 C5
Paternion A 72 B3
Paternò I 109 B3
Paternópoli I . . . 103 C8
Patersdorf D . . . 62 A3
Paterswolde NL . . 42 B3
Patitiri GR 116 C5
Patmos GR . . . 119 E1
Patna GB 24 C3
Patnow PL 54 A3
Patoniva FIN . . 113 C16
Patopirtti FIN . . 113 E18
Patos AL 105 C5
Patra = Patras GR . 117 D3
Patras = Patra GR . 117 D3
Patreksfjörður IS . 111 B2
Patrickswell IRL . . 20 B3
Patrimonio F . . . 102 A2
Patrington GB . . . 27 B5
Pattada I 110 B2
Pattensen
 Niedersachsen D . 44 B2
 Niedersachsen D . 51 A5
Patterdale GB . . . 26 A3
Patti I 109 A3
Páty H 74 A3
Pau F 76 C2
Pauillac F 66 C4
Paularo I 72 B3
Paulhaguet F . . . 68 C3
Paulhan F 78 C2
Paulilátino I . . . 110 B1
Paullo I 71 C4
Paulstown IRL . . 21 B4
Pausa D 52 C1
Pauträsk S . . . 115 C14
Pavia
 I 71 C4
 P 92 C2
Pavias E 96 B2
Pavilly F 58 A1
Pāvilosta LV . . . 6 C6
Pavullo nel Frignano
I 81 B4
Pawłowice PL . . . 54 B2
Pawłowice PL . . . 54 D3
Paxi GR 116 C2
Payallar TR . . . 119 F6
Payerne CH . . . 70 B1
Paymogo E 98 B3
Payrac F 77 B4
Pazardzhik BG . . 11 E8
Pazaryeri TR . . . 118 B4
Paziols F 78 D1
Pčelić HR 74 C2
Pçinja KOS . . . 85 C6
Pçeli KOS 85 D6
Peal de Becerro E . 100 B2
Peñaranda P . . . 31 D4
Peañasmarsh GB . 31 D4
Penzance GB . . . 28 C2
Penzberg D 62 C2
Penzlin D 45 B5
Pepelow D 44 A3
Pepinster B 50 C1
Peqin AL 105 B5
Pér H 74 A2
Pera Boa P 92 A3
Perachora GR . . 117 D4
Perafita P 87 C2
Peraleda de la Mata E . 93 B5
Peraleda del Zaucejo
E 93 C5
Peraleda de San Román
E 93 B5
Perales del Alfambra
E 90 C1
Perales del Puerto E . 93 A4
Perales de Tajuña E . 95 B3
Peralta E 89 B5
Peralta de la Sal E . 90 B3
Peralva P 98 B3

Pechenizhyn UA . . 11 B8
Pecica RO 75 B6
Pečinci SRB . . . 85 B4
Pecka SRB 85 B4
Peckelsheim D . . 51 B5
Pečory RUS 7 C9
Pécs H 74 B3
Pécsvárad H . . . 74 B3
Pećúrice MNE . . . 105 A5
Peczniew PL . . . 54 B3
Pedaso I 82 C2
Pedavena I 72 B1
Pedérobba I . . . 72 C1
Pedescala I 71 C6
Pedrafita E 86 B3
Pedrajas de San Esteban
E 88 C2
Pedralba E 96 B2
Pedralba de la Pradería
E 87 B4
Pedraza E 94 A3
Pedreguer E . . . 96 C3
Pedro Abad E . . . 100 B1
Pedro Bernardo E . 94 B2
Pedroche E . . . 100 A1
Pedrógão P 98 A3
Pedrógão P 92 B2
Pedrógão Grande P . 92 B2
Pedrola E 90 B1
Pedro-Martínez E . 100 B2
Pedro Muñoz E . . 95 C4
Pedrosa del Rey E . 88 C1
Pedrosa del Río Urbel
E 88 B3
Pedrosa de Tobalina
E 89 B3
Pedrosillo de los Aires
E 94 B1
Pedrosillo el Ralo E . 94 A1
Pędzewo PL . . . 47 B4
Peebles GB 25 C4
Peel GB 26 A1
Peenemünde D . . 45 A5
Peer B 49 B6
Pega P 93 A3
Pegalajar E 100 B2
Pegau D 52 B2
Peggau A 73 A5
Pegli I 80 B2
Pegnitz D 62 A2
Pego E 96 C2
Pegões-Estação P . 92 C2
Pegões Velhos P . . 92 C2
Pęgów PL 54 B1
Pegswood GB . . . 25 C6
Peguera E 97 B2
Pehlivanköy TR . . 118 A1
Peine D 51 A6
Peisey-Nancroix F . 70 C1
Peissenberg D . . . 62 C2
Peiting D 62 C1
Peitz D 53 B4
Péjo I 71 B5
Pelagićevo BIH . . 84 B3
Pelahustán E . . . 94 B2
Pełczyce PL . . . 46 B1
Pelhřimov CZ . . . 63 A6
Pélissanne F . . . 79 C4
Pelkosenniemi FIN . 113 E16
Pellegrino Parmense
I 81 B3
Pellegrue F 76 B3
Pellérd H 74 B3
Pellestrina I . . . 72 C2
Pellevoisin F . . . 67 B6
Pellizzano I . . . 71 B5
Pello
 FIN 113 F13
 S 113 F12
Peloche E 93 B5
Pełplin PL 47 B4
Pelussin F 69 C4
Pély H 75 A5
Pembroke GB . . . 28 B3
Pembroke Dock GB . 28 B3
Peñacerrada E . . 89 B4
Penacova P 92 A2
Peña de Cabra P . . 94 B1
Peñafiel E 88 C2
Penafiel P 87 C2
Peñaflor E 99 B5
Peñalba de Santiago
E 86 B4
Peñalsordo E . . . 93 C5
Penalva do Castelo P . 92 A3
Penamacôr P . . . 93 A3
Peñaparda E . . . 93 A4
Peñaranda de
 Bracamonte E . . 94 B1
Peñaranda de Duero
E 89 C3
Peñarroya de Tastavins
E 90 C3
Peñarroya-Pueblonuevo
E 93 C5
Peñarrubia E . . . 93 C5
Penarth GB 29 B4
Peñascosa E . . . 101 A3
Peñas de San Pedro
E 101 A4
Peñausende E . . . 88 C1
Penc H 65 C5
Pencoed GB . . . 29 B4
Pendalofos GB . . 116 B3
Pendeen GB . . . 28 C2
Pendine GB 28 B3
Pendueles E . . . 88 A2
Penedono P 87 D3
Penela P 92 A2
Pénestin F 56 C3
Penha Juntas P . . 87 C4
Peniche P 92 B1
Penicuik GB . . . 25 C4
Penig D 52 C2
Penilhos P 98 B3
Peñíscola E . . . 90 C3
Penistone GB . . . 27 B4
Penkridge GB . . . 26 C3
Penkun D 45 B6
Penmarch F . . . 56 C1
Pennabilli I 82 C1
Penne F 103 A6
Penne-d'Agenais F . 77 B3
Pennes IRL . . . 20 C3
Penpont GB . . . 25 C4
Penrhyndeudraeth
GB 26 C1
Penrith GB 26 A3
Penryn GB 28 C2
Pentraeth GB . . . 26 B1
Penybontfawr GB . 26 C2
Penygroes
 Carmarthenshire
 GB 28 B3
 Gwynedd GB . . 26 B1
Penzance GB . . .

Peralveche E . . . 95 B4
Perama GR . . . 117 G6
Perast MNE . . . 105 A4
Perbál H 65 C4
Perchtoldsdorf A . 64 B2
Percy F 57 B4
Perdasdefogu I . . 110 C2
Perdiguera E . . . 90 B2
Perdiguera E . . . 90 B2
Peregu Mare RO . 75 B5
Pereiro
 Faro P 98 B3
 Guarda P . . . 87 D3
 Santarém P . . 92 B2
Pereiro de Aguiar E . 91 A6
Perelada E 91 A6
Perelejos de las Truchas
E 95 B5
Pereña E 87 C4
Pereruela E . . . 88 C1
Pereyaslav-Khmelnytskyy
UA 11 A11
Pérfugas I 110 B1
Perg A 63 B5
Pérgine Valsugana I . 71 B6
Pérgola I 82 C1
Pergusa I 109 B3
Periam RO . . . 100 C1
Periana E 100 C1
Périers F 57 A4
Périgueux F . . . 67 C5
Perino I 80 B3
Perjasica HR . . . 73 C5
Perkáta H 74 A3
Perković HR . . . 83 C5
Perleberg D . . . 44 B3
Perlez SRB 75 C5
Përmet AL 116 B2
Pernarec CZ . . . 62 A4
Pernek SK 64 B3
Pernes F 78 B2
Pernes-les-Fontaines
F 79 B4
Pernik BG 11 E7
Pernink CZ 52 C2
Pernitz A 64 C1
Peroguarda P . . . 98 A2
Pérols F 78 C2
Péronne F 58 A3
Péronnes B 49 C5
Pero Pinheiro P . . 92 C1
Perorrubio E . . . 94 A3
Perosa Argentina I . 79 B6
Perozinho P . . . 87 C2
Perpignan F . . . 91 A5
Perranporth GB . . 28 C2
Perranzabuloe GB . 28 C2
Perrecy-les-Forges F . 69 B4
Perrero I 79 B6
Perrignier F . . . 69 B6
Perros-Guirec F . . 56 B2
Persan F 58 A3
Persberg S 34 C6
Persenbeug A . . . 63 B6
Pershore GB . . . 29 A5
Perstorp S 41 C3
Perth GB 25 B4
Pertisau A 72 A1
Pertočą SLO . . . 73 B6
Pertuis F 79 C4
Peručac SRB . . . 85 C4
Perúgia I 82 C1
Perušić HR 83 B4
Péruwelz B 49 C4
Pervomaysk UA . . 11 B11
Perwez B 49 C5
Pesadas de Burgos E . 88 B3
Pesaguero E . . . 88 A2
Pésaro I 82 C1
Pescantina I . . . 71 C5
Pescara I 103 A7
Pescasséroli I . . . 103 B6
Peschici I 104 B2
Peschiera del Garda I . 71 C5
Péscia I 81 C4
Pescina I 103 A6
Pesco Sannita I . . 103 B7
Peshkopi AL . . . 116 A2
Peshtera BG . . . 11 E8
Pesmes F 69 A5
Pesnica SLO . . . 73 B5
Peso da Régua P . 87 C3
Pesquera de Duero E . 88 C2
Pessac F 76 B2
Pestovo RUS . . . 7 B13
Petalidi GR . . . 117 F3
Pétange L 60 A1
Petas GR 116 C3
Peteranec HR . . . 74 B1
Peterborough GB . 30 B3
Peterculter GB . . 23 D6
Peterhead GB . . 23 D7
Peterlee GB . . . 25 D6
Petersfield GB . . 31 C3
Petershagen
 Brandenburg D . 45 C5
 Brandenburg D . 45 C6
 Nordrhein-Westfalen
 D 51 A4
Petershausen D . . 62 B2
Peterswell IRL . . 20 A3
Pétervására H . . . 65 B6
Petilia Policastro I . 107 B3
Petín E 87 B3
Pétfürdő H 74 A3
Petkus D 52 B3
Petlovača SRB . . 85 B4
Petöfiszallás H . . 75 B4
Petra E 97 B3
Petralia Sottana I . 109 B3
Petrčane HR . . . 83 B4
Petreto-Bicchisano
F 102 B1
Petrich BG 116 A5
Petrijevci HR . . . 74 C3
Petrinja HR . . . 73 C6
Petrodvorets RUS . 7 B10
Petrola E 96 C1
Petronà I 107 B3
Petroşani RO . . . 11 D7
Petrovac
 MNE 105 A4
 SRB 85 B6
Petrovaradin SRB . 75 C4
Petrovice
 BIH 84 B3
 CZ 53 C3
Pettenbach A . . . 63 C5
Pettigo IRL . . . 19 B4
Petworth GB . . . 31 D3
Peuerbach A . . . 63 B4
Peuntenansa E . . 88 A2
Peurasuvanto FIN . 113 E15
Pevensey Bay GB . 31 D4
Peveragno I . . . 80 B1
Pewsey GB 29 B6
Pewsum D 43 B4
Peyrat-le-Château F . 68 C1
Peyrehorade F . . 76 C1
Peyriac-Minervois F . 77 C5
Pér H 99 A4
Peyrins F 79 A4
Peyrissac F 67 C6
Peyrolles-en-Provence
F 79 C4
Peyruis F 79 B4
Pézarches F . . . 78 C3
Pézenas F 78 C2
Pezuls F 77 B3
Pfaffenhausen D . 61 B6
Pfaffenhofen
 Bayern D . . . 61 B6
 Bayern D . . . 62 B2
Pfaffenhoffen F . . 60 B3
Pfäffikon CH . . . 70 A3
Pfarrkirchen D . . 62 B3

Pfeffenhausen D . . 62 B2
Pfetterhouse F . . 70 A2
Pforzheim D . . . 61 B4
Pfreimd D 62 A3
Pfronten D 61 C6
Pfullendorf D . . . 61 C5
Pfullingen D . . . 61 B5
Pfunds A 71 B5
Pfungstadt D . . . 61 A4
Pyrch CH 60 B2
Phalsbourg F . . . 60 B3
Philippeville B . . . 49 C5
Philippsreut D . . . 63 B4
Philippsthal D . . . 51 C5
Piacenza I 81 A3
Piacenza d'Adige I . 72 C1
Piádena I 71 C5
Piana F 102 A1
Piana Crixia I . . . 80 B2
Piana degli Albanesi
I 108 B2
Piana di Monte Verna
I 103 B7
Piancastagnáio I . . 81 D5
Piandelagotti I . . 81 B4
Pianella
 Abruzzi I . . . 103 A7
 Toscana I . . . 81 C5
Pianello Val Tidone I . 80 B3
Pianoro I 81 B5
Pians A 71 A5
Pias
 E 87 B4
 P 98 A3
Piasek PL 45 C6
Piaseczno PL . . . 55 A6
Piasek PL 47 A5
Piastów PL 55 A5
Piaszczyna PL . . . 46 A3
Piątek PL 55 A4
Piatra Neamț RO . 11 C9
Piazza al Sérchio I . 81 B4
Piazza Armerina I . 109 B3
Piazza Brembana I . 71 C4
Piazze I 81 D5
Piazzola sul Brenta I . 72 C1
Picassent E . . . 96 B2
Piccione I 82 C1
Picerno I 104 C1
Picher D 44 B3
Pickering GB . . . 27 A5
Pico I 103 B6
Picón E 94 C2
Picquigny F . . . 58 A3
Piechowice PL . . 53 C5
Piedicavallo I . . . 70 C2
Piedicroce F . . . 102 A2
Piedimonte Etneo I . 109 B4
Piedimonte Matese I . 103 B7
Piedimulera I . . . 70 B3
Piedrabuena E . . 94 C2
Piedraescrita E . . 94 C2
Piedrafita E . . . 88 A1
Piedrahita E . . . 93 A5
Piedralaves E . . . 94 B2
Piedras Albas E . . 93 B4
Piedras Blancas E . 88 A1
Piegaro I 82 D1
Piekary SI. PL . . . 54 C3
Piekoszów PL . . . 55 C5
Pieksämäki FIN . . 3 E27
Pielenhofen D . . . 62 A2
Pielgrzymka PL . . 53 B5
Pieńsk PL 53 B5
Pienza I 81 C5
Piera E 91 B4
Pieranie PL . . . 47 C4
Pierowall GB . . . 23 B6
Pierre-Buffière F . 67 C6
Pierrecourt F . . . 60 C1
Pierre-de-Bresse F . 69 B5
Pierrefeu-du-Var F . 79 C5
Pierrefitte-Nestalas F . 76 D2
Pierrefitte-sur-Aire F . 59 B6
Pierrefonds F . . . 59 A3
Pierrefontaine-les-Varans
F 69 A6
Pierrefort F 78 B1
Pierrelatte F . . . 78 B3
Pierrepont
 Aisne F 59 A4
 Meurthe-et-Moselle F . 60 A1
Piesendorf A . . . 72 A2
Pieštany SK . . . 64 B3
Pieszkowo PL . . . 47 A6
Pieszyce PL . . . 54 C1
Pietarsaari FIN . . 3 E25
Pietragalla I . . . 104 C1
Pietra Ligure I . . 80 B2
Pietralunga I . . . 82 C1
Pietramelara I . . 103 B7
Pietraperzia I . . . 109 B3
Pietrasanta I . . . 81 C4
Pietravairano I . . 103 B7
Pieve di Cádore I . 72 B2
Pieve di Bono I . . 71 C5
Pieve di Cadore I . 72 B2
Pieve di Cento I . . 81 B5
Pieve di Soligo I . . 72 C2
Pieve di Teco I . . 80 B1
Pievepélago I . . . 81 B4
Pieve Santo Stefano I . 82 C1
Pieve Torina I . . . 82 C2
Piffonds F 59 C4
Pigadia GR . . . 119 G2
Pigeranos GR . . 119 F2
Piglio I 102 B6
Pignan F 78 C2
Pignataro Maggiore
I 103 B7
Pijnacker NL . . . 49 A5
Pikalevo RUS . . . 7 B13
Pila
 I 72 C2
 PL 46 B2
Pilar de la Horadada
E 101 A5
Pilas E 99 B4
Pilastri I 81 B5
Pilawa PL 55 B6
Piława Górna PL . . 54 C1
Piławki PL 47 B5
Pilchowice PL . . 54 C2
Pilchowitz Nowy PL . 54 C2
Píleo I 109 A4
Píles E 96 C2
Pilgrimstad S . . 115 E12
Pili
 Dodekanisa GR . 119 F2
 Trikala GR . . . 116 C3
Pilica PL 55 C4
Pilis H 75 A4
Piliscsaba H . . . 65 C4
Piliszántó H . . . 65 C4
Pilisvörösvár H . . 65 C4
Pilos GR 117 F3
Pilsting D 62 B3
Pilszcz PL 54 C2
Piltene LV 6 C6
Pilterud N 34 C2
Pilu RO 75 B6
Pina de Ebro E . . 90 B2
Pinar E 100 B2
Pınarbaşı TR . . . 118 C1
Pinarhisar TR . . 118 A2
Pinas F 77 C3
Pincehely H . . . 74 B3
Pinchbeck GB . . 30 B3
Pinczów PL 55 C5
Pineda de la Sierra E . 89 B3
Pineda de Mar E . 91 B5
Pinerella I 82 B1
Pinerolo I 79 B6
Pineta Grande I . . 103 B6
Pineto I 103 A7
Piney F 59 B5
Pinhal Novo P . . 92 C2
Pinhão P 87 C3
Pinheiro
 Aveiro P 87 C2
 Aveiro P 87 D2
Pinheiro Grande P . 92 B2
Pinhel P 87 D3
Pinhoe GB 29 C4

Pinilla E 101 A4
Pinilla de Toro E . 88 C1
Pinkafeld A . . . 73 A6
Pinneberg D . . . 43 B6
Pinnow D 53 B4
Pino E 102 A2
Pino de Val E . . . 86 B2
Pinofranqueado E . 93 A4
Pinols F 68 C3
Piñor E 86 B2
Pinos del Valle E . 100 C2
Pinoso E 101 A4
Pinos Puente E . . 100 B2
Pinsk BY 7 E9
Pinto E 94 B3
Pinzano al Tagliamento
I 72 B2
Pinzio P 93 A3
Pinzolo I 71 B5
Pióbbico I 82 C1
Piombino I 81 D4
Pionsat F 68 B2
Pióraco I 82 C1
Pirmasens D . . . 60 A3
Pirna D 53 C3
Pirnmill GB . . . 24 C2
Pirok MK 105 A6
Pirovac HR . . . 83 C4
Pirttikoski FIN . . 3 D26
Pisa I 81 C4
Pisany F 66 C4
Pisarovina HR . . 73 C5
Pirgi GR 117 D7
Pischelsdorf in der
 Steiermark A . . 73 A5
Píscia RO 75 C6
Pisciotta I 106 A2
Písek CZ 63 A5
Pisogne I 71 C5
Pissos F 76 B2
Pissouri CY . . . 120 B1
Pisticci I 104 C2
Pistóia I 81 C4
Piteå S 3 D24
Piteşti RO 11 D8
Pithiviers F . . . 58 B3
Pitigliano I . . . 102 A4
Pitlochry GB . . . 25 B4
Pitsomača HR . . . 74 C2
Pitres E 100 C2
Pittentrail GB . . 23 D4
Pitvaros H . . . 75 B5
Pivka SLO 73 C4
Pivnice SRB . . . 75 C4
Piwniczna PL . . 65 A6
Pizarra E 100 C1
Pizzano I 71 B5
Pizzighettone I . . 71 C4
Pizzo I 106 C3
Pizzolungo I . . . 108 A1
Pjätteryd S 40 C4
Plabennec F . . . 56 B1
Placencia E . . . 89 A4
Plaffeien CH . . . 70 B2
Plaisance
 Gers F 76 C3
 Haute-Garonne F . 77 C4
 Tarn F 77 C5
Plaka GR 116 C7
Plan E 90 A3
Planá CZ 62 A3
Planánd Lužnici CZ . 63 A5
Plaňany CZ . . . 53 C5
Planchez F 68 A4
Plancoët F 57 B3
Plancy-l'Abbaye F . 59 B4
Plan-de-Baix F . . 79 B4
Plandište SRB . . 75 C5
Plan-d'Orgon F . . 78 C3
Plánice CZ 63 A4
Planina
 SLO 73 B5
 SLO 73 C4
Plankenfels D . . 62 A2
Plasencia E . . . 93 A4
Plasenzuela E . . 93 B4
Plaški HR 83 A4
Plassen
 Buskerud N . . 32 B4
 Hedmark N . . 34 A4
Plášťovce SK . . . 65 B5
Plasy CZ 63 A4
Plat HR 84 D3
Plátamonas I . . . 116 B4
Platanata I . . . 106 B3
Platania I 106 B3
Platanos GR . . . 117 G5
Plati I 106 C3
Platičevo SRB . . 85 B4
Platja d'Aro E . . 91 B6
Plattling D 62 B3
Plau D 44 B4
Plaue
 Brandenburg D . 44 C4
 Thüringen D . . 51 C6
Plauen D 52 C2
Plavecký Mikuláš SK . 64 B3
Plavinas LV . . . 7 C8
Plavna SRB . . . 85 B6
Plavnica HR . . . 83 B5
Plavsk RUS . . . 7 E14
Playben F 56 B2
Pleaux F 68 C2
Pléboulle F . . . 57 B3
Pléchâtel F . . . 57 C4
Pleine-Fougères F . 57 B4
Pleinfeld D . . . 62 A1
Pleinting D 62 B4
Plélan-le-Grand F . 57 C3
Plélan-le-Petit F . 57 B3
Plémet F 56 B3
Plélauff F 56 B2
Plérin F 56 B3
Plešin SRB 85 C5
Plešivec SK . . . 65 B6
Plessa D 52 B3
Plessé F 66 A3
Plestin-les-Grèves F . 56 B2
Pleszew PL . . . 54 B2
Pleterska HR . . . 74 C1
Plettenberg D . . 50 B3
Pleubian F . . . 56 B2
Pleumartin F . . . 67 B5
Pleumeur-Bodou F . 56 B2
Pleven BG 11 E8
Plevnik-Drienové SK . 64 A4
Pleyben F 56 B2
Pléyber-Christ F . 56 B2
Pliego E 101 B4
Pliešovce SK . . . 65 B5
Plitvička Jezera HR . 83 B4
Plitvički Ljeskovac
HR 83 B4
Ploaghe I 110 B1
Ploče HR 84 C2
Plochingen D . . . 61 B5
Plock PL 47 C5
Ploemeur F . . . 56 C2

Ploërmel F 56 C2
Ploeuc-sur-Lie F . 56 B3
Plogastel St Germain
F 56 C1
Plogoff F 56 B1
Ploiești RO . . . 11 D9
Plomari GR . . . 118 D1
Plombières-les-Bains
F 60 C2
Plomin HR 82 A3
Plön D 44 A2
Plonéour-Lanvern F . 56 C1
Płonia PL 45 B6
Płońsk PL 47 C6
Płoskinia PL . . . 47 A5
Plössberg D . . . 62 A3
Ploty PL 45 B7
Plouagat F 56 B2
Plouaret F 56 B2
Plouarzel F . . . 56 B1
Plouay F 56 C2
Ploubalay F . . . 57 B3
Ploubazlanec F . . 56 B2
Ploudalmézeau F . 56 B1
Ploudiry F 56 B1
Plouénan F . . . 56 B1
Plouescat F . . . 56 B1
Plouézec F 56 B2
Plougasnou F . . 56 B2
Plougastel-Daoulas F . 56 B1
Plougonver F . . . 56 B2
Plougonvelin F . . 56 B1
Plougrescant F . . 56 B2
Plouguenast F . . 56 B3
Plouguerneau F . . 56 B1
Plouha F 56 B3
Plouhinec F . . . 56 B1
Plouigneau F . . . 56 B2
Ploumanac'h F . . 56 B2
Plounévez-Quintin F . 56 B2
Plouray F 56 B2
Plouzévédé F . . . 56 B1
Plovdiv BG . . . 11 E8
Plozévet F 56 C1
Pluméliau F . . . 56 C3
Plumieux F . . . 56 B3
Plumlov CZ . . . 64 A3
Plungė LT 6 D7
Pluty PL 47 A6
Pluvigner F . . . 56 C3
Plužine
 BIH 84 C3
 MNE 84 C3
Płużnica PL . . . 47 B4
Plymouth GB . . 28 C3
Plympton GB . . 28 C3
Plymstock GB . . 28 C3
Plyusa RUS . . . 7 B10
Plzeň CZ 63 A4
Pniewy PL 46 C2
Pobes E 89 B4
Poběžovice CZ . . 62 A3
Pobiedziska PL . . 46 C3
Pobierowo PL . . 45 A6
Pobla de Segur E . 91 A4
Pobladura del Valle E . 88 B1
Pobla-Tornesa E . 96 A3
Pobo de Dueñas E . 95 B5
Pobra de Trives E . 87 B3
Pobra do Brollón E . 86 B3
Pobra do Caramiñal
E 86 B2
Počátky CZ . . . 63 A6
Poceirão P . . . 92 C2
Pöchlarn A . . . 63 B6
Pociecha PL . . . 55 B5
Pockau D 52 C3
Pocking D 63 B4
Pocklington GB . . 27 B5
Poda MNE 85 C4
Podbořany CZ . . 52 C3
Podbrdo SLO . . . 72 B3
Podbrezová SK . . 65 B5
Podčetrtek SLO . . 73 B5
Poddębice PL . . 54 B3
Poděbrady CZ . . 53 C5
Podence P 87 C4
Podensac F . . . 76 B2
Podenzano I . . . 80 B3
Podersdorf am See A . 64 C2
Podgaje PL . . . 46 B2
Podgora HR . . . 84 C2
Podgóra PL . . . 55 B6
Podgorač HR . . . 74 C3
Podgorica MNE . . 105 A5
Podgrad SLO . . . 73 C4
Podhájska SK . . 64 B4
Podkova BG . . . 116 A7
Podlapača HR . . 83 B4
Podlejki PL . . . 47 B6
Podnovlje BIH . . 84 B3
Podolie SK 64 B3
Podolínec SK . . . 65 A6
Podolsk RUS . . . 7 D14
Podporozhy RUS . 7 A13
Podromanija BIH . 84 C3
Podturen HR . . . 74 B1
Podujevo KOS . . 85 C6
Podwilk PL . . . 65 A5
Poetto I 110 C2
Poggendorf D . . 45 A5
Poggiardo I . . . 107 A5
Póggibonsi I . . . 81 C5
Póggio a Caiano I . 81 C5
Poggio Imperiale I . 103 B8
Póggio Mirteto I . 102 A5
Póggio Moiano I . 102 A5
Póggio Renatico I . 81 B5
Póggio Rusco I . . 81 B5
Pöggstall A . . . 63 B6
Pogny F 59 B5
Pogorzela PL . . . 54 B2
Pogorzelice PL . . 46 A3
Pogradec AL . . . 116 B2
Pogrodzie PL . . 47 A5
Pohorelá SK . . . 65 B6
Pohořelice CZ . . 64 B2
Pohronská Polhora
SK 65 B5
Poiares P 92 A2
Poio E 87 B2
Poirino I 80 B1
Poissons F 59 B6
Poisson F 68 B4
Poissy F 58 B3
Poitiers F 67 B5
Poix-de-Picardie F . 58 A2
Poix-Terron F . . 59 A5
Pokka FIN 113 D14
Pokój PL 54 C2
Pokupsko HR . . 73 C5
Pol
 E 86 A3
 SK 65 B6
Pola RUS 7 C11
Pola de Allande E . 86 A4
Pol a Charra GB . . 22 D1
Pola de Laviana E . 88 A1
Pola de Lena E . . 88 A1
Pola de Siero E . . 88 A1
Pola de Somiedo E . 86 A4
Polaincourt-et-
 Clairefontaine F . 60 C2
Połajewo PL . . . 46 C2
Polán E 94 C2
Polanco E 88 A2
Polanica-Zdrój PL . 54 C1
Polaniec PL . . . 55 C6
Polanów PL . . . 46 A2
Polati TR 118 C7
Polatsk BY 7 D10
Polch D 50 C3
Połczyno PL . . . 47 A4
Polczyn-Zdrój PL . 46 B1
Polegate GB . . . 31 D4
Poległa I 31 D4
Polessk RUS . . . 6 D6
Polgárdi H 74 A3
Polhov Gradec SLO . 73 B4
Police PL 45 B6

Police nad Metuji CZ . 53 C6
Polichnitos GR . . 116 C8
Polička CZ 64 A2
Poličnik HR . . . 83 B4
Policoro I 106 A3
Policzna PL . . . 55 B6
Poligiros GR . . . 116 B5
Polignano a Mare I . 104 C3
Poligny F 69 B5
Polis CY 120 A1
Polistena I . . . 106 C3
Polizzi Generosa I . 109 B3
Poljana SRB . . . 85 B6
Poljanák HR . . . 83 B4
Poljčane SLO . . . 73 B5
Poljice
 BIH 83 B5
 BIH 84 C2
Poljna SRB . . . 85 C6
Polkowice PL . . 53 B6
Polla I 104 C1
Pollas E 88 C1
Pølla N 73 A5
Polleben D . . . 52 B1
Pollença E 97 B3
Pollenfeld D . . . 62 B2
Pollfoss N 114 F4
Póllica I 106 A2
Polminhac F . . . 77 B5
Polná CZ 63 A6
Polna RUS 7 B10
Polne PL 46 B2
Polomka SK . . . 65 B5
Polonne UA . . . 11 A9
Polperro GB . . . 28 C3
Polruan GB . . . 28 C3
Pöls A 73 A4
Polska Cerekiew PL . 54 C3
Poltár SK 65 B5
Põltsamaa EST . . 7 B8
Polyarny RUS . . 3 B30
Polyarnyye Zori RUS . 3 C30
Polzela SLO . . . 73 B5
Pomarance I . . . 81 C4
Pomarez F 76 C2
Pomárico I . . . 104 C2
Pomáz H 65 C5
Pombal P 92 B2
Pomeroy GB . . . 19 B5
Pomézia I 102 B5
Pomichna UA . . 11 B11
Pommard F . . . 69 A4
Pommelsbrunn D . 62 A2
Pomonte I 81 D4
Pomorie BG . . . 11 E9
Pomos CY 120 A1
Pompei I 103 C7
Pompey F 60 B2
Poncin F 69 B5
Pondorf D 62 B2
Ponferrada E . . 86 B4
Pongoma RUS . . 3 D31
Poniec PL 54 B1
Poniky SK 65 B5
Ponsacco I . . . 81 C4
Ponsul P 93 B3
Pont I 70 C2
Pont-a-Celles B . . 49 C5
Pontacq F 76 C2
Pontailler-sur-Saône
F 69 A5
Pont-à-Marcq F . . 49 C4
Pont-à-Mousson F . 60 B2
Pontão P 92 B2
Pontardawe GB . . 28 B4
Pontarddulais GB . 28 B3
Pontarion F . . . 68 C1
Pontassieve I . . . 81 C5
Pontaubault F . . 57 B4
Pont-Audemer F . 58 A1
Pontaumur F . . . 68 C2
Pont-Aven F . . . 56 C2
Pont Canavese I . . 70 C2
Pontcharra F . . . 69 C6
Pontcharra-sur-Turdine
F 69 C4
Pontchâteau F . . 66 A2
Pont-Croix F . . . 56 B1
Pont-d'Ain F . . . 69 B5
Pont-de-Beauvoisin F . 69 C5
Pont-de-Buis-lès-
 Quimerch F . . 56 B1
Pont-de-Chéruy F . 69 C5
Pont-de-Dore F . 68 C3
Pont-de-Labeaume F . 78 B3
Pont-de-l'Arche F . 58 A2
Pont de Molins E . 91 A5
Pont-de-Roide F . 70 A1
Pont-de-Salars F . 78 B1
Pont-d'Espagne F . 76 D2
Pont de Suert E . 90 A3
Pont-de-Vaux F . 69 B4
Pont-de-Veyle F . 69 B4
Pont d'Ouilly F . 57 B5
Pont-du-Château F . 68 C3
Pont-du-Navoy F . 69 B5
Ponte a Moriano I . 81 C4
Ponte Arche I . . 71 B5
Pontebba I . . . 72 B3
Ponte-Caldelas E . 87 B2
Ponteceso E . . . 86 A2
Pontecesures E . 87 B2
Pontecorvo I . . . 103 B6
Ponte da Barca P . 87 C2
Pontedássio I . . . 80 C2
Pontedécimo I . . 80 B2
Ponte de Lima P . 87 C2
Ponte dell'Ólio I . 81 B3
Pontedera I . . . 81 C4
Ponte de Sor P . . 92 B2
Pontedeume E . . 86 A2
Ponte di Barbarano I . 72 C1
Ponte di Legno I . 71 B5
Ponte di Nava I . 80 B1
Ponte di Piave I . 72 C2
Ponte Felcino I . . 82 C1
Pontefract GB . . 27 B4
Ponte Gardena I . 72 B1
Ponteginori I . . . 81 C4
Pontelagoscuro I . 81 B5
Ponteland GB . . 25 C6
Ponte-Leccia F . . 102 A2
Pontelongo I . . . 72 C2
Ponte nelle Alpi I . 72 B2
Pont-en-Royans F . 79 A4
Ponter Farces F . 57 B4
Pontes-e-Forças F . 87 B4
Pont Farcy F . . . 57 B4
Pontfaverger-Moronvillers
F 59 A5
Pontgibaud F . . . 68 C2
Ponthierry F . . . 58 B3
Pontigny F 59 C4
Pontínia I 102 B6
Pontinvrea I . . . 80 B2
Pontivy F 56 B3
Pont-l'Abbé F . . 56 C1
Pont-l'Évêque F . 58 A1
Pontlevoy F . . . 67 A6
Pontones E . . . 101 A3
Pontonx-sur-l'Adour
F 76 C2
Pontoon IRL . . . 18 C2
Pontorson F . . . 57 B4

Pontrémoli I 81 B3
Pont-Rémy F 48 C2
Pontresina CH 71 B4
Pontrhydfendigaid
  GB 28 A4
Pontrieux F 56 B2
Ponts E 91 B4
Ponts-aux-Dames F . .59 B3
Pont Scorff F 56 C2
Pöntsö FIN 113 E13
Pont-Ste Maxence F .58 A3
Pont-St Esprit F 78 B3
Pont-St Mamet F 77 B3
Pont-St Martin
  F 66 A3
  I 70 C2
Pont-St Vincent F 60 B2
Pont-sur-Yonne F 59 B4
Pontvallain F 57 C6
Pontypool GB 29 B4
Pontypridd GB 29 B4
Ponza I 102 C5
Poo E 88 A2
Poole GB 29 C6
Poolewe GB 22 D3
Poperinge B 48 C3
Pópoli I 103 A6
Popovac SRB 85 C6
Popovača HR 74 C1
Popow PL 55 A4
Poppel B 49 B6
Poppenhausen
  Bayern D 51 C6
  Hessen D 51 C5
Poppi I 81 C5
Popučke SRB 85 B4
Pópulo P 87 C3
Populonia I 81 C4
Pórbölly H 74 B3
Porcuna E 100 B1
Pordenone I 72 C2
Pordic F 56 B3
Poręba PL 55 C4
Poreč HR 72 C3
Pori FIN 3 F24
Porjus S 112 F8
Porkhov RUS 7 C10
Porlezza I 71 B4
Porlock GB 29 B4
Pörnbach D 62 B2
Pornic F 66 A2
Pornichet F 66 A2
Porodin SRB 85 B6
Poronin PL 65 A5
Poros
  Attiki GR 117 E5
  Kefalonia GR 117 D2
Porozina HR 82 A3
Porquerolles F 79 D5
Porrentruy CH 70 A2
Porreres E 97 B3
Porretta Terme I 81 B4
Porsgrunn N 35 C1
Porspoder F 56 B1
Port-a-Binson F 59 A4
Portadown GB 19 B5
Portaferry GB 19 B6
Portaje E 93 B4
Portalegre P 92 B3
Portarlington IRL 21 A4
Port Askaig GB 24 C1
Portavadie GB 24 C2
Portavogie GB 19 B6
Portball F 57 A4
Port Bannatyne GB . . .24 C2
Port-Barcarès F 78 D2
Portbou E 91 A6
Port-Camargue F 78 C3
Port Charlotte GB 24 C1
Port d'Andratx E 97 B2
Port-de-Bouc F 78 C3
Port-de-Lanne F 76 C1
Port de Pollença E 97 B3
Port-des-Barques F . . .66 C3
Port de Sóller E 97 B2
Portegrandi I 72 C2
Portel P 92 C3
Portela P 92 A2
Port Ellen GB 24 C1
Portelo P 87 C4
Portemouro E 86 B2
Port-en-Bessin F 57 A5
Port Erin GB 26 A1
Portes-lès-Valence F . .78 B3
Portets F 76 B2
Port Eynon GB 28 B3
Portezuelo E 93 B4
Port Glasgow GB 24 C3
Portglenone GB 19 B5
Porthcawl GB 28 B4
Port Henderson GB . . .22 D3
Porthleven GB 28 C2
Porthmadog GB 26 C1
Porticcio F 102 B1
Portici I 103 C7
Portico di Romagna I . .81 B5
Portilla de la Reina E . .88 A2
Portillo E 88 C2
Portimão P 98 B2
Portinatx E 97 B1
Portinho da Arrabida
  P 92 C1
Port Isaac GB 28 C3
Portishead GB 29 B5
Port-Joinville F 66 B2
Portknockie GB 23 D6
Port-la-Nouvelle F 78 C2
Portlaoise IRL 21 A4
Portlethen GB 23 D6
Port Logan GB 24 D3
Port Louis F 56 C2
Portmagne IRL 20 C1
Portmahomack GB 23 D5
Portman E 101 B5
Port Manech F 56 C2
Portnacroish GB 24 B2
Portnahaven GB 24 C1
Port Nan Giuran GB . . .22 C2
Port-Navalo F 66 A2
Port Nis GB 22 C2
Porto
  F 102 A1
  P 87 C2
Porto-Alto P 92 C2
Porto Azzurro I 81 D4
Portocannone I 103 B8
Porto Cerésio I 70 C3
Porto Cervo I 110 A2
Porto Cesáreo I 107 A4
Porto Colom E 97 B3
Porto Covo P 98 B2
Porto Cristo E 97 B3
Porto d'Ascoli I 82 D2
Porto de Lagos P 98 B2
Porto de Mos P 92 B2
Porto de Rei P 92 C2
Porto do Son E 86 B2
Portoferráio I 81 D4
Portofino I 80 B3
Porto Garibaldi I 82 B1
Portogruaro I 72 C2
Portokhelion GR 117 E5
Portomaggiore I 81 B5
Portomarin E 86 B3
Portonovo E 87 B2
Portopalo di Capo
  Passero I 109 C4
Portør N 33 D6
Porto Petro I 97 B3
Porto Pino I 110 D1
Porto Potenza Picena
  I 82 C2

Porto San Giórgio I . . .82 C2
Porto Sant'Elpídio I . . .82 C2
Porto Santo Stéfano
  I 102 A4
Portoscuso I 110 C1
Porto Tolle I 82 B1
Porto Tórres I 110 B1
Porto-Vecchio F 102 B2
Portovénere I 81 B3
Portpatrick GB 24 D2
Portree GB 22 D2
Portroe IRL 20 B3
Portrush GB 19 A5
Port St Mary GB 26 A1
Portsall F 56 B1
Portsmouth GB 31 D2
Portsoy GB 23 D6
Port-Ste Marie F 77 B3
Portstewart GB 19 A5
Port-St-Louis-du-Rhône
  F 78 C3
Portugalete E 89 A4
Portumna IRL 20 A3
Port-Vendres F 91 A6
Précy-sur-Thil F . . . . . .69 A4 (?)
Porvoo FIN 7 A8
Porzuna E 94 C2
Posada
  Oviedo E 88 A1
  Oviedo E 88 A2
  I 110 B2
Posada de Valdeón E . .88 A1
Posadas E 99 B5
Poschiavo CH 71 B5
Posedarje HR 83 B4
Positano I 103 C7
Possagno I 72 C1
Posseck D 52 C2
Possesse F 59 B5
Pössneck D 52 C1
Posta I 102 A6
Posta I 71 B6
Posta Piana I 104 B1
Postbauer-Heng D 62 A2
Posterholt NL 50 B2
Postiglione I 103 C8
Postioma I 72 C2
Postira HR 83 C5
Postojna SLO 73 C4
Postoloprty CZ 53 C3
Postomino PL 46 A2
Posušje BIH 84 C2
Potamos
  Attiki GR 117 F4
  Attiki GR 117 G5
Potegowo PL 46 A3
Potenza I 104 C1
Potenza Picena I 82 C2
Přerov CZ 64 A3
Prerow D 45 A4
Presencio E 88 B3
Presicce I 107 B5
Presly F 68 A2
Prešov SK 10 B6
Pressac F 67 B5
Pressath D 62 A2
Pressbaum A 64 B2
Prestatyn GB 26 B2
Prestebakke N 35 D3
Presteigne GB 29 A4
Přeštice CZ 63 A4
Preston
  Lancashire GB 26 B3
  Scottish Borders GB .25 C5
Prestonpans GB 25 C5
Prestwick GB 24 C3
Prettin D 52 B2
Pretoro I 103 A6
Pretzchendorf D 52 C3
Pretzier D 44 C3
Pretzsch D 52 B2
Preuilly-sur-Claise F . .67 B5
Prevalje SLO 73 B4
Prevenchères F 78 B2
Préveranges F 68 B2
Preveza GR 116 D2
Prevršac HR 73 C6
Prezid HR 73 C4
Priaranza del Bierzo
  E 86 B4
Priay F 69 B5
Pribeta SK 64 C4
Priboj
  BIH 84 B3
  SRB 85 C4
Přibor CZ 64 A4
Příbram CZ 63 A5
Pribylina SK 65 A5
Přibyslav CZ 63 A6
Pričević SRB 85 B4
Pridjel BIH 84 B3
Priego E 95 B4
Priego de Córdoba
  E 100 B1
Priekule LV 6 C6
Prien D 62 C3
Prienai LT 6 D7
Prievidza SK 65 B4
Prigradica HR 84 D1
Prigrevica SRB 75 C4
Prijeboj HR 83 B4
Prijedor BIH 83 B5
Prijepolje SRB 85 C4
Prilep MK 116 A3
Priluka BIH 84 C1
Primda CZ 62 A3
Primel-Trégastel F 56 B2
Primišlje HR 73 C5
Primorsko
  Kaliningrad RUS . . .47 A6
  Severo-Zapadnyy
    RUS 7 A10
Primošten HR 83 C4
Primstal D 60 A2
Princes Risborough
  GB 31 C3
Princetown GB 28 C3
Principina a Mare I . . .81 F29 (?)
Priolo Gargallo I 109 B4
Prioro E 88 B2
Priozersk RUS . . . . .3 F29 (?)
Prirechnyy RUS 113 C19
Prisoje BIH 84 C2
Pristen RUS 7 F14
Priština KOS 85 D6
Pritzerbe D 44 C4
Pritzier D 44 B3
Pritzwalk D 44 B4
Privas F 78 B3
Priverno I 102 B6
Privlaka
  Vukovarsko-Srijemska
    HR 74 C3
  Zadarska HR 83 B3
Prizna HR 83 B3
Prizren KOS 10 E6
Prizzi I 108 B2
Prnjavor
  BIH 84 B2
  HR 73 C5
  SRB 85 B4
Proaza E 86 A4
Probištip MK . . . . .116 A4 (?)
Probstzella D 52 C1
Probus GB 28 C3
Próchnik PL . . . . .55 D4 (?)
Prochowice PL 54 B1
Prócida I 103 C7
Prodhromos CY 120 B1
Prodo I 82 D1
Proença-a-Nova P 92 B3
Proença-a-Velha P 92 A3
Profondeville B 49 C5
Profitis GR . . . . .116 B5 (?)
Prokuplje SRB 10 E6
Propriano F 102 B1
Prosec CZ 64 A2
Prösen D 52 B3
Prosenjakovci SLO 73 B6
Prosotsani GR 116 A5
Prostějov CZ 64 A3
Prószków PL 54 C2
Proszowice PL 55 C5
Protić BIH 84 B1
Protivanov CZ 63 A5
Protivin CZ 63 A5
Prötzel D 45 C5
Provins F 59 B4
Prozor BIH 84 C2
Prrenjas AL 116 A2
Prudhoe GB 25 D6
Prudnik PL 54 C2
Pruggern A 72 A3
Prüm D 50 C2
Pruna E 99 C5
Prunelli-di-Fiumorbo
  F 102 A2
Prunetta I 81 B4
Pruniers F 68 B2
Prusce PL 54 B1
Prusice SK . . . . .64 A4 (?)
Pruszce PL 47 B4
Pruszcz Gdański PL . . .47 A4
Pruszków PL 55 A5
Prutz A 71 A5
Prüzen D 44 B4
Pruzhany BY 6 E8
Pruzilly UA 11 A12
Przylęg PL . . . . .46 C1 (?)
Przechlewo PL 46 B3
Przecław PL 55 C6
Przedbórz PL 55 B4
Przedecz PL 54 A3
Przejęslaw PL . . . . .53 B5 (?)
Przemków PL 53 B5
Przemocze PL 45 B6
Przemyśl PL 11 B7
Przerab PL . . . . .55 B4 (?)
Przewodnik PL 47 B4
Przewóz PL 53 B4
Przezmark PL 47 B5
Przodkowo PL 47 A4
Przybiernów PL 45 B6
Przyborowice PL . . . . .77 C3 (?)
Przyborowie PL . . . . . .77 C3 (?)
Przybyszew PL 55 B5
Przybyszów PL 55 B4
Przylep PL . . . . .46 C1 (?)
Przysucha PL 55 B5
Przytoczna PL 46 C1
Przyrów PL 55 B4
Przywidz PL 47 A4
Psachna GR 116 D5
Psara GR 116 D7
Psary PL 54 B3
Pskov RUS 7 C10
Pszczew PL 46 C1
Pszczółki PL 47 A4
Pszczyna PL 54 D3
Pszów PL 54 C3
Pszleos GR 116 B3
Ptolemaida GR 116 B3
Ptuj SLO 73 B5
Ptusza PL 46 B2
Puch A 62 C4
Puchberg am Schneeberg
  A 64 C1
Puchevillers F 48 C3
Púchov SK 64 A4
Pučišća HR 83 C5
Puck PL 47 A4
Puçol E 96 B2
Pučonci SLO 73 B6
Pudasjärvi FIN 3 D27
Puderbach D 50 C3
Puebla de Albortón E . .90 B2
Puebla de Alcocer E . .93 C5
Puebla de Beleña E . . .95 B3
Puebla de Don Fadrique
  E 101 B3
Puebla de Don Rodrigo
  E 94 C2
Puebla de Guzmán E . .98 B3
Puebla de la Calzada
  E 93 C4
Puebla de la Reina E . .93 C4
Puebla de Lillo E 88 A1
Puebla del Maestre E . .99 A4
Puebla del Príncipe
  E 100 A3
Puebla de Obando E . .93 B4
Puebla de Sanabria E . .87 B4
Puebla de Sancho Pérez
  E 93 C4
Puente Almuhey E 88 B2
Puente de Domingo
  Flórez E 86 B4
Puente de Génave E . .101 A3
Puente del Congosto
  E 93 A5
Puente Duero E 88 C2
Puente-Genil E 100 B1
Puente la Reina E 89 B5
Puente la Reina de Jaca
  E 90 A2
Puentelarra E 89 B3
Puente Mayorga E 99 C5
Puente Viesgo E 88 A3
Puertas
  Asturias E 88 A2
  Salamanca E 87 C4
Puerto de Mazarrón
  E 101 B4
Puerto de Santa Cruz
  E 94 C1
Puerto de San Vicente
  E 94 C1
Puerto-Lápice E 95 C3
Puertollano E 100 A1
Puerto Lumbreras E . .101 B4
Puerto Moral E 99 B4
Puerto Real E 99 C4
Puerto Rey E 94 C1
Puerto Seguro E 87 D4
Puerto Serrano E 99 C5
Puget-Sur-Argens F . . .79 C5
Puget-Théniers F 79 C5
Puget-ville F 79 C5
Pugnochiuso I 104 B2
Puig reig E 91 B4
Puigcerdà E 91 A4
Puigpunyent E 97 B2
Puillon F 76 C2
Puimichel F 79 C5
Puimoisson F 79 C5
Puiseaux F 58 B3
Puisieux F 48 C3
Puissalicon F . . . . .78 C2 (?)
Puisserguier F 78 C2
Puivert F 77 D5
Pujols F 76 B2
Pukanec SK 65 B4
Pukavik S 41 C4
Pukë AL 105 A5
Pula
  HR 82 B2
  I 110 C1
Puławy PL 10 A6
Pulborough GB 31 D3
Pulfero I 72 B3
Pulgar E 94 C2
Pulheim D 50 B2
Pulkau A 63 B6
Pulpi E 101 B4
Pulsano I 104 C3
Pulsnitz D 53 B4
Pułtusk PL 6 E6
Pumpuänt GR . . . . . . .28 A4 (?)
Punat HR 83 A3
Punta Marina I 82 B1
Punta Prima I 97 B4
Punta Sabbioni I 72 C2
Puntas de Calnegre
  E 101 B4
Punta Umbria E 99 B4
Puolanka FIN 3 D27
Puottaure S . . . . .112 F9 (?)
Puračić BIH 84 B3
Purbach am Neusiedler
  See A 64 C2
Purchena E 101 B3

Purfleet GB 31 C4
Purgstall A 63 B6
Purkersdorf A 64 B2
Purmerend NL 42 C1
Purullena E 100 B2
Pushkin RUS 7 B11
Pushkino RUS 7 C14
Püspökladány H 75 A6
Pусте Ulany SK 64 B3
Pустoshka RUS 7 C10
Puszcza Mariańska
  PL 55 A5
Pусzczykowo PL 54 A1
Pусzтаmagyaród H . . .74 B1
Pусzтаmonostor H . . .75 A4
Pусzтаszaboцs H 74 A3
Pусzтаváм H 74 A3
Putanges-Pont-Ecrepin
  F 57 B5
Putbus D 45 A5
Putignano I 104 C3
Putlitz D 44 B4
Putnok H 65 B6
Putte B 49 B5
Puttelange-aux-Lacs
  F 60 A2
Putten NL 49 A6
Puttgarden D 44 A3
Püttlingen D 60 A2
Putzu Idu I 110 B1
Puy-Guillaume F 68 C3
Puylaroque F 77 B4
Puylaurens F 77 C5
Puy-l'Évêque F 77 B4
Puymirol F 77 B3
Puyôo F 76 C2
Puyrolland F 67 B4
Pyatikhatky UA 11 B12
Pyetrikaw BY 7 E10
Pyhäjärvi FIN 3 E26
Pyla CY 120 A2
Pyla-sur-Mer F 76 B1
Pyrzycyn UA 11 A12
Pyrzyce PL 45 B6
Pysely CZ 63 A5
Pyskowice PL 54 C3
Pytalovo RUS 7 C9
Pyzdry PL 54 A2

Q

Quakenbrück D 43 C4
Quarngento I 80 B2
Quarré-les-Tombes F . .68 A3
Quarteira P 98 B2
Quartu Sant'Élena I . .110 C2
Quatre-Champs F 59 A5
Quedlinburg D 52 B1
Queensferry
  Edinburgh GB 25 C4
  Flintshire GB 26 B2
Queige F 69 C6
Queipo E 99 B4
Queixans E 91 A4
Quel E 89 B5
Queljada P 87 C2
Quemada E 89 C3
Queralbs E 91 A5
Quercianella I 81 C4
Querfurt D 52 B1
Quérigut F 77 D5
Quero
  E 95 C3
  I 72 C1
Querqueville F 57 A4
Quesada E 100 B2
Questembert F 56 C3
Quettehou F 57 A4
Quevauvillers F 58 A3
Quévy B 49 C5
Quiaiós P 92 A2
Quiberon F 66 A1
Quiberville F 58 A1
Quickborn D 44 B1
Quiévrain B 49 C4
Quillan F 77 D5
Quillebeuf F 58 A1
Quimper F 56 B1
Quimperlé F 56 C2
Quincampoix F 58 A2
Quincoces de Yuso E . .89 B3
Quincy F 68 A2
Quinéville F 57 A4
Quingey F 69 A5
Quinson F 79 C5
Quinssaines F 68 B2
Quinta-Grande P 92 C2
Quintana de la Serena
  E 93 C5
Quintana del Castillo
  E . . . . .88 B1 (?)
Quintana del Marco E . .88 B1
Quintana del Puente
  E 88 B2
Quintana-Martín Galíndez
  E 89 B3
Quintanapalla E 89 B3
Quintanar de la Orden
  E 95 C3
Quintanar de la Sierra
  E 89 C3
Quintanar del Rey E . . .95 C5
Quintana Redonda
  E . . . . .89 C4 (?)
Quintanilla de la Mata
  E 88 C3
Quintanilla del Coco
  E 89 C3
Quintanilla de Onésimo
  E 88 C2
Quintanilla de Somoza
  E 87 B4
Quintas de Valdelucio
  E 88 B2
Quintela P 87 D3
Quintin F 56 B3
Quinto E 90 B2
Quinzano d'Oglio I 71 C5
Quiroga E 86 B3
Quismondo E 94 B2
Quissac F 78 C2
Quistello I 81 A4

R

Raab A 63 B4
Raabs an der Thaya
  A 63 B6
Raahe FIN 3 D26
Raajärvi FIN 113 F15
Raalte NL 42 C3
Raamsdonksveer NL .49 B5
Raanujärvi FIN 113 F13
Raattama FIN 113 D13
Rab HR 83 B3
Rabac HR 82 A3
Rábade E 86 A3
Rábafüzes H 73 B6
Rábahidvég H 74 A1
Rabanales E 87 C4
Rábapatona H 64 C3
Rabapordány H 74 A2
Rabastens F 77 C4
Rabastens-de-Bigorre
  F 76 C3
Rabat = Victoria 107 C5
Rabat M 107 C5
Rabča SK 65 A5
Rábcakapi H . . . . .64 C3 (?)
Rabe SRB 75 B5
Rabino RUS . . . . .46 B1 (?)
Rabka PL 65 A5
Rabrovo SRB 85 B6
Rača
  Srbija SRB 85 B6
  Srbija SRB 85 C6
Rácale I 107 B5
Rácalmás H 74 A3

Racalmuto I 108 B2
Racconigi I 80 B1
Rače SLO 73 B5
Rachecourt-sur-Marne
  F 59 B6
Raciąż PL 47 C6
Racibórz PL 54 C3
Račinovci HR 84 B3
Ráckeve H 75 A3
Racławice PL 55 C5
Racławice Śląskie
  PL 54 C2
Racot PL 54 A1
Rада
  Skaraborg S 35 D5
  Värmland S 34 B5
Radaljub SRB 85 B4
Rădăuți RO 11 C8
Radda in Chianti I 81 C5
Raddusa I 109 B3
Radeberg D 53 B3
Radeburg D 52 B3
Radeče SLO 73 B5
Radekhiv UA 11 A8
Radenci SLO 73 B5
Radenthein A 72 B3
Radevormwald D 50 B3
Radicófani I 81 D5
Radičondoli I 81 C5
Radišići BIH 84 C2
Radizel SLO 73 B5
Radków PL 54 C1
Radlje ob Dravi SLO . . .73 B5
Radłów PL 55 C5
Radmer an der Stube
  A 73 A4
Radnejaur S 115 B15
Radnice CZ 63 A4
Radohova BIH 84 B2
Radojevo SRB 75 C5
Radolfzell D 61 C4
Radom PL 55 B6
Radomice PL 47 C5
Radomin PL 47 B5
Radomsko PL 55 B4
Radomyśl UA 11 A10
Radomyśl Wielki PL . . .55 C6
Radošina SK 64 B3
Radošovce SK 64 B3
Radostowo PL 47 A5
Radoszyce PL 55 B5
Radoszyn PL . . . . .53 A5 (?)
Radotin CZ 53 D4
Radoviš MK 116 A4
Radovljica SLO 73 B4
Radowo Wielkie PL . . .46 B1 (?)
Radstadt A 72 A3
Radstock GB 29 B5
Raduc HR 83 B4
Radviliškis LT 6 D7
Radzanów
  Mazowieckie PL . . .47 C6
  Mazowieckie PL . . .55 B5
Radziejów PL 47 C4
Radziejowice PL 55 A5
Radzovce SK 65 B5
Radzyń Chełmiński
  PL 47 B4
 Raeren B 50 C2
Raesfeld D 50 B2
Raffadali I 108 B2
Rafina GR 117 D5
Rafsbotn N 113 B12
Ragachow BY 7 E11
Ragály H 65 B6
Rägelin D . . . . .41 C2 (?)
Raglan GB 29 B5
Ragnitz A 73 B5
Ragusa I 109 C3
Rahden D 43 C5
Ráhólt H . . . . .34 B1 (?)
Raiano I 103 A6
Raigada E 87 B3
Rain D 62 B2
Rainbach im Mühlkreis
  A 63 B5
Rainham GB 31 C4
Rairiz de Veiga E 87 B3
Raisdorf D 44 A2
Raisio FIN 6 A7
Raitovaara FIN 3 E28
Raja-Jooseppi FIN .113 D17
Rajala FIN 113 E15
Rajcza PL 65 A4
Rajec SK 65 A4
Rajec-Jestřebí CZ 64 A2
Rajevo Selo HR 84 B3
Rajhrad CZ 64 A2
Rajić HR 74 C2
Rajka H 64 C3
Rakaca H 65 B6
Rakek SLO 73 C4
Rakhiv UA 11 B8
Rakitna SLO 73 C4
Rakitovo BG . . . . .11 E8 (?)
Rakkestad N 35 C3
Rákóczifalva H 75 A5
Rakoniewice PL 53 A6
Rakoszyce PL 54 B1
Rakov Czech . . . . .11 B12 (?)
Rakova BIH 84 B3
Rakovčan HR . . . . .83 B4 (?)
Rakovnik CZ 53 C3
Rakovo . . . . .84 B3 (?)
Rakow D . . . . .55 C6 (?)
Raków PL 55 C6
Rakvere EST 7 B9
Ralja SRB 85 B5
Rälla S 41 C6
Ramacastañas E 94 B1
Ramacca I 109 B3
Ramales de la Victoria
  E 89 A3
Ramberg N 112 D2
Rambervillers F 60 B2
Rambouillet F 58 B2
Rambucourt F 60 B1
Ramdala S 41 C5
Ramerupt F 59 B5
Ramingstein A 72 A3
Ramirás E 87 B2
Ramiswil CH 70 A2
Ramkvilla S 40 B4
Ramme DK 38 C1
Rämmen S 34 B6
Ramnäs S 36 C3
Râmnicu Vâlcea RO . .11 D8
Ramonville-St Agne
  F 77 C4
Rampside GB 26 A2
Ramsau D 62 C3
Ramsbeck D 51 B4
Ramsberg S 36 C2
Ramsey
  Cambridgeshire GB .30 B3
  Isle of Man GB 26 A1
Ramseycleuch GB 25 C4
Ramsgate GB 31 C5
Ramsjö S 115 E12
Ramstein-Meisenbach
  D 60 A3
Ramsund N 112 D5
Ramundberget S . . .114 E9
Ramvik S 115 E14
Ranalt A 71 A6
Rånäs S 36 C5
Rånåsfoss N 34 B3
Rance B 49 C5
Ránchio I 82 C1
Randaberg N 33 D2
Randalstown GB 19 B5
Randan F 68 B3
Randazzo I 109 B3
Rånddalen S 115 E10
Randegg A 63 B5
Randers DK 38 C3
Randijaur S 112 F8
Randin E 87 C3
Randsverk N 114 F6
Rânes F 57 B5
Rångedala S 40 B3
Rankweil A 71 A4
Rånnaväg S 40 B3
Rännelöv S 40 C3
Rannoch Station GB . .24 B3
Ranovac SRB 85 B6
Ransäter S 34 C5
Ransbach-Baumbach
  D 50 C3
Ranshofen A . . . . .62 B3 (?)
Ranskill GB . . . . .27 B5 (?)
Ransta S 36 C3
Ranttila FIN 113 C14
Ranua FIN 3 D27
Ranum DK 38 C2
Raon-l'Étape F 60 B2
Ráossi I 71 C6
Rapallo I 80 B3
Rapla EST 6 B8
Rapness GB 23 B6
Rapolano Terme I 81 C5
Rapolla I 104 C1
Raposa P 92 B2
Rapperswil CH 70 A3
Raša I 82 A3
Rasal E 90 A2
Rascafría E 94 B3
Rasdorf D 51 C5
Raseiniai LT 6 D7
Rasines E 89 A3
Rasquera E 90 B3
Rássina I 81 C5
Rastatt D 61 B4
Rastede D 43 B5
Rastenberg D 52 B1
Rastošnica BIH 84 B3
Rastovac MNE . . . . . . .84 D3 (?)
Rasueros E 94 A1
Rasy PL 55 B4
Raszków PL 54 B2
Rataje SRB 85 C6
Rätan S 115 E11
Rateče SLO 72 B3
Ratekau D 44 B2
Ratež SLO 73 C5
Rathangan IRL 21 A5
Rathcoole IRL 21 A5
Rathcormack IRL 20 B3
Rathdrum IRL 21 B5
Rathebur D 45 B5
Rathenow D 44 C4
Rathfriland GB 19 B5
Rathkeale IRL 20 B3
Rathmelton IRL 19 A4
Rathmolyon IRL 21 A5
Rathmore IRL 20 B2
Rathmullan IRL 19 A4
Rathnew IRL 21 B5
Rathvilly IRL 21 B5
Ratibořské Hory CZ . . .63 A5
Ratingen D 50 B2
Ratková SK 65 B6
Ratkovo SRB 75 C4
Ratne UA 6 F8
Ratoath IRL 21 A5
Rattelsdorf D 51 C6
Ratten A 73 A5
Rattosjärvi FIN 113 F13
Rattray GB 25 B4
Rättvik S 36 B2
Ratzeburg D 44 B2
Rätzlingen D 44 C3
Raucourt-et-Flaba F . . .59 A5
Raudeberg N 114 F2
Raufarhöfn IS 111 A10
Raufoss N 34 B2
Rauha FIN . . . . .3 C11 (?)
Rauhala FIN 113 D13
Rauland N 33 C5
Raulhac F 77 B5
Raulia N 115 B11
Rauma FIN 3 F24
Raundal N 32 B3
Raunds GB 30 B3
Rauris A 72 A3
Rautas S 112 E8
Rautavaara FIN 3 E28
Rautjärvi FIN 3 F28
Ravanusa I 108 B2
Rava-Rus'ka UA 11 A7
Ravča HR 84 C2
Ravda BG 11 E9
Ravels B 49 B5
Ravenglass GB 26 A2
Ravenna I 82 B1
Ravensburg D 61 C5
Rävlanda S 40 B2
Ravna Gora HR 73 C4
Ravne na Koroškem
  SLO 73 B4
Ravnište SRB 85 C6
Ravno BIH 84 D2
Ravno Selo SRB 75 C4
Rawa Mazowiecka PL .55 B5
Rawicz PL 54 B1
Rawtenstall GB 26 B3
Rayleigh GB 31 C4
Rayol F 79 C5
Ražana SRB 85 B4
Ražanac HR 83 B4
Razbojna SRB 85 C6
Razes F . . . . .67 B6 (?)
Razgrad BG 11 E9
Razkrižje SLO 73 B6
Razo E 86 A2
Reading GB 31 C3
Réalmont F 77 C5
Reboly RUS 3 E29
Rebordelo P 87 C3
Recanati I 82 C2
Recas
  E 94 B3
  RO 10 D6
Recco I 80 B3
Recess IRL 18 C2
Recey-sur-Ource F . . . .59 C5 (?)
Rechnitz A 73 A6
Rechytsa BY 7 E11
Recke D 43 C4
Recklinghausen D 50 B3
Recoaro Terme I 71 C6
Recogne B 60 A1
Recoules-Prévinquières
  F 78 B1
Recz PL 46 B1
Reczno PL 55 B4
Reda PL 47 A4
Redalen N 34 B2
Redange L 60 A1
Redcar GB 27 A4
Red Point GB 22 D3
Redditch GB 29 A6
Redefin D 44 B3
Redhill GB 31 C3
Redics H 74 B1
Redkino RUS 7 C14
Redland GB 23 B5
Redlin D 44 B4
Redon F 57 C3
Redondela E 87 B2
Redondo P 92 C3
Redruth GB 28 C2
Reepham GB 30 B5
Rees D 50 B2
Reeth GB 26 A4
Reetz D 44 C4
Reftele S 40 B3
Regalbuto I 109 B3
Regen D 62 A4
Regensburg D 62 A3
Regenstauf D 62 A3
Reggello I 81 C5

Réggio di Calábria I . .109 A4
Reggiolo I 81 B4
Réggio nell'Emília I . . .81 B4
Reghin RO 11 C8
Régil E 89 A4
Regna S 37 D2
Regniéville F 60 B1
Regny F 69 C4
Rego da Leirosa P 92 A2
Regöly H 74 B3
Regueiro E 86 B2
Reguengo
  Portalegre P 92 B3
  Santarém P 92 B2
Reguengos de Monsaraz
  P 92 C3
Rehau D 52 C2
Rehburg D 43 C6
Rehden D 43 C5
Rehna D 44 B3
Reichelsheim D 61 A4
Reichelshofen D 61 A6
Reichenau CH . . . . . . .64 C1 (?)
Reichenbach
  Sachsen D 52 C2
  Sachsen D 53 B4
Reichenfels A 73 A4
Reichensachsen D 51 B6
Reichertshofen D 62 B2
Reichshoffen F 60 B3
Reiden CH 70 A2
Reigada
  E 86 A4
  P 87 D4
Reigate GB 31 C3
Reillanne F 79 C4
Reillo E 95 C5
Reims F 59 A5
Reinach CH 70 A3
Reinbek D 44 B2
Reinberg D 45 A5
Reine N 112 E2
Reinfeld D 44 B2
Reinheim D 61 A4
Reinli N 32 B6
Reinosa E 88 A2
Reinstorf D 44 B2
Reinsvoll N 34 B2
Reisach A 72 B3
Reiss GB 23 C5
Reitan N 114 E8
Reit im Winkl D 62 C3
Rejmyre S 37 D2
Rekavice BIH 84 B2
Rekovac SRB 85 C6
Relleu E 96 C2
Rém H 75 B4
Remagen D 50 C3
Rémalard F 58 B1
Rembercourt-aux-Pots
  F 59 B6
Remedios P 92 B1
Remels D 43 B4
Remetea Mare RO 75 C6
Remich L 60 A2
Rémilly F 60 A2
Remiremont F 60 C2
Remolinos E 90 B1
Remoulins F 78 C3
Remscheid D 50 B3
Rémuzat F 79 B4
Rena N 34 A3
Renaison F 68 B3
Renazé F 57 C4
Renchen D 61 B4
Rende I 106 B3
Rendsburg D 44 A1
Renedo E 88 C2
Renens CH 69 B6
Renfrew GB 24 C3
Rengsjö S 36 A3
Reni UA 11 D10
Rennebu N 114 E6
Rennerod D 50 C4
Rennertshofen D 62 B2
Rennes F 57 B4
Rennes-les-Bains F . . .77 D5
Rennweg A 72 A3
Rens DK 39 E2
Rensjön S 112 D8
Rentería E 76 C1
Rentjärn S 115 B15
Repojelak H . . . . .74 A2 (?)
Repopelki FIN . . . . . . .3 E28 (?)
Repvåg N 113 B14
Requena E 96 B1
Requista F 77 B5
Rerik D 44 A3
Resana I 72 C1
Resarö S 37 C5
Reschen = Résia I 71 B5
Resen MK 116 A3
Resende P 87 C3
Résia = Reschen I 71 B5
Reşiţa RO 10 D6
Resko PL 46 B1
Resnik SRB 85 B5
Ressons-sur-Matz F . . .58 A3
Restábal E 100 C2
Resuttano I 109 B3
Retamal E 93 C4
Retford GB 27 B5
Rethel F 59 A5
Rethem D 43 C6
Rethimno GR 117 G6
Retie B 49 B6
Retiers F 57 C4
Retortillo E 87 D4
Retortillo de Soria E . . .89 C3
Retournac F 68 C4
Rétság H 65 C5
Retuerta del Bullaque
  E 94 C2
Retz A 64 B1
Retzbach D 61 A5
Reuden D 52 A2
Reuilly F 68 A2
Reus E 91 B4
Reusel NL 49 B6
Reuterstadt Stavenhagen
  D . . . . .45 B4 (?)
Reuth D . . . . .52 C2 (?)
Reutlingen D 61 B5
Reutte A 71 A5
Reuver NL 50 B2
Revel F 77 C4
Revello I 80 B1
Revenga E . . . . .94 B2 (?)
Revest-du-Bion F 79 B4
Révfülöp H 74 B2
Revigny-sur-Ornain F . .59 B5
Revin F 59 A5
Revine I 72 B2
Řevničov CZ 53 C3
Revo I 71 B6
Revolto (?) 86 B2
Revsnes N 32 A4
Revúca SK 65 B6
Rewal PL 45 A7
Rexbo S 36 B2
Reyðarfjörður IS 111 B11
Reykhólar IS 111 B3
Reykholt
  Árnessýsla IS 111 C5
  Borgarfjarðarsýsla
    IS 111 C4
Reykjahlíð IS 111 B9
Reykjavík IS 111 C4
Rezé F 66 A3
Rēzekne LV 7 C9
Rezovo BG 11 F10
Rezzato I 71 C5
Rezzato I (?) . . . . .80 B3 (?)
Rhade D 50 B2
Rhaunen D 60 A3
Rhayader GB 29 A4
Rheda-Wiedenbrück
  D 50 B4

Rhede
Niedersachsen D 43 B4
Nordrhein-Westfalen D 50 B2
Rheinau D 60 B3
Rheinbach D 50 C2
Rheinberg D 50 B2
Rheine D 50 A3
Rheinfelden D 70 A2
Rheinsberg D 45 B4
Rhêmes-Notre-Dame I 70 C2
Rhenen NL 49 B6
Rhens D 50 C3
Rheydt D 50 B2
Rhiconich GB 22 C4
Rhinow D 44 C4
Rhiw GB 26 C1
Rho I 70 C4
Rhodes GR 119 F3
Rhondda GB 29 B4
Rhosllanerchrugog GB 26 B2
Rhosneigr GB 26 B1
Rhossili GB 28 B3
Rhubodach GB 24 C2
Rhuddlan GB 26 B2
Rhyl GB 26 B2
Rhynie GB 23 D6
Riala S 37 C5
Riallé F 66 A3
Riaño E 88 B1
Riano I 102 A5
Rians F 79 C4
Rianxo E 86 B2
Riaza E 89 C3
Riba E 89 A3
Ribadavia E 87 B2
Ribadeo E 86 A3
Riba de Saelices E 95 B4
Ribadesella E 88 A1
Ribaflecha E 89 B4
Ribaforada E 89 C5
Ribare SRB 85 B6
Ribariće SRB 85 D5
Riba-roja d'Ebre E 90 B3
Riba-Roja de Turia E 96 B2
Ribe DK 39 D1
Ribeauvillé F 60 B3
Ribécourt-Dreslincourt F 59 A3
Ribeira da Pena P 87 C3
Ribeira de Piquín E 86 A3
Ribemont F 59 A4
Ribera I 108 B2
Ribérac F 67 C5
Ribera de Cardós E 91 A4
Ribera del Fresno E 93 C4
Ribesalbes E 96 A2
Ribes de Freser E 91 A5
Ribiers F 79 B4
Ribnica
BIH 84 B3
SLO 73 C4
SRB 85 C5
Ribnica na Potorju SLO 73 B5
Ribnik HR 73 C5
Rîbnița MD 11 C10
Ribnitz-Damgarten D 44 A4
Ribolla I 81 D5
Řicany CZ 64 A2
Ričany CZ 53 D4
Ríccia I 103 B7
Riccione I 82 B1
Ricco Del Golfo I 81 B3
Richebourg F 59 B6
Richelieu F 67 A5
Richisau CH 70 A3
Richmond
Greater London GB 31 C3
North Yorkshire GB 27 A4
Richtenberg D 45 A4
Richterswil CH 70 A3
Rickling D 44 A2
Rickmansworth GB 31 C3
Ricla E 89 C5
Riddarhyttan S 36 C2
Ridderkerk NL 49 B5
Riddes CH 70 B2
Ridjica SRB 75 C4
Riec-sur-Bélon F 56 C2
Ried A 63 B4
Riedenburg D 62 B2
Ried im Oberinntal A 71 A5
Riedlingen D 61 B5
Riedstadt D 61 A4
Riegersburg A 73 B5
Riego de la Vega E 88 B1
Riego del Camino E 88 C1
Riello E 88 B1
Riemst B 49 C6
Rienne B 49 D5
Riénsena E 88 A2
Riesa D 52 B3
Riese Pio X I 72 C1
Riesi I 109 B3
Riestedt D 52 B1
Rietberg D 51 B4
Rieti I 102 A5
Rietschen D 53 B4
Rieumes F 77 C4
Rieupeyroux F 77 B5
Rieux-Volvestre F 77 C4
Riez F 79 C5
Rīga LV 6 C8
Riggisberg CH 70 B2
Rignac F 77 B5
Rignano Gargánico I 104 B1
Rigolato I 72 B2
Rigside GB 25 C4
Rigutino I 81 C5
Riihimäki FIN 3 F26
Rijeka HR 73 C4
Rijeka Crnojeviča MNE 105 A5
Rijen NL 49 B5
Rijkevorsel B 49 B5
Rijssen NL 50 A2
Rilić BIH 84 C2
Rilievo I 108 B1
Rillé F 67 A5
Rillo de Gallo E 95 B5
Rimavská Baňa SK 65 B5
Rimavská Seč SK 65 B6
Rimavská Sobota SK 65 B6
Rimbo S 36 C5
Rimforsa S 37 D2
Rímini I 82 B1
Rîmnicu Sărat RO 11 D9
Rimogne F 59 A5
Rimpar D 61 A5
Rimske Toplice SLO 73 B5
Rincón de la Victoria E 100 C1
Rincón de Soto E 89 B5
Rindal N 114 D6
Rinde N 32 A3
Ringarum S 37 D3
Ringaskiddy IRL 20 C3
Ringe DK 39 D3
Ringebu N 34 A2
Ringkøbing DK 39 C1
Ringsaker N 34 B2
Ringsted DK 39 D4
Ringwood GB 29 C6
Rinkaby S 41 D4
Rinkabyholm S 40 C6
Rinlo E 86 A3
Rinn A 71 A6
Rinteln D 51 A5
Rio E 86 B3
Riobo E 86 B2
Riodeva E 96 A1
Rio do Coures P 92 B2
Rio Douro P 87 C3
Riofrio E 94 B2
Rio Frio P 92 C2
Riofrio de Aliste E 87 C4
Rio frio de Riaza E 95 A3
Riogordo E 100 C1
Rioja E 101 C3
Riola I 81 B5
Riola Sardo I 110 C1
Riolobos E 93 B4
Riom F 68 C3
Riomaggiore I 81 B3
Rio Maior P 92 B2
Rio Marina I 81 D4
Riom-ès-Montagnes F 68 C2
Rion-des-Landes F 76 C2
Rionegro del Puente E 87 B4
Rionero in Vúlture I 104 C1
Riopar E 101 A3
Riós E 87 C3
Rioseco E 88 A1
Rioseco de Tapia E 88 B1
Rio Tinto P 87 C2
Riotord F 69 C4
Riotorto E 86 A3
Rioz F 69 A6
Ripač BIH 83 B4
Ripacándida I 104 C1
Ripanj SRB 85 B5
Ripatransone I 82 D2
Ripley GB 27 B4
Ripoll E 91 A5
Ripon GB 27 A4
Riposto I 109 B4
Ripsa S 37 D3
Risan MNE 105 A4
Risbäck S 115 C12
Risca GB 29 B4
Rischenau D 51 B5
Riscle F 76 C2
Risebo S 40 A6
Risnes N 32 A2
Rišňovce SK 64 B3
Risør N 33 D6
Risøyhamn N 112 D4
Rissna S 115 D12
Ritsem S 112 E6
Ritterhude D 43 B5
Riutula FIN 113 D15
Riva del Garda I 71 C5
Riva Ligure I 80 C1
Rivanazzano I 80 B3
Rivarolo Canavese I 70 C2
Rivarolo Mantovano I 81 A4
Rive-de-Gier F 69 C4
Rivedoux-Plage F 66 B3
Rivello I 106 A2
Rivergaro I 80 B3
Rives F 69 C5
Rivesaltes F 78 D1
Rivignano I 72 C3
Rivne UA 11 A9
Rívoli I 80 A1
Rivolta d'Adda I 71 C4
Rixheim F 60 C3
Rixo S 35 D3
Riza GR 116 B5
Rizokarpaso CY 120 A3
Rjukan N 32 C5
Rø DK 41 D4
Rö S 37 C5
Roa
E 88 C3
N 34 B2
Roade GB 30 B3
Roager DK 39 D1
Roaldkvam N 33 C3
Roanne F 68 B4
Robakowo PL 47 B4
Róbbio I 70 C3
Röbel D 45 B4
Roberton GB 25 C5
Robertville B 50 C2
Robin Hood's Bay GB 27 A5
Robleda E 93 A4
Robledillo de Trujillo E 93 B5
Robledo
Albacete E 101 A3
Orense E 86 B4
Robledo de Chavela E 94 B2
Robledo del Buey E 94 C2
Robledo del Mazo E 94 C2
Robledollano E 93 B5
Robles de la Valcueva E 88 B1
Robliza de Cojos E 87 D5
Robres E 90 B2
Robres del Castillo E 89 B4
Rocafort de Queralt E 91 B4
Rocamadour F 77 B4
Roccabernarda I 107 B3
Roccabianca I 81 A4
Roccadáspide I 103 C8
Rocca di Mezzo I 103 A6
Rocca di Papa I 102 B5
Roccagorga I 102 B6
Rocca Imperiale I 106 A3
Roccalbegna I 81 D5
Roccalumera I 109 B4
Roccamena I 108 B2
Roccamonfina I 103 B6
Roccanova I 106 A3
Roccapalumba I 108 B2
Roccapassa I 103 A6
Rocca Priora I 82 C2
Roccaraso I 103 B7
Rocca San Casciano I 81 B5
Roccasecca I 103 B6
Rocca Sinibalda I 102 A5
Roccastrada I 81 C5
Roccatederighi I 81 C5
Roccella Iónica I 106 C3
Rocchetta Sant'António I 103 B8
Rocester GB 27 C4
Rochdale GB 26 B3
Rochechouart F 67 C5
Rochefort
B 49 C6
F 66 C4
Rochefort-en-Terre F 56 C3
Rochefort-Montagne F 68 C2
Rochefort-sur-Nenon F 69 A5
Roche-lez-Beaupré F 69 A6
Rochemaure F 78 B3
Rocheservière F 66 B3
Rochester
Medway GB 31 C4
Northumberland GB 25 C5
Rochlitz D 52 B2
Rociana del Condado E 99 B4
Rockenhausen D 60 A3
Rockhammar S 37 C2
Rockneby S 40 C6
Ročko Polje HR 73 C4
Ročov CZ 53 C3
Rocroi F 59 A5
Rodach D 51 C6
Roda de Bara E 91 B4
Roda de Ter E 91 B5
Rodalben D 60 A3
Rødberg N 32 B5
Rødby DK 44 A3
Rødbyhavn DK 44 A3
Rødding
Sonderjyllands Amt. DK 39 D2
Viborg Amt. DK 38 C1
Rödeby S 41 C5
Rodeiro E 86 B3
Rødekro DK 39 D2
Roden NL 42 B3
Ródenas E 95 B5
Rodenkirchen D 43 B5
Rödental D 52 C1
Rödermark D 51 D4
Rodewisch D 52 C2
Rodez F 77 B5
Rodi Gargánico I 104 B1
Roding D 62 A3
Rödjebro S 36 B4
Rødkærsbro DK 39 C2
Rodolivas GR 116 B5
Rodoñá E 91 B4
Rødvig DK 41 D2
Roermond NL 50 B1
Roesbrugge B 48 C3
Roeschwoog F 61 B4
Roeselare B 49 C4
Roetgen D 50 C2
Roffiac F 78 A2
Röfors S 37 D1
Rofrano I 106 A2
Rogač HR 83 C5
Rogačica SRB 85 B4
Rogalinek PL 54 A1
Rogaška Slatina SLO 73 B5
Rogatec SLO 73 B5
Rogatica BIH 84 C4
Rogatyn UA 11 B8
Rogätz D 52 A1
Roggendorf D 44 B3
Roggiano Gravina I 106 B3
Roghadal GB 22 D2
Rogliano
F 102 A2
I 106 B3
Rognan N 112 E4
Rogne N 32 A6
Rognes F 79 C4
Rogny-les-7-Ecluses F 59 C3
Rogowo PL 46 C3
Rogóz PL 47 A6
Rogoznica HR 83 C4
Rogoźnica PL 53 B6
Rogoźno PL 46 C2
Rohan F 56 B3
Röhlingen D 61 B6
Rohožnik SK 64 B3
Rohr D 51 C6
Rohrbach A 63 B4
Rohrbach-lès-Bitche F 60 A3
Rohrberg D 44 C3
Rohr im Gebirge A 63 C6
Röhrnbach D 63 B4
Roisel F 59 A4
Roja LV 6 C7
Rojales E 96 C2
Röjeråsen S 36 B1
Rojewo PL 47 C4
Rokiciny PL 55 B4
Rokietnica PL 46 C2
Rokiškis LT 7 D8
Rokitki PL 53 B5
Rokitno RUS 7 F13
Rokycany CZ 63 A4
Rolampont F 59 C6
Rold DK 38 C2
Røldal N 32 C3
Rolde NL 42 C3
Rollag N 32 B6
Rollán E 94 B1
Rolle CH 69 B6
Roma = Rome I 102 B5
Roma S 37 E5
Romagnano Sésia I 70 C3
Romagné F 57 B4
Romakloster S 37 E5
Roman RO 11 C9
Romana I 110 B1
Romanèche-Thorins F 69 B4
Romano di Lombardia I 71 C4
Romanshorn CH 71 A4
Romans-sur-Isère F 79 A4
Rombas F 60 A2
Rome = Roma I 102 B5
Romeán E 86 B3
Romenay F 69 B5
Romeral E 95 C3
Römerstein D 61 B5
Rometta I 109 A4
Romford GB 31 C4
Romhány H 65 C5
Römhild D 51 C6
Romilly-sur-Seine F 59 B4
Romny UA 11 A12
Romodan UA 11 B12
Romont CH 70 B1
Romorantin-Lanthenay F 68 A1
Romrod D 51 C5
Romsey GB 31 D2
Rømskog N 35 C3
Rønbjerg DK 38 C1
Roncal E 76 D2
Ronce-les-Bains F 66 C3
Ronchamp F 60 C2
Ronchi dei Legionari I 72 C3
Ronciglione I 102 A5
Ronco Canavese I 70 C2
Ronco Scrivia I 80 B2
Ronda E 99 C5
Rønde DK 39 C3
Rone S 37 E5
Ronehamn S 37 E5
Rong N 32 B1
Rönnäng S 38 B4
Rønne DK 41 D4
Ronneburg D 52 C2
Ronneby S 41 C5
Rönneshytta S 37 D2
Rönninge S 37 C4
Rönnöfors S 115 D10
Rönö S 37 D3
Ronov nad Doubravou CZ 63 A6
Ronse B 49 C4
Roosendaal NL 49 B5
Roosky IRL 19 C4
Ropczyce PL 55 C6
Ropeid N 33 C3
Ropinsalmi FIN 113 D10
Ropuerelos del Páramo E 88 B1
Roquebilière F 79 B6
Roquebrun F 78 C2
Roquecourbe F 77 C5
Roquefort F 76 B2
Roquemaure F 78 B3
Roquesteron F 79 C6
Roquetas de Mar E 101 C3
Roquetes E 90 C3
Roquevaire F 79 C4
Røra N 114 D8
Rörbäcksnäs S 34 A4
Rørbæk DK 38 C2
Rore BIH 83 B5
Röro S 38 B4
Røros N 114 E8
Rorschach CH 71 A4
Rørvig DK 39 D4
Rørvik N 114 C8
Rörvik S 40 B4
Rosà I 72 C1
Rosal de la Frontera E 98 B3
Rosalina Mare I 72 C2
Rosa Marina I 104 C3
Rosans F 79 B4
Rosário P 98 B2
Rosarno I 106 C2
Rosbach D 50 C3
Rosche D 44 C2
Rościszewo PL 47 C5
Roscoff F 56 B2
Roscommon IRL 18 C3
Roscrea IRL 21 B4
Rosdorf D 51 B5
Rose I 106 B3
Rosegg A 73 B4
Rosehall GB 22 D4
Rosehearty GB 23 D6
Rosel GB 57 A3
Rosell E 90 C3
Roselló E 90 B3
Rosendal N 32 C3
Rosenfeld D 61 B4
Rosenfors S 40 B5
Rosenheim D 62 C3
Rosenow D 45 B5
Rosenthal D 51 B4
Rosersberg S 37 C4
Roses E 91 A6
Roseto degli Abruzzi I 103 A7
Roseto Valfortore I 103 B8
Rosheim F 60 B3
Rosia I 81 C5
Rosice CZ 64 A2
Rosières-en-Santerre F 58 A3
Rosignano Maríttimo I 81 C4
Rosignano Solvay I 81 C4
Roşiori-de-Vede RO 11 D8
Roskhill GB 22 D2
Roskilde DK 39 D5
Roskovec AL 105 C5
Röslau D 52 C1
Roslavl RUS 7 E12
Roslev DK 38 C1
Rosmaninhal P 93 B3
Rosmult IRL 21 B4
Rosnowo PL 46 A2
Rosolini I 109 C3
Rosova MNE 85 C4
Rosoy F 59 B4
Rosporden F 56 C2
Rosquete P 92 B2
Rosrath D 50 C3
Rossa CH 71 B4
Rossano I 106 B3
Rossas
Aveiro P 87 D2
Braga P 87 C2
Rossdorf D 51 C6
Rossett GB 26 B3
Rosshaupten D 62 C1
Rossiglione I 80 B2
Rossignol B 60 A1
Rossla D 52 B1
Rosslare IRL 21 B5
Rosslare Harbour IRL 21 B5
Rosslau D 52 B2
Rosslea GB 19 B4
Rossleben D 52 B1
Rossön S 115 D13
Ross-on-Wye GB 29 B5
Rossoszyca PL 54 B3
Rosswein D 52 B3
Röstånga S 41 C3
Roštár SK 65 B6
Rostock D 44 A4
Rostrenen F 56 B2
Røsvik N 112 E4
Rosyth GB 25 B4
Röszke H 75 B5
Rot S 34 A6
Rota E 99 C4
Rota Greca I 106 B3
Rot am See D 61 A6
Rotberget N 34 B4
Rotella I 82 D2
Rotenburg
Hessen D 51 C5
Niedersachsen D 43 B6
Roth
Bayern D 62 A2
Rheinland-Pfalz D 50 C3
Rothbury GB 25 C6
Rothemühl D 45 B5
Röthenbach D 62 A2
Rothenburg D 53 B4
Rothenburg ob der Tauber D 61 A6
Rothéneuf F 57 B4
Rothenklempenow D 45 B6
Rothenstein D 62 B2
Rotherham GB 27 B4
Rothes GB 23 D5
Rothesay GB 24 C2
Rothwell GB 30 B3
Rotnes N 34 B2
Rotonda I 106 B3
Rotondella I 106 A3
Rotova E 96 C2
Rott
Bayern D 62 C1
Bayern D 62 C3
Rottach-Egern D 62 C2
Röttenbach D 62 A2
Rottenbuch D 62 C1
Rottenburg
Baden-Württemberg D 61 B4
Bayern D 62 B3
Rottenmann A 73 A4
Rotterdam NL 49 B5
Rotthalmünster D 63 B4
Rottingdean GB 31 D3
Röttingen D 61 A5
Rottleberode D 51 B6
Rottne S 40 B4
Rottneros S 34 C5
Rottofreno I 80 A3
Rottweil D 61 B4
Rötz D 62 A3
Roubaix F 49 C4
Roudnice nad Labem CZ 53 C4
Roudouallec F 56 B2
Rouen F 58 A2
Rouffach F 60 C3
Rougé F 57 C4
Rougemont F 69 A6
Rougemont le-Château F 60 C2
Rouillac F 67 C4
Rouillé F 67 B5
Roujan F 78 C2
Roulans F 69 A6
Roundwood IRL 21 A5
Rousínov CZ 64 A2
Roussac F 67 B6
Roussennac F 77 B5
Rousses F 78 B2
Roussillon F 69 C4
Rouvroy-sur-Audry F 59 A5
Rouy F 68 A3
Rovanieman maalaiskunta FIN 113 F14
Rovaniemi FIN 113 F14
Rovato I 71 C4
Rovensko pod Troskami CZ 53 C5
Roverbella I 71 C5
Rovereto I 71 C6
Rövershagen D 44 A4
Roverud N 34 B4
Rovigo I 81 A5
Rovinj HR 82 A2
Rovišce HR 74 C1
Rów PL 45 C6
Rowy PL 46 A3
Royal Leamington Spa GB 30 B2
Royal Tunbridge Wells GB 31 C4
Royan F 66 C3
Royat F 68 C3
Roybon F 69 C5
Roybridge GB 24 B3
Roye F 58 A3
Royère-de-Vassivière F 68 C1
Røykenvik N 34 B2
Royos E 101 B3
Røyrvik N 115 C10
Royston GB 30 B3
Rozadas E 86 A4
Rožaj MNE 85 D5
Rozalén del Monte E 95 C4
Rózańsko PL 45 C6
Rožanstvo SRB 85 C4
Rozay-en-Brie F 59 B3
Roždalovice CZ 53 C5
Rozdilna UA 11 C11
Rozental PL 47 B5
Rozhyshche UA 11 A8
Rožmitál pod Třemšínem CZ 63 A4
Rožňava SK 65 B6
Rožnov pod Radhoštěm CZ 64 A4
Rozoy-sur-Serre F 59 A5
Rozprza PL 55 B4
Roztoky CZ 53 C4
Rozvadov CZ 62 A3
Rozzano I 71 C4
Rranxë AL 105 B5
Rrëshen AL 105 B5
Rrogozhine AL 105 B5
Ruanes E 93 B5
Rubbestadnesset N 32 C2
Rubi E 91 B5
Rubiá E 86 B4
Rubiacedo de Abajo E 89 B3
Rubielos Bajos E 95 C4
Rubielos de Mora E 96 A2
Rubiera I 81 B4
Rubik AL 105 B5
Rucandio E 89 B3
Rud
Akershus N 34 B3
Buskerud N 34 B2
Ruda
PL 54 B3
S 40 B6
Rudabánya H 65 B6
Ruda Maleniecka PL 55 B5
Ruda Pilczycka PL 55 B5
Ruda Śl. PL 54 C3
Ruddervorde B 49 B4
Ruden A 73 B4
Rudersberg D 61 B5
Rudersdorf A 73 A6
Rüdersdorf D 45 C5
Ruderting D 63 B4
Rüdesheim D 50 D3
Rudkøbing DK 39 E3
Rudmanns A 63 B6
Rudna
CZ 53 C4
PL 53 B6
Rudnik
KOS 85 D5
SRB 85 B5
Rudniki
Opolskie PL 54 B3
Śląskie PL 55 C4
Rudno
Dolnośląskie PL 54 B1
Pomorskie PL 47 B4
Rudnya RUS 7 D11
Rudo BIH 85 C4
Rudolstadt D 52 C1
Rudowica PL 53 B5
Rudozem BG 116 A6
Rudskoga S 35 C6
Rudston GB 27 A5
Ruds Vedby DK 39 D4
Rudy PL 54 C3
Rue F 48 C2
Rueda E 88 C2
Rueda de Jalón E 90 B1
Ruelle-sur-Touvre F 67 C5
Ruerrero E 88 B3
Ruffano I 107 B5
Ruffec F 67 B5
Rufina I 81 C5
Rugby GB 30 B2
Rugeley GB 27 C4
Ruggstrop S 40 C6
Rugles F 58 B1
Rugozero RUS 3 D30
Rühen D 44 C2
Ruhla D 51 C6
Ruhland D 53 B3
Ruhle D 43 C4
Ruhpolding D 62 C3
Ruhstorf D 63 B4
Ruidera E 95 D4
Ruillé-sur-le-Loir F 58 C1
Ruinen NL 42 C3
Ruiselede B 49 B4
Rulles B 60 A1
Rülzheim D 61 A4
Rum H 74 A1
Ruma SRB 85 A4
Rumboci BIH 84 C2
Rumburk CZ 53 C4
Rumenka SRB 75 C4
Rumia PL 47 A4
Rumigny F 59 A5
Rumilly F 69 C5
Rumma S 37 D3
Rumney GB 29 B4
Rumont F 59 B6
Rumy PL 47 B6
Runa P 92 B1
Runcorn GB 26 B3
Rundmoen N 115 A11
Rungsted DK 41 D2
Runhällen S 36 B3
Runowo PL 47 A6
Runtuna S 37 D4
Ruokojärvi FIN 113 E13
Ruokolahti FIN 3 F28
Ruokto S 112 E8
Ruoms F 78 B3
Ruoti I 104 C1
Rupa HR 73 C4
Ruppichteroth D 50 C3
Rupt-sur-Moselle F 60 C2
Rus E 100 A2
Ruse BG 11 E9
Ruše SLO 73 B5
Rusele S 115 C15
Ruševo HR 74 C3
Rush IRL 21 A5
Rushden GB 30 B3
Rusiec PL 54 B3
Rusinowo
Zachodnio-Pomorskie PL 46 B1
Zachodnio-Pomorskie PL 46 B2
Ruskele S 115 C15
Ruski Krstur SRB 75 C4
Ruskington GB 27 B5
Rusovce SK 64 B3
Rüsselsheim D 51 D4
Russelv N 112 C9
Russi I 81 B6
Rust A 64 C2
Rustefjelbma N 113 B17
Rustrel F 79 C4
Ruszki PL 55 A5
Ruszów PL 53 B5
Rute E 100 B1
Rüthen D 51 B4
Rutherglen GB 24 C3
Ruthin GB 26 B2
Ruthven GB 23 D4
Ruthwell GB 25 D4
Rüti CH 70 A3
Rutigliano I 104 B3
Rutledal N 32 A2
Rutoši SRB 85 C4
Ruurlo NL 50 A2
Ruuvaoja FIN 113 E17
Ruvo del Monte I 104 C1
Ruvo di Púglia I 104 B2
Ruynes-en-Margeride F 78 B2
Ružic HR 83 C5
Ružomberok SK 65 A5
Ruzsa H 75 B4
Ry DK 39 C2
Rybany SK 64 B4
Rybina PL 47 A5
Rybinsk RUS 7 B15
Rybnik PL 54 C3
Rychliki PL 47 B5
Rychlocice PL 54 B3
Rychnov nad Kněžnou CZ 53 C6
Rychnowo PL 47 B6
Rychtal PL 54 B2
Rychwał PL 54 A3
Ryczywół PL 55 B6
Ryczywól PL 46 C2
Ryd S 40 C4
Rydaholm S 40 C4
Rydal S 40 B2
Rydbo S 37 C5
Rydboholm S 40 B2
Ryde GB 31 D2
Rydöbruk S 40 C3
Rydsgård S 41 D3
Rydsnäs S 40 B5
Rydultowy PL 54 C3
Rydzyna PL 54 B1
Rye GB 31 D4
Rygge N 35 C2
Ryjewo PL 47 B4
Rykene N 33 D5
Rylsk RUS 7 F13
Rymań PL 46 B1
Rýmařov CZ 64 A3
Rynarzewo PL 46 B3
Ryomgård DK 39 C3
Rypefjord N 113 B12
Rypin PL 47 B5
Rysjedalsvika N 32 A2
Ryssby S 40 C4
Rytel PL 46 B3
Rytro PL 65 A6
Rywociny PL 47 B6
Rzeczenica PL 46 B3
Rzeczniów PL 55 B6
Rzeczyca PL 55 B5
Rzęgnowo PL 47 B6
Rzejowice PL 55 B4
Rzemień PL 55 C6
Rzepin PL 45 C6
Rzesznikowo PL 46 B1
Rzeszów PL 10 A6
Rzgów PL 55 B4
Rzhev RUS 7 C13

S

Saal
Bayern D 51 C6
Bayern D 62 B2
Saalbach A 72 A2
Saalburg D 52 C1
Saales F 60 B3
Saalfeld D 52 C1
Saalfelden am Steinernen Meer A 72 A2
Saanen CH 70 B2
Saarbrücken D 60 A2
Saarburg D 60 A2
Saarijärvi FIN 3 E26
Saarlouis D 60 A2
Saas-Fee CH 70 B2
Šabac SRB 85 B4
Sabadell E 91 B5
Sabáudia I 102 B6
Sabbioneta I 81 B4
Sabero E 88 B1
Sabiñánigo E 90 A2
Sabiote E 100 A2
Sables-d'Or-les-Pins F 56 B3
Sablé-sur-Sarthe F 57 C5
Sabóia P 98 B2
Saborsko HR 83 A4
Sæbøvik N 32 C2
Sabres F 76 B2
Sabrosa P 87 C3
Sabugal P 93 A3
Sabuncu TR 118 C5
Sæby DK 38 B3
Săcălaz RO 75 C6
Sacecorbo E 95 B4
Saceda del Rio E 95 B4
Sacedón E 95 B4
Săcele RO 11 D8
Saceruela E 94 D2
Sachsenburg A 72 B3
Sachsenhagen D 43 C6
Sacile I 72 C2
Sacramenia E 88 C3
Sada E 86 A2
Sádaba E 90 A1
Saddell GB 24 C2
Sadernes E 91 A5
Sadki PL 46 B3
Sadkowice PL 55 B5
Sadlinki PL 47 B4
Sadów PL 53 A4
Sadská CZ 53 C4
Saelices E 95 C4
Saelices de Mayorga E 88 B1
Saerbeck D 50 A3
Saeul L 60 A1
Safaalan TR 118 A3
Safara P 98 A3
Säffle S 35 C4
Saffron Walden GB 31 B4
Safonovo RUS 7 D12
Safranbolu TR 16 A6
Säfsnäs S 36 B1
Şag RO 75 C6
Sagard D 45 A5
S'Agaro E 91 B6
Sågmyra S 36 B2
Sagone F 102 A1
Sagres P 98 C2
Ságújfalu H 65 B5
Sagunt E 96 B2
Sagvåg N 32 C2
Ságvár H 74 B3
Sagy F 69 B5
Sahagún E 88 B1
Šahy SK 65 B4
Saignelégier CH 70 A1
Saignes F 68 C2
Saija FIN 113 E17
Saillagouse F 91 A5
Saillans F 79 B4
Sains Richaumont F 59 A4
St Abb's GB 25 C5
St Affrique F 78 C1
St Agnan F 68 B3
St Agnant F 66 C4
St Agnes GB 28 C2
St Agrève F 78 A3
St Aignan F 67 A6
St Aignan-sur-Roë F 57 C4
St Albans GB 31 C3
St Alban-sur-Limagnole F 78 B2
St Amand-en-Puisaye F 68 A3
St Amand-les-Eaux F 49 C4
St Amand-Longpré F 58 C2
St Amand-Montrond F 68 B2
St Amans F 78 B2
St Amans-Soult F 77 C5
St Amant-Roche-Savine F 68 C3
St Amarin F 60 C2
St Ambroix F 78 B3
St Amé F 60 B2
St Amour F 69 B5
St André-de-Corcy F 69 C4
St André-de-Cubzac F 76 B2
St André-de-l'Eure F 58 B2
St André-de-Roquepertuis F 78 B3
St André-de-Sangonis F 78 C2
St Andre-de-Valborgne F 78 B2
St André-les-Alpes F 79 C5
St Andrews GB 25 B5
St Angel F 68 C2
St Anthème F 68 C3
St Antoine F 102 A2
St Antoine-de-Ficalba F 77 B3
St Antönien CH 71 B4
St Antonin-Noble-Val F 77 B4
St Août F 68 B1
St Armant-Tallende F 68 C3
St Arnoult F 58 B2
St Asaph GB 26 B2
St Astier F 67 C5
St Athan GB 29 B4
St Auban F 79 C5
St Aubin
CH 70 B1
F 69 A5
GB 57 A3
St Aubin-d'Aubigné F 57 B4
St Aubin-du-Cormier F 57 B4
St Aubin-sur-Aire F 60 B1
St Aubin-sur-Mer F 57 A5
St Aulaye F 67 C5
St Austell GB 28 C3
St Avit F 68 C2
St Avold F 60 A2
St Aygulf F 79 C5
St Bauzille-de-Putois F 78 C2
St Béat F 77 D3
St Beauzély F 78 B1
St Bees GB 26 A2
St Benim-d'Azy F 68 B3
St Benoît-du-Sault F 67 B6
St Benoit-en-Woëvre F 60 B1
St Berthevin F 57 B5
St Blaise-la-Roche F 60 B3
St Blazey GB 28 C3
St Blin F 59 B6
St Bonnet F 79 B5
St Bonnet Briance F 67 C6
St Bonnet-de-Joux F 69 B4
St Bonnet-le-Château F 68 C4
St Bonnet-le-Froid F 69 C4
St Brévin-les-Pins F 66 A2
St Briac-sur-Mer F 57 B3
St Brice-en-Coglès F 57 B4
St Brieuc F 56 B3
St Bris-le-Vineux F 59 C4
St Broladre F 57 B4
St Calais F 58 C1
St Cannat F 79 C4
St Cast-le-Guildo F 57 B3
St Céré F 77 B4
St Cergue CH 69 B6
St Cergues F 69 B6
St Cernin F 77 A5
St Chamant F 68 C1
St Chamas F 79 C4
St Chamond F 69 C4
St Chély-d'Apcher F 78 B2
St Chély-d'Aubrac F 78 B1
St Chinian F 78 C1
St Christol F 79 B4
St Christol-lès-Alès F 78 B3
St Christoly-Médoc F 66 C4
St Christophe-du-Ligneron F 66 B3
St Christophe-en-Brionnais F 69 B4
St Ciers-sur-Gironde F 67 C4
St Clair-sur-Epte F 58 A2
St Clar F 77 C3
St Claud F 67 C5
St Claude F 69 B5
St Clears GB 28 B3
St Columb Major GB 28 C3
St Come-d'Olt F 78 B1
St Cosme-en-Vairais F 58 B1
St Cyprien
Dordogne F 77 B4
Pyrenées-Orientales F 91 A6
St Cyr-sur-Loire F 67 A5
St Cyr-sur-Mer F 79 C4
St Cyr-sur-Methon F 69 B4
St David's GB 28 B2
St Denis F 58 B3
St Denis-d'Oléron F 66 B3
St Denis d'Orques F 57 B5
St Didier F 69 B4
St Didier-en-Velay F 69 C4
St Dié F 60 B2
St Dier-d'Auvergne F 68 C3
St Dizier F 59 B5
St Dizier-Leyrenne F 68 B1
St Dogmaels GB 28 A3
Ste Adresse F 57 A6
Ste Anne F 58 B1
Ste Anne-d'Auray F 56 C3
Ste Croix CH 69 B6
Ste Croix-Volvestre F 77 C4
Ste Engrâce F 76 C2
Ste Enimie F 78 B2
St Efflam F 56 B2
Ste Foy-de-Peyrolières F 77 C4
Ste Foy-la-Grande F 76 B3
Ste Foy l'Argentiere F 69 C4
Ste Gauburge-Ste Colombe F 58 B1
Ste Gemme la Plaine F 66 B3
Ste Geneviève F 58 A3
St Égrève F 69 C5
Ste Hélène F 76 B2
Ste Hélène-sur-Isère F 69 C6
Ste Hermine F 66 B3
Ste Jalle F 79 B4
Ste Livrade-sur-Lot F 77 B3
St Eloy-les-Mines F 68 B2
Ste Marie-aux-Mines F 60 B3
Ste Marie-du-Mont F 57 A4
Ste Maure-de-Touraine F 67 A5
Ste Maxime F 79 C5
Ste Ménéhould F 59 A5
Ste Mère-Église F 57 A4
St Emiland F 69 B4
St Émilion F 76 B2
St Enoder GB 28 C3
Sainteny F 57 A4
Ste Ode B 49 C6
Saintes F 67 C4
Ste Savine F 59 B5
Ste Sévère-sur-Indre F 68 B2
Ste Sigolène F 69 C4
St Esteben F 76 C1
St Estèphe F 66 C4
Ste Suzanne F 57 B5
St Étienne F 69 C4
St Etienne-de-Baigorry F 76 C1
St Étienne-de-Cuines F 69 C6
St Etienne-de-Fursac F 67 B6
St Etienne-de-Montluc F 66 A3
St Etienne-de-St Geoirs F 69 C5
St Étienne-de-Tinée F 79 B5
St Étienne-du-Bois F 69 B5
St Étienne-du-Rouvray F 58 A2
St Etienne-les-Orgues F 79 B4
Ste Tulle F 79 C4
St Fargeau F 59 C4
St Félicien F 78 A3
St Felix-de-Sorgues F 78 C1
St Félix-Lauragais F 77 C4
Saintfield GB 19 B6
St Fillans GB 24 B3
St Firmin F 79 B5
St Florent F 102 A2
St Florentin F 59 C4
St Florent-le-Vieil F 66 A3
St Florent-sur-Cher F 68 B2
St Flour F 78 A2
St Flovier F 67 B6
St Fort-sur-le-Né F 67 C4
St Fulgent F 66 B3
St Galmier F 69 C4
St Gaudens F 77 C3
St Gaultier F 67 B6
St Gély-du-Fesc F 78 C2
St Genest-Malifaux F 69 C4
St Gengoux-le-National F 69 B4
St Geniez F 79 B5
St Geniez-d'Olt F 78 B1
St Genis-de-Saintonge F 67 C4
St Genis-Pouilly F 69 B6
St Genix-sur-Guiers F 69 C5
St Georges Buttavent F 57 B5
St Georges-d'Aurac F 68 C3
St Georges-de-Commiers F 79 A4
St Georges-de-Didonne F 66 C4
St Georges-de-Luzençon F 78 B1
St Georges-de Mons F 68 C2
St Georges-de-Reneins F 69 B4
St Georges d'Oléron F 66 C3
St Georges-en-Couzan F 68 C3
St Georges-lès-Baillargeaux F 67 B5
St Georges-sur-Loire F 66 A4
St Georges-sur-Meuse B 49 C6
St Geours-de-Maremne F 76 C1
St Gérand-de-Vaux F 68 B3
St Gérand-le-Puy F 68 B3
St Germain F 60 C2
St Germain-Chassenay F 68 B3
St Germain-de-Calberte F 78 B2
St Germain-de-Confolens F 67 B5
St Germain-de-Joux F 69 B5
St Germain-des-Fossés F 68 B3
St Germain-du-Bois F 69 B5
St Germain-du-Plain F 69 B4
St Germain-du Puy F 68 A2
St Germain-en-Laye F 58 B3
St Germain-Laval F 68 C4
St Germain-Lembron F 68 C3
St Germain-les-Belles F 67 C6
St Germain-Lespinasse F 68 B3
St Germain-l'Herm F 68 C3
St Gervais-d'Auvergne F 68 B2
St Gervais-les-Bains F 70 C1
St Gervais-sur-Mare F 78 C2
St Gildas-de-Rhuys F 66 A2
St Gildas-des-Bois F 66 A2
St Gilles
Gard F 78 C3
Ille-et-Vilaine F 57 B4
St Gilles-Croix-de-Vie F 66 B3
St Gingolph F 70 B1
St Girons
Ariège F 77 D4
Landes F 76 C1
St Girons-Plage F 76 C1
St Gobain F 59 A4
St Gorgon-Main F 69 A6
St Guénolé F 56 C1
St Harmon GB 29 A4
St Helens GB 26 B3
St Helier GB 57 A3
St Herblain F 66 A3
St Hilaire
Allier F 68 B3
Aude F 77 C5
St Hilaire-de-Riez F 66 B3
St Hilaire-des-Loges F 67 B4
St Hilaire-de-Villefranche F 67 C4
St Hilaire-du-Harcouët F 57 B4
St Hilaire-du-Rosier F 79 A4
St Hippolyte
Aveyron F 77 B5
Doubs F 70 A1
St Hippolyte-du-Fort F 78 C2
St Honoré-les-Bains F 68 B3
St Hubert B 49 C6
St Imier CH 70 A2
St Issey GB 28 C3
St Ives
Cambridgeshire GB 30 B3
Cornwall GB 28 C2
St Izaire F 78 C1
St Jacques-de-la-Lande F 57 B4
St Jacut-de-la-Mer F 57 B3
St James F 57 B4
St Jaume d'Enveja E 90 C3
St Jean-Brévelay F 56 C3
St Jean-d'Angély F 67 C4
St Jean-de-Belleville F 69 C6
St Jean-de-Bournay F 69 C5
St Jean-de-Braye F 58 C2
St Jean-de-Côle F 67 C5
St Jean-de-Daye F 57 A4
St Jean de Losne F 69 A5
St Jean-de-Luz F 76 C1
St Jean-de-Maurienne F 69 C6
St Jean-de-Monts F 66 B2
St Jean-d'Illac F 76 B2
St Jean-du-Bruel F 78 B2
St Jean-du-Gard F 78 B2
St Jean-en-Royans F 79 A4
St Jean-la-Riviere F 79 C6
St Jean-Pied-de-Port F 76 C1
St Jean-Poutge F 77 C3
St Jeoire F 69 B6
St Joachim F 66 A2
St Johnstown IRL 19 B4
St Jorioz F 69 C6
St Joris Winge B 49 C5
St Jouin-de-Marnes F 67 B4
St Juéry F 77 C5
St Julien F 69 B5
St Julien-Chapteuil F 78 A3
St Julien-de-Vouvantes F 57 C4
St Julien-du-Sault F 59 B4
St Julien-du-Verdon F 79 C5
St Julien-en-Born F 76 B1
St Julien-en-Genevois F 69 B6
St Julien-l'Ars F 67 B5
St Julien la-Vêtre F 68 C3
St Julien-Mont-Denis F 69 C6
St Julien-sur-Reyssouze F 69 B5
St Junien F 67 C5

St Just
F 78 B3
GB 28 C2
St Just-en-Chaussée F 58 A3
St Just-en-Chevalet F 68 C3
St Justin F 76 C2
St Just-St Rambert F 69 C4
St Keverne GB 28 C2
St Lary-Soulan F 77 D3
St Laurent-d'Aigouze F 78 C3
St Laurent-de-Chamousset F 69 C4
St Laurent-de-Condel F 57 A5
St Laurent-de-la-Cabrerisse F 78 C1
St Laurent-de-la-Salanque F 78 D1
St Laurent-des-Autels F 66 A3
St Laurent-du-Pont F 69 C5
St Laurent-en-Caux F 58 A1
St Laurent-en-Grandvaux F 69 B5
St Laurent-Médoc F 76 A2
St Laurent-sur-Gorre F 67 C5
St Laurent-sur-Mer F 57 A5
St Laurent-sur-Sèvre F 66 B4
St Leger B 60 A1
St Léger-de-Vignes F 68 B3
St Léger-sous-Beuvray F 68 B4
St Léger-sur-Dheune F 69 B4
St Léonard-de-Noblat F 67 C6
St Leonards GB 31 D4
St Lô F 57 A4
St Lon-les-Mines F 76 C1
St Louis F 60 C3
St Loup F 68 B3
St Loup-de-la-Salle F 69 B4
St Loup-sur-Semouse F 60 C2
St Lunaire F 57 B3
St Lupicin F 69 B5
St Lyphard F 66 A2
St Lys F 77 C4
St Macaire F 76 B2
St Maclou F 58 A1
St Maixent-l'École F 67 B4
St Malo F 57 B3
St Mamet-la-Salvetat F 77 B5
St Mandrier-sur-Mer F 79 C4
St Marcel
Drôme F 78 B3
Saône-et-Loire F 69 B4
St Marcellin F 69 C5
St Marcellin sur Loire F 68 C4
St Marcet F 77 C3
St Mards-en-Othe F 59 B4
St Margaret's-at-Cliffe GB 31 C5
St Margaret's Hope GB 23 C6
St Mars-la-Jaille F 66 A3
St Martin-d'Ablois F 59 B4
St Martin-d'Auxigny F 68 A2
St Martin-de-Belleville F 69 C6
St Martin-de-Bossenay F 59 B4
St Martin-de-Crau F 78 C3
St Martin-de-Londres F 78 C2
St Martin-d'Entraunes F 79 B5
St Martin-de-Queyrières F 79 B5
St Martin-de-Ré F 66 B3
St Martin des Besaces F 57 A5
St Martin-d'Estreaux F 68 B3
St Martin-de-Valamas F 78 B3
St Martin-d'Hères F 69 C5
St Martin-du-Frêne F 69 B5
St Martin-en-Bresse F 69 B5
St Martin-en-Haut F 69 C4
St Martin-la-Méanne F 68 C1
St Martin-sur-Ouanne F 59 C4
St Martin-Valmeroux F 77 A5
St Martin-Vésubie F 79 B6
St Martory F 77 C3
St Mary's GB 23 C6
St Mathieu F 67 C5
St Mathieu-de-Tréviers F 78 C2
St Maurice CH 70 B1
St Maurice-Navacelles F 78 C2
St Maurice-sur-Moselle F 60 C2
St Mawes GB 28 C2
St Maximin-la-Ste Baume F 79 C4
St Méard-de-Gurçon F 76 B3
St Médard-de-Guizières F 76 A2
St Médard-en-Jalles F 76 B2
St Méen-le-Grand F 57 B3
St Menges F 59 A5
St Merløse DK 39 D4
St Město CZ 54 C1
St M'Hervé F 57 B4
St Michel
Aisne F 59 A5
Gers F 77 C3
St Michel-Chef-Chef F 66 A2
St Michel-de-Castelnau F 76 B2
St Michel-de-Maurienne F 69 C6
St Michel-en-Grève F 56 B2
St Michel-enl'Herm F 66 B3
St Michel-Mont-Mercure F 66 B4
St Mihiel F 60 B1
St Monance GB 25 B5
St Montant F 78 B3
St Moritz CH 71 B4
St Nazaire F 66 A2
St Nazaire-en-Royans F 79 A4
St Nazaire-le-Désert F 79 B4
St Nectaire F 68 C2
St Neots GB 30 B3
St Nicolas-de-Port F 60 B2
St Nicolas-de-Redon F 57 C3
St Nicolas-du-Pélem F 56 B2
St Niklaas B 49 B5
St Omer F 48 C3
St Pair-sur-Mer F 57 B4
St Palais F 76 C1
St Palais-sur-Mer F 66 C3
St Pardoux-la-Rivière F 67 C5
St Paul-Cap-de-Joux F 77 C4
St Paul-de-Fenouillet F 77 D5
St Paul-de-Varax F 69 B5
St Paulien F 68 C3
St Paul-le-Jeune F 78 B3
St Paul-lès-Dax F 76 C1
St Paul-Trois-Châteaux F 78 B3
St Pé-de-Bigorre F 76 C2
St Pée-sur-Nivelle F 76 C1
St Péravy-la-Colombe F 58 C2
St Péray F 78 B3
St Père-en-Retz F 66 A2
St Peter Port GB 56 A3
St Petersburg = Sankt-Peterburg RUS 7 B11
St Philbert-de-Grand-Lieu F 66 A3
St Pierre F 78 C1
St Pierre-d'Albigny F 69 C6
St Pierre-d'Allevard F 69 C6
St Pierre-de-Chartreuse F 69 C5
St Pierre-de-Chignac F 77 A3
St Pierre-de-la-Fage F 78 C2
St Pierre-d'Entremont F 69 C5
St Pierre-d'Oléron F 66 C3
St Pierre-Eglise F 57 A4
St Pierre-en-Port F 58 A1
St Pierre-le-Moûtier F 68 B3
St Pierre Montlimart F 66 A3
St Pierre-Quiberon F 66 A1
St Pierre-sur-Dives F 57 A5
St Pierreville F 78 B3
St Pieters-Leeuw B 49 C5
St Plancard F 77 C3
St Poix F 57 C4
St Pol-de-Léon F 56 B2
St Polgues F 68 C3
St Pol-sur-Ternoise F 48 C3
St Pons-de-Thomières F 78 C1
St Porchaire F 66 C4
St Pourçain-sur-Sioule F 68 B3
St Priest F 69 C4
St Privat F 68 C2
St Quay-Portrieux F 56 B3
St Quentin F 59 A4
St Quentin-la-Poterie F 78 B3
St Quentin-les-Anges F 57 C5
St Rambert d'Albon F 69 C4
St Rambert-en-Bugey F 69 C5
St Raphaël F 79 C5
St Rémy-de-Provence F 78 C3
St Rémy-du-Val F 57 B6
St Remy-en-Bouzemont F 59 B5
St Renan F 56 B1
St Révérien F 68 A3
St Riquier F 48 C2
St Romain-de-Colbosc F 58 A1
St Rome-de-Cernon F 78 B1
St Rome-de-Tarn F 78 B1
St Sadurni-d'Anoia E 91 B4
St Saëns F 58 A2
St Sampson GB 56 A3
St Samson-la-Poterie F 58 A2
St Saturnin-de-Lenne F 78 B2
St Saturnin-lès-Apt F 79 C4
St Sauflieu F 58 A3
St Saulge F 68 A3
St Sauveur
Finistère F 56 B2
Haute-Saône F 60 C2
St Sauveur-de-Montagut F 78 B3
St Sauveur-en-Puisaye F 59 C4
St Sauveur-en-Rue F 69 C4
St Sauveur-Lendelin F 57 A4
St Sauveur-le-Vicomte F 57 A4
St Sauveur-sur-Tinée F 79 B6
St Savin
Gironde F 76 A2
Vienne F 67 B5
St Savinien F 67 C4
St Savournin F 79 C4
St Seine-l'Abbaye F 69 A4
St Sernin-sur-Rance F 77 C5
St Sevan-sur-Mer F 57 B3
St Sever F 76 C2
St Sever-Calvados F 57 B4
St Sorlin-d'Arves F 69 C6
St Soupplets F 58 A3
St Sulpice F 77 C4
St Sulpice-Laurière F 67 B6
St Sulpice-les-Feuilles F 67 B6
St Symphorien F 76 B2
St Symphorien-de-Lay F 69 C4
St Symphorien d'Ozon F 69 C4
St Symphoriensur-Coise F 69 C4
St Teath GB 28 C3
St Thégonnec F 56 B2
St Thiébault F 60 B1
St Trivier-de-Courtes F 69 B5
St Trivier sur-Moignans F 69 B4
St Trojan-les-Bains F 66 C3
St Tropez F 79 C5
St Truiden B 49 C6
St Vaast-la-Hougue F 57 A4
St Valérien F 59 B4
St Valery-en-Caux F 58 A1
St Valéry-sur-Somme F 48 C2
St Vallier
Drôme F 69 C4
Saône-et-Loire F 69 B4
St Vallier-de-Thiey F 79 C5
St Varent F 67 B4
St Vaury F 68 B1
St Venant F 48 C3
St Véran F 79 B5
St Vincent I 70 C2
St Vincent-de-Tyrosse F 76 C1
St Vit F 69 A5
St Vith B 50 C2
St Vivien-de-Médoc F 66 C3
St Yan F 68 B4
St Ybars F 77 C4
St Yorre F 68 B3
St Yrieix-la-Perche F 67 C6
Saissac F 77 C5
Saja E 88 A2
Šajan SRB 75 C5
Šajkaš SRB 75 C5
Sajókaza H 65 B6
Sajószentpéter H 65 B6
Sajóvámos H 65 B6
Şakarya TR 118 B5
Šakiai LT 6 D7
Sakskøbing DK 39 E4
Sakule SRB 75 C5
Šala S 36 C3
Šal'a SK 64 B3
Sala Baganza I 81 B4
Sala Consilina I 104 C1
Salakovac SRB 85 B6
Salamanca E 94 B1
Salamina GR 117 E5
Salandra I 104 C2
Salaparuta I 108 B1
Salar E 100 B1
Salardú E 90 A3
Salas E 86 A4
Salas de los Infantes E 89 B3
Salau F 77 D4
Salavaux CH 70 B2
Salbertrand I 79 A5
Salbohed S 36 C3
Salbris F 68 A2
Salbu N 32 A2
Salce E 86 B4
Salching D 62 B3
Salcombe GB 28 C4
Saldaña E 88 B2
Saldus LV 6 C7
Sale I 80 B2
Saleby S 35 D5
Salem D 61 C5
Salemi I 108 B1
Salen
Argyll & Bute GB 24 B2
Highland GB 24 B2
N 114 C8
Sälen S 34 A5
Salernes F 79 C5
Salerno I 103 C7
Salers F 68 C2
Salford GB 26 B3
Salgótarján H 65 B5
Salgueiro P 92 B3
Salhus N 32 B2
Sali HR 83 C4
Sálice Salentino I 105 C3
Salientes E 86 B4
Salies-de-Béarn F 76 C2
Salies-du-Salat F 77 C3
Salignac-Eyvigues F 77 B4
Saligney-sur-Roudon F 68 B3
Salihli TR 119 D3
Salihorsk BY 7 E9
Salinas
Alicante E 101 A5
Huesca E 90 A3
Salinas de Medinaceli E 95 A4
Salinas de Pisuerga E 88 B2
Salindres F 78 B3
Saline di Volterra I 81 C4
Salins-les-Bains F 69 B5
Salir P 98 B2
Salisbury GB 29 B6
Salla
A 73 A4
FIN 113 F17
Sallachy GB 23 C4
Sallanches F 70 C1
Sallent E 91 B4
Sallent de Gállego E 76 D2
Salles F 76 B2
Salles-Curan F 78 B1
Salles-sur-l'Hers F 77 C4
Sallins IRL 21 A5
Sällsjö S 115 D10
Salmerón E 95 B4
Salmiech F 77 B5
Salmivaara FIN 113 F17
Salmoral E 94 B1
Salo FIN 6 A7
Salò I 71 C5
Salobreña E 100 C2
Salon-de-Provence F 79 C4
Salonica = Thessaloniki GR 116 B4
Salonta RO 10 C6
Salorino E 93 B3
Salornay-sur-Guye F 69 B4
Salorno I 71 B6
Salou E 91 B4
Šalovci SLO 73 B6
Salsbruket N 114 C8
Salses-le-Château F 78 D1
Salsomaggiore Terme I 81 B3
Salt E 91 B5
Saltaire GB 27 B4
Saltara I 82 C1
Saltash GB 28 C3
Saltburn-by-the-Sea GB 27 A5
Saltcoats GB 24 C3
Saltfleet GB 27 B6
Salto P 87 C3
Saltrød N 33 D5
Saltsjöbaden S 37 C5
Saltvik
FIN 36 B7
S 40 B6
Saludécio I 82 C1
Salussola I 70 C3
Saluzzo I 80 B1
Salvacañete E 95 B5
Salvada P 98 B3
Salvagnac F 77 C4
Salvaleon E 93 C4
Salvaterra de Magos P 92 B2
Salvaterra do Extremo P 93 B4
Salvatierra
Avila E 89 B4
Badajoz E 93 C4
Salvatierra de Santiago E 93 B4
Salviac F 77 B4
Salzburg A 62 C4
Salzgitter D 51 A6
Salzgitter Bad D 51 A6
Salzhausen D 44 B2
Salzhemmendorf D 51 A5
Salzkotten D 51 B4
Salzmünde D 52 B1
Salzwedel D 44 C3
Samadet F 76 C2
Samandıra TR 118 B4
Samassi I 110 C1
Samatan F 77 C3
Sambiase I 106 C3
Sambir UA 11 B7
Samborowo PL 47 B5
Sambuca di Sicilia I 108 B2
Samedan CH 71 B4
Samer F 48 C2
Sami GR 117 D2
Şamlı TR 118 C2
Sammichele di Bari I 104 C2
Samnaun CH 71 B5
Samobor HR 73 C5
Samoëns F 70 B1
Samogneux F 59 A6
Samokov BG 11 E7
Samora Correia P 92 C2
Šamorín SK 64 B3
Samos
E 86 B3
GR 119 E1
Samoš SRB 75 C5
Samothraki GR 116 B7
Samper de Calanda E 90 B2
Sampéyre I 79 B6
Sampieri I 109 C3
Sampigny F 60 B1
Samplawa PL 47 B5
Samproniano I 81 D5
Samtens D 45 A5
Samugheo I 110 C1
San Adrián E 89 B5
San Agustín E 101 C3
San Agustin de Guadalix E 94 B3
Sanaigmore GB 24 C1
San Alberto I 82 B1
San Amaro E 87 B2
Sânandrei RO 75 C6
San Andrês del Rabanedo E 88 B1
San Antanio di Santadi I 110 C1
San Antolín de Ibias E 86 A4
San Arcángelo I 104 C2
Sanary-sur-Mer F 79 C4
San Asensio E 89 B4
San Bartoloméde las Abiertas E 94 C2
San Bartoloméde la Torre E 99 B3
San Bartoloméde Pinares E 94 B2
San Bartolomeo in Galdo I 103 B8
San Benedetto del Tronto I 82 D2
San Benedetto in Alpe I 81 C5
San Benedetto Po I 81 A4
San Benito E 100 A1
San Benito de la Contienda E 93 C3
San Biágio Plátani I 108 B2
San Biágio Saracinisco I 103 B6
San Bonifacio I 71 C6
San Calixto E 99 B5
San Cándido I 72 B2
San Carlo
CH 70 B3
I 108 B2
San Carlos del Valle E 100 A2
San Casciano dei Bagni I 81 D5
San Casciano in Val di Pesa I 81 C5
San Cataldo
Puglia I 105 C4
Sicilia I 108 B2
San Cebrián de Castro E 88 C1
Sancergues F 68 A2
Sancerre F 68 A2
San Cesário di Lecce I 105 C4
Sancey-le-Long F 69 A6
Sanchiorian E 94 B2
San Chírico Raparo I 106 A3
Sanchonuño E 88 C2
San Cibrao das Viñas E 87 B3
San Cipirello I 108 B2
San Ciprián E 86 A3
San Clemente E 95 C4
San Clodio E 86 B3
Sancoins F 68 B2
San Colombano al Lambro I 71 C4
San Costanzo I 82 C2
San Crisóbal de Entreviñas E 88 B1
San Cristóbal de la Polantera E 88 B1
San Cristóbal de la Vega E 94 A2
San Cristovo E 87 C3
Sancti-Petri E 99 C4
Sancti-Spiritus E 87 D4
Sand
Hedmark N 34 B3
Rogaland N 33 C3
Sanda S 37 E5
San Damiano d'Asti I 80 B2
San Damiano Macra I 79 B6
Sandane N 114 F3
San Daniele del Friuli I 72 B3
Sandanski BG 116 A5
Sandared S 40 B2
Sandarne S 36 A4
Sandau D 44 C4
Sandbach
D 63 B4
GB 26 B3
Sandbank GB 24 C3
Sandbanks GB 29 C6
Sandbukt N 112 C10
Sandby DK 39 E4
Sande
D 43 B5
Sogn og Fjordane N 32 A2
Vestfold N 35 C2
Sandefjord N 35 C2
Sandeid N 33 C2
San Demétrio Corone I 106 B3
San Demétrio né Vestini I 103 A6
Sandersleben D 52 B1
Sanderstølen N 32 B6
Sandes N 33 D4
Sandesneben D 44 B2
Sandhead GB 24 D3
Sandhem S 40 B3
Sandhorst D 43 B4
Sandhurst GB 31 C3
Sandıklı TR 119 D5
Sandillon F 58 C3
Sandl A 63 B5
Sandnes N 33 D2
Sandness GB 22 A7
Sandnessjøen N 115 A9
Sando E 87 D4
Sandomierz PL 55 C6
San Dónaci I 105 C3
San Donàdi Piave I 72 C2
San Donato Val di Comino I 103 B6
Sándorfalva H 75 B5
Sandown GB 31 D2
Sandøysund N 35 C2
Sandrigo I 72 C1
Sandsele S 115 B14
Sandset N 112 D3
Sandsjöfors S 40 B4
Sandstad N 114 D6
Sandvatn N 33 D3
Sandvig-Allinge DK 41 D4
Sandvika
Akershus N 34 C2
Hedmark N 34 B4
Nord-Trøndelag N 114 D9
Sandviken S 36 B3
Sandvikvåy N 32 C2
Sandwich GB 31 C5
Sandy GB 30 B3
San Emiliano E 86 B5
San Enrique E 99 C5
San Esteban E 86 A4
San Esteban de Gormaz E 89 C3
San Esteban de la Sierra E 93 A5
San Esteban de Litera E 90 B3
San Esteban del Molar E 88 C1
San Esteban del Valle E 94 B2
San Esteban de Valdueza E 86 B4
San Fele I 104 C1
San Felice Circeo I 102 B6
San Felices E 88 B3
San Felices de los Gallégos E 87 D4
San Felice sul Panaro I 81 B5
San Ferdinando di Púglia I 104 B2
San Fernando E 99 C4
San Fernando de Henares E 95 B3
San Fili I 106 B3
San Foca I 105 C4
San Fratello I 109 B3
Sangatte F 48 C2
San Gavino Monreale I 110 C1
San Gémini Fonte I 102 A5
Sangerhausen D 52 B1
San Germano Vercellese I 70 C3
San Giácomo
Trentino Alto Adige I 72 B1
Umbria I 82 D1
San Gimignano I 81 C5
San Ginésio I 82 C2
Sangineto Lido I 106 B2
San Giórgio a Liri I 103 B6
San Giorgio della Richinvelda I 72 B2
San Giórgio del Sánnio I 103 B7
San Giórgio di Lomellina I 70 C3
San Giórgio di Nogaro I 72 C3
San Giorgio di Piano I 81 B5
San Giórgio Iónico I 104 C3
San Giovanni a Piro I 106 A2
San Giovanni Bianco I 71 C4
San Giovanni di Sinis I 110 C1
San Giovanni in Croce I 81 A4
San Giovanni in Fiore I 106 B3
San Giovanni in Persiceto I 81 B5
San Giovanni Reatino I 102 A5
San Giovanni Rotondo I 104 B1
San Giovanni Suérgiu I 110 C1
San Giovanni Valdarno I 81 C5
San Giuliano Terme I 81 C4
San Giustino I 82 C1
San Godenzo I 81 C5
Sangonera la Verde E 101 B4
San Gregorio Magno I 103 C8
Sangüesa E 90 A1
Sanguinet F 76 B1
San Guiseppe Jato I 108 B2
Sanica BIH 83 B5
Sanitz D 44 A4
San Javier E 101 B5
San Jorge P 92 B2
San José E 101 C3
San Juan E 89 B3
San Juan de Alicante E 96 C2
San Juan de la Nava E 94 B2
San Justo de la Vega E 86 B4
Sankt Aegyd am Neuwalde A 63 C6
Sankt Andrä A 73 B4
Sankt Andreasberg D 51 B6
Sankt Anna S 37 D3
Sankt Anna am Aigen A 73 B5
Sankt Anton am Arlberg A 71 A5
Sankt Anton an der Jessnitz A 63 C6
Sankt Augustin D 50 C3
Sankt Blasien D 61 C4
Sankt Englmar D 62 A3
Sankt Gallen
A 63 C5
CH 71 A4
Sankt Gallenkirch A 71 A4
Sankt Georgen
A 63 B5
D 61 B4
Sankt Georgen am Reith A 63 C5
Sankt Georgen ob Judenburg A 73 A4
Sankt Georgen ob Murau A 73 A4
Sankt Gilgen A 63 C4
Sankt Goar D 50 C3
Sankt Goarshausen D 50 C3
Sankt Ingbert D 60 A3
Sankt Jacob A 73 B4
Sankt Jakob in Defereggen A 72 B2
Sankt Johann am Tauern A 73 A4
Sankt Johann am Wesen A 63 B4
Sankt Johann im Pongau A 72 A3
Sankt Johann in Tirol A 72 A2
Sankt Katharein an der Laming A 73 A5
Sankt Kathrein am Hauenstein A 73 A5
Sankt Lambrecht A 73 A4
Sankt Leonhard am Forst A 63 B6
Sankt Leonhard im Pitztal A 71 A5
Sankt Lorenzen A 72 B2
Sankt Marein
Steiermark A 73 A5
Steiermark A 73 A5
Sankt Margarethen im Lavanttal A 73 B4
Sankt Margrethen CH 71 A4
Sankt Michael A 73 A5
Sankt Michael im Burgenland A 73 A6
Sankt Michael im Lungau A 72 A3
Sankt Michaelisdonn D 43 B6
Sankt Niklaus CH 70 B2
Sankt Nikolai im Sölktal A 73 A4
Sankt Olof S 41 D4
Sankt Oswald D 63 B4
Sankt Paul
A 73 B4
F 79 B5
Sankt Peter D 61 B4
Sankt Peter am Kammersberg A 73 A4
Sankt-Peterburg = St Petersburg RUS 7 B11
Sankt Peter-Ording D 43 A5
Sankt Pölten A 63 B6
Sankt Radegund A 73 A5
Sankt Ruprecht an der Raab A 73 A5
Sankt Salvator A 73 B4
Sankt Stefan A 73 B4
Sankt Stefan an der Gail A 72 B3
Sankt Stefan im Rosental A 73 B5
Sankt Valentin A 63 B5
Sankt Veit an der Glan A 73 B4
Sankt Veit an der Gölsen A 63 B6
Sankt Veit in Defereggen A 72 B2
Sankt Wendel D 60 A3
Sankt Wolfgang
A 63 C4
D 62 B3
San Lazzaro di Sávena I 81 B5
San Leo I 82 C1
San Leonardo de Yagüe E 89 C3
San Leonardo in Passiria I 71 B6
San Lorenzo al Mare I 80 C1
San Lorenzo a Merse I 81 C5
San Lorenzo Bellizzi I 106 B3
San Lorenzo de Calatrava E 100 A2
San Lorenzo de El Escorial E 94 B2
San Lorenzo de la Parrilla E 95 C4
San Lorenzo di Sebato I 72 B1
San Lorenzo in Campo I 82 C1
San Lorenzo Nuovo I 81 D5
San Lourenco P 98 A2
San Luca I 106 C3
Sanlúcar de Barrameda E 99 C4
Sanlúcar de Guadiana E 98 B3
Sanlúcar la Mayor E 99 B4
San Lúcido I 106 B3
Sanluri I 110 C1
San Marcello I 82 C2
San Marcello Pistoiese I 81 B4
San Marcial E 88 C1
San Marco I 103 C7
San Marco Argentano I 106 B3
San Marco dei Cavoti I 103 B7
San Marco in Lámis I 104 B1
San Marino RSM 82 C1
San Martín de Castañeda E 87 B4
San Martín de la Vega E 95 B3
San Martin de la Vega del Alberche E 93 A5
San Martín del Tesorillo E 99 C5
San Martin de Luiña E 86 A4
San Martin de Montalbán E 94 C2
San Martin de Oscos E 86 A4
San Martin de Pusa E 94 C2
San Martin de Unx E 89 B5
San Martín de Valdeiglesias E 94 B2
San Martino di Campagna I 72 B2
San Martino di Castrozza I 72 B1
San-Martino-di-Lota F 102 A2
San Martino in Pénsilis I 103 B8
San Mateo de Gallego E 90 B2
San Máuro Forte I 104 C2
San Michele all'Adige I 71 B6
San Michele di Ganzaria I 109 B3
San Michele Mondov ì I 80 B1
San Miguel de Aguayo E 88 A2
San Miguel de Bernuy E 88 C3
San Miguel del Arroyo E 88 C2
San Miguel de Salinas E 101 B5
Sânmihaiu Roman RO 75 C6
San Millán de la Cogolla E 89 B4
San Miniato I 81 C4
San Muñoz E 87 D4
Sänna S 37 D1
Sannazzaro de'Burgondi I 80 A2
Sanne D 44 C3
Sannicandro di Bari I 104 B2
Sannicandro Gargánico I 104 B1
San Nicola del'Alto I 107 B3
San Nicolás del Puerto E 99 B5
Sânnicolau Mare RO 75 B5
San Nicolò I 81 B5
San Nicolò Gerrei I 110 C2
Sannidal N 33 D6
Sanniki PL 47 C5
Sanok PL 11 B7
San Pablo de los Montes E 94 C2
San Pancrázio Salentino I 105 C3
San Pantaleo I 110 A2
San Páolo di Civitate I 103 B8
San Pawl il-Bahar M 107 C5
San Pedro
Albacete E 101 A3
Oviedo E 86 A4
San Pedro de Alcántara E 100 C1
San Pedro de Ceque E 87 B4
San Pedro del Arroyo E 94 B2
San Pedro de Latarce E 88 C1
San Pedro del Pinatar E 101 B5
San Pedro del Romeral E 88 A3
San Pedro de Merida E 93 C4
San Pedro de Valderaduey E 88 B2
San Pedro Manrique E 89 B4
San Pellegrino Terme I 71 C4
San Piero a Sieve I 81 C5
San Piero in Bagno I 81 C5
San Piero Patti I 109 A3
San Pietro I 109 B3
San Pietro in Casale I 81 B5
San Pietro in Gu I 72 C1
San Pietro in Palazzi I 81 C4
San Pietro in Volta I 72 C2
San Pietro Vara I 80 B3
San Pietro Vernótico I 105 C3
San Polo d'Enza I 81 B4
Sanquhar GB 25 C4
San Quírico d'Órcia I 81 C5
San Rafael del Rio E 90 C3
San Remo I 80 C1
San Román de Cameros E 89 B4
San Roman de Hernija E 88 C1
San Román de la Cuba E 88 B2
San Roman de los Montes E 94 B2
San Romao P 92 C3
San Roque E 99 C5
San Roque de Riomera E 88 A3
San Rufo I 104 C1
San Sebastián de los Ballesteros E 100 B1
San Salvador de Cantamuda E 88 B2
San Salvo I 103 A7
San Salvo Marina I 103 A7
San Sebastián de los Reyes E 94 B3
San Sebastiano Curone I 80 B3
San Secondo Parmense I 81 B4
Sansepolcro I 82 C1
San Serverino Marche I 82 C2
San Severino Lucano I 106 A3
San Severo I 103 B8
San Silvestre de Guzmán E 98 B3
Sanski Most BIH 83 B5
San Sosti I 106 B3
San Stéfano di Cadore I 72 B2
San Stino di Livenza I 72 C2
Santa Agnès E 97 B1
Santa Amalia E 93 B4
Santa Ana
Cáceres E 93 B5
Jaén E 100 B2
Santa Ana de Pusa E 94 C2
Santa Barbara E 90 C3
Santa Bárbara P 98 B2
Santa Barbara de Casa E 98 B3
Santa Bárbara de Padrões P 98 B3
Santacara E 89 B5
Santa Catarina P 98 B3
Santa Caterina di Pittinuri I 110 B1
Santa Caterina Villarmosa I 109 B3
Santa Cesárea Terme I 107 A5
Santa Clara-a-Nova P 98 B2
Santa Clara-a-Velha P 98 B2
Santa Clara de Louredo P 98 B3
Santa Coloma de Farners E 91 B5
Santa Coloma de Gramenet E 91 B5
Santa Coloma de Queralt E 91 B4
Santa Colomba de Curueño E 88 B1
Santa Colomba de Somoza E 86 B4
Santa Comba E 86 A2
Santa Comba Dáo P 92 A2
Santa Comba de Rossas P 87 C4
Santa Cristina I 71 C4
Santa Cristina de la Polvorosa E 88 B1
Santa Croce Camerina I 109 C3
Santa Croce di Magliano I 103 B7
Santa Cruz
E 86 A2
P 92 B1
Santa Cruz de Alhama E 100 B2
Santa Cruz de Campezo E 89 B4
Santa Cruz de Grio E 89 C5
Santa Cruz de la Salceda E 89 C3
Santa Cruz de la Sierra E 93 B5
Santa Cruz de la Zarza E 95 C3
Santa Cruz del Retamar E 94 B2
Santa Cruz del Valle E 94 B1
Santa Cruz de Moya E 96 B1
Santa Cruz de Mudela E 100 A2
Santa Cruz de Paniagua E 93 A4
Santadi I 110 C1
Santa Doménica Talao I 106 B2
Santa Doménica Vittória I 109 B3
Santa Elena E 100 A2
Santa Elena de Jamuz E 88 B1
Santaella E 100 B1
Santa Eufemia E 100 A1
Santa Eufémia d'Aspromonte I 106 C2
Santa Eulalia E 95 B5
Santa Eulália P 92 C3
Santa Eulalia de Oscos E 86 A3
Santa Eulàlia des Riu E 97 C1
Santa Fe E 100 B2
Santa Fiora I 81 D5
Sant'Ágata dei Goti I 103 B7
Sant'Ágata di Ésaro I 106 B2
Sant'Ágata di Puglia I 103 B8
Sant'Agata Feltria I 82 C1
Sant'Ágata Militello I 109 A3
Santa Gertrude I 71 B5
Santa Giustina I 72 B2
Sant Agust ide Lluçanès E 91 A5
Santa Iria P 98 B3
Santa Leocadia P 87 C2
Santa Lucia del Mela I 109 A4
Santa Lucia-de-Porto-Vecchio F 102 B2
Santa Luzia P 98 B2
Santa Maddalena Vallalta I 72 B2
Santa Magdalena de Polpis E 90 C3
Santa Margalida E 97 B3
Santa Margarida P 92 B2
Santa Margarida do Sado P 98 A2
Santa Margaridao de Montbui E 91 B4
Santa Margherita I 110 D1
Santa Margherita di Belice I 108 B2
Santa Margherita Ligure I 80 B3
Santa Maria
CH 71 B5
E 90 A2
Santa Maria al Bagno I 107 A4
Santa Maria Cápua Vétere I 103 B7
Santa Maria da Feira P 87 D2
Santa Maria de Cayón E 88 A3
Santa Maria de Corco E 91 A5
Santa Maria de Huerta E 95 A4
Santa Maria de la Alameda E 94 B2
Santa Maria de las Hoyas E 89 C3
Santa Maria del Camí E 97 B2
Santa Maria del Campo E 88 B3
Santa Maria del Campo Rus E 95 C4
Santa Maria della Versa I 80 B3
Santa Maria del Páramo E 88 B1
Santa Maria del Taro I 80 B3
Santa Maria de Mercadillo E 89 C3
Santa Maria de Nieva E 101 B4
Santa Maria de Trassierra E 100 B1
Santa Maria di Licodia I 109 B3
Santa Maria-di-Rispéscia I 81 D5
Santa Maria la Palma I 110 B1
Santa María la Real de Nieva E 94 A2
Santa Maria Maggiore I 70 B3
Santa Maria Ribarredonda E 89 B3
Santa Marina del Rey E 88 B1
Santa Marinella I 102 A4
Santa Marta
Albacete E 95 C4
Badajoz E 93 C4
Santa Marta de Magasca E 93 B4
Santa Marta de Penaguião P 87 C3
Santa Marta de Tormes E 94 B1
Santana
Évora P 92 C2
Setúbal P 92 C1
Santana da Serra P 98 B2
Sant'Ana de Cambas P 98 B3
Santana do Mato P 92 C2
Sant'Anastasia I 103 C7
Santander E 88 A3
Sant'Andrea Frius I 110 C2
Sant'Ángelo dei Lombardi I 103 C8
Sant'Angelo in Vado I 82 C1
Sant'Angelo Lodigiano I 71 C4
Santa Ninfa I 108 B1
Sant'Antíoco I 110 C1
Sant Antoni de Calonge E 91 B6
Sant Antoni de Portmany E 97 C1
Sant'Antonio-di-Gallura I 110 B2
Santanyí E 97 B3
Santa Olalla
Huelva E 99 B4
Toledo E 94 B2
Santa Pau E 91 A5
Santa Pola E 96 C2
Santa Ponça E 97 B2
Santarcángelo di Romagna I 82 B1
Santarém P 92 B2
Santa Severa
F 102 A2
I 102 A4
Santa Severina I 107 B3
Santas Martas E 88 B1
Santa Sofia I 81 C5
Santa Susana P 92 C2
Santa Suzana P 92 C3
Santa Teresa di Riva I 109 B4
Santa Teresa Gallura I 110 A2
Santa Uxía E 86 B2
Santa Valburga I 71 B5
Santa Vittória in Matenano I 82 C2
Sant Boi de Llobregat E 91 B5
Sant Carles de la Ràpita E 90 C3
Sant Carlos E 97 B1
Sant'Caterina I 81 D5
Sant Celoni E 91 B5
Sant Climent E 97 B4
Santed E 95 A5
Sant'Egídio alla Vibrata I 82 D2
Sant'Elia a Pianisi I 103 B7
Sant'Elia Fiumerapido I 103 B6
Santelices E 88 A3
San Telmo E 99 B4
Sant'Elpídio a Mare I 82 C2
Santéramo in Colle I 104 C2
Santervas de la Vega E 88 B2
Sant' Eufemia Lamezia I 106 C3
Sant Feliu E 91 B5
Sant Feliu de Codines E 91 B5
Sant Feliu de Guíxols E 91 B6
Sant Feliu Sasserra E 91 B5
Sant Ferran E 97 C1
Sant Francesc de Formentera E 97 C1
Sant Francesc de ses Salines E 97 C1
Santhià I 70 C3
Sant Hilari Sacalm E 91 B5
Sant Hipòlit de Voltregà E 91 A5
Santiago de Alcántara E 92 B3
Santiago de Calatrava E 100 B1
Santiago de Compostela E 86 B2
Santiago de la Espade E 101 A3
Santiago de la Puebla E 94 B1
Santiago de la Ribera E 101 B5
Santiago del Campo E 93 B4
Santiago de Litem P 92 B2
Santiago do Cacém P 98 B2
Santiago do Escoural P 92 C2
Santiago Maior P 92 C3
Santibáñez de Béjar E 93 A5
Santibáñez de la Peña E 88 B2
Santibáñez de Murias E 88 A1
Santibáñez de Vidriales E 87 B4
Santibáñez el Alto E 93 A4
Santibáñez el Bajo E 93 A4
Santillana E 88 A2
Santiponce E 99 B4
San Tirso de Abres E 86 A3
Santisteban del Puerto E 100 A2
Santiuste de San Juan Bautiste E 94 A2
Santiz E 94 A1
Sant Jaume dels Domenys E 91 B4
Sant Joan Baptista E 97 B1
Sant Joan de les Abadesses E 91 A5
Sant Jordi E 90 C3
Sant Josep de sa Talaia E 97 C1
Sant Juliáde Loria AND 91 A4
Sant'Ilario d'Enza I 81 B4
Sant Llorençde Morunys E 91 A4
Sant Llorençdes Carctassar E 97 B3
Sant Llorenç Savall E 91 B5
Sant Luis E 97 B4
Sant Mart ide Llemaná E 91 A5
Sant Marti de Maldá E 91 B4

Sant Marti Sarroca E 91 B4
Sant Mateu E 90 C3
Sant Miquel E 97 B1
Santo Aleixo P 98 A3
Santo Amado P 98 A3
Santo Amaro P 92 C3
Santo André P 98 A2
Santo Domingo E 93 C3
Santo Domingo de la Calzada E 89 B4
Santo Domingo de Silos E 89 C3
Santo Estêvão
Faro P 98 B3
Santarém P 92 C2
Santok PL 46 C1
Santomera E 101 A4
Santoña E 89 A3
Santo-Pietro-di Tenda F 102 A2
Sant'Oreste I 102 A5
Santo Spirito I 104 B2
Santo Stefano d'Aveto I 80 B3
Santo Stéfano di Camastra I 109 B3
Santo Stefano di Magra I 81 B3
Santo Stéfano Quisquina I 108 B2
Santo Tirso P 87 C2
Santotis E 88 A2
Santo Tomé E 100 A2
Santovenia
Burgos E 89 B3
Zamora E 88 C1
Sant Pau de Seguries E 91 A5
Santpedor E 91 B4
Sant Pere de Riudebitles E 91 B4
Sant Pere Pescador E 91 A6
Sant Pere Sallavinera E 91 B4
Sant Quirze de Besora E 91 A5
Sant Rafel E 97 C1
Sant Ramon E 91 B4
Santu Lussurgiu I 110 B1
Santutzi E 89 A3
Sant Vincençde Castellet E 91 B4
San Valentino alla Muta I 71 B5
San Venanzo I 82 D1
San Vicente de Alcántara E 93 B3
San Vicente de Arana E 89 B4
San Vicente de la Barquera E 88 A2
San Vicente de la Sonsierra E 89 B4
San Vicente de Toranzo E 88 A3
San Vietro E 87 C4
San Vigilio I 72 B1
San Vincente del Raspeig E 96 C2
San Vincenzo I 81 C4
San Vito I 110 C2
San Vito al Tagliamento I 72 C2
San Vito Chietino I 103 A7
San Vito dei Normanni I 104 C3
San Vito di Cadore I 72 B2
San Vito lo Capo I 108 A1
San Vito Romano I 102 B5
Sanxenxo E 86 B2
Sanza I 104 C1
São Aleixo P 92 C3
São Barnabé P 98 B2
São Bartoloméda Serra P 98 A2
São Bartolomeu de Messines P 98 B2
São Bento P 87 C2
São Brás P 98 B3
São Brás de Alportel P 98 B3
São Braz do Reguedoura P 92 C2
São Cristóvão P 92 C2
São Domingos P 98 B2
São Geraldo P 92 C2
São Jacinto P 92 A2
São João da Madeira P 87 D2
São João da Pesqueira P 87 C3
São João da Ribeira P 92 B2
São João da Serra P 87 D2
São João da Venda P 98 B3
São João dos Caldeireiros P 98 B3
São Julião P 92 B3
São Leonardo P 92 C3
São Luis P 98 B2
São Manços P 92 C3
São Marcos da Ataboeira P 98 B3
Saõ Marcos da Serra P 98 B2
São Marcos de Campo P 92 C3
São Martinho da Cortiça P 92 A2
São Martinho das Amoreiras P 98 B2
São Martinho do Porto P 92 B1
São Matias
Beja P 98 A3
Évora P 92 C2
São Miguel d'Acha P 92 A3
São Miguel de Machede P 92 C3
São Pedro da Torre P 87 C2
São Pedro de Cadeira P 92 B1
São Pedro de Moel P 92 B1
São Pedro de Solis P 98 B3
São Pedro do Sul P 87 D2
Saorge F 80 C1
São Romão P 92 C2
São Sebastião dos Carros P 98 B3
São Teotónio P 98 B2
São Torcato P 87 C2
Sapataria P 92 C1
Sapes GR 116 A7
Sapiãos P 87 C3
Sa Pobla E 97 B3
Sappada I 72 B2
Sappen N 112 C10
Sapri I 106 A2
Sarajevo BIH 84 C3
Saramon F 77 C3
Sarandë AL 116 C2
Saranovo SRB 85 B5
Saraorci SRB 85 B6
Sa Rapita E 97 B3
Saray TR 118 A2
Saraycık TR 118 C4
Sarayköy TR 119 E3
Saraylar TR 118 B2
Sarayönü TR 119 D7
Sarbia PL 46 C2
Sarbinowo
Zachodnio-Pomorskie PL 45 C6
Zachodnio-Pomorskie PL 46 A1
Sárbogárd H 74 B3
Sarcelles F 58 A3
Sarche I 71 B5
Sardara I 110 C1
Sardoal P 92 B2
Sardón de Duero E 88 C2
Sare F 76 C1
S'Arenal E 97 B2
Šarengrad HR 75 C4
Sarentino I 71 B6
Sarezzo I 71 C5
Sargans CH 71 A4
Sári H 75 A4
Sarıbeyler TR 118 C2
Sarıcakaya TR 118 B5
Sari-d'Orcino F 102 A1
Sarıgöl TR 119 D3
Sarıkaya TR 16 B7
Sarıköy TR 118 B2
Sarilhos Grandes P 92 C2
Sariñena E 90 B2
Sarıoba TR 118 C7
Sárisáp H 65 C4
Sariyer TR 118 A4
Sarkad H 75 B6
Sárkeresztes H 74 A3
Sárkeresztúr H 74 A3
Särkijärvi FIN 113 E12
Şarkikaraağaç TR 119 D6
Şarköy TR 118 B2
Sarlat-la-Canéda F 77 B4
Sarliac-sur-l'Isle F 67 C5
Sármellék H 74 B2
Särna S 115 F10
Sarnadas P 92 B3
Sarnano I 82 C2
Sarnen CH 70 B3
Sarnesfield GB 29 A5
Sárnico I 71 C4
Sarno I 103 C7
Sarnonico I 71 B6
Sarnow D 45 B5
Sarny UA 11 A9
Särö S 38 B4
Saronno I 70 C4
Sárosd H 74 A3
Šarovce SK 65 B4
Sarpoil F 68 C3
Sarpsborg N 35 C3
Sarracín E 88 B3
Sarral E 91 B4
Sarralbe F 60 A3
Sarrancolin F 77 D3
Sarras F 69 C4
Sarre I 70 C2
Sarreaus E 87 B3
Sarrebourg F 60 B3
Sarreguemines F 60 A3
Sárrétudvari H 75 A6
Sarre-Union F 60 B3
Sarria E 86 B3
Sarriàde Ter E 91 A5
Sarrión E 96 A2
Sarroca de Lleida E 90 B3
Sarroch I 110 C2
Sarron F 76 C2
Sársina I 82 C1
Særslev DK 39 D3
Sarstedt D 51 A5
Sárszentlörinc H 74 B3
Sárszentmihaly H 74 A3
Sárszentmiklós H 74 B3
Sarteano I 81 D5
Sartène F 102 B1
Sartilly F 57 B4
Sartirana Lomellina I 80 A2
Saruhanlı TR 118 D2
Sárvár H 74 A1
Sarvisvaara S 113 F10
Sarzana I 81 B3
Sarzeau F 66 A2
Sarzedas P 92 B3
Sasalli TR 119 D1
Sasamón E 88 B2
Sa Savina E 97 C1
Sásd H 74 B3
Sasino PL 46 A3
Sássari I 110 B1
Sassello I 80 B2
Sassenberg D 50 B4
Sassetta I 81 C4
Sassnitz D 45 A5
Sassocorvaro I 82 C1
Sasso d'Ombrone I 81 D5
Sassoferrato I 82 C1
Sassoleone I 81 B5
Sasso Marconi I 81 B5
Sassuolo I 81 B4
Sástago E 90 B2
Šaštinske Stráže SK 64 B3
Sas van Gent NL 49 B4
Såtåhaugen N 114 E7
Satão P 87 D3
Såtenäs S 35 D4
Säter S 36 B2
Sätila S 40 B2
Satillieu F 69 C4
Satnica Đakovačka HR 74 C3
Sátoraljaújhely H 10 B6
Satow D 44 B3
Sätra-brunn S 36 C3
Sætre N 35 C2
Satrup D 43 A6
Satteins A 71 A4
Satu Mare RO 11 C7
Saturnia I 102 A4
Saucats F 76 B2
Saucelle E 87 C4
Sauda N 33 C3
Sauðarkrókur IS 111 B6
Saudasjøen N 33 C3
Sauerlach D 62 C2
Saugues F 78 B2
Sauherad N 33 C6
Saujon F 66 C4
Sauland N 33 C5
Saulces Monclin F 59 A5
Saulgau D 61 B5
Saulgrub D 62 C2
Saulieu F 69 A4
Saulnot F 60 C2
Sault F 79 B4
Sault-Brénaz F 69 C5
Sault-de-Navailles F 76 C2
Saulx F 60 C2
Saulxures-sur-Moselotte F 60 C2
Saulzais-le-Potier F 68 B2
Saumos F 76 B1
Saumur F 67 A4
Saunavaara FIN 113 E16
Saundersfoot GB 28 B3
Saurat F 77 D4
Saurbær
Borgarfjarðarsýsla IS 111 C4
Dalasýsla IS 111 B4
Eyjafjarðarsýsla IS 111 B7
Sáuris I 72 B2
Sausset-les-Pins F 79 C4
Sauteyrargues F 78 C2
Sauvagnat F 68 C2
Sauve F 78 C2
Sauveterre-de-Béarn F 76 C2
Sauveterre-de-Guyenne F 76 B2
Sauviat-sur-Vige F 67 C6
Sauxillanges F 68 C3
Sauzet
Drôme F 78 B3
Lot F 77 B4
Sauzé-Vaussais F 67 B5
Sauzon F 66 A1
Sava I 104 C3
Sævareid N 32 B2
Savarsin RO 11 C7
Savaştepe TR 118 C2
Savci SLO 73 B6
Säve S 38 B4
Savelletri I 104 C3
Savelli I 107 B3
Savenay F 66 A3
Saverdun F 77 C4
Saverne F 60 B3
Savières F 59 B4
Savigliano I 80 B1
Savignac-les-Eglises F 67 C5
Savignano Irpino I 103 B8
Savignano sul Rubicone I 82 B1
Savigny-sur-Braye F 58 C1
Saviñán E 89 C5
Savines-le-lac F 79 B5
Savino Selo SRB 75 C4
Savio I 82 B1
Sävja S 36 C4
Šavnik MNE 85 D4
Savognin CH 71 B4
Savona I 80 B2
Savonlinna FIN 3 F28
Savournon F 79 B4
Sævråsvåg N 32 B2
Sävsjö S 40 B4
Savsjön S 36 C1
Sävsjöström S 40 B5
Savudrija HR 72 C3
Savukoski FIN 113 E17
Sawbridgeworth GB 31 C4
Sawtry GB 30 B3
Sax E 101 A5
Saxdalen S 36 B1
Saxilby GB 27 B5
Saxmundham GB 30 B5
Saxnäs S 115 C12
Saxthorpe GB 30 B5
Sayalonga E 100 C1
Sayatón E 95 B4
Sayda D 52 C3
Säytsjärvi FIN 113 C16
Śazava CZ 64 A1
Sázava CZ 63 A5
Scaër F 56 B2
Scafa I 103 A7
Scalasaig GB 24 B1
Scalby GB 27 A5
Scalea I 106 B2
Scaletta Zanclea I 109 A4
Scalloway GB 22 A7
Scamblesby GB 27 B5
Scandale I 107 B3
Scandiano I 81 B4
Scandicci I 81 C5
Scandolara Ravara I 81 A4
Scanno I 103 B6
Scansano I 81 D5
Scanzano Jónico I 104 C2
Scarborough GB 27 A5
Scardovari I 82 B1
Scardoy GB 22 D4
Scarinish GB 24 B1
Scarperia I 81 C5
Scarriff IRL 20 B3
Scey-sur-Saône et St Albin F 60 C1
Schachendorf A 73 A6
Schaffhausen CH 61 C4
Schafstädt D 52 B1
Schafstedt D 43 A6
Schäftlarn D 62 C2
Schagen NL 42 C1
Schalkau D 51 C7
Schangnau CH 70 B2
Schapbach D 61 B4
Scharbeutz D 44 A2
Schärding A 63 B4
Scharnitz A 71 A6
Scharrel D 43 B4
Schattendorf A 64 C2
Scheemda NL 42 B3
Scheessel D 43 B6
Schéggia I 82 C1
Scheibbs A 63 B6
Scheibenberg D 52 C2
Scheidegg D 61 C5
Scheifling A 73 A4
Scheinfeld D 61 A6
Schelklingen D 61 B5
Schenefeld
Schleswig-Holstein D 43 A6
Schleswig-Holstein D 44 B1
Schenklengsfeld D 51 C5
Scherfede D 51 B5
Schermbeck D 50 B2
Scherpenzeel NL 49 A6
Schesslitz D 52 D1
Scheveningen NL 49 A5
Schiedam NL 49 B5
Schieder-Schwalenberg D 51 B5
Schierling D 62 B3
Schiers CH 71 B4
Schildau D 52 B2
Schillingen D 60 A2
Schillingsfürst D 61 A6
Schilpário I 71 B5
Schiltach D 61 B4
Schiltigheim F 60 B3
Schio I 71 C6
Schirmeck F 60 B3
Schirnding D 52 C2
Schkeuditz D 52 B2
Schkölen D 52 B1
Schlabendorf D 53 B3
Schladen D 51 A6
Schladming A 72 A3
Schlangen D 51 B4
Schleiden D 50 C2
Schleiz D 52 C1
Schleswig D 43 A6
Schleusingen D 51 C6
Schlieben D 52 B3
Schliengen D 60 C3
Schliersee D 62 C2
Schlitz D 51 C5
Schloss Neuhans D 51 B4
Schlossvippach D 52 B1
Schlotheim D 51 B6
Schluchsee D 61 C4
Schlüchtern D 51 C5
Schmallenberg D 50 B4
Schmelz D 60 A2
Schmidmühlen D 62 A2
Schmiedeberg D 53 C3
Schmiedefeld D 51 C6
Schmirn A 72 A1
Schmölln
Brandenburg D 45 B6
Sachsen D 52 C2
Schnaittach D 62 A2
Schneeberg D 52 C2
Schneizlreuth D 62 C3
Schneverdingen D 44 B1
Schöder A 73 A4
Schoenburg B 50 C2
Schollene D 44 C4
Schöllkrippen D 51 C5
Schomberg D 61 B4
Schönach D 62 B3
Schönau
Baden-Württemberg D 60 C3
Bayern D 62 B3
Schönbeck D 45 B5
Schönberg
Bayern D 63 B4
Mecklenburg-Vorpommern D 44 B2
Schleswig-Holstein D 44 A2
Schönebeck D 52 A1
Schöneck D 52 C2
Schönecken- D 50 C2
Schönermark D 45 B5
Schönewalde D 52 B3
Schongau D 62 C1
Schöngrabern A 64 B2
Schönhagen D 51 B5
Schönhausen D 44 C4
Schöningen D 51 A6
Schönkirchen D 44 A2
Schönsee D 62 A3
Schöntal D 61 A5
Schönthal D 62 A3
Schonungen D 51 C6
Schönwalde D 44 A2
Schoondijke NL 49 B4
Schoonebeek NL 42 C3
Schoonhoven NL 49 B5
Schopfheim D 60 C3
Schöppenstedt D 51 A6
Schörfling A 63 C4
Schorndorf D 61 B5
Schortens D 43 B4
Schotten D 51 C5
Schramberg D 61 B4
Schraplau D 52 B1
Schrattenberg A 64 B2
Schrecksbach D 51 C5
Schrems A 63 B6
Schrobenhausen D 62 B2
Schröcken A 71 A5
Schrozberg D 61 A5
Schruns A 71 A4
Schüpfheim CH 70 B3
Schüttorf D 50 A3
Schwaan D 44 B4
Schwabach D 62 A2
Schwäbisch Gmünd D 61 B5
Schwäbisch Hall D 61 A5
Schwabmünchen D 62 B1
Schwadorf A 64 B2
Schwagstorf D 43 C4
Schwaigern D 61 A5
Schwalmstadt D 51 C5
Schwanberg A 73 B5
Schwanden CH 70 B4
Schwandorf D 62 A3
Schwanebeck D 52 B1
Schwanenstadt A 63 B4
Schwanewede D 43 B5
Schwanfeld D 61 A6
Schwangau D 62 C1
Schwarmstedt D 43 C6
Schwarza D 51 C6
Schwarzach im Pongau A 72 A3
Schwarzau im Gebirge A 63 C6
Schwarzenau A 63 B6
Schwarzenbach D 52 C1
Schwarzenbach am Wald D 52 C1
Schwarzenbek D 44 B2
Schwarzenberg D 52 C2
Schwarzenburg CH 70 B2
Schwarzenfeld D 62 A3
Schwarz-heide D 53 B3
Schwaz A 72 A1
Schwechat A 64 B2
Schwedt D 45 B6
Schwei D 43 B5
Schweich D 60 A2
Schweighausen D 60 B3
Schweinfurt D 51 C6
Schweinitz D 52 B3
Schweinrich D 45 B4
Schwelm D 50 B3
Schwemsal D 52 B2
Schwendt A 62 C3
Schwenningen D 61 B4
Schwepnitz D 53 B3
Schwerin D 44 B3
Schwerte D 50 B3
Schweskau D 44 C3
Schwetzingen D 61 A4
Schwyz CH 70 A3
Sciacca I 108 B2
Scicli I 109 C3
Ściechów PL 45 C6
Scigliano I 106 B3
Scilla I 109 A4
Ścinawa PL 54 B1
Scionzier F 69 B6
Scoglitti I 109 C3
Scole GB 30 B5
Sconser GB 22 D2
Scopello
Piemonte I 70 C3
Sicilia I 108 A1
Scordia I 109 B3
Scorzè I 72 C2
Scotch Corner GB 27 A4
Scotter GB 27 B5
Scourie GB 22 C3
Scousburgh GB 22 B7
Scrabster GB 23 C5
Screeb IRL 20 A2
Scremerston GB 25 C6
Scritto I 82 C1
Scunthorpe GB 27 B5
Scuol CH 71 B5
Scúrcola Marsicana I 103 A6
Seaford GB 31 D4
Seaham GB 25 D6
Seahouses GB 25 C6
Seascale GB 26 A2
Seaton GB 29 C4
Sebazac-Concourès F 77 B5
Sebečevo SRB 85 C5
Seben TR 118 B6
Sebersdorf A 73 A5
Sebezh RUS 7 C10
Sebnitz D 53 C4
Seborga I 80 C1
Seby S 41 C6
Seč
Vychodočeský CZ 63 A6
Západočeský CZ 63 A4
Sečanj SRB 75 C5
Secemin PL 55 C4
Séchault F 59 A5
Seckau A 73 A4
Seclin F 49 C4
Secondigny F 67 B4
Seda P 92 B3
Sedan F 59 A5
Sedano E 88 B3
Sedbergh GB 26 A3
Sedella E 100 C1
Séderon F 79 B4
Sedgefield GB 27 A4
Sedico I 72 B2
Sédilo I 110 B1
Sédini I 110 B1
Sedlarica HR 74 C2
Sedlčany CZ 63 A5
Sedlec-Prčice CZ 63 A5
Sedlice CZ 63 A4
Sędziejowice PL 55 B4
Sędziszów PL 55 C5
Sędziszów Małapolski PL 55 C6
Seebach F 60 B3
Seeboden A 72 B3
Seefeld
Brandenburg D 45 C5
Niedersachsen D 43 B5
Seefeld in Tirol A 71 A6
Seeg D 62 C1
Seehausen
Sachsen-Anhalt D 44 C3
Sachsen-Anhalt D 52 A1
Seeheim-Jugenheim D 61 A4
Seelbach D 60 B3
Seelow D 45 C6
Seelze D 43 C6
Seerhausen D 52 B3
Sées F 57 B6
Seesen D 51 B6
Seeshaupt D 62 C2
Seewalchen A 63 C4
Seferihisar TR 119 D1
Sefkerin SRB 85 A5
Segård N 34 B2
Segerstad S 35 C5
Segesd H 74 B2
Seglinge FIN 36 B7
Segmon S 35 C5
Segonzac F 67 C4
Segorbe E 96 B2
Segovia E 94 B2
Segré F 57 C5
Segura
E 89 B4
P 93 B3
Segura de León E 99 A4
Segura de los Baños E 90 C2
Ségur-les-Villas F 68 C2
Segurrilla E 94 B2
Sehnde D 51 A5
Seia P 92 A3
Seiches-sur-le-Loir F 67 A4
Seifhennersdorf D 53 C4
Seignelay F 59 C4
Seijo E 87 C2
Seilhac F 68 C1
Seilles B 49 C6
Seim N 32 B2
Seinäjoki FIN 3 E25
Seissan F 77 C3
Seitenstetten Markt A 63 B5
Seixal P 92 C1
Seiz A 73 A4
Seizthal A 73 A4
Sejerslev DK 38 C1
Seksna RUS 7 B15
Selárdalur IS 111 B1
Selárgius I 110 C2
Selb D 52 C2
Selby GB 27 B4
Selca HR 84 C1
Selcë AL 105 A5
Selce HR 73 C4
Selçuk TR 119 E2
Selde DK 38 C2
Selenča SRB 75 C4
Selendi
Manisa TR 118 D2
Manisa TR 118 D3
Selenicë AL 105 C5
Sélestat F 60 B3
Seleuš SRB 75 C5
Selevac SRB 85 B5
Selfoss IS 111 D5
Selgua E 90 B3
Selice SK 64 B3
Seligenstadt D 51 C4
Seligenthal D 51 C6
Selimiye TR 119 E2
Selizharovo RUS 7 C12
Selja S 36 A1
Selje N 114 E2
Seljelvnes N 112 C8
Seljord N 33 C5
Selkirk GB 25 C5
Sellano I 82 D1
Selles-St Denis F 68 A1
Selles-sur-Cher F 67 A6
Sellières F 69 B5
Sellin D 45 A5
Sellye H 74 C2
Selm D 50 B3
Selnica ob Dravi SLO 73 B5
Selongey F 59 C6
Selonnet F 79 B5
Selow D 44 B3
Selsey GB 31 D3
Selsingen D 43 B6
Selters D 50 C3
Seltso RUS 7 E13
Seltz F 61 B4
Selva E 97 B2
Selva di Cadore I 72 B2
Selva di Val Gardena I 72 B1
Selvik
Sogn og Fjordane N 32 A2
Vestfold N 35 C2
Selvino I 71 C4
Selyatyn UA 11 C8
Sem N 35 C2
Semeljci HR 74 C3
Semenovka
Chernihiv UA 7 E12
Kremenchuk UA 11 B12
Semič SLO 73 C5
Semide
F 59 A5
P 92 A2
Semily CZ 53 C5
Seminara I 106 C2
Semlac RO 75 B5
Şemmen-stedt D 51 A6
Šempeter SLO 73 B5
Semriach A 73 A5
Semur-en-Auxois F 69 A4
Sena E 90 B2
Sena de Luna E 88 B1
Senarpont F 58 A2
Sénas F 79 C4
Senćanski Trešnjevac SRB 75 C4
Sencelles E 97 B2
Senčur SLO 73 B4
Senden
Bayern D 61 B6
Nordrhein-Westfalen D 50 B3
Sendenhorst D 50 B3
Sendim P 87 C4
Senec SK 64 B3
Seneffe B 49 C5
Séneghe I 110 B1
Senés E 101 B3
Senez F 79 C5
Senftenberg D 53 B3
Sengouagnet F 77 D3
Sengwarden D 43 B5
Senica SK 64 B3
Senice na Hané CZ 64 A3
Senigállia I 82 C2
Senirkent TR 119 D5
Sénis I 110 C1
Senise I 106 A3
Senj HR 83 B3
Senje SRB 85 C6
Senjehopen N 112 C6
Senjski Rudnik SRB 85 C6
Senlis F 58 A3
Sennan S 40 C2
Sennecey-le-Grand F 69 B4
Sennen GB 28 C2
Senno BY 7 D10
Sénnori I 110 B1
Sennwald CH 71 A4
Sennybridge GB 29 B4
Senohrad SK 65 B5
Senonches F 58 B2
Senones F 60 B2
Senorb ì I 110 C2
Senovo SLO 73 B5
Senožeče SLO 73 C4
Senožeti SLO 73 B4
Sens F 59 B4
Sens-de-Bretagne F 57 B4
Senta SRB 75 C5
Senterada E 90 A3
Šentilj SLO 73 B5
Šentjernej SLO 73 C5
Šentjur SLO 73 B5
Senumstad N 33 D5
Seoane E 86 B3
Seon CH 70 A3
Sépeaux F 59 C4
Sépey CH 70 B2
Sepino I 103 B7
Sępólno Krajeńskie PL 46 B3
Seppenrade D 50 B3
Seppois F 70 A2
Septeuil F 58 B2
Sepúlveda E 88 C3
Sequals I 72 B2
Sequeros E 93 A4
Seraincourt F 59 A5
Seraing B 49 C6
Seravezza I 81 C4
Sered' SK 64 B3
Seredka RUS 7 B10
Şereflikoçhisar TR 16 B6
Seregélyes H 74 A3
Seregno I 71 C4
Sérent F 56 C3
Serfaus A 71 A5
Sergiyev Posad RUS 7 C15
Seriate I 71 C4
Sérifontaine F 58 A2
Serifos GR 117 E6
Sérignan F 78 C2
Serik TR 119 F6
Serina I 71 C4
Serinhisar TR 119 E4
Sermaises F 58 B3
Sermaize-les-Bains F 59 B5
Sérmide I 81 B5
Sermoneta I 102 B5
Sernache de Bonjardim P 92 B2
Sernancelhe P 87 D3
Serón E 101 B3
Serón de Najima E 89 C4
Serooskerke NL 49 B4
Seròs E 90 B3
Serpa P 98 B3
Serpukhov RUS 7 D14
Serracapriola I 103 B8
Serrada E 88 C2
Serra de Outes E 86 B2
Serradifalco I 108 B2
Serradilla E 93 B4
Serradilla del Arroyo E 93 A4
Serradilla del Llano E 93 A4
Serramanna I 110 C1
Serramazzoni I 81 B4
Serranillos E 94 B2
Serrapetrona I 82 C2
Serra San Bruno I 106 C3
Serra San Quírico I 82 C2
Serrastretta I 106 B3
Serravalle
Piemonte I 70 C3
Umbria I 82 D2
Serravalle di Chienti I 82 C1
Serravalle Scrívia I 80 B2
Serre I 103 C8
Serrejón E 93 B5
Serres
F 79 B4
GR 116 A5
Serrières F 69 C4
Serrières-de-Briord F 69 C5
Sersale I 106 B3
Sertã P 92 B2
Sertig Dörfli CH 71 B4
Servance F 60 C2
Serverette F 78 B2
Servia GR 116 B4
Servian F 78 C2
Serviers F 78 B3
Servigliano I 82 C2
Serzedelo P 87 C2
Seseña Nuevo E 95 B3
Sesimbra P 92 C1
Seskinore GB 19 B4
Sesma E 89 B4
Sessa Aurunca I 103 B6
Ses Salines E 97 B3
Şesta Godano I 80 B3
Šestanovac HR 84 C1
Sestao E 89 A4
Sestino I 82 C1
Sesto I 72 B2
Sesto Calende I 70 C3
Sesto Fiorentino I 81 C5
Séstola I 81 B4
Sesto San Giovanni I 71 C4
Sestriere I 79 B5
Sestri Levante I 80 B3
Sestroretsk RUS 7 A11
Sestu I 110 C2
Sesvete HR 73 C6
Setcases E 91 A5
Sète F 78 C2
Setenil E 99 C5
Şetermoen N 112 D7
Šetonje SRB 85 B6
Setskog N 34 C3
Settalsjølia N 114 E7
Séttimo Torinese I 70 C2
Settimo Vittone I 70 C2
Settle GB 26 A3
Setúbal P 92 C2
Seubersdort D 62 A2
Seúi I 110 C2
Seúlo I 110 C2
Seurre F 69 B5
Sevaster AL 105 C5
Sevel DK 38 C1
Sevenoaks GB 31 C4
Sévérac-le-Château F 78 B2
Sever do Vouga P 87 D2
Severin HR 73 C5
Severomorsk RUS 3 B30
Şéveso I 71 C4
Ševětin CZ 63 A5
Sevettijärvi FIN 113 C17
Sévigny F 59 A5
Sevilla = Seville E 99 B5
Sevilla la Nueva E 94 B2
Seville = Sevilla E 99 B5
Sevilleja de la Jara E 94 C2
Sevlievo BG 11 E8
Sevnica SLO 73 B5
Sevojno SRB 85 C4
Sevrier F 69 C6
Sevsk RUS 7 E13
Sexdrega S 40 B3
Seyches F 76 B3
Seyda D 52 B2
Seydişehir TR 119 E6
Seyðisfjörður IS 111 B12
Seyitgazi TR 118 C5
Seyitömer TR 118 C4
Seymen TR 118 A2
Seyne F 79 B5
Seynes F 78 B3
Seyssel F 69 C5
Sežana SLO 72 C3
Sézanne F 59 B4
Sezulfe P 87 C3
Sezze I 102 B6
Sfântu Gheorghe RO 11 D8
Sforzacosta I 82 C2
Sgarasta Mhor GB 22 D1
's-Gravendeel NL 49 B5
's-Gravenhage = The Hague NL 49 A5
's-Gravenzande NL 49 B5
Shaftesbury GB 29 B5
Shaldon GB 29 C4
Shanagolden IRL 20 B2
Shanklin GB 31 D2
Shannon IRL 20 B3
Shap GB 26 A3
Sharpness GB 29 B5
Shawbury GB 26 C3
Shchekino RUS 7 D14
Shchigry RUS 7 F14
Shchors UA 7 F11
's-Heerenberg NL 50 B2
Sheerness GB 31 C4
Sheffield GB 27 B4
Shefford GB 31 B3
Shenfield GB 31 C4
Shëngjergj AL 116 A2
Shëngjin AL 105 B5
Shepetivka UA 11 A9
Shepshed GB 27 C4
Shepton Mallet GB 29 B5
Sherborne GB 29 C5
Shercock IRL 19 C5
Sheringham GB 30 B5
's-Hertogenbosch NL 49 B6
Shiel Bridge GB 22 D3
Shieldaig GB 22 D3
Shijak AL 105 B5
Shillelagh IRL 21 B5
Shimsk RUS 7 B11
Shipston-on-Stour GB 29 A6
Shirgjan AL 105 B6
Shklow BY 7 D11
Shkodër AL 105 A5
Shoeburyness GB 31 C4
Shoreham-by-Sea GB 31 D3
Shostka UA 7 F12
Shotley Gate GB 31 C5
Shpola UA 11 B11
Shrewsbury GB 26 C3
Shugozero RUS 7 B13
Shumen BG 11 E9
Siabost GB 22 C2
Siamanna I 110 C1
Sianów PL 46 A2
Siatista GR 116 B3
Şiauges-St Romain F 78 A2
Šiauliai LT 6 D7
Sibari I 106 B3
Şibbhult S 41 C4
Šibenik HR 83 C4
Siberstedt D 43 A6
Sibinj HR 74 C2
Sibiu RO 11 D8
Sibnica SRB 85 B5
Sibsey GB 27 B6
Şiculiana I 108 B2
Šid SRB 85 A4
Sidari GR 116 C1
Siddeburen NL 42 B3
Sidensjö S 115 D15
Siderno I 106 C3
Sidirokastro GR 116 A5
Sidmouth GB 29 C4
Sidzina PL 65 A5
Siebe N 113 D12
Siebenlehn D 52 B3
Siedlce PL 6 E7
Siedlice PL 46 B1
Siedlinghausen D 51 B4
Siedlisko PL 46 C2
Siegburg D 50 C3
Siegen D 50 C4
Siegenburg D 62 B2
Sieghartskirchen A 64 B2
Siegsdorf D 62 C3
Siekierki PL 45 C6
Sielpia PL 55 B5
Siemiany PL 47 B5
Siena I 81 C5
Sieniawka PL 53 C4
Siennica PL 55 A6
Sienno PL 55 B6
Sieppijärvi FIN 113 E13
Sieradz PL 54 B3
Sieraków
Śląskie PL 54 C3
Wielkopolskie PL 46 C2
Sierakowice PL 46 A3
Sierck-les-Bains F 60 A2
Sierentz F 60 C3
Sierning A 63 B5
Sierpc PL 47 C5
Sierra de Fuentes E 93 B4
Sierra de Luna E 90 A2
Sierra de Yeguas E 100 B1
Sierre CH 70 B2
Siestrzeń PL 55 A5
Sietamo E 90 A2
Siewierz PL 55 C4
Sigdal N 34 B1
Sigean F 78 C1
Sigerfjord N 112 D4
Sighetu-Marmatiei RO 11 C7
Sighişoara RO 11 C8
Sigillo I 82 C1
Siglufjörður IS 111 A7
Sigmaringen D 61 B5
Signa I 81 C5
Signes F 79 C4
Signy-l'Abbaye F 59 A5
Signy-le-Petit F 59 A5
Sigogne F 67 C4
Sigri GR 116 C7
Sigtuna S 37 C4
Sigueiro E 86 B2
Sigüenza E 95 A4
Sigües E 90 A1
Sigulda LV 6 C8
Siilinjärvi FIN 3 E27
Sikenica SK 65 B4
Sikia GR 116 B5
Sikinos GR 117 F7
Sikkilsdalseter N 32 A6
Siklós H 74 C3
Sikórz PL 47 C5
Sikselet S 115 A14
Silandro I 71 B5
Silánus I 110 B1
Silbaš SRB 75 C4
Şile TR 118 A4
Šiles E 101 A3
Silgueiros P 92 A3
Silifke TR 16 C6
Silíqua I 110 C1
Silistra BG 11 D9
Silivri TR 118 A3
Siljan N 35 C1
Siljansnäs S 36 B1
Silkeborg DK 39 C2
Silla E 96 B2
Sillamäe EST 7 B9
Silleda E 86 B2
Sillé-le-Guillaume F 57 B5
Sillenstede D 43 B4
Sillerud S 35 C4
Sillian A 72 B2
Silloth GB 25 D4
Silno PL 46 B3
Silnowo PL 46 B2
Silo HR 73 C4
Sils E 91 B5
Silsand N 112 C6
Şilte S 37 E5
Šilute LT 6 D6
Silvalen N 114 B9
Silvaplana CH 71 B4
Silvares P 92 A3
Silvberg S 36 B2
Silverdalen S 40 B5
Silvermines IRL 20 B3
Silverstone GB 30 B2
Silverton GB 29 C4
Silves P 98 B2
Silvi Marina I 103 A7
Şimandre F 69 B4
Šimanovci SRB 85 B5
Simard F 69 B5
Simat de Valldigna E 96 B2
Simav TR 118 C3
Simbach
Bayern D 62 B3
Bayern D 62 B4
Simbário I 106 C3
Simeria RO 11 D7
Simi GR 119 F2
Simićevo SRB 85 B6
Simlångsdalen S 40 C3
Simmerath D 50 C2
Simmerberg D 61 C5
Simmern D 50 D3
Şimo FIN 3 D26
Šimonovce SK 65 B6
Simonsbath GB 28 B4
Simonstorp S 37 D3
Simontornya H 74 B3
Simplon CH 70 B3
Simrishamn S 41 D4
Sinaia RO 11 D8
Sinalunga I 81 C5
Sinanaj AL 105 C5
Sinarcas E 96 B1
Sincan TR 118 C7
Sincanlı TR 118 D5
Sindal DK 38 B3
Sindelfingen D 61 B5
Sindia I 110 B1
Sındırgı TR 118 C3
Sinekli TR 118 A3
Sines P 98 B2
Sinetta FIN 113 F14
Sineu E 97 B3
Singen D 61 C4
Singleton GB 31 D3
Singsås N 114 E7
Siniscóla I 110 B2
Sinj HR 83 C5
Sinlabajos E 94 A2
Sinn D 50 C4
Sínnai I 110 C2
Sinnes N 33 D3
Sinop TR 16 A7
Sins CH 70 A3
Sinsheim D 61 A4
Sint Annaland NL 49 B5
Sint Annaparochie NL 42 B2
Sint Athonis NL 50 B1
Sint Nicolaasga NL 42 C2
Sint Oedenrode NL 49 B6
Sintra P 92 C1
Sinzheim D 61 B4
Sinzig D 50 C3
Siófok H 74 B3
Sion CH 70 B2
Sion Mills GB 19 B4
Şiorac-en-Périgord F 77 B3
Šipanska Luka HR 84 D2
Šipovo BIH 84 B2
Sira N 33 D3
Siracusa I 109 B4
Siret RO 11 C9
Sirevåg N 33 D2
Sirig SRB 75 C4
Sirkka FIN 113 E13
Sirmione I 71 C5
Şirok H 65 C6
Široké SK 65 B6
Široki Brijeg BIH 84 C2
Sirolo I 82 C2
Siruela E 94 D1
Sisak HR 73 C6
Şisante E 95 C4
Šišljavić HR 73 C5
Sissach CH 70 A2
Sissonne F 59 A4
Sistelo P 87 C2
Sisteron F 79 B4
Sistiana I 72 C3
Sistranda N 114 D5
Sitasjaurestugorna S 112 E6
Sitges E 91 B4
Sitia GR 117 G8
Sittard NL 50 B1
Sittensen D 43 B6
Sittingbourne GB 31 C4
Sitzenroda D 52 B2
Sivac SRB 75 C4
Sivaslı TR 119 D4
Siverić HR 83 C5
Sivrihisar TR 118 C6
Sixt-Fer-á-Cheval F 70 B1
Siziano I 71 C4
Sizun F 56 B1
Sjenica SRB 85 C5
Sjoa N 114 F6
Sjøåsen N 114 C8
Sjöbo S 41 D3
Sjøenden
Hedmark N 34 A3
Hedmark N 34 B3
Sjøholt N 114 E3
Sjøli N 34 A3
Sjølstad N 114 C9
Sjölunda S 37 C2
Sjømarken S 40 B2
Sjørring DK 38 C1
Sjötofta S 40 B3
Sjötorp S 35 D5
Sjoutnäset S 115 C11
Sjøvegan N 112 D6
Sjuntorp S 35 D4
Skåbu N 32 A6
Skadovsk UA 11 C12
Skafså N 33 C5
Skaftafell IS 111 D9
Skagaströnd IS 111 B5
Skagen DK 38 B3
Skagersvik S 35 D6
Skaiå N 33 D4
Skaidi N 113 B13
Skala GR 117 D2
Skała PL 55 C4
Skaland N 112 C6
Skala Oropou GR 117 D5
Skala-Podilska UA 11 B9
Skalat UA 11 B8
Skalbmierz PL 55 C5
Skålevik N 33 D5
Skalica SK 64 B3
Skalité SK 65 A4
Skällinge S 40 B2
Skalná CZ 52 C2
Skals DK 38 C2
Skælskør DK 39 D4
Skalstugan S 114 D9
Skanderborg DK 39 C2
Skånes-Fagerhult S 41 C3
Skåne-Tranås S 41 D3
Skånevik N 33 C2
Skänninge S 37 D2
Skanör med Falsterbo S 41 D2
Skåpafors S 35 C4
Skąpe PL 53 A5
Skara S 35 D5
Skærbæk DK 39 D1
Skarberget N 112 D5
Skärblacka S 37 D2
Skarð IS 111 B3
Skarda S 115 C15
Skare N 32 C3
Skåre S 35 C5
Skärhamn S 38 B4
Skarnes N 34 B3
Skärplinge S 36 B4
Skarpnatö FIN 36 B6
Skarp Salling DK 38 C2
Skarrild DK 39 D1
Skarstad N 112 D5
Skärstad S 40 B4
Skarsvåg N 113 A14
Skarszewy PL 47 A4
Skårup DK 39 D3
Skärvången S 115 D11
Skarvsjöby S 115 C14
Skaryszew PL 55 B6
Skarżysko-Kamienna PL 55 B5
Skarzysko Ksiazece PL 55 B5
Skatøy N 33 D6
Skattkärr S 35 C5
Skattungbyn S 36 A1
Skatval N 114 D7
Skaulo S 112 E10
Skave DK 39 C1
Skawina PL 55 D4
Skebobruk S 36 C5
Skebokvarn S 37 C3
Skedala S 40 C2
Skedevi S 37 D2
Skedsmokorset N 34 B3
Skee S 35 D3
Skegness GB 27 B6
Skela SRB 85 B5
Skelani BIH 85 C4
Skellefteå S 3 D24
Skelleftehamn S 3 D24
Skelmersdale GB 26 B3
Skelmorlie GB 24 C3
Skelund DK 38 C3
Skender Vakuf BIH 84 B2
Skene S 40 B2
Skępe PL 47 C5
Skepplanda S 40 B2
Skeppshult S 40 B3
Skerries IRL 19 C5
Ski N 35 C2
Skiathos GR 116 C5
Skibbereen IRL 20 C2
Skibotn N 112 C9

Skidra GR 116 B4
Skien N 35 C1
Skierniewice PL 55 B5
Skillingaryd S 40 B4
Skillinge S 41 D4
Skillingmark S 34 C4
Skilloura CY 120 A2
Skinnarbol S 37 C5
Skinnskatteberg S . . .36 C2
Skipmannvik N 112 E4
Skipness GB 24 C2
Skipsea GB 27 B5
Skipton GB 26 B3
Skiptvet N 35 C3
Skiros GR 116 D6
Skivarp S 41 D3
Skive DK 38 C2
Skjånes N 113 B17
Skjærhalden N 35 C3
Skjeberg N 35 C3
Skjeggedal N 32 B3
Skjeljanger N 32 B1
Skjern DK 39 D1
Skjervøy N 112 B9
Skjold
  Rogaland N 33 C2
  Troms N 112 C8
Skjoldastraumen N . . .33 C2
Skjolden N 32 A4
Skjønhaug N 35 C3
Skjøtningsberg N 113 A16
Škocjan SLO 73 C5
Skoczów PL 65 A4
Škodborg DK 39 D2
Škofja Loka SLO 73 B4
Škofljica SLO 73 C4
Skog S 36 A3
Skoganvarre N 113 C14
Skøgen S 35 C4
Skogfoss N 113 C18
Skoghall S 35 C5
Skogly N 113 C18
Skogn N 114 D8
Skognes N 112 C8
Skogstorp
  Halland S 40 C2
  Södermanland S . . .37 C3
Skoki PL 46 C3
Sköldinge S 37 C3
Skole UA 11 B7
Skollenborg N 32 A4
Sköllersta S 37 C2
Skomlin PL 54 B3
Skonseng N 115 A11
Skopelos GR 116 C5
Skopje MK 10 E6
Skoppum N 35 C2
Skórcz PL 47 B4
Skorogoszcz PL 54 C2
Skoroszów PL 54 B2
Skorovatn N 115 C10
Skorped S 115 D14
Skørping DK 38 C2
Skotfoss N 33 C6
Skotniki PL 55 B4
Skotselv N 34 C4
Skotterud N 34 C4
Skottorp S 40 C2
Skovby DK 39 E2
Skövde S 35 D5
Skovsgård S 38 B2
Skrad HR 73 C4
Skradnik HR 83 C4
Skråmestø N 32 B1
Škrdlovice CZ 64 A1
Skrea S 40 C2
Skreia N 34 B2
Skrolsvik N 112 C5
Skruv S 40 C5
Skrwilno PL 47 B5
Skrydstrup DK 39 D2
Skucani BIH 84 C1
Skudeneshavn N 33 C2
Skui N 34 C2
Skulsk PL 47 C4
Skultuna S 37 C3
Skuodas LT 8 D2
Skurup S 41 D3
Skute N 34 B2
Skuteč CZ 64 A1
Skutskär S 36 B4
Skutvik N 112 D4
Skvyra UA 11 B10
Skwierzyna PL 46 C1
Skýcov SK 65 B4
Skyllberg S 37 D1
Skyttorp S 115 D12
Sládkovičovo SK 64 B3
Slagelse DK 39 D4
Slagharen NL 42 C3
Slagnäs S 115 B15
Slaidburn GB 26 B3
Slane IRL 19 C5
Slangerup DK 41 D2
Slano HR 84 D2
Slantsy RUS 7 B10
Slaný CZ 53 C4
Šlap SLO 72 B3
Šlapanice CZ 64 A2
Slåstad N 34 B3
Slatina
  BIH 84 C2
  HR 74 C2
  RO 11 D8
  SRB 85 C5
Slatiňany CZ 64 A1
Slatinice CZ 64 A3
Slättberg S 36 A1
Slattum N 34 C2
Slavičín CZ 64 A3
Slavkov CZ 64 B3
Slavkovica SRB 85 B5
Slavkov u Brna CZ . . .64 A2
Slavonice CZ 63 B6
Slavonski Brod HR . . .74 C3
Slavonski Kobas HR . .84 A2
Slavošovce SK 65 B6
Slavskoye RUS 47 A6
Slavuta UA 11 A9
Sława
  Lubuskie PL 53 B6
  Zachodnio-Pomorskie
  PL 46 B1
Sławharad BY 7 E11
Sławków PL 55 C4
Sławno
  Wielkopolskie PL . . .46 C3
  Zachodnio-Pomorskie
  PL 46 A2
Sławoborze PL 46 B1
Sl'ažany SK 64 B4
Sleaford GB 27 C5
Sleðbrjótur IS 111 B11
Sledmere GB 27 A5
Sleights GB 27 A5
Slemmestad N 34 C2
Slesin PL 47 C4
Sliač SK 65 B5
Sliema M 107 C5
Sligo IRL 18 B3
Slite S 37 E5
Slitu N 35 C3
Sliven BG 11 E9
Śliwice PL 47 B4
Slobozia RO 11 D9
Slochteren NL 42 B3
Slöinge S 40 C2
Słomniki PL 55 C5
Slonim BY 6 E8
Słońsk PL 45 C6
Slootdorp NL 42 C1
Slottsbron S 35 C5
Slough GB 31 C3
Slövåg N 32 B2

Slovenj Gradec SLO . .73 B5
Slovenska Bistrica
  SLO 73 B5
Slovenská L'upča SK . .65 B5
Slovenská-Ves SK . . .65 A6
Slovenské Darmoty
  SK 65 B5
Slovenske Konjice
  SLO 73 B5
Słubice
  Łódzkie PL 55 A4
  Lubuskie PL 53 A4
Sluis NL 49 B4
Šluknov CZ 53 B4
Sluni HR 83 A4
Słupca PL 54 A2
Słupia PL 55 B4
Słupiec PL 54 C1
Słupsk PL 46 A3
Slutsk BY 7 E9
Smałininkai LT 6 D7
Smalåsen N 115 B10
Smardzewo PL 53 A5
Smarhon BY 7 D9
Šmarje SLO 73 B5
Šmarjeta SLO 73 B4
Smečno CZ 53 C4
Smedby S 40 C6
Smědec CZ 63 B5
Smederevo SRB 85 B5
Smederevska Palanka
  SRB 85 B5
Smedjebacken S 36 B2
Smegorzów PL 55 C6
Smeland N 33 D5
Smidary CZ 53 C5
Śmigiel PL 54 A1
Smila UA 11 B11
Smilde NL 42 C3
Smiřice CZ 53 C5
Smithfield GB 25 D5
Smitovo PL 46 B2
Smogulec PL 46 B3
Smołdzino PL 46 A3
Smolenice SK 64 B3
Smolensk RUS 7 D12
Smolnik PL 55 B6
Smolyan BG 116 A6
Smuka SLO 73 C4
Smygehamn S 41 D3
Smykow PL 55 B5
Snainton GB 27 A5
Snaith GB 27 B4
Snaptun DK 39 D3
Snarby N 112 C8
Snarum N 34 B1
Snåsa N 115 C9
Snedsted DK 38 C1
Sneek NL 42 B2
Sneem IRL 20 C2
Snejbjerg DK 39 D1
Snihurivka UA 11 C12
Šnjegotina BIH 84 B2
Snøde DK 39 D3
Snøfjord N 113 B13
Snogebaek DK 41 D5
Snyatyn UA 11 B8
Soave I 71 C6
Sober E 86 B3
Sobernheim D 60 A3
Soběslav CZ 63 A5
Sobienie Jeziory PL . .55 B6
Sobota
  Dolnośląskie PL . . .53 B5
  Łódzkie PL 55 A4
Sobotište SK 64 B3
Sobotka CZ 53 C5
Sobótka
  Dolnośląskie PL . . .54 C1
  Wielkopolskie PL . . .54 B2
Sobra HR 84 D2
Sobrado
  Coruña E 86 A2
  Lugo E 86 B3
Sobral da Adiça P 98 A3
Sobral de Monte Agraço
  P 92 C1
Sobreira Formosa P . .92 B3
Søby DK 39 E3
Soca SLO 72 B3
Sočanica KOS 85 C5
Sochaczew PL 55 A5
Sochos GR 116 B5
Socodor RO 75 B6
Socol RO 85 B6
Socovos E 101 A4
Socuéllamos E 95 C4
Sodankylä FIN 113 E15
Söderåkra S 40 C6
Söderås S 36 A3
Söderbärke S 36 B2
Söderby-Karl S 36 C5
Söderfors S 36 B4
Söderhamn S 36 A4
Söderköping S 37 D3
Södertälje S 37 C4
Södingberg A 73 A5
Södra Finnö S 37 D3
Södra Ny S 35 C5
Södra Råda S 35 C6
Södra Sandby S 41 D3
Södra Vi S 40 B5
Sodražica SLO 73 C4
Sodupe E 89 A3
Soest
  D 50 B4
  NL 49 A6
Sofades GR 116 C4
Sofia B 11 E7
Sofikon GR 117 E5
Sofronea RO 75 B6
Sögel D 43 C4
Sogliano al Rubicone
  I 82 B1
Sogndalsfjøra N 32 A4
Søgne N 33 D4
Sögütköy TR 119 F3
Soham GB 30 B4
Sohland D 53 B4
Sohren D 60 A3
Soignies B 49 C5
Soissons F 59 A4
Söjtör H 74 B1
Sokal' UA 11 A8
Söke TR 119 E2
Sokna N 34 B1
Soknedal N 114 E7
Soko BIH 84 B3
Sokolac BIH 84 C3
Sokolov CZ 52 C2
Sokołów Podlaski PL . .6 E7
Sola N 33 D2
Solana de los Barros
  E 93 C4
Solana del Pino E . . .100 A1
Solánas E 110 C2
Solares E 89 A3
Solarino I 109 B4
Solarussa I 110 C1
Solas GB 22 D1
Solberg S 40 B4
Solber-gelva N 34 C2
Sölden A 71 B6
Solec Kujawski PL . . .47 B4
Solec nad Wisła PL . .55 B6
Soleils F 79 C5
Solenzara F 102 B2
Solesmes F 49 C4

Soleto I 107 A5
Solgne F 60 B2
Solheim N 32 B2
Solheimsvik N 33 C3
Solignac F 67 C6
Solihull GB 27 C4
Solin HR 83 C5
Solingen D 50 B3
Solivella E 91 B4
Solkan SLO 72 A2
Söll A 72 A2
Sollana E 96 B2
Sollebrunn S 35 D4
Solleftea S 115 D14
Sollenau A 64 C2
Sollen-tuna S 37 C4
Søller E 97 B2
Solleron S 36 B1
Sollia N 114 F8
Søllested DK 39 E4
Solliès-Pont F 79 C5
Sollihøgda N 34 C2
Solnechnogorsk RUS .7 C14
Solnice CZ 53 C6
Solofra I 103 C7
Solomiac F 77 C3
Solopaca I 103 B7
Solórzano E 89 A3
Solothurn CH 70 A2
Solre-le-Château F . . .49 C4
Solsona E 91 B4
Solsvik N 32 B1
Solt H 75 B4
Soltau D 44 C1
Soltsy RUS 7 B11
Soltszentimre H 75 B4
Soltvadkert H 75 B4
Solumsmoen N 34 C1
Solund N 32 A1
Solva GB 28 B2
Sölvesborg S 41 C4
Solymár H 65 C4
Soma I 118 C2
Somain F 49 C4
Somberek H 74 B3
Sombernon F 69 A4
Sombor SRB 75 C4
Sombreffe B 49 C5
Someren NL 50 B1
Somero FIN 6 A7
Somersham GB 30 B3
Somerton GB 29 B5
Sominy PL 46 A3
Somma Lombardo I . . .70 C3
Sommarøy N 112 C7
Sommarset N 112 E4
Sommatino I 109 B3
Sommeilles F 59 B6
Sommen S 37 D1
Sommepy-Tahure F . . .59 A5
Sömmerda D 52 B1
Sommerfeld D 45 C5
Sommersted DK 39 D2
Sommesous F 59 B5
Somme-Tourbe F 59 A5
Sommières F 78 C3
Sommières-du-Clain
  F 67 B5
Somo E 88 A3
Somogyfajsz H 74 B2
Somogyjád H 74 B2
Somogysámson H 74 B2
Somogysárd H 74 B2
Somogyszil H 74 B3
Somogyszob H 74 B2
Somogyvár H 74 B2
Somontín E 101 B3
Somosierra E 95 A3
Somosköújfalu H 65 B5
Sompolno PL 47 C4
Sompuis F 59 B5
Son NL 35 C2
Son Bou E 97 B4
Sonceboz CH 70 A2
Soncillo E 88 B3
Soncino I 71 C4
Sóndalo I 71 B5
Søndeled N 33 D6
Sønder Bjert DK 39 D2
Sønderborg DK 39 E2
Sønderby DK 39 E2
Sønder Felding DK . . .39 D1
Sønderho DK 39 D1
Sønder Hygum DK . . .39 D1
Sønder Omme DK 39 D1
Sondershausen D 51 B6
Sondervig DK 39 C1
Søndre Enningdal Kappel
  N 35 D3
Sóndrio I 71 B4
Soneja E 96 B2
Son en Breugel NL . . .49 B6
Songe N 33 D6
Songeons F 58 A2
Sonkamuotka FIN . . .113 D12
Sonkovo RUS 7 C14
Sönnarslöv S 41 D4
Sonneberg D 52 C1
Sonnefeld D 52 C1
Sonnewalde D 53 B3
Sonnino I 102 B6
Sonogno CH 70 B3
Sonsbeck D 50 B2
Sonseca E 94 C3
Son Servera E 97 B3
Sonsterud N 34 B4
Sonstorp S 37 D2
Sonta SRB 75 C4
Sontheim D 61 B6
Sonthofen D 71 A5
Sontra D 51 B5
Sopelana E 89 A4
Sopje HR 74 C2
Sopot
  PL 47 A4
  SRB 85 B5
Sopotnica MK 116 A3
Sopron H 64 C2
Šor SRB 85 C4
Sora I 103 B6
Soragna I 81 B4
Söråker S 115 E14
Sorano I 81 D5
Sorbara I 81 B5
Sorbas E 101 B3
Sórbolo I 81 B4
Sörbygden S 115 E13
Sore F 76 B2
Sörenberg CH 70 B3
Soresina I 71 C4
Sörforsa S 115 F14
Sørfjorden N 112 D4
Sörfors S 115 F14
Sorgono I 110 B2
Sorgues F 78 B3
Sørgutvik N 115 B9
Soria E 89 C4
Soriano Cálabro I . . .106 C3
Soriano nel Cimino I . .102 A5
Sorisdale GB 24 B1
Sørkjosen N 112 C9
Sørli N 115 C10
Sörmjöle S 115 D17
Sörmo N 112 D7
Sórnac F 68 C2
Soroca MD 11 B10
Sørreisa N 112 C7
Sorrento I 103 C7
Sorsele S 115 B14
Sörsjön S 34 A5
Sort E 91 A4
Sortavala RUS 3 F29

Sortino I 109 B4
Sortland N 112 D4
Sørum N 34 B2
Sørumsand N 34 C3
Sorunda S 37 C4
Sörup D 44 A1
Sørvær N 113 B11
Sørvágen N 112 E1
Sorvik S 36 B2
Sørvika N 114 E8
Sos F 76 B3
Sösdala S 41 C3
Sos del Rey Católico
  E 90 A1
Sošice HR 73 C5
Sosnica PL 46 B2
Sośnicowice PL 54 C3
Sośno PL 46 B3
Sosnovyy Bor RUS . . .7 B10
Sosnowiec PL 55 C4
Sospel F 80 C1
Šoštanj SLO 73 B5
Sotaseter N 114 F4
Sotillo de Adrada E . . .94 B2
Sotillo de la Ribera E . .88 C3
Sotin HR 75 C4
Sotkamo FIN 3 D28
Sotobañado y Priorato
  E 88 B2
Soto de la Marina E . . .88 A3
Soto del Barco E 86 A4
Soto de los Infantes
  E 86 A4
Soto de Real E 94 B3
Soto de Ribera E 88 A1
Sotoserrano E 93 A4
Soto y Amío E 88 B1
Sotresgudo E 88 B2
Sotrondio E 88 A1
Sottomarina I 72 C2
Sottrum D 43 B6
Sottunga FIN 36 B7
Sotuelamos E 95 C4
Souain F 59 A5
Soual F 77 C5
Soucy F 59 B4
Souda GR 117 G6
Soudron F 59 B5
Souesmes F 68 A2
Soufflenheim F 60 B3
Soufli GR 116 A8
Souillac F 77 B4
Souilly F 59 A6
Soulac-sur-Mer F 66 C3
Soulaines-Dhuys F . . .59 B5
Soulatgé F 77 D5
Soultz-Haut-Rhin F . . .60 C3
Soultz-sous-Forêts F . .60 B3
Soumagne B 50 C1
Soumoulou F 76 C2
Souppes-sur-Loing F . .58 B3
Sourdeval F 57 B5
Soure P 92 A2
Sournia F 77 D5
Souro Pires P 87 D3
Sourpi GR 116 C4
Sours F 58 B2
Sousceyrac F 77 B5
Sousel P 92 C3
Soustons F 76 C1
Söğüt
  Bilecik TR 118 B5
  Burdur TR 119 E4
Soutelo de Montes E . .86 B2
Southam GB 30 B2
Southampton GB 31 D2
Southborough GB 31 C4
South Brent GB 28 C4
South Cave GB 27 B5
Southend GB 24 C2
Southend-on-Sea GB . .31 C4
South Hayling GB 31 D3
South Molton GB 28 B4
South Ockendon GB . .31 C4
South Petherton GB . .29 C5
Southport GB 26 B2
South Shields GB 25 D6
South Tawton GB 28 C4
Southwell GB 27 B5
Southwold GB 30 B5
South Woodham Ferrers
  GB 31 C4
Söğütlü TR 118 B5
Souto P 92 A3
Soutochao E 87 C3
Souto da Carpalhosa
  P 92 B2
Souvigny F 68 B3
Souzay-Champigny F . .67 A4
Soverato I 106 C3
Soveria Mannelli I . . .106 B3
Sövestad S 41 D3
Sovetsk RUS 6 D7
Soviči BIH 84 C2
Sovicille I 81 C5
Søvik N 114 E3
Sowerby GB 27 A4
Soyaux F 67 C5
Sozopol BG 11 E9
Spa B 50 C1
Spadafora I 109 A4
Spaichingen D 61 B4
Spakenburg NL 49 A6
Spalding GB 30 B3
Spálene Poříčí CZ . . .63 A4
Spalt D 62 A1
Spangenberg D 51 B5
Spangereid N 33 D4
Spantekow D 45 B5
Sparanise I 103 B7
Sparbu N 114 D8
Sparkær DK 38 C2
Sparkford GB 29 B5
Sparreholm S 37 C3
Sparta = Sparti GR . . .117 E4
Spartà I 109 A4
Sparti = Sparta GR . . .117 E4
Spas-Demensk RUS . .7 D13
Spean Bridge GB 24 B3
Speicher D 60 A2
Speichersdorf D 52 A2
Speke GB 26 B3
Spello I 82 D1
Spenge D 51 A4
Spennymoor GB 25 D6
Spentrup DK 38 C3
Sperenberg D 52 A3
Sperlinga I 109 B3
Sperlonga I 103 B6
Spetalen N 35 C2
Spetses GR 117 E5
Speyer D 61 A4
Spézet F 56 B2

Spezzano Albanese
  I 106 B3
Spezzano della Sila
  I 106 B3
Spiddle IRL 20 A2
Spiegelau D 63 B4
Spiekeroog D 43 B4
Spiez CH 70 B2
Spigno Monferrato I . .80 B2
Spijk NL 42 B3
Spijkenisse NL 49 B5
Spilamberto I 81 B5
Spili GR 117 G6
Spilimbergo I 72 B2
Spilsby GB 27 B6
Spinazzola I 104 C2
Spincourt F 60 A1
Spind N 33 D3
Spindlerův-Mlyn CZ . .53 C5
Spinoso I 104 C1
Špišjč Bukovica HR . . .74 C2
Spišská Belá SK 65 A6
Spišská Nová Ves
  SK 65 B6
Spišská Stará Ves
  SK 65 A6
Spišské-Hanušovce
  SK 65 A6
Spišské Podhradie
  SK 65 B6
Spišské Vlachy SK . . .65 B6
Spišský-Štvrtok SK . . .65 B6
Spital A 63 C5
Spital am Semmering
  A 63 C6
Spittal an der Drau A . .72 B3
Spittle of Glenshee
  GB 25 B4
Spitz A 63 B6
Spjald DK 39 C1
Spjærøy N 35 C2
Spjelkavik N 114 E3
Spjutsbygd S 41 C5
Split HR 83 C5
Splügen CH 71 B4
Spodsbjerg DK 39 E3
Spofforth GB 27 B4
Spohle D 43 B5
Spoleto I 82 D1
Spoltore I 103 A7
Spondigna I 71 B5
Sponvika N 35 C3
Spornitz D 44 B3
Spotorno I 80 B2
Spraitbach D 61 B5
Sprakensehl D 44 C2
Spręcowo PL 47 B6
Spremberg D 53 B4
Spresiano I 72 C2
Sprimont B 49 C6
Springe D 51 A5
Sproatley GB 27 B5
Spuž MNE 105 A5
Spychowo PL 47 B6
Spydeberg N 35 C3
Spytkowice PL 55 B4
Squillace I 106 C3
Squinzano I 105 C4
Sračinec HR 73 B6
Srbac BIH 84 A2
Srbica KOS 85 D5
Srbobran SRB 75 C4
Srebrenica BIH 85 B4
Srebrenik BIH 84 B3
Sredets BG 11 E9
Središče SLO 73 B6
Śrem PL 54 A2
Sremska Mitrovica
  SRB 85 B4
Sremski Karlovci
  SRB 85 A4
Srní CZ 63 A4
Srnice Gornje BIH 84 B3
Srock PL 55 B4
Środa Śląska PL 54 B1
Środa Wielkopolski
  PL 54 A2
Srpska Crnja SRB . . .75 C5
Srpski Itebej SRB 75 C5
Srpski Miletić SRB . . .75 C4
Staatz A 64 B2
Stabbursnes N 113 B13
Staberdorf D 44 A3
Stabroek B 49 B5
Stachy CZ 63 A4
Staðarfell IS 111 B3
Stade D 43 B6
Stadl an der Mur A . . .72 A3
Stadskanaal NL 42 C3
Stadtallendorf D 51 C5
Stadthagen D 51 A5
Stadtilm D 52 C1
Stadtkyll D 50 C2
Stadtlauringen D 51 C6
Stadtlengsfeld D 51 C6
Stadtlohn D 50 B2
Stadtoldendorf D 51 B5
Stadtroda D 52 C1
Stadtsteinach D 52 C1
Stäfa CH 70 A3
Staffanstorp S 41 D3
Staffelstein D 51 C6
Staffin GB 22 D2
Stafford GB 26 C3
Stainach A 73 A4
Staindrop GB 27 A4
Staines-upon-Thames
  GB 31 C3
Stainville F 59 B6
Staithes GB 27 A5
Staiti I 106 D3
Stäket S 37 C4
Stakroge DK 39 D1
Štalac SRB 85 C6
Štalcerji SLO 73 C4
Stalden CH 70 B2
Stalham GB 30 B5
Stalheim N 32 B3
Stallarholmen S 37 C4
Ställberg S 36 C1
Ställdalen S 36 C1
Stallhofen A 73 A5
Stalon S 115 C12
Stalowa Wola PL 11 A7
Stamford GB 30 B3
Stamford Bridge GB . .27 B5
Stamnes N 32 B2
Stams A 71 A5
Stamsried D 62 A3
Stamsund N 112 D2
Stanford le Hope GB . .31 C4
Stånga S 37 E5
Stange N 34 B3
Stanghella I 72 C1
Stanhope GB 25 D5
Stanišić SRB 75 C4
Staňkov CZ 62 A4
Stankovci HR 83 C4
Stanley GB 25 D6
Stans CH 70 B3
Stansted Mountfitchet
  GB 31 C4
Stanzach A 71 A5
Stąpar SRB 75 C4
Stapar SRB 75 C4
Stapelburg D 51 B6
Staphorst NL 42 C3
Staporków PL 55 B5
Stara Baška HR 83 B3
Starachowice PL 55 B6
Stara Fužina SLO 72 B3
Stara Kamienica PL . .53 C5
Stara Kiszewa PL 47 B4
Stará L'ubovňa SK . . .65 A6
Stara Moravica SRB . .75 C4
Stara Novalja HR 83 B3
Stara Pazova SRB . . .85 B5
Stará Turá SK 64 B3
Staraya Russa RUS . .7 C11
Stara Zagora BG 11 E8
Stärbsnäs S 36 C6
Starčevo SRB 85 B5
Stare Dłutowo PL 47 B5
Stare Hamry CZ 65 A4
Staré Jablonki PL 47 B6
Stare Kurowo PL 46 C1
Stare Pole PL 47 A5
Stare Sedlo CZ 63 A5
Stare Stracze PL 53 B6
Stargard Szczeciński
  PL 45 B7
Stårheim N 114 F2
Stari Bar MNE 105 A5
Stari Banovci SRB . . .85 B5
Starigrad
  Ličko-Senjska HR . . .83 B3
  Splitsko-Dalmatinska
  HR 83 C5
Stari Gradac HR 74 C2
Starigrad-Paklenica
  HR 83 B4
Stari Majdan BIH 83 B5
Stari Mikanovci HR . . .74 C3
Stari Raušci KOS 85 D5
Staritsa RUS 7 C13
Starkenbach A 71 A5

Starnberg D 62 C2
Starodub RUS 7 E12
Starogard PL 46 B1
Starogard Gdański
  PL 47 B4
Starokonstyantyniv
  UA 11 B9
Staro Petrovo Selo
  HR 74 C2
Staro Selo
  HR 73 C5
  SRB 85 B6
Stary Brzozów PL 55 A5
Starý Dzierzgoń PL . . .47 B5
Starý Hrozenkov CZ . .64 B3
Stary Jaroslaw PL . . .46 A2
Starý Plzenec CZ 63 A4
Stary Sącz PL 65 A6
Starý Smokovec SK . .65 A6
Staryy Chartorysk
  UA 11 A8
Staško SK 65 A4
Stassfurt D 52 B1
Staszów PL 55 C6
Stathelle N 35 C1
Staufen D 60 C3
Staunton GB 29 B5
Stavaj SRB 85 C5
Stavang N 32 A2
Stavanger N 33 D2
Stavåsnäs S 34 B4
Stavby S 36 B5
Staveley GB 27 B4
Stavelot B 50 C1
Stavenisse NL 49 B5
Stavern N 35 C2
Stavnäs S 35 C4
Stavoren NL 42 C2
Stavros
  CY 120 A1
  GR 116 B5
Stavroupoli GR 116 A6
Stavseng N 32 A6
Stavsjø N 34 B2
Stavsnäs S 37 C5
Stawiszyn PL 54 B3
Steane N 33 C5
Steblevë AL 116 A2
Stechelberg CH 70 B2
Štěchovice CZ 63 A5
Stechow D 44 C4
Steckborn CH 61 C4
Stede Broek NL 42 C2
Steeg A 71 A5
Steenbergen NL 49 B5
Steenvoorde F 48 C3
Steenwijk NL 42 C3
Štefanje HR 74 C1
Steffisburg CH 70 B2
Stegaurach D 62 A1
Stege DK 39 E5
Stegelitz D 45 B5
Stegersbach A 73 A6
Stegna PL 47 A5
Steimbke D 43 C6
Stein
  GB 22 D2
Steinach
  A 71 A6
  Baden-Württemberg
  D 61 B4
  Bayern D 51 C6
  Thüringen D 52 C1
Stein an Rhein CH . . .61 C4
Steinau
  Bayern D 51 C5
  Niedersachsen D . . .43 B5
Steinbeck D 44 B2
Steinberg am Rofan
  A 72 A1
Steindorf A 73 B4
Steine N 32 B2
Steinen D 60 C3
Steinfeld
  A 72 B3
  Bayern D 61 B6
  Nordrhein-Westfalen
  D 50 A4
Steinfurt D 50 A3
Steingaden D 62 C1
Steinhagen D 51 A4
Steinheid D 52 C1
Steinheim
  Bayern D 61 B6
  Nordrhein-Westfalen
  D 51 B5
Steinhöfel D 45 C6
Steinhorst D 44 C2
Steinigtwolmsdorf D . .53 B4
Steinkjer N 114 C8
Steinsholt N 35 C1
Stekene B 49 B5
Stelle D 44 B2
Stellendam NL 49 B5
Stenay F 59 A6
Stenberga S 40 B5
Stendal D 44 C3
Stenhammar S 35 D5
Stenhamra S 37 C4
Stenhousemuir GB . . .25 B4
Stenlose DK 41 D2
Stensätra S 36 B3
Stensele S 115 B14
Stenstorp S 35 D5
Stenstrup DK 39 D3
Stenudden S 112 F6
Stenungsund S 38 A4
Štěpánov CZ 64 A3
Stepnica PL 45 B6
Stepojevac SRB 85 B5
Stepping DK 39 D2
Sterbfritz D 51 C5
Sternberg D 44 B3
Šternberk CZ 64 A3
Sterup D 44 A1
Stes Maries-de-la-Mer
  F 78 C3
Štěti CZ 53 C4
Stevenage GB 31 C3
Stewarton GB 24 C3
Steyerberg D 43 C6
Steyning GB 31 D3
Steyr A 63 C5
Stężyca PL 47 A4
Stezzano I 71 C4
Stia I 81 C5
Stibb Cross GB 28 C3
Sticciano Scalo I 81 D5
Stidsvig S 41 C3
Stiens NL 42 B2
Stigen S 35 D4
Stigliano I 104 C2
Stigtomta S 37 D3
Stilida GR 116 D4
Stilla N 113 C12
Stillington GB 27 A4
Stilo I 106 C3
Stintino I 110 B1
Stio I 103 C8
Štip MK 116 A4
Stira GR 117 D6
Stirling GB 25 B4
Štítnik SK 65 B6
Štíty CZ 54 D1
Stjärnhov S 37 C4
Stjärnsund S 36 B3
Stjørdalshalsen N . . .114 D8
Stobnica PL 55 B4
Stobno PL 46 B2
Stobreč HR 83 C5
Stockach D 61 C5
Stöckalp CH 70 B3
Stockaryd S 40 B4
Stockbridge GB 31 C2
Stockerau A 64 B2
Stockheim D 52 C1
Stockholm S 37 C5
Stockport GB 26 B3

Stocksbridge GB 27 B4
Stockton-on-Tees GB . .27 A4
Stöde S 115 E13
Stödvarfjörður IS 111 C12
Stoer GB 22 D3
Stoholm DK 38 C2
Stoke Ferry GB 30 B4
Stoke Fleming GB 29 C4
Stoke Mandeville GB . .31 C3
Stoke-on-Trent GB . . .26 B3
Stokesley GB 27 A4
Stokke N 35 C2
Stokkemarke DK 39 E4
Stokken N 33 D5
Stokkseyri IS 111 D4
Stokkvågen N 115 A9
Stokmarknes N 112 D3
Stolac BIH 84 C2
Stølaholmen N 32 A3
Stolberg D 50 C2
Stolin BY 7 F9
Stollberg D 52 C2
Stöllet S 34 B5
Stollhamm D 43 B5
Stolno PL 47 B4
Stolpen D 53 B4
Stolzenau D 43 C6
Stonehaven GB 25 B5
Stonehouse GB 25 C4
Stongfjorden N 32 A2
Stopanja SRB 85 C6
Stopnica PL 55 C5
Storå S 37 C2
Storås N 114 D6
Storby FIN 36 B6
Stordal
  Møre og Romsdal
  N 114 E4
  Nord-Trøndelag N . .114 D8
Store DK 23 B6
Storebø N 32 B2
Storebro S 40 B5
Store Damme DK 41 E2
Store Heddinge DK . . .41 D2
Store Herrestad S 41 D3
Store Levene S 35 D4
Store Molvik N 113 B17
Store Skedvi S 36 B2
Store Vika S 37 D4
Storfjellseter N 114 F7
Storfjord N 112 C9
Storfors S 35 C6
Storforshei N 112 F4
Storhøliseter N 32 A6
Storjord N 112 F4
Storkow
  Brandenburg D 53 A3
  Mecklenburg-
  Vorpommern D 45 B6
Storli N 114 E6
Storlien S 114 D9
Stornara I 104 B1
Stornoway GB 22 C2
Storo I 71 C5
Storozhynets UA 11 B8
Storrington GB 31 D3
Storseleby S 115 C13
Storsjön S 36 A3
Storslett N 112 C10
Storsteinnes N 112 C8
Storuman S 115 B14
Störvattnet S 115 E9
Storvik
  N 112 F2
  S 36 B3
Storvreta S 36 B4
Štos SK 65 B6
Stössen D 52 B1
Stötten D 62 C1
Stotternheim D 52 B1
Stouby DK 39 D2
Stourbridge GB 26 C3
Stourport-on-Severn
  GB 29 A5
Støvring DK 38 C2
Stow GB 25 C5
Stowbtsy BY 7 E9
Stowmarket GB 30 B5
Stow-on-the-Wold GB .29 B6
Straach D 52 B2
Strabane GB 19 B4
Strachan GB 25 B5
Strachur GB 24 B3
Strackholt D 43 B4
Stradbally IRL 20 B1
Stradella I 80 A3
Straelen D 50 B2
Stragari SRB 85 B5
Strakonice CZ 63 A4
Straldzha BG 11 E9
Stralsund D 45 A5
Strand
  N 114 D3
  S 34 A3
Stranda N 114 E3
Strandebarm N 32 B3
Strandhill IRL 18 B3
Strandlykkja N 34 B3
Strandvik N 32 B2
Strangford GB 19 B6
Strängnäs S 37 C4
Strångsjö S 37 D3
Stráni CZ 64 B3
Stranice SLO 73 B5
Stranorlar IRL 19 B4
Stranraer GB 24 D2
Strasatti I 108 B1
Strasbourg F 60 B3
Strasburg D 45 B5
Strašice CZ 63 A4
Stråssa S 37 C2
Strass im Steiermark
  A 73 B5
Strasskirchen D 62 B3
Strasswalchen A 63 C4
Stratford-upon-Avon
  GB 29 A6
Strathaven GB 25 C4
Strathdon GB 23 D5
Strathkanaird GB 22 D3
Strathpeffer GB 23 D4
Strathy GB 23 C5
Stratinska BIH 84 B1
Stratton GB 28 C3
Straubing D 62 B3
Straulas I 110 B2
Straume N 33 C6
Straumen
  Nordland N 112 E4
  Nord-Trøndelag N . .114 D8
Straumsjøen N 112 D3
Straupitz D 53 B4
Strausberg D 45 C5
Straussfurt D 52 B1
Strawczyn PL 55 C5
Straža
  SLO 73 C5
  SRB 85 B6
Strážnice Nezárkou
  CZ 63 A5
Strážnice CZ 64 B3
Strážný CZ 63 B4
Stráž Pod Ralskem
  CZ 53 C4
Street GB 29 B5

Strehla D 52 B3
Strekov SK 65 C4
Strem A 73 A6
Stremska-Rača SRB . .85 B4
Strengberg A 63 B5
Strengelvåg N 112 D4
Strenči LV 7 C8
Strendene N 112 D5
Streoci KOS 85 D5
Stresa I 70 C3
Streufdorf D 51 C6
Strib DK 39 D2
Stříbro CZ 62 A3
Strichen GB 23 D6
Strigno I 71 B6
Strijen NL 49 B5
Strizivojna HR 74 C3
Strmica HR 83 B5
Strmilov CZ 63 A6
Ströhen D 43 C5
Strokestown IRL 18 C3
Stromberg
  Nordrhein-Westfalen
  D 50 B4
  Rheinland-Pfalz D . .60 A3
Stromeferry GB 22 D3
Strömnäs S 115 C14
Stromness GB 23 C5
Strömsberg S 36 B4
Strömsbruk S 115 F14
Strömsfors S 37 D3
Strömsnäsbruk S 40 C3
Strömstad S 35 D3
Strömsund
  Jämtland S 115 D12
  Västerbotten S . . .115 B13
Stronachlachar GB . . .24 B3
Strongoli I 107 B4
Stronie Śląskie PL . . .54 C1
Strontian GB 24 B2
Stroppiana I 70 C3
Stroud GB 29 B5
Stroumbi CY 120 B1
Stróża PL 65 A5
Strücklingen D 43 B4
Struer DK 38 C1
Struga MK 116 A2
Strugi Krasnyye RUS . .7 B10
Strumica MK 116 A4
Strumien PL 65 A4
Struy GB 22 D4
Stružec HR 74 C1
Stryków PL 55 B4
Stryn N 114 F3
Stryy UA 11 B7
Strzałkowo PL 54 A2
Strzegocin PL 47 C6
Strzegom PL 54 C1
Strzegowo PL 47 C6
Strzelce
  PL 55 A4
Strzelce Krajeńskie
  PL 46 C1
Strzelce Kurowo PL . .46 C1
Strzelce Opolskie PL . .54 C3
Strzelin PL 54 C2
Strzelno PL 47 C4
Strzepcz PL 47 A4
Strzybnica PL 54 C3
Strzygi PL 47 B5
Strzyżów PL 11 A7
Stubbekøbing DK 39 E5
Stuben A 71 A5
Stubline SRB 85 B5
Studená CZ 63 A6
Studenci HR 84 C2
Studénka CZ 64 A4
Studenzen A 73 B5
Studienka SK 64 B3
Studland GB 29 C6
Studley GB 29 A6
Studzienice PL 46 A3
Stuer D 44 B4
Stugudal N 114 E8
Stugun S 115 D12
Stuhr D 43 B5
Stukenbrock D 51 B4
Stülpe D 52 A3
Stupava SK 64 B3
Stupnik HR 73 C5
Stupsk PL 47 B6
Sturminster Newton
  GB 29 C5
Šturovo SK 65 C4
Sturton GB 27 B5
Stuttgart D 61 B5
Stvolny CZ 52 C3
Stykkishólmur IS 111 B3
Styri N 34 B3
Stysö S 38 B4
Suances E 88 A2
Subbiano I 81 C5
Subiaco I 102 B6
Subotica SRB 75 B4
Subotište SRB 85 B4
Sučany SK 65 A4
Suceava RO 11 C9
Sucha-Beskidzka PL . .65 A5
Suchacz PL 47 A5
Suchań PL 46 B1
Suchdol nad Lužnice
  CZ 63 B5
Suchedniów PL 55 B5
Suchteln D 50 B2
Sucina E 101 B5
Suckow D 44 B3
Sućuraj HR 84 C2
Súðavík IS 111 A3
Sudbury GB 30 B4
Suddesjaur S 115 B16
Suden G 43 A5
Süderbrarup D 44 A1
Süderlügum D 39 E1
Sudoměřice u Bechyně
  CZ 63 A5
Sudovec HR 73 B6
Sueca E 96 B2
Suelli I 110 C2
Sugenheim D 61 A6
Sugères F 68 C3
Sugny B 59 A5
Suhl D 51 C6
Suhlendorf D 44 C2
Suhopolje HR 74 C2
Suhut TR 119 D5
Suica BIH 84 C1
Suippes F 59 A5
Sukhinichi RUS 7 D13
Sukobin MNE 105 A5
Sukošan HR 83 B4
Sükösd H 75 B3
Suków PL 55 C5
Šuľa SK 65 B5
Sулина RO 11 D10
Sulechów PL 53 A5
Sulęcin PL 53 A5
Sulęczyno PL 46 A3
Sulejów PL 55 B4
Sulejówek PL 55 A6
Sülfeld D 44 B2
Sulibórz PL 46 B1
Sulina RO 11 D10
Sulingen D 43 C5
Suliszewo PL 46 B1
Sulitjelma N 112 E5
Sułkowice PL 65 A5
Süller TR 119 D4
Sully-sur-Loire F 58 C3
Sulmierzyce
  Łódzkie PL 55 B4
  Wielkopolskie PL . . .54 B2
Sulmona I 103 A6
Süloğlu TR 118 A1
Sułoszowa PL 55 C4

Sulów PL 54 B2
Sulsdorf D 44 A3
Sultandağı TR 119 D6
Sülüklü TR 118 D7
Suloova TR 16 A7
Sulvik S 35 C4
Sülysáp H 75 A4
Sülz D 61 B4
Sulzbach
 Baden-Württemberg
 D 61 B3
 Baden-Württemberg
 D 61 B5
 Bayern D 61 A5
 Saarland D 60 A3
Sulzbach-Rosenberg
 D 62 A2
Sülze D 44 C2
Sulzfeld D 51 C6
Sumartin HR 84 C1
Sumburgh GB 22 B7
Sümeg H 74 B2
Šumiskaÿ CH 70 A2
Šumná CZ 64 B1
Šumperk CZ 54 D1
Šumvald CZ 64 A3
Sumy UA 7 F13
Sunbilla E 76 C1
Sünching D 62 B3
Sund
 FIN 36 B7
 S 35 C3
Sundborn S 36 B2
Sundby DK 38 C1
Sunde N 32 C2
Sunde bru N 33 D6
Sunderland GB 25 D6
Sundern D 50 B4
Sundhultsbrunn S . .40 B4
Sundnäs S 115 A14
Sunds DK 39 C2
Sundsfjord N 112 F3
Sundsvall S 115 E14
Sungurlu TR 16 A7
Suni I 110 B1
Sunja HR 74 C1
Sunnansjö S 36 B1
Sunnaryd S 40 B3
Sunndalsøra N 114 E5
Sunne 34 C5
Sunnemo S 34 C5
Sunnersberg S 35 D5
Suolovuopmio N . .113 C12
Suomussalmi FIN . . .3 D28
Suoyarvi RUS 3 E10
Super Sauze F 79 B5
Supetar HR 83 C5
Supetarska Draga HR .83 B3
Šupino I 102 B6
Supilja Stijena MNE .84 C4
Surahammar S 37 C3
Šurany SK 64 B4
Surazh
 BY 7 D11
 RUS 7 E12
Surbo I 105 C4
Surčin SRB 85 B5
Surgères F 66 B4
Surhuisterveen NL . .42 B3
Súria E 91 B4
Surin F 67 B5
Surka N 34 B2
Surnadalsøra N . . .114 E5
Sursee CH 70 A3
Surte S 38 B5
Surwold D 43 C4
Sury-le-Comtal F . . .69 C4
Šuša I 70 C2
Šušice CZ 63 A4
Sušnjevica HR 73 C4
Sussen D 61 B5
Susurluk TR 118 C3
Susz PL 47 B5
Sütçüler TR 119 E5
Sutivan HR 83 C5
Sutjeska SRB 75 C5
Sutomore MNE . . .105 A5
Sutri I 102 A5
Sutton GB 31 C3
Sutton Coldfield GB .27 C4
Sutton-in-Ashfield
 GB 27 B4
Sutton-on-Sea GB . .27 B6
Sutton-on-Trent GB .27 B5
Sutton Scotney GB . .31 C2
Sutton Valence GB . .31 C4
Suvaja BIH 83 B5
Suvereto I 81 C4
Suvorov RUS 7 D14
Suwałki PL 6 D7
Suze-la-Rousse F . . .78 B3
Suzzara I 81 B4
Svabensverk S 36 A3
Svalbardö IS 111 A10
Svalöv S 41 D3
Svanabyn S 115 C13
Svanberga S 36 C5
Svaneke DK 41 D5
Svanesund N 35 D3
Svängsta S 41 C4
Svannäs S 115 A15
Svanskog S 35 C4
Svanstein S 113 F12
Svappavaara S . . .112 E10
Svärdsjö S 36 B2
Svarstad N 35 C1
Svartå S 37 C1
Svärta S 37 C4
Svartå S 34 C5
Svärtinge S 37 D3
Svartnäs S 36 B3
Svartnes N 112 C8
Svarttjärn S 115 B13
Svatsum N 34 A1
Svätý Jur SK 64 B3
Svätý Peter SK 64 C4
Svedala S 41 D3
Sveg S 115 E11
Sveindal N 33 D4
Sveio N 33 C2
Svejbæk DK 39 C2
Svelgen N 114 F2
Svelvik N 35 C2
Svendborg DK 39 D3
Svene N 32 C6
Svenljunga S 40 B3
Svennevad S 37 C2
Svenstavik S 115 E11
Švermov CZ 53 C4
Sveti Ivan Zabno HR .74 C1
Sveti Ivan Zelina HR .73 C6
Sveti Nikola MNE . .105 B5
Sveti Rok HR 83 B4
Sveti Stefan MNE . .105 A4
Světlá nad Sázavou
 CZ 63 A6
Svetlyy RUS 47 A6
Svetvinčenat HR . . .82 A2
Švica HR 83 B4
Svidník SK 10 B6
Švihov CZ 63 A4
Svilajnac SRB 85 B6
Svilengrad BG 11 F9
Svindal N 35 C3
Svinhult S 40 B5
Svinna SK 64 B4
Svinninge
 DK 39 D4
 S 37 C5
Sviritsa RUS 7 A12
Svishtov BG 11 E8
Svislasch BY 6 E8
Svit SK 65 A6
Svitavy CZ 64 A2
Svitlovodsk UA 11 B12
Svodin SK 65 C4
Svolvær N 112 D3

Svortemyr N 32 A1
Svortland N 32 C2
Svratka CZ 64 A2
Svrčinovec SK 65 A4
Svullrya N 34 B4
Svyetlahorsk BY 7 E10
Swadlincote GB 27 C4
Swaffham GB 30 B4
Swanage GB 29 C6
Swanley GB 31 C4
Swanlinbar IRL 19 B4
Swansea GB 28 B4
Swarzęz PL 46 C3
Swatragh GB 19 B5
Świątki PL 47 B6
Świdnica
 Dolnośląskie PL . . .54 C1
 Lubuskie PL 53 B5
Świdnik PL 11 A7
Świdwin PL 46 B1
Świebodzice PL 53 C6
Świebodzin PL 53 A5
Świecie PL 47 B4
Świedziebnia PL . . .47 B5
Świerki PL 54 C1
Świerzawa PL 53 B5
Świerzno PL 45 B6
Święta Anna PL 55 C4
Święta PL 53 A6
Świętno PL 53 A6
Swiefterbant NL 42 C2
Swindon GB 29 B6
Swineshead GB 30 B3
Swinford IRL 18 C3
Świnoujście PL 45 B6
Swinton GB 25 C5
Swobnica PL 45 B6
Swords IRL 21 A5
Swornegacie PL 46 B3
Sya S 37 D2
Syasstroy RUS 7 A12
Sycewice PL 46 A2
Sychevka RUS 7 D13
Sycow PL 54 B2
Sycowice PL 53 A5
Sydnes N 33 C2
Syfteland N 32 B2
Syke D 43 C5
Sykkylven N 114 E3
Sylling N 34 C2
Sylte N 114 E4
Symbister GB 22 A7
Symington GB 25 C4
Symonds Yat GB . . .29 B5
Sypniewo
 Kujawsko-Pomorskie
 PL 46 B3
 Wielkopolskie PL . .46 B2
Syserum S 40 B6
Sysslebäck S 34 B4
Syväjärvi FIN 113 E14
Szabadbattyán H . . .74 A3
Szabadegyháza H . . .74 A3
Szabadszállás H . . .75 B4
Szadek PL 54 B3
Szajol H 75 A5
Szakály H 74 B3
Szakcs H 74 B3
Szakmár H 75 B4
Szalánta H 74 C3
Szałas PL 55 B5
Szalonna H 65 B6
Szamocin PL 46 B3
Szamotuły PL 46 C2
Szany H 74 A2
Szarvas H 75 B5
Szarvaskö H 65 C6
Szászvár H 74 B3
Százhalombatta H . .74 A3
Szczawa PL 65 A6
Szczawnica PL 65 A6
Szczecin PL 45 B6
Szczecinek PL 46 B2
Szczekociny PL 55 C4
Szczerców PL 55 B4
Szczucin PL 55 C6
Szczuczarz PL 46 B2
Szczurkowo PL 47 A6
Szczyrk PL 65 A5
Szczytna PL 54 C1
Szczytno PL 6 E6
Szczyty PL 54 B3
Szécsény H 65 B5
Szederkény H 74 C3
Szedres H 74 B3
Szeged H 75 B5
Szeghalom H 75 A6
Szegvár H 75 B5
Székesfehérvár H . . .74 A3
Székkutas H 75 B5
Szekszárd H 74 B3
Szemplino Czarne PL .47 B6
Szemud PL 47 A4
Szendehely H 65 C5
Szendrö H 65 B6
Szentendre H 65 C5
Szentes H 75 B5
Szentgotthárd H . . .73 B6
Szentlászló H 74 B2
Szentlörinc H 74 B2
Szentmártonkáta H . .75 A4
Szenyér H 74 B2
Szeremle H 74 B3
Szerencs H 65 B6
Szerep H 75 A6
Szigetszentmiklós H .75 A4
Szigetvár H 74 B2
Szikáncs H 75 B5
Szikszó H 65 B6
Szil H 74 A2
Szilvásvárad H 65 B6
Szklarska Poreba PL .53 C5
Szlichtyngowa PL . . .53 B6
Szob H 65 C4
Szolnok H 75 A5
Szombathely H 74 A1
Szorosad H 74 B3
Szprotawa PL 53 B5
Szreńsk PL 47 B6
Sztum PL 47 B5
Sztutowo PL 47 A5
Szubin PL 46 B3
Szücsi H 65 C5
Szulmierz PL 47 B6
Szulok H 74 B2
Szumanie PL 47 C5
Szwecja PL 46 B2
Szydłów
 Łódzkie PL 55 B5
 Świętokrzyskie PL . .55 C6
Szydłowiec PL 55 B5
Szydlowo PL 47 B6
Szydłowo PL 46 B2
Szymanów PL 55 A5
Szynkielów PL 54 B3
Szynwald PL 55 D6

T

Taastrup DK 41 D2
Tab H 74 B3
Tabanera la Luenga E .94 A2
Tabaqueros E 96 B1
Tábara E 88 C1
TabaS S 40 B4
Tabernas E 101 B4
Tabiano Bagni I 81 B4
Taboada E 86 B3
Taboadela E 87 B3
Tábor CZ 63 A5
Táborfalva H 75 A4
Taborište HR 73 C6
Tábua P 92 A2
Tabuaco P 87 C3
Tabuenca E 89 C5
Tabuyo del Monte E .87 B4

Tác H 74 A3
Tachov CZ 62 A3
Tadcaster GB 27 B4
Tadley GB 31 C2
Tafalla E 89 B5
Tafjord N 114 E4
Taganheira P 98 B2
Tågarp S 41 D2
Tággia I 80 C1
Tagliacozzo I 102 A6
Táglio di Po I 82 A1
Tagnon F 59 A5
Tahal E 101 B3
Tahitótfalu H 65 C5
Tahtaköprü TR 118 C4
Tahtaslü TR 118 C4
Tailfingen D 61 B5
Taillis F 57 B4
Tain GB 23 D4
Tain-l'Hermitage F . .78 A3
Taipadas P 92 C2
Taivalkoski FIN 3 D28
Takene S 35 C5
Takovo SRB 85 B5
Taksony H 75 A4
Tal E 86 B2
Talachyn BY 7 D10
Talamello I 82 C1
Talamone I 102 A4
Talant F 69 A4
Talarrubias E 93 B5
Talavera de la Reina
 E 94 C2
Talavera la Real E . .93 C4
Talayuela E 93 B5
Talayuelas E 96 B1
Talgarth GB 29 B4
Talgje N 33 C2
Talhadas P 92 A2
Táliga E 93 C3
Talizat F 78 A2
Tálknafjörður IS . . .111 B2
Talla I 81 C5
Talladale GB 22 D3
Tallaght IRL 21 A5
Tallard F 79 B4
Tällberg S 36 B1
Tallinn EST 6 B8
Talloires F 69 C6
Tallow IRL 21 B4
Talsjö S 115 C15
Talmay F 69 A5
Talmont-St Hilaire F .66 B3
Talmont-sur-Gironde
 F 66 C4
Talne UA 11 B11
Talsano I 104 C3
Talsi LV 6 C7
Talvik N 113 B11
Talybont GB 26 C2
Tal-Y-Llyn GB 26 C2
Tamajón E 95 B3
Tamame E 88 C1
Tamames E 93 A4
Tamarit de Mar E . . .91 B4
Tamarite de Litera E .90 B3
Tamarîu E 91 B6
Tamási H 74 B3
Tambach-Dietharz D .51 C6
Tameza E 86 A4
Tammisaari FIN 6 A7
Tampere FIN 3 F25
Tamsweg A 72 A3
Tamurejo E 94 D2
Tamworth GB 27 C4
Tana bru N 113 B17
Tañabueyes E 89 B3
Tanakajd H 74 A1
Tananger N 33 D2
Tananulla I 110 B2
Tancarville F 58 A1
Tandsjöborg S 115 F11
Tanga S 41 C2
Tangelic H 74 B3
Tangen N 34 B3
Tangerhütte D 44 C3
Tangermünde D 44 C3
Tanhua FIN 113 E16
Taninges F 69 B6
Tankavaara FIN . . .113 D16
Tann D 51 C6
Tanna D 52 C1
Tannadice GB 25 B5
Tännäs S 115 E9
Tannåker S 40 C3
Tannay
 Ardennes F 59 A5
 Nièvre F 68 A3
Tannenbergsthal D . .52 C2
Tännesberg D 62 A3
Tannheim A 71 A5
Tanowo PL 45 B6
Tanus F 77 B5
Tanvald CZ 53 C5
Taormina I 109 B4
Tapa EST 6 B8
Tapfheim D 62 B1
Tapia de Casariego E .86 A4
Tapio F 77 C4
Tápióbicske H 75 A4
Tápiógyörgye H 75 A4
Tápióság H 75 A4
Tápiószecső H 75 A4
Tápiószele H 75 A4
Tápiószentmárton H .75 A4
Tapolca H 74 B2
Tapolcafö H 74 A2
Tara HR 72 C3
Tarabo S 40 B2
Taradell E 91 B5
Taramundi E 86 A3
Tarancón E 95 B3
Táranto I 104 C3
Tarare F 69 C4
Tarascon F 78 C3
Tarascon-sur-Ariège
 F 77 D4
Tarashcha UA 11 B11
Tarazona E 89 C5
Tarazona de la Mancha
 E 95 C5
Tarbena E 96 C2
Tarbert
 IRL 20 B2
 GB 24 C2
Tarbes F 76 C3
Tarbet GB 24 B3
Tarbolton GB 24 C3
Tarcento I 72 B3
Tarčin BIH 84 C3
Tarczyn PL 55 B5
Tardajos E 88 B3
Tardelcuende E 89 C4
Tardets-Sorholus F . .76 C2
Tardienta E 90 B2
Tärendö S 113 E11
Targon F 76 B2
Târgovişte RO 11 D8
Târgu-Jiu RO 11 D7
Târgu Mureş RO . . .11 C8
Târgu Ocna RO 11 C9
Târgu Secuiesc RO . .11 D9
Tarifa E 99 C5
Tariquejas E 98 B3
Tarján H 65 C4
Tårnby DK 41 D2
Tarnobrzeg PL 55 C6

Tarnos F 76 C1
Tarnów
 Lubuskie PL 45 C6
 Małopolskie PL 55 D5
Tarnowo Podgórne
 PL 46 C2
Tarnowskie Góry PL . .54 C3
Tärnsjö S 36 B3
Tårnvik N 112 E4
Tarp D 43 A6
Tarquinia I 102 A4
Tarquinia Lido I . . .102 A4
Tarragona E 91 B4
Tàrrega E 91 B4
Tarrenz A 71 A5
Tårs
 Nordjyllands DK . . .38 B3
 Storstrøms DK 39 E4
Tarsia I 106 B3
Tarsus TR 16 C7
Tartas F 76 C2
Tartu EST 7 B9
Tarussa RUS 7 D14
Tarves GB 23 D6
Tarvisio I 72 B3
Taşağıl TR 119 F6
Täsch CH 70 B2
Taşköprü TR 16 A7
Tasov CZ 64 A2
Tasovčići BIH 84 C2
Taşucuo TR 16 C6
Tát H 65 C4
Tata H 65 C4
Tatabánya H 74 A3
Tataháza H 75 B4
Tatarbunary UA . . .11 D10
Tatárszentgyörgy H .75 A4
Tatranská-Lomnica
 SK 65 A6
Tau N 33 C2
Tauberbischofsheim
 D 61 A5
Taucha D 52 B2
Tauerchen F 60 A2
Teterow D 45 B4
Taufkirchen D 62 B3
Taufkirchen an der Pram
 A 63 B4
Taulé F 56 B2
Taulignan F 78 B3
Taulov DK 39 D2
Taunton GB 29 B4
Taunusstein D 50 C4
Tauragé LT 6 D7
Taurianova I 106 C3
Taurisano I 107 B5
Tauste E 90 B1
Tauves F 68 C2
Tavankut SRB 75 B4
Tavannes CH 70 A2
Tavarnelle val di Pesa
 I 81 C5
Tavas TR 119 E4
Tavaux F 69 A5
Tävelsås S 40 C4
Taverna I 106 B3
Taverne CH 70 B3
Tavernelle I 82 C1
Tavernes de la Valldigna
 E 96 B2
Tavérnola Bergamasca
 I 71 C5
Taverny F 58 A3
Tavescan E 91 A4
Taviano I 107 B5
Tavira P 98 B3
Tavistock GB 28 C3
Tavnik SRB 85 C5
Tavşanli TR 118 C4
Tayinloan GB 24 C2
Taynuilt GB 24 B2
Tayport GB 25 B5
Tázlár H 75 B4
Tazones E 88 A1
Tczew PL 47 A4
Tczów PL 55 B6
Teangue GB 22 D3
Teano I 103 B7
Teba E 100 C1
Tebay GB 26 A3
Techendorf A 72 B3
Tecklenburg D 50 A3
Tecko-matorp S 41 D3
Tecuci RO 11 D9
Tefenni TR 119 E4
Tegelsmora S 36 B4
Tegernsee D 62 C2
Teggiano I 104 C1
Tegoleto I 81 C5
Teichel D 52 C1
Teignmouth GB 29 C4
Teillay F 57 C4
Teillet F 77 C5
Teisendorf D 62 C3
Teistungen D 51 B6
Teixeiro E 86 A2
Tejada de Tiétar E . .93 A5
Tejado E 89 C4
Tejares E 94 B1
Tejn DK 41 D4
Teke TR 118 A4
Tekirdağ TR 118 B2
Tekovské-Lužany SK .65 B4
Telavåg N 32 B1
Telč CZ 63 A6
Telese Terme I 103 B7
Telford GB 26 C3
Telgárt SK 65 B5
Telgte D 50 B3
Tellingstedt D 43 A6
Telšiai LT 6 D7
Telti I 110 B2
Teltow D 45 C5
Tembleque E 95 C3
Temelin CZ 63 A5
Temerin SRB 75 C5
Temiño E 89 B3
Témpio Pausánia I . .110 B2
Templederry IRL . . .20 B3
Templemore IRL . . .21 B4
Temple Sowerby GB .26 A3
Templin D 45 B5
Temse B 49 B5
Tenay F 69 C5
Ten Boer NL 42 B3
Tenbury Wells GB . . .29 A5
Tenby GB 28 B3
Tende F 80 B1
Tende F 80 B1
Tenhult S 40 B4
Tenja HR 74 C3
Tenneville B 49 C6
Tennevoll N 112 D6
Tensta S 36 B4
Tenterden GB 31 C4
Teo E 86 B2
Teora I 103 C8
Tepasto FIN 113 E13
Teplá CZ 52 D2
Teplice CZ 53 C3
Teplička nad Váhom
 SK 65 A4
Tepsa FIN 113 E14
Ter Apel NL 43 C4
Terborg NL 50 B2
Terchová SK 65 A5
Terebovlya UA 11 B8
Teremia Mare RO . . .75 C5
Terena P 92 C3
Teresa de Cofrentes
 E 96 B1
Terešov CZ 63 A4
Terezín CZ 53 C4
Terezino Polje HR . .74 C2
Tergnier F 59 A4
Teriberka RUS 3 B31
Terlizzi I 104 B2
Termas de Monfortinho
 P 93 A4

Terme di Súio I 103 B6
Terme di Valdieri I . .79 B6
Termens E 90 B3
Termes F 78 B2
Términi Imerese I . .108 B2
Terminillo I 102 A5
Termoli I 103 B7
Termonfeckin IRL . . .19 C5
Ternberg A 63 C5
Terndrup DK 38 C3
Terneuzen NL 49 B4
Terni I 102 A5
Ternitz A 64 C2
Ternopil UA 11 B8
Terpni GR 116 B5
Terracina I 102 B6
Terråk N 115 B9
Terralba I 110 C1
Terranova di Pollino
 I 106 B3
Terranova di Sibari I .106 B3
Terras do Bouro P . .87 C2
Terrasini I 108 A2
Terrassa E 91 B5
Terrasson-Lavilledieu
 F 77 A4
Terrazos E 89 B3
Terriente E 95 B5
Terrugem P 92 C3
Tertenia I 110 C2
Teruel E 90 C1
Tervola FIN 3 D26
Tervuren B 49 C5
Terzaga E 95 B5
Tešanj BIH 84 B2
Teséani-Mlyňany SK .65 B4
Teslić BIH 84 B2
Tessin D 44 A4
Tessy-sur-Vire F 57 B4
Tét H 74 A2
Tetbury GB 29 B5
Teterchen F 60 A2
Teterow D 45 B4
Teteven BG 11 E8
Tetiyev UA 11 B10
Tetovo MK 10 E6
Tettau D 52 C1
Tettnang D 61 C5
Teublitz D 62 A3
Teuchern D 52 B2
Teulada
 E 96 C3
 I 110 D1
Teupitz D 45 C5
Teurajärvi S 113 F11
Teutschenthal D . . .52 B1
Tevel H 74 B3
Teviothead GB 25 C5
Tewkesbury GB 29 B5
Thale D 52 B1
Thalfang D 60 A2
Thalgau A 63 C4
Thalkirch CH 71 B4
Thalmässing D 62 A2
Thalwil CH 70 A3
Thame GB 31 C3
Thann F 60 C3
Thannhausen D 61 B6
Thaon-les-Vosges F .60 B2
Tharandt D 53 C3
Tharsis E 99 B3
Thasos GR 116 B6
Thatcham GB 31 C2
Thaxted GB 31 C4
Thayngen CH 61 C4
Theale GB 31 C2
The Barony GB 23 B5
Thebes = Thiva GR .117 D5
Theding-hausen D . .43 C6
Theessen D 52 A2
The Hague = 's-
 Gravenhage NL . . .49 A5
Themar D 51 C6
The Mumbles GB . . .28 B4
Thénezay F 67 B4
Thenon F 67 C6
Therouanne F 48 C3
Thessaloniki = Salonica
 GR 116 B4
Thetford GB 30 B4
Theth AL 105 A5
Theux B 49 C6
Thézar-les-Corbières
 F 78 C1
Thèze F 76 C2
Thiberville F 58 A1
Thibie F 59 B5
Thiéblemont-Farémont
 F 59 B5
Thiendorf D 53 B3
Thiene I 71 C6
Thierrens CH 70 B1
Thiers F 68 C3
Thiesi I 110 B1
Thiessow D 45 A5
Thiezac F 77 B5
Thimister B 80 A2
Thionville F 60 A2
Thira GR 117 F7
Thiron-Gardais F . . .58 B1
Thirsk GB 27 A4
Thiva = Thebes GR .117 D5
Thivars F 58 B2
Thiviers F 67 C5
Thizy F 69 B4
Tholen NL 49 B5
Tholey D 60 A3
Thomas Street IRL . .20 A3
Thomastown IRL . . .21 B4
Thônes F 69 C6
Thonnance-les-Joinville
 F 59 B6
Thonon-les-Bains F .69 B6
Thorame-Basse F . . .79 B5
Thorame-Haute F . . .79 B5
Thorens-Glières F . .69 C6
Thorigny-sur-Oreuse
 F 59 B4
Thörl A 73 A5
Þorlákshöfn IS 111 D4
Thornaby on Tees GB .27 A4
Thornbury GB 29 B5
Thorne GB 27 B5
Thornhill
 Dumfries & Galloway
 GB 25 C4
 Stirling GB 24 B3
Thornthwaite GB . . .26 A2
Thornton-le-Dale GB .27 A5
Þórshöfn IS 111 A10
Thouarcé F 67 A4
Thouars F 67 B4
Thrapston GB 30 B3
Threlkeld GB 26 A2
Thrumster GB 23 C5
Thueyts F 78 B3
Thuin B 49 C5
Thuir F 91 A5
Thumau D 52 C1
Thun CH 70 B2
Thuret F 68 C3
Thurey F 69 B5
Thüringen A 71 A4
Thurins F 69 C4
Thürkow D 44 B4
Thurles IRL 21 B4
Thurmaston GB 30 B2
Thurø By DK 39 D3
Thursby GB 25 D4
Thurso GB 23 C5
Thury-Harcourt F . . .57 B5
Thusis CH 71 B4
Thyborøn DK 38 C1
Þykkvibær IS 111 D5
Thyregod DK 39 D2
Tibi E 96 C2
Tibro S 35 D6
Tidaholm S 35 D5
Tidan S 35 D6

Tidersrum S 40 B5
Tiedra E 88 C1
Tiefenbach D 62 A3
Tiefencastel CH 71 B4
Tiefenort D 51 C6
Tiefensee D 45 C5
Tiel NL 49 B6
Tielmes E 95 B3
Tielt B 49 B4
Tienen B 49 C5
Tiengen D 61 C4
Tiercé F 57 C5
Tierga E 89 C5
Tiermas E 90 A1
Tiranë N 115 B9
Tierp S 36 B4
Tierrantona E 90 A3
Tighina MD 11 C10
Tighnabruaich GB . .24 C2
Tignes F 70 C1
Tigy F 58 C3
Tihany H 74 B2
Tijnje NL 42 B2
Tijola E 101 B3
Tikhvin RUS 7 B12
Tilberg S 37 C3
Tillac F 76 C3
Tilley B 49 C5
Tilloy Bellay F 59 A5
Tilly F 67 B6
Tilly-sur-Seulles F . .57 A5
Tim DK 39 C1
Timau I 72 B3
Timbaki GR 117 G6
Timişoara RO 75 C6
Timmele S 40 B3
Timmendorfer Strand
 D 44 B2
Timmernabben S . . .40 C6
Timmersdala S 35 D5
Timoleague IRL 20 C3
Timolin IRL 21 B5
Timrå S 115 E14
Timsfors S 40 C3
Timsgearraidh GB . .22 C1
Tinajas E 95 B4
Tinalhas P 92 B3
Tinchebray F 57 B5
Tincques F 48 C3
Tineo E 86 A4
Tinglev DK 39 E2
Tingsryd S 40 C4
Tingstäde S 37 E5
Tingvoll N 114 E5
Tinlot B 49 C6
Tinnoset N 33 C6
Tinos GR 117 E7
Tintagel GB 28 C3
Tinténiac F 57 B4
Tintern GB 29 B5
Tintigny B 60 A1
Tione di Trento I 71 B5
Tipperary IRL 20 B3
Tiptree GB 31 C4
Tirana = Tiranë AL . .105 B5
Tiranë = Tirana AL . .105 B5
Tirano I 71 B5
Tiraspol MD 11 C10
Tire TR 119 D2
Tirig E 90 C3
Tiriolo I 106 C3
Tirmavos GR 116 C4
Tirrénia I 81 C4
Tirschenreuth D 62 A3
Tirstrup DK 39 C3
Tirteafuera E 100 A1
Tisno HR 83 C4
Tišnov CZ 64 A2
Tisovec SK 65 B5
Tistedal N 35 C3
Tistelskog S 35 D4
Tistrup DK 39 D1
Tiszabö H 75 A5
Tiszabura H 75 A5
Tiszacsege H 75 A5
Tiszadorogma H 65 C6
Tiszaföldvár H 75 A5
Tiszafüred H 65 C6
Tiszajenő H 75 A5
Tiszakécske H 75 A5
Tiszakürt H 75 A5
Tiszalök H 75 A5
Tiszalúc H 65 B6
Tiszanána H 75 A5
Tiszaörs H 75 A5
Tiszaroff H 75 A5
Tiszasüly H 75 A5
Tiszasziget H 75 B5
Tiszaszőlős H 75 A5
Tiszaújváros H 113 E13
Tiszavasvári H 11 C9
Titaguas E 96 B1
Titel SRB 75 C5
Titisee-Neustadt D . .61 B4
Tito I 104 C1
Titova Korenica HR . .83 B4
Titran N 114 D5
Tittling D 63 B4
Tittmoning D 62 B3
Titz D 50 B2
Tiurajärvi FIN 113 E13
Tivat MNE 105 A4
Tived S 37 D1
Tiverton GB 29 C4
Tivisa E 90 B3
Tívoli I 102 B5
Tjåmotis S 112 F9
Tjæreborg DK 39 D1
Tjautjas S 112 E9
Tjeldstø N 32 B1
Tjentište BIH 84 C3
Tjöck FIN 3 E25
Tjøme N 35 C2
Tjong N 112 F2
Tjonnefoss N 33 D5
Tjörn IS 111 B5
Tjörnarp S 41 D3
Tjøtta N 115 B9
Tjurkö S 41 C5
Tjust S 40 C6
Tlmače SK 65 B4
Tłuchowo PL 47 C5
Tłumačov CZ 64 A3
Tłuszcz PL 55 A6
Tobarra E 101 A4
Tobercurry IRL 18 B3
Tobermore GB 19 B5
Tobermory GB 24 B1
Toberonochy GB . . .24 B2
Tobha Mor GB 22 D1
Tobo S 36 B4
Tocane-St Apre F . . .67 C5
Tocha P 92 A2
Tocina E 99 B5
Töcksfors S 35 C3
Tocón E 100 B2
Todai LV 114 C8
Todi I 102 A5
Todorici BIH 84 B2
Todtmoos D 61 C4
Todtnau D 60 C3
Toén E 87 B3
Tofta
 Gotland S 37 E5
 Skaraborg S 35 D5
Toftbyn S 36 B2
Tófte N 35 C2
Tófu I 74 B3
Töftedal S 35 D3
Tóftir FO 4 A3
Töftöl H 74 B3
Tohmo FIN 113 F16
Tokachi bho Thuath
 GB 22 C2
Tokaj H 65 B6
Tokod H 65 C4
Tököl H 75 A4
Tolastadh bho Thuath
 GB 22 C2
Tolcsva H 65 B6
Toldaos E 86 B3
Toledo E 94 C2

Tolentino I 82 C2
Tolfa I 102 A4
Tolg S 40 B4
Tolga N 114 E8
Tolkmicko PL 47 A5
Tolko PL 47 A6
Tollarp S 41 D3
Tølløse DK 39 D4
Tolmachevo RUS 7 B10
Tolmezzo I 72 B3
Tolmin SLO 72 B3
Tolna H 74 B3
Tolob GB 22 B7
Tolosa
 E 89 A4
 P 92 B3
Tolox E 100 C1
Tolva FIN 113 F17
Tolve I 104 C2
Tomar P 92 B2
Tomarza TR 16 B7
Tomaševac SRB 75 C5
Tomašica BIH 83 B5
Tomášikovo SK 64 B3
Tomašouka BY 6 F7
Tomaszów Mazowiecki
 PL 55 B5
Tombeboeuf F 77 B3
Tomdoun GB 22 D3
Tomelilla S 41 D3
Tomellosa E 95 B4
Tomelloso E 95 C3
Tomiño E 87 C2
Tomintoul GB 23 D5
Tomislavgrad BIH . . .84 C2
Tomisław PL 53 B5
Tomislawice PL 47 C4
Tomnavoulin GB . . .23 D5
Tompa H 75 B4
Tomra N 114 E3
Tomter N 35 C2
Tona E 91 B5
Tonara I 110 B2
Tonbridge GB 31 C4
Tondela P 92 A2
Tønder DK 39 E1
Tongeren B 49 C6
Tongue GB 23 C4
Tönisvorst D 50 B2
Tønjum N 32 A4
Tonkopuro FIN 113 F17
Tonnay-Boutonne F .67 C4
Tonnay-Charente F . .66 C4
Tonneins F 77 B3
Tonnerre F 59 C4
Tönning D 43 A5
Tonsåsen N 32 B6
Tønsberg N 35 C2
Tonstad N 33 D3
Toomyvara IRL 20 B3
Toormore IRL 20 C2
Topares E 101 B3
Topas E 94 A1
Töpchin D 45 C5
Topczewo PL 11 C8
Topola SRB 85 B5
Topólcani MK 116 A3
Topol'čany SK 64 B4
Topol'čianky SK 65 B4
Topolje HR 73 C6
Topólia GR 117 G5
Topolovac HR 74 C1
Topólniky SK 64 C3
Toponár H 74 B2
Toporów PL 53 A5
Topsham GB 29 C4
Topusko HR 73 C5
Toques E 86 B3
Torà E 91 B4
Toral de los Guzmanes
 E 88 B1
Toral de los Vados E .86 B4
Torbalı TR 119 D2
Torbjörntorp S 35 D5
Torbole I 71 C5
Torchiarolo I 105 C4
Torcross GB 29 C4
Torcy-le-Petit F 58 A2
Torda SRB 75 C5
Tørdal N 33 C5
Tordehumos E 88 C1
Tordera E 91 B5
Tordesillas E 88 C1
Tordesilos E 95 B5
Töreboda S 35 D6
Toreby DK 39 E4
Torekov S 41 C2
Torella dei Lombardi
 I 103 C8
Torello E 91 A5
Toreno E 86 B4
Torfou F 66 A3
Torgau D 52 B3
Torgelow D 45 B6
Torgueda P 87 C3
Torhamn S 41 C5
Torhop N 113 B16
Torhout B 48 B4
Torigni-sur-Vire F . . .57 A5
Torija E 95 B3
Toril E 96 A1
Torino = Turin I 80 A1
Toritto I 104 C2
Torkovichi RUS 7 B11
Torla E 90 A2
Tormac RO 75 C6
Törmänen FIN 113 D16
Törmänmäki FIN 3 D27
Tornada P 92 B1
Tornal'a SK 65 B5
Tornavacas E 93 A5
Tornby DK 38 B2
Tornesch D 43 B6
Torness GB 23 D4
Torniella I 81 C5
Tornimparte I 103 A6
Tornio FIN 3 D26
Tornjoš SRB 75 C5
Tornos E 90 C1
Toro E 88 C1
Törökszentmiklós H .75 A5
Toropets RUS 7 C11
Torpa S 40 C3
Torpè I 110 B2
Torphins GB 23 D6
Torpo N 32 B5
Torpoint GB 28 C3
Torpsbruk S 40 B4
Torquay GB 29 C4
Torquemada E 88 B2
Torralba E 95 B4
Torralba de Burgo E .89 C4
Torralba de Calatrava
 E 94 C3
Torrão P 92 C2
Torre Annunziata I . .103 C7
Torreblacos E 89 C4
Torreblanca E 90 C3
Torreblascopedro E . .100 A2
Torrecaballeros E . . .94 A2
Torrecampo E 100 A1
Torre Canne I 104 C3
Torre Cardela E 100 B2
Torrecilla E 95 B4
Torrecilla de la Jara
 E 94 C2
Torrecilla de la Orden
 E 94 A1
Torrecilla del Pinar E .88 C2
Torrecilla en Cameros
 E 89 B4
Torrecillas de la Tiesa
 E 93 B5
Torre das Vargens P .92 B3
Torre de Coelheiros
 P 92 C3

Torre de Dom Chama
 P 87 C3
Torre de Juan Abad
 E 100 A2
Torre de la Higuera E .99 B4
Torre del Bierzo E . .86 B4
Torre del Burgo E . . .95 B3
Torre del Campo E . .100 B2
Torre del Greco I . .103 C7
Torre del Lago Puccini
 I 81 C4
Torre dell'Orso I . . .105 C4
Torre de Miguel Sesmero
 E 93 C4
Torre de Moncorvo P .87 C3
Torre de Santa Maria
 E 93 B4
Torredembarra E . . .91 B4
Torredonjimeno E . .100 B2
Torre Faro I 109 A4
Torregrosa E 90 B3
Torreira P 87 D2
Torrejoncillo E 93 B4
Torrejón de Ardoz E .95 B3
Torrejón de la Calzada
 E 94 B3
Torrejón del Rey E . .95 B3
Torrejón el Rubio E . .93 B4
Torrelaguna E 95 B3
Torrelapaja E 89 C5
Torre la Ribera E . . .90 A3
Torrelavega E 88 A2
Torrelobatón E 88 C1
Torrelodones E 94 B3
Torre los Negros E . .90 C1
Torremaggiore I . . .103 B8
Torremanzanas E . . .96 C2
Torremayor E 93 C4
Torremezzo di Falconara
 I 106 B3
Torremocha E 93 B4
Torremolinos E 100 C1
Torrenieri I 81 C5
Torrenostra E 90 C3
Torrenova I 109 A3
Torrente E 96 B2
Torrenueva
 Ciudad Real E . . .100 A2
 Granada E 100 C2
Torreorgaz E 93 B4
Torre Orsáia I 104 C1
Torre-Pacheco E . . .101 B5
Torre Péllice I 79 B6
Torreperogil E 100 A2
Torres E 100 B2
Torres Novas P 92 B2
Torres Vedras P 92 B1
Torrevieja E 101 B5
Torricella I 104 C3
Torri del Benaco I . .71 C5
Torridon GB 22 D3
Torriglia I 80 B3
Torrijos E 94 C2
Torrita di Siena I 81 C5
Torroal P 92 C2
Torroella de Montgrí
 E 91 A6
Torrox E 100 C2
Torrskog S 35 C4
Torsåker S 36 B3
Torsang S 36 B2
Torsás S 41 C5
Torsby S 34 B5
Torsetra N 37 C3
Torshälla S 37 C3
Tórshavn FO 4 A3
Torslanda S 38 B4
Torsminde DK 39 C1
Torsnes N 32 B2
Törtel H 75 A4
Tórtola E 95 B4
Tórtoles de Esgueva
 E 88 C2
Tortol ì I 110 C2
Tortona I 80 B3
Tórtora I 106 B2
Tortoreto Lido I 103 A6
Tortorici I 109 A3
Tortosa E 90 C3
Tortosendo P 92 A3
Tortuera E 95 B5
Tortuna S 37 C3
Toruń PL 47 B4
Torup S 40 C3
Tor Vaìanica I 102 B5
Torver GB 26 A2
Tørvikbygde N 32 B3
Torviscón E 100 C2
Torzhok RUS 7 C13
Tosbotn N 115 B9
Toscolano-Maderno I .71 C5
Tosno RUS 7 B11
Tossa de Mar E 91 B5
Tossåsen S 115 E10
Tosse F 76 C1
Tösse S 35 D4
Tossicia I 103 A6
Tostedt D 43 B6
Tosya TR 16 A7
Tószeg H 75 A5
Toszek PL 54 C3
Totana E 101 B4
Totebo S 40 B6
Tôtes F 58 A2
Tótkomlós H 75 B5
Totland N 114 F2
Totnes GB 29 C4
Totouça P 92 B3
Toucy F 59 C4
Toul F 60 B1
Toulon F 79 C4
Toulon-sur-Allier F . .68 B3
Toulon-sur-Arroux F .69 B4
Toulouse F 77 C4
Tourcoing F 49 C4
Tour de la Parata F .102 B1
Tourlaville F 57 A4
Tournai B 49 C4
Tournan-en-Brie F . .58 B3
Tournay F 76 C3
Tournon-d'Agenais F .77 B3
Tournon-St Martin F .67 B5
Tournon-sur-Rhône
 F 78 A3
Tournus F 69 B4
Touro
 E 86 B2
 P 87 C3
Tourouvre F 58 B1
Tourriers F 67 C5
Tourteron F 59 A5
Tourves F 79 C4
Tourville-sur-Sienne
 F 57 A4
Toury F 58 B2
Touvedo P 87 C2
Touzim CZ 52 C2
Tovačov CZ 64 A3
Tovariševo SRB 75 C4
Tovarnik HR 75 C4
Tovdal N 33 D5
Tövsala FIN 36 B7
Towcester GB 30 B2
Town Yetholm GB . .25 C5

Tråastølen N 32 B4
Trabada E 86 A3
Trabadelo E 86 B4
Trabanca E 87 C4
Trabazos E 87 C4
Traben-Trarbach D . . .50 D3
Trabia I 108 B2
Tradate I 70 C3
Trädet S 40 B3
Trafaria P 92 C1
Tragacete E 95 B5
Tragwein A 63 B5
Traiguera E 90 C3
Trainel F 59 B4
Traisen A 63 B6
Traismauer A 64 B1
Traitsching D 62 A3
Trákhonas CY 120 A2
Tralee IRL 20 B2
Tramacastilla de Tena
  E 76 D2
Tramagal P 92 B2
Tramariglio I 110 B1
Tramatza I 110 B1
Tramelan CH 70 A2
Tramonti di Sopra I . . .72 B2
Tramore IRL 21 B4
Trampot F 60 B1
Trana I 80 A1
Tranås S 40 A4
Tranbjerg DK 39 C3
Tranby N 34 C2
Trancoso P 87 D3
Tranebjerg DK 39 D4
Tranekær DK 39 E3
Tranemo S 40 B3
Tranent GB 25 C5
Tranevåg N 33 D3
Trängslet S 34 A5
Tranhult S 40 B3
Trani I 104 B2
Trans-en-Provence F . .79 C5
Transtrand S 34 A5
Tranum DK 38 B2
Tranvik S 37 C5
Trapani I 108 A1
Trappes F 58 B3
Traryd S 40 C3
Trasacco I 103 B6
Trasierra E 99 A4
Träslövsläge S 40 B2
Trasmiras E 87 B3
Traspinedo E 88 C2
Trate SLO 73 B5
Trauchgau D 62 C1
Traun A 63 B5
Traunreut D 62 C3
Traunstein D 62 C3
Traunwalchen D 62 C3
Trávad S 35 D5
Travemünde D 44 B2
Traversétolo I 81 B4
Travnik
  BIH 84 B2
  SLO 73 C4
Travo
  F 102 B2
  I 80 B3
Trawsfynydd GB 26 C2
Trbovlje SLO 73 B5
Trbušani SRB 85 C5
Treban F 68 B3
Třebařov CZ 64 A2
Trebatsch D 53 A4
Trebbin D 52 A3
Třebechovice pod
  Orebem CZ 53 C5
Trebel D 44 C3
Třebenice CZ 53 C3
Trébeurden F 56 B2
Třebíč CZ 64 A1
Trebinje BIH 84 D3
Trebisacce I 106 B3
Trebitz D 52 B2
Trebnje SLO 73 C5
Třeboň CZ 63 A5
Třebovice CZ 64 A2
Trebsen D 52 B2
Trebujena E 99 C4
Trecastagni I 109 B4
Trecate I 70 C3
Trecenta I 81 A5
Tredegar GB 29 B4
Tredózio I 81 B5
Treffen A 72 B3
Treffort F 69 B5
Treffurt D 51 B6
Trefnant GB 26 B2
Tregaron GB 29 A4
Trégastel-Plage F 56 B2
Tregnago I 71 C6
Tregony GB 28 C3
Tréguier F 56 B2
Trégunc F 56 C2
Treharris GB 29 B4
Trehörningsjö S 115 D15
Tréia I 82 C2
Treignac F 68 C1
Treignat F 68 B2
Treignes B 49 C5
Treis-Karden D 50 C3
Trekanten S 40 C6
Trelazé F 67 A4
Trelech GB 28 B3
Trélissac F 67 C5
Trelleborg S 41 D3
Trélon F 49 C5
Trélou-sur-Marne F . . .59 A4
Tremblay-le-Vicomte
  F 58 B2
Tremés P 92 B2
Tremezzo I 71 C4
Třemošná CZ 63 A4
Tremp E 90 A3
Trenčianska Stankovce
  SK 64 B3
Trenčianska Turná
  SK 64 B3
Trenčianske Teplá
  SK 64 B4
Trenčianske Teplice
  SK 64 B4
Trenčín SK 64 B4
Trendelburg D 51 B5
Trengereid N 32 B2
Trensacq F 76 B2
Trent D 45 A5
Trento I 71 B6
Treorchy GB 29 B4
Trepča KOS 85 D5
Trept F 69 C5
Trepuzzi I 105 C4
Trescore Balneário I . .71 C4
Tresenda I 71 B5
Tresfjord N 114 E4
Tresigallo I 81 B5
Trešnjevica SRB 85 C6
Tresnuraghes I 110 B1
Trespaderne E 89 B3
Třešt CZ 63 A6
Trestina I 82 C1
Tretower GB 29 B4
Trets F 79 C4
Tretten N 34 A2
Treuchtlingen D 62 B1
Treuen D 52 C2
Treuenbrietzen D 52 A2
Treungen N 33 D5
Trevélez E 100 C2
Trevi I 82 D1
Treviana E 89 B3
Treviglio I 71 C4
Trevignano Romano
  I 102 A5
Treviso I 72 C2
Trévoux F 69 C4
Treysa D 51 C5
Trézelles F 68 B3

Trezzo sull'Adda I 71 C4
Trhová Kamenice CZ . .64 A1
Trhové Sviny CZ 63 B5
Triacastela E 86 B3
Triaize F 66 B3
Trianda GR 119 F3
Triaucourt-en-Argonne
  F 59 B6
Tribanj Krušćica HR . . .83 B4
Triberg D 61 B4
Tribsees D 45 A4
Tribute SLO 73 C5
Tricárico I 104 C2
Tricase I 107 B5
Tricésimo I 72 B3
Trieben A 73 A4
Triebes D 52 C2
Triepkendorf D 45 B5
Trier D 60 A2
Trieste I 72 C3
Triggiano I 104 B2
Trignac F 66 A2
Trigueros E 99 B4
Trigueros del Valle E . .88 C2
Trijebine SRB 85 C4
Trikala GR 116 C3
Trikeri GR 116 C5
Trilj HR 83 C5
Trillo E 95 B4
Trilport F 59 B3
Trim IRL 21 A5
Trimdon GB 25 D6
Trindade
  Beja P 98 B3
  Bragança P 87 C3
Tring GB 31 C3
Trinità d'Agultu I 110 B1
Trinitápoli I 104 B2
Trino I 70 C3
Trinta P 92 A3
Triora I 80 C1
Tripoli GR 117 E4
Triponzo I 82 D1
Triptis D 52 C1
Triste E 90 A2
Trittau D 44 B2
Trivento I 103 B7
Trivero I 70 C3
Trivigno I 104 C1
Trn BIH 84 B2
Trnava
  HR 74 C3
  SK 64 B3
Trnovec SK 64 B3
Trnovo BIH 84 C3
Trnovska vas SLO 73 B5
Troarn F 57 A5
Trochtelfingen D 61 B5
Tröbitz D 52 B3
Troense DK 39 D3
Trofa P 87 C2
Trofaiach A 73 A5
Trofors N 115 B10
Trogir HR 83 C5
Trøgstad N 35 C3
Tróia I 103 B8
Tróia P 92 C2
Troisdorf D 50 C3
Trois-Ponts B 50 C1
Troisvierges L 50 C2
Trojane SLO 73 B4
Trojanów PL 55 B6
Troldhede DK 39 D1
Trollhättan S 35 D4
Trolog BIH 84 C1
Tromello I 70 C3
Tromøy N 33 D5
Tromsø N 112 C8
Trondheim N 114 D7
Tronget F 68 B3
Trönning S 40 C2
Trönningeby S 40 B2
Trönö S 36 A3
Tronzano-Vercellese
  I 70 C3
Tróo F 58 C1
Troon GB 24 C3
Tropea I 106 C2
Tropojë AL 105 A6
Tropy Sztumskie PL . . .47 B5
Trosa S 37 D4
Trösken S 36 B3
Trosly-Breuil F 59 A4
Trossingen D 61 B4
Trostberg D 62 B3
Trostyanets UA 7 F13
Trouville-sur-Mer F . . .57 A6
Trowbridge GB 29 B5
Troyes F 59 B5
Trpanj HR 84 C2
Trpezi MNE 85 D5
Trpinja HR 74 C3
Tršće HR 73 C4
Trstice SK 64 A3
Trstin SK 64 B3
Trubchevsk RUS 7 E12
Trubia E 88 A1
Trubjela MNE 84 D3
Truchas E 87 B4
Trujillanos E 93 C4
Trujillo E 93 B5
Trumieje PL 47 B5
Trun
  CH 70 B3
  F 57 B6
Truro GB 28 C2
Trusetal D 51 C6
Truskavets' UA 11 B7
Trustrup DK 39 C3
Trutnov CZ 53 C5
Tryavna BG 11 E8
Trysil N 34 A4
Tryszczyn PL 46 B3
Trzcianka PL 46 B2
Trzciel PL 46 C1
Trzcińsko Zdrój PL . . .45 C6
Trzebiatów PL 45 A7
Trzebiel PL 53 B4
Trzebielino PL 46 A3
Trzebień PL 53 B5
Trzebiez PL 45 B6
Trzebinia PL 55 C4
Trzebnica PL 54 B2
Trzeciewiec PL 47 B4
Trzemeszno PL 46 C3
Trzemeszno-Lubuskie
  PL 46 C1
Trzetrzewina PL 65 A6
Tržič SLO 73 B4
Tsamandas GR 116 C2
Tschagguns A 71 A4
Tschernitz D 53 B4
Tsebrykove UA 11 C11
Tsvetkovo UA 11 B11
Tua P 87 C3
Tubbercurry IRL 18 B3
Tubbergen NL 42 C3
Tubilla del Lago E 89 C3
Tübingen D 61 B5
Tubize B 49 C5
Tučapy CZ 63 A5
Tučepi HR 84 C2
Tuchan F 78 D1
Tuchola PL 46 B3
Tuchów PL 65 A7

Tuczno PL 46 B2
Tuddal N 32 C5
Tudela E 89 B5
Tudela de Duero E 88 C2
Tudweiliog GB 26 C1
Tuejar E 96 B1
Tuffé F 58 B1
Tufsingdalen N 114 E8
Tuhaň CZ 53 C4
Tui E 87 B2
Tukums LV 6 C7
Tula
  I 110 B1
  RUS 7 D14
Tulcea RO 11 D10
Tul'chyn UA 11 B10
Tulette F 78 B3
Tuliszków PL 54 A3
Tulla IRL 20 B3
Tullamore IRL 21 A4
Tulle F 68 C1
Tullins F 69 C5
Tulln A 64 B2
Tullow IRL 21 B5
Tułowice PL 54 C2
Tulsk IRL 18 C3
Tumba S 37 C4
Tummel Bridge GB . . .24 B3
Tun S 35 D4
Tuna
  Kalmar S 40 B6
  Uppsala S 36 B5
Tuna Hästberg S 36 B2
Tunçbilek TR 118 C4
Tunes P 98 B2
Tungelsta S 37 C5
Tunie AL 105 C6
Tunnerstad S 40 A4
Tunnhovd N 32 B5
Tunstall GB 30 B5
Tuohikotti FIN 3 F27
Tuoro sul Trasimeno
  I 82 C1
Tupadły PL 47 C4
Tupanari BIH 84 B3
Tupik RUS 7 D12
Tuplice PL 53 B4
Tura H 65 C5
Turanj HR 83 C4
Turany SK 65 A5
Turbe BIH 84 B2
Turbenthal CH 70 A3
Turcia E 88 B1
Turčianske Teplice
  SK 65 B4
Turcifal P 92 B1
Turckheim F 60 B3
Turda RO 11 C7
Turégano E 94 A3
Turek PL 54 A3
Turgutlu TR 119 D2
Turi I 104 C3
Turin = Torino I 80 A1
Turis E 96 B2
Türje H 74 B2
Türkeve H 75 A5
Türkheim D 62 B1
Türkmenli TR 118 C1
Turku FIN 6 A7
Turleque E 94 C3
Turňa nad Bodvou
  SK 65 B6
Turnberry GB 24 C3
Turnhout B 49 B5
Türnitz A 63 C6
Turnov CZ 53 C5
Turnu Măgurele RO . .11 E8
Turón E 100 C2
Turoszów PL 53 C4
Turowo PL 47 B6
Turquel P 92 B1
Turri I 110 C1
Turries F 79 B5
Turriff GB 23 D6
Tursi I 104 C2
Turtmann CH 70 B2
Turze PL 54 B2
Turzovka SK 65 A4
Tusa I 109 B3
Tuscánia I 102 A4
Tuse DK 39 D4
Tušilovic HR 73 C5
Tuszyn PL 55 B4
Tutow D 45 B5
Tutrakan BG 11 D9
Tuttlingen D 61 C4
Tutzing D 62 C2
Tuzi MNE 105 A5
Tuzla
  BIH 84 B3
  TR 16 C7
Tuzlukçu TR 119 D6
Tvååker S 40 B2
Tväråbäck S 115 C16
Tväråträsk S 115 C16
Tvärskog S 40 C6
Tvedestrand N 33 D5
Tveit
  Hordaland N 32 B4
  Rogaland N 33 C3
Tver RUS 7 C13
Tverrelvmo N 112 D8
Tversted DK 38 B3
Tving S 41 C5
Tvrdošin SK 65 A5
Tvrdošovce SK 64 B4
Twardogóra PL 54 B2
Twatt GB 23 B5
Twello NL 50 A2
Twimberg A 73 B4
Twist D 43 C4
Twistringen D 43 C5
Tworóg PL 54 C3
Twyford
  Hampshire GB 31 C2
  Wokingham GB 31 C3
Tyachiv UA 11 B7
Tychówko PL 46 B2
Tychowo PL 46 B2
Tychy PL 54 C3
Tydal N 114 D8
Týec nad Labem CZ . .53 C5
Tyfors S 36 B1
Tygelsjö S 41 D2
Tykocin PL 6 E7
Tylden N 114 E7
Tylldal N 114 E7
Tylstrup DK 38 B2
Tymbark PL 65 A6
Tymowa PL 65 A6
Tyndrum GB 24 B3
Týnec nad Sázavou
  CZ 63 A5
Tynemouth GB 25 C6
Tyngsjö S 34 B5
Tyniště nad Orlicí CZ . .53 C6
Týn nad Vltavou CZ . . .63 A5
Tynset N 114 E7
Tyresö S 37 C5
Tyringe S 41 C3
Tyristrand N 34 B2
Tyrrellspass IRL 21 A4
Tysnes N 32 B2
Tysse N 32 B2
Tyssebotn N 32 B2
Tyssedal N 32 B3
Tystberga S 37 D4
Tysvær N 33 C2
Tywyn GB 26 C1
Tzermiado GR 117 G7
Tzummarum NL 42 B2

U

Ub SRB 85 B5
Úbby DK 39 D4
Úbeda E 100 A2
Überlingen D 61 C5
Ubidea E 89 A4
Ubli
  HR 84 D1
  MNE 105 A5
Ubrique E 99 C5
Ucero E 89 C3
Uchaud F 78 C3
Uchte D 43 C5
Uckerath D 50 C3
Uckfield GB 31 D4
Ucklum S 35 D3
Uclés E 95 C4
Ucria I 109 A3
Udbina HR 83 B4
Uddebo S 40 B3
Uddeholm S 34 B5
Uddevalla S 35 D3
Uddheden S 34 C4
Uden NL 49 B6
Uder D 51 B6
Údiča SK 65 A4
Údine I 72 B3
Udvar H 74 C3
Ueckermünde D 45 B6
Uelsen D 42 C3
Uelzen D 44 C2
Uetendorf CH 70 B2
Uetersen D 43 B6
Uetze D 44 C2
Uffculme GB 29 C4
Uffenheim D 61 A6
Ugarana E 89 A4
Ugento I 107 B5
Ugerløse DK 39 D4
Uggerby DK 38 B3
Uggiano la Chiesa I . .107 A5
Ugíjar E 100 C2
Ugine F 69 C6
Uglejevik BIH 84 B4
Uglenes N 32 B2
Uglich RUS 7 C15
Ugljane HR 83 C5
Ugod H 74 A2
Uherské Hradiště CZ . .64 A3
Uherský Brod CZ 64 A3
Uherský Ostroh CZ . . .64 B3
Uhingen D 61 B5
Uhliřské-Janovice
  CZ 63 A6
Uhřiněves CZ 53 C4
Uhyst D 53 B4
Uig GB 22 D2
Uitgeest NL 42 C1
Uithoorn NL 49 A5
Uithuizen NL 42 B3
Uithuizermeeden NL . .42 B3
Uivar RO 75 C5
Ujazd
  Łódzkie PL 55 B4
  Opolskie PL 54 C3
Ujezd u Brna CZ 64 A2
Ujhartyán H 75 A4
Újkigyós H 75 B6
Ujpetre H 74 C3
Újście PL 46 B2
Ujsolt H 75 B4
Újszász H 75 A5
Ujué E 89 B5
Ukanc SLO 72 B3
Ukmergé LT 6 D8
Ukna S 40 A6
Ula TR 119 E3
Ul'anka SK 65 B5
Ulaş TR 118 A2
Ulássai I 110 C2
Ulbjerg DK 38 C2
Ulbster GB 23 C5
Ulceby GB 27 B5
Ulcinj MNE 105 B5
Uldum DK 39 D2
Ulefoss N 33 C6
Uleila del Campo E . .101 B3
Ulëz AL 105 B5
Ulfborg DK 39 C1
Ulft NL 50 B2
Uljma SRB 85 A6
Ullånger S 115 D15
Ullapool GB 22 D3
Ullared S 40 B2
Ullatti S 113 E10
Ullatun N 33 C3
Ulldecona E 90 C3
Ulldemolins E 90 B3
Ullervad S 35 D5
Üllés H 75 B4
Üllő H 75 A4
Ulm D 61 B6
Ulme P 92 B2
Ulmen D 50 C2
Ulog BIH 84 C3
Ulricehamn S 40 B3
Ulrichstein D 51 C5
Ulrika S 37 D2
Ulriksfors S 115 D12
Ulrum NL 42 B3
Ulsberg N 114 E6
Ulsta GB 22 A7
Ulsted DK 38 B3
Ulsteinvik N 114 E2
Ulstrup
  Vestsjællands Amt.
    DK 39 D3
  Viborg Amt. DK 39 C2
Ulsvåg N 112 D4
Ulubey TR 119 D4
Uluborlu TR 119 D5
Ulukışla TR 16 C7
Ulverston GB 26 A2
Ulvik N 32 B3
Umag HR 72 C3
Uman UA 11 B11
Umba RUS 3 C31
Umbértide I 82 C1
Umbriático I 107 B3
Umčari SRB 85 B5
Umeå S 3 E24
Umgransele S 115 C15
Umhausen A 71 A5
Umka SRB 85 B5
Umljanovic HR 83 C5
Ummanás S 115 B13
Ummendorf D 61 B6
Umurbey TR 118 B1
Unaðsdalur IS 111 A3
Unapool GB 22 C3
Unari FIN 113 E14
Uncastillo E 90 A1
Undenäs S 37 D6
Undersaker S 115 D10
Undredal N 32 B4
Unecha RUS 7 E12
Unešić HR 83 C5
Úněšov CZ 63 A4
Ungheni MD 11 C9
Unhais da Serra P 92 A3
Unhošt CZ 53 C4
Unichowo PL 46 A3
Uničov CZ 64 A3
Uniejów PL 54 B3
Unisław PL 47 B4
Unken A 62 C3
Unna D 50 B3
Unnaryd S 40 C3
Unquera E 88 A2
Unterach A 63 C4
Unterägeri CH 70 A3
Unterammergau D 62 C2
Unterhaching D 62 B2
Unteriberg CH 70 A3
Unterkochen D 61 B6
Unter Langkampfen A .72 A2
Unterlaussa A 63 D5
Unterlüss D 44 C2
Untermünkheim D 61 A5
Unterschaching D 62 B2
Unterschleissheim D . .62 B2
Unterschwaningen D . .62 A1
Untersiemau D 51 C6
Unter-steinbach D 61 A6
Unterweissenbach A . .63 B5

Unterzell D 62 A3
Upavon GB 29 B6
Úpice CZ 53 C6
Upiłka PL 46 B3
Upphärad S 35 D4
Uppingham GB 30 B3
Upplands-Väsby S 37 C4
Uppsala S 36 C4
Upplsjøhytta N 34 A1
Upton-upon-Severn
  GB 29 A5
Ur F 91 A4
Ura e Shtrenjte AL . . .105 A5
Uras I 110 C1
Ura-Vajgurorë AL 105 C5
Uraz PL 54 B1
Urbánia I 82 C1
Urbino I 82 C1
Urçay F 68 B2
Urda E 94 C3
Urdax E 76 C1
Urdilde E 86 B2
Urdos F 76 D2
Urk NL 42 C2
Urkút H 74 A2
Urla TR 119 D1
Urlingford IRL 21 B4
Urnäsch CH 71 A4
Urnes N 32 A4
Uroševac KOS 10 E6
Urracal E 101 B3
Urries E 90 A1
Urroz E 76 C1
Ursensollen D 62 A2
Urshult S 40 C4
Uršna Sela SLO 73 C5
Urszulewo PL 47 C5
Ury F 58 B3
Urziceni RO 11 D9
Urzulei I 110 B2
Usagre E 93 C4
Uşak TR 118 D4
Ušče SRB 85 C5
Usedom D 45 B5
Useldange L 60 A1
Uséllus I 110 C1
Ushakovo RUS 47 A6
Usingen D 51 C4
Usini I 110 B1
Usk GB 29 B5
Úskedal N 32 C2
Üsküdar TR 118 A4
Uslar D 51 B5
Úsov CZ 64 A3
Usquert NL 42 B3
Ussássai I 110 C2
Usséf F 67 A5
Usséglio I 70 C2
Ussel
  Cantal F 78 A1
  Corrèze F 68 C2
Usson-du-Poitou F . . .67 B5
Usson-en-Forez F 68 C3
Usson-les-Bains F 77 D5
Ustaoset N 32 B5
Ustaritz F 76 C1
Úštěk CZ 53 C4
Uster CH 70 A3
Ústí CZ 64 A3
Ústibar BIH 85 C4
Ustikolina BIH 84 C3
Ústínad Labem CZ . . .53 C4
Ústínad Orlicí CZ 64 A2
Ustiprača BIH 84 C4
Ustka PL 46 A2
Ust Luga RUS 7 B10
Ustroń PL 65 A4
Ustronie Morskie PL . .46 A1
Ustyuzhna RUS 7 B14
Uszód H 74 B3
Utåker N 32 C2
Utansjö S 115 E14
Utebo E 90 B2
Utena LT 7 D8
Utery CZ 62 A4
Uthaug N 114 D7
Utiel E 96 B1
Utne N 32 B3
Utö S 37 D5
Utrecht NL 49 A6
Utrera E 99 B5
Utrillas E 90 C2
Utsjoki FIN 113 C16
Utstein kloster N 33 C2
Uttendorf A 72 A2
Uttenweiler D 61 B5
Utterslev DK 39 E4
Uttoxeter GB 27 C4
Utvälinge S 41 C2
Utvorda N 114 C7
Uusikaarlepyy FIN 3 E25
Uusikaupunki FIN 3 F24
Uvac BIH 85 C4
Uvaly CZ 53 C4
Uvdal N 32 B5
Uza F 76 B1
Uzdin SRB 75 C5
Uzdowo PL 47 B6
Uzel F 56 B3
Uzerche F 67 C6
Uzès F 78 B3
Uzhhorod UA 11 B7
Uzhok UA 11 B7
Užice SRB 85 C4
Uznach CH 70 A3
Uznové AL 105 C6
Uzümlü
  Konya TR 119 E6
  Muğla TR 119 E4
Uzunköprü TR 118 A1

V

Vaalajärvi FIN 113 E15
Vaas F 58 C1
Vaasa FIN 3 E24
Vaasen NL 50 A1
Vabre F 77 C5
Vác H 65 C5
Vacha D 51 C6
Váchartyán H 65 C5
Väckelsång S 40 C4
Vacqueyras F 78 B3
Vad S 36 B2
Vada I 81 C4
Väddö S 36 C5
Vadheim N 32 A2
Vadillo de la Sierra E . .93 A4
Vadillos E 95 B4
Vadla N 33 C3
Vado I 81 B5
Vado Lígure I 80 B2
Vadsø N 113 B18
Vadstena S 37 D1
Vadum DK 38 B2
Vaduz FL 71 A4
Vafos N 33 D6
Vågåmo N 114 F6
Væggerløse DK 39 E4
Vaggeryd S 40 B4
Vaghia GR 117 D5
Vaglia I 81 C5
Váglio Basilicata I . . .104 C1
Vagney F 60 B2
Vagnhärad S 37 D4
Vagnsunda S 37 C5
Vagos P 92 A2
Vai GR 117 G8
Vaiano I 81 C5
Vaiges F 57 B5
Vaihingen D 61 B5
Vaillant F 59 C6
Vailly-sur-Aisne F 59 A4
Vailly-sur-Sauldre F . . .68 A2
Vairano Scalo I 103 B7
Vaison-la-Romaine F . .79 B4
Vaite F 60 C1
Väjern S 35 D3

Vajszló H 74 C2
Vaksdal N 32 B2
Vál H 74 A3
Valaam RUS 3 F29
Valada P 92 B2
Váladalen S 115 D10
Valadares P 87 C2
Valado P 92 B1
Valandovo MK 116 A4
Valaská SK 65 B5
Valaská Belá SK 65 B4
Valaská Dubová SK . . .65 A5
Valašská Polanka CZ . .64 A3
Valašské Klobouky
  CZ 64 A4
Valašské Meziříčí CZ . .64 A3
Valberg F 79 B5
Vålberg S 35 C5
Valbo S 36 B4
Valbom P 87 C2
Valbondione I 71 B5
Valbonë AL 105 A5
Valbonnais F 79 B4
Valcabadillo E 88 B2
Valcani RO 75 C5
Valdagno I 71 C6
Valdahon F 69 A6
Valdaracete E 95 B3
Valday RUS 7 C12
Valdealgorfa E 90 C2
Valdecaballeros E 93 B5
Valdecabras E 95 B4
Valdecarros E 94 B1
Valdeconcha E 95 B4
Valdeflores E 99 B4
Valdefresno E 88 B1
Valdeganga E 95 C5
Valdelacasa E 93 A5
Valdelacasa de Tajo
  E 93 B5
Valdelarco E 99 B4
Valdelosa E 94 A1
Valdeltormo E 90 C3
Valdelugueros E 88 B1
Valdemanco de Esteras
  E 94 D2
Valdemarsvik S 37 D3
Valdemorillo E 94 B2
Valdemoro E 94 B3
Valdemoro Sierra E . . .95 B5
Valdenoceda E 89 B3
Valdeolivas E 95 B4
Valdeolleros E 94 B1
Valdepeñas E 100 A2
Valdepeñas de Jaén
  E 100 B2
Valdepiélago E 88 B1
Valdepolo E 88 B1
Valderas E 88 B1
Valdérice I 108 A1
Valderrobres E 90 C3
Valderrueda E 88 B2
Val de San Lorenzo E .87 B4
Val de Santo Domingo
  E 94 B2
Valdestillas E 88 C2
Valdetorres E 93 C4
Valdetorres de Jarama
  E 95 B3
Valdeverdeja E 93 B5
Valdevimbre E 88 B1
Valdieri I 80 B1
Valdilecha E 95 B3
Val-d'Isère F 70 C1
Valdobbiádene I 72 C1
Valdocondes E 89 C3
Valdoviño E 86 A2
Valdresfjella N 32 B5
Valdunquillo E 88 C1
Vale de Açor
  Beja P 98 B3
  Portalegre P 92 B3
Vale de Água P 98 B2
Vale de Cambra P 87 D2
Vale de Lobo P 98 B2
Vale de Prazeres P 92 A3
Vale de Reis P 92 C2
Vale de Rosa P 98 B3
Vale de Santarém P . . .92 B2
Vale do Peso P 92 B3
Valega P 87 D2
Váléggio sul Mincio I . .71 C5
Valeiro P 92 C2
Valença P 87 B2
Valençay F 67 A6
Valence
  Charente F 67 C5
  Drôme F 78 B3
Valence d'Agen F 77 B4
Valence-d'Albigeois
  F 77 B5
Valence-sur-Baïse F . . .77 C3
Valência I 96 B2
Valencia de Alcántara
  E 92 B3
Valencia de Don Juan
  E 88 B1
Valencia de las Torres
  E 93 C4
Valencia del Ventoso
  E 99 A4
Valencia de Mombuey
  E 98 A3
Valenciennes F 49 C4
Valensole F 79 C4
Valentano I 102 A4
Valentigney F 70 A1
Valentine F 77 C3
Valenza I 80 A2
Valenzuela E 100 B1
Valenzuela de Calatrava
  E 100 A2
Váler
  Hedmark N 34 B3
  Østfold N 35 C3
Valera de Abajo E 95 C4
Valeria E 95 C4
Valestrand N 33 C2
Valestrandsfossen N . .32 B2
Valevåg N 33 C2
Valga EST 7 C9
Valgorge F 78 B3
Valgrisenche I 70 C2
Valguarnera Caropepe
  I 109 B3
Valhelhas P 92 A3
Valjevo SRB 85 B4
Valka LV 7 C8
Valkeakoski FIN 3 F26
Valkenburg NL 50 C1
Valkenswaard NL 49 B6
Valko H 75 A4
Valla S 37 C3
Valladolid E 88 C2
Vallado E 86 A4
Vallåkra S 41 D2
Vallata I 103 B8
Vallberga S 40 C3
Vall d'Alba E 96 A2
Valldemossa E 97 B2
Valle N 33 C4
Valle Castellana I 82 D2
Valle de Abdalajís E . .100 C1
Valle de Cabuérniga
  E 88 A2
Valle de la Serena E . .93 C5
Valle de Matamoros
  E 93 C4
Valle de Santa Ana E . .93 C4
Valledoria I 110 B1
Vallelado E 88 C2
Vallelunga Pratameno
  I 108 B2
Vallendar D 50 C3
Vallentuna S 37 C5
Valleraugue F 78 B2
Vallermosa I 110 C1
Valletta M 107 C5
Valley GB 26 B1
Vallfogona de Riucorb
  E 91 B4
Valli del Pasúbio I 71 C6
Vallo della Lucánia I . .103 C8
Valloire F 69 C6
Vallombrosa I 81 C5
Vallon-Pont-d'Arc F . . .78 B3
Vallorbe CH 69 B6
Vallouise F 79 B5
Valls E 91 B4
Vallset N 34 B3
Vallsta S 36 A3
Vallstena S 37 E5
Valmadrid E 90 B2
Valmiera LV 7 C8
Valmojado E 94 B2
Valmont F 58 A1
Valmontone I 102 B5
Valö S 36 B5
Valognes F 57 A4
Valonga P 92 A2
Valongo P 87 C2
Válor E 100 C2
Valoria la Buena E 88 C2
Valøy N 114 C7
Valozhyn BY 7 D9
Valpaços P 87 C3
Valpelline I 70 C2
Valpiana I 81 C4
Valpovo HR 74 C3
Valras-Plage F 78 C2
Valréas F 78 B3
Vals CH 71 B4
Valsavarenche I 70 C2
Vålse DK 39 E4
Valsequillo E 93 C5
Valsjöbyn S 115 C11
Vals-les-Bains F 78 B3
Valsonne F 69 C4
Valstagna I 72 C1
Val-Suzon F 69 A4
Valtablado del Rio E . .95 B4
Valtberg D 62 A3
Valþjofsstaður IS 111 B11
Val Thorens F 69 C6
Valtice CZ 64 B2
Valtiendas E 88 C3
Valtierra E 89 B5
Valtopina I 82 C1
Valtorta I 71 C4
Valtournenche I 70 C2
Valverde E 89 C5

Vårsta S 37 C4
Vártdal N 114 E3
Vartofta S 40 A3
Varvarin SRB 85 C6
Várvik S 35 C4
Várvölgy H 74 B2
Varzi I 80 B3
Varzjära P 92 A2
Varzo I 70 B3
Varzy F 68 A3
Vasad H 75 A4
Väse S 35 C5
Vašica SRB 85 A4
Vasilevichi BY 7 E10
Väskinde S 37 E5
Vassenden N 32 A6
Vasvár H 74 A1
Vasylkiv UA 11 A11
Vatan F 68 A1
Vätö S 36 C5
Vatne N 114 E3
Vatnestrøm N 33 D5
Vättö S 36 C5
Vatra-Dornei RO 11 C8
Vatry F 59 B5
Vattholma S 36 B4
Vättis CH 71 B4
Vauchamps F 59 B4
Vaucouleurs F 60 B1
Vaudoy-en-Brie F 59 B4
Vaulen N 33 D2
Vaulruz CH 70 B1
Vaulx Vraucourt F 48 C3
Vaumas F 68 B3
Vausseroux F 67 B4
Vauvenargues F 79 C4
Vauvert F 78 C3
Vauvillers F 60 C2
Vaux-sur-Sûre B 60 A1
Vawkavysk BY 6 E8
Vaxholm S 37 C5
Väx jö S 40 C4
Växtorp S 41 C3
Vayrac F 77 B4
Vazec SK 65 A5
Veberöd S 41 D3
Vechelde D 51 A6
Vechta D 43 C5
Vecinos E 94 B1
Vecsés H 75 A4
Vedavågen N 33 C2
Veddige S 40 B2
Vedeseta I 71 C4
Vedevåg S 37 C2
Vedra E 86 B2
Veendam NL 42 B3
Veenendaal NL 49 A6
Vega
  Asturias E 88 A1
  Asturias E 88 A1
Vega de Espinareda
  E 86 B4
Vega de Infanzones E .88 B1
Vegadeo E 86 A3
Vega de Pas E 88 A3
Vega de Valcarce E . . .86 B4
Vega de Valdetronco
  E 88 C1
Vegårshei N 33 D5
Vegas de Coria E 93 A4
Vegas del Condado E .88 B1
Vegby S 40 B3
Vegger DK 38 C2
Veggli N 32 B6
Veghel NL 49 B6
Véglie I 105 C4
Vegset N 114 C9
Vejano I 102 A5
Vejbystrand S 41 C2
Vejen DK 39 D2
Vejer de la Frontera E .99 C5
Vejle DK 39 D2
Vejprty CZ 52 C3
Velada E 94 B2
Vela Luka HR 83 D5
Velayos E 94 B2
Velbert D 50 B3
Velburg D 62 A2
Velden
  Bayern D 62 A2
  Bayern D 62 B3
Velden am Worther See
  A 73 B4
Veldhoven NL 49 B6
Velefique E 101 B3
Velen D 50 B2
Velenje SLO 73 B5
Veles MK 116 A3
Velesevec HR 73 C6
Velešín CZ 63 B5
Velestino GR 116 C4
Vélez Blanco E 101 B3
Vélez de Benaudalla
  E 100 C2
Vélez-Málaga E 100 C1
Vélez Rubio E 101 B3
Velika
  HR 74 C2
  MNE 85 D5
Velika Drenova SRB . . .85 C6
Velika Gorica HR 73 C6
Velika Greda SRB 75 C5
Velika Ilova BIH 84 B2
Velika Kladuša BIH . . .73 C5
Velika Kopanica HR . . .74 C3
Velika Krsna SRB 85 B5
Velika Obarska BIH . . .84 B4
Velika Pisanica HR . . .74 C2
Velika Plana
  SRB 85 B6
  SRB 85 C6
Velika Zdenci HR 74 C2
Velike Lašče SLO 73 C4
Veliki Gaj SRB 75 C6
Veliki Popović SRB 85 B6
Veliki Šiljegovac SRB . .85 C6
Velikiy Ustyug RUS . . .7 C10
Veliko Gradište SRB . . .85 B6
Veliko Orašje SRB 85 B6
Veliko Selo SRB 85 B6
Veliko Tarnovo BG 11 E8
Velilla del Río Carríon
  E 88 B2

Velilla de San Antonio E . . .95 B3
Veli Lošinj HR . . .83 B3
Velipojë AL . . .105 B5
Velizh RUS . . .7 D11
Veljun HR . . .73 C5
Velká Bíteš CZ . . .64 A2
Velka Hled'scbe CZ . . .52 D2
Velká Lomnica SK . . .65 A6
Velkánad Veličkou CZ . . .64 B3
Velké Bystřice CZ . . .64 A3
Velké Heraltice CZ . . .54 C2
Velké Karlovice CZ . . .64 A4
Vel'ke'Kostol'any SK . . .64 B3
Vel'ké Leváre SK . . .64 B3
Velké Losiny CZ . . .54 C2
Velké Meziříčí CZ . . .64 A2
Velké Pavlovice CZ . . .64 B2
Vel'ké Rovné SK . . .65 A4
Vel'ké Uherce SK . . .65 B4
Vel'ké Zálužie SK . . .64 B3
Vel'ký Blahovec SK . . .65 B6
Velky Bor CZ . . .63 A4
Vel'ký Krtiš SK . . .65 B5
Vel'ký Meder SK . . .64 C3
Velky Ujezd CZ . . .64 A3
Vellahn D . . .44 B2
Vellberg D . . .61 A5
Velles F . . .67 B6
Velletri I . . .102 B5
Vellinge S . . .41 D3
Vellisca E . . .95 B4
Velliza E . . .88 C2
Vellmar D . . .51 B5
Velp NL . . .50 A1
Velten D . . .45 C5
Velvary CZ . . .53 C4
Velventos GR . . .116 B4
Vemb DK . . .39 C1
Vemdalen S . . .115 E10
Veme N . . .34 B2
Véménd H . . .74 B3
Vemmedrup DK . . .39 D5
Vena S . . .40 B5
Venaco F . . .102 A2
Venafro I . . .103 B7
Venarey-les-Laumes F . . .69 A4
Venaria I . . .70 C2
Venasca I . . .80 B1
Venčane SRB . . .85 B5
Vence F . . .79 C6
Venda Nova
  Coimbra P . . .92 A2
  Leiria P . . .92 B2
Vendas Novas P . . .92 C2
Vendays-Montalivet F 66 C3
Vendel S . . .36 B4
Vendelso S . . .37 C5
Vendeuil F . . .59 A4
Vendeuvre-sur-Barse F . . .59 B5
Vendoeuvres F . . .67 B6
Vendôme F . . .58 C2
Venelles F . . .79 C4
Veness GB . . .23 B6
Venézia = Venice I . . .72 C2
Venialbo E . . .88 C1
Venice = Venézia I . . .72 C2
Vénissieux F . . .69 C4
Venjan S . . .34 B5
Venlo NL . . .50 B2
Vennesla N . . .33 D4
Vennesund N . . .114 B9
Vennezey F . . .60 B2
Venn Green GB . . .28 C3
Venosa I . . .104 C1
Venray NL . . .50 B1
Vent A . . .71 B5
Venta de Baños E . . .88 C2
Venta del Moro E . . .96 B1
Venta de los Santos E . . .100 A2
Venta las Ranas E . . .88 A1
Ventanueva E . . .86 A4
Ventas de Huelma E . . .100 B2
Ventas de Zafarraya E . . .100 C1
Ventavon F . . .79 B4
Ventimiglia I . . .80 C1
Ventnor GB . . .31 D2
Ventosa de la Sierra E . . .89 C4
Ventosilla E . . .89 C4
Ventspils LV . . .6 C6
Venturina I . . .81 C4
Venzolasca F . . .102 A2
Venzone I . . .72 B3
Vép H . . .74 A1
Vera
  E . . .101 B4
  N . . .115 D9
Vera Cruz P . . .98 A3
Vera de Bidasoa E . . .76 C1
Vera de Moncayo E . . .89 C5
Verbánia I . . .70 C3
Verberie F . . .58 A3
Verbicaro I . . .106 B2
Verbier CH . . .70 B2
Vercelli I . . .70 C3
Vercel-Villedieu-le-Camp F . . .69 A6
Verchen D . . .45 B4
Vercheny F . . .79 B4
Verclause F . . .79 B4
Verdalsøra N . . .114 D8
Verden D . . .43 C6
Verdens Ende N . . .35 C2
Verdille F . . .67 C4
Verdú E . . .91 B4
Verdun-sur-Garonne F . . .77 C4
Verdun-sur-le-Doubs F . . .69 B5
Veresegyház H . . .65 C5
Verfeil F . . .77 C4
Vergato I . . .81 B5
Vergel E . . .96 C3
Vergeletto CH . . .70 B3
Verges F . . .91 A6
Vergiate I . . .70 C3
Vergt F . . .77 A3
Veria GR . . .116 B4
Verin E . . .87 C3
Veringenstadt D . . .61 B5
Verkhovye RUS . . .7 E14
Verl D . . .51 B4
Verma N . . .114 E5
Vermand F . . .59 A4
Vermelha P . . .92 B1
Vermenton F . . .59 C4
Vermosh AL . . .105 A5
Vernago I . . .71 B5
Vernante I . . .80 B1
Vernantes F . . .67 A5
Vernár SK . . .65 B6
Vernayaz CH . . .70 B2
Vernazza I . . .81 B3
Vern-d'Anjou F . . .57 C5
Vernéřice CZ . . .53 C4
Vernet F . . .77 C4
Vernet-les-Bains F . . .91 A5
Verneuil F . . .59 A4
Verneuil-sur-Avre F . . .58 B1
Vérnio I . . .81 B5
Vérnole I . . .105 C4
Vernon F . . .58 A2
Vernoux-en-Vivarais F . . .78 B3
Veróce H . . .65 C5
Verolanuova I . . .71 C5
Véroli I . . .103 B6
Verona I . . .71 C5
Verpelét H . . .65 C6
Verrabotn N . . .114 D7
Verrès I . . .70 C2

Verrey-sous-Salmaise F . . .69 A4
Verrières F . . .67 B5
Versailles F . . .58 B3
Versam CH . . .71 B4
Verseg H . . .65 C5
Versmold D . . .50 A4
Versoix CH . . .69 B6
Verteillac F . . .67 C5
Vértesacsa H . . .74 A3
Vertou F . . .66 A3
Vertus F . . .59 B4
Verviers B . . .50 C1
Vervins F . . .59 A4
Verwood GB . . .29 C6
Veryan GB . . .28 C3
Veržej SLO . . .73 B6
Verzy F . . .59 A5
Vescovato F . . .102 A2
Vése H . . .74 B2
Veselie BG . . .11 E9
Veselí nad Lužnicí CZ . . .63 A5
Veselí nad Moravou CZ . . .64 B3
Vésime I . . .80 B2
Veskoniemi FIN . . .113 C16
Vesoul F . . .60 C2
Vespolate I . . .70 C3
Vessigebro S . . .40 C2
Vestbygd N . . .33 D3
Vestenanova I . . .71 C6
Vester Husby S . . .37 D3
Vester Nebel DK . . .39 D2
Vesterhaven DK . . .38 B3
Vester Torp DK . . .39 D1
Vester Vedsted DK . . .39 D1
Vestervig DK . . .38 C1
Vestfossen N . . .35 C1
Vestmannaeyjar IS . . .111 D5
Vestmarka N . . .34 C3
Vestnes N . . .114 E4
Vestone I . . .71 C5
Vestre Gausdal N . . .34 A2
Vestre Jakobselv N . . .113 B18
Vestre Slidre N . . .32 A5
Vesvegønsk RUS . . .7 B14
Veszprém H . . .74 A2
Veszprémvarsány H . . .74 A2
Vésztő H . . .75 B6
Vetovo HR . . .74 C2
Vetralla I . . .102 A5
Větrný Jeníkov CZ . . .63 A6
Vétroz CH . . .70 B2
Vetschau D . . .53 B4
Vettasjärvi S . . .113 E10
Vetto I . . .81 B4
Vetulónia I . . .81 D4
Veules-les-Roses F . . .58 A1
Veulettes-sur-Mer F . . .58 A1
Veum N . . .33 D5
Veurne B . . .48 B3
Veverská Bítýška CZ . . .64 A2
Vevey CH . . .70 B1
Vevi GR . . .116 B3
Vevring N . . .32 A2
Vex CH . . .70 B2
Veynes F . . .79 B4
Veyre-Monton F . . .68 C3
Veyrier F . . .69 C6
Vézelay F . . .68 A3
Vézelise F . . .60 B2
Vézenobres F . . .78 B3
Vezins F . . .67 A4
Vézins-de-Lévézou F . . .78 B1
Vezirhan TR . . .118 B5
Vezirköprü TR . . .16 A7
Vezza di Óglio I . . .71 B5
Vezzani F . . .102 A2
Vezzano I . . .71 B6
Vezzano sul Cróstolo I . . .81 B4
Viadana I . . .81 B4
Via Gloria P . . .98 B3
Viana E . . .89 B4
Viana do Alentejo P . . .92 C2
Viana do Bolo E . . .87 B3
Viana do Castelo P . . .87 C2
Vianden L . . .60 A2
Viannos GR . . .117 G7
Viareggio I . . .81 C4
Viator E . . .101 C3
Vibble S . . .37 E5
Viborg DK . . .38 C2
Vibo Valéntia I . . .106 C3
Vibraye F . . .58 B1
Vic E . . .91 B5
Vicar E . . .101 C3
Vicarello I . . .81 C4
Vícari I . . .108 B2
Vicchio I . . .81 C5
Vicdessos F . . .77 D4
Vic-en-Bigorre F . . .76 C3
Vicenza I . . .71 C6
Vic-Fézensac F . . .76 C3
Vichy F . . .68 B3
Vickan S . . .38 B5
Vickerstown GB . . .26 A2
Vic-le-Comte F . . .68 C3
Vico F . . .102 A1
Vico del Gargano I . . .104 B1
Vico Equense I . . .103 C7
Vicopisano I . . .81 C4
Vicosoprano CH . . .71 B4
Vicovaro I . . .102 A5
Vic-sur-Aisne F . . .59 A4
Vic-sur-Cère F . . .77 B5
Victoria = Rabat M . . .107 C5
Vidago P . . .87 C3
Vidauban F . . .79 C5
Vide P . . .92 A3
Videbæk DK . . .39 C1
Videm SLO . . .73 C4
Videseter N . . .114 F4
Vidigueira P . . .98 A3
Vidin BG . . .11 E7
Vidlin GB . . .22 A7
Vidsy BY . . .7 D9
Viöchtach D . . .62 A3
Vidreres E . . .91 B5
Vidsel S . . .115 C16
Viduklē LT . . .6 D7
Viechtach D . . .62 A3
Vieira P . . .92 B2
Vieira do Minho P . . .87 C2
Vieiros P . . .92 C3
Vielha E . . .90 A3
Vielle-Aure F . . .77 D3
Viellespesse F . . .68 C3
Vielmur-sur-Agout F . . .77 C5
Vielsalm B . . .50 C1
Viels Maison F . . .59 B4
Vienenburg D . . .51 B6
Vienna = Wien A . . .64 B2
Vienne F . . .69 C4
Vieremä FIN . . .3 E26
Viernheim D . . .61 A4
Viersen D . . .50 B2
Vierville-sur-Mer F . . .57 A5
Vierzehnheiligen D . . .52 C1
Vierzon F . . .68 A2
Vieste I . . .104 B2
Vietas S . . .112 E7
Vietri di Potenza I . . .104 C1
Vietri sul Mare I . . .103 C7
Vieux-Boucau-les-Bains F . . .76 C1
Vif F . . .79 A4
Vig DK . . .39 D4
Vigásio I . . .71 C5
Vigaun A . . .63 C4
Vigeland N . . .33 D4
Vigeois F . . .67 C6
Vigévano I . . .70 C3
Viggianello I . . .106 B3
Viggiano I . . .104 C1
Vigliano I . . .102 A6
Vigmostad N . . .33 D4
Vignale I . . .80 A2
Vignanello I . . .102 A5

Vigneulles-lès-Hattonchâtel F . . .60 B1
Vignevieille F . . .77 D5
Vignola I . . .81 B5
Vignory F . . .59 B6
Vignoux-sur Barangeon F . . .68 A2
Vigo E . . .87 B2
Vigo di Fassa I . . .72 B1
Vigone I . . .80 B1
Vigrestad N . . .33 D2
Vihiers F . . .67 A4
Viitasaari FIN . . .3 E26
Vik IS . . .111 D6
Vik
  Nordland N . . .114 B9
  Rogaland N . . .33 D2
  Sogn og Fjordane N . . .32 A3
  S . . .41 D4
Vika S . . .36 B2
Vikajärvi FIN . . .113 F15
Vikane N . . .35 C2
Vikarbyn S . . .36 B2
Vike N . . .32 B2
Vikedal N . . .33 C2
Vikeland N . . .33 D4
Viken
  Jämtland S . . .115 C10
  Skåne S . . .41 C2
Viker N . . .34 B2
Vikersund N . . .34 C1
Vikeså N . . .33 D3
Vikevåg N . . .33 C2
Vikingstad S . . .37 D2
Vikmanshyttan S . . .36 B2
Vikna N . . .114 C7
Vikøy N . . .32 B3
Vikran
  Troms N . . .112 C7
  Troms N . . .112 D5
Viksjö S . . .115 E14
Viksøyri N . . .32 A3
Viksta S . . .36 B4
Vila Boim P . . .92 C3
Vila Chã de Ourique P . . .92 B2
Viladamat E . . .91 A6
Vila de Cruces E . . .86 B2
Vila de Rei P . . .92 B2
Vila do Bispo P . . .98 B2
Vila do Conde P . . .87 C2
Viladrau E . . .91 B5
Vila Flor P . . .87 C3
Vila Franca das Navas P . . .87 D3
Vilafranca del Maestrat E . . .90 C2
Vilafranca del Penedès E . . .91 B4
Vila Franca de Xira P . . .92 C1
Vila Fresca P . . .92 C1
Vilagarcía de Arousa E . . .86 B2
Vilajuiga E . . .91 A6
Vilamarín E . . .86 B3
Vilamartín de Valdeorras E . . .86 B3
Vila Nogueira P . . .92 C1
Vila Nova de Baronia P . . .92 A2
Vilanova de Castelló E . . .96 B2
Vila Nova de Cerveira P . . .87 C2
Vila Nova de Famalicão P . . .87 C2
Vila Nova de Foz Côa P . . .87 C3
Vila Nova de Gaia P . . .87 C2
Vila Nova de Milfontes P . . .98 B2
Vila Nova de Paiva P . . .87 D3
Vila Nova de São Bento P . . .98 B3
Vilanova de Sau E . . .91 B5
Vilanova i la Geltrú E . . .91 B4
Vilapedre E . . .86 A3
Vila Pouca de Aguiar P . . .87 C3
Vila Praia de Ancora P . . .87 C2
Vilar de Santos E . . .87 B3
Vilardevós E . . .87 C3
Vila Real P . . .87 C3
Vila-real de los Infantes E . . .96 B2
Vila Real de Santo António P . . .98 B3
Vilar Formoso P . . .93 A4
Vila-Rodona E . . .91 B4
Vila Ruiva P . . .98 A3
Vilasantar E . . .86 A2
Vilaseca E . . .91 B4
Vila Seca P . . .92 A2
Vilassar de Mar E . . .91 B5
Vilasund S . . .115 A11
Vila Velha de Ródão P . . .92 B3
Vila Verde
  Braga P . . .87 C2
  Lisboa P . . .92 B1
Vila Verde de Filcalho P . . .98 B3
Vila Viçosa P . . .92 C3
Vilches E . . .100 A2
Vildbjerg DK . . .39 C1
Vilémov CZ . . .63 A6
Vileyka BY . . .7 D9
Vilhelmina S . . .115 C13
Vília GR . . .117 D5
Viljandi EST . . .7 B8
Villabáñez E . . .88 C2
Villablanca E . . .98 B3
Villablino E . . .86 B4
Villabona E . . .89 A4
Villabragima E . . .88 C1
Villabuena del Puente E . . .88 C1
Villacadima E . . .95 A3
Villacañas E . . .95 C3
Villacarriedo E . . .88 A3
Villacarrillo E . . .100 A2
Villa Castelli I . . .104 C3
Villacastín E . . .94 B2
Villach A . . .72 B3
Villacidro I . . .110 C1
Villaconejos E . . .95 B3
Villaconejos de Trabaque E . . .95 B4
Vila Cova de Lixa P . . .87 C2
Villada E . . .88 B2
Villadangos del Páramo E . . .88 B1
Villadecanes E . . .86 B4
Villa del Prado E . . .94 B2
Villa del Río E . . .100 B1
Villadepera E . . .87 C4
Villa di Chiavenna I . . .71 B4
Villadiego E . . .88 B2
Villadompardo E . . .100 B1
Villadóssola I . . .70 B3
Villaeles de Valdavia E . . .88 B2
Villaescusa de Haro E . . .95 C4
Villafáfila E . . .88 C1
Villafeliche E . . .95 A5
Villaflores E . . .94 A1
Villafrades de Campos E . . .88 B2
Villafranca
  Ávila E . . .93 A5
  Navarra E . . .89 B5
Villafranca de Córdoba E . . .100 B1
Villafranca del Bierzo E . . .86 B4
Villafranca de los Barros E . . .93 C4
Villafranca de los Caballeros E . . .95 C3

Villafranca di Verona I . . .71 C5
Villafranca in Lunigiana I . . .81 B3
Villafranca-Montes de Oca E . . .89 B3
Villafranca Tirrena I . . .109 A4
Villafranco del Campo E . . .95 B5
Villafranco del Guadalquivir E . . .99 B4
Villafrati I . . .108 B2
Villafrechós E . . .88 C1
Villafruela E . . .88 C3
Villagarcia de las Torres E . . .93 C4
Villaggio Mancuso I . . .106 B3
Villagonzalo E . . .93 C4
Villagotón E . . .86 B4
Villagrains F . . .76 B2
Villaharta E . . .100 A1
Villahermosa E . . .100 A3
Villaherreros E . . .88 B2
Villahoz E . . .88 B3
Villaines-la-Juhel F . . .57 B5
Villajoyosa E . . .96 C2
Villalago I . . .103 B6
Villalba
  E . . .86 A3
  I . . .108 B2
Villalba de Calatrava E . . .100 A2
Villalba de Guardo E . . .88 B2
Villalba de los Alcores E . . .88 C2
Villalba de los Barros E . . .93 C4
Villalba del Rey E . . .95 B4
Villalcampo E . . .87 C4
Villalcázar de Sirga E . . .88 B2
Villalengua E . . .89 C5
Villalgordo del Júcar E . . .95 C4
Villalgordo del Marquesado E . . .95 C4
Villalmóndar E . . .89 B3
Villalón de Campos E . . .88 B1
Villalonga E . . .96 C2
Villalonso E . . .88 C1
Villalpando E . . .88 C1
Villaluenga E . . .94 B3
Villalumbroso E . . .88 B2
Villálvaro E . . .89 C3
Villamañán E . . .88 B1
Villamanin E . . .88 B1
Villamanrique E . . .100 A3
Villamanrique de la Condesa E . . .99 B4
Villamanta E . . .94 B2
Villamantilla E . . .94 B2
Villamar I . . .110 C1
Villamartín E . . .99 C5
Villamartín de Campos E . . .88 B2
Villamartín de Don Sancho E . . .88 B1
Villamassárgia I . . .110 C1
Villamayor E . . .88 A1
Villamayor de Calatrava E . . .100 A1
Villamayor de Campos E . . .88 C1
Villamayor de Santiago E . . .95 C4
Villamblard F . . .77 A3
Villamejil E . . .86 B4
Villamesías E . . .93 B5
Villaminaya E . . .94 C3
Villa Minozzo I . . .81 B4
Villamor de los Escuderos E . . .88 C1
Villamoronta E . . .88 B2
Villamuelas E . . .94 C3
Villamuriel de Cerrato E . . .88 C2
Villandraut F . . .76 B2
Villanova I . . .104 C3
Villanova d'Asti I . . .80 B1
Villanova del Battista I . . .103 B8
Villanova Mondov i I . . .80 B1
Villanova Monteleone I . . .110 B1
Villante E . . .88 B3
Villantério I . . .71 C4
Villanubla E . . .88 C2
Villanueva de Alcardete E . . .95 C3
Villanueva de Alcorón E . . .95 B4
Villanueva de Algaidas E . . .100 B1
Villanueva de Argaña E . . .88 B3
Villanueva de Bogas E . . .95 C3
Villanueva de Córdoba E . . .100 A1
Villanueva de Gállego E . . .90 B2
Villanueva del Aceral E . . .94 A2
Villanueva de la Concepción E . . .100 C1
Villanueva de la Fuente E . . .101 A3
Villanueva de la Jara E . . .95 C5
Villanueva de la Reina E . . .100 A2
Villanueva del Arzobispo E . . .100 A3
Villanueva de la Serena E . . .93 C5
Villanueva de la Sierra E . . .93 A4
Villanueva de las Manzanas E . . .88 B1
Villanueva de las Peras E . . .88 C1
Villanueva de las Torres E . . .100 B2
Villanueva de la Vera E . . .93 A5
Villanueva del Campo E . . .88 C1
Villanueva del Duque E . . .100 A1
Villanueva del Fresno E . . .93 C3
Villanueva del Huerva E . . .90 B1
Villanueva de los Castillejos E . . .98 B3
Villanueva de los Infantes E . . .100 A3
Villanueva del Rey E . . .99 A5
Villanueva del Río y Minas E . . .99 B5
Villanueva del Rosario E . . .100 C1
Villanueva del Trabuco E . . .100 B1
Villanueva de Mesia E . . .100 B2
Villanueva de Nia E . . .88 B2
Villanueva de Oscos E . . .86 A4
Villanueva de San Carlos E . . .100 A2
Villanueva de San Juan E . . .99 C5
Villanueva de Tapia E . . .100 B1
Villanueva de Valdegovia E . . .89 B3
Villány H . . .74 C3
Villaputzu I . . .110 C2

Villaquejida E . . .88 B1
Villaquilambre E . . .88 B1
Villaquiran de los Infantes E . . .88 B2
Villaralto E . . .100 A1
Villarcayo E . . .89 B3
Villard-de-Lans F . . .79 A4
Villar de Barrio E . . .87 B3
Villar de Chinchilla E . . .96 C1
Villar de Ciervo E . . .87 D4
Villardeciervos E . . .87 C4
Villar de Domingo Garcia E . . .95 B4
Villardefrades E . . .88 C1
Villar del Arzobispo E . . .96 B2
Villar del Buey E . . .87 C4
Villar del Cobo E . . .95 B5
Villar del Humo E . . .95 C5
Villar de los Navarros E . . .90 B1
Villar del Pedroso E . . .93 B5
Villar del Rey E . . .93 B4
Villar del Río E . . .89 C4
Villar del Saz de Navalón E . . .95 B4
Villar de Rena E . . .93 B5
Villarejo E . . .95 A3
Villarejo de Fuentes E . . .95 C4
Villarejo de Órbigo E . . .88 B1
Villarejo de Salvanes E . . .95 B3
Villarejo-Periesteban E . . .95 C4
Villares del Saz E . . .79 A6
Villaretto I . . .79 A6
Villargordo del Cabriel E . . .96 B1
Villarin de Campos E . . .88 C1
Villarino E . . .87 C4
Villarino de Conso E . . .87 B3
Villarluengo E . . .90 C2
Villarobe E . . .89 B3
Villarosa I . . .109 B3
Villar Perosa I . . .79 B6
Villarramiel E . . .88 B2
Villarreal de San Carlos E . . .93 B4
Villarrin de Campos E . . .88 C1
Villarrobledo E . . .95 C4
Villarroya de la Sierra E . . .89 C5
Villarroya de los Pinares E . . .90 C2
Villarrubia de los Ojos E . . .95 C3
Villarrubia de Santiago E . . .95 C3
Villarrubio E . . .95 C4
Villars-les-Dombes F . . .69 B5
Villarta E . . .95 C5
Villarta de los Montes E . . .94 C2
Villarta de San Juan E . . .95 C3
Villasana de Mena E . . .89 A3
Villasandino E . . .88 B2
Villa San Giovanni I . . .109 A4
Villa Santa Maria I . . .103 B7
Villasante E . . .89 A3
Villa Santina I . . .72 B2
Villasarracino E . . .88 B2
Villasayas E . . .89 C4
Villasdardo E . . .87 C4
Villaseca de Henares E . . .95 B4
Villaseca de Laciana E . . .86 B4
Villaseca de la Sagra E . . .94 C3
Villaseco de los Gamitos E . . .87 C4
Villaseco de los Reyes E . . .87 C4
Villasequilla de Yepes E . . .94 C3
Villasimíus I . . .110 C2
Villasmundo I . . .109 B4
Villasor I . . .110 C1
Villastar E . . .90 C1
Villastellone I . . .80 B1
Villatobas E . . .95 C3
Villatoya E . . .96 B1
Villatoro E . . .94 B2
Villavaliente E . . .96 B1
Villavelayo E . . .89 B4
Villavella E . . .87 B3
Villaver de de Guadalimar E . . .101 A3
Villaverde del Río E . . .99 B5
Villaviciosa E . . .88 A1
Villaviciosa de Córdoba E . . .99 A6
Villavieja de Yeltes E . . .87 D4
Villayón E . . .86 A4
Villé F . . .60 B3
Villebois-Lavalette F . . .67 C5
Villecerf F . . .59 B3
Villecomtal F . . .77 B5
Villedaigne F . . .78 C1
Villedieu-les-Poêles F . . .57 B4
Villedieu-sur-Indre F . . .67 B6
Ville-di-Pietrabugno F . . .102 A2
Villedómain F . . .67 A6
Villefagnan F . . .67 B5
Villefontaine F . . .69 C5
Villefort F . . .78 B2
Villefranche-d'Albigeois F . . .77 C5
Villefranche-d'Allier F . . .68 B2
Villefranche-de-Lauragais F . . .77 C4
Villefranche-de-Lonchat F . . .76 A3
Villefranche-de-Panat F . . .78 B1
Villefranche-de-Rouergue F . . .77 B5
Villefranche-du-Périgord F . . .77 B4
Villefranche-sur-Cher F . . .68 A1
Villefranche-sur-Mer F . . .80 C1
Villefranche-sur-Saône F . . .69 B4
Villegenon F . . .68 A2
Villel E . . .90 C1
Villemaur-sur-Vanne F . . .59 B4
Villemontais F . . .68 C3
Villemur-sur-Tarn F . . .77 C4
Villena E . . .96 C2
Villenauxe-la-Grande F . . .59 B4
Villenave-d'Ornon F . . .76 B2
Villeneuve
  CH . . .70 B1
  F . . .77 B5
Villeneuve-d'Ascq F . . .49 C4
Villeneuve-de-Berg F . . .78 B3
Villeneuve-de-Marsan F . . .76 C2
Villeneuve-de-Rivière F . . .77 C3
Villeneuve-la-Guyard F . . .59 B4
Villeneuve-l'Archevêque F . . .59 B4
Villeneuve-le-Comte F . . .59 B3
Villeneuve-lès-Avignon F . . .78 C3
Villeneuve-les-Corbières F . . .78 D1
Villeneuve-St Georges F . . .58 B3

Villeneuve-sur-Allier F . . .68 B3
Villeneuve-sur-Lot F . . .77 B3
Villeneuve-sur-Yonne F . . .59 B4
Villeréal F . . .77 B3
Villerías E . . .88 C2
Villeromain F . . .58 C2
Villers-Bocage
  Calvados F . . .57 A5
  Somme F . . .48 D3
Villers-Bretonneux F . . .48 D3
Villers-Carbonnel F . . .59 A3
Villers-Cotterêts F . . .59 A4
Villersexel F . . .60 C2
Villers-Farlay F . . .69 B5
Villers-Gambon B . . .49 C5
Villers-le-Lac F . . .70 A1
Villers-sur-Mer F . . .57 A6
Villerupt F . . .60 A1
Villerville F . . .57 A6
Villeseneux F . . .59 B5
Ville-sous-la-Ferté F . . .59 B5
Ville-sur-Tourbe F . . .59 A5
Villetrun F . . .58 C2
Villiers-St Benoit F . . .59 C4
Villiers-St Georges F . . .59 B4
Villingen D . . .61 B4
Villmar D . . .50 C4
Villoldo E . . .88 B2
Villon F . . .59 C5
Villoria E . . .94 B1
Vilnes N . . .32 A1
Vilnius LT . . .7 D8
Vils
  A . . .62 C1
  DK . . .38 C1
Vilsbiburg D . . .62 B3
Vilseck D . . .62 A2
Vilshofen D . . .63 B4
Vilshult S . . .41 C4
Vilusi MNE . . .84 D3
Vilvestre E . . .87 C4
Vilvoorde B . . .49 C5
Vimeiro P . . .92 B1
Vimercate I . . .71 C4
Vimianzo E . . .86 A1
Vimieiro P . . .92 C3
Vimioso P . . .87 C4
Vimmerby S . . .40 B5
Vimoutiers F . . .57 B6
Vimperk CZ . . .63 A4
Vinadi CH . . .71 B5
Vinadio I . . .79 B6
Vinaixa E . . .90 B3
Vinarós E . . .90 C3
Vinäs S . . .36 B1
Vinay F . . .79 A4
Vinberg S . . .40 C2
Vinca F . . .91 A5
Vinča SRB . . .85 B6
Vinchiaturo I . . .103 B7
Vinci I . . .81 C4
Vindeby DK . . .39 D3
Vindelgransele S . . .115 B15
Vindeln S . . .115 C16
Vinderup DK . . .38 C1
Vindsvik N . . .33 C3
Vinets F . . .59 B5
Vineuil F . . .58 C2
Vinga RO . . .75 B6
Vingåker S . . .37 C2
Vingnes N . . .34 A2
Vingrau F . . .78 D1
Vingrom N . . .34 A2
Vinhais P . . .87 C4
Vinica
  HR . . .73 B6
  SK . . .65 B6
  SLO . . .73 C5
Vinicka MNE . . .84 C3
Vinje
  Hordaland N . . .32 B3
  Sør-Trøndelag N . . .114 D6
  Telemark N . . .33 C4
Vinkovci HR . . .74 C3
Vinliden S . . .115 C14
Vinni EST . . .7 B9
Vinninga S . . .35 D5
Vinnytsya UA . . .11 B10
Vinon-sur-Verdon F . . .79 C4
Vinslöv S . . .41 C3
Vintjärn S . . .36 B3
Vintrosa S . . .37 C1
Viñuela E . . .100 C1
Viñuela de Sayago E . . .87 C5
Viñuelas E . . .95 B3
Vinuesa E . . .89 C4
Vinzelberg D . . .44 C3
Viöl D . . .43 A6
Véolo I . . .80 B1
Violay F . . .69 C4
Vípava SLO . . .72 C3
Vipiteno I . . .71 B6
Vipperow D . . .45 B4
Vir
  BIH . . .84 C2
  HR . . .83 B4
Vira CH . . .70 B3
Vire F . . .57 B5
Vireda S . . .40 B4
Vireux F . . .49 C5
Virgen A . . .72 B2
Virgen de la Cabeza E . . .100 A1
Virginia IRL . . .19 C4
Virieu F . . .69 C5
Virieu-le-Grand F . . .69 C5
Virje HR . . .74 B1
Virklund DK . . .39 C2
Virovitica HR . . .74 C2
Virpazar MNE . . .105 A5
Virsbo S . . .36 C3
Virserum S . . .40 B5
Virtaniemi FIN . . .113 D17
Virton B . . .60 A1
Virtsu EST . . .7 B7
Viry F . . .69 B6
Vis HR . . .83 C5
Visbek D . . .43 C5
Visby
  DK . . .39 D1
  S . . .37 E5
Visé B . . .50 C1
Višegrad BIH . . .85 C4
Viserba I . . .82 B1
Viševnica E . . .88 A1
Vişeu de Sus RO . . .11 C8
Vișna Gora SLO . . .73 C5
Višňan CZ . . .64 B2
Višňové CZ . . .64 B2
Viso del Marqués E . . .100 A2
Visoka
  BIH . . .84 C3
  SLO . . .73 B4
Visone I . . .80 B2
Visp CH . . .70 B2
Vissefjärda S . . .40 C5
Visselhövede D . . .43 C6
Vissenbjerg DK . . .39 D3
Visso I . . .82 D2
Vistabella del Maestrat E . . .90 C2
Vita I . . .108 B1
Vitanje SLO . . .73 B5
Vitanovac SRB . . .85 C5
Vitebsk = Vitsyebsk BY . . .7 D11
Viterbo I . . .102 A5
Vitez BIH . . .84 B2

Vithkuq AL . . .116 B2
Vitigudino E . . .87 C4
Vitina
  BIH . . .84 C2
  GR . . .117 E4
Vitis A . . .63 B6
Vítkov CZ . . .64 A3
Vitkovac SRB . . .85 C5
Vitomirica KOS . . .85 D5
Vitoria-Gasteiz E . . .89 B4
Vitré F . . .57 B4
Vitrey-sur-Mance F . . .60 C1
Vitry-en-Artois F . . .48 C3
Vitry-le-François F . . .59 B5
Vitry-sur-Seine F . . .58 B3
Vitsand S . . .34 B4
Vitsyebsk = Vitebsk BY . . .7 D11
Vittangi S . . .113 E10
Vittaryd S . . .40 C3
Vitteaux F . . .69 A4
Vittel F . . .60 B1
Vittinge S . . .36 C4
Vittória I . . .109 C3
Vittório Véneto I . . .72 C2
Vitträsk FIN . . .3 F27
Viù I . . .70 C2
Viul N . . .34 B2
Vivario F . . .102 A2
Viveiro E . . .86 A3
Vivel del Rio Martin E . . .90 C2
Viver E . . .96 B2
Viverols F . . .68 C3
Viveros E . . .101 A3
Viviers F . . .78 B3
Vivonne F . . .67 B5
Vivy F . . .67 A4
Vize TR . . .118 A2
Vizille F . . .79 A4
Viziru RO . . .11 D9
Vizovice CZ . . .64 A3
Vizvár H . . .74 B2
Vizzavona F . . .102 A2
Vizzini I . . .109 B3
Vlachiotis GR . . .117 F4
Vlachovice CZ . . .64 A3
Vlachovo SK . . .65 B6
Vláchovo Březí CZ . . .63 A4
Vladimirci SRB . . .85 B4
Vladimirovac SRB . . .85 A5
Vladislav CZ . . .64 A1
Vlagtwedde NL . . .43 B4
Vlajkovac SRB . . .85 A6
Vlasenica BIH . . .84 B3
Vlašim CZ . . .63 A5
Vlatkovići BIH . . .84 B2
Vledder NL . . .42 C3
Vlissingen NL . . .49 B4
Vlkolínec SK . . .65 A5
Vllorë AL . . .105 C5
Vlotho D . . .51 A4
Vnanje Gorice SLO . . .73 C4
Vobarno I . . .71 C5
Vöcin HR . . .74 C2
Vöcklabruck A . . .63 B4
Vöcklamarkt A . . .63 C4
Vodanj SRB . . .85 B5
Voderady SK . . .64 B3
Vodice
  Istarska HR . . .73 C4
  Šibenska HR . . .83 C4
  SLO . . .73 B4
Vodňany CZ . . .63 A5
Vodnjan HR . . .82 B2
Vodskov DK . . .38 B3
Voe GB . . .22 A7
Voerså DK . . .38 B3
Voghera I . . .80 B3
Vogogna I . . .70 B3
Vogošća BIH . . .84 C3
Vogüé F . . .78 B3
Vohburg D . . .62 B2
Vohenstrauss D . . .62 A3
Vöhl D . . .51 B4
Vöhrenbach D . . .61 B4
Vöhringen D . . .61 B6
Void-Vacon F . . .60 B1
Voiron F . . .69 C5
Voise F . . .58 B2
Voisey F . . .60 C1
Voiteur F . . .69 B5
Voitsberg A . . .73 A5
Vojakkala FIN . . .3 D26
Vojens DK . . .39 D2
Vojka SRB . . .85 B5
Vojlovica SRB . . .85 B5
Vojnić HR . . .73 C5
Vojnik SLO . . .73 B5
Vojvoda Stepa SRB . . .75 C5
Volada GR . . .119 G2
Volargne I . . .71 C5
Volary CZ . . .63 B4
Volče SLO . . .72 B3
Volda N . . .114 E3
Volendam NL . . .42 C2
Volga RUS . . .7 B15
Volimes GR . . .117 E2
Volissos GR . . .116 D7
Volkach D . . .61 A6
Völkermarkt A . . .73 B4
Volkhov RUS . . .7 B12
Völklingen D . . .60 A2
Volkmarsen D . . .51 B5
Voll N . . .114 E4
Vollenhove NL . . .42 C2
Vollore-Montagne F . . .68 C3
Vollsjö S . . .41 D3
Volodymyr-Volyns'ky UA . . .11 A8
Volokolamsk RUS . . .7 C13
Volos GR . . .116 C4
Volosovo RUS . . .7 B10
Volovets UA . . .11 B7
Voltággio I . . .80 B2
Volta Mantovana I . . .71 C5
Volterra I . . .81 C4
Voltri I . . .80 B2
Voltturara Áppula I . . .103 B8
Volturara Irpina I . . .103 C7
Volvic F . . .68 C3
Volx F . . .79 C4
Volyne CZ . . .63 A4
Vonitsa GR . . .116 D2
Vönöck H . . .74 A2
Vonsild DK . . .39 D2
Voorschoten NL . . .49 A5
Voorst NL . . .50 A2
Voorthuizen NL . . .49 A6
Vopnafjörður IS . . .111 B11
Vorau A . . .73 A5
Vorbasse DK . . .39 D2
Vorchdorf A . . .63 C4
Vorden
  D . . .43 C5
  NL . . .50 A2
Vordingborg DK . . .39 D4
Vorë AL . . .105 B5
Vorey F . . .68 C3
Vorgod DK . . .39 C1
Vormsund N . . .34 B3
Voronezh RUS . . .7 F14
Voskopojë AL . . .116 B2
Voss N . . .32 B3
Votice CZ . . .63 A5
Voué F . . .59 B5
Vouillé F . . .67 B5
Voulx F . . .59 B3
Voussac F . . .68 B3
Vouvray F . . .67 A5
Vouzela P . . .87 D2
Vouziers F . . .59 A5
Voves F . . .58 B2
Voxna S . . .36 A2
Voy GB . . .23 B5
Voynitsa RUS . . .3 D28
Voznesenye RUS . . .7 A13

Vrå
  DK . . .38 B2
  GR . . .117 E4
Vráble SK . . .64 B4
Vračevšnica MNE . . .84 D3
Vračev Gaj SRB . . .85 B6
Vračevsnica SRB . . .85 B5
Vrádal N . . .33 C5
Vrakneika GR . . .117 D3
Vrana HR . . .83 B4
Vranduk BIH . . .84 B2
Vrångö S . . .38 B4
Vrani RO . . .85 A6
Vranić BIH . . .84 C3
Vraniči BIH . . .84 C3
Vranja HR . . .73 C4
Vranjak BIH . . .84 B3
Vranje SRB . . .10 E6
Vranov nad Dyje CZ . . .64 B1
Vransko SLO . . .73 B5
Vrapčići BIH . . .84 C2
Vratsa BG . . .11 E7
Vrbanja HR . . .84 B3
Vrbanjci BIH . . .84 B2
Vrbas SRB . . .75 C4
Vrbaška BIH . . .84 A2
Vrbnik
  Primorsko-Goranska HR . . .83 A3
  Zadarsko-Kninska HR . . .83 B5
Vrbno pod Pradědem CZ . . .54 C2
Vrboska HR . . .83 C5
Vrbov SK . . .65 A6
Vrbovce SK . . .64 B3
Vrbové SK . . .64 B3
Vrbovec HR . . .73 C6
Vrbovski SRB . . .85 B5
Vrbovsko HR . . .73 C5
Vrchlabí CZ . . .53 C5
Vrchovice CZ . . .64 A3
Vrdy CZ . . .63 A6
Vrebac HR . . .83 B4
Vreden D . . .50 A2
Vrela KOS . . .85 D5
Vreoci SRB . . .85 B5
Vretstorp S . . .37 C1
Vrhnika SLO . . .73 C4
Vrhovine HR . . .83 B4
Vrhpolje SRB . . .85 B4
Vriezenveen NL . . .42 C3
Vrigne-aux-Bois F . . .59 A5
Vrigstad S . . .40 B4
Vríka HR . . .83 C5
Vrlika HR . . .83 C5
Vrmbaje SRB . . .85 C5
Vrnjačka Banja SRB . . .85 C5
Vrnograč BIH . . .73 C5
Vron F . . .48 C2
Vroomshoop NL . . .42 C3
Vroutek CZ . . .52 C3
Vrpolje SRB . . .74 C3
Vršac SRB . . .85 A6
Vrsar HR . . .82 A2
Vrsi HR . . .83 B4
Vrtoče BIH . . .83 B5
Vrútky SK . . .65 A4
Všestary CZ . . .53 C5
Vsetín CZ . . .64 A3
Vučá MNE . . .85 D5
Vučitrn KOS . . .85 D6
Vučkovica SRB . . .85 C5
Vught NL . . .49 B6
Vukovar HR . . .75 C4
Vulcan RO . . .11 D7
Vulcănești MD . . .11 D10
Vuoggatjålme S . . .112 F5
Vuojärvi FIN . . .113 E15
Vuolijoki FIN . . .3 D27
Vuotso FIN . . .113 D16
Vuzenica SLO . . .73 B5
Vyartsilya RUS . . .3 E29
Vyazma RUS . . .7 D13
Vyborg RUS . . .3 F28
Vydrany SK . . .64 B3
Vyerkhnyadzvinsk BY . . .7 D9
Vyhne SK . . .65 B4
Vylkove UA . . .11 D10
Vynohradiv UA . . .11 B7
Vyshniy Volochek RUS . . .7 C13
Výškov CZ . . .64 A2
Vysoké Mýto CZ . . .53 D6
Vysokovsk RUS . . .7 C14
Vyšší Brod CZ . . .63 B5
Vytegra RUS . . .7 A14

W

Waabs D . . .44 A1
Waalwijk NL . . .49 B6
Waarschoot B . . .49 B4
Wabern D . . .51 B5
Wąbrzezno PL . . .47 B4
Wąchock PL . . .55 B6
Wachow D . . .45 C4
Wachów PL . . .54 C3
Wächtersbach D . . .51 C5
Wackersdorf D . . .62 A3
Waddington GB . . .27 B5
Waddinxveen NL . . .49 A5
Wadebridge GB . . .28 C3
Wadelsdorf D . . .53 B4
Wädenswil CH . . .70 A3
Wadern D . . .60 A2
Wadersloh D . . .51 B4
Wadhurst GB . . .31 C4
Wadlew PL . . .55 B4
Wadowice PL . . .65 A5
Wagenfeld D . . .43 C5
Wageningen NL . . .49 A6
Waghäusel D . . .61 A4
Waging D . . .62 C3
Wagrain A . . .72 A3
Wągrowiec PL . . .46 C3
Wahlsdorf D . . .45 C5
Wahlstedt D . . .44 B2
Wahrenholz D . . .44 C2
Waiblingen D . . .61 B5
Waidhaus D . . .62 A3
Waidhofen an der Thaya A . . .63 B6
Waidhofen an der Ybbs A . . .63 C5
Waimes B . . .50 C2
Wainfleet All Saints GB . . .27 B6